# The Official RED BOOK®

## A GUIDE BOOK OF

# UNITED STATES COINS

## R.S. YEOMAN

**EDITOR**
## KENNETH BRESSETT

**RESEARCH EDITOR**
## Q. DAVID BOWERS

**VALUATIONS EDITOR**
## JEFF GARRETT

### 60th Edition
Fully Illustrated Catalog and
Retail Valuation List—1616 to Date

A Guide Book of United States Coins™
THE OFFICIAL RED BOOK OF UNITED STATES COINS™

THE OFFICIAL RED BOOK and THE OFFICIAL RED BOOK OF UNITED STATES COINS
are trademarks of Whitman Publishing, LLC. Library of Congress Catalog Card No.: 47-22284

www.whitman**books**.com

Printed in the United States of America.
The WCG™ pricing grid used throughout this publication is patent pending.

© 2006 Whitman Publishing, LLC
3101 Clairmont Road • Suite C • Atlanta GA 30329

For a complete listing of numismatic reference books,
supplies, and storage products, visit us at
www.whitman**books**.com

# CONTENTS

# CONTRIBUTORS TO THE SIXTIETH EDITION

*Special Consultants: Q. David Bowers, Philip Bressett, Jeff Garrett, Tom Hallenbeck, Robert Rhue, and Mary Sauvain*

Gary Adkins
David Akers
Buddy Alleva
Richard S. Appel
Michael Aron
Richard M. August
Richard A. Bagg
Mitchell A. Battino
Lee J. Bellisario
Philip E. Benedetti
Mark R. Borckardt
J.H. Cline
Elizabeth W. Coggan
Gary Cohen
Silvano Di Genova
Sheridan Downey
Steven Ellsworth
Chuck Furjanic
Dennis M. Gillio
Ronald J. Gillio
Ira M. Goldberg
Lawrence S. Goldberg
Kenneth M. Goldman
J.R. Grellman
Ron Guth
James Halperin
John B. Hamrick
Steven Hayden

Brian Hendelson
Gene L. Henry
Karl D. Hirtzinger
Jesse Iskowitz
Steve Ivy
James J. Jelinski
Donald H. Kagin
Bradley S. Karoleff
Mike Kliman
John J. Kraljevich Jr.
Richard A. Lecce
Robert B. Lecce
Julian M. Leidman
Stuart Levine
Kevin Lipton
Denis W. Loring
Arnold Margolis
Chris McCawley
Robert T. McIntire
Dwight N. Manley
Harry Miller
Lee S. Minshull
Scott P. Mitchell
Michael C. Moline
Paul Montgomery
Richard Nachbar
Casey Noxon
Paul Nugget

Mike Orlando
John M. Pack
William Panitch
Robert M. Paul
William P. Paul
Thomas Payne
Joel Rettew Jr.
Joel Rettew Sr.
Greg Rohan
Maurice Rosen
Richard J. Schwary
Roger Siboni
James A. Simek
William J. Spencer
Lawrence Stack
David M. Sundman
Anthony J. Swiatek
Steve Tanenbaum
Anthony Terranova
Ben Todd
Jerry Treglia
Frank E. Van Valen
Fred Weinberg
Douglas Winter
David Wnuck
Mark S. Yaffe

***Special credit is due to the following for service and data in this book:*** Richard A. Bagg, Stewart Blay, Roger W. Burdette, Columbus–America Discovery Group, Charles Davis, Tom DeLorey, George B. Fitzgerald, Bill Fivaz, George Fuld, Charles Hoskins, Robert W. Julian, George F. Kolbe, David W. Lange, G.J. Lawson, Andy Lustig, Arnold Margolis, J.P. Martin, Eric P. Newman, Doug Plasencia, Len Roosmalen, P. Scott Rubin, Paul Rynearson, Neil Shafer, Robert W. Shippee, Arlie Slabaugh, Mark R. Vitunic, Holland Wallace, Weimar White, John Whitney, and John Wright.

***Special credit is due to the following for service in the past editions of this book:*** Philip E. Benedetti, George H. Blenker, Q. David Bowers, Larry Briggs, Bob Entlich, Dennis J. Forgue, Harry J. Forman, Mike Fuljenz, Henry G. Garrett, William G. Gay, Harry Gittelson, Brian H. Hendelson, John W. Highfill, Michael Hodder, Robert H. Jacobs, A.M. Kagin, Stanley Kesselman, Jerry Kimmel, Mike Kliman, Paul L. Koppenhaver, Ed Leventhal, Glenn E. Miller, Beth O. Piper, Andrew W. Pollock III, John C. Porter, Joel D. Rettew, Mike Ringo, Gerald R. Scherer Jr., J.S. Schreiber, Hugh J. Sconyers, Robert R. Shaw, Thomas J. Smith, Paul Spiegel, Maurice A. Storck Sr., Charles Surasky, Mark Van Winkle, Russell P. Vaughn.

***Special photo credits are due to the following:*** American Numismatic Rarities, Douglas F. Bird, Steve Contursi, Bill Fivaz, Ira & Larry Goldberg Coins & Collectibles, Tom Mulvaney, the Museum of the American Numismatic Association, Noyes–Lusk DVD Photo Project, Numismatic Guaranty Corporation of America (NGC), Brent Pogue, Sarasota Rare Coin Gallery, the Smithsonian Institution, heritagecoins.com, Rick Snow, Spectrum, Stack's Rare Coins of New York, Superior Galleries, Anthony Swiatek, and the United States Mint.

Coin values shown in this book are retail prices figured from data supplied by the listed contributors approximately two months prior to publication. The coin market is so active in some categories that values can easily change during that period. Values listed are shown as a guide and are not intended to serve as a price list for any dealer's stock. A dash appearing in a price column indicates that coins in that grade exist even though there are no current sales or auction records for them. The dash does *not* necessarily mean that such coins are exceedingly rare. Italicized prices indicate unsettled or speculative values. A number of listings of rare coins do not have prices or dashes in certain grades. This indicates that they are not available or not believed to exist in those grades.

Prices rise when (1) the economic trend is inflationary and speculators turn to tangible assets as a hedge, or when the number of collectors increases, while coin supplies remain stationary or decrease through attrition or melting; (2) dealers replace their stocks of coins only from collectors or other dealers, who expect a profit over what they originally paid; (3) speculators attempt to influence the market through selective buying; or (4) bullion (gold and silver) prices rise.

Prices decline when (1) changes in collecting habits or economic conditions alter demand for certain coins; (2) speculators sell in large quantities; (3) hoards or large holdings are suddenly released and cannot be quickly absorbed by the normal market; or (4) bullion (gold and silver) prices decline.

Those who edit, contribute to, and publish this book advocate the collecting of coins for pleasure and educational benefits. A secondary consideration is that of investment, the profits from which are usually realized over the long term based on careful purchases.

The *Handbook of United States Coins* (commonly called the Blue Book), by R.S. Yeoman, Whitman Publishing, Atlanta, GA, contains average prices dealers will pay for these coins, and is obtainable through most coin dealers, hobby shops, bookstores, and the Internet.

## ABBREVIATIONS USED IN THIS BOOK:

| Abbreviation | Meaning | Abbreviation | Meaning |
|---|---|---|---|
| Arr | Arrows | Med | Medium |
| Cap | Capped | NM | No Motto |
| Cl | Close | Nml | Normal |
| CN | Copper-Nickel | NS | No Stars |
| DblDie | Doubled-Die | Obv | Obverse |
| Drap | Drapery | Pf | Proof |
| Drpd | Draped | Pl | Plain |
| Dt | Date | Pt | Partial |
| HE | Heraldic Eagle | Rev | Reverse |
| Horiz | Horizontal | Rt | Right |
| Leg | Legend | SE | Small Eagle |
| Lg | Large | Sm | Small |
| Lib | Liberty | Sq | Square |
| Ltrs | Letters | Std | Seated |

A slash between words or letters represents an overdated or overmintmark: "3/2" is an abbreviation of "3 Over 2," "D/S" is "D Over S," etc.

Collectors should be aware that copies of certain American issues were made after 1850 to provide facsimiles of rarer issues that would otherwise have been unobtainable. Many crude imitations have also been made in recent years, as well as forgeries intended to deceive collectors. The specimens illustrated herein, however, are genuine.

## CONDITIONS OF COINS
### *Essential Elements of the ANA Grading System*

**PROOF**—A specially made coin distinguished by sharpness of detail and usually with a brilliant, mirrorlike surface. *Proof* refers to the method of manufacture and is not a grade. The term implies mint condition unless otherwise noted. See page 320 for details.

> **GEM PROOF (PF-65)**—Brilliant surfaces with no noticeable blemishes or flaws. A few scattered, barely noticeable marks or hairlines.
>
> **CHOICE PROOF (PF-63)**—Reflective surfaces with only a few blemishes in secondary focal places. No major flaws.
>
> **PROOF (PF-60)**—Surface may have several contact marks, hairlines, or light rubs. Luster may be dull and eye appeal lacking.

**MINT STATE**—The terms *Mint State (MS)* and *Uncirculated (Unc.)* are used interchangeably to describe coins showing no trace of wear. Such coins may vary to some degree because of blemishes, toning, or slight imperfections, as described in the following subdivisions:

> **PERFECT UNCIRCULATED (MS-70)**—Perfect new condition, showing no trace of wear. The finest quality possible, with no evidence of scratches, handling, or contact with other coins. Very few regular-issue coins are ever found in this condition.
>
> **GEM UNCIRCULATED (MS-65)**—An above average Uncirculated coin that may be brilliant or lightly toned and that has very few contact marks on the surface or rim.
>
> **CHOICE UNCIRCULATED (MS-63)**—Has some distracting contact marks or blemishes in prime focal areas. Luster may be impaired.
>
> **UNCIRCULATED (MS-60)**—Has no trace of wear but may show a number of contact marks, and surface may be spotted or lack some luster.

**CHOICE ABOUT UNCIRCULATED (AU-55)**—Evidence of friction on high points of design. Most of the mint luster remains.

**ABOUT UNCIRCULATED (AU-50)**—Traces of light wear on many of the high points. At least half of the mint luster is still present.

**CHOICE EXTREMELY FINE (EF-45)**—Light overall wear on highest points. All design details are very sharp. Some of the mint luster is evident.

**EXTREMELY FINE (EF-40)**—Light wear on design throughout, but all features sharp and well defined. Traces of luster may show.

**CHOICE VERY FINE (VF-30)**—Light, even wear on the surface and highest parts of the design. All lettering and major features are sharp.

**VERY FINE (VF-20)**—Moderate wear on high points of design. All major details are clear.

**FINE (F-12)**—Moderate to considerable even wear. Entire design is bold with overall pleasing appearance.

**VERY GOOD (VG-8)**—Well worn with main features clear and bold, although rather flat.

**GOOD (G-4)**—Heavily worn, with design visible but faint in areas. Many details are flat.

**ABOUT GOOD (AG-3)**—Very heavily worn with portions of lettering, date, and legend worn smooth. The date may be barely readable.

*Important:* Damaged coins, such as those that are bent, corroded, scratched, holed, nicked, stained, or mutilated, are worth less than those without defects. Flawless uncirculated coins are generally worth more than values quoted in this book. Slightly worn coins ("sliders") that have been cleaned and conditioned ("whizzed") to simulate uncirculated luster are worth considerably less than perfect pieces.

Unlike damage inflicted after striking, manufacturing defects do not always lessen values. Examples include colonial coins with planchet flaws and weakly struck designs; early silver and gold with weight-adjustment "file marks" (parallel cuts made prior to striking); and coins with "lint marks" (surface marks due to the presence of dust or other foreign matter during striking).

Brief guides to grading are placed before each major coin type in this book.

## AN INTRODUCTION TO UNITED STATES COINS
### The Spanish Milled Dollar

The Spanish milled dollar, valued at 8 *reales*, and otherwise known as the *pillar dollar* or *piece of eight*, has been given a place in romantic fiction unequaled by any other coin.

This time-honored piece and its fractional parts (one-half, one, two, and four *reales*) were the principal coins of the American colonists, and were the forerunners of our own silver dollar and its fractional divisions. Thomas Jefferson even recommended to the Continental Congress on September 2, 1776, that the new country adopt the silver Spanish milled dollar as its monetary unit of value.

The coin shown above bears the M̃ mintmark for Mexico City. Similar pieces with other mintmarks were struck in Bolivia, Chile, Colombia, Guatemala, and Peru. Average value for an 8 *reales* of common date and mint is about $150 in Fine to Very Fine condition. Dates range from 1732 to 1772. *Note that many modern copies of the 8* reales *exist. These are produced mostly as souvenirs and have little or no value.*

## Money of the Early Americans

The saga of American money covers a period of nearly four centuries, from 1620 to the present. It began when the early European settlers in New England started trading with Native Americans for furs and commodities that could be exported to Britain. The furs, tobacco, and lumber exports were used to purchase needed items that could not be produced locally. Trade was carried on with the Indians through the use of barter and strings of wampum, which were fashioned from mussel shells in the form of beads. Beaver skins, wampum, and, in Virginia, tobacco, soon became the commonly accepted local media of exchange for all other available commodities that were not bartered. The immigrants, in fact, had little use for coined money at first; but when merchandise arrived from Europe, coins were usually demanded in payment for goods.

Nearly all foreign coins were accepted for purchases. The most popular were French louis, English guineas, German thalers, Dutch ducats, and various Spanish coins, including doubloons and, particularly, the Spanish milled dollar, or piece of eight. The piece of eight continued to be a standard money unit throughout the entire colonial period. Even after the Revolutionary War ended (in 1783) and the United States Mint was established (in 1792), the Spanish dollar and its fractional parts circulated in this country with official sanction, until 1859. One *real* equaled 12-1/2 cents and was known as a *bit*. A quarter of the dollar thus became known as *two bits*, a term that is still understood to mean 25 cents.

Because of the shortage of small change, large coins were sometimes cut into smaller pieces for convenience. Spanish pistareens and Spanish-American milled dollars were often chopped into halves, quarters, or eighths. Fraudulent cutting into five or six "quarters" caused many to distrust these cut pieces.

England consistently ignored the plight of its American colonists and made no effort to provide gold or silver coins, or small change in any form, for their convenience. The English mercantile system relied on exports from the colonies, and sought to control trade by limiting the amount of "hard" money paid to them. Under these constraints, the colonists were able to trade only with England for necessities, and were left with very little coinage that could be used in other countries. The foreign coins that were sometimes available were a valuable commodity for purchases outside the normal English trade.

As a remedy for the dearth of circulating coinage, a wide assortment of foreign coins and tokens were pressed into use, but only a very few were made in America prior to 1783. Copper coins known as *Hogge Money* (from their design; see page 34) were privately made for the Sommer Islands, now known as Bermuda, about the year 1616. The first coins minted for the colonies in America were made by John Hull in Boston for the Massachusetts Bay Colony. The General Court of the colony granted him authority to begin coinage, despite the possibility of objection and recrimination by the King of England. Starting in 1652 the Massachusetts minter began producing the famous NE, Willow, Oak, and Pine Tree shillings, with their fractional parts, for the convenience of the colonists. This venture, which defied English law and lasted from 1652 to 1682, was in a sense the first declaration of independence for the colonies.

As time passed, coins and tokens of many types were introduced and employed by the colonists to supplement their use of barter. Lord Baltimore was responsible for a small issue of silver pieces struck in England in 1659 and sent to Maryland for use there. Mark Newby imported from Ireland coins known as *St. Patrick's halfpence*, for use in the province of New Jersey in 1682. Coins dated 1722 to 1724, known as *Rosa Americana* and *Hibernia* coppers, were produced by William Wood in England and were widely circulated in America. There were also a few other issues, such as the Hibernia–Voce Populi coins, and the Elephant tokens, which likely circulated among the early settlers.

Enterprising American individuals were responsible for some of the other copper pieces that circulated during the 18th century. The Gloucester token, about which little is known, was one of these. Samuel and John Higley of Granby, Connecticut, made an interesting series of threepence pieces during the period from 1737 to 1739. J. Chalmers, a silversmith in Annapolis, Maryland, issued silver shillings, sixpence, and threepence pieces in 1783. In 1787 Ephraim Brasher, a New York goldsmith, struck a gold piece of the value of a doubloon (about $15 in New York currency). Standish Barry of Baltimore, Maryland, made a curious silver threepence token in 1790.

Still other tokens, struck in England, reached our shores in Revolutionary times and were for the most part speculative ventures. These much-needed, small-denomination coppers were readily circulated because of the great scarcity of fractional coins. Included in this category were the Nova Constellatio coppers and various English merchants' tokens.

During the period of turmoil following America's War of Independence, from about 1781 to 1794, still more English copper pieces were added to the great variety of coins and tokens employed in the new nation. It was a time when Americans were suffering from postwar economic depression, a shortage of currency, high taxes, and foreclosures from bankruptcies. In 1787 the Nova Eborac pieces (known as *New York coppers*), the Georgivs Triumpho coppers, and the Auctori Plebis tokens found their way into circulation as small change, despite their unofficial nature.

Collectors of colonial coins also include other pieces that are interesting because of their close association with early America and its first president. These consist of the Kentucky, Myddelton, and Franklin Press tokens, and those pieces bearing the portrait of George Washington. Although most of these pieces are dated from 1783 to

1795, many of them were made in England around the turn of the 19th century, and few of them actually circulated in the United States.

## Coinage of the States

The Articles of Confederation, adopted March 1, 1781, provided that Congress should have the sole right to regulate the alloy and value of coin struck by its own authority or by that of the respective states. Each state, therefore, had the right to coin money, with Congress serving as a regulating authority. New Hampshire was the first state to consider coinage, but few if any of its copper coins were placed into circulation. The only specimens known bear the date 1776.

In the period from 1785 to 1788, Vermont, Connecticut, and New Jersey granted coining privileges to companies and individuals. Massachusetts erected its own mint in Boston, where copper coins were produced in 1787 and 1788. A number of interesting types and varieties of these state issues, most of which were struck in fairly large quantities, are still extant, and form the basis for many present-day collections and museum exhibits of early American coins.

## The Beginnings of United States Coinage

Throughout the years from 1620 to 1776, Americans were forced to rely on numerous European coins and denominations that had to be converted to some common value to facilitate transactions. Further compounding this mathematical obstacle was the variation of values from one colony to another. Merchants became accustomed to using the Spanish dollar and its fractional parts, the *real*, the *medio* (half-*real*), and other, similar denominations. In time, those coins became more familiar to them than the old English coins, which were always scarce. It was only natural, therefore, that when a national coinage was under consideration a dollar-size coin was the first choice.

Contracts, currency statutes, and prices in the colonies were usually quoted in English pounds or Spanish dollars. In 1767 Maryland took the lead and produced paper money that was denominated in dollars. Connecticut, Massachusetts, and Virginia soon passed laws making Spanish coins legal tender. The first issue of Continental paper money, May 10, 1775, offers further evidence that the dollar was to be the basic American money unit, for it provided that the notes should be payable in "Spanish Milled Dollars or the value thereof in gold or silver."

The assistant financier of the Confederation, Gouverneur Morris, proposed a decimal coinage ratio designed to make conversion of various foreign currencies easier to compute in terms of a dollar-size unit. His plan was incorporated into a report presented by Robert Morris, superintendent of finance, to the Congress, January 15, 1782. Plans for a mint were advanced, and a uniform national currency to relieve the confused money conditions was outlined. Morris's unit, 1/1,440 of a dollar, was calculated to agree without a fraction with all the different valuations of the Spanish milled dollar in the various states. Although a government mint was approved on February 21, 1782, no immediate action was taken. During 1784, Thomas Jefferson, then a member of the House of Representatives, brought in a report concerning the plan and expressed disagreement with Morris's complicated money unit. He advocated the simple dollar unit because he believed the dollar was already as familiar and convenient a unit of value as the British pound. He favored the decimal system, and remarked, "The most easy ratio of multiplication and division is that of ten." George Washington referred to it as 'a measure, which in my opinion, has become indispensably necessary.'"

The Grand Committee in May 1785 recommended a gold five-dollar piece; a dollar of silver with fractional coins of the same metal (in denominations of half, quarter, 10th, and 20th parts of a dollar); and copper pieces valued at 1/100 and 1/200 of a dollar.

In 1783 Robert Morris submitted a series of pattern pieces in silver that were designed by Benjamin Dudley to carry out the decimal idea for United States money. These are known as the Nova Constellatio patterns and consist of the "mark," or 1,000 units; the "quint," or 500 units; the "bit," or 100 units; and a copper "five." The unit was to be a quarter grain of silver. This was not the first attempt at a dollar coin, for the Continental Currency piece of dollar size, dated 1776, had been struck in such metals as brass, pewter, and silver. The variety in silver possibly saw limited service as a dollar, although there is a theory that the Continental Congress considered circulating pewter pieces as an emergency token coinage.

Congress gave formal approval to the basic dollar unit and decimal coinage ratio in its resolution of August 8, 1786, but other, more pressing matters delayed further action. Not until the Constitutional Convention of 1787 had placed the country on firm ground and the new nation had elected George Washington president did the Congress again turn attention to the subjects of currency, a mint, and a coinage system.

The Massachusetts cents and half cents struck in 1787 and 1788 were the first official coins to bear stated values in terms of decimal parts of the dollar unit in the United States. The cent represented a hundredth part of a Spanish dollar.

The first federally authorized coin was the Fugio cent (sometimes called the *Franklin cent*, as Benjamin Franklin is believed to have supplied the design and composed the legends). This piece, similar in design to the Continental Currency dollar of 1776, was privately struck in 1787 by contract with the government.

Alexander Hamilton, then secretary of the Treasury, reported his views on monetary matters on January 21, 1791. He concurred in all essentials with the decimal subdivisions and multiples of the dollar contained in the earlier resolutions, and urged the use of both gold and silver in U.S. standard money.

Congress passed a resolution on March 3, 1791, that a mint be established, and authorized President Washington to engage artists and procure machinery for the making of coins. No immediate steps were taken, but when President Washington delivered his third annual address, he recommended immediate establishment of a mint.

On April 2, 1792, a bill was finally passed providing "that the money of account of the United States should be expressed in dollars or units, dismes or tenths, cents or hundredths, and milles or thousandths; a disme being the tenth part of a dollar, a cent the hundredth part of a dollar, a mille the thousandth part of a dollar...."

Denominations specified in the act were as follows:

| | Value | Grains Pure | Grains Standard |
|---|---|---|---|
| Gold eagle | $10.00 | 247-4/8 | 270 |
| Gold half eagle | 5.00 | 123-6/8 | 135 |
| Gold quarter eagle | 2.50 | 61-7/8 | 67-4/8 |
| Silver dollar | 1.00 | 371-4/16 | 416 |
| Silver half dollar | .50 | 185-10/16 | 208 |
| Silver quarter dollar | .25 | 92-13/16 | 104 |
| Silver disme (dime) | .10 | 37-2/16 | 41-3/5 |
| Silver half disme | .05 | 18-9/16 | 20-4/5 |
| Copper cent | .01 | 11 pennyweights | |
| Copper half cent | .005 | 5-1/2 pennyweights | |

The word *pure* meant unalloyed metal; *standard* meant, in the case of gold, 11/12 fine, or 11 parts pure metal to one part alloy, which was mixed with the pure metal to improve the wearing qualities of the coins. The fineness for silver coins was 1,485/1,664, or approximately 892.43 thousandths, in contrast with the gold coins' 22 carats, or 916-2/3 thousandths fineness.

The law also provided for free coinage of gold and silver coins at the fixed ratio of

15 to 1, and a token coinage of copper cents and half cents. Under the free-coinage provision no charge was to be made for converting gold or silver bullion into coins "weight for weight." At the depositor's option, however, he could demand an immediate exchange of coins for his bullion, for which privilege a deduction of one-half of 1% was to be imposed.

President Washington appointed David Rittenhouse, a well-known scientist, as the first director of the Mint. Construction began on a mint building nearly four months after the passage of the Act of April 2, 1792. The building was located on Seventh Street near Arch in Philadelphia.

The first coin struck by the government was the half disme. Fifteen hundred of these pieces were produced during the month of July 1792 before the mint was completed. George Washington supplied some of his own silver in the form of bullion or tableware, in the value of about $100, to make those first coins. A few dismes were also struck at this time or a short while later. Silver and gold for coinage were to be supplied by the public, but copper for cents and half cents had to be provided by the government. This was accomplished by the Act of May 8, 1792, when the purchase of not over 150 tons was authorized. On September 11, 1792, six pounds of old copper were purchased, and probably used for the striking of patterns. Thereafter, planchets with upset rims for cents and half cents were purchased from Boulton and Watt of Birmingham, England, from 1798 to 1838.

Several pattern coins were prepared in 1792 before regular mint operations commenced. *Patterns* are test or trial pieces intended to show the size, form, and design of proposed coins. These included Henry Voigt's silver center cent, a piece smaller than that of regular issue. The small plug of silver, worth about three-quarters of a cent, was evidently intended to bring the intrinsic value of the coin up to the value of 1¢ and to permit production of a coin of more convenient size. Alexander Hamilton had mentioned a year before that the proposed "intrinsic value" cent would be too large, and suggested that the amount of copper could be reduced and a trace of silver added. The pattern cent with a silver center may have been designed to conform to this recommendation.

The cents by Robert Birch are equally interesting. These patterns are identified by their legends, which read LIBERTY PARENT OF SCIENCE AND INDUSTRY and TO BE ESTEEMED BE USEFUL. The quarter with an eagle on the reverse side, by Joseph Wright, belongs among the 1792 patterns devised before regular issues were struck.

The Bank of Maryland deposited the first silver, sending $80,715.73-1/2 in French coins to the mint on July 18, 1794. Moses Brown, a Boston merchant, deposited the first gold in the form of ingots (February 12, 1795) amounting to $2,276.22, receiving silver coin in payment. The first coins transferred to the treasurer consisted of 11,178 cents on March 1, 1793. The first return of coined silver was made on October 15, 1794, and the first gold coins (744 half eagles) were delivered July 31, 1795. The early Mint was constantly vigilant to see that the weights of these coins were up to standard. Blank planchets were filed and adjusted prior to striking, and many of the coins made prior to 1836 show file marks and blemishes from these adjustments.

## Regular Mint Issues

Cents and half cents, exclusively, were coined during the year 1793, and by 1799 approximately $50,000 in these coins had been placed in circulation. This amount proved insufficient for the requirements of commerce, and small-denomination coins of the states and of foreign countries continued in use well into the 19th century.

One of the most serious problems confronting commercial interests prior to 1857 was the failure of the government to provide a sufficient volume of circulating coins. The fault, contrary to popular opinion at the time, did not lie with any lack of effort on the part of the Mint. Other circumstances tended to interfere with the expected steady flow of new coinage into the channels of trade.

Free circulation of United States gold and silver coins was greatly hindered by speculators. For example, worn Spanish dollars of reduced weight and value were easily exchanged for U.S. silver dollars, which meant the export of most of the new dollars as fast as they were minted, and a complete loss to American trade channels.

Gold coins failed to circulate for similar reasons. The ratio of 15 to 1 between gold and silver was close to the world ratio when Alexander Hamilton recommended it in 1791, but by 1799 the ratio in European commercial centers had reached 15-3/4 to 1. At this rate, the undervalued gold coins tended to flow out of the country, or were melted for bullion. After 1800, therefore, United States gold coins were rarely seen in general circulation. As no remedy could be found, coinage of the gold eagle and the silver dollar was suspended by President Jefferson in 1804 and 1806, respectively. It is generally held that the silver dollar was discontinued in 1804, although the last coins minted for the period were dated 1803.

With the lack of gold coins and silver dollars, the half dollar became America's desirable coin for large transactions, bank reserves, and foreign payments. Until 1830, in fact, half dollars circulated very little as they were mainly transferred from bank to bank. This accounts for the relatively good supply of higher-condition half dollars of this period that is still available to collectors. A Senate committee of 1830 reported that United States silver coins were considered so much bullion and were accordingly "lost to the community as coins."

There was only a negligible coinage of quarters, dimes, and half dimes from 1794 to 1834. It has been estimated that there was less than one piece for each person in the country in the year 1830. This period has been described as one of chaotic currency made up of bank notes, underweight foreign gold coins, foreign silver coins of many varieties, and domestic fractional silver coins. Paper money of that time was equally bothersome. Privately issued bank notes sometimes had no backing and were apt to be worthless at the time of redemption. In this period, before national paper money commenced in 1861, notes of the so-called wildcat banks flooded the country and were much more common than silver coins.

On June 28, 1834, a new law was passed reducing the weight of standard gold, which had the effect of placing American money on a gold standard. Trade and finance greatly benefited from this act, which also proved a boon to the gold mines of Georgia and North Carolina. Branch mints in Dahlonega, Georgia, and Charlotte, North Carolina, were established in 1838 to handle the newly mined gold at the source. The Templeton Reid and Bechtler issues of private gold coins were struck in this area.

The law of January 18, 1837, completely revised and standardized the Mint and coinage laws. Legal standards, Mint charges, legal tender, Mint procedure, tolerance in coin weights, accounting methods, a bullion fund, standardization of gold and silver coins to 900 thousandths fineness, and other desirable regulations were covered by the new legislation. Results of importance to the collector were the changes in type for the various coin denominations and the resumption of coinage of the eagle in 1838 and larger quantities of silver dollars in 1840.

Prior to Andrew Jackson's election as president in 1828, the Second Bank of the United States had considerable control over the nation's currency. In 1832 Jackson vetoed a bill rechartering the bank, and transferred government deposits to state banks. The action took away some stability from an already shaky economy and eventually led to a national financial collapse. By 1836 the country was so deprived of circulating coinage that merchants resorted to making their own "hard times tokens" to facilitate trade. The few available government coins were hoarded or traded at a premium for unreliable private paper money.

The California gold discovery in 1848 was responsible for an interesting series of private, state, and territorial gold issues in the western states, culminating in the establishment of a branch mint at San Francisco in 1854.

Two new regular gold issues were adopted in 1849. In that year the double eagle and gold dollar joined the American family of coins. The California gold fields greatly influenced the world gold market, making the exportation of silver profitable. For example, the silver in two half dollars was worth $1.03-1/2 in gold. The newly introduced gold dollars soon took over the burden and hastened the disappearance of silver coins from trade channels. This was the situation when the new 3¢ postage rate brought about the bill authorized by Congress on March 3, 1851, calling for the coinage of a silver three-cent piece in 1851. This was the United States' first subsidiary coins in precious metals, for its value was intrinsically 86% of its face value, as an expedient designed to prevent its withdrawal from circulation.

The $3 gold piece was authorized by the Act of February 21, 1853. It was never a popular or necessary coin because of the existing $2.50 and $5 coins; it nevertheless was issued regularly from 1854 until 1889.

On February 21, 1853, fractional silver coins were made subsidiary by reduction of their weights. As the coins' face value now exceeded their bullion value, free coinage of silver was prohibited, and the Mint was authorized to purchase its silver requirements on its own account using the bullion fund of the Mint, and, according to law, "the profit of said coinage shall be…transferred to the account of the treasury of the United States."

To identify the new lightweight pieces, arrows were placed at the date on all silver coins except three-cent pieces, for which arrows were added to the reverse. Dollars, which were not reduced in weight, were not marked in any way. On the quarters and half dollars of 1853, rays were added on the reverse to denote the change of weight. In 1854, the rays were removed, and in 1856, the arrows disappeared from all but the silver three-cent coins. Production of silver coins in large quantities during this period greatly relieved the demands on gold dollars and three-cent pieces. Consequently, for the first time in the nation's history there was a supply of fractional coins in general circulation sufficient to facilitate commerce.

The Coinage Act of February 21, 1857, was designed primarily to reform the copper coinage. Although large cents and half cents are interesting and valuable in the eyes of the modern collector, they were unpopular with the American public in the 1850s because of their size. They also cost the Mint too much to produce.

The new law abolished the half cent, and reduced the size and changed the design of the cent. The new Flying Eagle cent contained 88% copper and 12% nickel. Nearly 1,000 pattern cents were stamped from dies bearing the date 1856, although no authority for the issue existed before 1857. Other important effects of the law were the retirement of Spanish silver coins from circulation, and dispersal of the new cents in such excessive quantities as to create a nuisance to business houses, particularly in the eastern cities. The Indian Head design replaced the Flying Eagle in 1859, and in 1864 the weight of the cent was further reduced and its composition changed to a proportion of 95% copper and 5% tin and zinc. (This bronze composition was the standard for the cent except for the years 1943 and 1944–1946. In 1962 the alloy was changed to 95% copper and 5% zinc. In 1982 the composition was changed to 97.5% zinc and 2.5% copper.)

The abundance of copper coins turned to scarcity following the outbreak of the Civil War. Anticipation of a scarcity of hard money, and depreciation of the value of paper money, induced hoarding. The large volume of greenbacks in circulation caused a premium on gold. Subsidiary silver, as a result of the sudden depreciation, quickly vanished from circulation. As an expediency, some people made use of postage stamps for small change. Merchants, banks, and individuals produced a wide variety of small-denomination paper scrip and promissory notes to meet their needs. In 1862 the government produced its first issue of "Postage Currency" and subsequent fractional notes. In 1863 a great number of privately issued copper tokens appeared to help fill the void. As with the tokens of 1837, they were of two general classes: tradesmen's tokens and imitations of official cents. Many of the latter were political or patriotic in character and carried slogans typical of the times. They not only served as a medium of exchange, but also often advertised merchants or products, and were usually produced at a profit.

The Coinage Act of April 22, 1864, which effected changes in the cent, provided also for the new bronze two-cent piece. The act, moreover, provided legal tender status for these two coins up to 10 times their face value. The two-cent piece was the first coin to bear the motto IN GOD WE TRUST. The new coin was at first readily accepted by the public, but proved an unnecessary denomination because of the competing three-cent coins, and production was halted after only nine years. Treasury Secretary Salmon P. Chase had issued a great many currency notes of the three-cent denomination early in 1865. The nickel interests seized upon this circumstance to fight for a new three-cent coin for redemption of the paper money. A law was quickly passed and signed by President Abraham Lincoln on March 3, 1865, providing for a three-cent coin of 75%-25% copper-nickel composition. The United States then possessed two types of three-cent pieces, although neither was seriously needed. The nickel three-cent piece was struck continuously until 1889, the silver three-cent piece until 1873.

The new copper-nickel alloy ratio was selected for the five-cent coin, adopted May 16, 1866, and thereafter known as a *nickel*. Again, the people had a coin denomination available to them in two forms. The silver half dime, like the three-cent piece, was retired from service in 1873 to curb the use of silver.

The great influx of silver from the Comstock Lode in Nevada increased the nation's supply of silver coins and taxed the Philadelphia Mint's capacity for production. Pressure from silver-mine interests in Nevada influenced the opening of a special mint in Carson City to assay and mint silver locally, rather than having it shipped to Philadelphia or San Francisco. Production was inefficient, costly, and slow. By 1893 the lode was virtually depleted, and minting activities ceased.

The Law of March 3, 1871, was a redemption measure and was passed to provide the United States Treasury with means for the disposal of millions of minor coins, which had accumulated in the hands of postmasters, merchants, and others. Small-denomination coins, because of this new law, were placed on an equal footing with silver and could be redeemed when presented in lots of $20.

There was a general revision of the coinage laws in 1873. Several years of study and debate preceded the final enactment. The legislative history of the bill occupies hundreds of pages of the *Congressional Globe*, and the result was considered by many a clumsy attempt and a failure. The law has sometimes been referred to as the "Crime of '73." One consequence of the bill, which achieved final enactment on February 12, 1873, was the elimination of the silver dollar. In its stead, the trade dollar of greater weight was provided for use in commerce with the Orient in competition with the Mexican dollar. The legal tender provision, which gave the trade dollar currency within U.S. borders, was repealed the following year to avoid profiteers' buying them overseas at a reduced rate. The trade dollar was thus the only United States coin ever demonetized. (Through an oversight, it was reinstated under the Coinage Act of 1965.)

It may be a surprise to some collectors to learn that silver dollars did not circulate to any great extent in the United States after 1803. The coin was turned out steadily since 1840, but for various reasons (such as exportation, melting, and holding in bank vaults), the dollar was virtually an unknown coin. The Law of 1853 in effect demonetized silver and committed the country to gold as a single standard. The silver-mining interests came to realize what had occurred a little later, and the ensuing quarter century of political and monetary history was filled with their voluble protests. There was a constant bitter struggle for the return to bimetallism.

From an economic point of view the inadequate supply of gold was responsible for a steady decline in prices worldwide. This brought about a gradual business depression in the United States, particularly in the South and Midwest. Private silver interests influenced great sections of the West for bimetallism as a remedy for the failing price level. Authorities have concluded that a worldwide adoption of bimetallism would have improved economic conditions; but, had the United States alone proceeded to place its money on a double standard at the old 16-to-1 ratio, the situation would only have worsened.

Of particular importance to collectors were those features of the Law of 1873 that affected the statuses and physical properties of the individual coins. The weights of the half dollar, quarter, and dime were slightly changed, and arrows were placed at the date for the ensuing two years to indicate the differences in weight. Silver three-cent pieces, half dimes, and two-cent pieces were abolished by the act, and the manufacture of minor coins was restricted to the Philadelphia Mint.

The short-lived twenty-cent piece was authorized March 3, 1875. It was created for the western states, where the Spanish "bit" had become equivalent to a U.S. dime. The five-cent piece did not circulate there, so when a quarter was offered for a "bit" purchase, only a dime was returned in change. The so-called double dime was frequently confused with the quarter dollar and was issued for circulation only in 1875 and 1876.

On February 28, 1878, Congress passed the Bland-Allison Act, which restored legal tender character to silver money. It required the Treasury to purchase at market price two to four million dollars' worth of silver each month and to coin it into silver dollars at a ratio to gold of 16 to 1. Proponents of "free silver" contended that with more money in circulation, workers would receive higher wages. Business leaders argued for the gold standard and against free silver because they believed that inflation would cheapen the value of money. The act was called by some "a wretched compromise."

The North and East so disliked the silver dollars that the coins did not actively circulate there and eventually found their way back to the Treasury, mostly through tax payments. Treasury Secretary Daniel Manning transferred ownership to the people and removed the coins from Treasury holdings by the simple expedient of issuing Silver Certificates in small bills to effect a wide circulation.

The Bland-Allison Act was repealed in 1890 and the Sherman Act took its place. Under this new law, 4,500,000 ounces of silver per month could be paid for with Treasury Notes that were to be legal tender, and redeemable in gold or silver dollars coined from the bullion purchased. Important in this case was the fact that the notes were constantly being redeemed for gold that mainly was exported. The measure was actually a government subsidy for a few influential silver miners, and as such it was marked for failure. It was hastily repealed. The Bland-Allison Act and the Sherman Act added a total of 570 million silver dollars to the nation's monetary stocks.

The Gold Standard Act of 1900 again gave the country a single standard, but reaffirmed the fiction that the silver dollar was a standard coin. It still enjoyed unlimited legal tender, but was as much a subsidiary coin, practically speaking, as the dime, for its value in terms of standard gold, even before the gold-surrender executive order, was far below its face value.

The lapse in coinage after 1904 and until 1921 was due to lack of demand. Legislation authorizing further metal supplies for silver dollars was not forthcoming until 1918, when the Pittman Act provided silver for more dollars.

Before the First World War the value of gold was equal to the value of gold coined into money. In order to encourage a steady flow of gold to the mints, the government (with the exception of the period 1853–1873) had adopted a policy of gratuitous

# WELCOME TO NUMISMATICS

coinage. The cost of converting gold into coin had generally been considered an expense chargeable to the government.

In practice, the Mint made fine bars for commercial use, or mint bars for coinage, at its discretion. The bars in later years were stored in vaults and Gold or Silver Certificates issued in place of the coins.

On April 5, 1933, President Franklin Roosevelt issued an order prohibiting banks from paying out gold and Gold Certificates without permission, and gold currency was thus kept for reserve purposes. The law was intended to stabilize the value of gold. In effect, it removed all gold from circulation and prevented it from being hoarded or even saved by collectors. Gold imports and newly mined domestic gold could be sold only to the government. Today, gold bullion and coins may be collected and saved by anyone, as all restrictions were removed in 1975.

Under the Coinage Act of 1965, the compositions of dimes, quarters, and half dollars were changed to eliminate or reduce the silver content of these coins because the price of silver had risen to above their face values. The replacement "clad" dimes and quarters were composed of an outer layer of copper-nickel (75%-25%) bonded to an inner core of pure copper. Beginning in 1971 the half dollar and dollar compositions were changed to that of the dime and quarter. All silver clad coins have an outer layer of 80% silver bonded to an inner core of 21% silver, with a total content of 40% silver.

By the Law of September 26, 1890, changes in designs of United States coins cannot be made more often than once every 25 years without congressional approval. Since that date, there have been design changes in all denominations, and there have been many gold and silver commemorative issues. In 1999, a 10-year program was started to honor each of the individual states by using special designs on the reverse of the quarter. The five-cent coin has also experienced recent design changes. These factors, and a growing awareness of the value and historical importance of older coins, are largely responsible for the ever-increasing interest in coin collecting in the United States.

## MINTS AND MINTMARKS

Mintmarks are small letters designating where coins were made. Coins struck at Philadelphia before 1979 (except 1942–1945 five-cent pieces) do not have mintmarks. Starting in 1979, a letter P was used on the dollar, and thereafter on all other denominations except the cent. Mintmark position is on the reverse of nearly all coins prior to 1965 (the cent is an exception), and on the obverse after 1967. Letters used are as follows:

    C—Charlotte, North Carolina (gold coins only; 1838–1861)
    CC—Carson City, Nevada (1870–1893)
    D—Dahlonega, Georgia (gold coins only; 1838–1861)
    D—Denver, Colorado (1906 to date)
    O—New Orleans, Louisiana (1838–1861; 1879–1909)
    P—Philadelphia, Pennsylvania (1793 to date; P not used in early years)
    S—San Francisco, California (1854 to date)
    W—West Point, New York (1984 to date)

All dies for United States coins were made at the Philadelphia Mint prior to 1996. Some dies are now made at the Denver Mint. Dies for use at other mints are made with the appropriate mintmarks before they are shipped to those mints. Because this was a hand operation prior to 1985, the exact positioning and size of the mintmarks may vary slightly, depending on where and how deeply the punches were impressed. This also accounts for double-punched and superimposed mintmarks such as the 1938 D Over D, and D Over S, Buffalo nickels. Polishing of dies may also alter the apparent size of fine details. Occasionally the mintmark is inadvertently left off a die sent to a branch mint, as was the case with some of the recent Proof dimes. Similarly, some 1982 dimes without mintmarks were made as circulation strikes. The mintmark M was used on coins made in Manila for the Philippines from 1925 through 1941.

Prior to 1900, punches for mintmarks varied greatly in size. This is particularly noticeable in the 1850 to 1880 period, in which the letters range from very small to very large. An attempt to standardize sizes started in 1892 with the Barber series, but exceptions are seen in the 1892-O half dollar and 1905-O dime, both of which have normal and "microscopic" mintmarks. A more or less standard-size, small mintmark was used on all minor coins starting in 1909, and on all dimes, quarters, and halves after the Barber series was replaced in 1916. Slight variations in mintmark size occur through 1945, with notable differences in 1928, when small and large S mintmarks were used.

In recent years a single D or S punch has been used to mark all branch-mint dies. The change to the larger D for Denver coins occurred in 1933. Nickels, dimes, half dollars, and dollars of 1934 exist with either the old, smaller-size mintmark or the new, larger-size D. All other denominations of 1934 and after are standard. The San Francisco mintmark was changed to a larger size during 1941 and, with the exception of the half dollar, all 1941-S coins are known with either small or large mintmarks. Halves were not changed until 1942, and the 1942-S and 1943-S pieces exist both ways. The 1945-S dime with "microscopic" S is an unexplained use of a punch originally intended for Philippine coins of 1907 through 1920. In 1979, the punches were replaced. Varieties of some 1979 coins appear with either the old- or new-shaped S or D. The S punch was again replaced in 1982 with a punch that yielded a more distinct letter.

Mintmark application technique for Proof coins was changed in 1985, and for circulation-strike production in 1990 and 1991, when the letter was applied directly to the production hub rather than being hand punched on each working die. At the same time, all the mintmark letters were made much larger and clearer than those of previous years.

## QUANTITIES OF COINS STRUCK

Collectors are cautioned that Mint reports are not always reliable for estimating the rarities of coins. In the early years of the Mint, dies of previous years were often used until they became worn or broken. It should also be emphasized that quantities reported, particularly for gold and silver, cover the number of coins struck and have no reference to the quantity reaching actual circulation. Many issues were deposited in the Treasury as backing for paper currency and were later melted.

Gold coins struck before August 1, 1834, are rare today, because from 1821 onward (and at times before 1821), the gold in the coins was worth more than their face values indicated. Such coins were struck as bullion and traded at a premium above face value.

The quantities reported by the Mint of three-dollar gold pieces from 1873 to 1877 and half cents from 1832 to 1836 are subject to doubt.

Coinage figures shown for 1964 through 1966 are for coins bearing those dates. Some of them were struck in more than one year and at various mints, both with and without mintmarks. In recent years, mintage figures reported by the Mint have been revised several times and remain uncertain as to precise amounts.

Mintage quantities are shown adjacent to each date throughout this book. Figures shown in italic are estimates based on the most accurate information available. Exact mintage figures for most Proof pre-1878 minor coins, and most pre-1860 silver and gold coins, are not known. Reported figures are occasionally revised when new information becomes available. Proof totals are shown in parentheses, and are not included with coins made for circulation.

## RARE COINS AS AN INVESTMENT

Investing in rare coins can be a rewarding experience for anyone who approaches the calling armed with the right attitude and background knowledge about this exciting field. It can just as easily become a costly mistake for anyone who attempts to profit from coins without giving serious thought to the idiosyncrasies of this unique market.

The best advice given to anyone considering investing in rare coins is to use common sense. No thinking person would consider buying a diamond ring from a street peddler, or an art masterpiece at a garage sale. It is just the same with rare coins, and the more careful you are in selecting a qualified dealer and making an educated evaluation of the coins you purchase, the greater will be your chance of making a profitable investment.

The opportunities for successful collecting and investing in quality numismatic items are as great today as at any time in the past. Inexperienced buyers can now purchase coins that have been graded and authenticated by third-party services to assure the quality of each item. Coins that are independently graded by these professional services are sealed in plastic holders, called *slabs*, to identify and protect them. There is also more written information available for beginners than ever before. The pricing of rare coins is very competitive in today's widespread market, where profit margins are often lower than in the past.

The shift in emphasis from collecting to investing has created a new market and demand for coins, resulting in more stringent grading methods and in pricing geared to the perceived rarity of coins in various levels of uncirculated perfection. Coins in high grades of condition that have been certified and encapsulated ("slabbed") may be valued at multiples of similar coins that have not been so treated. The "raw" (non-serviced) coins that are listed in this guidebook are valued at what collectors normally pay for such items without encapsulation, and in many cases will be lower than what is charged for "investment" (slabbed) coins.

For hundreds of years, rare coins and precious metals have proven themselves to be an excellent hedge against inflation and a source of ready money in times of disaster. There is no reason to think that this will change in the future. Gone are the days when coin collecting was only a passive hobby for those who would study the history and artistry of these enjoyable objects. The activity has grown to the point that speculation on the future demand for rare coins has made them a part of many investment portfolios.

With this change in attitude about collecting has come a measure of concern for those who purchase coins without the background or experience necessary to avoid costly mistakes. The buyer must beware of overpriced or overgraded coins that simply are not worth what is charged for them. This is especially true of coins that are offered for sale or at auction over the Internet, where it is often not possible to examine the items carefully enough to determine authenticity or grade. Extreme caution is advised for anyone considering an investment in expensive coins. Investigate the person or firm with whom you are dealing. Seek professional, unbiased help with grading determinations. Satisfy yourself that the coins you select are authentic and are not priced considerably higher than is being charged by other dealers.

Protecting valuable coins from deterioration is an important part of investing. They should also be insured and kept in a secure place. The best protection for keeping coins pristine is to store them in inert, airtight plastic holders (the encapsulated slabs are a good example), and away from paper products, cigarette smoke, wood, natural rubber, paint, and textiles such as wool or felt. Humidity greater than 75% can also be harmful and should be avoided.

Collectors and investors alike can profit by investigating the background and history of the coins they buy. Coins are a mirror of history and art, telling the story of mankind over the past 2,600 years and reflecting the economic struggles, wars, prosperity, and creativity of every major nation on earth. We are but the custodians of these historical relics; we must appreciate and care for them while they are in our possession. Those who treat rare coins with the consideration and respect they deserve will profit in many ways, not the least of which can be in the form of a sound financial return on one's investment of time and money.

## CHECKING YOUR COINS FOR AUTHENTICITY

Coin collectors occasionally encounter counterfeit coins, or coins that have been altered or changed so that they appear to be something other than what they really are. Any coin that does not seem to fit the description of similar pieces listed in this guide book should be looked upon with suspicion. Experienced coin dealers can usually tell quickly whether a coin is genuine, and would never knowingly sell spurious coins to a collector. Coins found in circulation or bought from a nonprofessional source should be examined carefully.

The risk of purchasing a spurious coin can be minimized through the use of common sense and an elementary knowledge of the techniques used by counterfeiters. It is well to keep in mind that the more popular a coin is among collectors and the public, the more likely it is that counterfeits and replicas will abound. Generally, collector coins valued at under $100 are rarely replicated because of the high cost of making such items. The same is true of counterfeits that are made to deceive the public. In modern times, few counterfeit coins have been made because it is more profitable for the fakers to print paper money.

### Replicas

Reproductions of famous and historical coins have been distributed for decades by marketing firms and souvenir vendors. These pieces are often tucked away by the original recipients as curios, and later are found in old furniture by others who believe they have discovered objects of great value. Most replicas are poorly made by the casting method, and are virtually worthless. They can sometimes be identified by a seam that runs around the edge of the piece where the two halves of the casting mold were joined together. Genuine specimens of extremely rare or valuable coins are almost never found in unlikely places.

### Counterfeits

For many centuries, counterfeiters have produced base-metal forgeries of gold and silver coins to deceive the public in the normal course of trade. These pieces are usually crudely made and easily detected on close examination. Crudely cast counterfeit copies of older coins are the most prevalent. These can usually be detected by the casting bubbles or pimples that can be seen with low-power magnification. Pieces struck from handmade dies are more deceptive, but the engravings do not match those of genuine Mint products.

More recently, as coin collecting has gained popularity and rare coin prices have risen, "numismatic" counterfeits have become more common. The majority of these are die-struck gold coin counterfeits that have been mass produced overseas since 1950. Forgeries exist of most U.S. gold coins dated between 1870 and 1933, as well as all issues of the gold dollar and three-dollar gold piece. Most of these are very well made, as they were intended to pass the close scrutiny of collectors. Few gold coins of earlier dates have been counterfeited, but false 1799 ten-dollar gold pieces and 1811 five-dollar coins have been made. Gold coins in less than Extremely Fine condition are seldom counterfeited.

Silver dollars dated 1804, Lafayette dollars, several of the low-mintage commemorative half dollars, and the 1795 half dimes have been forged in quantity. Minor-coin forgeries made in recent years are the 1909-S V.D.B., 1914-D and 1955 doubled die Lincoln cents, 1877 Indian Head cents, 1856 Flying Eagle cents, and, on a much smaller scale, a variety of dates of half cents and large cents. Nineteenth-century copies of colonial coins are also sometimes encountered.

## Alterations

Coins are occasionally altered by the addition, removal, or change of a design feature (such as a mintmark or date digit) or by the polishing, sandblasting, acid etching, toning, or plating of the surface of a genuine piece. Changes of this sort are usually done to deceive collectors. Among U.S. gold coins, only the 1927-D double eagle is commonly found with an added mintmark. On $2.50 and $5 gold coins, 1839 through 1856, New Orleans O mintmarks have been altered to C (for Charlotte, North Carolina) in a few instances.

Over a century ago, five-dollar gold pieces were imitated by gold plating 1883 Liberty Head five-cent coins without the word CENTS on the reverse. Other coins commonly created fraudulently through alteration include the 1799 large cent and the 1909-S, 1909-S V.D.B., 1914-D, 1922 "plain," and 1943 "copper" cents. The 1913 Liberty Head nickel has been extensively replicated by alteration of 1903 and 1912 nickels. Scarce, high-grade Denver and San Francisco Buffalo nickels of the 1920s; 1916-D and 1942 Over 1941 dimes; 1918 Over 1917-S quarters; 1932-D and -S quarters; and 1804 silver dollars have all been made by the alteration of genuine coins of other dates or mints.

## Detection

The best way to detect counterfeit coins is to compare suspected pieces with others of the same issue. Carefully check size, color, luster, weight, edge devices, and design details. Replicas generally have less detail than their genuine counterparts when studied under magnification. Modern struck counterfeits made to deceive collectors are an exception to this rule. Any questionable gold coin should be referred to an expert for verification.

Cast forgeries are usually poorly made and of incorrect weight. Base metal is often used in place of gold or silver, and the coins are lightweight and often incorrect in color and luster. Deceptive cast pieces have been made using real metal content and modern dental techniques, but these too usually vary in quality and color.

Detection of alterations sometimes involves comparative examination of the suspected areas of a coin (usually mintmarks and date digits) at magnification ranging from 10x to 40x.

Coins of exceptional rarity or value should never be purchased without a written guarantee of authenticity. Professional authentication of rare coins for a fee is available with the services offered by commercial grading services, and by some independent coin dealers.

# COINS FROM TREASURES AND HOARDS: A KEY TO UNDERSTANDING RARITY AND VALUE

*by Q. David Bowers*

## Elements of Rarity

In many instances, the mintage of a coin can be a determinant of its present-day rarity and value. However, across American numismatics there are many important exceptions, some very dramatic. Some of these situations are well known, others less so. On the following pages I discuss famous hoards, finds, and treasures as well as some that are not so well known.

## Perplexing Silver Dollars

As an introduction and example, if you peruse this issue of the *Guide Book* you will find many listings of Morgan silver dollars of 1878 through 1921 for which the mintage figure does not seem to correlate with a coin's price. For example, among such coins the 1901, of which 6,962,000 were made for circulation, is valued at $225,000 in MS-65. In the same series the 1884-CC, of which only 1,136,000 were struck, is listed at $500, or only a tiny fraction of the value of a 1901.

Why the difference? The explanation is that nearly all of the 6,962,000 dollars of 1901 were either placed into circulation at the time, and became worn, or were melted generations ago. Very few were saved by collectors, and today MS-65 coins are extreme rarities. On the other hand, of the 1,126,000 1885-CC silver dollars minted, relatively few went into circulation. Vast quantities were sealed in 1,000-coin cloth bags and put into government storage. Generations later, as coin collecting became popular, thousands were paid out by the Treasury Department. Years after that, in the early 1960s, when silver metal rose in value, there was a "run" on long-stored silver dollars, and it was learned in March 1964 that 962,638 1884-CC dollars—84.7% of the original mintage—were still in the hands of the Treasury Department!

With this information, the price disparities become understandable. Even though the 1901 had a high mintage, few were saved, and although worn coins are common, gem MS-65 coins are rarities. In contrast, nearly all of the low-mintage 1885-CC dollars were stored by the government, and today most of them still exist, including some in MS-65 grade.

There are many other situations in which mintages are not particularly relevant to the availability and prices of coins today. Often a special circumstance will lead to certain coins' being saved in especially large quantities, later dramatically affecting the availability and value of such pieces. The following are some of those circumstances.

## Excitement of a New Design

In the panorama of American coinage, some new designs have captured the fancy of the public, who saved them in large quantities when they were released. In many other instances new designs were ignored, and coins slipped into circulation unnoticed.

In 1909, much publicity was given to the new Lincoln portrait to be used on the one-cent piece, replacing the familiar Indian Head motif. On the reverse in tiny letters were the initials, V.D.B., of the coin's designer, Victor David Brenner. The occasion was the 100th anniversary of Lincoln's birth. Coinage commenced at the Philadelphia and San Francisco mints. In total, 27,995,000 1909 V.D.B. cents were struck and 484,000 of the 1909-S V.D.B.

On August 2, 1909, the new cents were released to the public. A mad scramble ensued, and soon, banks had to ration the number paid out to any single individual, this being particularly true in the East. Interest in the West was less intense, and fewer coins were saved. A controversy arose as to the V.D.B. initials, and some newspaper notices complained that as Brenner had been paid for his work, there was no point in giving his initials a prominent place on the coins. Never mind that artists' initials had been used on other coins for a long time. As examples, the M initial of George T. Morgan appeared on both the obverse and reverse of silver dollars from 1878 onward; Chief Engraver Charles E. Barber was memorialized by a B on the neck of Miss Liberty on dimes, quarters, and half dollars from 1892 onward; and the recent (1907 onward) double eagles bore the monogram of Augustus Saint-Gaudens prominently on the obverse. The offending V.D.B. initials were removed, and later 1909 and 1909-S cents were made without them.

Word spread that the cents with V.D.B. would be rare, and even more were saved. Today, the 1909 V.D.B. cents are readily available in Mint State. The 1909-S V.D.B., of lower mintage and of which far fewer were saved, lists for $2,200 in MS-63.

A few years later, at the Denver Mint, 1,193,000 1914-D cents were struck. Not much attention was paid to them, and today examples are rare, with an MS-63 listing for $3,000. Years later, only 866,000 1931-S cents were made. However, at this time there was a strong and growing interest in the numismatic hobby, and the low mintage figure was widely publicized; and although the mintage of the 1931-S is lower than for the 1914-D, an MS-63 1931-S is valued at just $125.

## Other Popular First-Year Coins

Among other United States coins struck since 1792, these first-year-of issue varieties (a partial list) were saved in large numbers and are especially plentiful today:

- **1943 zinc-coated steel cent.** The novel appearance of this coin resulted in many being saved as curiosities.
- **1883 Liberty Head nickel without cents.** The Mint expressed the value of this new design simply as "V," without mention of cents—not particularly unusual, as three-cent pieces of the era were simply denominated as "III." Certain people gold-plated the new nickels and passed them off as five-dollar gold coins of similar diameter. Soon, the Mint added CENTS. News accounts were printed that the "mistake" coins without CENTS would be recalled and would become very rare. So many were saved that today this variety is the most plentiful in Mint State of any Liberty Head nickel in the entire series from 1883 to 1913.
- **1913 Buffalo nickel.** These were saved in large quantities, and today there are more Mint State coins of this year in existence than for any other issue of the next 15 years.
- **1837 Liberty Seated, No Stars half dime.** Several thousand or more were saved, a large number for a half dime of the era. Apparently, their cameo-like appearance made them attractive curiosities at the time, the same being true of the dimes of the same year.
- **1837 Liberty Seated, No Stars dime.** Somewhat over a thousand were saved, a large number for a dime of the era.
- **1916 "Mercury" dime.** Quantities were saved of the 1916 and 1916-S, the first year of issue. However, for some reason the low-mintage 1916-D was generally overlooked and today is very rare in Mint State.
- **1932 Washington quarter.** At the Philadelphia Mint, 5,504,000 were minted, and it is likely that several hundred thousand were saved, making them plentiful today. The 1932-D quarter was struck to the extent of 436,800, but for some reason was overlooked by the public, with the result that Mint State coins are rare today. On the other hand, of the 408,000 1932-S quarters struck, thousands were saved. Today, Mint State 1932-S quarters are at least 10 to 20 times more readily available than are equivalent examples of the higher-mintage 1932-D.
- **1999 onward, state quarters.** Beginning in 1999, five different quarter dollar designs were produced each year, with motifs observing the states in the order that they joined the Union. These coins were highly publicized, and many were, and still are, saved as souvenirs.
- **1964 Kennedy half dollar.** The popularity of the assassinated president was such that although hundreds of millions were minted, it is likely that most were saved as souvenirs. This was also the last year of the 90% silver-content half dollar made for circulation, further increasing its popularity.

- **2000 Sacagawea "golden dollar."** These coins, intended to be a popular substitute for paper dollars and to last much longer in circulation, were launched with much fanfare in 2000, and more than just a few were saved by the public. However, the coin did not catch on for general use in commerce. Later issues have been made for sale to collectors, not for circulation.
- **MCMVII (1907) High-Relief gold twenty-dollar coin.** Although only about 12,000 were minted, at least 6,000 survive today, mostly in Mint State. Released in December 1907, the coin, by famous sculptor Augustus Saint-Gaudens, created a sensation, and soon the coins were selling for $30 each. Today, Mint State coins are plentiful, but as the demand for them is extremely strong, choice specimens sell for strong prices. An MS-63 coin lists for $26,500.
- **1892 and 1893 World's Columbian Exposition commemorative half dollars.** These, the first commemorative half dollars, were widely publicized, and hundreds of thousands were saved. Today they are very common.

## Coins Few People Noticed

In contrast to the above, most coins of new designs attracted no particular notice, and examples were not saved in unusual quantities. In sharp contrast to the ultra-popular Kennedy half dollar of 1964, its predecessor design, the Franklin half dollar (launched in 1948), generated very little interest, and even numismatists generally ignored them—perhaps preferring the old Liberty Walking design that had been a favorite for a long time.

Although a long list could be made, here are some first-year-of-issue coins that were not noticed in their own time. Consequently, specimens range from scarce to rare in Mint State today:

- **1793 cent and half cent.** As popular as these may be today, in 1793 there was no known instance in which a numismatist or museum deliberately saved pieces as souvenirs.
- **1794–1795 half dime, half dollar, and silver dollar.** The Flowing Hair coins, highly desired today, seem to have attracted little notice in their time, and again there is no record of any having been deliberately saved.
- **1807 and related Capped Bust coinages.** The Capped Bust and related coins of John Reich, assistant engraver at the Mint, were first used in 1807 on the silver half dollar and gold five-dollar piece, and later on certain other denominations. Today these are extremely popular with collectors, but in their time they were not noticed, and few were saved in Mint State.
- **1839 Liberty Seated half dollar.** Today, examples are very elusive, particularly the very first version without drapery at the elbow. The variety attracted no notice when it was first issued, nor did the with-drapery issue that followed it.
- **1840 Liberty Seated dollar.** Specimens are very scarce in Mint State today and are virtually unknown in gem preservation.
- **1892 Barber dime, quarter dollar, and half dollar.** In 1892 the new Liberty Head design by Charles E. Barber replaced the long-lived Liberty Seated motif. The new coins received bad press notices, this unattributed item published in an 1892 newspaper being representative: "During the week which closed last Saturday some of the new coins issued by the United States government crept into circulation and were commented on by beholders from different points of view.... On one side there appears a spread-eagle and on the other the profile of a head surmounted by the legend: 'In God We Trust.' The eagle is a meager and ill-fed specimen of our noble bird and the profile is that of a goddess of liberty, though it looks like the head of the ignoble Emperor Vitellius with a goiter. To be extremely frank, these new coins are not artistic. Even this mild statement is unduly flattering to the designers.... The nation has

poor luck in getting up designs for coins. The reason is not apparent unless it be that sufficient inducements are not offered to bring our really good designers into competition...." Another factor detracting from public interest was the wide attention focused on the forthcoming commemorative half dollars of the World's Columbian Exposition. Not many of the new Barber coins were saved.

- **1938 Jefferson nickel.** Although the numismatic hobby was dynamic at the time, the new nickel design attracted little notice, and no unusual quantities were saved. The market was still reeling from the burst bubble of the 1935 through 1936 commemorative craze, and there was little incentive to save coins for investment.

## The 1962–1964 Treasury Release

The Bland-Allison Act of February 28, 1878, a political boondoggle passed to accommodate silver-mining interests in the West, mandated that the Treasury Department buy millions of ounces of silver each year and convert it to silver dollars. At the time, the world price of silver bullion was dropping, and there were economic difficulties in the mining states. From 1878 to 1904 and again in 1921, silver dollars of the Morgan design were minted under this legislation and subsequent acts, to the extent of 656,989,387 pieces. From 1921 to 1935, silver dollars of the Peace design were produced in the amount of 190,577,279 pieces.

Although silver dollars were used in commerce in certain areas of the West, paper currency by and large served the needs of trade and exchange. As these hundreds of millions of newly minted dollars were not needed, most were put up in 1,000-coin canvas bags and stored in Treasury vaults. In 1918, under terms of the Pittman Act, 270,232,722 Morgan dollars were melted. At the time, the market for silver was temporarily strong, and there was a call for bullion to ship to India. No accounting was kept of the dates and mints involved in the destruction. Just the quantities were recorded (this procedure being typical when the Treasury melted old coins). However, hundreds of millions remained.

Now and again there was a call for silver dollars for circulation, especially in the West; and in the East and Midwest there was a modest demand for pieces for use as holiday and other gifts; in such instances many were paid out. The earlier example of the high-mintage 1901 dollar being rare in Mint State, as most were circulated, is reflective of this. Others coins were stored, such as the aforementioned low-mintage 1884-CC, of which 84.7% were still in the hands of the Treasury as late as 1964! At this time the Treasury decided to hold back bags that were marked as having Carson City dollars, although in records of storage no account was made of them earlier.

Beginning in a significant way in the 1950s, silver dollars became very popular with numismatists. The rarest of all Morgan silver dollars by 1962 was considered to be the 1903-O. In the *Guide Book*, an Uncirculated coin listed for $1,500, the highest price for any variety. Experts estimated that fewer than a dozen Mint State coins existed in all of numismatics. It was presumed that most had been melted in 1918 under the Pittman Act.

Then this:

In November 1962, during the normal payout of silver dollars as gifts for the holiday season, some long-sealed bags of coins were taken from a Philadelphia Mint vault that had remained under seal since 1929. It was soon found that brilliant 1903-O dollars were among these! A treasure hunt ensued, and hundreds of thousands of these former rarities were found. The rush was on!

From then until March 1964, hundreds of millions of Morgan and Peace dollars were emptied from government and bank storage. At one time a long line of people, some with wheelbarrows, formed outside of the Treasury Building in Washington, DC, to obtain bags of dollars. Finally, only about three million coins remained, mostly the aforementioned Carson City issues, which the Treasury decided to hold back. These were later sold at strong premiums in a series of auctions held by the General Services Administration.

In the meantime, Morgan and Peace dollars became very large and important sections of the coin hobby, as they remain today. However, as can be seen, the combined elements of some coins' having been melted in 1918, others having been placed into circulation generations ago, and still others existing in Mint State from long-stored hoards, results in silver dollar prices that often bear little relation to mintage figures.

## Other Famous Hoards

While the great Treasury release of 1962 through 1964 is the most famous of all hoards, quite a few others have attracted interest and attention over the years. Here are some of them:

• ***Castine Hoard of Early Silver Coins* (discovered in the 1840s).** From November 1840 through April 1841, Captain Stephen Grindle and his son Samuel unearthed many silver coins on their farm on the Bagaduce River about six miles from the harbor of Castine, Maine. The number of pieces found was not recorded, but is believed to have been between 500 and 2,000, buried in 1690 (the latest date observed) or soon afterward. Most pieces were foreign silver coins, but dozens of Massachusetts Pine Tree shillings and related silver coins were found. This hoard stands today as one of the most famous in American history.

• ***Bank of New York Hoard* (1856).** Circa 1856, a keg containing several thousand 1787 Fugio copper cents was found at the Bank of New York at 44 Wall Street. Each was in Mint State, most with brown toning. For many years these were given out as souvenirs and keepsakes to clients. By 1948, when numismatist Damon G. Douglas examined them, there were 1,641 remaining. Today, many remain at the bank and are appreciated for their history and value.

• ***Nichols Find of Copper Cents* (by 1859).** In the annals of American numismatics, one of the most famous hoards is the so-called Nichols Find, consisting of 1796 and 1797 copper cents, Mint State, perhaps about 1,000 in total. These were distributed in the late 1850s by David Nichols. All were gone as of 1863, by which time they were worth $3 to $4 each, or less than a thousandth of their present-day value.

• ***Randall Hoard of Copper Cents* (1860s).** Sometime soon after the Civil War, a wooden keg filled with as-new copper cents was located in the South and was said to have been beneath an old railroad platform in Georgia. Revealed were thousands of coins dated 1816 to 1820, with the 1818 and 1820 being the most numerous. Today, the Randall hoard accounts for most known Mint State examples of these particular dates.

• ***Colonel Cohen Hoard of 1773 Virginia Halfpennies* (by the 1870s).** Sometime in the 1870s or earlier, Colonel Mendes I. Cohen, a Baltimore numismatist, obtained a cache of at least 2,200 Uncirculated specimens of the 1773 Virginia halfpenny. These passed through several hands, and many pieces were dispersed along the way. As a result, today these are the only pre-colonial (pre-1776) American coins that can be easily obtained in Mint State.

* *Exeter Hoard of Massachusetts Silver* **(1876).** During the excavation of a cellar near the railroad station in Exeter, New Hampshire, a group of 30 to 40 Massachusetts silver shillings was found in the sand, amid the remains of what seemed to be a wooden box. All bore the date 1652 and were of the Pine Tree and Oak Tree types, plus, possibly, a rare Willow Tree shilling.

* *Economite Treasure* **(1878).** In 1878 a remarkable hoard of silver coins was found in a subterranean storage area at Economy, Pennsylvania, in a building erected years earlier by the Harmony Society, a utopian work-share community. The March 1881 issue of the *Coin Collector's Journal* gave this inventory: Quarter dollars: 1818 through 1828, 400 pieces. Half dollars: 1794, 150; 1795, 650; 1796, 2; 1797, 1; 1801, 300; 1802, 200; 1803, 300; 1805 Over '04, 25; 1805, 600; 1806, 1,500; 1807, 2,000; 1815, 100. Common half dollars: 1808 through 1836, 111,356. Silver dollars: 1794, 1; 1795, 800; 1796, 125; 1797, 80; 1798 Small Eagle reverse, 30; 1798 Large Eagle reverse, 560; 1799 5 stars facing, 12; 1799, 1,250; 1800, 250; 1801, 1802, and 1803, 600. Foreign silver (French, Spanish, and Spanish-American), total face value: $12,600. Total face value of the hoard: $75,000.00. Other information indicates that most of the coins had been taken from circulation and showed different degrees of wear.

* *Hoard of Miser Aaron White* **(before 1888).** Aaron White, a Connecticut attorney, distrusted paper money and even went so far as to issue his own token, inscribed NEVER KEEP A PAPER DOLLAR IN YOUR POCKET TILL TOMORROW. He had a passion for saving coins and accumulated more than 100,000 pieces. After his death the coins were removed to a warehouse. Later, they were placed in the hands of dealer Édouard Frossard, who sold most of them privately and others by auction on July 20, 1888, billing them as "18,000 American and foreign copper coins and tokens selected from the Aaron White hoard." An overall estimate of the White hoard, as it existed before it was given to Frossard, was made by Benjamin P. Wright, and included these: "250 colonial and state copper coins, 60,000 copper large cents (which were mainly 'rusted' and spotted; 5,000 of the nicest ones were picked out and sold for 2¢ each), 60,000 copper-nickel Flying Eagle and Indian cents (apparently most dated 1862 and 1863), 5,000 bronze two-cent pieces, 200 half dollars, 100 silver dollars, 350 gold dollars, and 20,000 to 30,000 foreign copper coins."

* *Collins Find of 1828 Half Cents* **(1894).** Circa 1894, Benjamin H. Collins, a Washington, DC, numismatist, acquired a bag of half cents dated 1828, of the 13-stars variety. It is believed that about 1,000 coins were involved, all bright Uncirculated. By the early 1950s all but a few hundred had been distributed in the marketplace, and by now it is likely that all have individual owners.

* *Chapman Hoard of 1806 Half Cents* **(1906).** About 1906, Philadelphia dealer Henry Chapman acquired a hoard of 1806 half cents. Although no figure was given out at the time, it is estimated that a couple hundred or so coins were involved. Most or all had much of their original mint red color, with toning to brown, and with light striking at the upper part of the wreath.

* *Baltimore Find* **(1934).** One of the most storied hoards in American numismatics is the Baltimore Find, a cache of at least 3,558 gold coins, all dated before 1857.

On August 31, 1934, two young boys were playing in the cellar of a rented house at 132 South Eden Street, Baltimore, and found these coins hidden in a wall. Later, more were found in the same location. On May 2, 1935, many of the coins were sold at auction, by which time others had been sold privately, some unofficially. This hoard included many choice and gem coins dated in the 1850s.

• **New Orleans Bank Find** (1982). A few minutes past noon, on October 29, 1982, a bulldozer unearthed a cache of long-hidden silver coins, believed to have been stored in three wooden boxes in the early 1840s. The pieces were mostly Spanish-American issues, but hundreds of United States coins, including 1840-O and 1841-O Liberty Seated quarters, were also found. A scrabble in the dirt and mud ensued, and men in business suits, ladies in dresses, and others scrambled to find treasure. The latest dated coin found was from 1842. This must have been a secret reserve of some long-forgotten merchant or bank.

• **Wells-Fargo Hoard of 1908 $20** (1990s). In the 1990s, dealer Ron Gillio purchased a hoard of 19,900 examples of the 1908 No Motto double eagle. For a time these were stored in a Wells Fargo Bank branch, giving the name to the cache. All were Mint State, and many were of choice and gem quality. Offered in the market, these were dispersed over a period of several years.

• **Gold coins from abroad** (turn of the 21st century). In the late 20th century and in the first years of the 21st, some exciting finds of Mint State double eagles were located in foreign banks. Involved were high-grade examples of some Carson City issues in the Liberty Head series and hundreds of scarce-mintmark varieties of double eagles after 1923. As is often the case when hoards are discovered, pieces were filtered into the market without any publicity or an accounting of specific varieties found.

## Sunken Treasure

Throughout American history, tens of thousands of ships have been lost at sea and on inland waters. Only a handful of these vessels were reported as having had significant quantities of coins aboard.

In the late 20th and early 21st centuries, numismatists were front-row center as coins from several side-wheel steamers lost in the 1850s and 1860s yielded rare coins. Sketches of four of these ships are given here. Two of these, the SS *Yankee Blade* and the SS *Central America*, carried coins from the California gold rush.

The other two treasure ships, the SS *Brother Jonathan* and the SS *Republic*, were lost off the coasts of California and Georgia, respectively; each had double eagles and other coins on board.

## SS Yankee Blade, *Lost October 1, 1854*

The SS *Yankee Blade*, launched in 1853, was in the service of the Independent Steamship Co. in 1854. On October 1 she was on a run from San Francisco south to Panama, carrying about 900 passengers and crew and an unknown amount of gold, but including about $152,000 in coins consigned by the banking house of Page, Bacon & Co. In heavy fog Captain Henry T. Randall, believing he was in deep water far at sea, proceeded at full speed ahead, trying to establish a speed record—certain to be beneficial in advertising.

The captain was wrong, and the steamer was amid the rockbound Channel Islands, off the coast of Santa Barbara, California. The ship smashed onto a rock, and was stranded at a tipsy angle. In time, she sank, but not before most people escaped. In the ensuing confusion, an estimated 17 to 50 passengers lost their lives.

As to what happened to the gold coins aboard, some were seemingly recovered soon after the disaster, in circumstances shrouded in mystery. Perhaps other coins were found later, over a long period of time. In any event, in 1948 the hull was found again, and afterward various divers visited the wreck. Circa 1977, extensive recoveries were made, and an estimated 200 to 250 1854-S double eagles came on the market. All showed microscopic granularity, possibly from the action of sea-bottom sand, and all had die cracks on the reverse. Little in the way of facts has ever reached print.

## *SS* Central America, *Lost September 12, 1857*

In contrast to the preceding, in the annals of undersea treasure hunting the SS *Central America* has been extremely well documented. On August 20, 1857, more than 400 people, plus crew, and about $2,600,000 in gold treasure left San Francisco aboard the steamer SS *Sonora*, headed for Panama. The destination was reached in due course, and the passengers and gold crossed 48 miles of land on the Panama Railroad and arrived at the port city of Aspinwall on the Atlantic side.

On Thursday, September 3, SS *Central America* left Aspinwall. A stop was made at Havana on Monday, September 7. On the next morning the ship continued north toward New York City, its destination, where the gold coins and ingots would be received.

On Wednesday, September 9, a day out of Havana, the second officer noted in his records that a fresh breeze was kicking up swells. A tropical storm was in progress, but sure to fade in a day or so. Meanwhile, the large ship could handle any type of weather. However, matters went from bad to worse, and on Thursday the SS *Central America* was in the grip of a monster hurricane, one of the strongest on record.

On Friday the storm still raged, and the ship developed leaks in several places, flooding the lower areas. On the lower deck, the rising water and the violent tossing of the vessel made it virtually impossible to continue feeding coal to the boilers. At 11:00 in the morning, Captain William Lewis Herndon enlisted the aid of male passengers to form a bucket line to bail water, which proved to be futile. The ship became swamped and was at the mercy of the waves hitting broadside. By the next morning the decks were awash, and it was feared that the ship would be lost. The captain directed that the American flag be flown upside-down, a signal of distress.

Early in the afternoon the sail of the brig *Marine* came into sight, and soon the small ship drew near. In the following hours nearly all of the women and children were transferred to the *Marine*, and some crew members went also. A few minutes after 8:00 in the evening a huge wave hit the ship; she shuddered, timbers splintered, and with Captain Herndon standing on the paddle box, the SS *Central America* slipped below the waves. Although some passengers and crew were later rescued from the water, about 435 lives were lost. The hull settled at the bottom, 7,200 feet below the surface.

Overshadowed by the Panic of 1857, the Civil War, and other matters of national importance, the SS *Central America* was largely forgotten. Its location was not known, except that it had gone down somewhere along the planned route. In 1980 Tommy Thompson, a Columbus, Ohio, scientist, directed his efforts to finding the wreck, and in 1985 a group of entrepreneurs and investors formed the Columbus-America Discovery Group. After much effort, including the guidance of scientist Bob Evans, the long-lost ship was found, and recovery of gold coins and ingots was accomplished through the aid of the *Nemo*, a remote-controlled underwater device with arms that could retrieve the treasure carefully. When all was said and done, more than 5,400 mint-fresh 1857-S double eagles, several hundred gold ingots, and other coins were recovered.

The California Gold Marketing Group, under the direction of Dwight Manley, began the sale of the treasure coins and ingots in 2000, and within the next few years all were sold, for an estimated $100,000,000. As part of the project, Q. David Bowers created the 1,050-page book *A California Gold Rush History*, with extensive illustrations and information. As no larger Gold Rush–era treasure was ever lost, by definition no greater treasure can ever be found, making the SS *Central America* find a unique event.

## SS Brother Jonathan, *Lost January 30, 1865*

In 1865, the side-wheel steamer SS *Brother Jonathan* was important in the coastwise trade from California north to Oregon and Washington. Shortly before noon on Friday, July 28, the 1,360-ton vessel headed from San Francisco to Portland, carrying 150 or more passengers, a crew of about 60, and a 500-ton cargo ranging from machinery for a woolen mill to casks of whiskey. Gold coins were aboard, of an unknown value.

Heading along the coast the ship ran into high winds and waves, and Captain Samuel J. DeWolf put the vessel into the harbor at Crescent City to spend the night. In the morning the sea would be calm, it was thought. On Sunday, January 30, the crew resumed the trip, but the open sea was still rough, and the captain ordered the ship to turn around and go back to Crescent City. Unexpectedly, the ship struck a submerged rock, a pinnacle hidden just below the waves. Only a few passengers survived. In the best seafaring tradition, the captain went down with the ship.

In following years, many efforts were made to find the lost ship, but without success. Finally, in the 1990s a group of investors and entrepreneurs formed Deep Sea Research, Inc., found the ship, and were able to recover more than 1,000 gold coins, a find dominated by Mint State 1865-S double eagles. Detailed records and photographs preserve every element of the recovery—a model of undersea archaeological technique.

## SS Republic, *Lost October 25, 1865*

Originally christened the SS *Tennessee* in 1853, this sidewheel steamer served in both the Confederate and Union navies during the Civil War. Just months after the war's end, the SS *Republic*, loaded with much-needed cargo and coins, left New York bound for New Orleans. Caught in a hurricane off the coast of Georgia, the ship sank to the bottom of the Atlantic with a reported $400,000 in specie on board.

In 2003, the numismatic world was startled and delighted to learn that Odyssey Marine Exploration, Inc., had located the wreckage, in about 1,700 feet of water. Strewn on the sea floor was an array of gold and silver coins, along with about 14,000 other artifacts (bottles, ceramic items, personal effects, etc.). Recovery began in November 2003 and was concluded in early 2005, by which time 262 dives had been logged. The recovery included more than 51,000 coins, among them more than 1,400 gold eagles, dating from 1838 to 1858. The most numerous were those dated 1847 (of which 221 were found, mostly in AU grade). Several thousand double eagles of all date and mintmark issues from 1850 to 1865, except the 1856-O, were found. The varieties for which more than 100 coins each were brought to the surface included 1852 (104 recovered and assigned various grades), 1861 (457), 1862-S (127), 1863-S (180), 1864-S (168), 1865 (320), and 1865-S (253). After careful conservation by Numismatic Conservation Services, nearly all of the gold coins were found to be in pristine condition, with no impairment from their immersion. Conditions ranged from worn, for earlier years, up to choice and gem Mint State for certain of the later issues. The most valuable single coin was a Mint State 1854-O $20, valued at more than a half-million dollars. The talents of numismatist John Albanese were tapped to supervise the care and distribution of the coins.

More than 180 different varieties of Liberty Seated half dollars were recovered from the shipwreck, including five 1861-O die combinations attributed to Confederate control of the New Orleans mint. Many of the silver halves show only slight evidence of their 140 years underwater. Some coins have microscopic coralline structures embedded in their surfaces or some saltwater etching, in many cases observable only under a microscope. Although not graded on a traditional scale, the coins are encapsulated and noted as having a "Shipwreck Effect." Many of them exhibit nearly full detail and have become very popular in the collectibles marketplace because of this provenance.

## BRITISH NEW WORLD ISSUES
### Sommer Islands (Bermuda)

This coinage, the first struck for the English colonies in America, was issued circa 1616. The coins were known as *Hogge Money* or *Hoggies*.

The pieces were made of copper, lightly silvered, in four denominations: shilling, sixpence, threepence, and twopence, each indicated by Roman numerals. The hog is the main device and appears on the obverse side of each. SOMMER ISLANDS is inscribed within beaded circles. The reverse shows a full-rigged galleon with the flag of St. George on each of four masts.

The islands were named for Sir George Sommers, who was shipwrecked there in 1609 while en route to the Virginia plantations. Shakespeare's *Tempest* was possibly based on this incident.

The Bermuda Islands, as they are known today, were named for Juan Bermudez, who is believed to have stopped there in 1515. A few hogs that he carried for delivery to the West Indies were left behind. When Sommers and his party arrived, the islands were overrun with the animals, which served as a welcome source of food for the expedition.

Twopence　　　　　　　　Threepence

Sixpence Obverse　　　Large Portholes Reverse　　　Small Portholes Reverse

Shilling Obverse　　　Small Sail Reverse　　　Large Sail Reverse

| | G | VG | F | VF | EF |
|---|---|---|---|---|---|
| Twopence, Large Star Between Legs . . . . . . . . . . . | $4,500. | $6,000. | $11,000. | $25,000. | $36,000. |
| Twopence, Small Star Between Legs . . . . . . . . . . . | 4,500. | 6,000. | 11,000. | 25,000. | 36,000. |
| Threepence *(very rare)* . . . . . . . . . . . . . . . . . . . | — | — | 80,000. | 110,000. | — |
| Sixpence, Small Portholes . . . . . . . . . . . . . . . . . | 3,500. | 5,250. | 8,500. | 27,500. | 45,000. |
| Sixpence, Large Portholes . . . . . . . . . . . . . . . . . | 3,500. | 5,250. | 8,500. | 27,500. | 45,000. |
| Shilling, Small Sail . . . . . . . . . . . . . . . . . . . . . . | 4,000. | 6,500. | 16,000. | 37,000. | 70,000. |
| Shilling, Large Sail . . . . . . . . . . . . . . . . . . . . . . | 4,500. | 7,000. | 17,000. | 40,000. | 75,000. |

## Massachusetts
### *"New England" Coinage (1652)*

The earliest authorized medium of exchange in the New England settlements was wampum. The General Court of Massachusetts in 1637 ordered "that wampamege should passe at 6 a penny for any sume under 12 d." Wampum consisted of shells of various colors, ground to the size of kernels of corn. A hole was drilled through each piece so it could be strung on a leather thong for convenience and adornment.

Corn, pelts, and bullets were frequently used in lieu of coins, which were rarely available. Silver and gold coins brought over from England, Holland, and other countries tended to flow back across the Atlantic to purchase needed supplies. The colonists, thus left to their own resources, dealt with the friendly Native Americans in kind. In 1661 the law making wampum legal tender was repealed.

Agitation for a standard coinage reached its height in 1651. England, recovering from a civil war between the Puritans and Royalists, ignored the colonists, who took matters into their own hands in 1652.

The General Court in 1652 ordered the first metallic currency—the New England silver threepence, sixpence, and shilling—to be struck in the English Americas (the Spaniards had established a mint in Mexico City in 1535). Silver bullion was procured principally from the West Indies. The mint was located in Boston, Massachusetts, and John Hull was appointed mintmaster; his assistant was Robert Sanderson (or Saunderson). At first, Hull received as compensation one shilling threepence for every 20 shillings coined. This fee was adjusted several times during his term as mintmaster.

NE Threepence                    NE Sixpence

NE Shilling

*Early American coins are rare in conditions better than those listed and are consequently valued much higher.*

|  | G | VG | F | VF |
|---|---|---|---|---|
| NE Threepence *(unique)* | | | | — |
| NE Sixpence *(8 known)* | $25,000. | $50,000. | $80,000. | $175,000. |
| NE Shilling | 35,000. | 65,000. | 90,000. | 210,000. |

*$345,000, VF, Stack's auction, Oct-05*

### *Willow Tree Coinage (1653–1660)*

The simplicity of the designs on the NE coins invited counterfeiting and clipping of the edges. Therefore, they were soon replaced by the Willow, Oak, and Pine Tree series. The Willow Tree coins were struck from 1653 to 1660, the Oak Trees from 1660 to 1667, and the Pine Trees from 1667 to 1682. All of them (with the exception of the Oak Tree twopence) bore the date 1652, which gives them the appearance of having been struck when Cromwell was in power, after the English civil war. The coinage was abandoned in 1682; a proposal to renew coinage in 1686 was rejected by the General Court.

Early American coins were produced from handmade dies that are often individually distinctive. The great number of die varieties that can be found and identified are of interest to collectors who value each according to individual rarity. Values shown for type coins in this guide are for the most common die variety.

Threepence

Sixpence

Shilling

| | G | VG | F | VF | EF |
|---|---|---|---|---|---|
| 1652 Willow Tree Threepence *(3 known)* ........ | — | — | — | | |
| 1652 Willow Tree Sixpence *(14 known)* ......... | $20,000. | $32,000. | $60,000. | $125,000. | $200,000. |
| *$253,000, Unc, Stack's auction, Nov-05* | | | | | |
| 1652 Willow Tree Shilling .................... | 20,000. | 35,000. | 80,000. | 160,000. | 225,000. |
| *$276,000, EF, Stack's auction, Oct-05* | | | | | |

## *Oak Tree Coinage (1660–1667)*

Twopence

Threepence

Sixpence

Shilling

| | G | VG | F | VF | EF | AU |
|---|---|---|---|---|---|---|
| 1662 Oak Tree Twopence, Small 2 | $575. | $1,000. | $2,200. | $4,200. | $7,000. | $10,000. |
| 1662 Oak Tree Twopence, Large 2 | 575. | 1,000. | 2,200. | 4,200. | 7,000. | 10,000. |
| 1652 Oak Tree Threepence, | | | | | | |
|    No IN on Obverse ......... | 650. | 1,100. | 2,750. | 5,750. | 9,000. | 12,000. |
| 1652 Oak Tree Threepence, | | | | | | |
|    IN on Obverse ............ | 650. | 1,200. | 3,000. | 6,000. | 10,000. | 15,000. |

|  | G | VG | F | VF | EF | AU |
|---|---|---|---|---|---|---|
| 1652 Oak Tree Sixpence, IN on Rev | $750. | $1,250. | $3,250. | $7,200. | $14,000. | $18,000. |
| 1652 Oak Tree Sixpence, IN on Obv | 750. | 1,250. | 3,000. | 7,000. | 13,000. | 17,000. |
| 1652 Oak Tree Shilling, IN at Left | 750. | 1,250. | 3,300. | 6,500. | 10,500. | 13,500. |
| 1652 Oak Tree Shilling, IN at Bottom | 750. | 1,250. | 3,000. | 6,000. | 10,000. | 13,000. |
| 1652 Oak Tree Shilling, ANDO | 850. | 1,800. | 4,000. | 8,000. | 14,000. | 19,000. |
| 1652 Oak Tree Shilling, Spiny Tree | 750. | 1,250. | 2,750. | 5,750. | 10,000. | 12,500. |

## Pine Tree Coinage (1667–1682)

The first Pine Tree coins were minted on the same size planchets as the Oak Tree pieces. Subsequent issues of the shilling were narrower and thicker to conform to the size of English coins. Large Planchet shillings ranged from 27 to 31 mm in diameter; Small Planchet shillings ranged from 22 to 26 mm in diameter.

**Threepence**

**Sixpence**

**Shilling, Large Planchet (1667–1674)**   **Shilling, Small Planchet (1675–1682)**

|  | G | VG | F | VF | EF | AU |
|---|---|---|---|---|---|---|
| 1652 Pine Tree Threepence, Pellets at Trunk ......... | $550. | $800. | $1,800. | $3,400. | $6,250. | $9,250. |
| 1652 Pine Tree Threepence, Without Pellets ......... | 550. | 800. | 1,800. | 3,400. | 6,250. | 9,250. |
| 1652 Pine Tree Sixpence, Pellets at Trunk ........... | 600. | 925. | 1,900. | 3,900. | 6,700. | 9,500. |
| 1652 Pine Tree Sixpence, Without Pellets ........... | 600. | 950. | 2,000. | 4,200. | 7,200. | 10,000. |
| 1652 Pine Tree Shilling, Large Planchet (27–31 mm) .. |  |  |  |  |  |  |
|    1652 Pine Tree Shilling, Pellets at Trunk .......... | 700. | 1,050. | 2,200. | 4,600. | 8,250. | 12,500. |
|    1652 Pine Tree Shilling, Without Pellets at Trunk .... | 700. | 1,050. | 2,200. | 4,600. | 8,250. | 12,500. |
|    1652 Pine Tree Shilling, No H in MASATUSETS ..... | 800. | 1,400. | 2,800. | 5,500. | 12,500. | 17,000. |
|    1652 Pine Tree Shilling, Monogrammed NE in Legend | 700. | 1,100. | 2,300. | 4,700. | 8,500. | 13,000. |
| 1652 Pine Tree Shilling, Small Planchet (22–26 mm) .. | 600. | 925. | 1,900. | 4,000. | 7,500. | 12,500. |

## Maryland
### Lord Baltimore Coinage

Cecil Calvert, the second Lord Baltimore, inherited from his father nearly absolute control over Maryland. Cecil believed he had the right to coin money for the colony, and in 1659 he ordered shillings, sixpences, and groats (four-penny pieces) from the Royal Mint in London and shipped samples to Maryland, to his brother Philip, who was then his secretary for the colony. Cecil's right to strike coins was challenged but upheld by Cromwell's government. The whole issue was small, and while his coins did circulate in Maryland at first, by 1700 they had largely disappeared.

Calvert's coins bear his portrait on the obverse, with a Latin legend calling him "Lord of Mary's Land." The reverses bear his family coat of arms and the denomination in Roman numerals. There are several die varieties of each. Many of these coins are found holed and repaired. The copper penny, or denarium, is the rarest denomination, with only six known specimens.

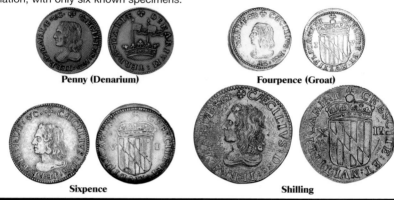

**Penny (Denarium)**        **Fourpence (Groat)**

**Sixpence**        **Shilling**

|  | G | VG | F | VF | EF | AU |
|---|---|---|---|---|---|---|
| Penny, copper *(6 known)* .................. | — | — | — | — |  | $125,000. |
| *$241,500, Proof, Stack's auction, May-04* |  |  |  |  |  |  |
| Fourpence ............................ | $2,000. | $3,750. | $6,750. | $15,000. | $22,000. | 36,000. |
| Sixpence ............................. | 1,600. | 2,600. | 5,250. | 9,000. | 14,500. | 20,000. |
| Shilling ............................. | 2,000. | 3,400. | 6,500. | 14,000. | 19,000. | 25,000. |

## New Jersey
### *St. Patrick or Mark Newby Coinage*

Mark Newby, who came to America from Dublin, Ireland, in November 1681, brought copper pieces believed by numismatists to have been struck in Dublin circa 1663 to 1672. These are called *St. Patrick coppers.*

The coinage was made legal tender by the General Assembly of New Jersey in May 1682. The legislature did not specify which size piece could circulate, only that the coin was to be worth a halfpenny in trade. Most numismatists believe the larger-size coin was intended. However, as many more farthing-size pieces are known than halfpennies, some believe that the smaller-size piece was meant. Copper coins often circulated in the colonies at twice what they would have been worth in England.

The obverses show a crowned king kneeling and playing a harp. The legend FLOREAT REX ("May the King Prosper") is separated by a crown. The reverse side of the halfpence shows St. Patrick with a crozier in his left hand and a trefoil in his right, and surrounded by people. At his left side is a shield. The legend is ECCE GREX ("Behold the Flock"). The farthing reverse shows St. Patrick driving away reptiles and serpents as he holds a metropolitan cross in his left hand. The legend reads QUIESCAT PLEBS ("May the People Be at Ease").

The large-size piece, called a *halfpenny*, bears the arms of the City of Dublin on the shield on the reverse; the smaller-size piece, called a *farthing*, does not. All of these pieces have a reeded edge.

The decorative brass insert found on the coinage, usually over the crown on the obverse, was put there to make counterfeiting more difficult. On some pieces this decoration has been removed or does not show. Numerous die variations exist.

St. Patrick "Farthing"    St. Patrick "Halfpenny"

| | G | VG | F | VF | EF | AU |
|---|---|---|---|---|---|---|
| St. Patrick "Farthing" ..................... | $125. | $300. | $750. | $2,200. | $4,500. | $8,500. |
| Similar, Halo Around Saint's Head ........... | 400. | 1,000. | 2,500. | 5,000. | — | — |
| Similar, No C in QUIESCAT ................. | 400. | 1,000. | 2,500. | 5,000. | — | — |
| St. Patrick "Farthing," silver ................. | 1,750. | 2,400. | 4,800. | 7,200. | 10,000. | 14,500. |
| St. Patrick "Farthing," gold *(unique) $184,000, AU, Stack's auction, Jan-05* | | | | | | — |
| St. Patrick "Halfpenny" ..................... | 400. | 1,000. | 1,800. | 3,750. | 10,000. | 15,000. |

# COINAGE AUTHORIZED BY BRITISH ROYAL PATENT
## American Plantations Tokens

These tokens, struck in nearly pure tin, were the first royally authorized coinage for the British colonies in America. They were made under a franchise granted in 1688 to Richard Holt. Most examples show black oxidation of the tin. Bright, unblemished specimens are more valuable. Restrikes were made about 1828 from original dies.

| | G | F | EF | AU | Unc. |
|---|---|---|---|---|---|
| (1688) James II Plantation Token Farthing | | | | | |
| 1/24 Part Real ..................... | $225. | $475. | $1,350. | $1,750. | $3,600. |
| 1/24 Part Real, ET. HB. REX ......... | 275. | 750. | 2,250. | 5,000. | 7,500. |
| 1/24 Part Real, Sidewise 4 in 24 ..... | 400. | 1,500. | 4,250. | 6,750. | — |
| 1/24 Part Real, Arms Transposed ..... | 600. | 1,900. | 5,500. | 7,250. | — |
| 1/24 Part Real, Restrike ............ | 120. | 300. | 700. | 1,000. | 1,750. |

## Coinage of William Wood
### Rosa Americana Coins

William Wood, an Englishman, obtained a patent from George I to make tokens for Ireland and the American colonies.

The first pieces struck were undated; others bear the dates 1722, 1723, 1724, and 1733. The Rosa Americana pieces were issued in three denominations—half penny, penny, and twopence—and were intended for America. This type had a full-blown rose on the reverse with the words ROSA AMERICANA UTILE DULCI ("American Rose—Useful and Pleasant").

The obverse, common to both Rosa Americana and Hibernia pieces, shows the head of George I and the legend GEORGIUS D:G MAG: BRI: FRA: ET. HIB: REX ("George, by the Grace of God, King of Great Britain, France, and Ireland") or abbreviations thereof. Rosa Americana tokens, however, were rejected by the American colonists. The coins are made of a brass composition of 75% copper, 24.7% zinc, and .3% silver (sometimes mistakenly referred to as *Bath metal*).

|  | VG | F | VF | EF | AU | Unc. |
|---|---|---|---|---|---|---|
| (No date) Twopence, Motto in Ribbon *(illustrated)* | $175. | $400. | $725. | $1,250. | $3,000. | $5,500. |
| (No date) Twopence, Motto Without Ribbon *(3 known)* | — | — | — | | | |

|  | VG | F | VF | EF | AU | Unc. |
|---|---|---|---|---|---|---|
| 1722 Halfpenny, VTILE DVLCI | $925. | $2,500. | $3,800. | $6,200. | $7,250. | |
| 1722 Halfpenny, D.G.REX ROSA AMERI. UTILE DULCI | 150. | 260. | 550. | 1,100. | 2,250. | $4,200. |
| 1722 Halfpenny, DEI GRATIA REX UTILE DULCI | 150. | 260. | 525. | 1,000. | 1,900. | 3,600. |

|  | VG | F | VF | EF | AU | Unc. |
|---|---|---|---|---|---|---|
| 1722 Penny, GEORGIVS | | | $9,250. | — | — | |
| 1722 Penny, VTILE DVLCI | $170. | $275. | 800. | $1,300. | $2,750. | $5,250. |
| 1722 Penny, UTILE DULCI | 150. | 260. | 500. | 1,000. | 1,750. | 3,800. |

# COLONIAL ISSUES

| | VG | F | VF | EF | AU | Unc. |
|---|---|---|---|---|---|---|
| 1722 Twopence, Period After REX . . . . . . . . . . . . . | $170. | $275. | $700. | $1,200. | $2,750. | $5,250. |
| 1722 Twopence, No Period After REX . . . . . . . . . | 170. | 275. | 700. | 1,200. | 2,750. | 5,250. |

| | VG | F | VF | EF | AU | Unc. |
|---|---|---|---|---|---|---|
| 1723 Halfpenny, Uncrowned Rose . . . . . . . . . . . . . | $900. | $1,750. | $3,500. | $5,000. | $6,250. | — |
| 1723 Halfpenny, Crowned Rose . . . . . . . . . . . . . . | 115. | 170. | 450. | 1,000. | 2,200. | $4,400. |

| | VG | F | VF | EF | AU | Unc. |
|---|---|---|---|---|---|---|
| 1723 Penny . . . . . . . . . . . . . . . . . . . . . . . . . . . | $115. | $170. | $400. | $900. | $1,500. | $3,300. |
| 1723 Twopence *(illustrated)* . . . . . . . . . . . . . . . . | 175. | 300. | 550. | 1,200. | 1,950. | 3,600. |

| | EF | AU | Unc. |
|---|---|---|---|
| 1724, 4 Over 3 Penny (pattern), DEI GRATIA . . . . . . . . . . . . . . . . . . . . . . . | $7,000. | $13,500. | $17,000. |
| 1724, 4 Over 3 Penny (pattern), D GRATIA . . . . . . . . . . . . . . . . . . . . . . . . . | 8,200. | 17,000. | 30,000. |
| (Undated) (1724) Penny, ROSA: SINE: SPINA. *(5 known)* | | | |
| *$21,850, VF, Stack's auction, May-05* . . . . . . . . . . . . . . . . . . . . . . . . . | 28,000. | 35,000. | — |

1724 Twopence (pattern) *$25,300, Choice AU, Stack's auction, May-05* . . . . . . . . . . . . . . . . . . . . . . . . . . . .

The 1733 twopence is a pattern piece and bears the bust of George II facing to the left. It was issued by the successors to the coinage patent, as William Wood had died in 1730.

1733 Twopence (pattern), Proof *$63,250, Gem Proof, Stack's auction, May-05* . . . . . . . . . . . . . . . . . . . . .

## *Wood's Hibernia Coinage*

The type intended for Ireland had a seated figure with a harp on the reverse side and the word HIBERNIA. Denominations struck were farthing and halfpenny, with dates 1722, 1723, and 1724. Hibernia coins were unpopular in Ireland, so some of them were sent to the American colonies.

|  | **First Type** | **Second Type** |  | **1723 Over 22** |  |
|---|---|---|---|---|---|
|  | VG | F | VF | EF | AU | Unc. |
| 1722 Farthing, D: G: REX . . . . . . . . . . . . . . . . . . . . | $420. | $575. | $1,100. | $2,200. | $3,400. | $6,500. |
| 1722 Halfpenny, D: G: REX, Rocks at Right (pattern) | — | — | 3,500. | 8,250. | | |
| 1722 Halfpenny, First Type, Harp at Left . . . . . . . . | 125. | 175. | 325. | 700. | 1,000. | 1,600. |
| 1722 Halfpenny, Second Type, Harp at Right . . . . . | 90. | 125. | 310. | 600. | 750. | 1,425. |
| 1722 Halfpenny, Second Type, DEII (blunder) . . . . . | 145. | 300. | 725. | 1,300. | 1,750. | 2,450. |
| 1723 Farthing, D.G.REX . . . . . . . . . . . . . . . . . . . . | 115. | 165. | 275. | 600. | 750. | 1,425. |
| 1723 Farthing, DEI. GRATIA. REX . . . . . . . . . . . . . | 65. | 95. | 175. | 325. | 500. | 900. |
| 1723 Farthing (silver pattern) . . . . . . . . . . . . . . . . | 1,700. | 2,300. | 4,000. | 5,000. | 6,750. | 9,500. |

**1724, Hibernia Farthing**      **1724, Hibernia Halfpenny**

| | VG | F | VF | EF | AU | Unc. |
|---|---|---|---|---|---|---|
| 1723 Halfpenny, 23 Over 22 . . . . . . . . . . . . . . . . . | $80. | $140. | $350. | $700. | $1,100. | $1,750. |
| 1723 Halfpenny . . . . . . . . . . . . . . . . . . . . . . . . | 50. | 75. | 175. | 325. | 500. | 850. |
| 1723 Halfpenny (silver pattern) . . . . . . . . . . . . . | — | — | — | — | — | — |
| 1724 Farthing . . . . . . . . . . . . . . . . . . . . . . . . . | 125. | 225. | 550. | 1,200. | 1,800. | 3,250. |
| 1724 Halfpenny . . . . . . . . . . . . . . . . . . . . . . . | 90. | 150. | 350. | 725. | 1,000. | 2,000. |
| 1724 Halfpenny, DEI Above Head . . . . . . . . . . . . | 140. | 300. | 900. | 1,350. | 1,700. | 3,000. |

# Virginia Halfpennies

In 1773, coinage of a copper halfpenny was authorized for Virginia by the Crown. The pattern, in Proof struck on a large planchet with a wide milled border, is often referred to as a penny.

The silver piece dated 1774 is referred to as a shilling, but may have been a pattern or trial for a halfpenny or a guinea.

*Red uncirculated pieces without spots are worth considerably more.*

| | VG | F | VF | EF | AU | Unc. |
|---|---|---|---|---|---|---|
| 1773 Halfpenny, Period After GEORGIVS . . . . . . . | $50. | $110. | $240. | $425. | $600. | $1,100. |
| 1773 Halfpenny, No Period After GEORGIVS . . . . . | 75. | 125. | 270. | 500. | 750. | 1,350. |

**1773, "Penny"**      **1774, "Shilling"**

| Date | PF |
|---|---|
| 1773 "Penny" . . . . . . . . . . . . . . . . . . . . . . . . . . . . . . . . . . . . . . . . . . . . . . . . . . . . . . . | $20,000. |
| 1774 "Shilling" *(6 known)* . . . . . . . . . . . . . . . . . . . . . . . . . . . . . . . . . . . . . . . . . . . . . . . . | *125,000.* |

## EARLY AMERICAN AND RELATED TOKENS
### Elephant Tokens
#### *London Elephant Tokens*

The London Elephant tokens were struck circa 1672 to 1694. Although they were undated, two examples are known to have been struck over 1672 British halfpennies. Most were struck in copper, but one was made of brass. The legend on this piece, GOD PRESERVE LONDON, is probably just a general plea for divine aid and not a specific reference to the outbreak of plague in 1665 or the great fire of 1666.

These pieces were not struck for the colonies, and probably did not circulate widely in America, although a few may have been carried there by colonists. They are associated with the 1694 Carolina and New England Elephant tokens, through a shared obverse die.

| | VG | F | VF | EF | AU | Unc. |
|---|---|---|---|---|---|---|
| (1694) Halfpenny, GOD PRESERVE LONDON, Thick Planchet | $300. | $500. | $1,000. | $1,700. | $2,400. | $3,800. |
| (1694) Halfpenny, GOD PRESERVE LONDON, Thin Planchet | 500. | 900. | 2,200. | 3,500. | 5,250. | 9,000. |
| Similar, Brass *(unique)* | | | | — | | |
| (1694) Halfpenny, GOD PRESERVE LONDON, Diagonals in Center of Shield | 600. | 1,000. | 3,000. | 4,500. | 6,500. | 11,000. |
| (1694) Halfpenny, similar, Sword in Second Quarter of Shield | — | — | 11,500. | — | — | — |
| (1694) Halfpenny, LON DON | 850. | 2,100. | 3,500. | 5,600. | 9,000. | 13,500. |

#### *Carolina Elephant Tokens*

Although no law is known authorizing coinage for Carolina, two very interesting pieces known as *Elephant tokens* were made with the date 1694. These copper tokens were of halfpenny denomination. The reverse reads GOD PRESERVE CAROLINA AND THE LORDS PROPRIETERS 1694.

The second and more available variety has the last word spelled PROPRIETORS. The correction was made on the original die, for the E shows plainly beneath the O. The elephant's tusks nearly touch the milling on the second variety.

The Carolina pieces were probably struck in England and perhaps intended only as tokens, or possibly as advertising to heighten interest in the Carolina Plantation.

# COLONIAL ISSUES

|  | VG | F | VF | EF | AU |
|---|---|---|---|---|---|
| 1694 PROPRIETERS ................ | $5,000. | $6,500. | $13,500. | $20,000. | $30,000. |
| 1694 PROPRIETERS, O Over E ........ | 4,500. | 6,000. | 11,000. | 17,500. | 25,000. |

## *New England Elephant Tokens*

Like the Carolina tokens, the New England Elephant tokens are believed to have been struck in England as promotional pieces to increase interest in the American colonies.

|  | VG | F | VF | EF | AU |
|---|---|---|---|---|---|
| 1694 NEW ENGLAND ............... | $25,000. | $35,000. | $47,500. | $62,500. | — |

## New Yorke in America Token

The New Yorke in America token is a farthing or halfpenny token intended for New York, issued by Francis Lovelace, who was governor from 1668 until 1673. The token uses the older spelling with a final "e" (YORKE), which predominated before 1710. The obverse shows Cupid pursuing the butterfly-winged Psyche—a rebus on the name Lovelace. The reverse shows a heraldic eagle, identical to the one displayed in fesse, raguly (i.e., on a crenellated bar) on the Lovelace coat of arms. In weight, fabric, and die axis the tokens are similar to the 1670 farthing tokens of Bristol, England, where they may have been struck. There is no evidence that any of these pieces ever circulated in America.

|  | VG | F | VF | EF |
|---|---|---|---|---|
| (Undated) Brass ........................... | $5,500. | $12,500. | $21,000. | $35,000. |
| (Undated) Pewter .......................... | 6,000. | 14,000. | 27,500. | 45,000. |

## Gloucester Tokens

S.S. Crosby, in his book *The Early Coins of America*, stated that this coin appears to have been intended as a pattern for a shilling—a private coinage by Richard Dawson of Gloucester (county), Virginia. The only specimens known are struck in brass, although the denomination XII indicates that a silver coinage (one shilling) may have been planned. The building may represent some public building, possibly the courthouse.

Although neither of the two known examples shows the full legends, combining the pieces shows GLOVCESTER COVRTHOVSE VIRGINIA/RIGHAVLT DAWSON. ANNO.DOM. 1714. This recent discovery has provided a new interpretation of the legends, as a Righault family once owned land near the Gloucester courthouse. A similar, but somewhat smaller, piece dated 1715 exists. The condition of this unique piece is too poor for positive attribution.

| | F |
|---|---|
| 1714 Shilling, brass *(2 known)* .................................................. | $75,000. |

## Higley or Granby Coppers

Dr. Samuel Higley owned a private copper mine near Granby, Connecticut. He worked the mine as an individual, smelting his own ore and making his own dies for the coins that he issued. After his death in 1737 his brother John continued the coinage.

The Higley coppers were never officially authorized. All the tokens were made of pure copper. There were seven obverse and four reverse dies. The first issue, in 1737, bore the legend THE VALUE OF THREEPENCE. After a time, the quantity exceeded the local demand, and a protest arose against the value of the piece. Higley, a resourceful individual, promptly created a new design, still with the Roman III, but with the inscription VALUE ME AS YOU PLEASE. On the reverse appeared the words I AM GOOD COPPER. Electrotypes and casts exist.

| | G | VG | F | VF |
|---|---|---|---|---|
| 1737 THE VALVE OF THREE PENCE, CONNECTICVT, 3 Hammers ............... | $10,000. | $18,000. | $36,000. | $80,000. |
| 1737 THE VALVE OF THREE PENCE, I AM GOOD COPPER, 3 Hammers ................... | 10,500. | 19,000. | 38,000. | 82,000. |
| 1737 VALUE ME AS YOU PLEASE, I AM GOOD COPPER, 3 Hammers ................... | 10,000. | 18,000. | 36,000. | 80,000. |

# COLONIAL ISSUES

| | G | VG | F | VF |
|---|---|---|---|---|
| 1737 VALVE • ME • AS • YOU • PLEASE, | | | | |
|     I • AM • GOOD • COPPER, 3 Hammers *(3 known)* | *$218,500, EF, Stack's auction, May-04* | | | |
| (1737) VALUE • ME • AS • YOU • PLEASE, | | | | |
|     J • CUT • MY • WAY • THROUGH, Broad Axe .. | $10,000. | $18,000. | $36,000. | $80,000. |
| (1737) THE • WHEELE • GOES • ROUND, | | | | |
|     Reverse as Above *(unique)* .............. | | | 125,000. | |
| 1739 VALUE • ME • AS • YOU • PLEASE, | | | | |
|     J • CUT • MY • WAY • THROUGH, Broad Axe .. | 13,000. | 22,000. | 40,000. | 100,000. |

## Hibernia–Voce Populi Coins

These coins, struck in the year 1760, were prepared by Roche, of King Street, Dublin, who was at that time engaged in the manufacture of buttons for the army. Like other Irish tokens, some of these pieces found their way to colonial America and possibly circulated in the colonies with numerous other counterfeit halfpence and "bungtown tokens."

There are two distinct issues. Coins from the first, with a "short bust" on the obverse, range in weight from 87 to 120 grains. Those from the second, with a "long bust" on the obverse, range in weight from 129 to 154 grains. Most of the "long bust" varieties have the letter P on the obverse. None of the "short bust" varieties bear the letter P, and judging from their weight, may have been contemporary counterfeits.

**Large-Letter Variety Farthing**

**Halfpenny**

**Halfpenny, "P" Before Face**

**VOOE POPULI**

| | G | VG | F | VF | EF | AU | Unc. |
|---|---|---|---|---|---|---|---|
| 1760 Farthing, Large Letters .... | $250. | $350. | $675. | $1,700. | $3,000. | $4,500. | $8,250. |
| 1760 Farthing, Small Letters .... | 650. | 1,300. | 2,750. | 6,500. | 13,000. | — | — |
| 1760 Halfpenny .............. | 70. | 130. | 175. | 375. | 700. | 1,300. | 2,400. |
| 1760 Halfpenny, VOOE POPULI .. | 80. | 150. | 250. | 450. | 800. | 1,500. | 3,500. |
| 1760 Halfpenny, P Below Bust .. | 110. | 190. | 300. | 650. | 1,600. | 3,500. | 7,000. |
| 1760 Halfpenny, P in Front of Face | 100. | 165. | 275. | 600. | 1,300. | 2,500. | 5,500. |

## Pitt Tokens

William Pitt, who endeared himself to America, is the subject of these pieces, probably intended as commemorative medalets. The so-called halfpenny served as currency during a shortage of regular coinage. The reverse legend (THANKS TO THE FRIENDS OF LIBERTY AND TRADE) refers to Pitt's efforts to have the Stamp Act repealed. The Pitt farthing-size tokens, struck in brass or copper, are rare.

**Farthing**          **Halfpenny**

| | VG | F | VF | EF | AU | Unc. |
|---|---|---|---|---|---|---|
| 1766 Farthing | | $8,200. | $22,000. | $32,000. | — | |
| 1766 Halfpenny | $425. | 700. | 1,450. | 2,750. | $4,250. | $7,250. |
| 1766 Halfpenny, silvered | | | 2,100. | 4,500. | 6,500. | 11,500. |

## Rhode Island Ship Medals

The obverse type shows the flagship of British Admiral Lord Richard Howe at anchor, while the reverse depicts the retreat of American forces from Rhode Island in 1778. The inscriptions show that the coin was meant for a Dutch-speaking audience. It is believed the medal was struck in England circa 1779 or 1780 for the Dutch market, as propaganda to persuade the Dutch not to sign the Treaty of Armed Neutrality (December 1780). Specimens are known in brass, copper, and pewter.

**Rhode Island Ship Medal (1778–1779)**

| | VF | EF | AU | Unc. |
|---|---|---|---|---|
| VLUGTENDE ("Fleeing") Below Ship, brass or copper | | $16,000. | | |
| Wreath Below Ship, brass or copper | $1,050. | 2,000. | $2,750. | $4,400. |
| Without Wreath Below Ship, brass or copper | 1,000. | 1,750. | 2,400. | 3,750. |
| Similar, pewter | 5,000. | 7,500. | 10,000. | 12,000. |

## John Chalmers Issues

John Chalmers, a silversmith, struck a series of silver tokens at Annapolis in 1783. The shortage of change and the refusal of the people to use underweight cut Spanish coins, or "bits," prompted the issuance of these pieces.

On the Chalmers threepence and shilling obverses, two clasped hands are shown, symbolizing unity of the several states; the reverse of the threepence has a branch encircled by a wreath. A star within a wreath is placed on the obverse of the sixpence, with hands clasped upon a cross utilized as the reverse type. On this denomination, the designer's initials TS (for Thomas Sparrow, a fellow silversmith of Chalmers') can be found in the crescents that terminate the horizontal arms of the cross. The reverse of the more common shilling varieties displays two doves competing for a worm underneath a hedge and a snake. There are only a few known examples of the shilling type with 13 interlinked rings, from which a liberty cap on a pole arises.

|  | VG | F | VF | EF | AU |
|---|---|---|---|---|---|
| 1783 Threepence ................... | $1,500. | $3,000. | $5,000. | $9,000. | $12,500. |
| 1783 Sixpence, Small Date ........... | 2,500. | 5,500. | 12,000. | 19,000. | 26,000. |
| 1783 Sixpence, Large Date ........... | 2,250. | 5,000. | 10,000. | 18,000. | 24,000. |

|  | VG | F | VF | EF | AU |
|---|---|---|---|---|---|
| 1783 Shilling, Birds, Long Worm | | | | | |
|   (illustrated) ................... | $1,300. | $2,400. | $4,500. | $8,000. | $13,000. |
| 1783 Shilling, Birds, Short Worm ....... | 1,300. | 2,400. | 4,250. | 7,500. | 12,000. |
| 1783 Shilling, Rings ................ | — | — | 175,000. | — | — |

# FRENCH NEW WORLD ISSUES

None of the coins of the French regime relate to territories that later became part of the United States. They were all general issues for the French colonies of the New World. The coinage of 1670 was authorized by an edict of Louis XIV dated February 19, 1670, for use in New France, Acadia, the French settlements in Newfoundland, and the French West Indies. The copper coinage of 1717 to 1722 was authorized by edicts of 1716 and 1721 for use in New France, Louisiana, and the French West Indies.

## Coinage of 1670

The coinage of 1670 consisted of silver 5 and 15 sols and copper 2 deniers (or "doubles"). A total of 200,000 of the 5 sols and 40,000 of the 15 sols was struck at Paris. Nantes was to have coined the copper, but did not; the reasons for this may never be known, since the archives of the Nantes Mint before 1700 were destroyed. The only known specimen is a pattern struck at Paris. The silver coins were raised in value by a third in 1672 to keep them circulating, but in vain. They rapidly disappeared, and by 1680 none were to be seen. Later they were restored to their original values. This rare issue should not be confused with the common 1670-A 1/12 ecu with reverse legend SIT. NOMEN. DOMINI. BENEDICTUM.

The 1670-A double de l'Amerique Françoise was struck at the Paris Mint along with the 5- and 15-sols denominations of the same date. All three were intended to circulate in France's North American colonies. Probably due to an engraving error, very few 1670-A doubles were actually struck. Today, only one is known to survive.

**Copper Double**      **Silver 5 Sols**

|  | VG | F | VF | EF | AU |
|---|---|---|---|---|---|
| 1670-A Copper Double *(unique)* . . . . . . . . |  |  | $85,000. |  |  |
| 1670-A 5 Sols . . . . . . . . . . . . .(200,000) | $650. | $1,100. | 2,400. | $4,400. | $8,000. |
| 1670-A 15 Sols . . . . . . . . . . . . .(40,000) | 10,000. | 24,000. | 45,000. | 69,500. | — |

## Coinage of 1717–1720

The copper 6 and 12 deniers of 1717 were authorized by an edict of Louis XV dated December 1716, to be struck at Perpignan (mintmark Q). The order could not be carried out, for the supply of copper was too brassy. A second attempt in 1720 also failed, probably for the same reason.

|  | F | EF |
|---|---|---|
| 1717-Q 6 Deniers, No Crowned Arms on Reverse *(ex. rare)* . . . . . . . . |  | — |
| 1717-Q 12 Deniers, No Crowned Arms on Reverse . . . . . . . . . . . . . . |  | $44,000. |
| 1720-A 6 Deniers, Crowned Arms on Reverse *(illustrated)* . . . . . . . . | $150. | 750. |
| 1720-A 20 Sols, silver . . . . . . . . . . . . . . . . . . . . . . . . . . . . . . . . . . . | 375. | 1,200. |

## Billon Coinage of 1709–1760

The piece of 30 deniers was called a *mousquetaire*, and was coined at Metz and Lyon. The 15 deniers was coined only at Metz. The sou marque and the half sou were coined at almost every French mint, those of Paris being commonest. The half sou of 1740 is the only commonly available date. Specimens of the sou marque dated after 1760 were not used in North America. A unique specimen of the 1712-AA 30 deniers is known in the size and weight of the 15-denier coins.

**30 Deniers "Mousquetaire"**     **Sou Marque (24 Deniers)**

| | VG | F | VF | EF | AU |
|---|---|---|---|---|---|
| 1711–1713-AA 15 Deniers . . . . . . . . . . . | $135. | $275. | $550. | $1,100. | $2,400. |
| 1709–1713-AA 30 Deniers . . . . . . . . . . . | 85. | 175. | 325. | 650. | 1,550. |
| 1709–1713-D 30 Deniers . . . . . . . . . . . . | 85. | 175. | 325. | 650. | 1,550. |
| 1738–1748 Half Sou Marque, various mints . . . . . . . . . . . . . . . | 75. | 150. | 300. | 600. | 1,550. |
| 1738–1760 Sou Marque, various mints . . | 70. | 120. | 175. | 400. | 650. |

## Coinage of 1721–1722

The copper coinage of 1721 and 1722 was authorized by an edict of Louis XV dated June 1721. The coins were struck on copper blanks imported from Sweden. Rouen and La Rochelle struck pieces of nine deniers in 1721 and 1722. New France received 534,000 pieces, mostly from the mint of La Rochelle, but only 8,180 were successfully put into circulation, as the colonists disliked copper. In 1726 the rest of the issue was sent back to France.

### *Copper Sou or Nine Deniers*

| | VG | F | VF | EF |
|---|---|---|---|---|
| 1721-B (Rouen) . . . . . . . . . . . . . . . . . . . . . . . . . . . | $200. | $450. | $850. | $1,400. |
| 1721-H (La Rochelle) . . . . . . . . . . . . . . . . . . . . . . | 90. | 200. | 450. | 850. |
| 1722-H . . . . . . . . . . . . . . . . . . . . . . . . . . . . . . . . . | 90. | 200. | 450. | 850. |
| 1722-H, 2 Over 1 . . . . . . . . . . . . . . . . . . . . . . . . . | 175. | 300. | 550. | 1,100. |

## French Colonies in General

These were coined for use in the French colonies and only unofficially circulated in Louisiana along with other foreign coins and tokens. Most were counterstamped RF (République Française) for use in the West Indies. The mintmark A signifies the Paris Mint.

| | VG | VF | EF | AU |
|---|---|---|---|---|
| 1767 French Colonies, Sou . . . . . . . . . . . . . . . . . . . . | $100. | $400. | $800. | $1,800. |
| 1767 French Colonies, Sou, counterstamped RF . . . . | 85. | 200. | 450. | 850. |

# SPECULATIVE ISSUES, TOKENS, AND PATTERNS
## Nova Constellatio Coppers

The Nova Constellatio coppers, dated 1783 and 1785 and without denomination, were struck in fairly large quantities in Birmingham, England, beginning in 1785, and were shipped to New York where they entered circulation. Apparently they resulted from a private coinage venture undertaken by Constable, Rucker & Co., a trading business formed by William Constable, John Rucker, Robert Morris, and Gouverneur Morris as equal partners. The designs and legends were copied from the denominated patterns dated 1783 made in Philadelphia. A few additional coppers dated 1786 were made by an inferior diesinker.

1783,
CONSTELLATIO
Pointed Rays, Small U.S.

1783,
CONSTELLATIO
Pointed Rays, Large U.S.

1783,
CONSTELATIO
Blunt Rays

1785,
CONSTELATIO
Blunt Rays

1785,
CONSTELLATIO
Pointed Rays

| | VG | F | VF | EF | AU | Unc. |
|---|---|---|---|---|---|---|
| 1783, CONSTELLATIO, Pointed Rays, Small U.S. . . . . . . . . . . | $100. | $220. | $450. | $1,000. | $1,950. | $3,500. |
| 1783, CONSTELLATIO, Pointed Rays, Large U.S. . . . . . . . . . . | 110. | 250. | 600. | 1,400. | 3,000. | 6,000. |
| 1783, CONSTELATIO, Blunt Rays . . | 110. | 250. | 575. | 1,250. | 2,500. | 5,000. |
| 1785, CONSTELATIO, Blunt Rays . . | 110. | 250. | 600. | 1,400. | 3,200. | 6,000. |
| 1785, CONSTELLATIO, Pointed Rays | 100. | 220. | 525. | 1,100. | 2,000. | 3,750. |
| 1785, Similar, Sm, Close Date . . . . | 375. | 750. | 3,300. | 6,000. | 8,000. | |
| 1786, Similar, Small Date . . . . . . . . | — | — | | | | |

## Immune Columbia Pieces

These are considered experimental or unofficial pieces. No laws describing them are known. There are several types bearing the seated figure of Justice. These dies were possibly the work of George Wyon. The Immune Columbia device with liberty cap and scale replaced the LIBERTAS and JUSTITIA on the Nova Constellatio coppers.

**1785, Silver,
13 Stars**

**1785, Pointed Rays,
CONSTELLATIO**

| | VF |
|---|---|
| 1785, Copper, 13 Stars ................................................. | $23,000. |
| 1785, Silver, 13 Stars ................................................. | 38,500. |
| 1785, Pointed Rays, CONSTELLATIO, Extra Star in Reverse Legend, copper .............. | 23,500. |
| 1785, Blunt Rays, CONSTELLATIO, copper *(2 known)* ............................. | — |
| 1785, Blunt Rays, CONSTELATIO, gold *(unique)* ................................. | — |

*Note:* A gold specimen in the National Numismatic Collection (now in the Smithsonian) was acquired in 1843 from collector Matthew A. Stickney in exchange for an 1804 dollar.

**1785, George III Obverse**

| | G | VG | F |
|---|---|---|---|
| 1785, George III Obverse ............................... | $5,000. | $7,000. | $9,500. |
| 1785, VERMON AUCTORI Obverse, IMMUNE COLUMBIA ......... | 5,500. | 8,000. | 9,250. |

**1787, IMMUNIS COLUMBIA, Eagle Reverse**

| | VG | F | VF | EF | AU | Unc. |
|---|---|---|---|---|---|---|
| 1787, IMMUNIS COLUMBIA, Eagle Reverse .......... | $700. | $1,500. | $3,500. | $6,750. | $10,000. | $14,000. |

*Note:* Believed to be a prototype for federal coinage; some were coined after 1787.

## Confederatio Coppers

The Confederatio coppers are experimental or pattern pieces. This will explain why the die with the CONFEDERATIO legend was combined with other designs, such as the bust of George Washington, Libertas et Justitia of 1785, Immunis Columbia of 1786, the New York "Excelsiors," Inimica Tyrannis Americana, and others. In all, 13 dies were struck in 14 combinations. Some of the dies may have been made by George Wyon of Birmingham, England.

There are two types of the Confederatio reverse. In one instance the stars are contained in a small circle; in the other, larger stars are in a larger circle.

**Typical Obverse**    **Small Circle Reverse**    **Large Circle Reverse**

| | VF |
|---|---|
| 1785, Stars in Small Circle, Various Obverses | $40,000. |
| 1785, Stars in Small Circle, silver | — |
| 1785, Stars in Large Circle, Various Obverses | 35,000. |

## Speculative Patterns

The motto-and-shield design used on some of these patterns was later adopted for use on the New Jersey copper coins.

**1786, IMMUNIS COLUMBIA**    **Eagle Reverse**    **Shield Reverse**

| | VF |
|---|---|
| 1786, IMMUNIS COLUMBIA, Eagle Reverse | $50,000. |
| 1786, IMMUNIS COLUMBIA, Shield Reverse | 38,000. |

**Washington Obverse**    **Eagle Reverse**    **Shield Reverse**

(No date) (1786) Washington Obverse, Shield Reverse  *$253,000, AU, Stack's auction, Oct-03*
1786, Eagle Obverse, Shield Reverse *(unique)  $37,500, Unc., B&R auction, 1980* . . . . . . . . . .   —
1786, Washington Obverse, Eagle Reverse *(2 known)* . . . . . . . . . . . . . . . . . . . . . . . . . . . . . . .   —

# COINAGE OF THE STATES
## New Hampshire

New Hampshire was the first of the states to consider the subject of coinage following the Declaration of Independence.

William Moulton was empowered to make a limited quantity of coins of pure copper authorized by the State House of Representatives in 1776. Although cast patterns were prepared, it is believed that they were not approved. Little of the proposed coinage was ever actually circulated.

Other purported patterns are of doubtful origin. These include a unique engraved piece and a rare struck piece with large initials WM on the reverse.

| | VG |
|---|---|
| 1776 New Hampshire Copper . . . . . . . . . . . . . . . . . . . . . . . . . . . . . . . . . . . . . . . . . . . . . . . . . . . | $30,000. |

## Massachusetts
### *Massachusetts Unofficial Coppers*

Nothing is known regarding the origin of the Pine Tree piece dated 1776. The obverse has a crude pine tree with "1d LM" at its base and the inscription MASSACHUSETTS STATE. The reverse has a figure probably intended to represent the Goddess of Liberty, seated on a globe and holding a liberty cap and staff. A dog sits at her feet. The legend LIBERTY AND VIRTUE surrounds the figure.

| | VF |
|---|---|
| 1776 Pine Tree Copper *(unique)* . . . . . . . . . . . . . . . . . . . . . . . . . . . . . . . . . . . . . . . . . . . . . . | — |

A similar piece, probably from the same source, has a Native American with a bow on the obverse, and seated figure on the reverse.

| | VG |
|---|---|

1776 Indian Copper *(unique)* .................................................... —

This piece is sometimes called the *Janus copper*. On the obverse are three heads, facing left, front, and right, with the inscription STATE OF MASSA. 1/2 D. The reverse shows the Goddess of Liberty facing right, resting against a globe inscribed GODDESS LIBERTY 1776.

| | F |
|---|---|

1776 Halfpenny, 3 Heads on Obverse *(unique)* $42,000, B&R auction, Nov-79 ............. —

## Massachusetts Authorized Issues

An "Act for establishing a mint for the coinage of gold, silver and copper" was passed by the Massachusetts General Court on October 17, 1786. The next year, the council directed that the design should incorporate "the figure of an Indian with a bow and arrow and a star at one side, with the word 'Commonwealth,' the reverse, a spread eagle with the words 'of Massachusetts A.D. 1787.' "

The coinage of Massachusetts copper cents and half cents in 1787 and 1788 was under the direction of Joshua Witherle. These were the first coins bearing the denomination *cent* as established by Congress. Many varieties exist, the most valuable being that with arrows in the eagle's right talon.

Most of the dies for these coppers were made by Joseph Callender. Jacob Perkins of Newburyport also engraved some of the dies.

The mint was abandoned early in 1789, in compliance with the newly ratified Constitution.

**1787 Half Cent**

| | 1787 Cent, Obverse | Arrows in Right Talon | | Arrows in Left Talon | |

| | G | F | VF | EF | AU | Unc. |
|---|---|---|---|---|---|---|
| 1787 Half Cent | $100. | $250. | $575. | $1,200. | $2,000. | $3,500. |
| 1787 Cent, Arrows in Right Talon | 10,000. | 23,000. | 45,000. | — | — | 300,000. |
| 1787 Cent, Arrows in Left Talon | 100. | 250. | 650. | 1,400. | 3,000. | 6,000. |
| 1787 Cent, "Horn"(die break) From Eagle's Head | 110. | 275. | 700. | 1,500. | 3,250. | 6,500. |

1788 Half Cent          1788 Cent, Period After MASSACHUSETTS

| | G | F | VF | EF | AU | Unc. |
|---|---|---|---|---|---|---|
| 1788 Half Cent | $125. | $300. | $600. | $1,300. | $2,600. | $4,000. |
| 1788 Cent, Period After MASSACHUSETTS | 100. | 250. | 550. | 1,200. | 2,600. | 4,500. |
| 1788 Cent, No Period After MASSACHUSETTS | 115. | 275. | 700. | 1,500. | 2,800. | 5,500. |

Early American coins were produced from handmade dies, which are often individually distinctive. The great number of die varieties that can be found and identified are of interest to collectors who value each according to individual rarity. Values shown for type coins in this guidebook are for the most common die variety of each.

## Connecticut

Authority for establishing a mint near New Haven was granted by the state to Samuel Bishop, Joseph Hopkins, James Hillhouse, and John Goodrich in 1785.

Available records indicate that most of the Connecticut coppers were coined under a subcontract by Samuel Broome and Jeremiah Platt, former New York merchants. Abel Buell and James Atlee were probably the principal diesinkers.

1785 Copper, Bust Facing Left

*See next page for chart.*

**1785 Copper, Bust Facing Right**  **1785 Copper, African Head**  **1786 Copper, ETLIB INDE**

**1786 Copper, Large Head
Facing Right**

**1786 Copper, Mailed
Bust Facing Left**

**1786 Copper,
Draped Bust**

**1786 Copper, Mailed Bust
Facing Left, Hercules Head**

|  | G | VG | F | VF | EF | AU |
|---|---|---|---|---|---|---|
| 1785 Copper, Bust Facing Left . . . . . . . | $225. | $375. | $695. | $1,750. | $3,800. | $8,000. |
| 1785 Copper, Bust Facing Right . . . . . | 60. | 100. | 220. | 675. | 1,750. | 3,500. |
| 1785 Copper, African Head . . . . . . . . . | 75. | 150. | 550. | 1,300. | 3,500. | 7,000. |
| 1786 Copper, ETLIB INDE . . . . . . . . . . | 85. | 170. | 375. | 950. | 2,200. | 4,500. |
| 1786 Copper, Large Head Facing Right | 125. | 275. | 750. | 2,500. | 5,500. |  |

# POST-COLONIAL ISSUES

| | G | VG | F | VF | EF | AU |
|---|---|---|---|---|---|---|
| 1786 Copper, Mailed Bust Facing Left . . . | $60. | $100. | $190. | $550. | $1,350. | $2,750. |
| 1786 Copper, Draped Bust . . . . . . . . . . . | 100. | 200. | 500. | 1,250. | 2,800. | 5,750. |
| 1786 Copper, Mailed Bust Facing Left, Hercules Head . . . . . . . . . . . . . . . . . | 120. | 225. | 600. | 2,000. | 4,500. | |

The Connecticut coppers, especially those dated 1787 and 1788, were usually crudely struck and on imperfect planchets.

**1787 Copper, Small Head Facing Right, ETLIB INDE**

**1787 Copper, Muttonhead Variety**

| | G | VG | F | VF | EF | AU |
|---|---|---|---|---|---|---|
| 1787 Copper, Small Head Facing Right, ETLIB INDE . . . . . . . . . . . . . . . . . | $120. | $200. | $400. | $1,550. | $3,500. | $7,000. |
| 1787 Copper, Liberty Std Right *(2 known)* | | — | | | | |
| 1787 Copper, Mailed Bust Facing Right, INDE ET LIB . . . . . . . . . . . . . . . . . | 120. | 200. | 500. | 2,250. | 4,500. | |
| 1787 Copper, Muttonhead . . . . . . . . . . | 100. | 175. | 450. | 1,900. | 4,000. | 8,250. |

**1787 Copper, Mailed Bust Facing Left**

**1787 Copper, Horned Bust**

**1787 Copper, Laughing Head**

**1787 Copper, Reverse**

| | G | VG | F | VF | EF | AU |
|---|---|---|---|---|---|---|
| 1787 Copper, Mailed Bust Facing Left . . . . . . . . . . . . . . | $60. | $90. | $170. | $525. | $1,500. | $2,700. |
| 1787 Copper, Mailed Bust Facing Left, Laughing Head . . | 60. | 110. | 200. | 600. | 1,750. | 3,000. |
| 1787 Copper, Mailed Bust Facing Left, Hercules Head *(see 1786)* . . . . . . . . . . . . . . . . . . . . | 325. | 650. | 1,400. | 3,300. | 5,500. | — |
| 1787 Copper, Mailed Bust Facing Left, Dated 1787 Over 1877 . . . . . . . . . . . . . . . . . . . . | 90. | 175. | 550. | 1,550. | 4,350. | — |
| 1787 Copper, Mailed Bust Facing Left, Dated 1787 Over 1788 . . . . . . . . . . . . . . . . . . . . | 140. | 225. | 750. | 1,750. | 4,600. | — |
| 1787 Copper, Mailed Bust Facing Left, Horned Bust . . . . | 50. | 75. | 175. | 450. | 1,175. | 2,200. |
| 1787 Copper, Mailed Bust Facing Left, CONNECT . . . . . . | 60. | 125. | 250. | 700. | 1,950. | 2,750. |

**1787 Copper,
Draped Bust
Facing Left**

| | G | VG | F | VF | EF | AU |
|---|---|---|---|---|---|---|
| 1787 Copper, Draped Bust Facing Left .............. | $50. | $85. | $140. | $400. | $975. | $1,900. |
| 1787 Copper, Draped Bust Facing Left, AUCIORI ...... | 50. | 85. | 170. | 500. | 1,100. | 2,300. |
| 1787 Copper, Draped Bust Facing Left, AUCTOPI ...... | 60. | 100. | 220. | 700. | 1,750. | 3,000. |
| 1787 Copper, Draped Bust Facing Left, AUCTOBI ...... | 60. | 100. | 220. | 675. | 1,700. | 2,900. |
| 1787 Copper, Draped Bust Facing Left, CONNFC ...... | 55. | 85. | 175. | 550. | 1,200. | 2,300. |
| 1787 Copper, Draped Bust Facing Left, CONNLC ...... | 85. | 190. | 375. | 875. | 2,000. | 3,200. |
| 1787 Copper, Draped Bust Facing Left, FNDE ......... | 60. | 90. | 190. | 550. | 1,450. | 2,650. |
| 1787 Copper, Draped Bust Facing Left, ETLIR ....... | 55. | 90. | 190. | 550. | 1,450. | 2,650. |
| 1787 Copper, Draped Bust Facing Left, ETIIB ......... | 60. | 90. | 190. | 550. | 1,450. | 2,650. |
| 1787 Copper, GEORGIVS III Obv (Rev as Below) ...... | 1,150. | 2,200. | 4,900. | — | — | — |

| **1788 Copper, Mailed Bust Facing Right** | **1788 Copper, Mailed Bust Facing Left** | **1788 Copper, Draped Bust Facing Left** |
|---|---|---|

| | G | VG | F | VF | EF | AU |
|---|---|---|---|---|---|---|
| 1788 Copper, Mailed Bust Facing Right ............. | $50. | $100. | $220. | $600. | $1,550. | $2,750. |
| 1788 Copper, GEORGIVS III Obv (Rev as Above) ...... | 120. | 225. | 550. | 1,500. | 3,000. | — |
| 1788 Copper, Small Head (see 1787) .............. | 1,100. | 2,450. | 3,900. | 9,000. | 17,000. | — |
| 1788 Copper, Mailed Bust Facing Left .............. | 50. | 80. | 175. | 550. | 1,150. | 2,225. |
| 1788 Copper, Mailed Bust Facing Left, CONNLC ....... | 70. | 145. | 300. | 700. | 2,200. | 3,450. |
| 1788 Copper, Draped Bust Facing Left .............. | 55. | 85. | 220. | 550. | 1,350. | 2,500. |
| 1788 Copper, Draped Bust Facing Left, CONNLC ...... | 95. | 220. | 550. | 1,375. | 2,750. | 4,000. |
| 1788 Copper, Draped Bust Facing Left, INDL ET LIB ... | 90. | 155. | 350. | 825. | 1,975. | 3,500. |

## New York and Related Issues
### *Brasher Doubloons*

Perhaps the most famous pieces coined before establishment of the U.S. Mint at Philadelphia were those produced by the well-known New York goldsmith and jeweler Ephraim Brasher, who was a neighbor and friend of George Washington.

The gold pieces Brasher made weighed about 408 grains and were valued at $15 in New York currency. They were approximately equal to the Spanish doubloon, which was equal to 16 Spanish dollars.

Pieces known as *Lima Style doubloons* were dated 1742, but it is almost certain that they were produced in 1786, and were the first efforts of Brasher to make a circulating coin for local use. Neither of the two known specimens shows the full legends; but weight, gold content, and punchmark are all identical to those for the other Brasher coins. An analogous cast imitation Lima style doubloon dated 1735 bears a hallmark attributed to Standish Barry of Baltimore, Maryland, circa 1787.

An original design was used on the 1787 doubloon with an eagle on one side and the arms of New York on the other. In addition to his impressed hallmark, Brasher's name appears in small letters on each of his coins. The unique 1787 gold half doubloon is struck from doubloon dies on an undersized planchet that weighs half as much as the larger coins.

It is uncertain why Brasher produced these pieces. He was later commissioned to test and verify other gold coins then in circulation. His hallmark EB was punched on each coin as evidence of his testing and its value. In some cases the foreign coins have been weight-adjusted by clipping.

"1742" (1786) Lima Style gold doubloon *(2 known)  $690,000, EF, Heritage auction, Jan-05* . . .   $700,000.

| | |
|---|---:|
| 1787 New York gold doubloon, EB on Breast  *$2,990,000, EF, Heritage auction, Jan-05* | $3,000,000. |
| 1787 New York gold doubloon, EB on Wing  *$2,415,000, AU, Heritage auction, Jan-05* . . | 2,450,000. |
| 1787 New York gold half doubloon *(unique, in Smithsonian Collection)* . . . . . . . . . . . . . | — |
| Various foreign gold coins with Brasher's EB hallmark . . . . . . . . . . . . . . . . . . . . . . . . . | 10,000.+ |

## Copper Coinage

Several individuals petitioned the New York legislature in early 1787 for the right to coin copper for the state, but a coinage was never authorized. Instead, a law was passed to regulate the copper coins already in use. Nevertheless, various unauthorized copper pieces were issued within the state, principally by two private mints.

One firm, known as Machin's Mills, was organized by Thomas Machin and situated near Newburgh. Shortly after this mint was formed, on April 18, 1787, it was merged with the Rupert, Vermont, mint operated by Reuben Harmon Jr. Harmon held a coinage grant from the Republic of Vermont. The combined partnership agreed to conduct their business in New York, Vermont, Connecticut, or elsewhere if they could benefit by it.

The operations at Machin's Mills were conducted in secret and were looked upon with suspicion by the local residents. They minted several varieties of imitation George III halfpence, as well as coppers of Connecticut, Vermont, and New Jersey.

The other mints, located in or near New York City, were operated by John Bailey and Ephraim Brasher. They had petitioned the legislature on February 12, 1787, for a franchise to coin copper. The extent of their partnership, if any, and details of their operation are unknown. Studies of the state coinage show that they produced primarily the EXCELSIOR and NOVA EBORAC pieces of New York, and the "running fox" New Jersey coppers.

*Believed to be the bust of Washington.*

|  | G | VG | F | VF |
| --- | --- | --- | --- | --- |
| 1786, NON VI VIRTUTE VICI .................. | $5,000. | $7,250. | $13,500. | $27,500. |

**1787 EXCELSIOR**
Copper, Eagle on
Globe Facing Right

**1787 EXCELSIOR**
Copper, Large Eagle
on Obverse

|  | G | F | VF | EF |
| --- | --- | --- | --- | --- |
| 1787 EXCELSIOR Copper, Eagle on Globe Facing Right | $2,200. | $7,000. | $16,000. | $31,000. |
| 1787 EXCELSIOR Copper, Eagle on Globe Facing Left | 2,100. | 6,600. | 15,000. | 29,500. |
| 1787 EXCELSIOR Copper, Large Eagle on Obverse, Arrows and Branch Transposed .............. | 4,500. | 14,000. | 30,000. | 40,000. |

# POST-COLONIAL ISSUES

**1787, George Clinton**

**1787, Indian and NY Arms**

**1787, Indian and Eagle on Globe**

**1787, Indian and George III Reverse**

|  | G | VG | F | VF | EF |
|---|---|---|---|---|---|
| 1787, George Clinton . . . . . . . . . . . . | $7,500. | $12,500. | $21,000. | $38,500. | $80,000. |
| 1787, Indian and New York Arms . . . | 6,250. | 9,500. | 16,500. | 33,000. | 62,500. |
| 1787, Indian and Eagle on Globe . . . . | 11,500. | 15,500. | 27,500. | 52,000. | 115,000. |
| 1787, Indian and George III Reverse | | | | | |
|    (3 known) . . . . . . . . . . . . . . . . | | 42,000. | | | |

## Imitation British Halfpence
### (Machin's Mills and Other Coinage of 1786–1789)

The most common coin used for small transactions in early America was the copper British halfpenny. Wide acceptance and the non–legal tender status of these copper coins made them a prime choice for unauthorized reproduction by private individuals. Many such counterfeits were made in this country by casting or other crude methods. Some were made in England and imported to this country. Pieces dated 1781 and 1785 seem to have been made specifically for this purpose, while others were circulated in both countries.

During the American state coinage era, James F. Atlee and/or others engraved dies used to mint unauthorized, lightweight, imitation British halfpence. These American-made British halfpence have the same devices, legends, and, in some cases, dates as genuine regal halfpence. There are three distinct groups of these halfpence, all linked to the regular state coinage. The first group was probably struck in New York City prior to 1786. The second group was minted in New York City in association with John Bailey and Ephraim Brasher during the first half of 1787. The third group was struck at Machin's Mills during the second half of 1787 and into 1788. Pieces dated 1784 are believed to have been struck elsewhere in New England.

Dates used on these pieces were often evasive and are as follows: 1771, 1772, and 1774 through 1776 for the first group; 1747 and 1787 for the second group; and 1776, 1778, 1787, and 1788 for the third group. Pieces generally attributed to Atlee can be identified by a single outline in the crosses (British Union) of Britannia's shield and large triangular denticles along the coin's circumference. These pieces are not to be confused with the similar, English-made George III counterfeits (some of which have identical dates), or with genuine British halfpence (dated 1770 to 1775).

## *Georgivs/Britannia*
### Machin's Mills Copper Halfpennies

| | | Group I | Group II | Group III | | |
|---|---|---|---|---|---|---|
| | **G** | **VG** | **F** | **VF** | **EF** | **AU** |
| 1747, GEORGIVS II | $190. | $330. | $800. | $2,400. | $4,400. | — |
| 1771, GEORGIVS III | 100. | 150. | 380. | 1,000. | 2,700. | $4,600. |
| 1772, GEORGIVS III | 100. | 160. | 450. | 1,100. | 3,100. | 5,500. |
| 1772, GEORGIUS III | 200. | 375. | 850. | 2,250. | 4,400. | — |
| 1774, GEORGIVS III | 65. | 120. | 300. | 850. | 2,300. | 4,000. |
| 1774, GEORGIUS III | 80. | 160. | 350. | 950. | 2,600. | 4,200. |
| 1775, GEORGIVS III | 80. | 130. | 300. | 900. | 2,300. | 3,800. |
| 1776, GEORGIVS III | 200. | 325. | 850. | 1,850. | 4,000. | — |
| 1776, Small Date, CEORCIVS | 900. | 2,000. | 4,400. | 9,500. | — | — |
| 1778, GEORGIVS III | 75. | 125. | 300. | 800. | 2,600. | 4,200. |
| 1784, GEORGIVS III | 375. | 800. | 1,750. | 3,250. | — | — |
| 1787, GEORGIVS III | 65. | 110. | 250. | 700. | 2,100. | 3,600. |
| 1788, GEORGIVS III | 70. | 120. | 300. | 800. | 2,400. | 3,800. |

*Note:* See related George III combinations under Connecticut, Vermont, and New York.

## *Nova Eborac Coinage for New York*

**1787, NOVA EBORAC,**
**Reverse: Seated Figure Facing Right**

**1787, NOVA EBORAC,**
**Reverse: Seated Figure Facing Left**

**1787, NOVA EBORAC, Small Head**        **1787, NOVA EBORAC, Large Head**

|  | Fair | G | F | VF | EF | AU |
|---|---|---|---|---|---|---|
| 1787, NOVA EBORAC, Seated Figure Facing Right ......... |  | $125. | $375. | $1,150. | $2,650. | $3,800. |
| 1787, NOVA EBORAC, Seated Figure Facing Left .......... |  | 110. | 350. | 900. | 1,750. | 3,000. |
| 1787, NOVA EBORAC, Small Head | $1,200. | 3,700. | 7,500. | 19,000. |  |  |
| 1787, NOVA EBORAC, Large Head | 200. | 700. | 2,000. | 7,250. |  |  |

## New Jersey

On June 1, 1786, the New Jersey colonial legislature granted to Thomas Goadsby, Albion Cox, and Walter Mould authority to coin some three million coppers weighing six pennyweight and six grains apiece, not later than June 1788, on condition that they delivered to the Treasurer of the State "one-tenth part of the full sum they shall strike and coin," in quarterly installments. These coppers were to pass current at 15 to the shilling.

In an operation of this kind, the contractors purchased the metal and assumed all expenses of coining. The difference between these expenses and the total face value of the coins issued represented the profit.

Later, Goadsby and Cox asked authority to coin two thirds of the total independently. Their petition was granted November 22, 1786. Mould was known to have produced his coins at Morristown, while Cox (and probably Goadsby) operated in Rahway. Coins were also minted in Elizabethtown and New York.

The series offers many varieties. The obverse shows a horse's head with plow and the legend NOVA CAESAREA ("New Jersey"). The reverse has a United States shield and legend E PLURIBUS UNUM ("One Composed of Many").

**1786, Date Under Draw Bar,**        **1786, Date Under Plow,**
**No Coulter**        **No Coulter**

|  | G | F | VF |
|---|---|---|---|
| 1786, Date Under Draw Bar, No Coulter .................... |  | $40,000. | $90,000. |
| 1786, Date Under Plow, No Coulter ...................... | $900. | 2,750. | 7,500. |

**1786, Narrow Shield**  **Sprig Above Plow**  **1786, Wide Shield**

| | G | F | VF | EF | AU |
|---|---|---|---|---|---|
| 1786, Narrow Shield, Straight Plow Beam .............. | $60. | $220. | $575. | $1,450. | $2,500. |
| 1786, Narrow Shield, Curved Plow Beam .............. | 65. | 230. | 600. | 1,650. | 2,700. |
| 1786, Wide Shield .............. | 70. | 240. | 650. | 2,200. | 3,200. |
| 1786, Wide Shield, Bridle ......... | 70. | 240. | 650. | 2,200. | 3,200. |

**1787, PLURIBS, Large Planchet**  **Small Planchet**  **Outlined Shield**

| | G | F | VF | EF | AU |
|---|---|---|---|---|---|
| 1787, Pronounced Outline to Shield ... | $60. | $220. | $550. | $1,275. | $2,300. |
| 1787, Wide Shield, Sprig Above Plow .. | 60. | 220. | 550. | 1,200. | 2,200. |
| 1787, Narrow Shield, Sprig Above Plow | 60. | 220. | 550. | 1,200. | 2,200. |
| 1787, Small Planchet, Plain Shield .... | 60. | 220. | 550. | 1,200. | 2,200. |
| 1787, Large Planchet, Plain Shield .... | 65. | 220. | 700. | 1,650. | 2,700. |
| 1787, Large Planchet, Plain Shield, PLURIBS .................. | 125. | 475. | 1,300. | 3,275. | 6,500. |
| 1787, Similar, Second U Over S in PLURIBUS .................. | 200. | 500. | 1,400. | 3,275. | 6,500. |
| 1787, Similar, PLURIRUS ........... | 170. | 425. | 925. | 2,725. | 4,450. |
| 1787, Date Over 1887 .............. | 450. | 1,950. | 4,325. | 8,000. | — |

**Camel Head**  **Serpent Head**  **Running Fox Variety**

|  | **G** | **F** | **VF** | **EF** | **AU** |
|---|---|---|---|---|---|
| 1787, "Camel Head" (Snout in High Relief) | $70. | $220. | $800. | $1,500. | $2,750. |
| 1787, Serpent Head ............... | 85. | 350. | 1,400. | 3,250. | 5,250. |
| 1787, WM Above Plow .............. |  |  | — |  |  |
| 1788, Horse's Head Facing Right ...... | 60. | 200. | 750. | 1,400. | 3,000. |
| 1788, Horse's Head Facing Right, |  |  |  |  |  |
|     Running Fox Before Legend ...... | 150. | 575. | 2,100. | 4,450. | 8,500. |
| 1788, Similar, Indistinct Coulter ....... | 450. | 2,250. | 5,500. | 12,000. | — |
| 1788, Horse's Head Facing Left ....... | 400. | 1,600. | 4,300. | 8,000. | — |

## Vermont

Reuben Harmon Jr., of Rupert, Vermont, was granted permission to coin copper pieces for a period of two years beginning July 1, 1785. The well-known Vermont "Landscape" coppers were first produced in that year. The franchise was extended for eight years in 1786.

Harmon's mint was located in the northeast corner of Rupert near a stream known as Millbrook. Colonel William Coley, a New York goldsmith, made the first dies. Some of the late issues were made near Newburgh, New York, by the Machin's Mills coiners.

Most Vermont coppers are struck on poor and defective planchets. Well-struck coins on smooth, full planchets command higher prices.

**1785, IMMUNE COLUMBIA**

**1785, VERMONTS**       **1785, Reverse**       **1785, VERMONTIS**

**1786, VERMONTENSIUM**       **1786, Baby Head**

*See next page for chart.*

| | | **Bust Left** | **1786, Reverse** | | **1787, Reverse** |
|---|---|---|---|---|---|

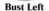

| | G | VG | F | VF | EF | AU |
|---|---|---|---|---|---|---|
| 1785, IMMUNE COLUMBIA ...... | $5,500. | $8,000. | $9,250. | $27,500. | — | — |
| 1785, VERMONTS ............. | 300. | 625. | 1,275. | 3,200. | $7,250. | $12,000. |
| 1785, VERMONTIS ............ | 325. | 750. | 1,500. | 3,750. | 9,500. | 16,000. |
| 1786, VERMONTENSIUM ....... | 250. | 500. | 900. | 2,400. | 3,900. | 8,500. |
| 1786, Baby Head .............. | 350. | 625. | 1,200. | 4,200. | 8,500. | — |
| 1786, Bust Left ............... | 175. | 350. | 850. | 2,500. | 4,500. | — |
| 1787, Bust Left .............. | 4,000. | 9,500. | 23,000. | 38,000. | — | |

**1787, BRITANNIA**

| | G | VG | F | VF | EF | AU |
|---|---|---|---|---|---|---|
| 1787, BRITANNIA ............. | $120. | $160. | $300. | $650. | $1,750. | $3,250. |

*Note:* The reverse of this coin is always weak.

**1787, 1788, Bust Right (Several Varieties)**

| | G | VG | F | VF | EF | AU |
|---|---|---|---|---|---|---|
| 1787, Bust Right (several varieties) | $150. | $250. | $550. | $1,300. | $2,750. | $4,300. |
| 1788, Bust Right (several varieties) | 120. | 170. | 425. | 950. | 1,700. | 3,300. |
| 1788, Backward C in AUCTORI .. | 4,500. | 6,750. | 14,000. | — | — | |
| 1788, *ET LIB* *INDE ........ | 350. | 675. | 1,400. | 4,250. | 13,000. | — |

**1788, GEORGIVS III REX**

| | G | VG | F | VF | EF | AU |
|---|---|---|---|---|---|---|
| 1788, GEORGIVS III REX . . . . . . . . | $550. | $900. | $2,400. | $4,250. | $12,000. | |

*Note:* This piece should not be confused with the common English halfpence with similar design and reverse legend BRITANNIA.

# PRIVATE TOKENS AFTER CONFEDERATION
## North American Tokens

This piece was struck in Dublin, Ireland. The obverse shows the seated figure of Hibernia facing left. The date of issue is believed to have been much later than that shown on the token. Like many Irish tokens, this issue found its way to America in limited quantities and was accepted near the Canadian border.

| | VG | F | VF | EF | AU |
|---|---|---|---|---|---|
| 1781, copper or brass . . . . . . . . . . . . | $70. | $140. | $325. | $775. | $1,600. |

## Bar Coppers

The Bar copper is undated and of uncertain origin. It has 13 parallel and unconnected bars on one side. On the other side is the large roman-letter USA monogram. The design was supposedly copied from a Continental button.

The significance of the design is clearly defined by its extreme simplicity. The separate 13 states (bars) unite into a single entity as symbolized by the interlocking letters (USA).

This piece is believed to have first circulated in New York during November 1785, and may have been made in England.

On the less valuable struck copy made by J.A. Bolen (circa 1862) the A passes under, instead of over, the S.

| | VG | F | VF | EF | AU | Unc. |
|---|---|---|---|---|---|---|
| (Undated) (Circa 1785) Bar Copper | $1,500. | $2,750. | $4,500. | $7,000. | $9,000. | — |

## Auctori Plebis Tokens

This token is sometimes included with the coins of Connecticut, as it greatly resembles issues of that state. It was struck in England by an unknown maker, possibly for use in America.

|  | G | VG | F | VF | EF | AU | Unc. |
|---|---|---|---|---|---|---|---|
| 1787, AUCTORI PLEBIS | $100. | $160. | $325. | $700. | $1,300. | $2,400. | $6,250. |

## Mott Store Cards

This item has long been considered an early token because of its date (1789). Some scholars believe it was most likely produced no earlier than 1807 as a commemorative of the founding of the Mott Company, and probably served as a business card. The firm, operated by Jordan Mott, was located at 240 Water Street, a fashionable section of New York at that time.

|  | F | VF | EF | AU | Unc. |
|---|---|---|---|---|---|
| 1789, Mott Token, Thick Planchet | $260. | $450. | $800. | $1,350. | $2,000. |
| 1789, Mott Token, Thin Planchet | 350. | 600. | 1,300. | 2,300. | 3,500. |
| 1789, Mott Token, Entire Edge Engrailed | 450. | 700. | 1,750. | 2,900. | 4,500. |

## Standish Barry Threepence

Standish Barry, of Baltimore, circulated a silver threepence in 1790. He was a watch-and clockmaker, an engraver, and, later, a silversmith. The tokens are believed to have been an advertising venture at a time when small change was scarce. The precise date on this piece may indicate that Barry intended to commemorate Independence Day, but there are no records to prove this. The head on the obverse is probably that of George Washington. The legend BALTIMORE TOWN JULY 4, 90, appears in the border. Also see the gold doubloon attributed to Barry (p. 61).

|  | F | VF |
|---|---|---|
| 1790 Threepence | $15,000. | $30,000. |

## Albany Church Pennies

The First Presbyterian Church of Albany, New York, authorized an issue of 1,000 copper uniface tokens in 1790. These passed at 12 to a shilling and were used to stop contributions of worn and counterfeit coppers. Two varieties were made, one with the addition of a large D (the British abbreviation for penny) above the word CHURCH.

| | VG | F |
|---|---|---|
| (Undated) (1790) Without D ............................................... | $6,250. | $14,500. |
| (Undated) (1790) With D Added ........................................ | 6,200. | 13,500. |

## Kentucky Tokens

These tokens were struck in England circa 1792 to 1794. Each star in the triangle represents a state, identified by its initial letter. These pieces are usually called *Kentucky cents* because the letter K (for Kentucky) happens to be at the top. Some of the edges are plain; others are engrailed with an oblique reeding; and some have edge lettering that reads PAYABLE IN LANCASTER LONDON OR BRISTOL or PAYABLE AT BEDWORTH NUNEATON OR HINKLEY.

| | VF | EF | AU | Unc. |
|---|---|---|---|---|
| (1792–1794) Copper, Plain Edge .............. | $215. | $400. | $700. | $1,200. |
| (1792–1794) Copper, Engrailed Edge .......... | 550. | 950. | 1,600. | 3,500. |
| (1792–1794) Copper, Lettered Edge, PAYABLE AT BEDWORTH, etc. ...................... | — | — | — | — |
| (1792–1794) Copper, Lettered Edge, PAYABLE IN LANCASTER, etc. .................... | 250. | 450. | 800. | 1,300. |
| (1792–1794) Copper, Lettered Edge, PAYABLE AT I. FIELDING, etc. .................... | — | — | — | — |

## Franklin Press Tokens

This piece is an English tradesman's token, but, being associated with Benjamin Franklin, has accordingly been included in American collections.

|  | VF | EF | AU | Unc. |
|---|---|---|---|---|
| 1794 Franklin Press Token .................... | $275. | $450. | $750. | $1,300. |
|   Similar, Edge Reads AN ASYLUM FOR THE | | | | |
|     OPPRESS'D OF ALL NATIONS *(unique)* ....... | | | | |
|   Similar, Edge Diagonally Reeded *(unique)* ....... | | | | |

## Talbot, Allum & Lee Cents

Talbot, Allum & Lee, engaged in the India trade and located at 241 Pearl Street, New York, placed a large quantity of English-made coppers in circulation during 1794 and 1795. ONE CENT appears on the 1794 issue, and the legend PAYABLE AT THE STORE OF on the edge. The denomination is not found on the 1795 reverse but the edge legend was changed to read WE PROMISE TO PAY THE BEARER ONE CENT. Rare plain-edged specimens of both dates exist. Exceptional pieces have edges ornamented or with lettering CAMBRIDGE BEDFORD AND HUNTINGDON.X.X. Many of these tokens were later cut down and used by the U.S. Mint as planchets for coining 1795 and 1797 half cents.

**1794 Cent, With NEW YORK**

**1795 Cent**

|  | VG | VF | EF | AU | Unc. |
|---|---|---|---|---|---|
| 1794 Cent, With NEW YORK ........ | $85. | $275. | $450. | $750. | $1,600. |
| 1794 Cent, Without NEW YORK ..... | 575. | 2,250. | 5,000. | 7,000. | |
| 1795 Cent .................... | 80. | 245. | 400. | 650. | 1,250. |

## Myddelton Tokens

These tokens were struck at the Soho Mint of Boulton and Watt near Birmingham, England, but they were never actually issued for circulation in Kentucky. They are unsurpassed in beauty and design by any piece of this period.

| | PF |
| --- | --- |
| 1796, copper . . . . . . . . . . . . . . . . . . | $20,000. |

| | PF |
| --- | --- |
| 1796, silver . . . . . . . . . . . . . . . . . . | $20,000. |

## Copper Company of Upper Canada Tokens

The obverse of this piece is the same as that of the Myddelton token. The new reverse refers to a Canadian firm and may have been made for numismatic purposes, or as part of coiner's samples.

| | PF |
| --- | --- |
| 1796, copper . . . . . . . . . . . . . . . . . . . . . . . . . . . . . . . . . . . . . . . . . . . . . . . | $9,000. |

## Castorland Medals

These medals, or "jetons," are dated 1796 and allude to a proposed French settlement known as Castorland in Carthage, New York, at the time of the French Revolution. They were given to directors of the colonizing company for their attendance at board meetings.

Copy dies are still available and have been used at the Paris Mint for restriking throughout the years. Restrikes have a more modern look. Their metallic content (in French) is impressed on the edge: ARGENT (silver), CUIVRE (copper), and OR (gold).

*See next page for chart.*                     **73**

| | EF | AU | Unc. |
|---|---|---|---|
| 1796, Original, silver (Reeded Edge, Unbroken Dies) .......... | $5,000. | $7,000. | $10,000. |
| 1796, Original, silver or bronze (Reverse Rusted and Broken) .... | 200. | 225. | 550. |
| (1796) Undated, Restrike, silver (Paris Mint Edge Marks) ....... | | 30. | 70. |
| (1796) Undated, Restrike, bronze (Paris Mint Edge Marks) ...... | | 20. | 40. |

## Theatre at New York Tokens

These token pennies were issued by Skidmore of London and illustrate the Park Theatre, New York, circa 1797.

| | EF | PF |
|---|---|---|
| Penny, THE THEATRE AT NEW YORK AMERICA ................ | $8,000. | $14,000. |

## New Spain (Texas) Jola Tokens

These copper tokens were authorized by the military governor of San Antonio in 1818. Eight thousand pieces were coined by José Antonio de la Garza (JAG). Large- and small-planchet varieties exist, and all are very rare.

| | F | VF | EF |
|---|---|---|---|
| 1818 1/2 Real ........................................ | $6,500. | $9,000. | $18,000. |

## North West Company Tokens

These tokens were probably valued at one beaver skin and struck in Birmingham in 1820 by John Walker & Co. All but two known specimens are holed, and most have been found in the region of the lower Columbia River valley in Oregon.

| | G | VG | F | VF |
|---|---|---|---|---|
| 1820, copper or brass ..................... | $750. | $2,000. | $4,000. | $7,500. |

# WASHINGTON PIECES

Coins and tokens in this interesting series dated from 1783 to 1795 bear the portrait of George Washington. The likenesses in most instances were faithfully reproduced and were designed to honor the first president. Many of these pieces were of English origin and were made later than their dates indicate.

The legends generally signify a strong unity among the states and the marked display of patriotism that pervaded the new nation during that period. We find among these tokens an employment of what were soon to become the nation's official coin devices, namely, the American eagle, the United States shield, and stars. The denomination ONE CENT is used in several instances, while on some of the English pieces HALFPENNY will be found. Several of these pieces were private patterns for proposed coinage contracts.

## Georgivs Triumpho Tokens

Although the head shown on this token bears a strong resemblance to that on some coins of George III, many collectors consider the Georgivs Triumpho (Triumphant George) a token intended to commemorate the successful termination of the Revolutionary War.

The reverse side shows the Goddess of Liberty behind a framework of 13 bars and fleurs-de-lis. Holding an olive branch in her right hand and staff of liberty in her left, she is partially encircled by the words VOCE POPOLI ("By the Voice of the People") 1783.

| | VG | F | VF | EF | AU | Unc. |
|---|---|---|---|---|---|---|
| 1783, GEORGIVS TRIUMPHO . . . . . | $125. | $275. | $650. | $1,300. | $2,450. | $6,500. |

## Washington Portrait Pieces

**Large Military Bust, Point of Bust Close to W**

| | F | VF | EF | AU | Unc. |
|---|---|---|---|---|---|
| 1783, Large Military Bust . . . . . . . . . . . . | $90. | $190. | $450. | $1,000. | $2,750. |
| 1783, Small Military Bust, Plain Edge . . . | 95. | 220. | 550. | 1,350. | 3,400. |
| 1783, Small Military Bust, Engrailed Edge | 150. | 300. | 750. | 1,900. | 3,800. |

| | F | VF | EF | AU | Unc. | PF |
|---|---|---|---|---|---|---|
| 1783, Draped Bust, No Button (illustrated) . . . . . . . . . . . . . . | $95. | $200. | $425. | $850. | $2,400. | |
| 1783, Draped Bust, With Button (on Drapery at Neck) . . . . . . . | 150. | 350. | 650. | 1,050. | 4,500. | |
| 1783, Draped Bust, Copper Restrike, Plain Edge . . . . . . . . | | | | | | $900. |
| 1783, Draped Bust, Copper Restrike, Engrailed Edge . . . . | | | | | | 700. |
| 1783, Draped Bust, Silver Restrike, Engrailed Edge . . . . | | | | | | 1,600. |

| | VG | VF | EF | AU | Unc. |
|---|---|---|---|---|---|
| 1783, UNITY STATES . . . . . . . . . . . . . | $115. | $275. | $550. | $1,100. | $2,600. |

| | F | VF | EF | AU | Unc. |
|---|---|---|---|---|---|
| (Undated) Double-Head Cent . . . . . . . . | $100. | $275. | $550. | $1,100. | $3,000. |

**Satirical Medal Presumably of American Origin**

| | G |
|---|---|
| 1784, Ugly Head, Copper *$20,000, Stack's auction, Dec-83* .......................... | $60,000. |
| 1784, Ugly Head, Pewter *(unique)* ................................................ | |

### 1791 Cent, Edge Lettered UNITED STATES OF AMERICA

| **Obverse** | **Large Eagle Reverse** | | **Small Eagle Reverse** | |
|---|---|---|---|---|
| | **F** | **EF** | **AU** | **Unc.** |
| 1791 Cent, Large Eagle (Date on Obverse) ...... | $500. | $950. | $1,750. | $2,800. |
| 1791 Cent, Small Eagle (Date on Reverse) ....... | 525. | 1,000. | 2,000. | 3,300. |

| | **F** | **EF** | **AU** |
|---|---|---|---|
| 1791 Liverpool Halfpenny, Lettered Edge .................... | $1,400. | $4,000. | $6,500. |

**1792, Eagle With Stars Reverse**

*See next page for chart.*

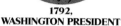

**1792,**
**WASHINGTON PRESIDENT**

**Legend Reverse**

**(1792) Undated,**
**WASHINGTON BORN VIRGINIA**

| | VG | F | VF | EF |
|---|---|---|---|---|
| 1792, WASHINGTON PRESIDENT, Eagle With Stars Reverse | | | | |
| PRESIDENT at Side of Bust, copper | | | | — |
| PRESIDENT Extends Below Bust, copper | | | | — |
| PRESIDENT Extends Below Bust, silver | | | $125,000. | — |
| PRESIDENT Extends Below Bust, gold *(unique)* | | | — | |
| 1792, WASHINGTON PRESIDENT, Legend on Reverse | | | | |
| Plain Edge, copper | $2,750. | $7,000. | 13,000. | |
| Lettered Edge, copper | — | — | — | — |
| (1792) Undated, WASHINGTON BORN VIRGINIA, Eagle With Stars Reverse, copper *(3 known)* | | — | | |
| (1792) Undated, WASHINGTON BORN VIRGINIA, Legend on Reverse | | | | |
| Copper | 2,000. | 4,000. | 7,000. | $11,000. |
| Silver | — | — | — | |

*Note:* Uniface restrike of lettered obverse exists, made from transfer dies by Albert Collis, 1959.

## *Getz Patterns*

Dies engraved by Peter Getz of Lancaster, Pennsylvania, were probably intended for the half dollar and cent, but were rejected by the president, who did not want his portrait on the first United States coinage.

| | VG | F | VF | EF |
|---|---|---|---|---|
| 1792, Small Eagle, silver *$241,500, AU, Stack's auction, May-04* | — | — | — | $250,000. |
| 1792, Sm Eagle, copper *$54,625, EF, Stack's auction, May-04* | $5,500. | $10,000. | $20,000. | 50,000. |
| 1792, Small Eagle, Ornamented Edge (Circles and Squares), copper *$149,500, EF, Stack's auction, May-04* | — | — | — | 150,000. |
| 1792, Small Eagle, Ornamented Edge, silver *(4 known)* *$391,000, Unc, Stack's auction, May-04* | — | — | — | 100,000. |
| 1792, Large Eagle, silver *$34,500, EF, Stack's auction, May-04* | — | — | 34,500. | |

**1792 Cent, Roman Head, Lettered Edge: UNITED STATES OF AMERICA**

| | PF |
|---|---|
| 1792 Cent, Roman Head, Lettered Edge UNITED STATES OF AMERICA, Proof . . . . . . . . . . . . . . . | *$35,000.* |

**1793 Ship Halfpenny, Lettered Edge**

| | F | VF | EF | AU | Unc. |
|---|---|---|---|---|---|
| 1793 Ship Halfpenny, Lettered Edge . . | $220. | $450. | $800. | $1,300. | $3,000. |
| 1793 Ship Halfpenny, Plain Edge *(rare)* | | — | — | | |

**1795 Halfpenny, Grate Token**
*Large Coat Buttons variety shown.*

| | VF | EF | AU | Unc. |
|---|---|---|---|---|
| 1795, Large Buttons, Lettered Edge . . . . . . . . . . . . . | $425. | $850. | $1,600. | $2,300. |
| 1795, Large Buttons, Reeded Edge . . . . . . . . . . . . . | 210. | 425. | 650. | 1,000. |
| 1795, Small Buttons, Reeded Edge . . . . . . . . . . . . . | 275. | 575. | 900. | 1,800. |

## *Liberty and Security Tokens*

*See next page for chart.*

| | F | VF | EF | AU | Unc. |
|---|---|---|---|---|---|
| 1795 Halfpenny, Plain Edge . . . . . . . . | $160. | $350. | $675. | $1,300. | $3,250. |
| 1795 Halfpenny, LONDON Edge . . . . . . | 150. | 325. | 650. | 1,100. | 3,000. |
| 1795 Halfpenny, BIRMINGHAM Edge | 170. | 375. | 750. | 1,600. | 3,450. |
| 1795 Halfpenny, ASYLUM Edge . . . . . . | 300. | 650. | 1,500. | 2,400. | 4,000. |
| 1795 Penny, ASYLUM Edge . . . . . . . . | — | — | | | |

**(1795) Undated, Liberty and Security Penny**

| | F | VF | EF | AU | Unc. |
|---|---|---|---|---|---|
| (1795) Undated, Liberty and Security Penny . . . . | $300. | $525. | $1,000. | $1,700. | $3,400. |
| Same, Corded Outer Rims . . . . . . . . . . . . . . . . . | 650. | 1,075. | 2,100. | 3,750. | 5,500. |

## *North Wales Halfpennies*

| | G | F | VF | EF | AU |
|---|---|---|---|---|---|
| 1795, NORTH WALES Halfpenny . . . . . | $110. | $275. | $600. | $1,450. | $2,750. |
| 1795, Lettered Edge . . . . . . . . . . . . . . | 550. | 1,500. | 3,800. | 6,500. | — |
| 1795, Two Stars at Each Side of Harp | 2,500. | 6,000. | 14,000. | | |

## *Success Medals*

| | F | VF | EF | AU | Unc. |
|---|---|---|---|---|---|
| (Undated) SUCCESS Medal, Large, Plain or Reeded Edge . . . . | $270. | $525. | $975. | $2,200. | $3,900. |
| (Undated) SUCCESS Medal, Small, Plain or Reeded Edge . . . . | 325. | 650. | 1,200. | 2,400. | 4,250. |

*Note:* These pieces are struck in copper or brass and are believed to have been made in the mid-19th century. Specimens with original silvering are rare and are valued 20 to 50% higher. Varieties exist.

## CONTINENTAL CURRENCY

The Continental Currency pieces probably had some value at the time they were issued, but the exact nature of their monetary role is still unclear. They were the first silver dollar–sized coins ever proposed for the United States, and may have been intended as a substitute for the paper dollar. One obverse die was engraved by someone whose initials were E.G. (undoubtedly Elisha Gallaudet) and is marked EG FECIT ("EG Made It"). Studies of the coinage show that there may have been two separate emissions made at different mints. The link design on the reverse was suggested by Benjamin Franklin.

Varieties result from differences in the spelling of the word CURRENCY and the addition of EG FECIT on the obverse. These coins were struck in pewter, brass, and silver. Pewter pieces probably served as a dollar, substituting for paper currency of this design that was never issued. Brass and silver pieces may have been experimental or patterns. Pewter pieces in original bright Uncirculated condition are worth an additional premium.

Numerous copies and replicas of these coins have been made over the years. Authentication is recommended for all pieces.

CURRENCY             CURENCY

| | G | F | VF | EF | AU | Unc. |
|---|---|---|---|---|---|---|
| 1776 CURENCY, Pewter *(2 varieties)* | $7,000. | $11,000. | $19,000. | $27,500. | $37,500. | $55,000. |
| 1776 CURENCY, Brass *(2 varieties)* | 22,000. | 35,000. | 55,000. | 80,000. | — | — |
| 1776 CURENCY, Silver *(2 known)* | | | | | | |
|    $345,000. VF, Stack's auction, Jan-05 | | 250,000. | 350,000. | | | |
| 1776 CURRENCY, Pewter . . . . . . . . | 7,250. | 12,000. | 20,000. | 29,000. | 39,000. | 57,500. |
| 1776 CURRENCY, EG FECIT, Pewter | 7,500. | 13,000. | 22,000. | 31,000. | 42,000. | 60,000. |
| 1776 CURRENCY, EG FECIT, Silver | | | | | | |
|    *(2 known)* $425,500. EF, | | | | | | |
|    Stack's auction, Oct-03 . . . . . | — | — | — | 430,000. | — | — |
| 1776 CURRENCEY, Pewter . . . . . . . | — | — | — | — | 100,000. | — |
| 1776 CURRENCY, Ornament After Date *(2 known)* | | | | | | |

## NOVA CONSTELLATIO PATTERNS

These Nova Constellatio pieces undoubtedly represent the first patterns for a coinage of the United States. They were designed by Benjamin Dudley for Gouverneur Morris to carry out his ideas for a decimal coinage system. The 1,000-unit designation he called a *mark*, the 500 a *quint*. These denominations, together with the small 100-unit piece, were designed to standardize the many different coin values among the several states. These pattern pieces represent the first attempt at a decimal ratio, and were the forerunners of our present system of money values. Neither the proposed denominations nor the coins advanced beyond the pattern stage. These unique pieces are all dated 1783. There are two types of the quint. The enigmatic copper "five" was first brought to the attention of collectors in 1980. Electrotypes exist.

5 Units

Bit (100 Units)

Quint (Type 1)

Reverse

Quint (Type 2)

Mark

| | | |
|---|---|---|
| 1783 (Five) "5," Copper | ................................................................ | *(unique)* |
| 1783 (Bit) "100," Silver, Decorated Edge *$97,500, Unc, B&R auction, Nov-79* | ............... | *(2 known)* |
| 1783 (Bit) "100," Silver, Plain Edge | ....................................................... | *(unique)* |
| 1783 (Quint) "500," Silver, Type 1 *$165,000, Unc, B&R auction, Nov-79* | .................... | *(unique)* |
| 1785 (Quint) "500," Silver, Type 2 *$55,000, Unc, B&R auction, Nov-79* | ..................... | *(unique)* |
| 1785 (Mark) "1000," Silver *$190,000, Unc, B&R auction, Nov-79* | .......................... | *(unique)* |

## FUGIO CENTS

The first coins issued by authority of the United States were the "Fugio" cents. Entries in the *Journal of Congress* supply interesting information about proceedings relating to this coinage. For example, the entry of Saturday, April 21, 1787, reads as follows: "That the board of treasury be authorized to contract for three hundred tons of copper coin of the federal standard, agreeable to the proposition of Mr. James Jarvis.... That it be coined at the expense of the contractor, etc."

On Friday, July 6, 1787, it was "[r]esolved, that the board of treasury direct the contractor for the copper coinage to stamp on one side of each piece the following device, viz: thirteen circles linked together, a small circle in the middle, with the words 'United States,' around it; and in the centre, the words 'We are one'; on the other side of the same piece the following device, viz: a dial with the hours expressed on the face of it; a meridian sun above on one side of which is the word 'Fugio,' [the intended meaning is *time flies*] and on the other the year in figures '1787,' below the dial, the words 'Mind Your Business.'"

The legends have been credited to Benjamin Franklin, and the coin, as a consequence, has sometimes been referred to as the Franklin cent.

These cents were coined in New Haven, Connecticut, and possibly elsewhere. Most of the copper used in this coinage came from military stores, and in fact, is believed to have consisted of the copper bands that held together the powder kegs sent to America by the French. The dies were made by Abel Buell of New Haven.

**Cross After Date**   **Label With Raised Rims**   **American Congress Pattern**

| | VG | F | VF | EF | AU | Unc. |
|---|---|---|---|---|---|---|
| Obv No Cinquefoils, Cross After Date | | | | | | |
| Reverse Rays and AMERICAN CONGRESS .. | | | — | $240,000. | | |
| Reverse Label with Raised Rims *(ex. rare)* .. | | | | 22,000. | | |
| Reverse STATES UNITED ............... | $750. | $1,500. | $4,000. | 7,000. | $12,000. | — |
| Reverse UNITED STATES ............... | 700. | 1,400. | 3,750. | 6,500. | 10,000. | — |

**Cinquefoil After Date**

| | VG | F | VF | EF | AU | Unc. |
|---|---|---|---|---|---|---|
| STATES UNITED at Sides of Circle, Cinquefoils on Label ............ | $300. | $550. | $900. | $1,500. | $2,000. | $3,400. |
| STATES UNITED, 1 Over Horiz 1 ....... | 450. | 950. | 2,500. | 5,000. | | |
| UNITED STATES, 1 Over Horiz 1 ....... | 400. | 875. | 2,500. | 5,000. | | |
| UNITED STATES at Sides of Circle ...... | 300. | 575. | 900. | 1,700. | 2,000. | 3,500. |
| STATES UNITED, Label With Raised Rims, Large Letters in WE ARE ONE | 550. | 1,000. | 2,400. | 5,250. | 10,000. | 18,000. |
| STATES UNITED, 8 Pointed Stars on Label ..................... | 500. | 700. | 1,200. | 2,500. | 4,500. | 8,500. |
| UNITED Above, STATES Below *(rare)* ... | 1,500. | 3,000. | 7,500. | 10,000. | 15,000. | — |

*Note: These types, with pointed rays, have regular obverses punctuated with four cinquefoils (five-leafed ornaments).*

## 1787 With Club Rays

| | VG | F | VF | EF | AU |
|---|---|---|---|---|---|
| Club Rays, Rounded Ends ................. | $475. | $1,000. | $2,200. | $4,000. | $7,500. |
| Club Rays, Concave Ends to Rays, FUCIO (C instead of G) *(ex. rare)* ............... | 3,250. | 7,000. | 17,000. | 26,000. | |
| Club Rays, Concave Ends, FUGIO, UNITED STATES | 4,000. | 8,250. | 20,000. | — | — |
| Club Rays, Similar, STATES UNITED Reverse ..... | — | — | | — | — |

So-called New Haven "restrikes" are believed to have been made from dies created in the 1860s. A story circulated at that time that these were old dies found by 14-year-old C. Wylls Betts in 1858 on the site of the Broome & Platt store in New Haven, where the original coins were made.

**New Haven Restrike**
*Note narrow rings.*

| | EF | AU | Unc. |
|---|---|---|---|
| Gold *(2 known)* ......................................... | — | — | — |
| Silver ................................................. | $1,250. | $1,750. | $2,950. |
| Copper or Brass ......................................... | 400. | 600. | 1,000. |

## 1792 PROPOSED COINAGE

Many members of the House favored a representation of the president's head on the obverse of each coin; others considered the idea a monarchical practice. Washington is believed to have expressed disapproval of the use of his portrait on American coins.

The majority considered a figure emblematic of Liberty more appropriate, and the Senate finally concurred in this opinion. Robert Birch was an engraver employed at designing proposed devices for American coins. He, perhaps together with others, engraved the dies for the disme and half disme. He has also been associated with a large copper cent of unusual design known as the Birch cent.

## 1792 SILVER CENTER CENT

| | F | VF | EF | AU |
|---|---|---|---|---|
| Cent, Silver Center (13 known, including one unique specimen without plug) | $140,000. | $250,000. | $375,000. | $450,000. |
| Cent, Without Silver Center (9 known) | 175,000. | 450,000. | 700,000. | 850,000. |

## 1792 BIRCH CENT

G.W.Pt.

| | F | VF | EF |
|---|---|---|---|
| Copper, Lettered Edge, TO BE ESTEEMED * BE USEFUL* (8 known) | $100,000. | $300,000. | $375,000. |
| Copper, Plain Edge (2 known) | | 300,000. | |
| Copper, Lettered Edge, TO BE ESTEEMED BE USEFUL * (2 known) | | | — |
| White Metal, G*W.Pt. (George Washington President) Below Wreath (unique) | | | 475,000. |

## 1792 HALF DISME

| | G | VG | F | VF | EF | AU | Unc. |
|---|---|---|---|---|---|---|---|
| Silver | $14,000. | $23,000. | $35,000. | $65,000. | $95,000. | $160,000. | $350,000. |
| Copper (unique) | | | | — | | | |

## 1792 DISME

| | VF | EF | Unc. |
|---|---|---|---|
| Silver (3 known) | $500,000. | $750,000. | — |
| Copper (about 15 known; illustrated) | 100,000. | 180,000. | $400,000. |

## 1792 QUARTER DOLLAR

Joseph Wright, an accomplished artist in the private sector, designed this attractive, pattern quarter dollar intended for the original United States coins. He was George Washington's choice for the position of first chief engraver of the United States Mint, and designed the 1793 Liberty Cap cent in that capacity, but died in September 1793 before being confirmed by Congress. Unique uniface trials of the quarter dollar pattern obverse and reverse also exist.

| | |
|---|---|
| 1792, Copper *(illustrated)* | *(2 known)* |
| 1792, White Metal | *(4 known)* |

## A SKETCH OF COIN COLLECTING IN AMERICA

When the Philadelphia Mint was constructed in 1792 and produced its first coins for general circulation in 1793, there was no community of numismatists in the United States.

In June 1838, the Mint Cabinet was established. Adam Eckfeldt, an old-timer who had been at the Mint since 1792, contributed some coins he had set aside in recent years. Before this, there had been no effort to save pieces for posterity. This is why many early United States coins made in quantity are very rare or even nonexistent in Mint State today. Year by year more people became attracted to the hobby, probably to the extent of several hundred enthusiasts by the 1850s.

In 1857, the discontinuation of the copper half cent and cent prompted a wave of nostalgia for these coins that had been around since childhood. Many people tried to find as many different dates as possible, before they all disappeared. In 1858, the American Numismatic Society was formed, and in that era several other collecting groups were organized as well. The first coin-collecting magazine was the *American Journal of Numismatics*, 1866. The American Numismatic Association began in 1891 and soon adopted *The Numismatist* (which had been published since 1888) as its official magazine.

In the 1930s, coin collecting took a great leap forward with the introduction of popular albums by Wayte Raymond and, in 1934, "penny boards" by J.K. Post, whose business later became a part of Whitman Publishing. The first *Guide Book of United States Coins* appeared in 1946 (with a cover date of 1947). Today, it has been estimated that several million collectors buy coins from the U.S. Mint and otherwise acquire pieces of interest—colonial and pre-federal, such as in the sections discussed above, or more modern, as in the sections to follow. With the continuing parade of new commemoratives and other coin designs, collector interest remains high, making numismatics one of the most dynamic and popular hobbies in the United States today.

The half cent is the lowest face value coin struck by the United States. All half cents are scarce, and this series is beginning to enjoy the popularity of large cents and certain other early series. Prices for the common dates and varieties have remained at reasonable levels for many years.

This denomination was authorized on April 2, 1792. Originally the weight was to have been 132 grains, but this was changed to 104 grains by the Act of January 14, 1793, before coinage commenced. The weight was again changed to 84 on January 26, 1796, by presidential proclamation in conformity with the Act of March 3, 1795. Coinage was discontinued by the Act of February 21, 1857. All were coined at the Philadelphia Mint.

There were various intermissions in coinage. During the period from 1836 through 1848, coinage consisted entirely of Proofs and in very small quantities, causing a very noticeable lapse in the series for most collectors. While 1796 is the most valuable date, the original and restrike Proofs of 1831, 1836, and 1840 through 1848, along with other rare varieties, are all difficult to obtain.

## TYPE COIN VALUES

| | G-4 | F-12 | EF-40 | AU-50 | MS-60 | MS-63 | MS-65 | PF-60 | PF-63 | PF-65 |
|---|---|---|---|---|---|---|---|---|---|---|
| Liberty Cap, 1793 | $2,200.+ | $5,000.+ | $18,500.+ | $27,500.+ | $40,000.+ | $65,000.+ | $100,000. | | | |
| Liberty Cap, 1794–1797 | 375.+ | 800.+ | 3,400.+ | 7,500.+ | 15,000. | 20,000. | 50,000. | | | |
| Draped Bust, 1800–1808 | 60.+ | 100.+ | 325.+ | 600.+ | 1,000.+ | 2,000. | 6,500. | | | |
| Classic Head, 1809–1836 | 45.+ | 60.+ | 100.+ | 175.+ | 350.+ | 500. | 2,000. | $4,500. | $5,000. | $7,500. |
| Braided Hair, 1840–1857 | 45.+ | 60.+ | 95.+ | 150.+ | 245.+ | 400. | 2,250. | 2,500. | 4,000. | 7,000. |

+ or – indicates change from previous year

## LIBERTY CAP, HEAD FACING LEFT (1793)

*Designer probably Joseph Wright; weight 6.74 grams; composition, copper; approx. diameter 22 mm; edge: TWO HUNDRED FOR A DOLLAR.*

**AG-3 ABOUT GOOD**—Clear enough to identify.
**G-4 GOOD**—Outline of bust of Liberty clear, no details. Date readable. Reverse lettering incomplete.
**VG-8 VERY GOOD**—Some hair details. Reverse lettering complete.
**F-12 FINE**—Most of hair detail visible. Leaves worn, but all visible.
**VF-20 VERY FINE**—Hair near ear and forehead worn, other areas distinct. Some details in leaves visible.
**EF-40 EXTREMELY FINE**—Light wear on highest parts of head and wreath.
**AU-50 ABOUT UNCIRCULATED**—Only a trace of wear on Liberty's face.

*Values shown are for coins with attractive surfaces and color consistent with the amount of normal wear. Minor imperfections are permissible for grades below Fine. Coins that are porous, corroded, or similarly defective are worth significantly lower prices.*

| | Mintage | AG-3 | G-4 | VG-8 | F-12 | VF-20 | EF-40 | AU-50 |
|---|---|---|---|---|---|---|---|---|
| 1793 | 35,334 | $1,200. | $2,200. | $3,500. | $5,000. | $8,750. | $18,500. | $27,500. |

## LIBERTY CAP, HEAD FACING RIGHT (1794–1797)

*1794—Designer Robert Scot; weight 6.74 grams; composition, copper; approx. diameter 23.5 mm; edge: TWO HUNDRED FOR A DOLLAR. 1795—Designer John Smith Gardner; weight 6.74 grams; composition, copper; approx. diameter 23.5 mm; edge: TWO HUNDRED FOR A DOLLAR. 1795–1797 (thin planchet)—Weight 5.44 grams; composition, copper; approx. diameter 23.5 mm; edge: plain (some 1797 are either lettered or gripped).*

**AG-3–AU-50**—See previous type for grading details.

**Normal Head** **High-Relief Head**

*See next page for chart.*

| | Mintage | AG-3 | G-4 | VG-8 | F-12 | VF-20 | EF-40 | AU-50 |
|---|---|---|---|---|---|---|---|---|
| 1794, All kinds ......81,600 | | | | | | | | |
| 1794, Normal Head ...... | | $260. | $500. | $700. | $1,300. | $2,200. | $4,750. | $9,000. |
| 1794, High-Relief Head ... | | 285. | 525. | 750. | 1,400. | 2,400. | 5,000. | 9,250. |

**Pole to Cap**

**Punctuated Date**

**No Pole to Cap**

| | Mintage | AG-3 | G-4 | VG-8 | F-12 | VF-20 | EF-40 | AU-50 |
|---|---|---|---|---|---|---|---|---|
| 1795, All kinds ......139,690 | | | | | | | | |
| 1795, Lettered Edge, With Pole ............. | | $225. | $425. | $675. | $1,100. | $2,000. | $4,500. | $8,000. |
| 1795, Lettered Edge, Punctuated Date ........ | | 225. | 425. | 675. | 1,100. | 2,000. | 4,500. | 8,000. |
| 1795, Plain Edge, Punctuated Date ........ | | 175. | 375. | 550. | 800. | 1,500. | 4,000. | 7,500. |
| 1795, Plain Edge, No Pole **(a)** | | 175. | 375. | 550. | 800. | 1,500. | 4,000. | 7,500. |
| 1796, With Pole **(b)** ....1,390 | | 6,500. | 10,000. | 15,000. | 20,000. | 35,000. | 50,000. | 75,000. |
| 1796, No Pole .............* | | 12,000. | 26,000. | 37,500. | 55,000. | 100,000. | | |

* Included in number above. **a.** Many are struck on cut-down cents, or are on planchets cut from Talbot, Allum & Lee tokens (see page 72). **b.** The deceptive "Dr. Edwards" struck copy of this coin has a different head and larger letters.

**1797, 1 Above 1**

**1797, Low Head**

| | Mintage | AG-3 | G-4 | VG-8 | F-12 | VF-20 | EF-40 | AU-50 |
|---|---|---|---|---|---|---|---|---|
| 1797, All kinds **(a)** ....127,840 | | | | | | | | |
| 1797, 1 Above 1, Pl Edge ... | | $200. | $400. | $575. | $850. | $1,600. | $3,400. | $5,500. |
| 1797, Plain Edge ......... | | 220. | 450. | 600. | 1,100. | 2,200. | 4,500. | 6,000. |
| 1797, Pl Edge, Low Head ... | | 275. | 475. | 675. | 1,600. | 2,500. | 8,500. | — |
| 1797, Lettered Edge ....... | | 650. | 1,400. | 2,500. | 5,500. | 11,000. | 26,000. | 57,500. |
| 1797, Gripped Edge ....... | | 8,200. | 20,000. | 50,000. | 65,000. | — | — | — |

**a.** Many are struck on cut-down cents, or are on planchets cut from Talbot, Allum & Lee tokens (see page 72).

## DRAPED BUST (1800–1808)

*Designer Robert Scot; weight 5.44 grams; composition, copper; diameter 23.5 mm; plain edge.*

**AG-3 ABOUT GOOD**—Clear enough to identify.
**G-4 GOOD**—Outline of bust of Liberty clear, few details, date readable. Reverse lettering worn and incomplete.
**VG-8 VERY GOOD**—Some drapery visible. Date and legends complete.
**F-12 FINE**—Shoulder drapery and hair over brow worn smooth.
**VF-20 VERY FINE**—Only slight wear in previously mentioned areas. Slight wear on reverse.
**EF-40 EXTREMELY FINE**—Light wear on highest parts of head and wreath.
**AU-50 ABOUT UNCIRCULATED**—Wear slight on hair above forehead.

# HALF CENTS

**1st Reverse
(Style of 1800)**

**2nd Reverse
(Style of 1803)**

| | Mintage | AG-3 | G-4 | VG-8 | F-12 | VF-20 | EF-40 | AU-50 |
|---|---|---|---|---|---|---|---|---|
| 1800 . . . . . . . . . . . . . .202,908 | | $35. | $60. | $75. | $135. | $240. | $600. | $850. |
| 1802, 2/0, Rev of 1800 . . . . . .* | 8,500. | 20,000. | 30,000. | 44,000. | 55,000. | — | — |
| 1802, 2/0, 2nd Rev . . . . .20,266 | 325. | 650. | 1,400. | 3,300. | 9,000. | 22,000. | — |
| 1803 . . . . . . . . . . . . . . . . . . .* | 30. | 60. | 85. | 140. | 275. | 800. | 1,200. |
| 1803, Widely Spaced 3 . .92,000 | 30. | 60. | 85. | 140. | 275. | 800. | 1,200. |

* Included in number below.

**Plain 4**      **Crosslet 4**      **Stemless Wreath**      **Stems to Wreath**

| | Mintage | AG-3 | G-4 | VG-8 | F-12 | VF-20 | EF-40 | AU-50 |
|---|---|---|---|---|---|---|---|---|
| 1804, All kinds . . . . . 1,055,312 | | | | | | | | |
| 1804, Plain 4, Stems to Wreath. . . . . . . . | $35. | $70. | $100. | $180. | $325. | $850. | $1,650. |
| 1804, Plain 4, Stemless Wreath. . . . . . . . | 30. | 60. | 75. | 100. | 175. | 325. | 575. |
| 1804, Crosslet 4, Stemless. . . . . . . . . . . . . | 30. | 60. | 75. | 100. | 175. | 325. | 575. |
| 1804, Crosslet 4, Stems . . . . | 30. | 60. | 75. | 100. | 175. | 325. | 575. |
| 1804, "Spiked Chin" . . . . . . . | 35. | 70. | 85. | 110. | 220. | 375. | 650. |

**1804, "Spiked Chin"**      **Small 5**      **Medium 5**      **Large 5**

| | Mintage | AG-3 | G-4 | VG-8 | F-12 | VF-20 | EF-40 | AU-50 |
|---|---|---|---|---|---|---|---|---|
| 1805, All kinds. . . . . . . 814,464 | | | | | | | | |
| 1805, Med 5, Stemless. . . . . | $30. | $60. | $75. | $100. | $170. | $325. | $575. |
| 1805, Sm 5, Stems. . . . . . . . | 275. | 700. | 1,300. | 2,600. | 5,000. | 9,500. | 16,000. |
| 1805, Lg 5, Stems . . . . . . . . | 30. | 60. | 75. | 100. | 170. | 325. | 575. |

| | | Large 6 | | Small 6 | | 1808, 8 Over 7 | Normal Date |

| | Mintage | AG-3 | G-4 | VG-8 | F-12 | VF-20 | EF-40 | AU-50 |
|---|---|---|---|---|---|---|---|---|
| 1806, All kinds .....356,000 | | | | | | | | |
| 1806, Small 6, Stems ...... | | $80. | $220. | $375. | $650. | $1,300. | $2,850. | $6,500. |
| 1806, Small 6, Stemless ... | | 30. | 60. | 80. | 90. | 135. | 275. | 600. |
| 1806, Large 6, Stems ...... | | 30. | 60. | 80. | 90. | 135. | 275. | 600. |
| 1807 .............476,000 | | 30. | 60. | 80. | 100. | 175. | 450. | 900. |
| 1808, All kinds ......400,000 | | | | | | | | |
| 1808, 8 Over 7 ........... | | 65. | 135. | 275. | 600. | 1,300. | 3,400. | 9,000. |
| 1808, Normal Date ........ | | 30. | 60. | 80. | 100. | 175. | 450. | 900. |

## CLASSIC HEAD (1809–1836)

*Designer John Reich. Standards same as for previous issue.*

**G-4 GOOD**—LIBERTY only partly visible on hair band. Lettering, date, stars, worn but visible.
**VG-8 VERY GOOD**—LIBERTY entirely visible on hair band. Lower curls worn.
**F-12 FINE**—Only partial wear on LIBERTY, and hair at top worn in spots.
**VF-20 VERY FINE**—Lettering clear-cut. Hair only slightly worn.
**EF-40 EXTREMELY FINE**—Light wear on highest points of hair and leaves.
**AU-50 ABOUT UNCIRCULATED**—Sharp hair detail with only a trace of wear on higher points.
**MS-60 UNCIRCULATED**—Typical brown to red surface. No trace of wear.
**MS-63 CHOICE UNCIRCULATED**—Well-defined color, brown to red. No traces of wear.

**1811, Wide Date**

**1809, 9 Over Inverted 9**   **1809, Small o Inside 0**   **1809, Normal Date**   **1811, Close Date**

| | Mintage | G-4 | VG-8 | F-12 | VF-20 | EF-40 | AU-50 | MS-60 | MS-63 |
|---|---|---|---|---|---|---|---|---|---|
| 1809, All kinds .......1,154,572 | | | | | | | | | |
| 1809, Small o Inside 0 ........ | | $45. | $55. | $80. | $120. | $325. | $500. | $900. | $1,400. |
| 1809, 9 Over Inverted 9 ....... | | 45. | 70. | 85. | 110. | 250. | 700. | 1,000. | 1,800. |
| 1809, Normal Date .......... | | 45. | 55. | 70. | 90. | 120. | 220. | 600. | 800. |
| 1810 ................215,000 | | 45. | 65. | 110. | 220. | 450. | 800. | 1,750. | 2,750. |
| 1811, All kinds .........63,140 | | | | | | | | | |
| 1811, Wide Date ............ | | 165. | 375. | 650. | 1,500. | 5,000. | 6,000. | 10,000. | 13,500. |
| 1811, Close Date ............ | | 150. | 325. | 600. | 1,400. | 4,500. | 5,500. | 7,500. | 10,000. |
| 1811, Rev of 1802, Unofficial Restrike *(ex. rare)* ........ | | | | | | — | — | | |
| 1825 ..................63,000 | | 45. | 55. | 70. | 85. | 165. | 375. | 850. | 1,300. |
| 1826 ................234,000 | | 45. | 55. | 70. | 85. | 135. | 275. | 500. | 700. |

**13 Stars** **12 Stars**

| | Mintage | G-4 | VG-8 | F-12 | VF-20 | EF-40 | AU-50 | MS-60 | MS-63 |
|---|---|---|---|---|---|---|---|---|---|
| 1828, All kinds........ 606,000 | | | | | | | | | |
| 1828, 13 Stars ............. | | $45. | $55. | $65. | $90. | $100. | $160. | $375. | $500. |
| 1828, 12 Stars ............. | | 45. | 55. | 65. | 100. | 220. | 320. | 1,200. | 1,650. |
| 1829 ............... 487,000 | | 45. | 55. | 65. | 90. | 135. | 185. | 350. | 600. |

Beginning in 1831, new coinage equipment and modified dies produced a raised rim on each side of these coins. Proofs and restrikes were made at the Mint for sale to collectors. Restrikes are believed to have been struck circa 1858 through 1861.

**Reverse (1831–1836)** **Reverse (1840–1857)**

| | Mintage | PF-40 | PF-60 | PF-63 |
|---|---|---|---|---|
| 1831, Original *(beware of altered date)* ................2,200 | | $11,000. | $14,000. | $22,000. |
| 1831, Restrike, Large Berries (Reverse of 1836) .............. | | — | 5,500. | 11,000. |
| 1831, Restrike, Small Berries (Reverse of 1840–1857) ........ | | — | 7,500. | 16,000. |

| | Mintage | VG-8 | F-12 | VF-20 | EF-40 | AU-50 | MS-60 | PF-63 |
|---|---|---|---|---|---|---|---|---|
| 1832 **(a)** ........... 51,000 | | $45. | $60. | $70. | $100. | $165. | $350. | $4,800. |
| 1833 **(a)** .......... 103,000 | | 45. | 60. | 70. | 100. | 165. | 350. | 4,800. |
| 1834 **(a)** .......... 141,000 | | 45. | 60. | 70. | 100. | 165. | 350. | 4,800. |
| 1835 **(a)** .......... 398,000 | | 45. | 60. | 70. | 100. | 165. | 350. | 4,800. |
| 1836, Original ............. | | | | | | | | 8,000. |
| 1836, Restrike (Reverse of 1840–1857)........ | | | | | | | | 13,500. |

**a.** The figures given here are thought to be correct, although official Mint records report these quantities for 1833 through 1836 rather than 1832 through 1835.

No half cents were struck in 1837. Because of the great need for small change, however, a large number of tokens similar in size to current large cents were issued privately by businessmen who needed them in commerce. Thousands of half cent tokens were issued of the variety listed and illustrated below.

| | G-4 | VG-8 | F-12 | VF-20 | EF-40 | AU-50 | MS-60 |
|---|---|---|---|---|---|---|---|
| 1837 Token *(not a coin)* ..... | $35. | $50. | $60. | $100. | $175. | $300. | $550. |

## BRAIDED HAIR (1840–1857)

Both originals and restrikes use the reverse of 1840 to 1857. Most originals have large berries and most restrikes have small berries in the wreath.

*Designer Christian Gobrecht; weight 5.44 grams; composition, copper; diameter 23 mm; plain edge.*

**VG-8 VERY GOOD**—Beads in hair uniformly distinct. Hair lines visible in spots.
**F-12 FINE**—Hair lines above ear worn. Beads sharp.
**VF-20 VERY FINE**—Lowest curl worn; hair otherwise distinct.
**EF-40 EXTREMELY FINE**—Light wear on highest points of hair and on leaves.
**AU-50 ABOUT UNCIRCULATED**—Very slight trace of wear on hair above Liberty's ear.
**MS-60 UNCIRCULATED**—No trace of wear. Clear luster.
**MS-63 CHOICE UNCIRCULATED**—No trace of wear.
**PF-63 CHOICE PROOF**—Nearly perfect.

*Brilliant red Uncirculated half cents are worth more than prices shown.*

| | PF-63 | PF-65 | | PF-63 | PF-65 |
|---|---|---|---|---|---|
| 1840, Original | $5,500. | $8,000. | 1845, Original | $5,500. | $8,000. |
| 1840, Restrike | 5,000. | 7,500. | 1845, Restrike | 5,000. | 7,500. |
| 1841, Original | 5,000. | 7,500. | 1846, Original | 5,500. | 8,000. |
| 1841, Restrike | 4,500. | 7,000. | 1846, Restrike | 5,000. | 7,500. |
| 1842, Original | 5,500. | 8,000. | 1847, Original | 5,500. | 8,500. |
| 1842, Restrike | 5,000. | 7,500. | 1847, Restrike | 4,500. | 7,000. |
| 1843, Original | 5,500. | 7,500. | 1848, Original | 6,000. | 8,500. |
| 1843, Restrike | 5,000. | 7,500. | 1848, Restrike | 5,000. | 7,500. |
| 1844, Original | 5,500. | 8,000. | 1849, Original, Sm Dt | 5,500. | 8,000. |
| 1844, Restrike | 5,000. | 7,500. | 1849, Restrike, Sm Dt | 6,000. | 8,500. |

**1849, Small Date**     **1849, Large Date**

*Brilliant red Uncirculated half cents are worth more than prices shown.*

| | Mintage | VG-8 | F-12 | VF-20 | EF-40 | AU-50 | MS-60 | MS-63 | PF-63 |
|---|---|---|---|---|---|---|---|---|---|
| 1849, Large Date | 39,864 | $50. | $65. | $80. | $140. | $220. | $400. | $550. | — |
| 1850 | 39,812 | 50. | 65. | 80. | 140. | 220. | 400. | 650. | $4,800. |
| 1851 | 147,672 | 45. | 60. | 70. | 95. | 145. | 245. | 425. | 4,800. |
| 1852, Original | | | | | | | | | — |
| 1852, Restrike | | | | | | | | | 4,800. |
| 1853 | 129,694 | 45. | 60. | 70. | 95. | 145. | 245. | 425. | |
| 1854 | 55,358 | 45. | 60. | 70. | 95. | 145. | 245. | 425. | 4,800. |
| 1855 | 56,500 | 45. | 60. | 70. | 95. | 145. | 245. | 425. | 4,800. |
| 1856 | 40,430 | 45. | 70. | 75. | 110. | 160. | 275. | 475. | 4,800. |
| 1857 | 35,180 | 65. | 90. | 120. | 150. | 220. | 340. | 525. | 4,800. |

Cents and half cents were the first coins struck for circulation under the authority of the United States government. Coinage began in 1793 with laws specifying that the cent should weigh exactly twice as much as the half cent. Large cents were coined every year from 1793 to 1857 with the exception of 1815, when a lack of copper prevented production. All were coined at the Philadelphia Mint. Mintage records in some cases may be inaccurate, as many of the early pieces were struck later than the dates shown on the coins. Varieties listed are those most significant to collectors. Numerous other die varieties may be found because each of the early dies was individually made. Values of varieties not listed in this guide depend on collector interest, rarity, and demand. Proof large cents were first made in 1817; all Proofs are rare, as they were not made available to the general public before the mid-1850s.

## TYPE COIN VALUES

| | G-4 | F-12 | EF-40 | MS-60 | MS-63 | MS-65 | PF-60 | PF-65 |
|---|---|---|---|---|---|---|---|---|
| Chain, 1793 | $6,800.+ | $15,000.+ | $50,000.+ | $100,000. | $150,000. | $350,000. | | |
| Wreath, 1793 | 1,900.+ | 4,250.+ | 11,000.+ | 40,000. | 50,000. | 150,000. | | |
| Liberty Cap, 1793–1796 | 275.+ | 625.+ | 2,800.+ | 7,000. | 8,000. | 17,500. | | |
| Draped Bust, 1796–1807 | 45.+ | 165.+ | 900.+ | 2,500. | 4,000. | 9,500. | | |
| Classic Head, 1808–1814 | 45.+ | 240.+ | 1,200.+ | 4,000. | 6,000. | 12,500. | | |
| Matron Head, 1816–1836 | 18.+ | 28.+ | 140.+ | 350.+ | 550. | 1,450. | $7,000. | $13,000. |
| Matron Head Modified, 1837–1839 | 18.- | 30.+ | 100. | 300. | 400. | 950. | 7,000. | 13,000. |
| Braided Hair, 1839–1857 | 16.+ | 24.+ | 55.+ | 165.+ | 250.+ | 600. | 4,250. | 6,500. |
| + or – indicates change from previous year | | | | | | | | |

## FLOWING HAIR

**AG-3 ABOUT GOOD**—Date and devices clear enough to identify.
**G-4 GOOD**—Lettering worn but readable. No detail on bust.
**VG-8 VERY GOOD**—Date and lettering distinct, some details of head visible.
**F-12 FINE**—About half of hair and other details visible.
**VF-20 VERY FINE**—Ear visible, most details visible.
**EF-40 EXTREMELY FINE**—Wear evident on highest points of hair and back of temple.

### Chain Reverse (1793)

*Designer Henry Voigt; weight 13.48 grams; composition, copper; approx. diameter 26–27 mm; edge: bars and slender vine with leaves.*

**Obverse** **AMERI. Reverse** **AMERICA Reverse**

*Values shown for Fine and better copper coins are for those with attractive surfaces and color consistent with the amount of normal wear. Coins that are porous, corroded, or similarly defective are worth significantly lower prices.*

| | Mintage | AG-3 | G-4 | VG-8 | F-12 | VF-20 | EF-40 |
|---|---|---|---|---|---|---|---|
| 1793 Chain, All kinds | 36,103 | | | | | | |
| 1793, AMERI. in Legend | | $2,750. | $8,000. | $13,500. | $19,000. | $37,500. | $65,000. |
| 1793, AMERICA **(a)** | | 2,400. | 6,800. | 12,000. | 15,000. | 30,000. | 50,000. |

**a.** Varieties with or without periods after date and LIBERTY.

## Wreath Reverse (1793)

The reverse of this type bears a single-bow wreath, as distinguished from the wreath tied with a double bow on the following type. A three-leaf sprig appears above the date on the obverse, and both sides have borders of small beads.

Introduction of this reverse answered criticism of the chain design, but the stronger modeling of the face and hair still failed to gain acceptance as representative of Liberty. After three months' production the design was abandoned in favor of the Liberty Cap type.

Instead of the normal sprig above the date, the rare strawberry-leaf variety has a spray of trefoil leaves and a small blossom. The trefoils match those found on the normal wreath reverse. It is not clear why this variety was created. All four known specimens are badly worn.

*Designer Henry Voigt; weight 13.48 grams; composition, copper; approx. diameter 26–28 mm; edge: vine and bars, or lettered ONE HUNDRED FOR A DOLLAR followed by either a single or a double leaf.*

**Wreath Type**                    **Strawberry Leaf Variety**

| | Mintage | AG-3 | G-4 | VG-8 | F-12 | VF-20 | EF-40 | AU-50 |
|---|---|---|---|---|---|---|---|---|
| 1793, Wreath, All kinds . . . . .63,353 | | | | | | | | |
| 1793, Vine/Bars Edge . . . . . . . . . . | | $550. | $1,900. | $2,650. | $4,250. | $6,500. | $11,000. | $23,000. |
| 1793, Lettered Edge . . . . . . . . . . | | 750. | 2,200. | 3,000. | 4,500. | 7,000. | 13,500. | 25,000. |
| 1793, Strawberry Leaf *(4 known)* | | — | — | \$414,000, Fine, ANR auction, Nov-04 | | | | |

# LIBERTY CAP (1793–1796)

Another major change was made in 1793 to satisfy continuing objections to the obverse portrait. This version appears to have been more successful, as it was continued into 1796. The 1793 pieces had beaded borders, but a border of denticles (or "teeth") was adopted in 1794. A famous 1794 variety is the probably whimsical "starred" reverse, with a border of 94 tiny, five-pointed stars among the denticles.

Portrait variations listed for 1794 are the result of several changes of die engravers. The so-called Jefferson Head of 1795 is now thought to be a sample for a proposed coinage contract by a private manufacturer, John Harper.

Planchets became too thin for edge lettering after the weight reduction ordered in late 1795. The variety with reeded edge was probably an experimental substitute, rejected in favor of a plain edge.

*1793–1795 (thick planchet)—Designer Joseph Wright; weight 13.48 grams; composition, copper; approx. diameter 29 mm; edge: ONE HUNDRED FOR A DOLLAR followed by a single leaf. 1795–1796 (thin planchet)—Designer John Smith Gardner; weight 10.89 grams; composition, copper; approx. diameter 29 mm; plain edge.*

**1793, Vine and Bars Edge**          **Lettered Edge (1793–1795)**
*Chain and Wreath types only.*          **ONE HUNDRED FOR A DOLLAR**

**Beaded Border (1793)**

**Head of 1793 (1793–1794)**
*Head in high, rounded relief.*

**Head of 1794 (1794)**
*Well-defined hair;*
*hook on lowest curl.*

**Head of 1795 (1794–1796)**
*Head in low relief;*
*no hook on lowest curl.*

**1794, Starred Reverse**

| | Mintage | AG-3 | G-4 | VG-8 | F-12 | VF-20 | EF-40 | AU-50 |
|---|---|---|---|---|---|---|---|---|
| 1793, Liberty Cap | 11,056 | $1,700. | $3,500. | $7,000. | $11,000. | $25,000. | $50,000. | — |
| 1794, All kinds | 918,521 | | | | | | | |
|    1794, Head of 1793 | | 500. | 1,250. | 2,500. | 3,750. | 8,500. | 22,000. | — |
|    1794, Head of 1794 | | 120. | 300. | 450. | 750. | 1,400. | 3,200. | — |
|    1794, Head of 1795 | | 120. | 300. | 450. | 700. | 1,300. | 3,000. | — |
|    1794, Starred Reverse | | 4,500. | 9,000. | 14,000. | 32,000. | 55,000. | — | — |
|    1794, No Fraction Bar | | 110. | 300. | 500. | 850. | 1,800. | 5,500. | — |
| 1795, Lettered Edge | 37,000 | 140. | 325. | 500. | 850. | 1,800. | 4,800. | — |
| 1795, Plain Edge | 501,500 | 80. | 275. | 375. | 625. | 1,300. | 2,800. | — |
| 1795, Reeded Edge *(4 known)* | | | | | | | | |

**Reeded Edge**

**"Jefferson" Head**

**1796–1807**
*This head was modified slightly*
*in 1798. See page 97 for details.*

| | Mintage | AG-3 | G-4 | VG-8 | F-12 | VF-20 | EF-40 | AU-50 |
|---|---|---|---|---|---|---|---|---|
| 1795, Jefferson Head *(not a regular Mint issue)*, Plain Edge | | $5,000. | $11,500. | $16,500. | $27,500. | $55,000. | | |
| 1795, Jefferson Head, Lettered Edge *(3 known)* | | — | — | | | | | |
| 1796, Liberty Cap | 109,825 | 140. | 325. | 475. | 1,000. | 2,000. | $5,000. | — |

# DRAPED BUST (1796–1807)

*Designer Robert Scot; weight 10.89 grams; composition, copper; approx. diameter 29 mm; plain edge.*

**AG-3 ABOUT GOOD**—Clear enough to identify.
**G-4 GOOD**—Lettering worn, but clear; date clear. Bust lacking in detail.
**VG-8 VERY GOOD**—Drapery on Liberty partly visible. Less wear in date and lettering.
**F-12 FINE**—Hair over brow smooth; some detail showing in other parts of hair.
**VF-20 VERY FINE**—Hair lines slightly worn. Hair over brow better defined.
**EF-40 EXTREMELY FINE**—Hair above forehead and left of eye outlined and detailed. Only slight wear on olive leaves.

| **Reverse of 1794** | **Reverse of 1795** | **Reverse of 1797** |
|---|---|---|
| **(1794–1796)** | **(1795–1798)** | **(1796–1807)** |
| *Note double leaf at top right; 14–16 leaves on left, 16–18 leaves on right.* | *Note single leaf at top right; 17–21 leaves on left, 16–20 leaves on right.* | *Note double leaf at top right; 16 leaves on left, 19 leaves on right.* |

**LIHERTY**
Error

| | Mintage | AG-3 | G-4 | VG-8 | F-12 | VF-20 | EF-40 |
|---|---|---|---|---|---|---|---|
| 1796, Draped Bust, All kinds . . .363,375 | | | | | | | |
| 1796, Reverse of 1794 . . . . . . . . . . . . | | $110. | $240. | $550. | $850. | $2,200. | $4,500. |
| 1796, Reverse of 1795 . . . . . . . . . . . . | | 90. | 165. | 285. | 600. | 1,600. | 3,200. |
| 1796, Reverse of 1797 . . . . . . . . . . . . | | 90. | 165. | 285. | 600. | 1,500. | 3,000. |
| 1796, LIHERTY Error . . . . . . . . . . . . . | | 165. | 300. | 700. | 1,300. | 3,750. | 7,200. |
| 1796, Stemless Reverse *(2 known)* . . | | | | | | | |

| **Gripped Edge** | **With Stems** | **Stemless** |
|---|---|---|

| | Mintage | AG-3 | G-4 | VG-8 | F-12 | VF-20 | EF-40 |
|---|---|---|---|---|---|---|---|
| 1797, All kinds . . . . . . . . . . . . . .897,510 | | | | | | | |
| 1797, Gripped Edge, 1796 Reverse . . . | | $50. | $135. | $240. | $400. | $850. | $2,750. |
| 1797, Plain Edge, 1796 Reverse . . . . . | | 55. | 145. | 265. | 425. | 875. | 2,800. |
| 1797, 1797 Reverse, Stems . . . . . . . . | | 45. | 110. | 190. | 275. | 635. | 1,750. |
| 1797, 1797 Reverse, Stemless . . . . . . | | 55. | 135. | 265. | 540. | 1,350. | 4,400. |

# LARGE CENTS

**Style 1 Hair** **Style 2 Hair** **1798, 8 Over 7**

*Style 1 hair: all 1796–1797 and many 1798 varieties,
and on 1800 over 1798. Style 2 hair: 1798–1807
(extra curl near shoulder).*

| | Mintage | AG-3 | G-4 | VG-8 | F-12 | VF-20 | EF-40 |
|---|---|---|---|---|---|---|---|
| 1798, All kinds ............1,841,745 | | | | | | | |
| 1798, 8 Over 7 .................. | | $55. | $135. | $275. | $550. | $1,750. | $4,350. |
| 1798, Reverse of 1796 ............ | | 45. | 115. | 275. | 600. | 1,600. | 5,750. |
| 1798, Style 1 Hair ................ | | 35. | 90. | 130. | 250. | 575. | 1,750. |
| 1798, Style 2 Hair ................ | | 32. | 85. | 120. | 250. | 550. | 1,675. |

**1799, 9 Over 8** **1800 Over 1798** **1800, 80 Over 79**

| | Mintage | AG-3 | G-4 | VG-8 | F-12 | VF-20 | EF-40 |
|---|---|---|---|---|---|---|---|
| 1799, 9 Over 8 **(a)** ................ | | $1,500. | $2,800. | $5,000. | $11,500. | $27,500. | — |
| 1799, Normal Date ................ | | 1,200. | 2,400. | 4,500. | 10,000. | 25,000. | — |
| 1800, All kinds ...........2,822,175 | | | | | | | |
| 1800/1798 Style 1 Hair ............ | | 30. | 70. | 135. | 265. | 1,000. | $3,750. |
| 1800, 80/79, Style 2 Hair .......... | | 30. | 70. | 115. | 225. | 550. | 2,000. |
| 1800, Normal Date ............... | | 30. | 70. | 115. | 225. | 500. | 1,750. |

**a.** Mintage for 1799 is included with the 1798 figure.

**Fraction 1/000** **Corrected Fraction** **1801 Reverse, 3 Errors**

*Error-fraction dies appear on cents of 1801–1803, but all of these dies originated in 1801, possibly from
the same engraver.*

*See next page for chart.*

| | Mintage | AG-3 | G-4 | VG-8 | F-12 | VF-20 | EF-40 |
|---|---|---|---|---|---|---|---|
| 1801, All kinds ...........1,362,837 | | | | | | | |
| 1801, Normal Reverse ............ | | $30. | $55. | $85. | $190. | $440. | $1,100. |
| 1801, 3 Errors: 1/000, | | | | | | | |
| One Stem, and IINITED ......... | | 60. | 175. | 350. | 775. | 1,800. | 7,250. |
| 1801, Fraction 1/000 .............. | | 30. | 65. | 100. | 240. | 500. | 1,750. |
| 1801, 1/100 Over 1/000 .......... | | 30. | 75. | 135. | 265. | 700. | 1,950. |
| 1802, All kinds ...........3,435,100 | | | | | | | |
| 1802, Normal Reverse ............ | | 30. | 55. | 85. | 190. | 375. | 975. |
| 1802, Fraction 1/000 .............. | | 30. | 65. | 110. | 220. | 450. | 1,500. |
| 1802, Stemless Wreath ........... | | 30. | 55. | 85. | 190. | 375. | 1,000. |

**1803, Small Date, Blunt 1**    **1803, Large Date, Pointed 1**    **Small Fraction**    **Large Fraction**

*All Small Date varieties have blunt 1 in date.*
*Large Dates have pointed 1 and noticeably larger 3.*

*Values shown for Fine and better copper coins are for those with attractive surfaces and color consistent with the amount of normal wear. Coins that are porous, corroded, or similarly defective are worth significantly lower prices.*

| | Mintage | AG-3 | G-4 | VG-8 | F-12 | VF-20 | EF-40 |
|---|---|---|---|---|---|---|---|
| 1803, All kinds .................3,131,691 | | | | | | | |
| 1803, Small Date, Small Fraction ........... | | $30. | $55. | $90. | $165. | $340. | $900. |
| 1803, Small Date, Large Fraction ........... | | 30. | 55. | 90. | 165. | 340. | 900. |
| 1803, Large Date, Small Fraction ........... | | 2,400. | 4,500. | 8,000. | 14,500. | 22,000. | |
| 1803, Large Date, Large Fraction ........... | | 35. | 80. | 165. | 340. | 900. | 2,750. |
| 1803, 1/100 Over 1/000 ................. | | 30. | 80. | 120. | 240. | 500. | 1,500. |
| 1803, Stemless Wreath .................. | | 30. | 80. | 120. | 240. | 500. | 1,500. |

**Broken Dies**

*All genuine 1804 cents have crosslet 4 in date and a large fraction.*
*The 0 in date is in line with O in OF on reverse.*

| | Mintage | AG-3 | G-4 | VG-8 | F-12 | VF-20 | EF-40 |
|---|---|---|---|---|---|---|---|
| 1804 (a) ...................96,500 | | $600. | $900. | $2,000. | $3,500. | $4,750. | $10,000. |

a. Values shown are for coins with normal or broken dies.

A restrike 1804 was manufactured from discarded mint dies. An altered 1803 die was used for the obverse and a die of the 1820 cent used for the reverse. They were struck circa 1860 to satisfy the demand for this rare date. Known as the "restrike," the product actually is a combination of two unrelated dies and cannot be confused with the genuine.

**Restrike of 1804 Cent**

| | Mintage | AG-3 | G-4 | VG-8 | F-12 | VF-20 | EF-40 |
|---|---|---|---|---|---|---|---|
| 1804, Unofficial Restrike of 1860 *(Uncirculated)* . . . . . . . . . . | | | | | | | $1,000. |
| 1805 . . . . . . . . . . . . . . . . . . . . . . . . . . . . . . . . . . . | 941,116 | $30. | $60. | $85. | $175. | $350. | 1,000. |
| 1806 . . . . . . . . . . . . . . . . . . . . . . . . . . . . . . . . . . . | 348,000 | 30. | 70. | 115. | 225. | 500. | 1,700. |

**Small 1807, 7 Over 6 (Blunt 1)**     **Large 1807, 7 Over 6 (Pointed 1)**     **"Comet" Variety**
*Note die break behind head.*

| | Mintage | AG-3 | G-4 | VG-8 | F-12 | VF-20 | EF-40 |
|---|---|---|---|---|---|---|---|
| 1807, All kinds . . . . . . . . . . . . . . . . . . . | 829,221 | | | | | | |
| 1807, Small 7 Over 6, Blunt 1 . . . . . . . . . . . . | | $1,200. | $2,500. | $4,250. | $8,500. | $17,500. | $32,500. |
| 1807, Large 7 Over 6 . . . . . . . . . . . . . . . . . | | 30. | 55. | 80. | 165. | 400. | 1,000. |
| 1807, Small Fraction . . . . . . . . . . . . . . . . . | | 30. | 55. | 80. | 185. | 425. | 1,300. |
| 1807, Large Fraction . . . . . . . . . . . . . . . . . | | 30. | 55. | 80. | 185. | 375. | 950. |
| 1807, "Comet" Variety . . . . . . . . . . . . . . . . . | | 30. | 55. | 100. | 225. | 525. | 2,500. |

## CLASSIC HEAD (1808–1814)

This group (1808–1814) does not compare in sharpness and quality to those struck previously (1793–1807) nor to those struck later (from 1816 on). The copper used was softer, having less metallic impurity. This impaired the wearing quality of the series. For this reason, collectors find greater difficulty in obtaining these dates in choice condition.

*Designer John Reich; standards same as for previous issue.*

**AG-3 ABOUT GOOD**—Details clear enough to identify.
**G-4 GOOD**—Legends, stars, and date worn, but plain.
**VG-8 VERY GOOD**—LIBERTY all readable. Liberty's ear visible. Details worn but plain.
**F-12 FINE**—Hair on forehead and before ear nearly smooth. Ear and hair under ear sharp.
**VF-20 VERY FINE**—Some detail in all hair lines. Slight wear on leaves on reverse.
**EF-40 EXTREMELY FINE**—All hair lines sharp. Very slight wear on high points.

*See next page for chart.*

|  | Mintage | AG-3 | G-4 | VG-8 | F-12 | VF-20 | EF-40 |
|---|---|---|---|---|---|---|---|
| 1808 ..................1,007,000 | | $25. | $50. | $135. | $300. | $550. | $1,500. |
| 1809 ......................222,867 | | 50. | 120. | 235. | 460. | 1,150. | 3,000. |

| 1810, 10 Over 09 | Normal Date | 1811, Last 1 Over 0 | Normal Date |
|---|---|---|---|

|  | Mintage | AG-3 | G-4 | VG-8 | F-12 | VF-20 | EF-40 |
|---|---|---|---|---|---|---|---|
| 1810, All kinds ............1,458,500 | | | | | | | |
| 1810, 10 Over 09 ............... | | $25. | $50. | $120. | $240. | $550. | $1,400. |
| 1810, Normal Date .............. | | 25. | 50. | 90. | 240. | 525. | 1,200. |
| 1811, All kinds .............218,025 | | | | | | | |
| 1811, Last 1 Over 0 ............. | | 35. | 85. | 135. | 465. | 1,400. | 4,350. |
| 1811, Normal Date .............. | | 40. | 100. | 150. | 375. | 950. | 1,900. |

| 1812, Small Date | 1812, Large Date | 1814, Plain 4 | 1814, Crosslet 4 |
|---|---|---|---|

|  | Mintage | AG-3 | G-4 | VG-8 | F-12 | VF-20 | EF-40 |
|---|---|---|---|---|---|---|---|
| 1812, All kinds ............1,075,500 | | | | | | | |
| 1812, Small Date ................. | | $20. | $45. | $85. | $240. | $550. | $1,200. |
| 1812, Large Date ................. | | 20. | 45. | 85. | 240. | 550. | 1,200. |
| 1813 ......................418,000 | | 25. | 55. | 120. | 265. | 600. | 1,500. |
| 1814, All kinds .............357,830 | | | | | | | |
| 1814, Plain 4 .................... | | 20. | 45. | 85. | 240. | 550. | 1,200. |
| 1814, Crosslet 4 ................. | | 20. | 45. | 85. | 240. | 550. | 1,200. |

# LIBERTY HEAD (1816–1857)

*Designer Robert Scot or John Reich; weight 10.89 grams; composition, copper; approx. diameter 28–29 mm; plain edge.*

**G-4 GOOD**—Details on Liberty's head partly visible. Even wear in date and legends.
**VG-8 VERY GOOD**—LIBERTY, date, stars, and legends clear. Part of hair cord visible.
**F-12 FINE**—All hair lines visible. Hair cords uniformly visible.
**VF-20 VERY FINE**—Hair cords only slightly worn. Hair lines only partly worn, all well defined.
**EF-40 EXTREMELY FINE**—Both hair cords stand out sharply. All hair lines sharp.
**AU-50 ABOUT UNCIRCULATED**—Only traces of wear on hair and highest points on leaves and bow.
**MS-60 UNCIRCULATED**—Typical brown surface. No trace of wear.
**MS-63 CHOICE UNCIRCULATED**—Some distracting contact marks or blemishes in prime focal areas. Impaired luster possible.

## Matron Head (1816–1836)

**Standard Design**                    **15 Stars**

*The values shown for all MS-60 and MS-63 Matron Head large cents are for average condition; red to bright red Uncirculated pieces with attractive surfaces (not cleaned) command higher prices. Beware of slightly worn copper coins that have been cleaned and recolored to simulate uncirculated luster. Cents in VF or better condition with attractive surface and tone may also command higher prices than those listed here.*

| | Mintage | G-4 | VG-8 | F-12 | VF-20 | EF-40 | AU-50 | MS-60 | MS-63 |
|---|---|---|---|---|---|---|---|---|---|
| 1816 . . . . . . . . . . . . . .2,820,982 | | $18. | $25. | $40. | $90. | $190. | $300. | $500. | $700. |
| 1817, All kinds . . . . .3,948,400 | | | | | | | | | |
| 1817, 13 Stars . . . . . . . . . . . | | 18. | 24. | 38. | 75. | 135. | 240. | 450. | 600. |
| 1817, 15 Stars . . . . . . . . . . . | | 20. | 35. | 50. | 135. | 500. | 800. | 2,400. | 3,500. |
| 1818 . . . . . . . . . . . . .3,167,000 | | 19. | 25. | 35. | 70. | 135. | 200. | 525. | 650. |

**1819, 9 Over 8**          **1819, Large Date**          **1819, Small Date**

| | Mintage | G-4 | VG-8 | F-12 | VF-20 | EF-40 | AU-50 | MS-60 | MS-63 |
|---|---|---|---|---|---|---|---|---|---|
| 1819, All kinds . . . . . .2,671,000 | | | | | | | | | |
| 1819, 9 Over 8 . . . . . . . . . . . | | $19. | $27. | $35. | $85. | $240. | $350. | $750. | $1,100. |
| 1819, Large Date . . . . . . . . . | | 18. | 24. | 30. | 65. | 140. | 300. | 450. | 700. |
| 1819, Small Date . . . . . . . . . | | 18. | 24. | 30. | 65. | 140. | 300. | 450. | 700. |

**1820, 20 Over 19**
*Note 1 under 2.*

**1820, Large Date**
*Note plain-topped 2.*

**1820, Small Date**
*Note curl-topped 2.*

| | Mintage | G-4 | VG-8 | F-12 | VF-20 | EF-40 | AU-50 | MS-60 | MS-63 |
|---|---|---|---|---|---|---|---|---|---|
| 1820, All kinds . . . . . .4,407,550 | | | | | | | | | |
| 1820, 20 Over 19 . . . . . . . . . | $18. | $24. | $45. | $110. | $335. | $550. | $1,000. | $1,500. |
| 1820, Large Date . . . . . . . . . | 18. | 23. | 30. | 70. | 175. | 250. | 400. | 600. |
| 1820, Small Date . . . . . . . . . | 18. | 23. | 30. | 70. | 175. | 275. | 450. | 800. |
| 1821 . . . . . . . . . . . . . .389,000 | 32. | 55. | 135. | 375. | 1,300. | 2,300. | 7,500. | — |
| 1822 . . . . . . . . . . . . .2,072,339 | 18. | 23. | 45. | 100. | 275. | 550. | 1,000. | 1,750. |

**1823, 3 Over 2**

**1823, Restrike**

| | Mintage | G-4 | VG-8 | F-12 | VF-20 | EF-40 | AU-50 | MS-60 | MS-63 |
|---|---|---|---|---|---|---|---|---|---|
| 1823, 3 Over 2 . . . . . . . . . . .(a) | $60. | $120. | $300. | $675. | $2,200. | $4,000. | $7,500. | — |
| 1823, Normal Date . . . . . . . .(a) | 65. | 140. | 325. | 800. | 3,000. | 5,750. | 8,500. | — |
| 1823, Unofficial Restrike, | | | | | | | | |
| from broken obverse die . . | | | | 400. | 500. | 900. | 1,200. | |

**a.** Included with 1824.

The 1823 unofficial restrike was made at the same time and by the same people as the 1804 "restrike" (see page 98), using a discarded 1823 obverse and an 1813 reverse die. The dies are heavily rusted (producing lumps on the coins) and most examples have both dies cracked across.

**1824, 4 Over 2**

**1826, 6 Over 5**

| | Mintage | G-4 | VG-8 | F-12 | VF-20 | EF-40 | AU-50 | MS-60 | MS-63 |
|---|---|---|---|---|---|---|---|---|---|
| 1824, All kinds ......1,262,000 | | | | | | | | | |
| 1824, 4 Over 2 ............ | | $25. | $40. | $85. | $260. | $1,450. | $2,750. | $5,500. | $7,000. |
| 1824, Normal Date ......... | | 18. | 25. | 45. | 165. | 500. | 850. | 2,400. | 3,750. |
| 1825 .............1,461,100 | | 18. | 24. | 30. | 100. | 325. | 650. | 2,000. | 2,750. |
| 1826, All kinds ......1,517,425 | | | | | | | | | |
| 1826, 6 Over 5 ............ | | 24. | 45. | 100. | 250. | 900. | 1,350. | 2,750. | 5,000. |
| 1826, Normal Date ......... | | 18. | 24. | 30. | 100. | 250. | 450. | 900. | 1,400. |
| 1827 .............2,357,732 | | 18. | 24. | 30. | 100. | 225. | 400. | 750. | 1,300. |

**Date Size, Through 1828**     **Date Size, 1828 and Later**

| | Mintage | G-4 | VG-8 | F-12 | VF-20 | EF-40 | AU-50 | MS-60 | MS-63 |
|---|---|---|---|---|---|---|---|---|---|
| 1828, All kinds .......2,260,624 | | | | | | | | | |
| 1828, Lg Narrow Date ........ | | $18. | $24. | $35. | $75. | $185. | $400. | $1,200. | $1,750. |
| 1828, Small Wide Date ....... | | 19. | 28. | 50. | 120. | 275. | 525. | 1,900. | 2,250. |

**Large Letters (1808–1834)**     **Medium Letters (1829–1837)**
*Note individual*                *Note isolation*
*letter size and proximity.*     *of letters, esp. STATES.*

| | Mintage | G-4 | VG-8 | F-12 | VF-20 | EF-40 | AU-50 | MS-60 | MS-63 |
|---|---|---|---|---|---|---|---|---|---|
| 1829, All kinds .......1,414,500 | | | | | | | | | |
| 1829, Large Letters ......... | | $18. | $22. | $28. | $85. | $185. | $375. | $550. | $1,200. |
| 1829, Medium Letters ....... | | 19. | 27. | 110. | 340. | 440. | 2,200. | 5,500. | |
| 1830, All kinds .......1,711,500 | | | | | | | | | |
| 1830, Large Letters ......... | | 18. | 22. | 30. | 70. | 190. | 300. | 450. | 850. |
| 1830, Medium Letters ....... | | 22. | 37. | 160. | 450. | 1,200. | 3,250. | 9,500. | |
| 1831, All kinds .......3,359,260 | | | | | | | | | |
| 1831, Large Letters ......... | | 18. | 22. | 28. | 65. | 140. | 250. | 375. | 700. |
| 1831, Medium Letters ....... | | 18. | 22. | 28. | 65. | 175. | 275. | 425. | 800. |
| 1832, All kinds .......2,362,000 | | | | | | | | | |
| 1832, Large Letters ......... | | 18. | 22. | 28. | 65. | 140. | 250. | 375. | 650. |
| 1832, Medium Letters ....... | | 18. | 22. | 28. | 65. | 140. | 250. | 375. | 650. |
| 1833 .............2,739,000 | | 18. | 22. | 28. | 65. | 140. | 250. | 350. | 600. |

| **Large 8 and Stars** | **Large 8, Small Stars** | **Small 8, Large Stars** |

| Mintage | G-4 | VG-8 | F-12 | VF-20 | EF-40 | AU-50 | MS-60 | MS-63 |
|---|---|---|---|---|---|---|---|---|
| 1834, All kinds . . . . . .1,855,100 | | | | | | | | |
| 1834, Large 8, Stars,<br>and Reverse Letters . . . . . . | $18. | $30. | $75. | $190. | $525. | $800. | $2,200. | $3,750. |
| 1834, Large 8 and Stars,<br>Medium Letters . . . . . . . . . | 160. | 325. | 500. | 1,000. | 3,000. | 5,500. | — | — |
| 1834, Large 8, Small Stars,<br>Medium Letters . . . . . . . . . | 18. | 24. | 30. | 65. | 140. | 250. | 275. | 650. |
| 1834, Small 8, Large Stars,<br>Medium Letters . . . . . . . . . | 18. | 24. | 30. | 65. | 140. | 250. | 275. | 600. |

| **Large 8 and Stars,<br>Matron Head** | **Small 8 and Stars,<br>Matron Head** | **1835, Head of 1836** |

| Mintage | G-4 | VG-8 | F-12 | VF-20 | EF-40 | AU-50 | MS-60 | MS-63 |
|---|---|---|---|---|---|---|---|---|
| 1835, All kinds . . . . . . . . . . . .3,878,400 | | | | | | | | |
| 1835, Large 8 and Stars . . . . . . . . . . | $18. | $24. | $30. | $65. | $225. | $400. | $750. | $1,400. |
| 1835, Small 8 and Stars . . . . . . . . . . | 18. | 24. | 30. | 65. | 175. | 275. | 375. | 675. |
| 1835, Head of 1836 . . . . . . . . . . . . . . | 18. | 24. | 30. | 55. | 125. | 250. | 350. | 525. |
| 1836 . . . . . . . . . . . . . . . . . . . . .2,111,000 | 18. | 24. | 30. | 55. | 125. | 250. | 350. | 525. |

## Matron Head Modified (1837–1839)

*Designer Christian Gobrecht; weight 10.89 grams; composition, copper; diameter 27.5 mm; plain edge.*

**G-4 GOOD**—Considerably worn. LIBERTY readable.
**VG-8 VERY GOOD**—Hairlines smooth but visible; outline of ear clearly defined.
**F-12 FINE**—Hairlines at top of head and behind ear worn but visible. Braid over brow plain; ear clear.
**VF-20 VERY FINE**—All details sharper than for F-12. Only slight wear on hair over brow.
**EF-40 EXTREMELY FINE**—Hair above ear detailed, but slightly worn.
**AU-50 ABOUT UNCIRCULATED**—Trace of wear on high points of hair above ear and eye and on highest points on leaves and bow.
**MS-60 UNCIRCULATED**—Typical brown surface. No trace of wear.
**MS-63 CHOICE UNCIRCULATED**—Some distracting contact marks or blemishes in prime focal areas. Impaired luster possible.

# LARGE CENTS

**1829–1837**
*Medium letters;
note letter spacing.*

**Head of 1838**
*Note slim bust
with beaded cords.*

**1837–1839**
*Small letters;
note letter spacing.*

*The values shown for all MS-60 and MS-63 Young Head large cents are for average condition; red to bright red Uncirculated large cents with attractive surfaces (not cleaned) command higher prices. Beware of slightly worn copper coins that have been cleaned and recolored to simulate uncirculated luster. Cents in VF or better condition with attractive surface and tone may also command higher prices than those listed here.*

| | Mintage | G-4 | VG-8 | F-12 | VF-20 | EF-40 | AU-50 | MS-60 | MS-63 |
|---|---|---|---|---|---|---|---|---|---|
| 1837, All kinds ......5,558,300 | | | | | | | | | |
| 1837, Plain Cord, Medium Letters ......... | | $18. | $24. | $30. | $50. | $110. | $225. | $325. | $550. |
| 1837, Plain Cord, Small Letters ........... | | 18. | 24. | 30. | 50. | 120. | 250. | 375. | 600. |
| 1837, Head of 1838 .......... | | 18. | 24. | 30. | 45. | 100. | 185. | 300. | 450. |
| 1838 .............6,370,200 | | 18. | 24. | 30. | 45. | 100. | 175. | 300. | 425. |

**1839 Over 1836**
*Note closed 9,
plain cords.*

**Silly Head**
*Note lock at
forehead.*

**Booby Head**
*Note shoulder tip.*

| | Mintage | G-4 | VG-8 | F-12 | VF-20 | EF-40 | AU-50 | MS-60 | MS-63 |
|---|---|---|---|---|---|---|---|---|---|
| 1839, All kinds ......3,128,661 | | | | | | | | | |
| 1839, 9 Over 6, Plain Cords ............. | | $225. | $440. | $1,200. | $2,400. | $8,000. | $11,500. | — | — |
| 1839, Head of 1838, Beaded Cords .......... | | 18. | 24. | 30. | 50. | 110. | 225. | $325. | $550. |
| 1839, Silly Head ........... | | 19. | 25. | 35. | 75. | 165. | 300. | 850. | 1,200. |
| 1839, Booby Head **(a)** ...... | | 18. | 25. | 35. | 60. | 120. | 275. | 650. | 1,100. |

**a.** The 1839 Booby Head variety has a modified reverse that omits the line under CENT (see 1837–1839 Small Letters photo above).

## Braided Hair (1839–1857)

**1840, Large Date**     **1840, Small Date**     **Small Date Over Large 18**

| | Mintage | G-4 | VG-8 | F-12 | VF-20 | EF-40 | AU-50 | MS-60 | MS-63 |
|---|---|---|---|---|---|---|---|---|---|
| 1839 . . . . . . . . . . . . . . . . . .(b) | | $18. | $23. | $28. | $50. | $110. | $265. | $400. | $650. |
| 1840, All kinds . . . . . .2,462,700 | | | | | | | | | |
|   1840, Large Date . . . . . . . . . | | 16. | 20. | 24. | 35. | 75. | 150. | 300. | 550. |
|   1840, Small Date . . . . . . . . . | | 16. | 20. | 24. | 35. | 75. | 150. | 300. | 550. |
|   1840, Small Date, Lg 18 . . . . . | | 17. | 22. | 27. | 45. | 160. | 370. | 650. | 1,300. |
| 1841, Small Date . . . .1,597,367 | | 16. | 20. | 24. | 40. | 120. | 240. | 450. | 925. |

**b.** Mintage included in "1839, All kinds" on prior page.

**1842, Small Date**     **1842, Large Date**     **Small Letters (1839–1843)**

| | Mintage | G-4 | VG-8 | F-12 | VF-20 | EF-40 | AU-50 | MS-60 | MS-63 |
|---|---|---|---|---|---|---|---|---|---|
| 1842, All kinds . . . . . .2,383,390 | | | | | | | | | |
|   1842, Small Date . . . . . . . . . | | $16. | $20. | $24. | $35. | $85. | $220. | $400. | $650. |
|   1842, Large Date . . . . . . . . . | | 16. | 20. | 24. | 35. | 85. | 150. | 300. | 500. |

**Head of 1840**
*Petite head (1839–1843)*     **Head of 1844**
*Mature head (1843–1857)*     **Large Letters (1843–1857)**

| | Mintage | G-4 | VG-8 | F-12 | VF-20 | EF-40 | AU-50 | MS-60 | MS-63 |
|---|---|---|---|---|---|---|---|---|---|
| 1843, All kinds . . . . . .2,425,342 | | | | | | | | | |
|   1843, Petite, Sm Ltrs . . . . . . . | | $16. | $20. | $24. | $35. | $80. | $140. | $300. | $450. |
|   1843, Petite, Lg Ltrs . . . . . . . | | 18. | 27. | 45. | 80. | 210. | 320. | 825. | 1,400. |
|   1843, Mature, Lg Ltrs . . . . . . . | | 17. | 22. | 27. | 45. | 150. | 275. | 550. | 1,000. |
| 1844, Normal Date . . .2,398,752 | | 16. | 20. | 24. | 40. | 85. | 160. | 250. | 500. |
| 1844, 44 Over 81 . . . . . . . . . . * | | 27. | 30. | 50. | 90. | 210. | 450. | 1,100. | 2,250. |

* Included in number above.

**1846, Small Date**
*Note squat date,
closed 6.*

**1846, Medium Date**
*Note Medium height,
ball-top 6.*

**1846, Tall Date**
*Note vertically stretched
date, open-mouthed 6.*

| | Mintage | G-4 | VG-8 | F-12 | VF-20 | EF-40 | AU-50 | MS-60 | MS-63 |
|---|---|---|---|---|---|---|---|---|---|
| 1845 | 3,894,804 | $16. | $20. | $24. | $32. | $70. | $120. | $225. | $385. |
| 1846, All kinds | 4,120,800 | | | | | | | | |
| 1846, Small Date | | 16. | 20. | 24. | 30. | 65. | 120. | 225. | 350. |
| 1846, Medium Date | | 16. | 20. | 24. | 30. | 70. | 130. | 210. | 450. |
| 1846, Tall Date | | 16. | 22. | 24. | 38. | 100. | 165. | 375. | 820. |
| 1847 | 6,183,669 | 16. | 20. | 24. | 30. | 65. | 120. | 225. | 375. |
| 1847, 7 Over "Small 7" | * | 20. | 26. | 38. | 65. | 135. | 385. | 1,000. | 2,000. |

* Included in number above.

| | Mintage | G-4 | VG-8 | F-12 | VF-20 | EF-40 | AU-50 | MS-60 | MS-63 |
|---|---|---|---|---|---|---|---|---|---|
| 1848 (c) | 6,415,799 | $16. | $20. | $24. | $30. | $65. | $120. | $225. | $375. |
| 1849 | 4,178,500 | 16. | 20. | 24. | 30. | 80. | 135. | 275. | 440. |
| 1850 | 4,426,844 | 16. | 20. | 24. | 30. | 60. | 110. | 175. | 275. |

c. The 1848 Small Date cent is a rare contemporary counterfeit.

The following are not true overdates, but are some of the more spectacular of several date-punch blunders of the 1844 through 1854 period. The so-called overdates of 1844 and 1851 each have the date punched upside down, then corrected normally.

**1844, 44 Over 81**

**1851, 51 Over 81**

**1847, 7 Over "Small" 7**

| | Mintage | G-4 | VG-8 | F-12 | VF-20 | EF-40 | AU-50 | MS-60 | MS-63 |
|---|---|---|---|---|---|---|---|---|---|
| 1851, Normal Date | 9,889,707 | $16. | $20. | $24. | $30. | $55. | $110. | $175. | $275. |
| 1851, 51 Over 81 | * | 20. | 28. | 38. | 55. | 135. | 200. | 450. | 750. |
| 1852 | 5,063,094 | 16. | 20. | 24. | 30. | 55. | 110. | 175. | 275. |
| 1853 | 6,641,131 | 16. | 20. | 24. | 30. | 55. | 110. | 175. | 275. |
| 1854 | 4,236,156 | 16. | 20. | 24. | 38. | 55. | 110. | 175. | 275. |

* Included in number above.

Original sketches of engraver James B. Longacre's work reveal that the slanting 5's in the following pieces were a peculiarity of his. The figure punch for an upright 5 was probably the work of an apprentice.

**1855, Upright 5's**          **1855, Slanting 5's**          **1855, Knob on Ear**

| | Mintage | G-4 | VG-8 | F-12 | VF-20 | EF-40 | AU-50 | MS-60 | MS-63 |
|---|---|---|---|---|---|---|---|---|---|
| 1855, All kinds . . . . . .1,574,829 | | | | | | | | | |
| 1855, Upright 5's . . . . . . . . . | $16. | $22. | $24. | $30. | $55. | $110. | $165. | $250. |
| 1855, Slanting 5's . . . . . . . . . | 16. | 22. | 24. | 30. | 55. | 110. | 190. | 300. |
| 1855, Slanting 5's, | | | | | | | | | |
| Knob on Ear . . . . . . . . . . . | 18. | 23. | 28. | 45. | 85. | 165. | 340. | 540. |
| 1856, All kinds . . . . . .2,690,463 | | | | | | | | | |
| 1856, Upright 5 . . . . . . . . . . . | 16. | 20. | 24. | 30. | 55. | 110. | 165. | 250. |
| 1856, Slanting 5 . . . . . . . . . . | 16. | 20. | 24. | 30. | 55. | 110. | 165. | 250. |

**1857, Large Date**                    **1857, Small Date**

| | Mintage | G-4 | VG-8 | F-12 | VF-20 | EF-40 | AU-50 | MS-60 | MS-63 |
|---|---|---|---|---|---|---|---|---|---|
| 1857, All kinds . . . . . . . .333,546 | | | | | | | | | |
| 1857, Large Date . . . . . . . . . | $50. | $70. | $90. | $110. | $150. | $235. | $340. | $550. |
| 1857, Small Date . . . . . . . . . | 55. | 75. | 100. | 120. | 160. | 260. | 365. | 650. |

## PASSING OF THE LARGE CENT AND HALF CENT

By 1857, the cost of making and distributing copper coins had risen. Mint Director Snowden reported that they "barely paid expenses." Both cents and half cents had become unpopular; in fact, they hardly circulated outside the larger cities. The practice of issuing subsidiary silver coins, which began in 1853, brought about a reform of the copper coinage. The half cent was abandoned and a smaller cent was introduced in 1857.

The law of 1857 brought important benefits to the citizens. By its terms, Spanish coins were redeemed and melted at the mint in exchange for new, small cents. The decimal system became popular and official thereafter, and the old method of reckoning in *reales*, *medios*, shillings, and so on was gradually given up (although the terms *two bits* and *penny* were still commonly used). The new, convenient small cent won popular favor and soon became a useful instrument of retail trade and a boon to commerce.

In 1868, some large cent pieces of the 1843 to 1857 design were created as numismatic specimens.

The Act of February 21, 1857, provided for the coinage of the new copper-nickel small cent. It also called for Spanish and Mexican coins and old copper cents and half cents in circulation to be brought in and exchanged for U.S. silver coins and the new cents. The cent weighed 72 grains, with a metallic composition of 88% copper and 12% nickel.

The 1856 Flying Eagle cent, a pattern, was made to show Congress how the new cent would look. Additional Proof pieces were struck for sale to collectors. It is believed that between 1,500 and 2,500 pieces were struck in all. These have always been collected as regular issues because of their early widespread popularity. A few 1856 Flying Eagle cents probably went into circulation during the Civil War.

Some 1858-dated cents have been altered to read 1856. They are easy to spot because the shape of the 5 is different on the 1858 than it is on the 1856.

Many varieties are known for 1857 and 1858. In particular, 1858 is found with two major variations. In the Large Letter design, the A and M in AMERICA are joined, while in the Small Letter design they are separated; minor variations of the reverse designs of corn, wheat, cotton, and tobacco also appear. The 1858, 8 Over 7 variety can be identified by a small dot in the field above the first 8—during production, the die was ground down until the 7 was invisible. Coins with the 7 showing are more desirable.

## TYPE COIN VALUES

| | G-4 | F-12 | EF-40 | MS-60 | MS-63 | MS-65 | PF-63 | PF-65 |
|---|---|---|---|---|---|---|---|---|
| Flying Eagle, 1857–1858 | $22.00+ | $34.00+ | $140.+ | $320.+ | $650.+ | $3,400.+ | $8,200.+ | $25,000. |
| Indian, CN, 1859 | 15.00+ | 25.00+ | 110.+ | 240.+ | 500.+ | 2,800.+ | 1,600.+ | 5,000. |
| Indian, CN, 1860–1864 | 10.00+ | 20.00+ | 45.+ | 100.+ | 160.+ | 900.+. | 700. | 3,500. |
| Indian, 1864–1909 | 2.00+ | 4.00+ | 10.+ | 35.+ | 55.+ | 80.+ | 300.+ | 400.+ |
| Lincoln, 1909, V.D.B. | 4.50+ | 5.50+ | 7.+ | 15.+ | 18.+ | 60.+ | 2,200.+ | 4,500. |
| + or – indicates change from previous year | | | | | | | | |

# FLYING EAGLE (1856–1858)

*Designer James B. Longacre; weight 4.67 grams; composition .880 copper, .120 nickel; diameter 19 mm; plain edge. All coined at Philadelphia Mint.*

**G-4 GOOD**—All details worn, but readable.
**VG-8 VERY GOOD**—Details in eagle's feathers and eye evident, but worn.
**F-12 FINE**—Eagle-head details and feather tips sharp.
**VF-20 VERY FINE**—Considerable detail visible in feathers in right wing and tail.
**EF-40 EXTREMELY FINE**—Slight wear, all details sharp.
**AU-50 ABOUT UNCIRCULATED**—Slight wear on eagle's left wing and breast.
**MS-60 UNCIRCULATED**—No trace of wear. Light blemishes.
**MS-63 CHOICE UNCIRCULATED**—Some distracting contact marks or blemishes in prime focal areas. Some impairment of luster possible.
**PF-63 CHOICE PROOF**—Nearly perfect.

**1858, 8 Over 7**  **Large Letters**  **Small Letters**

*See next page for chart.*

| | Mintage | G-4 | VG-8 | F-12 | VF-20 | EF-40 | AU-50 | MS-60 | MS-63 | PF-63 |
|---|---|---|---|---|---|---|---|---|---|---|
| 1856 . . . . . . . . . . . . . . .2,000 | | $6,200. | $6,800. | $7,500. | $8,750. | $10,000. | $12,000. | $14,000. | $18,500. | $20,000. |
| 1857 . . . .(485) 17,450,000 | | 22. | 24. | 34. | 50. | 140. | 180. | 320. | 650. | 8,200. |
| 1858, All kinds . .24,600,000 | | | | | | | | | | |
| 1858, Lg Letters . . . .(80) | | 22. | 24. | 34. | 50. | 140. | 180. | 320. | 650. | 8,200. |
| 1858, Sm Ltrs . . . . .(200) | | 22. | 24. | 34. | 50. | 140. | 180. | 320. | 650. | 8,200. |
| 1858, 8 Over 7 . . . . . . . . | | 75. | 100. | 200. | 400. | 800. | 1,400. | 3,250. | 10,000. | |

# INDIAN HEAD

The "Indian Head" design first issued in 1859 is actually a representation of Liberty wearing an Indian headdress, not an actual Indian. The first year featured a laurel wreath on the reverse. This was changed after one year to the oak wreath with a small shield. Coins of 1859 and early 1860 show a pointed bust. Those made from late 1860 until 1864 have a more rounded bust. Prior to the issuance of five-cent nickel pieces in 1866, these coins were commonly referred to as *nickels* or *nicks*. Later, they were called *white cents*.

**G-4 GOOD**—No LIBERTY visible.
**VG-8 VERY GOOD**—At least some letters of LIBERTY readable on headband.
**F-12 FINE**—LIBERTY mostly visible.
**VF-20 VERY FINE**—Slight but even wear on LIBERTY.
**EF-40 EXTREMELY FINE**—LIBERTY sharp. All other details sharp. Only slight wear on ribbon end.
**AU-50 ABOUT UNCIRCULATED**—Very slight trace of wear above the ear and the lowest curl of hair.
**MS-60 UNCIRCULATED**—No trace of wear. Light blemishes.
**MS-63 CHOICE UNCIRCULATED**—Some distracting contact marks or blemishes in prime focal areas. Impaired luster possible.

## Variety 1 – Copper-Nickel, Laurel Wreath Reverse (1859)

*Designer James B. Longacre; weight 4.67 grams; composition .880 copper, .120 nickel; diameter 19 mm; plain edge. All coined at Philadelphia Mint.*

**Laurel Wreath Reverse, Without Shield (1859 Only)**

*Spotted, cleaned, or discolored pieces are worth less than values shown.*

| | Mintage | G-4 | VG-8 | F-12 | VF-20 | EF-40 | AU-50 | MS-60 | MS-63 | PF-63 |
|---|---|---|---|---|---|---|---|---|---|---|
| 1859 (800) . .36,400,000 | | $15. | $20. | $25. | $60. | $110. | $200. | $240. | $500. | $1,600. |

## Variety 2 – Copper-Nickel, Oak Wreath With Shield (1860–1864)

*Standards same as for Variety 1.*

**Oak Wreath Reverse, With Shield (1860–1909)**

| | Mintage | G-4 | VG-8 | F-12 | VF-20 | EF-40 | AU-50 | MS-60 | MS-63 | PF-63 |
|---|---|---|---|---|---|---|---|---|---|---|
| 1860 ....(1,000)....20,566,000 | | $12. | $15. | $20. | $25. | $55. | $85. | $150. | $225. | $800. |
| 1860, Pointed Bust ...........* | | 18. | 20. | 25. | 40. | 85. | 150. | 275. | 500. | |
| 1861 ....(1,000)....10,100,000 | | 22. | 35. | 45. | 60. | 100. | 175. | 225. | 275. | 1,000. |
| 1862......(550)....28,075,000 | | 10. | 15. | 20. | 25. | 45. | 70. | 100. | 160. | 700. |
| 1863......(460)....49,840,000 | | 10. | 15. | 20. | 25. | 45. | 70. | 100. | 160. | 700. |
| 1864......(370)....13,740,000 | | 20. | 25. | 35. | 45. | 75. | 90. | 160. | 200. | 750. |

* Included in number above.

## Variety 3 – Bronze (1864–1909)

*Designer James B. Longacre; weight 3.11 grams; composition .950 copper, .050 tin and zinc; diameter 19 mm; plain edge; mints: Philadelphia, San Francisco.*

During the Civil War, nearly all gold and silver, and eventually the copper-nickel cent, disappeared from circulation. In larger cities, thin, copper, cent-sized tokens began to be issued by merchants to fill the void left by the missing cents. The government stepped in and with the Act of April 22, 1864, issued its own thin, bronze coin and made the issuance of the merchants' tokens illegal.

The obverse was redesigned near the end of 1864. A slightly sharper portrait included the designer's initial L (for Longacre) on the lower ribbon behind the neck. If the coin is turned slightly (so Indian faces observer) the highlighted details of the L will appear to better advantage. The tip of the bust is pointed on the variety with L, and rounded on the variety without L. This design continued until 1909, when the design was replaced with the Lincoln cent.

**Indian Head Cent With L**

| | Mintage | G-4 | VG-8 | F-12 | VF-20 | EF-40 | AU-50 | MS-60 | MS-63 | PF-63 |
|---|---|---|---|---|---|---|---|---|---|---|
| 1864, All kinds .....39,233,714 | | | | | | | | | | |
| 1864, No L (150+).......... | | $10. | $15. | $25. | $40. | $70. | $85. | $100. | $140. | $1,000. |
| 1864, With L (20+).......... | | 60. | 85. | 150. | 175. | 275. | 350. | 400. | 650. | 24,000. |
| 1865 **(a)** (500+).35,429,286 | | 10. | 15. | 20. | 30. | 45. | 65. | 90. | 135. | 475. |
| 1866 (725+)..9,826,500 | | 50. | 60. | 75. | 100. | 185. | 240. | 275. | 330. | 475. |
| 1867 (625+)..9,821,000 | | 50. | 60. | 80. | 135. | 225. | 265. | 290. | 350. | 475. |
| 1868 (600+).10,266,500 | | 45. | 50. | 70. | 100. | 170. | 220. | 250. | 300. | 475. |
| 1869, 9 Over 9 .............* | | 120. | 165. | 275. | 375. | 550. | 650. | 700. | 850. | |
| 1869 (600+)..6,420,000 | | 65. | 85. | 220. | 275. | 375. | 475. | 480. | 600. | 625. |
| 1870 (1,000+)..5,275,000 | | 55. | 75. | 200. | 260. | 350. | 400. | 450. | 565. | 575. |
| 1871 (960+)..3,929,500 | | 65. | 80. | 260. | 300. | 375. | 435. | 480. | 600. | 625. |
| 1872 (950+)..4,042,000 | | 80. | 100. | 300. | 340. | 450. | 550. | 600. | 925. | 950. |

* Included in number below. **a.** One variety of 1865 appears to show traces of a 4 under the 5 in the date. On other varieties, the tip of the 5 is either plain or curved. The 9 is doubled on some varieties of the 1869; on others it appears to be over an 8, although it is actually a doubled 9. None of these varieties is a true overdate. Varieties of 1870, 1871, 1872, and 1873 Close 3 have either a bold or a shallow N in CENT. 1871 and 1872 with shallow N are scarce.

*Chart continued on next page.*

| | Close 3 | | Open 3 | | | | | | | |
|---|---|---|---|---|---|---|---|---|---|---|
| | Mintage | G-4 | VG-8 | F-12 | VF-20 | EF-40 | AU-50 | MS-60 | MS-63 | PF-63 |
| 1873, All kinds ........11,676,500 | | | | | | | | | | |
| 1873, Cl 3 *(1,100+)* ......... | | $25.00 | $35.00 | $60. | $120. | $180. | $225. | $425. | $550. | $575. |
| 1873, Doubled | | | | | | | | | | |
| LIBERTY ................. | | 200.00 | 325.00 | 700. | 1,200. | 2,400. | 4,200. | 7,500. | 13,000. | |
| 1873, Open 3 ............... | | 20.00 | 30.00 | 50. | 85. | 160. | 190. | 250. | 325. | |
| 1874 .........*(700)* 14,187,500 | | 18.00 | 20.00 | 40. | 50. | 100. | 140. | 225. | 250. | 425. |
| 1875 .........*(700)* 13,528,000 | | 18.00 | 20.00 | 40. | 50. | 100. | 140. | 225. | 250. | 425. |
| 1876 .......*(1,150)* 7,944,000 | | 35.00 | 40.00 | 55. | 80. | 160. | 225. | 300. | 380. | 450. |
| 1877 .........*(900)* ...852,500 | | 625.00 | 800.00 | 1,200. | 1,600. | 2,200. | 2,600. | 3,400. | 4,000. | 4,000. |
| 1878 .......*(2,350)* 5,797,500 | | 32.00 | 40.00 | 55. | 80. | 160. | 225. | 300. | 380. | 450. |
| 1879 .......*(3,200)* 16,228,000 | | 8.00 | 12.00 | 18. | 38. | 70. | 80. | 90. | 120. | 375. |
| 1880 .......*(3,955)* 38,961,000 | | 5.00 | 7.00 | 8. | 11. | 26. | 90. | 110. | 130. | 325. |
| 1881 .......*(3,575)* 39,208,000 | | 5.00 | 6.00 | 7. | 10. | 20. | 30. | 60. | 90. | 325. |
| 1882 .......*(3,100)* 38,578,000 | | 5.00 | 6.00 | 7. | 10. | 20. | 30. | 60. | 90. | 325. |
| 1883 .......*(6,609)* 45,591,500 | | 5.00 | 6.00 | 7. | 10. | 20. | 30. | 60. | 90. | 325. |
| 1884 .......*(3,942)* 23,257,800 | | 5.50 | 6.50 | 9. | 14. | 27. | 38. | 75. | 120. | 325. |
| 1885 .......*(3,790)* 11,761,594 | | 8.00 | 9.00 | 15. | 28. | 65. | 75. | 110. | 200. | 325. |
| 1886, All kinds (4,290) 17,650,000 | | | | | | | | | | |
| 1886, Var 1 ................. | | 6.00 | 8.00 | 20. | 55. | 140. | 160. | 200. | 225. | 325. |
| 1886, Var 2 ................. | | 7.50 | 12.00 | 25. | 75. | 190. | 220. | 325. | 475. | 1,000. |

On coins minted from 1859 through mid-1886, the last feather of the headdress points between I and C of AMERICA; on the second variety, from mid-1886 through 1909, it points between C and A.

**1888, Last 8 Over 7**
*A less prominent similar variety exists but is valued lower than the clear overdate.*

| | Mintage | G-4 | VG-8 | F-12 | VF-20 | EF-40 | AU-50 | MS-60 | MS-63 | PF-63 |
|---|---|---|---|---|---|---|---|---|---|---|
| 1887 (2,960) 45,223,523 | | $3.00 | $4.00 | $5.00 | $7.00 | $18.00 | $27.50 | $55. | $80. | $325. |
| 1888 (4,582) 37,489,832 | | 3.00 | 3.50 | 5.00 | 7.50 | 22.00 | 27.00 | 65. | 125. | 325. |
| 1888, 8/7 .. 37,494,414 | | 1,000.00 | 1,300.00 | 1,600.00 | 3,200.00 | 6,500.00 | 16,000. | 22,000. | 27,500. | |
| 1889 (3,336) 48,866,025 | | 3.00 | 3.50 | 5.00 | 7.00 | 20.00 | 25.00 | 60. | 80. | 325. |
| 1890 (2,740) 57,180,114 | | 3.00 | 3.50 | 5.00 | 7.00 | 22.00 | 27.00 | 60. | 80. | 325. |
| 1891 (2,350) 47,070,000 | | 3.00 | 3.50 | 5.00 | 7.00 | 22.00 | 27.00 | 60. | 80. | 325. |
| 1892 (2,745) 37,647,087 | | 3.00 | 3.50 | 5.00 | 7.00 | 22.00 | 27.00 | 60. | 80. | 325. |
| 1893 (2,195) 46,640,000 | | 3.00 | 3.50 | 5.00 | 7.00 | 22.00 | 27.00 | 60. | 80. | 325. |
| 1894 (2,632) 16,749,500 | | 5.00 | 6.00 | 10.00 | 15.00 | 45.00 | 55.00 | 85. | 115. | 325. |
| 1894, Dbl Dt .........* | | 30.00 | 40.00 | 65.00 | 130.00 | 225.00 | 350.00 | 550. | 950. | |
| 1895 (2,062) 38,341,574 | | 3.00 | 4.00 | 5.00 | 7.00 | 15.00 | 25.00 | 40. | 65. | 325. |
| 1896 (1,862) 39,055,431 | | 3.00 | 4.00 | 5.00 | 7.00 | 15.00 | 25.00 | 40. | 65. | 325. |
| 1897 (1,938) 50,464,392 | | 3.00 | 4.00 | 5.00 | 7.00 | 15.00 | 25.00 | 40. | 65. | 325. |
| 1898 (1,795) 49,821,284 | | 3.00 | 4.00 | 5.00 | 7.00 | 15.00 | 25.00 | 40. | 65. | 325. |
| 1899 (2,031) 53,598,000 | | 3.00 | 4.00 | 5.00 | 7.00 | 15.00 | 25.00 | 40. | 65. | 325. |

* Included in number above.

| | Mintage | G-4 | VG-8 | F-12 | VF-20 | EF-40 | AU-50 | MS-60 | MS-63 | PF-63 |
|---|---|---|---|---|---|---|---|---|---|---|
| 1900 ....(2,262) | 66,831,502 | $2. | $3. | $4. | $5. | $10. | $20. | $35. | $55. | $300. |
| 1901 ....(1,985) | 79,609,158 | 2. | 3. | 4. | 5. | 10. | 20. | 35. | 55. | 300. |
| 1902 ....(2,018) | 87,374,704 | 2. | 3. | 4. | 5. | 10. | 20. | 35. | 55. | 300. |
| 1903 ....(1,790) | 85,092,703 | 2. | 3. | 4. | 5. | 10. | 20. | 35. | 55. | 300. |
| 1904 ....(1,817) | 61,326,198 | 2. | 3. | 4. | 5. | 10. | 20. | 35. | 55. | 300. |
| 1905 ....(2,152) | 80,717,011 | 2. | 3. | 4. | 5. | 10. | 20. | 35. | 55. | 300. |
| 1906 ....(1,725) | 96,020,530 | 2. | 3. | 4. | 5. | 10. | 20. | 35. | 55. | 300. |
| 1907 ....(1,475) | 108,137,143 | 2. | 3. | 4. | 5. | 10. | 20. | 35. | 55. | 300. |

**Location of Mintmark S on Reverse of
Indian Cent (1908 and 1909 Only)**

| | Mintage | G-4 | VG-8 | F-12 | VF-20 | EF-40 | AU-50 | MS-60 | MS-63 | PF-63 |
|---|---|---|---|---|---|---|---|---|---|---|
| 1908.... (1,620) | .... 32,326,367 | $2.00 | $3. | $4. | $5. | $10. | $20. | $35. | $55. | $300. |
| 1908S ............. | 1,115,000 | 65.00 | 75. | 85. | 100. | 150. | 225. | 275. | 375. | |
| 1909.... (2,175) | .... 14,368,470 | 3.50 | 4. | 5. | 6. | 18. | 22. | 37. | 60. | 300. |
| 1909S............. | 309,000 | 350.00 | 400. | 435. | 450. | 500. | 600. | 700. | 900. | |

## LINCOLN, WHEAT EARS REVERSE (1909–1958)

Victor D. Brenner designed this cent, which was issued to commemorate the 100th anniversary of Lincoln's birth. The designer's initials (V.D.B.) appear on the reverse of a limited quantity of cents of 1909. The initials were restored, in 1918, to the obverse side on Lincoln's shoulder, as illustrated on page 114. The Lincoln type was the first cent to have the motto IN GOD WE TRUST.

Matte Proof coins were made for collectors from 1909 through 1916, and an exceptional specimen dated 1917 is also reported to exist.

**G-4 GOOD**—Date worn but apparent. Lines in wheat heads missing. Full rims.
**VG-8 VERY GOOD**—Half of lines visible in upper wheat heads.
**F-12 FINE**—Wheat lines worn but visible.
**VF-20 VERY FINE**—Lincoln's cheekbone and jawbone worn but separated. No worn spots on wheat heads.
**EF-40 EXTREMELY FINE**—Slight wear. All details sharp.
**AU-50 ABOUT UNCIRCULATED**—Slight wear on cheek and jaw and on wheat stalks.
**MS-60 UNCIRCULATED**—No trace of wear. Light blemishes or discoloration.
**MS-63 CHOICE UNCIRCULATED**—No trace of wear. Slight blemishes. Red-brown color.
**MS-65 GEM UNCIRCULATED**—No trace of wear. Barely noticeable blemishes. Nearly full red color.

## Lincoln, Wheat Ears Reverse, V.D.B. (1909)

**Designer's Initials V.D.B.
(1909 Reverse Only)**

**No V.D.B. on Reverse
(1909–1958)**

**Mintmark Location**

*See next page for chart.*

# Lincoln, Wheat Ears Reverse (1909–1958)
## Variety 1 – Bronze (1909–1942)

*Designer Victor D. Brenner; weight 3.11 grams; composition .950 copper, .050 tin and zinc; diameter 19 mm; plain edge; mints: Philadelphia, Denver, San Francisco.*

*Brilliant choice Uncirculated cents command higher prices. Discolored (brown) or weakly struck pieces are worth less.*

| Mintage | G-4 | VG-8 | F-12 | VF-20 | EF-40 | AU-50 | MS-60 | MS-63 |
|---|---|---|---|---|---|---|---|---|
| 1909, V.D.B. . . . . . . .27,995,000 | $4.50 | $5.00 | $5.50 | $6.00 | $7.00 | $9. | $15. | $18. |
| 1909, V.D.B., Pf **(a)** . .(1,194) . . . . . . . . | | | | | | | | 2,200. |
| 1909S, V.D.B. . . . . . . . .484,000 | 600.00 | 700.00 | 750.00 | 825.00 | 1,000.00 | 1,150. | 1,350. | 2,200. |
| 1909 . . . . . . . . . . .72,702,618 | 1.75 | 2.00 | 2.50 | 3.00 | 4.00 | 9. | 16. | 22. |
| 1909, Pf . . .(2,352) . . . . . . . . | | | | | | | | 400. |
| 1909S . . . . . . . . . . .1,825,000 | 75.00 | 80.00 | 100.00 | 140.00 | 200.00 | 240. | 275. | 350. |
| 1909S, S Over Horiz S . . . . . . . . . . . . . | 80.00 | 85.00 | 110.00 | 150.00 | 220.00 | 250. | 300. | 375. |
| 1910 . . . . . . . . . .146,801,218 | 0.30 | 0.40 | 0.60 | 1.00 | 2.25 | 6. | 16. | 25. |
| 1910, Pf **(a)** (4,083) . . . . . . . . | | | | | | | | 335. |
| 1910S . . . . . . . . . . .6,045,000 | 8.00 | 10.00 | 12.00 | 15.00 | 30.00 | 65. | 85. | 100. |
| 1911 . . . . . . . . . .101,177,787 | 0.25 | 0.40 | 1.00 | 1.50 | 5.00 | 8. | 20. | 50. |
| 1911, Pf **(a)** (2,411) . . . . . . . . | | | | | | | | 350. |
| 1911D . . . . . . . . . .12,672,000 | 5.00 | 6.00 | 8.00 | 14.00 | 42.00 | 70. | 90. | 120. |
| 1911S . . . . . . . . . . .4,026,000 | 18.00 | 20.00 | 24.00 | 28.00 | 55.00 | 95. | 165. | 260. |
| 1912 . . . . . . . . . . .68,153,060 | 1.25 | 1.50 | 2.00 | 5.00 | 10.00 | 18. | 32. | 45. |
| 1912, Pf **(a)** (2,145) . . . . . . . . | | | | | | | | 350. |
| 1912D . . . . . . . . . .10,411,000 | 6.00 | 7.00 | 9.00 | 20.00 | 50.00 | 80. | 140. | 210. |
| 1912S . . . . . . . . . . .4,431,000 | 12.00 | 15.00 | 18.00 | 23.00 | 55.00 | 85. | 140. | 180. |
| 1913 . . . . . . . . . . .76,532,352 | 0.75 | 1.00 | 1.50 | 3.50 | 15.00 | 18. | 30. | 50. |
| 1913, Pf **(a)** (2,848) . . . . . . . . | | | | | | | | 375. |
| 1913D . . . . . . . . . .15,804,000 | 2.50 | 3.00 | 4.00 | 9.00 | 30.00 | 65. | 100. | 180. |
| 1913S . . . . . . . . . . .6,101,000 | 7.00 | 8.00 | 9.00 | 14.00 | 35.00 | 75. | 140. | 250. |
| 1914 . . . . . . . . . . .75,238,432 | 0.50 | 0.75 | 1.50 | 4.00 | 14.00 | 32. | 50. | 65. |
| 1914, Pf **(a)** (1,365) . . . . . . . . | | | | | | | | 425. |
| 1914D **(b)** . . . . . . . .1,193,000 | 135.00 | 185.00 | 260.00 | 340.00 | 600.00 | 1,200. | 1,600. | 3,000. |
| 1914S . . . . . . . . . . .4,137,000 | 12.00 | 14.00 | 15.00 | 27.00 | 60.00 | 140. | 275. | 475. |
| 1915 . . . . . . . . . . .29,092,120 | 1.50 | 2.00 | 4.50 | 11.00 | 45.00 | 65. | 90. | 140. |
| 1915, Pf **(a)** (1,150) . . . . . . . . | | | | | | | | 575. |
| 1915D . . . . . . . . . .22,050,000 | 1.75 | 2.00 | 2.50 | 4.00 | 15.00 | 42. | 80. | 110. |
| 1915S . . . . . . . . . . .4,833,000 | 7.00 | 8.00 | 10.00 | 14.00 | 47.00 | 110. | 175. | 250. |
| 1916 . . . . . . . . . .131,833,677 | 0.20 | 0.25 | 0.35 | 1.00 | 4.00 | 10. | 16. | 32. |
| 1916, Pf **(a)** (1,050) . . . . . . . . | | | | | | | | 800. |
| 1916D . . . . . . . . . .35,956,000 | 0.75 | 0.90 | 1.50 | 4.00 | 9.00 | 22. | 65. | 120. |
| 1916S . . . . . . . . . .22,510,000 | 1.00 | 1.50 | 2.00 | 3.00 | 12.00 | 30. | 80. | 150. |

* Included in number above. **a.** Matte Proof; valuations are for PF-63 coins. **b.** Beware of altered mintmark. No V.D.B. on shoulder of genuine 1914-D cent.

**Doubled-Die Variety of 1917**

**Doubled-Die Variety of 1936**

*Designer's initials placed on Lincoln's shoulder next to rim, starting 1918.*

# SMALL CENTS

| Mintage | G-4 | VG-8 | F-12 | VF-20 | EF-40 | AU-50 | MS-60 | MS-63 |
|---|---|---|---|---|---|---|---|---|
| 1917 . . . . . . . .196,429,785 | $0.20 | $0.25 | $0.30 | $1.00 | $3.00 | $8.00 | $16.00 | $32.00 |
| 1917, DblDie Obv . . . . . . . . | | | 140.00 | 290.00 | 575.00 | 850.00 | 1,250.00 | 2,200.00 |
| 1917, Matte Proof . . . . . . . . | | | | | | | — | |
| 1917D . . . . . . .55,120,000 | 0.30 | 0.40 | 1.00 | 2.50 | 9.50 | 24.00 | 70.00 | 140.00 |
| 1917S . . . . . . .32,620,000 | 0.50 | 0.65 | 0.85 | 2.00 | 8.00 | 20.00 | 70.00 | 150.00 |
| 1918 . . . . . . . .288,104,634 | 0.20 | 0.25 | 0.40 | 0.85 | 2.50 | 6.00 | 15.00 | 32.00 |
| 1918D . . . . . . .47,830,000 | 0.30 | 0.50 | 1.00 | 2.00 | 8.50 | 18.00 | 65.00 | 125.00 |
| 1918S . . . . . . .34,680,000 | 0.30 | 0.50 | 1.00 | 2.00 | 8.50 | 30.00 | 75.00 | 160.00 |
| 1919 . . . . . . . .392,021,000 | 0.15 | 0.25 | 0.40 | 0.65 | 3.00 | 5.00 | 13.00 | 26.00 |
| 1919D . . . . . . .57,154,000 | 0.25 | 0.30 | 0.45 | 1.30 | 5.00 | 30.00 | 55.00 | 110.00 |
| 1919S . . . . . .139,760,000 | 0.16 | 0.30 | 1.00 | 1.50 | 4.50 | 14.00 | 40.00 | 90.00 |
| 1920 . . . . . . . .310,165,000 | 0.16 | 0.25 | 0.35 | 0.40 | 2.00 | 4.00 | 14.00 | 26.00 |
| 1920D . . . . . .49,280,000 | 0.25 | 0.35 | 0.60 | 1.50 | 8.00 | 25.00 | 70.00 | 120.00 |
| 1920S . . . . . .46,220,000 | 0.25 | 0.35 | 0.60 | 1.00 | 6.00 | 28.00 | 95.00 | 210.00 |
| 1921 . . . . . . . .39,157,000 | 0.20 | 0.35 | 0.60 | 1.25 | 4.00 | 16.00 | 45.00 | 80.00 |
| 1921S . . . . . . . .15,274,000 | 1.00 | 1.40 | 1.75 | 4.00 | 22.00 | 65.00 | 125.00 | 200.00 |
| 1922D . . . . . . . .7,160,000 | 9.00 | 10.00 | 12.00 | 15.00 | 27.00 | 45.00 | 90.00 | 145.00 |
| 1922, No D (c) . . . . . . . .* | 475.00 | 600.00 | 800.00 | 1,000.00 | 2,000.00 | 4,000.00 | 7,500.00 | 27,500.00 |
| 1922, Weak D . . . . . . . . .* | 35.00 | 40.00 | 55.00 | 80.00 | 190.00 | 225.00 | 375.00 | 675.00 |
| 1923 . . . . . . . . .74,723,000 | 0.15 | 0.20 | 0.35 | 0.75 | 3.00 | 7.00 | 15.00 | 30.00 |
| 1923S . . . . . . . .8,700,000 | 2.00 | 2.50 | 4.00 | 6.50 | 25.00 | 70.00 | 220.00 | 435.00 |
| 1924 . . . . . . . .75,178,000 | 0.15 | 0.20 | 0.35 | 0.60 | 3.50 | 8.50 | 24.00 | 50.00 |
| 1924D . . . . . . . .2,520,000 | 14.00 | 17.00 | 22.00 | 35.00 | 95.00 | 180.00 | 310.00 | 425.00 |
| 1924S . . . . . . .11,696,000 | 1.00 | 1.25 | 1.75 | 3.00 | 15.00 | 65.00 | 120.00 | 235.00 |
| 1925 . . . . . . . .139,949,000 | 0.15 | 0.25 | 0.35 | 0.50 | 2.00 | 6.00 | 10.00 | 25.00 |
| 1925D . . . . . . .22,580,000 | 0.25 | 0.35 | 0.45 | 1.50 | 8.00 | 25.00 | 65.00 | 100.00 |
| 1925S . . . . . . .26,380,000 | 0.20 | 0.25 | 0.35 | 1.00 | 8.00 | 20.00 | 75.00 | 165.00 |
| 1926 . . . . . . . .157,088,000 | 0.15 | 0.20 | 0.30 | 0.45 | 1.50 | 4.00 | 8.00 | 18.00 |
| 1926D . . . . . . .28,020,000 | 0.25 | 0.35 | 0.60 | 1.30 | 7.00 | 20.00 | 65.00 | 100.00 |
| 1926S . . . . . . . .4,550,000 | 2.25 | 3.00 | 5.00 | 6.50 | 15.00 | 55.00 | 125.00 | 275.00 |
| 1927 . . . . . . . .144,440,000 | 0.15 | 0.20 | 0.30 | 0.55 | 1.50 | 3.50 | 10.00 | 20.00 |
| 1927D . . . . . . .27,170,000 | 0.25 | 0.35 | 0.50 | 0.85 | 4.00 | 12.00 | 55.00 | 80.00 |
| 1927S . . . . . . .14,276,000 | 0.65 | 0.80 | 1.40 | 2.50 | 10.00 | 25.00 | 80.00 | 140.00 |
| 1928 . . . . . . . .134,116,000 | 0.15 | 0.20 | 0.30 | 0.55 | 1.50 | 3.00 | 10.00 | 20.00 |
| 1928D . . . . . . .31,170,000 | 0.20 | 0.30 | 0.40 | 0.90 | 3.00 | 10.00 | 32.00 | 80.00 |
| 1928S (d) . . . . .17,266,000 | 0.35 | 0.50 | 0.75 | 1.25 | 4.50 | 15.00 | 65.00 | 115.00 |
| 1929 . . . . . . . .185,262,000 | 0.15 | 0.20 | 0.30 | 0.60 | 1.50 | 4.00 | 8.00 | 14.00 |
| 1929D . . . . . . .41,730,000 | 0.15 | 0.25 | 0.35 | 0.70 | 3.00 | 6.00 | 20.00 | 40.00 |
| 1929S . . . . . . .50,148,000 | 0.15 | 0.25 | 0.35 | 0.60 | 2.50 | 5.00 | 14.00 | 25.00 |
| 1930 . . . . . . . .157,415,000 | 0.10 | 0.15 | 0.25 | 0.40 | 1.00 | 2.00 | 6.00 | 11.00 |
| 1930D . . . . . . .40,100,000 | 0.15 | 0.20 | 0.30 | 0.45 | 2.50 | 4.00 | 12.00 | 28.00 |
| 1930S . . . . . . .24,286,000 | 0.15 | 0.20 | 0.30 | 0.50 | 1.50 | 6.00 | 10.00 | 16.00 |
| 1931 . . . . . . . .19,396,000 | 0.35 | 0.45 | 0.60 | 1.00 | 2.00 | 6.00 | 20.00 | 40.00 |
| 1931D . . . . . . . .4,480,000 | 3.00 | 4.00 | 5.00 | 6.00 | 10.00 | 35.00 | 60.00 | 90.00 |
| 1931S . . . . . . . . . .866,000 | 60.00 | 65.00 | 70.00 | 75.00 | 90.00 | 100.00 | 110.00 | 125.00 |
| 1932 . . . . . . . . .9,062,000 | 1.50 | 1.75 | 2.00 | 2.50 | 3.00 | 10.00 | 20.00 | 27.50 |
| 1932D . . . . . . .10,500,000 | 0.70 | 0.90 | 1.20 | 1.75 | 2.50 | 7.00 | 16.00 | 32.00 |
| 1933 . . . . . . . .14,360,000 | 0.75 | 0.90 | 1.25 | 1.50 | 3.00 | 9.00 | 17.00 | 32.00 |

\* Included in number above. **c.** 1922 cents with a weak or missing mintmark were made from extremely worn dies that originally struck normal 1922D cents. Three different die pairs were involved; two of them produced "Weak D" coins. One die pair (no. 2, identified by a "strong reverse") is acknowledged as striking "No D" coins. Weak D cents are worth considerably less. Beware of removed mintmark. **d.** Large and small mintmark varieties; see page 20.

*Chart continued on next page.*

| | Mintage | G-4 | VG-8 | F-12 | VF-20 | EF-40 | AU-50 | MS-60 | MS-63 |
|---|---|---|---|---|---|---|---|---|---|
| 1933D | 6,200,000 | $2.00 | $2.25 | $2.50 | $3.50 | $6.00 | $11.00 | $25.00 | $30.00 |
| 1934 | 219,080,000 | 0.10 | 0.12 | 0.15 | 0.30 | 1.00 | 4.00 | 8.00 | 11.00 |
| 1934D | 28,446,000 | 0.15 | 0.25 | 0.30 | 0.45 | 2.00 | 5.00 | 20.00 | 27.50 |
| 1935 | 245,388,000 | 0.10 | 0.12 | 0.15 | 0.20 | 0.50 | 1.00 | 6.00 | 8.00 |
| 1935D | 47,000,000 | 0.10 | 0.12 | 0.15 | 0.25 | 0.50 | 2.00 | 8.00 | 10.00 |
| 1935S | 38,702,000 | 0.10 | 0.15 | 0.25 | 0.50 | 2.00 | 5.00 | 16.00 | 22.00 |
| 1936 | (5,569) | 309,632,000 | 0.10 | 0.15 | 0.25 | 0.50 | 1.50 | 3.00 | 8.00 | 10.00 |
| 1936, DblDie Obv | * | — | — | 55.00 | 90.00 | 100.00 | 250.00 | 1,000.00 | |
| 1936D | 40,620,000 | 0.10 | 0.20 | 0.30 | 0.50 | 1.00 | 4.00 | 9.00 | |
| 1936S | 29,130,000 | 0.10 | 0.25 | 0.40 | 0.55 | 2.00 | 4.00 | 9.00 | |
| 1937 | (9,320) | 309,170,000 | 0.10 | 0.15 | 0.30 | 0.50 | 1.00 | 3.00 | 7.50 | 75.00 (e) |
| 1937D | 50,430,000 | 0.10 | 0.15 | 0.25 | 0.40 | 1.00 | 3.00 | 9.50 | |
| 1937S | 34,500,000 | 0.10 | 0.20 | 0.30 | 0.40 | 1.00 | 3.00 | 10.00 | |
| 1938 | (14,734) | 156,682,000 | 0.10 | 0.15 | 2.00 | 3.00 | 1.00 | 2.00 | 8.50 | 60.00 (e) |
| 1938D | 20,010,000 | 0.20 | 0.30 | 0.50 | 0.80 | 1.25 | 5.00 | 13.00 | |
| 1938S | 15,180,000 | 0.35 | 0.45 | 0.55 | 0.75 | 1.10 | 4.00 | 11.00 | |
| 1939 | (13,520) | 316,466,000 | 0.10 | 0.12 | 0.15 | 0.25 | 0.50 | 1.00 | 6.50 | 55.00 (e) |
| 1939D | 15,160,000 | 0.45 | 0.55 | 0.65 | 0.85 | 1.25 | 5.00 | 12.00 | |
| 1939S | 52,070,000 | 0.15 | 0.20 | 0.30 | 0.75 | 1.00 | 2.50 | 11.00 | |
| 1940 | (15,872) | 586,810,000 | 0.10 | 0.12 | 0.15 | 0.40 | 0.60 | 2.00 | 6.50 | 45.00 (e) |
| 1940D | 81,390,000 | 0.10 | 0.15 | 0.25 | 0.60 | 0.75 | 2.00 | 6.50 | |
| 1940S | 112,940,000 | 0.10 | 0.12 | 0.15 | 0.50 | 1.00 | 1.75 | 6.75 | |
| 1941 | (21,100) | 887,018,000 | 0.10 | 0.12 | 0.15 | 0.30 | 0.60 | 1.50 | 6.50 | 40.00 (e) |
| 1941D | 128,700,000 | 0.10 | 0.12 | 0.15 | 0.50 | 1.00 | 3.00 | 9.50 | |
| 1941S (d) | 92,360,000 | 0.10 | 0.15 | 0.30 | 0.50 | 1.00 | 4.00 | 12.50 | |
| 1942 | (32,600) | 657,796,000 | 0.10 | 0.12 | 0.15 | 0.20 | 0.50 | 0.75 | 5.50 | 42.00 (e) |
| 1942D | 206,698,000 | 0.10 | 0.12 | 0.15 | 0.25 | 0.50 | 0.85 | 6.50 | |
| 1942S | 85,590,000 | 0.15 | 0.25 | 0.30 | 0.85 | 1.25 | 5.50 | 17.00 | |

* Included in number above. **d.** Large and small mintmark varieties; see page 20. **e.** Valuations are for PF-63 coins.

## Variety 2 – Zinc-Coated Steel (1943)

Owing to a shortage of copper during the critical war year 1943, the Treasury Department resorted to the use of zinc-coated steel for cents. No bronze cents were officially issued in 1943. A few specimens struck on bronze planchets by error are known to exist. Through a similar error, a few of the 1944 cents were struck on steel planchets.

*1943—Weight 2.70 grams; composition, steel coated with zinc; diameter 19 mm; plain edge.*

**1943-D, Boldly Doubled Mintmark**          **1944-D, D Over S**

| | Mintage | F-12 | VF-20 | EF-40 | AU-50 | MS-63 | MS-65 |
|---|---|---|---|---|---|---|---|
| 1943 | 684,628,670 | $0.25 | $0.30 | $0.40 | $0.50 | $2.00 | $6.00 |
| 1943D | 217,660,000 | 0.25 | 0.35 | 0.45 | 0.75 | 2.75 | 8.00 |
| 1943D, Boldly Doubled Mintmark | * | 6.00 | 12.00 | 20.00 | 25.00 | 30.00 | 75.00 |
| 1943S | 191,550,000 | 0.35 | 0.50 | 0.60 | 1.00 | 4.00 | 15.00 |

* Included in number above.

## Variety 1 (Bronze) Resumed (1944–1958)

Cartridge cases were salvaged for coinage of 1944 through 1946. Although the color was slightly different for uncirculated specimens, the coins proved satisfactory in every respect.

*1944–1946—Weight, 3.11 grams; composition .950 copper, .050 zinc; diameter 19 mm; plain edge. 1947–1958—Weight 3.11 grams; composition .950 copper, .050 tin and zinc; diameter 19 mm.*

# SMALL CENTS

| | Mintage | VF-20 | EF-40 | AU-50 | MS-63 | MS-65 | PF-65 |
|---|---|---|---|---|---|---|---|
| 1944 . . . . . . . . . . . . . . .1,435,400,000 | | $0.10 | $0.20 | $0.35 | $0.75 | $2.00 | |
| 1944D . . . . . . . . . . . . . . .430,578,000 | | 0.10 | 0.20 | 0.35 | 0.75 | 2.00 | |
| 1944D, D Over S . . . . . . . . . . . . . . .* | | 125.00 | 175.00 | 225.00 | 440.00 | 1,850.00 | |
| 1944S . . . . . . . . . . . . . .282,760,000 | | 0.10 | 0.20 | 0.35 | 0.75 | 6.00 | |
| 1945 . . . . . . . . . . . . . . .1,040,515,000 | | 0.10 | 0.20 | 0.35 | 0.75 | 2.00 | |
| 1945D . . . . . . . . . . . . . . .266,268,000 | | 0.10 | 0.20 | 0.35 | 0.75 | 2.00 | |
| 1945S . . . . . . . . . . . . . . .181,770,000 | | 0.10 | 0.20 | 0.35 | 0.75 | 6.00 | |
| 1946 . . . . . . . . . . . . . . . .991,655,000 | | 0.10 | 0.15 | 0.35 | 0.50 | 2.00 | |
| 1946D . . . . . . . . . . . . . . .315,690,000 | | 0.10 | 0.20 | 0.35 | 0.50 | 4.00 | |
| 1946S . . . . . . . . . . . . . . .198,100,000 | | 0.10 | 0.20 | 0.35 | 0.50 | 5.00 | |
| 1946S, S Over D . . . . . . . . . . . . . . .* | | 25.00 | 75.00 | 125.00 | 225.00 | 575.00 | |
| 1947 . . . . . . . . . . . . . . .190,555,000 | | 0.10 | 0.20 | 0.40 | 0.80 | 3.00 | |
| 1947D . . . . . . . . . . . . . . .194,750,000 | | 0.10 | 0.20 | 0.40 | 0.50 | 3.00 | |
| 1947S . . . . . . . . . . . . . . .99,000,000 | | 0.15 | 0.25 | 0.50 | 0.75 | 6.00 | |
| 1948 . . . . . . . . . . . . . . .317,570,000 | | 0.10 | 0.20 | 0.35 | 0.75 | 2.00 | |
| 1948D . . . . . . . . . . . . . . .172,637,500 | | 0.10 | 0.20 | 0.35 | 0.50 | 3.00 | |
| 1948S . . . . . . . . . . . . . . .81,735,000 | | 0.15 | 0.30 | 0.35 | 0.80 | 6.00 | |
| 1949 . . . . . . . . . . . . . . .217,775,000 | | 0.10 | 0.20 | 0.35 | 1.00 | 4.00 | |
| 1949D . . . . . . . . . . . . . . .153,132,500 | | 0.10 | 0.20 | 0.35 | 1.00 | 4.00 | |
| 1949S . . . . . . . . . . . . . . .64,290,000 | | 0.20 | 0.30 | 0.35 | 2.00 | 6.00 | |
| 1950 . . . . .(51,386) . . . . 272,635,000 | | 0.10 | 0.20 | 0.35 | 0.75 | 2.00 | $75.00 |
| 1950D . . . . . . . . . . . . . . .334,950,000 | | 0.10 | 0.20 | 0.35 | 0.50 | 2.00 | |
| 1950S . . . . . . . . . . . . . . .118,505,000 | | 0.10 | 0.25 | 0.35 | 0.75 | 2.75 | |
| 1951 . . . . . .(57,500) . . . .284,576,000 | | 0.10 | 0.25 | 0.35 | 0.60 | 2.75 | 75.00 |
| 1951D . . . . . . . . . . . . . . .625,355,000 | | 0.10 | 0.12 | 0.35 | 0.50 | 2.00 | |
| 1951S . . . . . . . . . . . . . . .136,010,000 | | 0.15 | 0.25 | 0.50 | 1.00 | 3.00 | |
| 1952 . . . . . .(81,980) . . . . 186,775,000 | | 0.10 | 0.15 | 0.35 | 1.00 | 3.00 | 55.00 |
| 1952D . . . . . . . . . . . . . . .746,130,000 | | 0.10 | 0.15 | 0.25 | 0.50 | 3.00 | |
| 1952S . . . . . . . . . . . . . . .137,800,004 | | 0.10 | 0.20 | 0.35 | 2.00 | 6.00 | |
| 1953 . . . . . .(128,800) . . . . 256,755,000 | | 0.10 | 0.15 | 0.20 | 0.25 | 2.00 | 50.00 |
| 1953D . . . . . . . . . . . . . . .700,515,000 | | 0.10 | 0.15 | 0.20 | 0.25 | 2.00 | |
| 1953S . . . . . . . . . . . . . . .181,835,000 | | 0.10 | 0.15 | 0.20 | 0.50 | 2.00 | |
| 1954 . . . . . .(233,300) . . . . . 71,640,050 | | 0.25 | 0.35 | 0.45 | 0.50 | 2.00 | 18.00 |
| 1954D . . . . . . . . . . . . . . .251,552,500 | | 0.10 | 0.12 | 0.20 | 0.25 | 1.00 | |
| 1954S . . . . . . . . . . . . . . .96,190,000 | | 0.10 | 0.12 | 0.20 | 0.25 | 1.00 | |

\* Included in number above.

The popular 1955 doubled-die error coins (illustrated below) were made from improperly prepared dies that show a fully doubled outline of date and legend. Do not confuse these with less valuable pieces showing only minor traces of doubling. Counterfeits exist.

**1955, Doubled-Die Error**

| | Mintage | VF-20 | EF-40 | AU-50 | MS-63 | MS-65 | PF-65 |
|---|---|---|---|---|---|---|---|
| 1955 . . .(378,200) . . .330,580,000 | | $0.10 | $0.12 | $0.15 | $0.25 | $0.75 | $18.00 |
| 1955, DblDie Obv . . . . . . . . . . . . .* | | 1,100.00 | 1,200.00 | 1,350.00 | 2,800.00(a) | 11,500.00 | |
| 1955D . . . . . . . . . . . . .563,257,500 | | 0.10 | 0.10 | 0.15 | 0.25 | 0.50 | |
| 1955S . . . . . . . . . . . . .44,610,000 | | 0.20 | 0.30 | 0.40 | 0.75 | 2.00 | |
| 1956 . . .(669,384) . . .420,745,000 | | 0.10 | 0.12 | 0.15 | 0.25 | 0.50 | 4.00 |
| 1956D . . . . . . . . . . .1,098,201,100 | | 0.10 | 0.12 | 0.15 | 0.25 | 0.50 | |
| 1956D, D Above Shadow D . . . . . .* | | 10.00 | 25.00 | 30.00 | 35.00 | 75.00 | |
| 1957 (1,247,952) . . .282,540,000 | | 0.10 | 0.12 | 0.15 | 0.25 | 0.50 | 4.00 |
| 1957D . . . . . . . . . . .1,051,342,000 | | 0.10 | 0.12 | 0.15 | 0.25 | 0.50 | |
| 1958 . . .(875,652) . . .252,525,000 | | 0.10 | 0.12 | 0.15 | 0.25 | 0.50 | 5.00 |
| 1958 DblDie Obv (2 known) . . . . . . . | | | | | — | — | |
| 1958D . . . . . . . . . . . . .800,953,300 | | 0.10 | 0.12 | 0.15 | 0.25 | 0.50 | |

\* Included in number above.  **a.** Value for MS-60 is $1,900.

## LINCOLN, MEMORIAL REVERSE (1959 TO DATE)

Frank Gasparro designed the Lincoln Memorial reverse, which was introduced in 1959 on the 150th anniversary of Lincoln's birth.

### Copper (1959–1982)

*Designer V.D. Brenner (obv) Frank Gasparro (rev); mints: Philadelphia, Denver, San Francisco. 1959–1962—Weight 3.11 grams; composition .950 copper, .050 tin and zinc; diameter 19 mm; plain edge. 1962–1982—Weight 3.11 grams; composition .950 copper, .050 zinc. 1982 to date—Weight 2.5 grams; composition copper-plated zinc (core: .992 zinc, .008 copper, with a plating of pure copper; total content .975 zinc, .025 copper).*

| | | 1960, Small Date | 1960, Large Date |
| | Mintage | MS-63 | MS-65 | PF-65 |
|---|---|---|---|---|
| 1959 . . . . . . . . . . . . . . . . . . . . . .(1,149,291). . . . . . 609,715,000 | | $0.20 | $0.30 | $3.00 |
| 1959D . . . . . . . . . . . . . . . . . . . . . . . . . . . . . . .1,279,760,000 | | 0.50 | 0.55 | |
| 1960, Large Date . . . . . . . . . . . .(1,691,602). . . . . . 586,405,000 | | 0.20 | 0.30 | 2.00 |
| 1960, Small Date  . . . . . . . . . . . . . . . . . . . . .* . . . . . . . . . . * | | 3.00 | 7.00 | 20.00 |
| 1960D, Large Date . . . . . . . . . . . . . . . . . . . .1,580,884,000 | | 0.20 | 0.30 | |
| 1960D, Small Date  . . . . . . . . . . . . . . . . . . . . . . . . . . . . . . * | | 0.20 | 0.30 | |
| 1960, D Over D, Lg Over Sm Dt . . . . . . . . . . . . . . . . . . . . .* | | 200.00 | 300.00 | |
| 1961 . . . . . . . . . . . . . . . . . . . . .(3,028,244). . . . . . 753,345,000 | | 0.10 | 0.30 | 1.50 |
| 1961D . . . . . . . . . . . . . . . . . . . . . . . . . . . . . . .1,753,266,700 | | 0.10 | 0.30 | |
| 1962 . . . . . . . . . . . . . . . . . . . . .(3,218,019). . . . . . 606,045,000 | | 0.10 | 0.30 | 1.50 |
| 1962D . . . . . . . . . . . . . . . . . . . . . . . . . . . . . . .1,793,148,140 | | 0.10 | 0.30 | |
| 1963 . . . . . . . . . . . . . . . . . . . . .(3,075,645). . . . . . 754,110,000 | | 0.10 | 0.30 | 1.50 |
| 1963D . . . . . . . . . . . . . . . . . . . . . . . . . . . . . . .1,774,020,400 | | 0.10 | 0.30 | |
| 1964 . . . . . . . . . . . . . . . . . . . . .(3,950,762) . . . . 2,648,575,000 | | 0.10 | 0.30 | 1.50 |
| 1964D . . . . . . . . . . . . . . . . . . . . . . . . . . . . . . .3,799,071,500 | | 0.10 | 0.30 | |
| 1965 . . . . . . . . . . . . . . . . . . . . . . . . . . . . . . .1,497,224,900 | | 0.20 | 0.50 | |
| 1966 . . . . . . . . . . . . . . . . . . . . . . . . . . . . . . .2,188,147,783 | | 0.20 | 0.50 | |
| 1967 . . . . . . . . . . . . . . . . . . . . . . . . . . . . . . .3,048,667,100 | | 0.20 | 0.50 | |
| 1968 . . . . . . . . . . . . . . . . . . . . . . . . . . . . . . .1,707,880,970 | | 0.25 | 0.60 | |
| 1968D . . . . . . . . . . . . . . . . . . . . . . . . . . . . . . .2,886,269,600 | | 0.10 | 0.40 | |
| 1968S . . . . . . . . . . . . . . . . . .(3,041,506). . . . . . 258,270,001 | | 0.10 | 0.40 | 1.00 |

\* Included in number above.

In 1969, the dies were modified to strengthen the design, and Lincoln's head was made slightly smaller. In 1973, dies were further modified and the engraver's initials FG made larger. The initials were reduced slightly in 1974. During 1982 the dies were again modified and the bust, lettering, and date made slightly smaller. One variety of the 1984 cent shows Lincoln's ear doubled. Some 1,579,324 cents dated 1974 were struck in aluminum as experimental pieces. None were placed in circulation, and most were later destroyed. One was preserved for the National Collection in the Smithsonian Institution. Other 1974 experimental cents were struck in bronze-clad steel.

1972, Doubled-Die Error

1969-S, Doubled-Die Error

1970, Small Date (High 7)

1970, Large Date (Low 7)

1971-S, Proof Doubled Die

**1981, Clear S**

**1982, Large Date**

**1982, Small Date**

| | Mintage | MS-65 | PF-65 |
|---|---|---|---|
| 1969 . . . . . . .1,136,910,000 | $0.70 | |
| 1969D . . . . . .4,002,832,200 | 0.30 | |
| 1969S . . . . . . . .(2,934,631) | | $1.00 |
| . . . . . . . .544,375,000 | 0.30 | |
| 1969S DblDie Obv . . . . . .* | — | |
| 1970 . . . . . . .1,898,315,000 | 0.50 | |
| 1970D . . . . . .2,891,438,900 | 0.20 | |
| 1970S, All kinds (2,632,810) | | |
| . . . . . . . .690,560,004 | | |
| 1970S, Sm Dt (High 7)  * | 65.00 | 70.00 |
| 1970S, Lg Dt (Low 7) . .* | 0.30 | 1.00 |
| 1970S DblDie Obv . . . . .* | — | |
| 1971 . . . . . . .1,919,490,000 | 0.80 | |
| 1971D . . . . . .2,911,045,600 | 0.80 | |
| 1971S . . . . . . .(3,220,733) | | 1.00 |
| . . . . . . . .525,133,459 | 0.80 | |
| 1971S, DblDie Obv . . . . . .* | | 650.00 |
| 1972, DblDie Obv (a) . . . .** | 700.00 | |
| 1972 . . . . . . .2,933,255,000 | 0.20 | |
| 1972D . . . . . .2,665,071,400 | 0.25 | |
| 1972S . . . . . . .(3,260,996) | | 1.00 |
| . . . . . . . .376,939,108 | 0.30 | |
| 1973 . . . . . . .3,728,245,000 | 0.20 | |
| 1973D . . . . . .3,549,576,588 | 0.20 | |
| 1973S . . . . . . . .(2,760,339) | | 1.00 |
| . . . . . . . .317,177,295 | 0.30 | |
| 1974 . . . . . .4,232,140,523 | 0.20 | |
| 1974D . . . . . .4,235,098,000 | 0.20 | |
| 1974S . . . . . . .(2,612,568) | | 1.00 |
| . . . . . . . .409,426,660 | 0.30 | |

| | Mintage | MS-65 | PF-65 |
|---|---|---|---|
| 1975 . . . . . .5,451,476,142 | $0.20 | |
| 1975D . . . . . .4,505,275,300 | 0.20 | |
| 1975S . . . . . . . .(2,845,450) | | $3.50 |
| 1976 . . . . . .4,674,292,426 | 0.20 | |
| 1976D . . . . . .4,221,592,455 | | 0.20 |
| 1976S . . . . . . . .(4,149,730) | | 3.20 |
| 1977 . . . . . .4,469,930,000 | 0.20 | |
| 1977D . . . . . .4,194,062,300 | 0.20 | |
| 1977S . . . . . . . .(3,251,152) | | 2.50 |
| 1978 . . . . . .5,558,605,000 | 0.20 | |
| 1978D . . . . . .4,280,233,400 | 0.20 | |
| 1978S . . . . . . . .(3,127,781) | | 2.50 |
| 1979 . . . . . .6,018,515,000 | 0.20 | |
| 1979D . . . . . .4,139,357,254 | 0.20 | |
| 1979S, Filled S  (3,677,175) | | 4.00 |
| 1979S, Clear S . . . . . . . . .* | | 4.25 |
| 1980 . . . . . .7,414,705,000 | 0.20 | |
| 1980D . . . . . .5,140,098,660 | | 0.20 |
| 1980S . . . . . . . .(3,554,806) | | 2.00 |
| 1981 . . . . . .7,491,750,000 | | 0.20 |
| 1981D . . . . . .5,373,235,677 | | 0.20 |
| 1981S, Filled S. . (4,063,083) | | 2.00 |
| 1981S, Clear S . . . . . . . . .* | | 65.00 |
| 1982, Lg Dt  10,712,525,000 | 0.20 | |
| 1982, Sm Dt . . . . . . . . . .* | 0.30 | |
| 1982D . . . . . .6,012,979,368 | 0.20 | |
| 1982S . . . . . . . .(3,857,479) | | 2.50 |

\* Included in number above. \*\* Included in number below. **a.** Other slightly doubled varieties (worth far less) exist.

## Copper-Plated Zinc (1982 to Date)

*The composition for this period changed to copper-plated zinc. The core is 99.2% zinc, 0.8% copper, with a plating of pure copper; the weight is 2.5 grams (approximately 20% lighter than the copper cents).*

| | Mintage | MS-65 | PF-65 |
|---|---|---|---|
| 1982, Large Date . . . . . .(a) | $1.00 | |
| 1982, Small Date . . . . . .(a) | 1.25 | |

| | Mintage | MS-65 | PF-65 |
|---|---|---|---|
| 1982D, Large Date . . . . .(a) | $0.25 | |
| 1982D, Small Date . . . . .(a) | 0.10 | |

**a.** Included in previous chart.

**1983, Doubled-Die Reverse**

**Double Ear Variety**

*See next page for chart.*

| Mintage | MS-65 | PF-65 | Mintage | MS-65 | PF-65 |
|---|---|---|---|---|---|
| 1983 . . . . . . .7,752,355,000 | $0.20 | | 1995, DblDie Obv . . . . . . . .* | $45.00 | |
| 1983, DblDie Rev . . . . . . . .* | 300.00 | | 1995D . . . . . .7,128,560,000 | 0.20 | |
| 1983D . . . . . .6,467,199,428 | 0.20 | | 1995S . . . . . . . .(2,797,481) | | $9.00 |
| 1983S . . . . . . .(3,279,126) | | $3.00 | 1996 . . . . . . .6,612,465,000 | 0.20 | |
| 1984 . . . . . . .8,151,079,000 | 0.20 | | 1996D . . . . . .6,510,795,000 | 0.20 | |
| 1984, Doubled Ear . . . . . . .* | 200.00 | | 1996S . . . . . . . .(2,525,265) | | 4.50 |
| 1984D . . . . . .5,569,238,906 | 0.50 | | 1997 . . . . . . .4,622,800,000 | 0.20 | |
| 1984S . . . . . . .(3,065,110) | | 4.00 | 1997D . . . . . .4,576,555,000 | 0.20 | |
| 1985 . . . . . . .5,648,489,887 | 0.20 | | 1997S . . . . . . . .(2,796,678) | | 10.00 |
| 1985D . . . . . .5,287,339,926 | 0.20 | | 1998 . . . . . . .5,032,155,000 | 0.20 | |
| 1985S . . . . . . .(3,362,821) | | 5.00 | 1998, Wide AM **(a)** . . . . . .* | 10.00 | |
| 1986 . . . . . . .4,491,395,493 | | 0.50 | 1998D . . . . . .5,225,353,500 | 0.20 | |
| 1986D . . . . . .4,442,866,698 | 0.20 | | 1998S . . . . . . . .(2,086,507) | | 9.00 |
| 1986S . . . . . . .(3,010,497) | | 6.50 | 1998S, Close AM **(a)** . . . . .* | | — |
| 1987 . . . . . . .4,682,466,931 | 0.20 | | 1999 . . . . . . .5,237,600,000 | 0.20 | |
| 1987D . . . . . .4,879,389,514 | 0.20 | | 1999, Wide AM **(a)** . . . . . .* | 500.00 | |
| 1987S . . . . . . .(4,227,728) | | 5.00 | 1999D . . . . . .6,360,065,000 | 0.20 | |
| 1988 . . . . . . .6,092,810,000 | 0.20 | | 1999S . . . . . . . .(3,347,966) | | 5.00 |
| 1988D . . . . . .5,253,740,443 | 0.20 | | 1999S, Close AM **(a)** . . . . .* | | — |
| 1988S . . . . . . .(3,262,948) | | 9.00 | 2000 . . . . . . .5,503,200,000 | 0.20 | |
| 1989 . . . . . . .7,261,535,000 | 0.20 | | 2000, Wide AM **(a)** . . . . . .* | 5.00 | |
| 1989D . . . . . .5,345,467,111 | 0.20 | | 2000D . . . . . .8,774,220,000 | 0.20 | |
| 1989S . . . . . . .(3,220,194) | | 9.00 | 2000S . . . . . . . .(4,047,993) | | 3.00 |
| 1990 . . . . . . .6,851,765,000 | 0.20 | | 2001 . . . . . . .4,959,600,000 | 0.20 | |
| 1990D . . . . . .4,922,894,533 | 0.20 | | 2001D . . . . . .5,374,990,000 | 0.20 | |
| 1990S . . . . . . .(3,299,559) | | 5.00 | 2001S . . . . . . . .(3,184,606) | | 3.00 |
| 1990, Pf, No S . . . . . . . . . .* | | 3,000.00 | 2002 . . . . . . .3,260,800,000 | 0.20 | |
| 1991 . . . . . . .5,165,940,000 | 0.20 | | 2002D . . . . . .4,028,055,000 | 0.20 | |
| 1991D . . . . . .4,158,446,076 | 0.20 | | 2002S . . . . . . . .(3,211,995) | | 3.00 |
| 1991S . . . . . . .(2,867,787) | | 22.00 | 2003 . . . . . . .3,300,000,000 | 0.20 | |
| 1992 . . . . . . .4,648,905,000 | 0.20 | | 2003D . . . . . .3,548,000,000 | 0.20 | |
| 1992D . . . . . .4,448,673,300 | 0.20 | | 2003S . . . . . . . .(3,298,439) | | 3.00 |
| 1992D, Close AM **(a)** . . . . .* | 500.00 | | 2004 . . . . . . .3,379,600,000 | 0.20 | |
| 1992S . . . . . . .(4,176,560) | | 4.00 | 2004D . . . . . .3,456,400,000 | 0.20 | |
| 1993 . . . . . . .5,684,705,000 | 0.20 | | 2004S . . . . . . . .(2,992,069) | | 3.00 |
| 1993D . . . . . .6,426,650,571 | 0.20 | | 2005 . . . . . . .3,935,600,000 | 0.20 | |
| 1993S . . . . . . .(3,394,792) | | 9.00 | 2005D . . . . . .3,764,450,000 | 0.20 | |
| 1994 . . . . . . .6,500,850,000 | 0.20 | | 2005S . . . . . . . .(3,273,000) | | 3.00 |
| 1994D . . . . . .7,131,765,000 | 0.20 | | 2006 . . . . . . . . . . . . . . . . . | 0.20 | |
| 1994S . . . . . . .(3,269,923) | | 8.00 | 2006D . . . . . . . . . . . . . . . . | 0.20 | |
| 1995 . . . . . . .6,411,440,000 | 0.20 | | 2006S . . . . . . . . . . . . . . . . | | 3.00 |

* Included in number above. **a.** Varieties were made using Proof dies that have a wide space between A and M in AMERICA. The letters nearly touch on other uncirculated cents after 1993.

Some of the cents minted since 1994 show the faint trace of a mintmark, believed to be the result of the letter's having been removed from the master die during production of working dies for coinage. So-called phantom mintmark pieces were produced in Philadelphia but show traces of either a D or an S. Values for such pieces vary according to date and condition but are not significantly higher than for normal pieces.

# TWO-CENT PIECES

The Act of April 22, 1864, which changed the weight and composition of the cent, included a provision for a bronze two-cent piece. The weight was specified as 96 grains, the alloy being the same as for the cent. The two-cent piece is one of the shortest lived issues of United States coinage. The motto IN GOD WE TRUST appeared for the first time on the new coin, due largely to increased religious sentiment during the Civil War crisis. There are two varieties for the first year of issue, 1864: the Small Motto, which is scarce, and the Large Motto. See illustrations below.

**1864, Small Motto**

**1864, Large Motto**

On the obverse, the D in GOD is narrow on the Large Motto. The stem to the leaf shows plainly on the Small Motto variety. There is no stem on the Large Motto. The first T in TRUST is very close to the ribbon crease at left on the Small Motto variety; there is a 1 mm gap on the Large Motto variety. The shield device is very similar to that on the nickel five-cent piece introduced in 1866. Listed Proof mintages are estimates.

## TYPE COIN VALUES

| | G-4 | F-12 | EF-40 | MS-60 | MS-63 | MS-65 | PF-63 | PF-65 |
|---|---|---|---|---|---|---|---|---|
| 1864–1873 | $16.+ | $25.+ | $45.+ | $85.+ | $150. | $425. | $475.+ | $1,000. |

+ or – indicates change from previous year

*Designer James B. Longacre; weight 6.22 grams; composition .950 copper, .050 tin and zinc; diameter 23 mm; plain edge. All coined at Philadelphia Mint.*

**G-4 GOOD**—At least part of IN GOD visible.
**F-12 FINE**—Complete motto visible. The word WE weak.
**EF-40 EXTREMELY FINE**—The word WE bold.
**AU-50 ABOUT UNCIRCULATED**—Traces of wear visible on leaf tips, arrow points, and the word WE.
**MS-60 UNCIRCULATED**—No trace of wear. Light blemishes.
**MS-63 UNCIRCULATED**—Some distracting contact marks or blemishes in prime focal areas. Some impairment of luster possible.

*Brilliant red choice Uncirculated and Proof coins command higher prices. Spotted, cleaned, or discolored pieces are worth less.*

| | Mintage | G-4 | F-12 | VF-20 | EF-40 | AU-50 | MS-60 | MS-63 | PF-63 |
|---|---|---|---|---|---|---|---|---|---|
| 1864, Small Motto . . . . . . . . . . * | | $120. | $250. | $375. | $525. | $650. | $800. | $1,100. | $16,500. |
| 1864, Lg Motto *(100+)* | 19,847,500 | 16. | 25. | 30. | 45. | 65. | 85. | 150. | 600. |
| 1865 **(a)** . . . . .*(500+)* | 13,640,000 | 16. | 25. | 30. | 45. | 65. | 85. | 150. | 475. |
| 1866 . . . . . . . .*(725+)* | 3,177,000 | 16. | 25. | 30. | 45. | 65. | 85. | 150. | 475. |
| 1867 . . . . . . . .*(625+)* | 2,938,750 | 16. | 25. | 30. | 45. | 65. | 85. | 150. | 475. |
| 1867, Doubled Die . . . . . . . . . . * | — | — | 160. | 225. | 275. | 450. | 650. | |
| 1868 . . . . . . . .*(600+)* | 2,803,750 | 18. | 30. | 40. | 55. | 90. | 140. | 225. | 475. |
| 1869 . . . . . . . .*(600+)* | 1,546,500 | 19. | 32. | 42. | 60. | 110. | 160. | 225. | 475. |
| 1870 . . . . . . .*(1,000+)* . . | 861,250 | 20. | 40. | 50. | 85. | 135. | 240. | 280. | 600. |
| 1871 . . . . . . . .*(960+)* . . | 721,250 | 25. | 42. | 60. | 110. | 160. | 275. | 350. | 750. |
| 1872 . . . . . . . .*(950+)*. . . . | 65,000 | 285. | 400. | 575. | 720. | 800. | 1,000. | 1,500. | 1,000. |
| 1873, Close 3, Pf only . . . . .*(600)* | | 1,200. | 1,300. | 1,400. | 1,500. | | | | 2,000. |
| 1873, Open 3, Restrike . . . .*(500)* | | 1,000. | 1,100. | 1,300. | 1,600. | | | | 2,300. |

* Included in regular mintage. **a.** One variety appears to show traces of a 4 under the 5 in the date. Other varieties show the tip of the 5 either plain or curved.

# SILVER THREE-CENT PIECES (TRIMES) (1851–1873)

This smallest of United States silver coins was authorized by Congress March 3, 1851. The first three-cent silver pieces had no lines bordering the six-pointed star. From 1854 through 1858 there were three lines, while issues of the final 15 years show only two lines. Issues from 1854 through 1873 have an olive sprig over the III and a bundle of three arrows beneath. Nearly the entire production of non-Proof coins from 1863 to 1872 was melted in 1873.

## TYPE COIN VALUES

|  | G-4 | F-12 | EF-40 | MS-60 | MS-63 | MS-65 | PF-63 | PF-65 |
|---|---|---|---|---|---|---|---|---|
| Variety 1, 1851–1853 | $25.+ | $35.+ | $60.+ | $160.+ | $270.+ | $1,000. |  |  |
| Variety 2, 1854–1858 | 25.+ | 35.+ | 100.+ | 280. | 600. | 2,750. | $2,750. | $7,000. |
| Variety 3, 1859–1873 | 25.+ | 35.+ | 65. | 160. | 275. | 850. | 500. | 1,500. |

+ or – indicates change from previous year

*Designer James B. Longacre. 1851–1853—Weight .80 gram; composition .750 silver, .250 copper; diameter 14 mm; plain edge; mints: Philadelphia, New Orleans. 1854–1873—Weight .75 gram; composition .900 silver, .100 copper; diameter 14 mm; plain edge. All coined at Philadelphia Mint.*

**G-4 GOOD**—Star worn smooth. Legend and date readable.
**VG-8 VERY GOOD**—Outline of shield defined. Legend and date clear.
**F-12 FINE**—Only star points worn smooth.
**VF-20 VERY FINE**—Only partial wear on star ridges.
**EF-40 EXTREMELY FINE**—Ridges on star points visible.
**AU-50 ABOUT UNCIRCULATED**—Trace of wear visible at each star point. Center of shield possibly weak.
**MS-60 UNCIRCULATED**—No trace of wear. Light blemishes.
**MS-63 CHOICE UNCIRCULATED**—Some distracting contact marks or blemishes in prime focal areas. Some impairment of luster possible.

   ← *Mintmark location.*

**Variety 1 (1851–1853)**          **Variety 2 (1854–1858)**

**Variety 3 (1859–1873)**                    **1862, 2 Over 1**

*Well-struck specimens of Variety 2 command higher prices.*

| | Mintage | G-4 | VG-8 | F-12 | VF-20 | EF-40 | AU-50 | MS-60 | MS-63 | PF-63 |
|---|---|---|---|---|---|---|---|---|---|---|
| 1851 | .......5,447,400 | $25. | $30. | $35. | $40. | $65. | $150. | $175. | $275. | — |
| 1851O | ..........720,000 | 35. | 40. | 45. | 85. | 150. | 220. | 350. | 500. | |
| 1852, 1/Inv 2 | ..........* | | | | — | | | | | |
| 1852 | .......18,663,500 | 25. | 30. | 35. | 40. | 60. | 150. | 160. | 270. | — |
| 1853 | .......11,400,000 | 25. | 30. | 35. | 40. | 60. | 150. | 160. | 270. | |
| 1854 | ..........671,000 | 25. | 30. | 35. | 45. | 100. | 220. | 350. | 650. | $14,000. |
| 1855 | ..........139,000 | 30. | 45. | 55. | 100. | 180. | 300. | 550. | 950. | 5,000. |
| 1856 | .......1,458,000 | 25. | 30. | 35. | 50. | 100. | 250. | 280. | 600. | 4,300. |
| 1857 | .......1,042,000 | 25. | 30. | 35. | 50. | 100. | 250. | 300. | 600. | 3,750. |
| 1858 | ..(300+) 1,603,700 | 25. | 30. | 35. | 50. | 100. | 180. | 280. | 600. | 2,750. |
| 1859 | ...(800) .364,200 | 25. | 30. | 35. | 45. | 65. | 150. | 160. | 275. | 500. |
| 1860 | ..(1,000) ..286,000 | 25. | 30. | 35. | 45. | 65. | 150. | 160. | 275. | 500. |
| 1861 | ..(1,000) ..497,000 | 25. | 30. | 35. | 45. | 65. | 150. | 160. | 275. | 500. |
| 1862, 2/1 | ..........* | 25. | 30. | 35. | 45. | 70. | 150. | 180. | 375. | |
| 1862 | ...(550) ..343,000 | 25. | 30. | 35. | 45. | 65. | 150. | 165. | 300. | 525. |
| 1863, So-Called 3/2 | ..........* | | | | | | | | | |
| 1863 | ...(460) ...21,000 | 300. | 325. | 350. | 375. | 435. | 550. | 650. | 1,000. | 650. |
| 1864 | ...(470) ...12,000 | 300. | 325. | 350. | 375. | 435. | 550. | 650. | 1,000. | 650. |
| 1865 | ...(500) ....8,000 | | | 425. | 450. | 475. | 500. | 625. | 975. | 640. |

* Included in number below.

| | Mintage | G-4 | VG-8 | F-12 | VF-20 | EF-40 | AU-50 | MS-60 | MS-63 | PF-63 |
|---|---|---|---|---|---|---|---|---|---|---|
| 1866 | ....(725) . .22,000 | | | $350. | $400. | $435. | $480. | $630. | $950. | $650. |
| 1867 | ....(625) . . .4,000 | | | 425. | 450. | 475. | 500. | 650. | 1,000. | 650. |
| 1868 | ....(600) . . .3,500 | | | 425. | 450. | 475. | 500. | 650. | 1,000. | 650. |
| 1869 | ....(600) . . .4,500 | | | 425. | 450. | 475. | 500. | 650. | 1,000. | 650. |
| 1870 | ...(1,000) . . .3,000 | | | 425. | 450. | 475. | 500. | 650. | 1,000. | 650. |
| 1871 | ....(960) . . .3,400 | | | 425. | 450. | 475. | 500. | 650. | 1,000. | 650. |
| 1872 | ....(950) . . .1,000 | | | 450. | 475. | 485. | 550. | 750. | 1,400. | 650. |
| 1873 (Cl 3, Pf only) | | | | | | | | | | |
| | (600) . . . . . . . | | | | | 825. | | | | 1,200. |

# NICKEL THREE-CENT PIECES (1865–1889)

Nickel three-cent pieces were struck to replace the silver version.

## TYPE COIN VALUES

| | G-4 | F-12 | EF-40 | MS-60 | MS-63 | MS-65 | PF-63 | PF-65 |
|---|---|---|---|---|---|---|---|---|
| 1865–1889 | $15.+ | $25.+ | $35.+ | $100. | $150. | $700. | $325. | $600. |

+ or − indicates change from previous year

*Designer James B. Longacre; weight 1.94 grams; composition .750 copper, .250 nickel; diameter 17.9 mm; plain edge. All coined at Philadelphia Mint.*

**G-4 GOOD**—Date and legends complete though worn. III smooth.
**VG-8 VERY GOOD**—III half worn. Rims complete.
**VF-20 VERY FINE**—Three-quarters of hair details visible.
**EF-40 EXTREMELY FINE**—Slight, even wear.
**AU-50 ABOUT UNCIRCULATED**—Slight wear on hair curls, above forehead, and on wreath and numeral III.
**MS-60 UNCIRCULATED**—No trace of wear. Light blemishes.
**MS-63 CHOICE UNCIRCULATED**—Some distracting contact marks or blemishes in prime focal areas. Some impairment of luster possible.

| | Mintage | G-4 | VG-8 | VF-20 | EF-40 | AU-50 | MS-60 | MS-63 | PF-63 |
|---|---|---|---|---|---|---|---|---|---|
| 1865 . . . . . . . .(500+) | 11,382,000 | $15. | $18. | $25. | $35. | $55. | $100. | $150. | $1,500. |
| 1866 . . . . . . .(725+) | 4,801,000 | 15. | 18. | 25. | 35. | 55. | 100. | 150. | 325. |
| 1867 . . . . . . .(625+) | 3,915,000 | 15. | 18. | 25. | 35. | 55. | 100. | 150. | 325. |
| 1868 . . . . . . .(600+) | 3,252,000 | 15. | 18. | 25. | 35. | 55. | 100. | 150. | 325. |
| 1869 . . . . . . .(600+) | 1,604,000 | 15. | 18. | 25. | 35. | 55. | 100. | 175. | 325. |
| 1870 . . . . . .(1,000+) | 1,335,000 | 15. | 18. | 25. | 35. | 55. | 110. | 175. | 325. |
| 1871 . . . . . . .(960+) | 604,000 | 15. | 18. | 25. | 35. | 55. | 120. | 175. | 325. |
| 1872 . . . . . . .(950+) | 862,000 | 15. | 18. | 25. | 35. | 55. | 120. | 175. | 325. |
| 1873, Cl 3 . .(1,100+) | 390,000 | 15. | 18. | 25. | 35. | 55. | 130. | 175. | 325. |
| 1873, Open 3. . . . . . . | 783,000 | 15. | 18. | 25. | 35. | 55. | 120. | 165. | |
| 1874 . . . . . . .(700+) | 790,000 | 15. | 18. | 25. | 35. | 55. | 120. | 175. | 325. |
| 1875 . . . . . . .(700+) | 228,000 | 15. | 18. | 26. | 40. | 75. | 150. | 200. | 325. |
| 1876 . . . . . .(1,150+) | 162,000 | 15. | 18. | 30. | 42. | 100. | 175. | 225. | 325. |
| 1877, Pf only (510+) | . . . . . . . . | | | 1,100. | 1,200. | | | | 1,700. |
| 1878, Pf only (2,350) | . . . . . . . . | | | 500. | 600. | | | | 900. |
| 1879 . . . . . . .(3,200) | . . .38,000 | 55. | 65. | 85. | 100. | 135. | 250. | 400. | 400. |
| 1880 . . . . . . .(3,955) | . . . .21,000 | 85. | 100. | 120. | 140. | 160. | 275. | 350. | 400. |
| 1881 . . . . . . .(3,575) | 1,077,000 | 15. | 18. | 25. | 35. | 55. | 100. | 175. | 350. |
| 1882 . . . . . . .(3,100) | . . .22,200 | 85. | 90. | 110. | 135. | 170. | 275. | 400. | 425. |
| 1883 . . . . . . .(6,609) | . . . .4,000 | 150. | 175. | 250. | 300. | 350. | 375. | 750. | 450. |
| 1884 . . . . . . .(3,942) | . . . .1,700 | 325. | 350. | 500. | 550. | 600. | 800. | 1,100. | 500. |
| 1885 . . . . . . .(3,790) | . . . .1,000 | 400. | 425. | 560. | 650. | 675. | 900. | 1,100. | 500. |
| 1886, Pf only (4,290) | . . . . . . . . | | | 325. | 375. | | | | 450. |
| 1887 . . . . . . .(2,960) | . . . .5,001 | 250. | 300. | 325. | 350. | 400. | 475. | 500. | 450. |
| 1887, 7/6 . . . . . . . . | * | | | 350. | 400. | | | | 500. |
| 1888 . . . . . . .(4,582) | . . .36,501 | 45. | 50. | 60. | 75. | 120. | 250. | 335. | 350. |
| 1889 . . . . . . .(3,436) | . . .18,125 | 75. | 85. | 110. | 150. | 190. | 250. | 375. | 375. |

* Included in number above.

## TYPE COIN VALUES

| | G-4 | F-12 | EF-40 | MS-60 | MS-63 | MS-65 | PF-63 | PF-65 |
|---|---|---|---|---|---|---|---|---|
| Shield, Rays, 1866–1867 | $25.00+ | $45.00+ | $160.00+ | $275.+ | $450.+ | $2,400.+ | $2,200.+ | $3,800.+ |
| Shield, No Rays, 1867–1883 | 15.00 | 22.00+ | 40.00+ | 120.+ | 180.+ | 675.+ | 325.+ | 575.+ |
| Liberty, No Cents, 1883 | 6.00+ | 8.00+ | 10.00+ | 35.+ | 50.+ | 150.+ | 300.+ | 1,100.+ |
| Liberty, Cents, 1883–1912 | 2.00 | 4.50 | 26.00 | 65. | 100. | 650.+ | 250.+ | 550.+ |
| Buffalo, Var 1, 1913 | 9.00+ | 14.00 | 22.00+ | 45.+ | 60.+ | 165.+ | 1,400.+ | 3,750.+ |
| Buffalo, Var 2, 1913–1938 | 1.00 | 1.75 | 3.00+ | 20. | 40.+ | 60.+ | 1,000. | 1,750. |
| Jefferson, War, 1942–1945 | 0.60 | 0.70 | 1.25 | 5. | 7. | 13.+ | 100. | 250. |

+ or − indicates change from previous year

# SHIELD (1866–1883)

The Shield type nickel was made possible by the Act of May 16, 1866. Its weight was set at 77-16/100 grains (5 grams), with the same composition as the nickel three-cent piece that was authorized in 1865, and a design similar to that of the two-cent coin. In 1866 the coin was designed with rays between the stars on the reverse. Some of the pieces minted in 1867 have the same details, but later the rays were eliminated, creating two varieties for that year. There was no further change in the type until it was replaced by the Liberty Head design in 1883. Only Proof pieces were struck in 1877 and 1878.

*Designer James B. Longacre; weight 5 grams; composition .750 copper, .250 nickel; diameter 20.5 mm; plain edge. All coined at Philadelphia Mint.*

**G-4 GOOD**—All letters in motto readable.
**VG-8 VERY GOOD**—Motto clear and stands out. Rims slightly worn but even. Part of shield lines visible.
**F-12 FINE**—Half of each olive leaf worn smooth.
**EF-40 EXTREMELY FINE**—Slight wear to leaf tips and cross over shield.
**AU-50 ABOUT UNCIRCULATED**—Traces of light wear on only the high points of the design. Half of mint luster present.
**MS-60 UNCIRCULATED**—No trace of wear. Light blemishes.
**MS-63 CHOICE UNCIRCULATED**—Some distracting contact marks or blemishes in prime focal areas. Impaired luster possible.

**Variety 1,**
**Rays Between Stars (1866–1867)**

**1866, Repunched Date**

*Sharply struck Uncirculated coins are valued higher than the prices shown here.*

| | Mintage | G-4 | VG-8 | F-12 | EF-40 | AU-50 | MS-60 | MS-63 | PF-63 |
|---|---|---|---|---|---|---|---|---|---|
| 1866, Rays *(600+)* . . .14,742,500 | | $25. | $40. | $45. | $160. | $240. | $275. | $450. | $2,200. |
| 1866, Repunched Date . . . . . . . . . | | 55. | 75. | 135. | 260. | 365. | 575. | 1,100. | |
| 1867, Rays . .*(25+)* . . . .2,019,000 | | 35. | 50. | 60. | 190. | 285. | 375. | 475. | 34,000. |

**Variety 2,**
**Without Rays (1867–1883)**

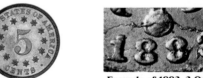

**Example of 1883, 3 Over 2**
*Other varieties exist,*
*as well as pieces with recut 3.*

| | Mintage | G-4 | VG-8 | F-12 | EF-40 | AU-50 | MS-60 | MS-63 | PF-63 |
|---|---|---|---|---|---|---|---|---|---|
| 1867, No Rays *(600+)* | 28,890,500 | $15. | $20. | $24. | $45. | $75. | $125. | $200. | $425. |
| 1868 ........*(600+)* | 28,817,000 | 15. | 20. | 24. | 45. | 75. | 125. | 200. | 425. |
| 1869 ........*(600+)* | 16,395,000 | 15. | 20. | 24. | 45. | 75. | 125. | 200. | 425. |
| 1870 ......*(1,000+)* | 4,806,000 | 20. | 25. | 35. | 65. | 120. | 185. | 260. | 425. |
| 1871 ........*(960+)* ... 561,000 | | 55. | 65. | 100. | 220. | 275. | 375. | 575. | 475. |
| 1872 ........*(950+)* | 6,036,000 | 22. | 25. | 38. | 70. | 120. | 200. | 300. | 425. |
| 1873, Cl 3 ...*(1,100+)* ... 436,050 | | 25. | 35. | 40. | 135. | 190. | 325. | 550. | 425. |
| 1873, Open 3 .........4,113,950 | | 22. | 25. | 40. | 75. | 135. | 200. | 300. | |
| 1873, Lg Over Sm 3............* | | | | | | | — | — |
| 1874 ........*(700+)* | 3,538,000 | 25. | 35. | 55. | 90. | 130. | 200. | 320. | 425. |
| 1875 ........*(700+)* | 2,097,000 | 30. | 40. | 65. | 110. | 150. | 235. | 350. | 525. |
| 1876 ......*(1,150+)* | 2,530,000 | 30. | 40. | 65. | 110. | 150. | 235. | 300. | 475. |
| 1877, Pf only ..*(510+)*.......... | | | | | 1,850. | | | | 2,500. |
| 1878, Pf only (2,350).......... | | | | | 1,100. | | | | 1,350. |
| 1879 ........*(3,200)* ....25,900 | | 350. | 450. | 550. | 650. | 700. | 800. | 900. | 700. |
| 1879, 9 Over 8 ......*.......... | | | | | | | | | 725. |
| 1880 ........*(3,955)* ....16,000 | | 450. | 550. | 650. | 1,200. | 1,750. | 3,800. | 7,000. | 725. |
| 1881 ........*(3,575)* ....68,800 | | 250. | 300. | 400. | 500. | 650. | 750. | 950. | 525. |
| 1882 ........*(3,100)* 11,472,900 | | 15. | 20. | 22. | 40. | 75. | 120. | 180. | 325. |
| 1883 ........*(5,419)* 1,451,500 | | 15. | 22. | 30. | 55. | 85. | 135. | 185. | 375. |
| 1883, 3 Over 2................* | | 160. | 220. | 260. | 540. | 665. | 825. | 1,200. | |

* Included in number above.

# LIBERTY HEAD (1883–1912)

In 1883, the nickel design was changed to the Liberty Head. This type first appeared without the word CENTS on the coin, merely a large letter V. Some of these "CENTS-less" coins were gold plated and passed for $5. Later in that year the word CENTS was added to discourage the fraudulent practice.

Five 1913 Liberty Head nickels were originally owned by Colonel E.H.R. Green (son of the famous Hetty Green, the "Witch of Wall Street"). These have since been dispersed and are now held in various public and private collections. These were not a regular issue and were never placed in circulation.

*Designer Charles E. Barber; weight 5 grams; composition .750 copper, .250 nickel; diameter 21.2 mm; plain edge; mints: Philadelphia, Denver, San Francisco.*

**G-4 GOOD**—No details in head. LIBERTY obliterated.
**VG-8 VERY GOOD**—Some letters in LIBERTY legible.
**F-12 FINE**—All letters in LIBERTY legible.
**VF-20 VERY FINE**—LIBERTY bold, including letter L.
**EF-40 EXTREMELY FINE**—LIBERTY sharp. Corn grains at bottom of wreath visible on reverse.
**AU-50 ABOUT UNCIRCULATED**—Traces of light wear on only high points of design. Half of mint luster present.
**MS-60 UNCIRCULATED**—No trace of wear, but many contact marks possible. Surface may be spotted, or luster faded.
**MS-63 CHOICE UNCIRCULATED**—No trace of wear. Light blemishes.

**Variety 1, Without CENTS (1883 Only)**

*See next page for chart.*

*Sharply struck Uncirculated coins are valued higher than the prices shown; dull or weakly struck pieces are worth less.*

| | Mintage | G-4 | VG-8 | F-12 | VF-20 | EF-40 | AU-50 | MS-60 | MS-63 | PF-63 |
|---|---|---|---|---|---|---|---|---|---|---|
| 1883, Without CENTS | | | | | | | | | | |
| (5,219) | 5,474,300 | $6. | $7. | $8. | $9. | $10. | $14. | $35. | $50. | $300. |

**Variety 2, With CENTS (1883–1913)**

↑ **Mintmark Location**

| | Mintage | G-4 | VG-8 | F-12 | VF-20 | EF-40 | AU-50 | MS-60 | MS-63 | PF-63 |
|---|---|---|---|---|---|---|---|---|---|---|
| 1883, With CENTS | | | | | | | | | | |
| (6,783) | 16,026,200 | $14.00 | $16.00 | $30.00 | $45. | $75. | $100. | $140. | $200. | $275. |
| 1884 (3,942) | 11,270,000 | 18.00 | 30.00 | 35.00 | 50. | 80. | 110. | 190. | 275. | 250. |
| 1885 (3,790) | 1,472,700 | 475.00 | 550.00 | 700.00 | 800. | 1,000. | 1,200. | 1,500. | 2,000. | 1,200. |
| 1886 (4,290) | 3,326,000 | 200.00 | 280.00 | 375.00 | 460. | 650. | 760. | 875. | 1,100. | 625. |
| 1887 (2,960) | 15,260,692 | 10.00 | 15.00 | 30.00 | 45. | 70. | 90. | 135. | 185. | 250. |
| 1888 (4,582) | 10,167,901 | 25.00 | 35.00 | 50.00 | 85. | 125. | 175. | 225. | 300. | 250. |
| 1889 (3,336) | 15,878,025 | 6.00 | 12.00 | 24.00 | 35. | 60. | 100. | 125. | 165. | 250. |
| 1890 (2,740) | 16,256,532 | 6.00 | 12.00 | 24.00 | 35. | 60. | 100. | 160. | 200. | 250. |
| 1891 (2,350) | 16,832,000 | 6.00 | 12.00 | 24.00 | 35. | 60. | 100. | 160. | 200. | 250. |
| 1892 (2,745) | 11,696,897 | 6.00 | 10.00 | 20.00 | 25. | 60. | 100. | 130. | 160. | 250. |
| 1893 (2,195) | 13,368,000 | 6.00 | 10.00 | 20.00 | 25. | 60. | 100. | 130. | 160. | 250. |
| 1894 (2,632) | 5,410,500 | 12.00 | 20.00 | 80.00 | 140. | 200. | 275. | 300. | 400. | 250. |
| 1895 (2,062) | 9,977,822 | 5.00 | 8.00 | 22.00 | 35. | 65. | 100. | 140. | 200. | 250. |
| 1896 (1,862) | 8,841,058 | 8.00 | 15.00 | 32.00 | 55. | 80. | 125. | 180. | 235. | 250. |
| 1897 (1,938) | 20,426,797 | 4.00 | 5.00 | 10.00 | 20. | 40. | 65. | 100. | 160. | 250. |
| 1898 (1,795) | 12,530,292 | 4.00 | 5.00 | 10.00 | 20. | 40. | 70. | 150. | 185. | 250. |
| 1899 (2,031) | 26,027,000 | 2.25 | 2.75 | 8.00 | 16. | 30. | 55. | 90. | 130. | 250. |
| 1900 (2,262) | 27,253,733 | 2.00 | 2.50 | 7.50 | 12. | 28. | 50. | 85. | 135. | 250. |
| 1901 (1,985) | 26,478,228 | 2.00 | 2.50 | 4.50 | 10. | 26. | 50. | 70. | 125. | 250. |
| 1902 (2,018) | 31,487,561 | 2.00 | 2.50 | 4.50 | 10. | 26. | 50. | 70. | 125. | 250. |
| 1903 (1,790) | 28,004,935 | 2.00 | 2.50 | 4.50 | 10. | 26. | 50. | 70. | 125. | 250. |
| 1904 (1,817) | 21,403,167 | 2.00 | 2.50 | 4.50 | 10. | 26. | 50. | 70. | 125. | 250. |
| 1905 (2,152) | 29,825,124 | 2.00 | 2.50 | 4.50 | 10. | 26. | 50. | 70. | 125. | 250. |
| 1906 (1,725) | 38,612,000 | 2.00 | 2.50 | 4.50 | 10. | 26. | 50. | 70. | 125. | 250. |
| 1907 (1,475) | 39,213,325 | 2.00 | 2.50 | 4.50 | 10. | 26. | 50. | 70. | 125. | 250. |
| 1908 (1,620) | 22,684,557 | 2.00 | 2.50 | 4.50 | 10. | 26. | 50. | 70. | 125. | 250. |
| 1909 (4,763) | 11,585,763 | 2.50 | 3.00 | 5.00 | 12. | 30. | 60. | 85. | 135. | 250. |
| 1910 (2,405) | 30,166,948 | 2.00 | 2.50 | 4.50 | 10. | 26. | 42. | 65. | 100. | 250. |
| 1911 (1,733) | 39,557,639 | 2.00 | 2.50 | 4.50 | 10. | 26. | 42. | 65. | 100. | 250. |
| 1912 (2,145) | 26,234,569 | 2.00 | 2.50 | 4.50 | 10. | 26. | 42. | 65. | 100. | 250. |
| 1912D | 8,474,000 | 3.00 | 4.00 | 10.00 | 35. | 75. | 160. | 300. | 375. | |
| 1912S | 238,000 | 140.00 | 175.00 | 250.00 | 450. | 800. | 1,250. | 1,500. | 1,800. | |
| 1913 Liberty Head *(5 known)* | | | $1,840,000, PF-66, Superior auction, Mar-01 | | | | | 3,000,000. | | |

## INDIAN HEAD OR BUFFALO (1913–1938)

These pieces are known as Buffalo, Bison, or Indian Head nickels. In the first year of issue, 1913, there were two distinct varieties, the first showing the bison on a mound, and the second with the base redesigned to a thinner, straight line.

James E. Fraser designed this nickel, employing three different Indians as models. His initial F is beneath the date. The bison was supposedly modeled after "Black Diamond" in the New York Central Park Zoo.

Matte Proof coins were made for collectors from 1913 to 1916. Specimen strikings of 1917 are reported.

*Designer James Earle Fraser; weight 5 grams; composition .750 copper, .250 nickel; diameter 21.2 mm; plain edge; mints: Philadelphia, Denver, San Francisco.*

**G-4 GOOD**—Legends and date readable. Buffalo's horn does not show.
**VG-8 VERY GOOD**—Horn worn nearly flat.
**F-12 FINE**—Horn and tail smooth but partially visible. Obverse rim intact.
**VF-20 VERY FINE**—Much of horn visible. Indian's cheekbone worn.
**EF-40 EXTREMELY FINE**—Horn lightly worn. Slight wear on Indian's hair ribbon.
**AU-50 ABOUT UNCIRCULATED**—Traces of light wear on only the high points of the design. Half of mint luster present.
**MS-60 UNCIRCULATED**—No trace of wear. May have several blemishes.
**MS-63 CHOICE UNCIRCULATED**—No trace of wear. Light blemishes.

### Variety 1 – FIVE CENTS on Raised Ground (1913)

| | Mintage | G-4 | VG-8 | F-12 | VF-20 | EF-40 | AU-50 | MS-60 | MS-63 | MATTE PF-63 |
|---|---|---|---|---|---|---|---|---|---|---|
| 1913, Var 1 | | | | | | | | | | |
| (1,520) | 30,992,000 | $9. | $12. | $14. | $16. | $22. | $32. | $45. | $60. | $1,400. |
| 1913D, Var 1 | 5,337,000 | 12. | 15. | 18. | 24. | 35. | 50. | 65. | 75. | |
| 1913S, Var 1 | 2,105,000 | 35. | 40. | 45. | 55. | 75. | 95. | 120. | 160. | |

### Variety 2 – FIVE CENTS in Recess (1913–1938)

**Mintmark Below FIVE CENTS**     **1916, Doubled-Die Obverse**     **1918-D, 8 Over 7**

| | Mintage | G-4 | VG-8 | F-12 | VF-20 | EF-40 | AU-50 | MS-60 | MS-63 | MATTE PF-63 |
|---|---|---|---|---|---|---|---|---|---|---|
| 1913, Var 2 | | | | | | | | | | |
| (1,514) | 29,857,186 | $8. | $9. | $10. | $12. | $18. | $25. | $30. | $65. | $1,000. |
| 1913D, Var 2 | 4,156,000 | 95. | 115. | 140. | 170. | 190. | 210. | 250. | 350. | |
| 1913S, Var 2 | 1,209,000 | 275. | 325. | 375. | 425. | 475. | 550. | 700. | 1,000. | |

*Chart continued on next page.*

# NICKEL FIVE-CENT PIECES

| | Mintage | G-4 | VG-8 | F-12 | VF-20 | EF-40 | AU-50 | MS-60 | MS-63 | PF-63 |
|---|---|---|---|---|---|---|---|---|---|---|
| 1914, 4 Over 3 ......* | | | | $350.00 | $550.00 | $850. | $1,800. | | | |
| 1914 (1,275) 20,664,463 | $15.00 | $17.00 | 20.00 | 22.00 | 30. | 40. | $50. | $80. | $900. |
| 1914D ......3,912,000 | 70.00 | 90.00 | 115.00 | 160.00 | 250. | 300. | 375. | 500. | |
| 1914S ......3,470,000 | 20.00 | 30.00 | 40.00 | 55.00 | 80. | 140. | 185. | 425. | |
| 1915 (1,050) 20,986,220 | 5.00 | 6.00 | 7.00 | 10.00 | 22. | 40. | 50. | 75. | 1,100. |
| 1915D ......7,569,000 | 15.00 | 20.00 | 30.00 | 50.00 | 100. | 140. | 250. | 325. | |
| 1915S ......1,505,000 | 32.00 | 50.00 | 85.00 | 165.00 | 385. | 450. | 575. | 850. | |
| 1916   (600) 63,497,466 | 4.00 | 5.00 | 6.00 | 7.00 | 10. | 15. | 42. | 70. | 1,650. |
| 1916, DblDie Obv ..... | 1,800.00 | 3,750.00 | 7,000.00 | 10,000.00 | 13,000. | 30,000. | 45,000. | 135,000. | |
| 1916D ......13,333,000 | 10.00 | 15.00 | 20.00 | 32.00 | 80. | 110. | 150. | 250. | |
| 1916S ......11,860,000 | 6.50 | 11.00 | 17.00 | 30.00 | 70. | 100. | 175. | 280. | |
| 1917 ......51,424,019 | 4.00 | 5.00 | 6.00 | 7.00 | 13. | 30. | 50. | 125. | — |
| 1917D ......9,910,000 | 15.00 | 20.00 | 35.00 | 70.00 | 125. | 230. | 300. | 750. | |
| 1917S ......4,193,000 | 20.00 | 35.00 | 65.00 | 90.00 | 175. | 300. | 375. | 1,250. | |
| 1918 ......32,086,314 | 4.00 | 5.00 | 6.00 | 12.00 | 30. | 45. | 95. | 300. | |
| 1918D, 8/7 .........* | 1,000.00 | 1,500.00 | 2,700.00 | 5,500.00 | 9,500. | 12,000. | 28,000. | 60,000. | |
| 1918D ......8,362,000 | 15.00 | 25.00 | 40.00 | 100.00 | 200. | 325. | 375. | 1,200. | |
| 1918S ......4,882,000 | 12.00 | 25.00 | 42.00 | 90.00 | 185. | 300. | 500. | 3,000. | |
| 1919 ......60,868,000 | 1.50 | 2.00 | 2.50 | 6.00 | 12. | 30. | 45. | 100. | |
| 1919D (a) ...8,006,000 | | | | | | | | | |
| 1919S (a) ...7,521,000 | 8.00 | 20.00 | 40.00 | 100.00 | 250. | 350. | 500. | 1,800. | |
| 1920 ......63,093,000 | 1.50 | 2.00 | 2.50 | 5.00 | 12. | 25. | 50. | 125. | |
| 1920D (a) ...9,418,000 | 7.00 | 15.00 | 25.00 | 100.00 | 275. | 325. | 500. | 1,800. | |
| 1920S ......9,689,000 | 4.00 | 7.00 | 20.00 | 90.00 | 175. | 300. | 500. | 2,000. | |
| 1921 ......10,663,000 | 3.00 | 4.00 | 6.00 | 20.00 | 50. | 75. | 100. | 300. | |
| 1921S ......1,557,000 | 70.00 | 110.00 | 175.00 | 525.00 | 850. | 1,200. | 1,500. | 2,200. | |
| 1923 ......35,715,000 | 2.00 | 2.50 | 3.00 | 6.00 | 13. | 30. | 50. | 150. | |
| 1923S (a) ...6,142,000 | 6.00 | 8.00 | 18.00 | 125.00 | 275. | 350. | 450. | 900. | |
| 1924 ......21,620,000 | 1.50 | 2.00 | 5.00 | 10.00 | 20. | 45. | 65. | 150. | |
| 1924D ......5,258,000 | 7.00 | 8.00 | 25.00 | 75.00 | 225. | 300. | 350. | 1,000. | |
| 1924S ......1,437,000 | 15.00 | 30.00 | 100.00 | 475.00 | 1,250. | 1,800. | 2,400. | 4,000. | |
| 1925 ......35,565,100 | 3.00 | 3.50 | 4.00 | 8.00 | 15. | 30. | 40. | 100. | |
| 1925D (a) ...4,450,000 | 8.00 | 15.00 | 35.00 | 90.00 | 175. | 250. | 400. | 750. | |
| 1925S ......6,256,000 | 5.00 | 10.00 | 18.00 | 85.00 | 180. | 250. | 450. | 2,200. | |
| 1926 ......44,693,000 | 1.00 | 1.50 | 2.50 | 4.00 | 10. | 20. | 35. | 75. | |
| 1926D (a) ...5,638,000 | 6.00 | 12.00 | 24.00 | 90.00 | 175. | 275. | 300. | 550. | |
| 1926S ........970,000 | 18.00 | 30.00 | 75.00 | 450.00 | 900. | 2,800. | 4,500. | 8,000. | |
| 1927 ......37,981,000 | 1.00 | 1.25 | 2.50 | 4.00 | 10. | 20. | 35. | 75. | |
| 1927D ......5,730,000 | 2.50 | 5.00 | 7.00 | 30.00 | 75. | 125. | 150. | 300. | |
| 1927S ......3,430,000 | 1.50 | 3.00 | 5.00 | 32.00 | 90. | 175. | 500. | 2,500. | |
| 1928 ......23,411,000 | 1.00 | 1.25 | 2.50 | 5.00 | 10. | 25. | 30. | 75. | |
| 1928D ......6,436,000 | 1.50 | 2.50 | 5.00 | 15.00 | 40. | 45. | 50. | 100. | |
| 1928S ......6,936,000 | 2.00 | 2.25 | 3.00 | 12.00 | 27. | 100. | 250. | 650. | |
| 1929 ......36,446,000 | 1.00 | 1.50 | 2.50 | 4.00 | 10. | 20. | 35. | 70. | |
| 1929D ......8,370,000 | 1.25 | 2.00 | 2.50 | 8.00 | 35. | 45. | 60. | 125. | |
| 1929S ......7,754,000 | 1.00 | 1.50 | 2.00 | 2.50 | 14. | 25. | 50. | 75. | |
| 1930 ......22,849,000 | 1.00 | 1.50 | 2.50 | 4.00 | 10. | 20. | 30. | 70. | |
| 1930S ......5,435,000 | 1.00 | 1.50 | 2.50 | 3.00 | 12. | 30. | 50. | 110. | |
| 1931S ......1,200,000 | 15.00 | 16.00 | 18.00 | 20.00 | 22. | 40. | 60. | 80. | |
| 1934 ......20,213,003 | 1.00 | 1.50 | 2.50 | 4.00 | 10. | 18. | 50. | 60. | |

* Included in number below. **a.** Uncirculated pieces with full, sharp details are worth considerably more.

| | Mintage | G-4 | VG-8 | F-12 | VF-20 | EF-40 | AU-50 | MS-60 | MS-63 | PF-63 |
|---|---|---|---|---|---|---|---|---|---|---|
| 1934D . . . . . . . . . .7,480,000 | | $1.00 | $1.50 | $2.50 | $5.00 | $15.00 | $40. | $70. | $100. | |
| 1935 . . . . . . . . . .58,264,000 | | 1.00 | 1.50 | 1.75 | 2.00 | 3.00 | 9. | 20. | 40. | |
| 1935, DblDie Rev . . . . . . . . .* | | 40.00 | 50.00 | 90.00 | 150.00 | 400.00 | 1,600. | | | |
| 1935D **(b)** . . . . . . .12,092,000 | | 1.00 | 1.50 | 2.50 | 6.00 | 15.00 | 40. | 60. | 75. | |
| 1935S . . . . . . . . . .10,300,000 | | 1.00 | 1.50 | 2.00 | 2.50 | 4.00 | 15. | 50. | 70. | |
| 1936 . . . .(4,420) 118,997,000 | | 1.00 | 1.50 | 1.75 | 2.00 | 3.00 | 9. | 20. | 40. | $1,200. |
| 1936D, . . . . . . . . .24,814,000 | | 1.00 | 1.50 | 1.75 | 2.00 | 4.00 | 12. | 35. | 40. | |
| 1936D, 3-1/2 Legs . . . . . . . .* | | 250.00 | 300.00 | 400.00 | 900.00 | 1,000.00 | | | | |
| 1936S . . . . . . . . . .14,930,000 | | 1.00 | 1.50 | 1.75 | 2.00 | 3.50 | 12. | 35. | 40. | |
| 1937 . . . .(5,769) 79,480,000 | | 1.00 | 1.50 | 1.75 | 2.00 | 3.00 | 9. | 20. | 40. | 1,000. |

\* Included in number above. **b.** Large and small mintmark varieties exist; see page 20.

**1937-D, "3-Legged" Variety**
*A similar variety exists for 1936-D.*

**1938-D, D Over S**

| | Mintage | G-4 | VG-8 | F-12 | VF-20 | EF-40 | AU-50 | MS-60 | MS-63 |
|---|---|---|---|---|---|---|---|---|---|
| 1937D . . . . . . . . . . . .17,826,000 | | $1.00 | $1.50 | $1.75 | $3.00 | $4.00 | $10. | $30. | $40. |
| 1937D, 3-Legged . . . . . . . . . . . .* | | 450.00 | 575.00 | 750.00 | 850.00 | 1,000.00 | 1,400. | 2,500. | 5,500. |
| 1937S . . . . . . . . . . . . .5,635,000 | | 1.00 | 1.50 | 1.75 | 3.00 | 3.50 | 10. | 30. | 40. |
| 1938D . . . . . . . . . . . . .7,020,000 | | 2.00 | 2.50 | 3.00 | 3.25 | 3.75 | 10. | 20. | 40. |
| 1938D, D Over S . . . . . . . . . . . .* | | 5.00 | 7.50 | 10.00 | 15.00 | 18.00 | 30. | 50. | 75. |

\* Included in number above.

# JEFFERSON (1938 TO DATE)

The obverse of this nickel was designed by Felix Schlag, who won an award of $1,000 in a competition with some 390 artists. His design established the definite public approval of portrait and pictorial themes rather than symbolic devices on our coinage.

*Designer Felix Schlag; weight 5 grams; composition (1938–1942, 1946 to date), .750 copper, .250 nickel, (1942–1945), .560 copper, .350 silver, .090 manganese, with net weight .05626 oz. pure silver; diameter 21.2 mm; plain edge; mints: Philadelphia, Denver, San Francisco.*

**VG-8 VERY GOOD**—Second porch pillar from right nearly gone, other three still visible but weak.
**F-12 FINE**—Jefferson's cheekbone worn flat. Hair lines and eyebrow faint. Second pillar weak, especially at bottom.
**VF-20 VERY FINE**—Second pillar plain and complete on both sides.
**EF-40 EXTREMELY FINE**—Cheekbone, hair lines, eyebrow slightly worn but well defined. Base of triangle above pillars visible but weak.
**AU-50 ABOUT UNCIRCULATED**—Traces of light wear on only high points of design. Half of mint luster present.
**MS-60 UNCIRCULATED**—No trace of wear. Light blemishes.
**MS-65 CHOICE UNCIRCULATED**—No trace of wear. Barely noticeable blemishes.

**1939, Doubled MONTICELLO and FIVE CENTS**

*See next page for chart.*

*Uncirculated pieces with fully struck steps have higher value.*

| | Mintage | VF-20 | EF-40 | AU-50 | MS-60 | MS-63 | MS-65 | PF-65 |
|---|---|---|---|---|---|---|---|---|
| 1938 . . .(19,365) . . .19,496,000 | | $0.50 | $1.00 | $1.50 | $2.50 | $3.50 | $11. | $125. |
| 1938D . . . . . . . . . . . .5,376,000 | | 1.50 | 2.00 | 3.00 | 4.00 | 7.00 | 14. | |
| 1938S . . . . . . . . . . . .4,105,000 | | 2.50 | 3.00 | 3.50 | 4.50 | 7.50 | 15. | |
| 1939 . . .(12,535) . .120,615,000 | | 0.25 | 0.50 | 0.75 | 1.50 | 2.50 | 4. | 125. |
| 1939, Doubled MONTICELLO, | | | | | | | | |
| FIVE CENTS . . . . . . . . . .* | | 70.00 | 85.00 | 125.00 | 160.00 | 325.00 | 650. | |
| 1939D . . . . . . . . . . . .3,514,000 | | 6.00 | 12.00 | 25.00 | 55.00 | 75.00 | 100. | |
| 1939S . . . . . . . . . . . .6,630,000 | | 1.50 | 4.00 | 9.00 | 16.00 | 22.00 | 38. | |
| 1940 . . .(14,158) . .176,485,000 | | 0.25 | 0.40 | 0.75 | 1.00 | 1.50 | 4. | 125. |
| 1940D . . . . . . . . . . .43,540,000 | | 0.35 | 0.50 | 1.00 | 2.00 | 2.50 | 6. | |
| 1940S . . . . . . . . . . .39,690,000 | | 0.35 | 0.50 | 1.00 | 2.25 | 3.00 | 6. | |
| 1941 . . .(18,720) . .203,265,000 | | 0.20 | 0.30 | 0.50 | 0.75 | 1.50 | 6. | 125. |
| 1941D . . . . . . . . . . .53,432,000 | | 0.25 | 0.40 | 1.50 | 2.50 | 3.50 | 6. | |
| 1941S (a) . . . . . . . .43,445,000 | | 0.30 | 0.50 | 1.50 | 3.00 | 4.00 | 7. | |
| 1942 . . .(29,600) . . .49,789,000 | | 0.30 | 0.45 | 1.25 | 4.00 | 6.00 | 10. | 125. |
| 1942D . . . . . . . . . . .13,938,000 | | 1.00 | 2.00 | 5.00 | 27.00 | 36.00 | 55. | |
| 1942D Over Horiz D . . . . . . . . .* | | 50.00 | 75.00 | 125.00 | 260.00 | 360.00 | 1,000. | |

* Included in number above. **a.** Large and small mintmark varieties; see page 20.

## Wartime Silver Alloy (1942–1945)

On October 8, 1942, the wartime five-cent piece composed of copper (56%), silver (35%), and manganese (9%) was introduced to eliminate nickel, a critical war material. A larger mintmark was placed above the dome of Monticello. The letter P (Philadelphia) was used for the first time, indicating the change of alloy.

**Mintmark Location**

**1943, 3 Over 2**

**1943, Doubled Eye**

| | Mintage | VF-20 | EF-40 | AU-50 | MS-60 | MS-63 | MS-65 | PF-65 |
|---|---|---|---|---|---|---|---|---|
| 1942P (27,600) . . .57,873,000 | | $1.00 | $1.50 | $3.00 | $7. | $10. | $16. | $250. |
| 1942S . . . . . . . . . .32,900,000 | | 1.00 | 1.50 | 3.00 | 7. | 10. | 16. | |
| 1943P, 3/2 . . . . . . . . . . . . . .* | | 50.00 | 90.00 | 125.00 | 180. | 260. | 620. | |
| 1943P . . . . . . . . .271,165,000 | | 0.90 | 1.25 | 2.50 | 5. | 7. | 13. | |
| 1943P, Doubled Eye . . . . . . . .* | | 30.00 | 50.00 | 75.00 | 100. | 160. | 360. | |
| 1943D . . . . . . . . . .15,294,000 | | 1.00 | 1.50 | 2.50 | 6. | 10. | 15. | |
| 1943S . . . . . . . . .104,060,000 | | 0.90 | 1.25 | 2.50 | 5. | 7. | 13. | |
| 1944P . . . . . . . . .119,150,000 | | 0.90 | 1.25 | 3.00 | 7. | 10. | 20. | |
| 1944D . . . . . . . . . .32,309,000 | | 0.90 | 1.25 | 3.00 | 6. | 10. | 18. | |
| 1944S . . . . . . . . . .21,640,000 | | 0.90 | 1.25 | 2.50 | 5. | 8. | 16. | |
| 1945P . . . . . . . . .119,408,100 | | 0.90 | 1.25 | 2.50 | 5. | 7. | 18. | |
| 1945P, DblDie Rev . . . . . . . . .* | | 20.00 | 30.00 | 50.00 | 75. | 125. | 300. | |
| 1945D . . . . . . . . . .37,158,000 | | 0.90 | 1.25 | 2.50 | 5. | 7. | 16. | |
| 1945S . . . . . . . . . .58,939,000 | | 0.90 | 1.25 | 2.50 | 5. | 7. | 16. | |

*Note:* 1944 nickels without mintmarks are counterfeits. Genuine pieces of other wartime dates struck in nickel by error are known to exist. * Included in regular mintage.

## Prewar Composition,
## Mintmark Style Resumed (1946–1967)

| | Mintage | VF-20 | EF-40 | AU-50 | MS-60 | MS-63 | MS-65 |
|---|---|---|---|---|---|---|---|
| 1946 | 161,116,000 | $0.25 | $0.30 | $0.35 | $0.70 | $2.00 | $6.00 |
| 1946D | 45,292,200 | 0.35 | 0.40 | 0.45 | 0.90 | 2.00 | 6.00 |
| 1946S | 13,560,000 | 0.40 | 0.45 | 0.50 | 1.00 | 1.50 | 3.50 |
| 1947 | 95,000,000 | 0.25 | 0.30 | 0.35 | 0.70 | 1.50 | 3.50 |
| 1947D | 37,822,000 | 0.30 | 0.35 | 0.40 | 0.80 | 1.50 | 3.50 |
| 1947S | 24,720,000 | 0.40 | 0.45 | 0.50 | 1.00 | 1.50 | 3.50 |

| | Mintage | MS-60 | MS-63 | MS-65 | PF-65 |
|---|---|---|---|---|---|
| 1948 | 89,348,000 | $1.00 | $1.50 | $3.50 | |
| 1948D | 44,734,000 | 1.50 | 2.00 | 4.50 | |
| 1948S | 11,300,000 | 1.50 | 2.00 | 4.50 | |
| 1949 | 60,652,000 | 2.50 | 4.00 | 7.50 | |
| 1949D | 36,498,000 | 1.50 | 2.00 | 5.50 | |
| 1949D, D Over S | * | 150.00 | 200.00 | 350.00 | |
| 1949S | 9,716,000 | 1.75 | 2.50 | 5.50 | |
| 1950 | (51,386) .... 9,796,000 | 2.00 | 3.25 | 6.00 | $65.00 |
| 1950D | 2,630,030 | 12.00 | 15.00 | 18.50 | |
| 1951 | (57,500) .... 28,552,000 | 3.00 | 4.00 | 8.50 | 55.00 |
| 1951D | 20,460,000 | 4.00 | 5.00 | 9.50 | |
| 1951S | 7,776,000 | 1.50 | 2.00 | 4.50 | |
| 1952 | (81,980) .... 63,988,000 | 1.00 | 1.50 | 3.50 | 40.00 |
| 1952D | 30,638,000 | 3.50 | 5.00 | 8.50 | |
| 1952S | 20,572,000 | 1.00 | 1.50 | 3.50 | |
| 1953 | (128,800) .... 46,644,000 | 0.25 | 0.50 | 1.50 | 36.00 |
| 1953D | 59,878,600 | 0.25 | 0.50 | 1.50 | |
| 1953S | 19,210,900 | 0.75 | 1.00 | 2.00 | |

\* Included in number above.

**1954-S, S Over D**     **1955-D, D Over S** [a]

| | Mintage | MS-60 | MS-63 | MS-65 | PF-65 |
|---|---|---|---|---|---|
| 1954 | (233,300) .... 47,684,050 | $1.00 | $1.50 | $3.00 | $20.00 |
| 1954D | 117,183,060 | 0.60 | 1.00 | 1.50 | |
| 1954S | 29,384,000 | 1.75 | 2.00 | 3.00 | |
| 1954S, S Over D | * | 25.00 | 40.00 | 75.00 | |
| 1955 | (378,200) .... 7,888,000 | 0.75 | 1.00 | 2.00 | 14.00 |
| 1955D | 74,464,100 | 0.50 | 0.75 | 1.10 | |
| 1955D, D Over S **(a)** | * | 35.00 | 55.00 | 85.00 | |
| 1956 | (669,384) .... 35,216,000 | 0.50 | 0.75 | 1.00 | 3.00 |
| 1956D | 67,222,940 | 0.50 | 0.75 | 1.00 | |
| 1957 | (1,247,952) .... 38,408,000 | 0.50 | 0.75 | 1.00 | 3.00 |
| 1957D | 136,828,900 | 0.50 | 0.70 | 1.00 | |

\* Included in number above. **a.** Varieties exist; value is for the variety illustrated.

*Chart continued on next page.*    

# NICKEL FIVE-CENT PIECES

| | Mintage | MS-60 | MS-63 | MS-65 | PF-65 |
|---|---|---|---|---|---|
| 1958 | (875,652) 17,088,000 | $0.60 | $0.80 | $1.50 | $4.00 |
| 1958D | 168,249,120 | 0.40 | 0.50 | 1.00 | |
| 1959 | (1,149,291) 27,248,000 | 0.25 | 0.50 | 0.80 | 2.00 |
| 1959D | 160,738,240 | 0.25 | 0.50 | 0.80 | |
| 1960 | (1,691,602) 55,416,000 | 0.25 | 0.50 | 0.80 | 1.50 |
| 1960D | 192,582,180 | 0.25 | 0.50 | 0.80 | |
| 1961 | (3,028,144) 73,640,100 | 0.25 | 0.50 | 0.80 | 1.00 |
| 1961D | 229,342,760 | 0.25 | 0.50 | 0.80 | |
| 1962 | (3,218,019) 97,384,000 | 0.25 | 0.50 | 0.80 | 1.00 |
| 1962D | 280,195,720 | 0.25 | 0.50 | 0.80 | |
| 1963 | (3,075,645) 175,776,000 | 0.25 | 0.50 | 0.80 | 1.00 |
| 1963D | 276,829,460 | 0.25 | 0.50 | 0.80 | |
| 1964 | (3,950,762) 1,024,672,000 | 0.25 | 0.50 | 0.80 | 1.00 |
| 1964D | 1,787,297,160 | 0.25 | 0.50 | 0.80 | |
| 1965 | 136,131,380 | 0.25 | 0.50 | 0.80 | |

## 1966 Through 2003

*The designer's initials FS were added below the bust starting in 1966, and dies were further remodeled to strengthen the design in 1971, 1972, 1977, and 1982. The mintmark position was moved to the obverse starting in 1968.*

| | Mintage | MS-63 | MS-65 | PF-65 | | | Mintage | MS-63 | MS-65 | PF-65 |
|---|---|---|---|---|---|---|---|---|---|---|
| 1966 | 156,208,283 | $0.25 | $0.50 | (a) | | 1976S | (4,149,730) | | | $2.00 |
| 1967 | 107,325,800 | 0.25 | 0.50 | $0.80 | | 1977 | 585,376,000 | $0.25 | $0.50 | |
| 1968D | 91,227,880 | 0.25 | 0.50 | | | 1977D | 297,313,422 | 0.50 | 1.00 | |
| 1968S | (3,041,506) | | | 1.00 | | 1977S | (3,251,152) | | | 1.50 |
| | 100,396,004 | 0.25 | 0.50 | | | 1978 | 391,308,000 | 0.25 | 0.50 | |
| 1969D | 202,807,500 | 0.25 | 0.50 | | | 1978D | 313,092,780 | 0.25 | 0.50 | |
| 1969S | (2,934,631) | | | 1.00 | | 1978S | (3,127,781) | | | 1.50 |
| | 120,165,000 | 0.25 | 0.50 | | | 1979 | 463,188,000 | 0.25 | 0.50 | |
| 1970D | 515,485,380 | 0.25 | 0.50 | | | 1979D | 325,867,672 | 0.25 | 0.50 | |
| 1970S | (2,632,810) | | | 1.00 | | 1979S | (3,677,175) | | | |
| | 238,832,004 | 0.25 | 0.50 | | | 1979S, Filled S | | | | 1.50 |
| 1971 | 106,884,000 | 0.75 | 1.50 | | | 1979S, Clear S | | | | 1.75 |
| 1971D | 316,144,800 | 0.30 | 0.60 | | | 1980P | 593,004,000 | 0.25 | 0.50 | |
| 1971, No S (b) | | | | 1,000.00 | | 1980D | 502,323,448 | 0.25 | 0.50 | |
| 1971S | (3,220,733) | | | 2.00 | | 1980S | (3,554,806) | | | 1.50 |
| 1972 | 202,036,000 | 0.25 | 0.50 | | | 1981P | 657,504,000 | 0.25 | 0.50 | |
| 1972D | 351,694,600 | 0.25 | 0.50 | | | 1981D | 364,801,843 | 0.25 | 0.50 | |
| 1972S | (3,260,996) | | | 2.00 | | 1981S | (4,063,083) | | | 2.00 |
| 1973 | 384,396,000 | 0.25 | 0.50 | | | 1982P | 292,355,000 | 2.50 | 5.50 | |
| 1973D | 261,405,000 | 0.25 | 0.50 | | | 1982D | 373,726,544 | 1.75 | 3.00 | |
| 1973S | (2,760,339) | | | 1.50 | | 1982S | (3,857,479) | | | 3.00 |
| 1974 | 601,752,000 | 0.25 | 0.50 | | | 1983P | 561,615,000 | 1.50 | 4.00 | |
| 1974D | 277,373,000 | 0.25 | 0.50 | | | 1983D | 536,726,276 | 1.25 | 2.35 | |
| 1974S | (2,612,568) | | | 2.00 | | 1983S | (3,279,126) | | | 3.00 |
| 1975 | 181,772,000 | 0.50 | 1.00 | | | 1984P | 746,769,000 | 1.00 | 2.00 | |
| 1975D | 401,875,300 | 0.25 | 0.50 | | | 1984D | 517,675,146 | 0.25 | 0.50 | |
| 1975S | (2,845,450) | | | 2.00 | | 1984S | (3,065,110) | | | 4.00 |
| 1976 | 367,124,000 | 0.45 | 0.90 | | | 1985P | 647,114,962 | 0.50 | 1.00 | |
| 1976D | 563,964,147 | 0.45 | 0.90 | | | 1985D | 459,747,446 | 0.50 | 1.00 | |

**a.** Two presentation pieces were given to the designer. **b.** 1971 Proof nickels without mintmark were made in error. See pages 20 and 321.

| | Mintage | MS-63 | MS-65 | PF-65 | | Mintage | MS-63 | MS-65 | PF-65 |
|---|---|---|---|---|---|---|---|---|---|
| 1985S | (3,362,821) | | | $3.00 | 1995P | 774,156,000 | $0.25 | $0.50 | |
| 1986P | 536,883,483 | $0.50 | $1.00 | | 1995D | 888,112,000 | 0.50 | 1.00 | |
| 1986D | 361,819,140 | 1.00 | 1.75 | | 1995S | (2,797,481) | | | $5.00 |
| 1986S | (3,010,497) | | | 7.00 | 1996P | 829,332,000 | 0.25 | 0.50 | |
| 1987P | 371,499,481 | 0.25 | 0.50 | | 1996D | 817,736,000 | 0.25 | 0.50 | |
| 1987D | 410,590,604 | | | | 1996S | (2,525,265) | | | 3.00 |
| 1987S | (4,227,728) | | | 3.00 | 1997P | 470,972,000 | 0.50 | 1.00 | |
| 1988P | 771,360,000 | 0.25 | 0.50 | | 1997P, Special | | | | |
| 1988D | 663,771,652 | 0.25 | 0.50 | |    Unc **(c)** | 25,000 | 200.00 | 250.00 | |
| 1988S | (3,262,948) | | | 5.00 | 1997D | 466,640,000 | 1.00 | 2.00 | |
| 1989P | 898,812,000 | 0.25 | 0.45 | | 1997S | (2,796,678) | | | 3.00 |
| 1989D | 570,842,474 | 0.25 | 0.45 | | 1998P | 688,272,000 | 0.35 | 0.70 | |
| 1989S | (3,220,194) | | | 4.00 | 1998D | 635,360,000 | 0.35 | 0.70 | |
| 1990P | 661,636,000 | 0.25 | 0.50 | | 1998S | (2,086,507) | | | 3.00 |
| 1990D | 663,938,503 | 0.25 | 0.50 | | 1999P | 1,212,000,000 | 0.25 | 0.50 | |
| 1990S | (3,299,559) | | | 4.00 | 1999D | 1,066,720,000 | 0.25 | 0.50 | |
| 1991P | 614,104,000 | 0.30 | 0.60 | | 1999S | (3,347,966) | | | 3.50 |
| 1991D | 436,496,678 | 0.30 | 0.60 | | 2000P | 846,240,000 | 0.25 | 0.50 | |
| 1991S | (2,867,787) | | | 4.50 | 2000D | 1,509,520,000 | 0.25 | 0.50 | |
| 1992P | 399,552,000 | 1.50 | 2.50 | | 2000S | (4,047,993) | | | 3.00 |
| 1992D | 450,565,113 | 0.25 | 0.70 | | 2001P | 675,704,000 | 0.25 | 0.50 | |
| 1992S | (4,176,560) | | | 4.00 | 2001D | 627,680,000 | 0.25 | 0.50 | |
| 1993P | 412,076,000 | 0.25 | 0.60 | | 2001S | (3,184,606) | | | 3.00 |
| 1993D | 406,084,135 | 0.25 | 0.60 | | 2002P | 539,280,000 | 0.25 | 0.50 | |
| 1993S | (3,394,792) | | | 4.00 | 2002D | 691,200,000 | 0.25 | 0.50 | |
| 1994P | 722,160,000 | 0.25 | 0.50 | | 2002S | (3,211,995) | | | 3.00 |
| 1994P, Special | | | | | 2003P | 441,840,000 | 0.25 | 0.50 | |
|    Unc **(c)** | 167,703 | 60.00 | 100.00 | | 2003D | 383,040,000 | 0.25 | 0.50 | |
| 1994D | 715,762,110 | 0.25 | 0.50 | | 2003S | (3,298,439) | | | 3.00 |
| 1994S | (3,269,923) | | | 4.00 | | | | | |

**c.** Special "frosted" uncirculated pieces were included in the 1993 Thomas Jefferson commemorative dollar packaging (sold in 1994) and the 1997 Botanic Garden sets. They resemble Proof coins.

## "Westward Journey" Nickels

The United States Mint began the Westward Journey Nickel Series™ in 2004. The coins in this special program commemorate the bicentennial of the Louisiana Purchase and the journey of Meriwether Lewis and William Clark to explore the vast area recently acquired by the American government.

The 2004 Louisiana Purchase/Peace Medal design was adapted from the reverse of certain of the original Indian Peace Medals commissioned for the expedition. These medals bear a portrait of President Jefferson on one side, and symbols of peace and friendship on the other. They were presented to Native American chiefs and other important leaders as tokens of the goodwill of the United States.

The 2004 Keelboat design features an angled side view of the keelboat that transported the Lewis and Clark expedition and their supplies through the rivers of the Louisiana Territory. Built to Captain Lewis's specifications, this 55-foot keelboat could be sailed, rowed, poled like a raft, or towed from the riverbank.

The 2005 nickels feature a new likeness of President Thomas Jefferson. The "Liberty" inscription on the coin was based on his handwriting. The new portrait was inspired by the marble bust of Jefferson completed in 1789 by French sculptor Jean-Antoine Houdon.

The 2005 American Bison design features a bison standing in profile. Journals from the Lewis and Clark expedition described this large animal, which held great significance to many American Indian cultures. (The design also hearkens to the Indian Head/Buffalo nickel of 1913 to 1938, a popular numismatic motif.)

The 2005 "Ocean in View" design captures the expedition's joy at finally seeing the Pacific Ocean after many months of arduous travel. It shows a cliffs-and-ocean scene and an inscription inspired by an excited entry in the journal of Captain William Clark, from November 7, 1805: "Ocean in view! O! The joy!"

The 2006 "Monticello" design shows a facing portrait of Jefferson and the traditional depiction of Monticello.

| 2004 Obverse | Peace Medal | Keelboat |
| 2005 Obverse | American Bison | Ocean in View |
| 2006 Obverse | Monticello | |

| | Mintage | MS-63 | MS-65 | PF-65 |
|---|---|---|---|---|
| 2004P, Peace Medal | 361,440,000 | $0.25 | $0.50 | |
| 2004D, Peace Medal | 372,000,000 | 0.25 | 0.50 | |
| 2004S, Peace Medal | (2,992,069) | | | $5.00 |
| 2004P, Keelboat | 366,720,000 | 0.25 | 0.50 | |
| 2004D, Keelboat | 344,880,000 | 0.25 | 0.50 | |
| 2004S, Keelboat | (2,992,069) | | | 5.00 |
| 2005P, American Bison | 448,320,000 | 0.25 | 0.50 | |
| 2005D, American Bison | 487,680,000 | 0.25 | 0.50 | |
| 2005S, American Bison | (3,273,000) | | | 5.00 |
| 2005P, Ocean in View | (411,120,000) | 0.25 | 0.50 | |
| 2005D, Ocean in View | (394,080,000) | 0.25 | 0.50 | |
| 2005S, Ocean in View | (3,273,000) | | | 5.00 |
| 2006P, Monticello | | 0.25 | 0.50 | |
| 2006D, Monticello | | 0.25 | 0.50 | |
| 2006S, Monticello | | | | 5.00 |

Half dimes have the same general designs as larger United States silver coins. Authorized by the Act of April 2, 1792, they were not struck until February 1795, although some were dated 1794. At first the weight was 20.8 grains, and fineness .8924. By the Act of January 18, 1837, the weight was reduced to 20-5/8 grains and the fineness changed to .900. The weight was later reduced to 19.2 grains by the Act of February 21, 1853. Half dimes offer many varieties in the early dates.

## TYPE COIN VALUES

|  | G-4 | F-12 | EF-40 | MS-60 | MS-63 | MS-65 | PF-63 | PF-65 |
|---|---|---|---|---|---|---|---|---|
| Flowing Hair, 1794–1795 | $1,050.+ | $1,750.+ | $4,750.+ | $12,500.+ | $16,500.+ | $39,000.+ |  |  |
| Drpd Bust, SE, 1796–1797 | 1,100.+ | 2,100.+ | 6,250.+ | 14,500.+ | 25,000. | 100,000.+ |  |  |
| Drpd Bust, HE, 1800–1805 | 725.+ | 1,750.+ | 3,750.+ | 11,000.+ | 20,000.+ | 42,500.+ |  |  |
| Cap Bust, 1829–1837 | 35.+ | 60.+ | 145.+ | 375.+ | 800.+ | 3,100.+ | $9,800.+ | $35,000.+ |
| Lib Std, NS, 1837–1838 | 38.+ | 70.+ | 220.+ | 750.+ | 1,000. | 4,100.+ | 16,500.+ | 45,000.+ |
| Lib Std, Stars, 1838–1859 | 16.+ | 22.+ | 65.+ | 185.+ | 310.+ | 1,500.+ | 1,750.+ | 5,000.+ |
| Lib Std, Arr, 1853–1855 | 16.+ | 22.+ | 65.+ | 210.+ | 300. | 2,350.+ | 8,200.+ | 20,000.+ |
| Lib Std, Leg, 1860–1873 | 16.+ | 22.+ | 48.+ | 160.+ | 225. | 1,150.+ | 625.+ | 2,700.+ |

+ or – indicates change from previous year

# FLOWING HAIR (1794–1795)

*Designer Robert Scot; weight 1.35 grams; composition .8924 silver, .1076 copper; approx. diameter 16.5 mm; reeded edge. All coined at Philadelphia Mint.*

**AG-3 ABOUT GOOD**—Details clear enough to identify.

**G-4 GOOD**—Eagle, wreath, bust outlined but lack details.

**VG-8 VERY GOOD**—Some details on face. All lettering legible.

**F-12 FINE**—Hair ends visible. Hair at top smooth.

**VF-20 VERY FINE**—Hair lines at top visible. Hair about ear defined.

**EF-40 EXTREMELY FINE**—Hair above forehead and at neck well defined but shows some wear.

**AU-50 ABOUT UNCIRCULATED**—Slight wear on high waves of hair, near ear and face, and on head and tips of eagle's wings.

**MS-60 UNCIRCULATED**—No trace of wear. Light blemishes.

**MS-63 CHOICE UNCIRCULATED**—Some distracting marks or blemishes in prime focal areas. Some impairment of luster possible.

| | Mintage | AG-3 | G-4 | VG-8 | F-12 | VF-20 | EF-40 | AU-50 | MS-60 | MS-63 |
|---|---|---|---|---|---|---|---|---|---|---|
| 1794 | 86,416 | $750. | $1,350. | $1,700. | $2,250. | $3,250. | $5,500. | $9,000. | $15,000. | $25,000. |
| 1795 | * | 450. | 1,050. | 1,250. | 1,750. | 2,750. | 4,750. | 6,500. | 12,500. | 16,500. |

* Included in number above.

# DRAPED BUST (1796–1797)

*Designer Robert Scot; weight 1.35 grams; composition .8924 silver, .1076 copper; approx. diameter 16.5 mm; reeded edge. All coined at Philadelphia Mint.*

**AG-3 ABOUT GOOD**—Details clear enough to identify.

**G-4 GOOD**—Date, stars, LIBERTY readable. Bust of Liberty outlined, but no details.

**VG-8 VERY GOOD**—Some details visible.

**F-12 FINE**—Hair and drapery lines worn, but visible.

**VF-20 VERY FINE**—Only left side of drapery indistinct.

**EF-40 EXTREMELY FINE**—Details visible in all hair lines.

**AU-50 ABOUT UNCIRCULATED**—Slight wear on bust, shoulder, and hair; wear on eagle's head and top of wings.

**MS-60 UNCIRCULATED**—No trace of wear. Light blemishes.

**MS-63 CHOICE UNCIRCULATED**—Some distracting marks or blemishes in prime focal areas. Impaired luster possible.

## Small Eagle Reverse (1796–1797)

*See next page for chart.*

| | Mintage | AG-3 | G-4 | VG-8 | F-12 | VF-20 | EF-40 | AU-50 | MS-60 | MS-63 |
|---|---|---|---|---|---|---|---|---|---|---|
| 1796, 6 Over 5 . . . | 10,230 | $650. | $1,150. | $1,500. | $2,250. | $3,750. | $6,750. | $13,500. | $23,500. | $42,500. |
| 1796 . . . . . . . . . . . . . . * | | 550. | 1,100. | 1,400. | 2,100. | 3,500. | 6,500. | 11,000. | 14,500. | 27,500. |
| 1796, LIKERTY . . . . . . . * | | 550. | 1,150. | 1,500. | 2,150. | 3,500. | 6,500. | 11,500. | 15,500. | 30,000. |
| 1797, 15 Stars . . . | 44,527 | 550. | 1,100. | 1,400. | 2,100. | 3,500. | 6,250. | 10,500. | 14,500. | 25,000. |
| 1797, 16 Stars . . . . . . . * | | 550. | 1,100. | 1,400. | 2,100. | 3,500. | 6,250. | 10,500. | 14,500. | 25,000. |
| 1797, 13 Stars . . . . . . . * | | 650. | 1,150. | 1,850. | 2,500. | 3,750. | 8,000. | 14,000. | 26,000. | 30,000. |

\* Included in number above.

## Heraldic Eagle Reverse (1800–1805)

**1800, LIBEKTY**

| | Mintage | AG-3 | G-4 | VG-8 | F-12 | VF-20 | EF-40 | AU-50 | MS-60 | MS-63 |
|---|---|---|---|---|---|---|---|---|---|---|
| 1800 . . . . . . . . . . | 24,000 | $350. | $725. | $950. | $1,750. | $2,400. | $3,750. | $7,750. | $11,000. | $20,000. |
| 1800, LIBEKTY . . . | 16,000 | 350. | 725. | 950. | 1,750. | 2,400. | 3,750. | 7,750. | 11,000. | 20,000. |
| 1801 . . . . . . . . . . | 27,760 | 350. | 725. | 1,150. | 1,900. | 2,600. | 4,000. | 8,000. | 14,000. | 22,500. |
| 1802 . . . . . . . . . . . | 3,060 | 12,500. | 22,500. | 34,000. | 42,500. | 85,000. | 100,000. | | | |
| 1803, Large 8 . . . . | 37,850 | 400. | 850. | 1,150. | 1,850. | 2,750. | 4,500. | 8,500. | 14,500. | 22,500. |
| 1803, Small 8 . . . . . . . * | | 400. | 850. | 1,200. | 1,950. | 2,950. | 4,500. | 8,500. | 14,500. | 22,500. |
| 1805 . . . . . . . . . . | 15,600 | 400. | 850. | 1,200. | 1,950. | 3,000. | 5,500. | 13,500. | | |

\* Included in number above.

## CAPPED BUST (1829–1837)

*Designer William Kneass; weight 1.35 grams; composition .8924 silver, .1076 copper; approx. diameter 15.5 mm; reeded edge. All coined at Philadelphia Mint.*

**G-4 GOOD**—Bust of Liberty outlined, no detail. Date and legend legible.
**VG-8 VERY GOOD**—Complete legend and date plain. At least three letters of LIBERTY on edge of cap show clearly.
**F-12 FINE**—All letters in LIBERTY visible.
**VF-20 VERY FINE**—Full rims. Ear and shoulder clasp show plainly.
**EF-40 EXTREMELY FINE**—Ear very distinct; eyebrow and hair well defined.
**AU-50 ABOUT UNCIRCULATED**—Traces of light wear on many of the high points. At least half of mint luster still present.
**MS-60 UNCIRCULATED**—No trace of wear. Light blemishes.
**MS-63 CHOICE UNCIRCULATED**—No trace of wear. Light blemishes. Attractive mint luster.

| | Mintage | G-4 | VG-8 | F-12 | VF-20 | EF-40 | AU-50 | MS-60 | MS-63 |
|---|---|---|---|---|---|---|---|---|---|
| 1829. . . . . . . . . . . . . . | 1,230,000 | $35. | $45. | $60. | $85. | $145. | $225. | $375. | $800. |
| 1830. . . . . . . . . . . . . . | 1,240,000 | 35. | 45. | 60. | 85. | 145. | 225. | 375. | 800. |
| 1831. . . . . . . . . . . . . . | 1,242,700 | 35. | 45. | 60. | 85. | 145. | 225. | 375. | 800. |
| 1832. . . . . . . . . . . . . . | 965,000 | 35. | 45. | 60. | 85. | 145. | 225. | 375. | 800. |
| 1833. . . . . . . . . . . . . . | 1,370,000 | 35. | 45. | 60. | 85. | 145. | 225. | 375. | 800. |
| 1834. . . . . . . . . . . . . . | 1,480,000 | 35. | 45. | 60. | 85. | 145. | 225. | 375. | 800. |
| 1834, 3 Over Inv 3 . . . . . . . . . . * | | 40. | 50. | 75. | 135. | 250. | 500. | 600. | 1,000. |
| 1835, All kinds. . . . . . . | 2,760,000 | | | | | | | | |
|    1835, Lg Dt and 5c . . . . . . . . . | | 35. | 45. | 60. | 85. | 145. | 225. | 375. | 800. |
|    1835, Lg Dt, Sm 5c . . . . . . . . . | | 35. | 45. | 60. | 85. | 145. | 225. | 375. | 800. |
|    1835, Sm Dt, Lg 5c . . . . . . . . . | | 35. | 45. | 60. | 85. | 145. | 225. | 375. | 800. |
|    1835, Sm Dt and 5c. . . . . . . . . | | 35. | 45. | 60. | 85. | 145. | 225. | 375. | 800. |
| 1836, Small 5c. . . . . . . | 1,900,000 | 35. | 45. | 60. | 85. | 145. | 225. | 375. | 800. |
| 1836, Large 5c. . . . . . . . . . . . . * | | 35. | 45. | 60. | 85. | 145. | 225. | 375. | 800. |
| 1836, 3 Over Inv 3 . . . . . . . . . . . * | | 40. | 50. | 75. | 145. | 250. | 475. | 600. | 1,000. |
| 1837, Small 5c . . . . . . . . | 871,000 | 40. | 50. | 75. | 125. | 200. | 400. | 950. | 2,000. |
| 1837, Large 5c. . . . . . . . . . . . . * | | 35. | 45. | 60. | 85. | 145. | 225. | 375. | 800. |

\* Included in number above.

# LIBERTY SEATED (1837–1873)

*Designer Christian Gobrecht; weight 1.34 grams; composition .900 silver, .100 copper; diameter 15.5 mm; reeded edge; mints: Philadelphia, New Orleans.*

**G-4 GOOD**—LIBERTY on shield smooth. Date and letters legible.
**VG-8 VERY GOOD**—At least three letters in LIBERTY visible.
**F-12 FINE**—Entire LIBERTY visible, weak spots.
**VF-20 VERY FINE**—Entire LIBERTY strong and even.
**EF-40 EXTREMELY FINE**—LIBERTY and scroll edges distinct.
**AU-50 ABOUT UNCIRCULATED**—Traces of light wear on many of the high points. At least half of mint luster still present.
**MS-60 UNCIRCULATED**—No trace of wear. Light blemishes.
**MS-63 CHOICE UNCIRCULATED**—No trace of wear. Light blemishes. Attractive mint luster.

## Variety 1 – No Stars on Obverse (1837–1838)

| | Mintage | G-4 | VG-8 | F-12 | VF-20 | EF-40 | AU-50 | MS-60 | MS-63 |
|---|---|---|---|---|---|---|---|---|---|
| 1837, Small Date | 1,405,000 | $38. | $48. | $70. | $135. | $220. | $475. | $900. | $1,200. |
| 1837, Large Date | * | 38. | 48. | 70. | 135. | 220. | 425. | 750. | 1,000. |
| 18380, No Stars | 70,000 | 80. | 130. | 220. | 425. | 725. | 1,100. | 1,750. | 7,200. |

* Included in number above.

## Variety 2 – Stars on Obverse (1838–1853)

From 1838 through 1859, the mintmark is located above the bow on the reverse. Large, medium, or small mintmark varieties occur for several dates.

**No Drapery From Elbow (1837–1840)**

**Drapery From Elbow (Starting 1840)**

| | Mintage | G-4 | VG-8 | F-12 | VF-20 | EF-40 | AU-50 | MS-60 | MS-63 |
|---|---|---|---|---|---|---|---|---|---|
| 1838, No Drapery | 2,225,000 | $16. | $20. | $27. | $32. | $75. | $160. | $260. | $420. |
| 1838, Small Stars | * | 20. | 30. | 55. | 100. | 185. | 360. | 620. | 1,100. |
| 1839, No Drapery | 1,069,150 | 16. | 20. | 27. | 32. | 75. | 160. | 260. | 420. |
| 18390, No Drapery | 1,034,039 | 20. | 22. | 27. | 35. | 80. | 170. | 525. | 1,850. |
| 1840, No Drapery | 1,034,000 | 16. | 20. | 27. | 32. | 75. | 160. | 260. | 420. |
| 18400, No Drapery | 695,000 | 16. | 20. | 28. | 37. | 80. | 235. | 725. | 2,100. |
| 1840, Drapery | 310,085 | 22. | 37. | 55. | 120. | 210. | 360. | 460. | 825. |
| 18400, Drapery | 240,000 | 32. | 55. | 110. | 160. | 410. | 1,250. | 3,100. | 8,200. |
| 1841 | 1,150,000 | 16. | 20. | 27. | 32. | 75. | 160. | 210. | 320. |
| 18410 | 815,000 | 17. | 22. | 35. | 47. | 110. | 285. | 665. | 1,525. |
| 1842 | 815,000 | 16. | 20. | 27. | 32. | 75. | 160. | 210. | 325. |
| 18420 | 350,000 | 30. | 37. | 65. | 185. | 525. | 825. | 1,275. | 2,100. |
| 1843 | 1,165,000 | 16. | 20. | 27. | 32. | 75. | 160. | 210. | 325. |
| 1844 | 430,000 | 16. | 20. | 27. | 32. | 75. | 160. | 210. | 325. |
| 18440 | 220,000 | 80. | 115. | 200. | 550. | 1,100. | 3,200. | 5,600. | 13,000. |
| 1845 | 1,564,000 | 16. | 20. | 27. | 32. | 75. | 160. | 210. | 325. |
| 1846 | 27,000 | 220. | 365. | 650. | 800. | 2,200. | 4,400. | 11,000. | 18,500. |
| 1847 | 1,274,000 | 16. | 20. | 21. | 32. | 75. | 160. | 275. | 525. |
| 1848, Medium Date | 668,000 | 15. | 18. | 25. | 30. | 70. | 150. | 210. | 325. |
| 1848, Large Date | * | 22. | 32. | 45. | 65. | 130. | 285. | 565. | 1,600. |

* Included in number above.

*Chart continued on next page.*

| | Mintage | G-4 | VG-8 | F-12 | VF-20 | EF-40 | AU-50 | MS-60 | MS-63 |
|---|---|---|---|---|---|---|---|---|---|
| 1848O | 600,000 | $20. | $22. | $32. | $55. | $120. | $250. | $410. | $720. |
| 1849, All kinds | 1,309,000 | | | | | | | | |
| 1849, 9 Over 6 | | 22. | 32. | 37. | 55. | 120. | 225. | 410. | 1,425. |
| 1849, 9 Over 8 | | 27. | 37. | 47. | 55. | 135. | 260. | 620. | 1,850. |
| 1849, Normal Date | | 16. | 20. | 26. | 35. | 75. | 150. | 235. | 520. |
| 1849O | 140,000 | 27. | 37. | 75. | 220. | 475. | 1,200. | 2,500. | 4,200. |
| 1850 | 955,000 | 16. | 20. | 26. | 35. | 75. | 150. | 210. | 350. |
| 1850O | 690,000 | 20. | 27. | 32. | 65. | 110. | 310. | 750. | 1,650. |
| 1851 | 781,000 | 16. | 20. | 26. | 35. | 75. | 150. | 210. | 310. |
| 1851O | 860,000 | 20. | 22. | 26. | 48. | 110. | 235. | 520. | 850. |
| 1852 | 1,000,500 | 16. | 20. | 26. | 35. | 75. | 150. | 210. | 310. |
| 1852O | 260,000 | 27. | 37. | 65. | 135. | 260. | 525. | 865. | 1,850. |
| 1853, No Arrows | 135,000 | 32. | 42. | 65. | 135. | 235. | 475. | 765. | 1,200. |
| 1853O, No Arrows | 160,000 | 180. | 265. | 365. | 625. | 1,500. | 2,750. | 6,200. | 12,000. |

## Variety 3 – Arrows at Date (1853–1855)

As on the dimes, quarters, and halves, arrows were placed at the sides of the date for a short period starting in 1853. They were placed there to denote the reduction of weight under the terms of the Act of February 21, 1853.

*Weight 1.24 grams; composition .900 silver, .100 copper; diameter 15.5 mm; reeded edge; mints: Philadelphia, New Orleans, San Francisco.*

| | Mintage | G-4 | VG-8 | F-12 | VF-20 | EF-40 | AU-50 | MS-60 | MS-63 | PF-63 |
|---|---|---|---|---|---|---|---|---|---|---|
| 1853 | 13,210,020 | $16. | $20. | $22. | $32. | $65. | $130. | $210. | $310. | |
| 1853O | 2,200,000 | 18. | 25. | 35. | 45. | 75. | 150. | 275. | 925. | |
| 1854 | 5,740,000 | 16. | 20. | 22. | 32. | 65. | 140. | 230. | 325. | |
| 1854O | 1,560,000 | 18. | 22. | 32. | 42. | 70. | 155. | 275. | 725. | |
| 1855 | 1,750,000 | 16. | 20. | 22. | 32. | 65. | 130. | 210. | 300. | $8,200. |
| 1855O | 600,000 | 18. | 24. | 32. | 55. | 175. | 200. | 560. | 1,100. | |

## Variety 2 Resumed (1856–1859: Weight Standard of 1853)

**1858 Over Inverted Date**

| | Mintage | G-4 | VG-8 | F-12 | VF-20 | EF-40 | AU-50 | MS-60 | MS-63 | PF-63 |
|---|---|---|---|---|---|---|---|---|---|---|
| 1856 | 4,880,000 | $16. | $20. | $22. | $32. | $65. | $130. | $185. | $320. | $5,250. |
| 1856O | 1,100,000 | 16. | 20. | 22. | 55. | 110. | 265. | 575. | 1,000. | |
| 1857 | 7,280,000 | 16. | 20. | 22. | 32. | 65. | 130. | 185. | 320. | 4,250. |
| 1857O | 1,380,000 | 16. | 20. | 22. | 42. | 70. | 210. | 375. | 500. | |
| 1858 | 3,500,000 | 16. | 20. | 22. | 32. | 65. | 130. | 185. | 320. | 2,000. |
| 1858, Repunched High Dt | * | 40. | 55. | 80. | 120. | 235. | 365. | 750. | 1,600. | |
| 1858, Over Inverted Dt | * | 35. | 50. | 75. | 100. | 220. | 325. | 700. | 1,400. | |
| 1858O | 1,660,000 | 16. | 20. | 27. | 47. | 80. | 155. | 265. | 450. | |
| 1859 | 340,000 | 16. | 20. | 27. | 42. | 85. | 130. | 220. | 425. | 1,750. |
| 1859O | 560,000 | 20. | 22. | 32. | 47. | 130. | 210. | 285. | 375. | |

* Included in number above.

A new die was utilized in 1859 at the Philadelphia Mint, in which the stars are hollow in the center and the arms of Liberty are slimmer. During the years 1859 and 1860 interesting half dime patterns were made which do not bear our nation's identity. These are transitional pieces, not made for circulation, but struck at the time the inscription UNITED STATES OF AMERICA was being transferred from the reverse to the obverse.

| | Mintage | MS-60 | MS-63 | PF-63 |
|---|---|---|---|---|
| 1859, Obverse of 1859, Reverse of 1860 ...............*20* | | | | $25,000. |
| 1860, Obverse of 1859, Reverse of 1860 (With Stars) .....*100* | | $2,500. | $3,750. | |

## Variety 4 – Legend On Obverse (1860–1873)

| So-Called 1861, 1 Over 0 | Mintmark Below Bow (1860–1869, 1872–1873) | Mintmark Above Bow (1870–1872) |
|---|---|---|

| | Mintage | G-4 | VG-8 | F-12 | VF-20 | EF-40 | AU-50 | MS-60 | MS-63 | PF-63 |
|---|---|---|---|---|---|---|---|---|---|---|
| 1860, Legend | | | | | | | | | | |
| (1,000) ...798,000 | | $16. | $20. | $22. | $27. | $48. | $80. | $160. | $225. | $625. |
| 1860O ..........1,060,000 | | 16. | 20. | 22. | 27. | 48. | 100. | 200. | 320. | |
| 1861 ...(1,000) ..3,360,000 | | 16. | 20. | 22. | 27. | 48. | 80. | 160. | 225. | 625. |
| 1861, 1 Over 0 .......... | | 32. | 45. | 65. | 135. | 265. | 525. | 600. | 900. | |
| 1862 .....(550) ..1,492,000 | | 22. | 30. | 45. | 55. | 65. | 110. | 180. | 260. | 625. |
| 1863 .....(460) ....18,000 | | 160. | 185. | 235. | 300. | 475. | 625. | 750. | 950. | 775. |
| 1863S ...........100,000 | | 27. | 40. | 45. | 55. | 160. | 320. | 750. | 1,000. | |
| 1864 .....(470) ...48,000 | | 325. | 440. | 475. | 700. | 925. | 1,100. | 1,200. | 1,350. | 775. |
| 1864S ...........90,000 | | 45. | 55. | 100. | 135. | 275. | 440. | 725. | 1,400. | |
| 1865 .....(500) ....13,000 | | 275. | 325. | 425. | 550. | 650. | 750. | 850. | 1,200. | 775. |
| 1865S ...........120,000 | | 27. | 40. | 50. | 65. | 160. | 525. | 925. | 2,000. | |
| 1866 .....(725) ....10,000 | | 320. | 375. | 425. | 550. | 650. | 675. | 775. | 1,200. | 675. |
| 1866S ...........120,000 | | 27. | 40. | 50. | 65. | 160. | 375. | 475. | 950. | |
| 1867 .....(625) .....8,000 | | 450. | 525. | 625. | 750. | 850. | 925. | 1,100. | 1,400. | 775. |
| 1867S ...........120,000 | | 22. | 35. | 50. | 65. | 160. | 325. | 575. | 1,200. | |
| 1868 .....(600) ....88,600 | | 55. | 65. | 120. | 185. | 325. | 475. | 675. | 900. | 775. |
| 1868S ...........280,000 | | 16. | 20. | 27. | 32. | 42. | 130. | 320. | 600. | |
| 1869 .....(600) ...208,000 | | 16. | 20. | 27. | 32. | 42. | 160. | 260. | 320. | 625. |
| 1869S ...........230,000 | | 16. | 20. | 27. | 32. | 42. | 130. | 320. | 800. | |
| 1870 ...(1,000) ...535,000 | | 16. | 20. | 22. | 27. | 42. | 80. | 150. | 275. | 625. |
| 1870S *(unique)  $661,250, MS-63, B&M auction, Jul-04* | | | | | | | | 675,000. | | |
| 1871 .....(960) ..1,873,000 | | 16. | 20. | 22. | 27. | 42. | 80. | 150. | 275. | 625. |
| 1871S ...........161,000 | | 18. | 22. | 32. | 65. | 80. | 180. | 310. | 500. | |
| 1872 .....(950) ..2,947,000 | | 16. | 20. | 22. | 27. | 42. | 80. | 150. | 250. | 625. |
| 1872S, All kinds ....837,000 | | | | | | | | | | |
| 1872S, Mintmk above bow | | 16. | 20. | 22. | 27. | 42. | 80. | 150. | 275. | |
| 1872S, Mintmk below bow | | 16. | 20. | 22. | 27. | 42. | 80. | 150. | 275. | |
| 1873 (Cl 3 only) | | | | | | | | | | |
| (600) ...712,000 | | 16. | 20. | 22. | 27. | 42. | 80. | 150. | 275. | 625. |
| 1873S (Cl 3 only) ...324,000 | | 16. | 20. | 22. | 27. | 42. | 80. | 150. | 275. | |

The designs of the dimes, first coined in 1796, follow closely those of the half dimes up through the Liberty Seated type. The dimes in each instance weigh twice as much as the half dimes.

## TYPE COIN VALUES

| | G-4 | F-12 | EF-40 | MS-60 | MS-63 | MS-65 | PF-63 | PF-65 |
|---|---|---|---|---|---|---|---|---|
| Drpd Bust, SE, 1796–1797 | $1,750.00+ | $2,750.00+ | $7,000.00+ | $16,000.00+ | $27,500.00+ | $70,000.00+ | — | — |
| Drpd Bust, HE, 1798–1807 | 470.00+ | 900.00+ | 1,850.00+ | 4,750.00+ | 9,750.00+ | 37,000.00+ | — | — |
| Cap Bust, 1809–1828 | 35.00+ | 110.00+ | 650.00+ | 2,250.00+ | 2,500.00+ | 13,000.00+ | — | — |
| Cap Bust, 1828–1837 | 25.00 | 40.00+ | 300.00+ | 850.00+ | 1,600.00+ | 7,250.00+ | $11,500.00+ | $31,500.00+ |
| Lib Std, NS, 1837–1838 | 35.00+ | 90.00+ | 500.00 | 1,100.00+ | 1,800.00 | 8,250.00+ | 12,500.00 | 30,000.00+ |
| Lib Std, Stars, 1838–1860 | 18.00+ | 30.00+ | 60.00+ | 300.00 | 700.00 | 3,250.00+ | 1,500.00 | 4,250.00+ |
| Lib Std, Arr, 1853–1855 | 15.00 | 20.00 | 50.00 | 300.00 | 675.00 | 2,800.00+ | 12,000.00- | 30,000.00 |
| Lib Std, Motto, 1860–1891 | 15.00+ | 18.00+ | 30.00+ | 150.00 | 250.00 | 925.00+ | 550.00- | 1,500.00+ |
| Lib Std, Arr, 1873–1874 | 15.00 | 25.00 | 140.00+ | 550.00 | 900.00 | 4,500.00+ | 1,200.00 | 6,250.00+ |
| Barber, 1892–1916 | 2.50+ | 4.00 | 22.00+ | 110.00+ | 170.00+ | 725.00+ | 450.00+ | 1,750.00+ |
| Mercury, 1916–1945 | 0.80+ | 1.00+ | 2.00+ | 10.00 | 12.00+ | 30.00+ | 180.00 | 400.00 |
| Roosevelt, 1946–1964 | 0.70+ | 0.75+ | 1.00+ | 1.10+ | 1.25+ | 6.00+ | 1.50+ | 2.00+ |

+ or − indicates change from previous year

# DRAPED BUST (1796–1807)
## Small Eagle Reverse (1796–1797)

*Designer Robert Scot; weight 2.70 grams; composition .8924 silver, .1076 copper; approx. diameter 19 mm; reeded edge. All coined at Philadelphia Mint.*

**AG-3 ABOUT GOOD**—Details clear enough to identify.
**G-4 GOOD**—Date legible. Bust outlined, but no detail.
**VG-8 VERY GOOD**—All but deepest drapery folds worn smooth. Hair lines nearly gone and curls lacking in detail.
**F-12 FINE**—All drapery lines visible. Hair partly worn.
**VF-20 VERY FINE**—Only left side of drapery indistinct.
**EF-40 EXTREMELY FINE**—Hair well outlined with details visible.
**AU-50 ABOUT UNCIRCULATED**—Traces of light wear on many of the high points. At least half of mint luster still present.
**MS-60 UNCIRCULATED**—No trace of wear. Light blemishes.
**MS-63 CHOICE UNCIRCULATED**—Some distracting marks or blemishes in prime focal areas. Impaired luster possible.

|  | 1796 | | 1797, 16 Stars | | 1797, 13 Stars |

| | Mintage | AG-3 | G-4 | VG-8 | F-12 | VF-20 | EF-40 | AU-50 | MS-60 | MS-63 |
|---|---|---|---|---|---|---|---|---|---|---|
| 1796 . . . . . . . . . 22,135 | | $850. | $1,750. | $2,250. | $2,750. | $4,000. | $7,000. | $10,000. | $16,000. | $27,500. |
| 1797, All kinds . . 25,261 | | | | | | | | | | |
|   1797, 16 Stars . . . . . . | | 850. | 1,750. | 2,350. | 2,850. | 4,750. | 8,000. | 11,000. | 18,500. | 32,500. |
|   1797, 13 Stars . . . . . . | | 850. | 1,750. | 2,350. | 2,850. | 4,750. | 8,000. | 11,000. | 18,500. | 29,500. |

## Heraldic Eagle Reverse (1798–1807)

| | Mintage | AG-3 | G-4 | VG-8 | F-12 | VF-20 | EF-40 | AU-50 | MS-60 | MS-63 |
|---|---|---|---|---|---|---|---|---|---|---|
| 1798, All kinds | 27,550 | | | | | | | | | |
| 1798, 98 Over 97, 16 Stars on Rev | | $300. | $625. | $950. | $1,150. | $1,850. | $2,900. | $4,000. | $6,500. | $14,500. |
| 1798, 98 Over 97, 13 Stars on Rev | | 700. | 1,800. | 2,750. | 3,750. | 6,000. | 8,500. | | | |
| 1798 | | 300. | 625. | 875. | 1,100. | 1,750. | 2,750. | 3,500. | 6,000. | 14,500. |
| 1798, Small 8 | | 350. | 725. | 1,000. | 1,400. | 2,100. | 3,850. | 5,250. | 10,000. | 15,000. |
| 1800 | 21,760 | 300. | 550. | 800. | 1,150. | 2,000. | 3,500. | 4,250. | 6,500. | 14,500. |
| 1801 | 34,640 | 300. | 550. | 850. | 1,450. | 2,750. | 5,500. | 8,500. | 17,500. | 30,000. |
| 1802 | 10,975 | 400. | 950. | 1,350. | 2,200. | 3,750. | 7,500. | 12,500. | 25,000. | |
| 1803 | 33,040 | 250. | 550. | 850. | 1,150. | 2,150. | 5,250. | 8,500. | 12,500. | |
| 1804, All kinds | 8,265 | | | | | | | | | |
| 1804, 13 Stars on Rev | | 650. | 1,250. | 2,000. | 3,250. | 5,250. | 13,500. | 27,500. | — | |
| 1804, 14 Stars on Rev | | 675. | 1,350. | 2,500. | 4,000. | 7,500. | 18,500. | 28,500. | 37,500. | |
| 1805, All kinds | 120,780 | | | | | | | | | |
| 1805, 4 Berries | | 225. | 475. | 700. | 900. | 1,250. | 1,850. | 2,750. | 4,750. | 9,750. |
| 1805, 5 Berries | | 225. | 475. | 700. | 900. | 1,250. | 1,850. | 2,750. | 5,750. | 10,000. |
| 1807 | 165,000 | 225. | 475. | 700. | 900. | 1,250. | 1,850. | 2,750. | 4,750. | 9,750. |

# CAPPED BUST (1809–1837)

*Designer John Reich; weight 2.70 grams; composition .8924 silver, .1076 copper; approx. diameter (1809–1827) 18.8 mm, (1828–1837) 18.5 mm; reeded edge. All coined at Philadelphia Mint.*

**AG-3 ABOUT GOOD**—Details clear enough to identify.
**G-4 GOOD**—Date, letters, and stars discernible. Bust outlined, no details.
**VG-8 VERY GOOD**—Legends and date plain. Some letters in LIBERTY visible.
**F-12 FINE**—Clear LIBERTY. Ear and shoulder clasp visible. Part of rim visible on both sides.
**VF-20 VERY FINE**—LIBERTY distinct. Full rim. Ear and clasp plain and distinct.
**EF-40 EXTREMELY FINE**—LIBERTY sharp. Ear distinct. Hair above eye well defined.
**AU-50 ABOUT UNCIRCULATED**—Traces of light wear on only the high points of the design. Half of mint luster present.
**MS-60 UNCIRCULATED**—No trace of wear. Light blemishes.
**MS-63 CHOICE UNCIRCULATED**—Some distracting marks or blemishes in prime focal areas. Impaired luster possible.

## Variety 1 – Wide Border (1809–1828)

**1811 Over 09**

| | Mintage | G-4 | VG-8 | F-12 | VF-20 | EF-40 | AU-50 | MS-60 | MS-63 |
|---|---|---|---|---|---|---|---|---|---|
| 1809 | 51,065 | $125. | $185. | $350. | $625. | $1,300. | $2,000. | $4,250. | $6,750. |
| 1811/9 | 65,180 | 110. | 150. | 275. | 550. | 1,150. | 1,800. | 3,400. | 6,000. |

**1814, Small Date**          **1814, Large Date**

*See next page for chart.*

| | Mintage | G-4 | VG-8 | F-12 | VF-20 | EF-40 | AU-50 | MS-60 | MS-63 |
|---|---|---|---|---|---|---|---|---|---|
| 1814, All kinds ........421,500 | | | | | | | | | |
| 1814, Small Date .......... | | $50. | $80. | $100. | $225. | $550. | $950. | $2,000. | $4,500. |
| 1814, Large Date .......... | | 30. | 40. | 55. | 160. | 450. | 650. | 1,100. | 2,500. |
| 1814, STATESOFAMERICA ... | | 55. | 80. | 120. | 300. | 550. | 1,000. | 2,000. | 4,500. |

**1820, Large O**

**1820, Small O**

**1821, Small Date**

**1821, Large Date**

| | Mintage | G-4 | VG-8 | F-12 | VF-20 | EF-40 | AU-50 | MS-60 | MS-63 |
|---|---|---|---|---|---|---|---|---|---|
| 1820, All kinds .......942,587 | | | | | | | | | |
| 1820, Large 0 ............. | | $30. | $35. | $50. | $110. | $400. | $650. | $1,100. | $2,250. |
| 1820, Small 0 ............. | | 30. | 35. | 50. | 130. | 450. | 700. | 1,200. | 2,500. |
| 1820, STATESOFAMERICA ... | | 35. | 45. | 80. | 200. | 500. | 1,100. | 2,000. | 4,250. |
| 1821, All kinds .....1,186,512 | | | | | | | | | |
| 1821, Small Date .......... | | 27. | 40. | 60. | 150. | 500. | 750. | 1,400. | 2,900. |
| 1821, Large Date .......... | | 27. | 40. | 55. | 125. | 450. | 700. | 1,200. | 2,200. |
| 1822 ................100,000 | | 450. | 700. | 1,100. | 1,600. | 2,800. | 6,000. | 12,000. | 17,500. |

**1823, 3 Over 2**

**Small E's**

**Large E's**

| | Mintage | G-4 | VG-8 | F-12 | VF-20 | EF-40 | AU-50 | MS-60 | MS-63 |
|---|---|---|---|---|---|---|---|---|---|
| 1823, 3/2, All kinds ....440,000 | | | | | | | | | |
| 1823, 3/2, Small E's ........ | | $27. | $40. | $55. | $120. | $450. | $700. | $1,200. | $2,500. |
| 1823, 3/2, Large E's ........ | | 27. | 40. | 55. | 120. | 450. | 700. | 1,200. | 2,500. |

**1824, 4 Over 2**

**1828, Large Date**

**1828, Small Date**

| | Mintage | G-4 | VG-8 | F-12 | VF-20 | EF-40 | AU-50 | MS-60 | MS-63 |
|---|---|---|---|---|---|---|---|---|---|
| 1824, 4 Over 2 .......510,000 | | $30. | $50. | $100. | $375. | $650. | $1,300. | $2,000. | $3,700. |
| 1825 ....................* | | 27. | 40. | 55. | 125. | 425. | 700. | 1,100. | 2,600. |
| 1827 .............1,215,000 | | 27. | 40. | 55. | 125. | 425. | 700. | 1,100. | 2,500. |
| 1828, Both varieties ....125,000 | | | | | | | | | |
| 1828, Lg Dt, Curl Base 2 ..... | | 50. | 80. | 130. | 300. | 625. | 1,000. | 2,200. | 4,000. |

* Included in number above.

## Variety 2 – Modified Design (1828–1837)

New Mint equipment was used to make the Small Date 1828 dimes and subsequent issues. Unlike earlier coinage, these have beaded borders and a uniform diameter. Large Date has curl base knob 2; Small Date has square base knob 2.

| 1829, Small 10c. | 1829, Large 10c. | 1829, Curl Base 2 | 1830, 30 Over 29 |
|---|---|---|---|

| | Mintage | G-4 | VG-8 | F-12 | VF-20 | EF-40 | AU-50 | MS-60 | MS-63 |
|---|---|---|---|---|---|---|---|---|---|
| 1828, Sm Dt, Sq Base 2 ....* | | $35. | $45. | $75. | $150. | $400. | $650. | $1,300. | $2,100. |
| 1829, All kinds ........770,000 | | | | | | | | | |
| 1829, Curl Base 2 .......... | | 4,000. | 6,000. | 10,000. | 20,000. | | | | |
| 1829, Small 10c ........... | | 25. | 35. | 40. | 80. | 300. | 425. | 850. | 1,600. |
| 1829, Medium 10c ......... | | 25. | 35. | 40. | 80. | 300. | 425. | 850. | 1,600. |
| 1829, Large 10c ........... | | 25. | 35. | 55. | 110. | 325. | 450. | 950. | 1,700. |
| 1830, All kinds ........510,000 | | | | | | | | | |
| 1830, 30 Over 29 ......... | | 35. | 50. | 110. | 200. | 425. | 650. | 1,250. | 3,250. |
| 1830, Large 10c ........... | | 25. | 35. | 40. | 80. | 300. | 425. | 850. | 1,600. |
| 1830, Small 10c ........... | | 25. | 35. | 40. | 80. | 300. | 425. | 850. | 1,600. |
| 1831 ................771,350 | | 25. | 35. | 40. | 80. | 300. | 425. | 850. | 1,600. |
| 1832 ...............522,500 | | 25. | 35. | 40. | 80. | 300. | 425. | 850. | 1,600. |
| 1833, All kinds ........485,000 | | | | | | | | | |
| 1833 ................... | | 25. | 35. | 40. | 80. | 300. | 425. | 850. | 1,600. |
| 1833, Last 3 High .......... | | 25. | 35. | 40. | 80. | 300. | 425. | 850. | 1,600. |
| 1834, All kinds ........635,000 | | 25. | 35. | 40. | 80. | 300. | 425. | 850. | 1,600. |
| 1834, Small 4 ............ | | 25. | 35. | 40. | 80. | 300. | 425. | 900. | 1,700. |
| 1834, Large 4 ............ | | 25. | 35. | 40. | 80. | 300. | 425. | 850. | 1,600. |
| 1835 .............1,410,000 | | 25. | 35. | 40. | 80. | 300. | 425. | 850. | 1,600. |
| 1836 .............1,190,000 | | 25. | 35. | 40. | 80. | 300. | 425. | 850. | 1,600. |
| 1837 ...............359,500 | | 25. | 35. | 40. | 80. | 300. | 425. | 850. | 1,600. |

* Included in listing in previous chart.

# LIBERTY SEATED (1837–1891)
## Variety 1 – No Stars on Obverse (1837–1838)

*Designer Christian Gobrecht; weight 2.67 grams; composition .900 silver, .100 copper; diameter 17.9 mm; reeded edge; mints: Philadelphia, New Orleans.*

**G-4 GOOD**—LIBERTY on shield smooth. Date and letters legible.
**F-12 FINE**—LIBERTY visible, weak spots.
**VF-20 VERY FINE**—LIBERTY strong and even.
**EF-40 EXTREMELY FINE**—LIBERTY and scroll edges distinct.
**AU-50 ABOUT UNCIRCULATED**—Wear on Liberty's shoulder and hair high points.
**MS-60 UNCIRCULATED**—No trace of wear. Light blemishes.
**MS-63 CHOICE UNCIRCULATED**—Some distracting contact marks or blemishes in prime focal areas. Impaired luster possible.

| No Drapery From Elbow<br>No Stars on Obverse | Mintmarks on Liberty Seated dimes on reverse, within or<br>below the wreath. Size of mintmark varies on many dates. |
|---|---|

| | Mintage | G-4 | F-12 | VF-20 | EF-40 | AU-50 | MS-60 | MS-63 |
|---|---|---|---|---|---|---|---|---|
| 1837, All kinds ....682,500 | | | | | | | | |
| 1837, Large Date ........ | | $35. | $90. | $300. | $500. | $700. | $1,100. | $1,800. |
| 1837, Small Date ........ | | 40. | 95. | 325. | 525. | 725. | 1,200. | 2,000. |
| 1838O ...........406,034 | | 45. | 125. | 400. | 750. | 1,200. | 2,800. | 6,000. |

## Variety 2 – Stars on Obverse (1838–1853)

**No Drapery From Elbow, Tilted Shield
(1838–1840)**

**Drapery From Elbow, Upright Shield
(1840–1891)**

**1838, Small Stars**     **1838, Large Stars**               **Obverse**               **Reverse**

| | Mintage | G-4 | F-12 | VF-20 | EF-40 | AU-50 | MS-60 | MS-63 |
|---|---|---|---|---|---|---|---|---|
| 1838, All kinds . . . . . 1,992,500 | | | | | | | | |
| 1838, Small Stars . . . . . . . . . | | $25. | $55. | $80. | $175. | $400. | $700. | $1,350. |
| 1838, Large Stars . . . . . . . . . | | 20. | 30. | 40. | 120. | 250. | 350. | 850. |
| 1838, Partial Drapery . . . . . . | | 25. | 50. | 100. | 200. | 500. | 850. | 2,000. |
| 1839, No Drapery . . . 1,053,115 | | 18. | 30. | 40. | 110. | 250. | 400. | 850. |
| 1839O, No Drapery . . 1,323,000 | | 22. | 35. | 45. | 120. | 275. | 450. | 1,200. |
| 1840, No Drapery . . . . 981,500 | | 18. | 20. | 40. | 110. | 250. | 400. | 850. |
| 1840O, No Drapery . . 1,175,000 | | 20. | 40. | 55. | 150. | 350. | 1,200. | 2,500. |
| 1840, Drapery . . . . . . 377,500 | | 30. | 90. | 165. | 300. | 450. | 900. | 5,000. |
| 1841 **(a)** . . . . . . . . . 1,622,500 | | 18. | 30. | 35. | 55. | 140. | 350. | 650. |
| 1841O . . . . . . . . . . . 2,007,500 | | 20. | 35. | 50. | 85. | 225. | 900. | 1,800. |
| 1842 . . . . . . . . . . . . 1,887,500 | | 18. | 30. | 35. | 50. | 125. | 400. | 650. |
| 1842O . . . . . . . . . . . 2,020,000 | | 20. | 35. | 70. | 225. | 1,300. | 2,500. | 6,000. |
| 1843 . . . . . . . . . . . . 1,370,000 | | 18. | 30. | 35. | 50. | 125. | 400. | 800. |
| 1843O . . . . . . . . . . . . 150,000 | | 40. | 100. | 225. | 600. | 2,000. | 5,000. | — |
| 1844 . . . . . . . . . . . . . . 72,500 | | 200. | 450. | 700. | 1,200. | 1,800. | 4,000. | 9,000. |
| 1845 . . . . . . . . . . . . 1,755,000 | | 18. | 30. | 35. | 50. | 125. | 400. | 800. |
| 1845O . . . . . . . . . . . . 230,000 | | 20. | 60. | 200. | 550. | 1,200. | 3,500. | — |
| 1846 . . . . . . . . . . . . . . 31,300 | | 75. | 200. | 350. | 950. | 2,500. | 5,500. | 16,000. |
| 1847 . . . . . . . . . . . . . 245,000 | | 18. | 40. | 65. | 125. | 350. | 950. | 2,500. |
| 1848 . . . . . . . . . . . . . 451,500 | | 20. | 30. | 45. | 85. | 150. | 550. | 850. |
| 1849 . . . . . . . . . . . . . 839,000 | | 18. | 30. | 40. | 60. | 125. | 300. | 900. |
| 1849O . . . . . . . . . . . . 300,000 | | 20. | 45. | 125. | 300. | 750. | 2,500. | 6,000. |
| 1850 . . . . . . . . . . . 1,931,500 | | 18. | 30. | 40. | 60. | 125. | 300. | 700. |
| 1850O . . . . . . . . . . . . 510,000 | | 20. | 35. | 80. | 150. | 350. | 1,000. | 2,500. |
| 1851 . . . . . . . . . . . 1,026,500 | | 18. | 30. | 40. | 60. | 125. | 350. | 800. |
| 1851O . . . . . . . . . . . . 400,000 | | 20. | 40. | 80. | 175. | 450. | 2,250. | 3,500. |
| 1852 . . . . . . . . . . . 1,535,500 | | 18. | 30. | 40. | 60. | 125. | 300. | 700. |
| 1852O . . . . . . . . . . . . 430,000 | | 25. | 45. | 140. | 250. | 350. | 1,600. | 2,750. |
| 1853, No Arrows . . . . . . 95,000 | | 50. | 125. | 225. | 300. | 450. | 800. | 1,100. |

**a.** 1841, Small Stars, No Drapery, Upright Shield: two examples known (one Proof and one VF).

## Variety 3 – Arrows at Date (1853–1855)

*Weight 2.49 grams; composition .900 silver, .100 copper; diameter 17.9 mm; reeded edge; mints: Philadelphia,
New Orleans, San Francisco, Carson City.*

**Arrows at Date (1853–1855)**               **Small Date, Arrows Removed (1856–1860)**

# DIMES

| | Mintage | G-4 | F-12 | VF-20 | EF-40 | AU-50 | MS-60 | MS-63 | PF-63 |
|---|---|---|---|---|---|---|---|---|---|
| 1853, With Arrows | 12,078,010 | $15. | $20. | $30. | $50. | $175. | $300. | $675. | |
| 1853O | 1,100,000 | 15. | 25. | 50. | 125. | 350. | 1,100. | 3,250. | |
| 1854 | 4,470,000 | 15. | 20. | 30. | 50. | 175. | 300. | 675. | $12,000. |
| 1854O | 1,770,000 | 15. | 20. | 45. | 85. | 200. | 450. | 1,100. | |
| 1855 | 2,075,000 | 15. | 20. | 30. | 60. | 185. | 300. | 1,000. | 12,000. |

## Variety 2 Resumed (1856–1860)

| | Mintage | G-4 | F-12 | VF-20 | EF-40 | AU-50 | MS-60 | MS-63 | PF-63 |
|---|---|---|---|---|---|---|---|---|---|
| 1856, All kinds | 5,780,000 | | | | | | | | |
| 1856, Large Date | | $17. | $22. | $35. | $60. | $160. | $310. | $750. | |
| 1856, Small Date | | 15. | 20. | 30. | 50. | 130. | 300. | 700. | $4,000. |
| 1856O | 1,180,000 | 15. | 20. | 30. | 60. | 250. | 800. | 1,500. | |
| 1856S | 70,000 | 100. | 350. | 575. | 900. | 1,400. | 3,500. | 15,000. | |
| 1857 | 5,580,000 | 15. | 20. | 30. | 50. | 130. | 300. | 700. | 3,750. |
| 1857O | 1,540,000 | 15. | 20. | 30. | 70. | 200. | 425. | 750. | |
| 1858 | (300+) 1,540,000 | 15. | 20. | 30. | 50. | 130. | 300. | 700. | 2,000. |
| 1858O | 290,000 | 22. | 35. | 85. | 135. | 300. | 600. | 1,000. | |
| 1858S | 60,000 | 90. | 200. | 400. | 800. | 1,400. | 3,500. | 14,000. | |
| 1859 | (800) 429,200 | 18. | 20. | 30. | 60. | 130. | 300. | 700. | 1,500. |
| 1859O | 480,000 | 20. | 25. | 60. | 95. | 275. | 400. | 900. | |
| 1859S | 60,000 | 100. | 275. | 425. | 1,000. | 2,000. | 10,000. | 25,000. | |
| 1860S | 140,000 | 30. | 60. | 150. | 350. | 800. | 2,500. | 4,500. | |
| 1859, Obverse of 1859 (With Stars), Reverse of 1860 | | | | | | | | 10,000. | 18,500. |

In 1859 (see the last row of the previous chart), an interesting dime pattern was made that does not bear the nation's identity. It is a "transitional" piece, not made for circulation, but struck at the time the inscription UNITED STATES OF AMERICA was being transferred from the reverse to the obverse.

## Variety 4 – Legend on Obverse (1860–1873)

| | Mintage | G-4 | F-12 | VF-20 | EF-40 | AU-50 | MS-60 | MS-63 | PF-63 |
|---|---|---|---|---|---|---|---|---|---|
| 1860 | (1,000) 606,000 | $15. | $20. | $30. | $40. | $100. | $250. | $600. | $700. |
| 1860O | 40,000 | 320. | 800. | 1,700. | 4,000. | 6,000. | 12,000. | — | |
| 1861 (a) | (1,000) 1,883,000 | 15. | 20. | 30. | 40. | 100. | 225. | 400. | 700. |
| 1861S | 172,500 | 40. | 110. | 200. | 400. | 500. | 1,500. | 4,000. | |
| 1862 | (550) 847,000 | 15. | 20. | 25. | 40. | 80. | 225. | 350. | 700. |
| 1862S | 180,750 | 40. | 70. | 175. | 250. | 325. | 1,200. | 3,250. | |
| 1863 | (460) 14,000 | 275. | 525. | 650. | 750. | 900. | 1,200. | 1,400. | 800. |
| 1863S | 157,500 | 35. | 55. | 100. | 180. | 325. | 1,200. | 3,250. | |
| 1864 | (470) 11,000 | 220. | 400. | 550. | 850. | 1,000. | 1,200. | 1,400. | 850. |
| 1864S | 230,000 | 25. | 40. | 90. | 125. | 300. | 900. | 1,300. | |
| 1865 | (500) 10,000 | 250. | 550. | 700. | 800. | 900. | 1,100. | 1,300. | 900. |
| 1865S | 175,000 | 25. | 50. | 140. | 225. | 750. | 2,500. | 5,500. | |
| 1866 | (725) 8,000 | 300. | 550. | 700. | 850. | 1,200. | 1,400. | 1,600. | 750. |

**a.** Dies modified slightly during 1861. First variety with only five vertical lines in top of shield is scarcer than the later variety.

*Chart continued on next page.*

| | Mintage | G-4 | F-12 | VF-20 | EF-40 | AU-50 | MS-60 | MS-63 | PF-63 |
|---|---|---|---|---|---|---|---|---|---|
| 1866S . . . . . . . . . . . . . . 135,000 | | $40. | $70. | $120. | $225. | $325. | $1,000. | $3,250. | |
| 1867 . . . . . . . (625) . . . . . . 6,000 | | 400. | 750. | 950. | 1,100. | 1,300. | 1,500. | 1,800. | $800. |
| 1867S . . . . . . . . . . . . . . 140,000 | | 30. | 70. | 120. | 225. | 550. | 1,200. | 2,250. | |
| 1868 . . . . . . . (600) . . . . 464,000 | | 15. | 25. | 40. | 65. | 150. | 300. | 800. | 650. |
| 1868S . . . . . . . . . . . . . . 260,000 | | 15. | 35. | 70. | 125. | 225. | 400. | 1,000. | |
| 1869 . . . . . . . (600) . . . . 256,000 | | 15. | 30. | 65. | 100. | 200. | 400. | 875. | 650. |
| 1869S . . . . . . . . . . . . . . 450,000 | | 15. | 25. | 35. | 65. | 150. | 375. | 775. | |
| 1870 . . . . . . (1,000) . . . . 470,500 | | 15. | 20. | 25. | 50. | 100. | 200. | 450. | 600. |
| 1870S . . . . . . . . . . . . . . . 50,000 | | 250. | 400. | 450. | 550. | 850. | 1,800. | 2,500. | |
| 1871 . . . . . . . (960) . . . . 906,750 | | 15. | 20. | 25. | 50. | 150. | 300. | 425. | 600. |
| 1871CC . . . . . . . . . . . . . . 20,100 | | 1,000. | 2,500. | 5,000. | 8,000. | 13,000. | — | | |
| 1871S . . . . . . . . . . . . . . 320,000 | | 15. | 20. | 25. | 50. | 100. | 200. | 450. | |
| 1872 . . . . . . . (950) . . 2,395,500 | | 15. | 20. | 25. | 40. | 90. | 175. | 300. | 600. |
| 1872, DblDie Rev *(rare)* . . . . . . . * | | | | | | | | | |
| 1872CC . . . . . . . . . . . . . . 35,480 | | 400. | 1,300. | 3,000. | 6,000. | 16,000. | — | | |
| 1872S . . . . . . . . . . . . . . 190,000 | | 25. | 85. | 140. | 225. | 400. | 1,200. | 2,500. | |
| 1873, Cl 3 . . (1,100) . . 1,506,900 | | 15. | 20. | 25. | 40. | 90. | 150. | 250. | 600. |
| 1873, Open 3 . . . . . . . . . 60,000 | | 20. | 45. | 75. | 130. | 200. | 600. | 1,200. | |
| 1873CC *(unique)* **(a)** . . . . . 12,400 | | | | | | | | 1,000,000.**(b)** | |

*$891,250, MS-65, B&M auction, Jul-04*

\* Included in number above. **a.** Most of the mintage was melted after the law of 1873 was passed. **b.** MS-65.

## Variety 5 – Arrows at Date (1873–1874)

In 1873 the dime was increased in weight to 2.50 grams. Arrows at the date in 1873 and 1874 indicate this change.

*Weight 2.50 grams; composition .900 silver, .100 copper; diameter 17.9 mm; reeded edge; mints: Philadelphia, New Orleans, San Francisco, Carson City.*

| | Mintage | G-4 | F-12 | VF-20 | EF-40 | AU-50 | MS-60 | MS-63 | PF-63 |
|---|---|---|---|---|---|---|---|---|---|
| 1873 . . . . . . (800) . . 2,377,700 | | $15. | $25. | $55. | $140. | $300. | $550. | $900. | $1,200. |
| 1873, DblDie Obv . . . . . . . . . . . * | | 65. | 200. | 500. | 1,000. | | | | |
| 1873CC . . . . . . . . . . . . . . 18,791 | | 900. | 3,300. | 6,000. | 16,000. | 30,000. | — | — | |
| 1873S . . . . . . . . . . . . . . 455,000 | | 20. | 35. | 60. | 175. | 450. | 1,000. | 2,100. | |
| 1874 . . . . . . (700) . . 2,939,300 | | 15. | 25. | 55. | 140. | 310. | 600. | 900. | 1,200. |
| 1874CC . . . . . . . . . . . . . . 10,817 | | 2,500. | 5,000. | 12,000. | 18,000. | 30,000. | — | — | |
| 1874S . . . . . . . . . . . . . . 240,000 | | 25. | 65. | 110. | 225. | 500. | 900. | 2,000. | |

\* Included in number above.

## Variety 4 Resumed (1875-1891)

| | Mintage | G-4 | F-12 | VF-20 | EF-40 | AU-50 | MS-60 | MS-63 | PF-63 |
|---|---|---|---|---|---|---|---|---|---|
| 1875 . . . . . . . (700) . .10,350,000 | | $15. | $18. | $20. | $30. | $80. | $150. | $250. | $550. |
| 1875CC, All kinds . . . .4,645,000 | | | | | | | | | |
| 1875CC, Below Bow . . . . . . . . | | 15. | 18. | 30. | 50. | 90. | 275. | 450. | |
| 1875CC, Above Bow . . . . . . . . | | 15. | 20. | 30. | 60. | 100. | 300. | 500. | |
| 1875S, All kinds . . . . . 9,070,000 | | | | | | | | | |
| 1875S, Below Bow . . . . . . . . . . | | 15. | 18. | 20. | 30. | 80. | 150. | 250. | |
| 1875S, Above Bow . . . . . . . . | | 15. | 18. | 20. | 40. | 85. | 160. | 250. | |

| | Mintage | G-4 | F-12 | VF-20 | EF-40 | AU-50 | MS-60 | MS-63 | PF-63 |
|---|---|---|---|---|---|---|---|---|---|
| 1876 .....(1,150) ... 1,145,000 | | $15. | $18. | $20. | $30. | $80. | $150. | $250. | $550. |
| 1876CC ...........8,270,000 | | 15. | 18. | 25. | 50. | 90. | 225. | 450. | |
| 1876S ...........10,420,000 | | 15. | 18. | 20. | 35. | 80. | 150. | 250. | |
| 1877 ......(510) ... 7,310,000 | | 15. | 18. | 20. | 30. | 80. | 150. | 250. | 600. |
| 1877CC ...........7,700,000 | | 15. | 18. | 30. | 50. | 95. | 225. | 400. | |
| 1877S ............2,340,000 | | 15. | 18. | 20. | 30. | 80. | 150. | 250. | |
| 1878 ......(800) ... 1,677,200 | | 15. | 18. | 20. | 30. | 80. | 150. | 250. | 550. |
| 1878CC .............200,000 | | 50. | 125. | 200. | 400. | 575. | 1,100. | 1,750. | |
| 1879 ....(1,100)...... 14,000 | | 200. | 325. | 400. | 500. | 550. | 625. | 700. | 550. |
| 1880 ....(1,355)..... 36,000 | | 150. | 250. | 350. | 400. | 500. | 600. | 700. | 550. |
| 1881 .....(975)..... 24,000 | | 150. | 250. | 375. | 425. | 525. | 625. | 725. | 550. |
| 1882 ....(1,100) ... 3,910,000 | | 15. | 18. | 20. | 30. | 80. | 150. | 250. | 550. |
| 1883 ....(1,039) ... 7,674,673 | | 15. | 18. | 20. | 30. | 80. | 150. | 250. | 550. |
| 1884 ......(875) ... 3,365,505 | | 15. | 18. | 20. | 30. | 80. | 150. | 250. | 550. |
| 1884S ..............564,969 | | 20. | 30. | 50. | 90. | 300. | 750. | 1,200. | |
| 1885 ......(930) ... 2,532,497 | | 15. | 18. | 20. | 30. | 80. | 150. | 250. | 550. |
| 1885S ...............43,690 | | 400. | 800. | 1,400. | 2,200. | 4,000. | 5,500. | 9,000. | |
| 1886 ......(886) ... 6,376,684 | | 15. | 18. | 20. | 30. | 80. | 150. | 250. | 550. |
| 1886S ..............206,524 | | 30. | 50. | 75. | 135. | 200. | 600. | 1,200. | |
| 1887 ......(710) ... 11,283,229 | | 15. | 18. | 20. | 30. | 80. | 150. | 250. | 550. |
| 1887S ............4,454,450 | | 15. | 18. | 20. | 30. | 80. | 150. | 250. | |
| 1888 ......(832) ... 5,495,655 | | 15. | 18. | 20. | 30. | 80. | 150. | 250. | 550. |
| 1888S ............1,720,000 | | 15. | 18. | 20. | 30. | 110. | 300. | 750. | |
| 1889 ......(711) ... 7,380,000 | | 15. | 18. | 20. | 30. | 80. | 150. | 250. | 550. |
| 1889S ..............972,678 | | 18. | 30. | 50. | 80. | 150. | 450. | 900. | |
| 1890 ......(590) ... 9,910,951 | | 15. | 18. | 20. | 30. | 80. | 150. | 250. | 550. |
| 1890S, Lg S ........1,423,076 | | 17. | 25. | 55. | 85. | 150. | 350. | 700. | |
| 1890S, Sm S (rare) .......... | | | | — | — | | | | |
| 1891 ......(600) .. 15,310,000 | | 15. | 18. | 20. | 30. | 80. | 150. | 250. | 600. |
| 1891O ............4,540,000 | | 15. | 18. | 25. | 50. | 110. | 200. | 350. | |
| 1891O, 0/0 ................* | | 60. | 120. | 150. | 225. | — | — | | |
| 1891S ............3,196,116 | | 15. | 18. | 20. | 30. | 80. | 175. | 300. | |

* Included in number above.

# BARBER OR LIBERTY HEAD (1892–1916)

Designed by Charles E. Barber, chief engraver of the Mint, who also designed the twenty-five- and fifty-cent pieces. His initial B is at the truncation of the neck.

*Designer Charles E. Barber; weight 2.50 grams; composition .900 silver, .100 copper (net weight: .07234 oz. pure silver); diameter 17.9 mm; reeded edge; mints: Philadelphia, Denver, New Orleans, San Francisco.*

**G-4 GOOD**—Date and letters plain. LIBERTY obliterated.
**VG-8 VERY GOOD**—Some letters visible in LIBERTY.
**F-12 FINE**—Letters in LIBERTY visible, though some weak.
**VF-20 VERY FINE**—Letters of LIBERTY evenly plain.
**EF-40 EXTREMELY FINE**—All letters in LIBERTY sharp, distinct. Headband edges distinct.
**AU-50 ABOUT UNCIRCULATED**—Slight traces of wear on hair cheekbone and on leaf tips in wreath.
**MS-60 UNCIRCULATED**—No trace of wear. Light blemishes.
**MS-63 CHOICE UNCIRCULATED**—Some distracting marks or blemishes in prime focal areas. Impaired luster possible.

**Mintmark location is on reverse, below wreath.**

*See next page for chart.*

| Mintage | G-4 | VG-8 | F-12 | VF-20 | EF-40 | AU-50 | MS-60 | MS-63 | PF-63 |
|---|---|---|---|---|---|---|---|---|---|
| 1892 (1,245) 12,120,000 | $4.50 | $6.00 | $17. | $25. | $30. | $75. | $125. | $200. | $450. |
| 1892O . . . . . . .3,841,700 | 10.00 | 14.00 | 32. | 50. | 70. | 95. | 175. | 300. | |
| 1892S . . . . . . . .990,710 | 60.00 | 110.00 | 190. | 240. | 280. | 330. | 425. | 775. | |
| 1893, 3/2 . . . . . . . . . . .* | 125.00 | 140.00 | 150. | 165. | 200. | 300. | 700. | 1,800. | 900. |
| 1893 . .(792)  3,339,940 | 8.00 | 12.00 | 20. | 30. | 45. | 75. | 150. | 225. | 450. |
| 1893O . . . . . . .1,760,000 | 30.00 | 45.00 | 120. | 150. | 190. | 230. | 325. | 650. | |
| 1893S . . . . . . .2,491,401 | 13.00 | 25.00 | 35. | 45. | 80. | 150. | 290. | 700. | |
| 1894 . .(972)  1,330,000 | 25.00 | 40.00 | 110. | 150. | 180. | 210. | 325. | 500. | |
| 1894O . . . . . . . .720,000 | 65.00 | 90.00 | 190. | 275. | 400. | 600. | 1,450. | 2,500. | |
| 1894S . . . . . . . . . . . .24 | *$1,322,500, PF-66, DLRC auction, Mar-05* | | | | | | | | 1,400,000. |
| 1895 . .(880) . . .690,000 | 80.00 | 160.00 | 325. | 475. | 550. | 625. | 725. | 1,500. | 550. |
| 1895O . . . . . . . .440,000 | 350.00 | 500.00 | 800. | 1,150. | 2,250. | 3,400. | 6,000. | 8,500. | |
| 1895S . . . . . . .1,120,000 | 40.00 | 55.00 | 125. | 180. | 240. | 310. | 500. | 1,200. | |
| 1896 . .(762)  2,000,000 | 10.00 | 22.00 | 50. | 75. | 100. | 120. | 175. | 500. | 450. |
| 1896O . . . . . . . .610,000 | 75.00 | 150.00 | 290. | 350. | 450. | 650. | 1,000. | 2,400. | |
| 1896S . . . . . . . .575,056 | 80.00 | 140.00 | 280. | 335. | 400. | 550. | 850. | 1,500. | |
| 1897 . .(731) 10,868,533 | 2.50 | 3.50 | 8. | 15. | 30. | 70. | 135. | 200. | 450. |
| 1897O . . . . . . . .666,000 | 65.00 | 110.00 | 280. | 375. | 475. | 600. | 900. | 1,700. | |
| 1897S . . . . . . .1,342,844 | 18.00 | 35.00 | 90. | 120. | 170. | 250. | 450. | 1,000. | |
| 1898 . .(735) 16,320,000 | 3.00 | 4.00 | 7. | 12. | 26. | 75. | 115. | 170. | 450. |
| 1898O . . . . . . .2,130,000 | 12.00 | 26.00 | 85. | 130. | 190. | 280. | 450. | 1,200. | |
| 1898S . . . . . . .1,702,507 | 8.00 | 10.00 | 30. | 45. | 80. | 150. | 375. | 1,200. | |
| 1899 . .(846) 19,580,000 | 3.00 | 4.00 | 7. | 12. | 25. | 70. | 125. | 170. | 450. |
| 1899O . . . . . . .2,650,000 | 9.00 | 18.00 | 65. | 95. | 140. | 225. | 400. | 1,150. | |
| 1899S . . . . . . .1,867,493 | 8.00 | 15.00 | 30. | 35. | 45. | 110. | 300. | 750. | |
| 1900 . .(912) 17,600,000 | 3.00 | 4.00 | 7. | 12. | 25. | 70. | 110. | 170. | 450. |
| 1900O . . . . . . .2,010,000 | 18.00 | 35.00 | 100. | 150. | 220. | 350. | 600. | 1,000. | |
| 1900S . . . . . . .5,168,270 | 5.00 | 6.00 | 12. | 20. | 30. | 70. | 175. | 400. | |
| 1901 . .(813) 18,859,665 | 2.50 | 3.00 | 7. | 10. | 26. | 70. | 110. | 170. | 450. |
| 1901O . . . . . . .5,620,000 | 3.50 | 5.50 | 15. | 25. | 65. | 180. | 450. | 950. | |
| 1901S . . . . . . . .593,022 | 75.00 | 140.00 | 340. | 425. | 550. | 625. | 1,000. | 1,650. | |
| 1902 . .(777) 21,380,000 | 2.50 | 3.00 | 5. | 7. | 22. | 70. | 110. | 170. | 450. |
| 1902O . . . . . . .4,500,000 | 3.00 | 5.00 | 15. | 32. | 65. | 150. | 400. | 1,000. | |
| 1902S . . . . . . .2,070,000 | 8.00 | 20.00 | 55. | 80. | 140. | 200. | 400. | 1,000. | |
| 1903 . .(755) 19,500,000 | 2.50 | 3.00 | 5. | 7. | 22. | 70. | 110. | 170. | 450. |
| 1903O . . . . . . .8,180,000 | 4.00 | 5.00 | 14. | 25. | 50. | 110. | 275. | 550. | |
| 1903S . . . . . . . .613,300 | 80.00 | 130.00 | 350. | 450. | 700. | 850. | 1,200. | 1,800. | |
| 1904 . .(670) 14,600,357 | 2.50 | 4.00 | 6. | 9. | 22. | 70. | 110. | 170. | 450. |
| 1904S . . . . . . . .800,000 | 40.00 | 70.00 | 150. | 225. | 325. | 475. | 800. | 1,500. | |
| 1905 . .(727) 14,551,623 | 2.50 | 3.00 | 5. | 7. | 22. | 70. | 110. | 170. | 450. |
| 1905O . . . . . . .3,400,000 | 4.00 | 6.00 | 32. | 55. | 90. | 150. | 300. | 500. | |
| 1905O, Micro O (a) . . . .* | 12.00 | 25.00 | 90. | 140. | 220. | 400. | 900. | 1,700. | |
| 1905S . . . . . . .6,855,199 | 3.00 | 4.00 | 9. | 20. | 40. | 90. | 250. | 325. | |
| 1906 . .(675) 19,957,731 | 2.50 | 3.00 | 4. | 7. | 22. | 70. | 110. | 170. | 450. |
| 1906D . . . . . . .4,060,000 | 4.00 | 5.00 | 8. | 15. | 35. | 80. | 175. | 400. | |
| 1906O . . . . . . .2,610,000 | 5.00 | 14.00 | 45. | 75. | 95. | 130. | 200. | 325. | |
| 1906S . . . . . . .3,136,640 | 3.00 | 5.00 | 13. | 25. | 45. | 110. | 275. | 550. | |
| 1907 . .(575) 22,220,000 | 2.50 | 3.00 | 4. | 7. | 22. | 70. | 110. | 170. | 450. |
| 1907D . . . . . . .4,080,000 | 2.50 | 4.00 | 9. | 18. | 45. | 110. | 300. | 900. | |
| 1907O . . . . . . .5,058,000 | 3.00 | 7.00 | 30. | 45. | 70. | 110. | 210. | 375. | |

* Included in regular mintage. **a.** Normal and "microscopic" mintmark varieties; see page 20.

# DIMES

| | Mintage | G-4 | VG-8 | F-12 | VF-20 | EF-40 | AU-50 | MS-60 | MS-63 | PF-63 |
|---|---|---|---|---|---|---|---|---|---|---|
| 1907S | .......3,178,470 | $2.50 | $6.00 | $15. | $25. | $60. | $140. | $400. | $750. | |
| 1908 | (545) 10,600,000 | 2.50 | 3.00 | 4. | 7. | 22. | 70. | 110. | 170. | $450. |
| 1908D | .......7,490,000 | 2.50 | 3.00 | 6. | 10. | 28. | 70. | 130. | 300. | |
| 1908O | .......1,789,000 | 5.00 | 12.00 | 40. | 60. | 90. | 140. | 300. | 600. | |
| 1908S | .......3,220,000 | 2.50 | 5.00 | 12. | 22. | 45. | 170. | 350. | 800. | |
| 1909 | (650) 10,240,000 | 2.50 | 3.00 | 4. | 7. | 22. | 70. | 110. | 170. | 450. |
| 1909D | ........954,000 | 8.00 | 20.00 | 60. | 90. | 140. | 225. | 500. | 1,000. | |
| 1909O | .......2,287,000 | 4.00 | 8.00 | 13. | 22. | 50. | 90. | 200. | 500. | |
| 1909S | .......1,000,000 | 8.00 | 20.00 | 80. | 130. | 180. | 310. | 550. | 1,200. | |
| 1910 | (551) 11,520,000 | 2.50 | 3.00 | 4. | 7. | 22. | 70. | 110. | 170. | 450. |
| 1910D | .......3,490,000 | 2.50 | 4.00 | 9. | 18. | 45. | 90. | 220. | 450. | |
| 1910S | .......1,240,000 | 5.00 | 9.00 | 50. | 70. | 100. | 180. | 425. | 700. | |
| 1911 | (543) 18,870,000 | 2.50 | 3.00 | 4. | 7. | 22. | 70. | 110. | 170. | 450. |
| 1911D | ......11,209,000 | 2.50 | 3.00 | 4. | 7. | 22. | 70. | 110. | 170. | |
| 1911S | .......3,520,000 | 2.50 | 4.00 | 9. | 20. | 40. | 100. | 200. | 400. | |
| 1912 | (700) 19,349,300 | 2.50 | 3.00 | 4. | 7. | 22. | 70. | 110. | 170. | 450. |
| 1912D | .....11,760,000 | 2.50 | 3.00 | 4. | 7. | 22. | 70. | 110. | 170. | |
| 1912S | .......3,420,000 | 2.50 | 3.00 | 6. | 12. | 32. | 90. | 170. | 300. | |
| 1913 | (622) 19,760,000 | 2.50 | 3.00 | 4. | 7. | 22. | 70. | 110. | 170. | 450. |
| 1913S | ........510,000 | 16.00 | 30.00 | 75. | 130. | 240. | 320. | 500. | 750. | |
| 1914 | (425) 17,360,230 | 2.50 | 3.00 | 4. | 7. | 22. | 70. | 110. | 170. | 450. |
| 1914D | .....11,908,000 | 2.50 | 3.00 | 4. | 7. | 22. | 70. | 110. | 170. | |
| 1914S | .......2,100,000 | 2.50 | 4.00 | 10. | 18. | 40. | 80. | 175. | 350. | |
| 1915 | (450) 5,620,000 | 2.50 | 3.00 | 4. | 7. | 22. | 70. | 110. | 170. | 450. |
| 1915S | ........960,000 | 7.00 | 11.00 | 32. | 45. | 65. | 140. | 275. | 475. | |
| 1916 | ......18,490,000 | 2.50 | 3.00 | 4. | 7. | 22. | 70. | 110. | 170. | |
| 1916S | .......5,820,000 | 2.50 | 3.00 | 4. | 7. | 22. | 70. | 110. | 170. | |

# WINGED LIBERTY HEAD OR "MERCURY" (1916–1945)

Although this coin is commonly called the *Mercury dime*, the main device is in fact a representation of Liberty. The wings crowning her cap are intended to symbolize liberty of thought. The designer's monogram AW is to the right of the neck.

*Designer Adolph A. Weinman; weight 2.50 grams; composition .900 silver, .100 copper (net weight: .07234 oz. pure silver); diameter 17.9 mm; reeded edge; mints: Philadelphia, Denver, San Francisco.*

**G-4 GOOD**—Letters and date clear. Lines and bands in fasces obliterated.
**VG-8 VERY GOOD**—Half of sticks discernible in fasces.
**F-12 FINE**—All sticks in fasces defined. Diagonal bands worn nearly flat.
**VF-20 VERY FINE**—Diagonal bands definitely visible.
**EF-40 EXTREMELY FINE**—Only slight wear on diagonal bands. Braids and hair before ear clearly visible.
**AU-50 ABOUT UNCIRCULATED**—Slight trace of wear. Most mint luster present.
**MS-63 CHOICE UNCIRCULATED**—No trace of wear. Light blemishes. Attractive mint luster.
**MS-65 GEM UNCIRCULATED**—Only light, scattered marks that are not distracting. Strong luster, good eye appeal.

*Mintmark location is on reverse, left of fasces.*

*See next page for chart.*

*Uncirculated values shown are for average pieces with minimum blemishes; those with sharp strikes and split bands on reverse are worth much more.*

| | Mintage | G-4 | VG-8 | F-12 | VF-20 | EF-40 | AU-50 | MS-63 | MS-65 |
|---|---|---|---|---|---|---|---|---|---|
| 1916 | 22,180,080 | $3.00 | $4.00 | $6.00 | $8. | $10. | $25. | $45. | $120. |
| 1916D | 264,000 | 850.00 | 1,250.00 | 2,500.00 | 4,000. | 6,000. | 9,000. | 18,000. | 30,000. |
| 1916S | 10,450,000 | 4.00 | 6.00 | 9.00 | 12. | 20. | 25. | 65. | 250. |
| 1917 | 55,230,000 | 2.00 | 2.50 | 3.00 | 6. | 8. | 12. | 55. | 165. |
| 1917D | 9,402,000 | 4.50 | 6.00 | 11.00 | 22. | 45. | 95. | 350. | 1,200. |
| 1917S | 27,330,000 | 2.00 | 2.50 | 4.00 | 7. | 12. | 30. | 180. | 550. |
| 1918 | 26,680,000 | 2.50 | 4.00 | 6.00 | 12. | 25. | 40. | 125. | 450. |
| 1918D | 22,674,800 | 2.50 | 4.00 | 6.00 | 12. | 24. | 50. | 250. | 650. |
| 1918S | 19,300,000 | 2.50 | 3.00 | 5.00 | 10. | 18. | 40. | 275. | 700. |
| 1919 | 35,740,000 | 2.50 | 3.00 | 4.00 | 6. | 10. | 30. | 120. | 350. |
| 1919D | 9,939,000 | 4.00 | 7.00 | 12.00 | 24. | 35. | 75. | 450. | 2,000. |
| 1919S | 8,850,000 | 3.50 | 4.00 | 8.00 | 16. | 35. | 75. | 450. | 1,100. |
| 1920 | 59,030,000 | 1.75 | 2.00 | 3.00 | 5. | 8. | 15. | 75. | 250. |
| 1920D | 19,171,000 | 3.00 | 3.50 | 4.50 | 8. | 20. | 45. | 350. | 800. |
| 1920S | 13,820,000 | 3.00 | 4.00 | 5.00 | 8. | 18. | 45. | 300. | 1,300. |
| 1921 | 1,230,000 | 45.00 | 75.00 | 125.00 | 300. | 575. | 900. | 1,750. | 3,500. |
| 1921D | 1,080,000 | 65.00 | 125.00 | 200.00 | 400. | 750. | 1,200. | 2,000. | 3,500. |
| 1923 (a) | 50,130,000 | 1.75 | 2.50 | 3.00 | 5. | 7. | 16. | 45. | 125. |
| 1923S | 6,440,000 | 2.50 | 4.00 | 8.00 | 15. | 65. | 105. | 400. | 1,200. |
| 1924 | 24,010,000 | 1.75 | 2.50 | 4.00 | 6. | 14. | 27. | 100. | 200. |
| 1924D | 6,810,000 | 3.00 | 4.50 | 7.00 | 16. | 50. | 110. | 500. | 1,200. |
| 1924S | 7,120,000 | 3.00 | 4.00 | 6.00 | 10. | 45. | 110. | 500. | 1,250. |
| 1925 | 25,610,000 | 1.75 | 3.00 | 4.00 | 5. | 8. | 20. | 85. | 225. |
| 1925D | 5,117,000 | 4.00 | 5.00 | 12.00 | 40. | 110. | 200. | 800. | 1,800. |
| 1925S | 5,850,000 | 3.00 | 4.00 | 8.00 | 15. | 65. | 110. | 500. | 1,500. |
| 1926 | 32,160,000 | 1.50 | 2.00 | 2.50 | 4. | 7. | 16. | 65. | 250. |
| 1926D | 6,828,000 | 3.00 | 4.50 | 6.00 | 10. | 25. | 50. | 275. | 600. |
| 1926S | 1,520,000 | 9.00 | 11.00 | 25.00 | 60. | 250. | 450. | 1,500. | 3,000. |
| 1927 | 28,080,000 | 1.50 | 2.00 | 3.00 | 4. | 7. | 15. | 60. | 150. |
| 1927D | 4,812,000 | 3.50 | 5.00 | 8.00 | 20. | 65. | 90. | 400. | 1,300. |
| 1927S | 4,770,000 | 2.50 | 4.00 | 6.00 | 9. | 24. | 50. | 550. | 1,500. |
| 1928 | 19,480,000 | 1.50 | 2.00 | 3.00 | 5. | 7. | 18. | 50. | 130. |
| 1928D | 4,161,000 | 4.00 | 5.00 | 8.00 | 19. | 45. | 80. | 350. | 900. |
| 1928S (b) | 7,400,000 | 2.00 | 3.00 | 4.00 | 5. | 16. | 45. | 300. | 500. |
| 1929 | 25,970,000 | 1.50 | 2.00 | 3.00 | 4. | 6. | 12. | 35. | 75. |
| 1929D | 5,034,000 | 2.50 | 3.50 | 5.00 | 6. | 15. | 25. | 40. | 75. |
| 1929S | 4,730,000 | 1.75 | 2.50 | 3.50 | 5. | 10. | 20. | 45. | 125. |
| 1930 (a) | 6,770,000 | 1.75 | 2.00 | 3.00 | 5. | 8. | 16. | 50. | 125. |
| 1930S | 1,843,000 | 2.50 | 4.00 | 5.00 | 7. | 15. | 45. | 120. | 210. |
| 1931 | 3,150,000 | 2.00 | 3.00 | 4.00 | 6. | 10. | 22. | 70. | 150. |
| 1931D | 1,260,000 | 8.00 | 9.00 | 12.00 | 20. | 35. | 50. | 140. | 280. |
| 1931S | 1,800,000 | 4.00 | 4.50 | 5.50 | 8. | 16. | 40. | 150. | 300. |

**a.** Dimes dated 1923-D or 1930-D are counterfeit. **b.** Large and small mintmarks; see page 20.

| | Mintage | F-12 | VF-20 | EF-40 | MS-63 | MS-65 | PF-65 |
|---|---|---|---|---|---|---|---|
| 1934 | 24,080,000 | $1.20 | $1.50 | $3.50 | $30. | $50. | |
| 1934D (b) | 6,772,000 | 2.00 | 2.50 | 8.00 | 60. | 85. | |
| 1935 | 58,830,000 | 1.20 | 1.50 | 2.50 | 15. | 35. | |
| 1935D | 10,477,000 | 2.00 | 2.50 | 8.00 | 50. | 90. | |

**b.** Large and small mintmarks; see page 20.

| | Mintage | F-12 | VF-20 | EF-40 | MS-63 | MS-65 | PF-65 |
|---|---|---|---|---|---|---|---|
| 1935S ................ 15,840,000 | | $1.20 | $1.50 | $5.00 | $30. | $40. | |
| 1936 ........(4,130) .... 87,500,000 | | 1.20 | 2.50 | 3.50 | 18. | 30. | $2,100. |
| 1936D ................. 16,132,000 | | 1.70 | 3.50 | 6.00 | 35. | 55. | |
| 1936S ................. 9,210,000 | | 1.20 | 2.50 | 3.50 | 30. | 35. | |
| 1937 ........(5,756) .... 56,860,000 | | 1.20 | 1.50 | 2.50 | 15. | 30. | 850. |
| 1937D ................. 14,146,000 | | 1.20 | 2.50 | 4.00 | 30. | 45. | |
| 1937S ................. 9,740,000 | | 1.20 | 2.50 | 3.50 | 30. | 40. | |
| 1938 ........(8,728) .... 22,190,000 | | 1.20 | 2.50 | 3.00 | 15. | 30. | 550. |
| 1938D ................. 5,537,000 | | 2.00 | 3.00 | 4.00 | 25. | 35. | |
| 1938S ................. 8,090,000 | | 1.20 | 2.50 | 3.50 | 28. | 40. | |
| 1939 ........(9,321) .... 67,740,000 | | 1.20 | 1.50 | 2.50 | 12. | 25. | 450. |
| 1939D ................. 24,394,000 | | 1.20 | 1.50 | 2.50 | 12. | 25. | |
| 1939S ................. 10,540,000 | | 1.75 | 2.25 | 3.00 | 25. | 40. | |
| 1940 ........(11,827) .... 65,350,000 | | 1.00 | 1.25 | 2.00 | 12. | 30. | 400. |
| 1940D ................. 21,198,000 | | 1.00 | 1.25 | 2.00 | 14. | 30. | |
| 1940S ................. 21,560,000 | | 1.00 | 1.25 | 2.00 | 15. | 30. | |
| 1941 ........(16,557) ... 175,090,000 | | 1.00 | 1.25 | 2.00 | 12. | 30. | 400. |
| 1941D ................. 45,634,000 | | 1.00 | 1.25 | 2.00 | 14. | 25. | |
| 1941S (b) .............. 43,090,000 | | 1.00 | 1.25 | 2.00 | 12. | 30. | |

b. Large and small mintmarks; see page 20.

1942, 2 Over 1

1942-D, 2 Over 1

| | Mintage | F-12 | VF-20 | EF-40 | MS-63 | MS-65 | PF-65 |
|---|---|---|---|---|---|---|---|
| 1942, 2 Over 1 .................. * | | $625.00 | $800.00 | $900. | $4,250. | $15,000. | |
| 1942 ........(22,329) ... 205,432,329 | | 1.00 | 1.25 | 2. | 12. | 30. | $400. |
| 1942D, 2 Over 1 ................ * | | 675.00 | 850.00 | 950. | 4,500. | 8,000. | |
| 1942D ................. 60,740,000 | | 1.00 | 1.25 | 2. | 15. | 30. | |
| 1942S ................. 49,300,000 | | 1.00 | 1.25 | 2. | 20. | 35. | |
| 1943 ................. 191,710,000 | | 1.00 | 1.25 | 2. | 12. | 25. | |
| 1943D ................. 71,949,000 | | 1.00 | 1.25 | 2. | 15. | 30. | |
| 1943S ................. 60,400,000 | | 1.00 | 1.25 | 2. | 16. | 30. | |
| 1944 ................. 231,410,000 | | 1.00 | 1.25 | 2. | 12. | 25. | |
| 1944D ................. 62,224,000 | | 1.00 | 1.25 | 2. | 15. | 30. | |
| 1944S ................. 49,490,000 | | 1.00 | 1.25 | 2. | 15. | 30. | |
| 1945 ................. 159,130,000 | | 1.00 | 1.25 | 2. | 12. | 28. | |
| 1945D ................. 40,245,000 | | 1.00 | 1.25 | 2. | 12. | 30. | |
| 1945S ................. 41,920,000 | | 1.00 | 1.25 | 2. | 12. | 30. | |
| 1945S, Micro S ................. * | | 1.50 | 2.50 | 6. | 40. | 100. | |

* Included in regular mintage.

## ROOSEVELT (1946 TO DATE)

John R. Sinnock (whose initials, JS, are at the truncation of the neck) designed this dime showing a portrait of Franklin D. Roosevelt. The design has heavier lettering and a more modernistic character than preceding types.

Mintmark on
reverse 1946–1964.

Mintmark on
obverse starting 1968.

### Silver Coinage (1946–1964)

*Designer John R. Sinnock; weight 2.50 grams; composition .900 silver, .100 copper (net weight .07234 oz. pure silver); diameter 17.9 mm; reeded edge; mints: Philadelphia, Denver, San Francisco, West Point.*

**EF-40 EXTREMELY FINE**—All lines of torch, flame, and hair very plain.
**MS-63 CHOICE UNCIRCULATED**—Some distracting contact marks or blemishes in prime focal areas. Impaired luster possible.
**MS-65 GEM UNCIRCULATED**—Only light scattered marks that are not distracting. Strong luster, good eye appeal.
**PF-65 GEM PROOF**—Nearly perfect.

| | Mintage | EF-40 | MS-63 | MS-65 | PF-65 |
|---|---|---|---|---|---|
| 1946 | 255,250,000 | $1.00 | $3.00 | $12.00 | |
| 1946D | 61,043,500 | 1.00 | 3.00 | 14.00 | |
| 1946S | 27,900,000 | 1.00 | 4.50 | 20.00 | |
| 1947 | 121,520,000 | 1.00 | 6.00 | 12.00 | |
| 1947D | 46,835,000 | 1.00 | 6.50 | 12.00 | |
| 1947S | 34,840,000 | 1.00 | 6.00 | 12.00 | |
| 1948 | 74,950,000 | 1.00 | 4.00 | 12.00 | |
| 1948D | 52,841,000 | 1.00 | 6.00 | 12.00 | |
| 1948S | 35,520,000 | 1.00 | 5.50 | 12.00 | |
| 1949 | 30,940,000 | 1.50 | 25.00 | 30.00 | |
| 1949D | 26,034,000 | 1.25 | 10.00 | 18.00 | |
| 1949S | 13,510,000 | 3.00 | 40.00 | 50.00 | |
| 1950 ........(51,386) | 50,130,114 | 1.00 | 12.00 | 14.00 | $45.00 |
| 1950D | 46,803,000 | 1.00 | 6.00 | 12.00 | |
| 1950S | 20,440,000 | 1.00 | 35.00 | 40.00 | |
| 1951 ........(57,500) | 103,880,102 | 1.00 | 2.50 | 10.00 | 45.00 |
| 1951D | 56,529,000 | 1.00 | 2.25 | 10.00 | |
| 1951S | 31,630,000 | 1.00 | 12.00 | 20.00 | |
| 1952 ........(81,980) | 99,040,093 | 1.00 | 2.00 | 10.00 | 35.00 |
| 1952D | 122,100,000 | 1.00 | 2.50 | 6.00 | |
| 1952S | 44,419,500 | 1.00 | 8.00 | 12.00 | |
| 1953 ........(128,800) | 53,490,120 | 1.00 | 3.00 | 8.00 | 35.00 |
| 1953D | 136,433,000 | 1.00 | 3.00 | 8.00 | |
| 1953S | 39,180,000 | 1.00 | 2.50 | 8.00 | |
| 1954 ........(233,300) | 114,010,203 | 1.00 | 2.50 | 8.00 | 18.00 |
| 1954D | 106,397,000 | 1.00 | 2.50 | 8.00 | |
| 1954S | 22,860,000 | 1.00 | 2.50 | 8.00 | |
| 1955 ........(378,200) | 12,450,181 | 1.00 | 2.50 | 8.00 | 15.00 |
| 1955D | 13,959,000 | 1.00 | 2.50 | 8.00 | |
| 1955S | 18,510,000 | 1.00 | 2.50 | 8.00 | |
| 1956 ........(669,384) | 108,640,000 | 1.00 | 2.00 | 7.00 | 5.00 |
| 1956D | 108,015,100 | 1.00 | 2.00 | 7.00 | |

**1960, Proof Doubled-Die Obverse**

**1964-D, Doubled-Die Reverse**

|  | Mintage | EF-40 | MS-63 | MS-65 | PF-65 |
|---|---|---|---|---|---|
| 1957 . . . . . . . . . . . . .(1,247,952) . . . 160,160,000 | | $1.00 | $2.00 | $7.00 | $4.00 |
| 1957D. . . . . . . . . . . . . . . . . . . . . 113,354,330 | | 1.00 | 2.50 | 7.00 | |
| 1958 . . . . . . . . . . . . . .(875,652) . . . . 31,910,000 | | 1.00 | 2.00 | 8.00 | 4.00 |
| 1958D. . . . . . . . . . . . . . . . . . . . . 136,564,600 | | 1.00 | 2.00 | 8.00 | |
| 1959 . . . . . . . . . . . . .(1,149,291) . . . . 85,780,000 | | 1.00 | 2.00 | 7.00 | 2.00 |
| 1959D. . . . . . . . . . . . . . . . . . . . . 164,919,790 | | 1.00 | 2.00 | 7.00 | |
| 1960 . . . . . . . . . . . . .(1,691,602) . . . . 70,390,000 | | 1.00 | 2.00 | 7.00 | 2.00 |
| 1960, Doubled-Die Obv . . . . . . . . . . . . . . . . . . . * | | | | | 300.00 |
| 1960D. . . . . . . . . . . . . . . . . . . . . 200,160,400 | | 1.00 | 1.25 | 6.00 | |
| 1961 . . . . . . . . . . . . .(3,028,244) . . . 93,730,000 | | 1.00 | 1.25 | 6.00 | 2.00 |
| 1961D. . . . . . . . . . . . . . . . . . . . . 209,146,550 | | 1.00 | 1.25 | 6.00 | |
| 1962 . . . . . . . . . . . . .(3,218,019) . . . . 72,450,000 | | 1.00 | 1.25 | 6.00 | 2.00 |
| 1962D. . . . . . . . . . . . . . . . . . . . . 334,948,380 | | 1.00 | 1.25 | 6.00 | |
| 1963 . . . . . . . . . . . . .(3,075,645) . . . 123,650,000 | | 1.00 | 1.25 | 6.00 | 2.00 |
| 1963, Doubled-Die Rev . . . . . . . . . . . . . . . . . . . * | | | | | 400.00 |
| 1963D. . . . . . . . . . . . . . . . . . . . . 421,476,530 | | 1.00 | 1.25 | 6.00 | |
| 1964 . . . . . . . . . . . . .(3,950,762) . . . 929,360,000 | | 1.00 | 1.25 | 6.00 | 2.00 |
| 1964D **(a)** . . . . . . . . . . . . . . . . . . . . 1,357,517,180 | | 1.00 | 1.25 | 6.00 | |
| 1964D, Doubled-Die Rev **(a)** . . . . . . . . . . . . . . . . * | | 50.00 | 250.00 | 300.00 | |

\* Included in number above. **a.** Variations of 9 in date have pointed or straight tail.

## Clad Coinage and Silver Proofs (1965 to Date)

*Weight 2.27 grams; composition, outer layers of copper-nickel (.750 copper, .250 nickel) bonded to inner core of pure copper; diameter 17.9 mm; reeded edge. Silver Proofs: pre-1965 standards.*

| | Mintage | MS-65 | PF-65 | | Mintage | MS-65 | PF-65 |
|---|---|---|---|---|---|---|---|
| 1965 . . . . . . .1,652,140,570 | | $1.50 | | 1972S . . . . . . . .(3,260,996) | | | $1.50 |
| 1966 . . . . . . .1,382,734,540 | | 1.25 | | 1973 . . . . . . . .315,670,000 | | $1.00 | |
| 1967 . . . . . . .2,244,007,320 | | 1.00 | | 1973D . . . . . . .455,032,426 | | 1.00 | |
| 1968 . . . . . . .424,470,400 | | 1.00 | | 1973S . . . . . . . .(2,760,339) | | | 1.50 |
| 1968D . . . . . . .480,748,280 | | 1.00 | | 1974 . . . . . . . .470,248,000 | | 1.00 | |
| 1968S **(a)** . . . . .(3,041,506) | | | $1.50 | 1974D . . . . . . .571,083,000 | | 1.00 | |
| 1969 . . . . . . . .145,790,000 | | 2.00 | | 1974S . . . . . . . .(2,612,568) | | | 1.50 |
| 1969D . . . . . . .563,323,870 | | 1.00 | | 1975 . . . . . . . .585,673,900 | | 1.00 | |
| 1969S . . . . . . .(2,394,631) | | | 1.50 | 1975D . . . . . . .313,705,300 | | 1.00 | |
| 1970 . . . . . . . .345,570,000 | | 1.00 | | 1975S **(a)** . . . . .(2,845,450) | | | 2.00 |
| 1970D . . . . . . .754,942,100 | | 1.00 | | 1976 . . . . . . . .568,760,000 | | 1.00 | |
| 1970S **(a)** . . . . .(2,632,810) | | | 1.50 | 1976D . . . . . . .695,222,774 | | 1.00 | |
| 1971 . . . . . . . .162,690,000 | | 1.50 | | 1976S . . . . . . . .(4,149,730) | | | 2.00 |
| 1971D . . . . . . .377,914,240 | | 1.25 | | 1977 . . . . . . . .796,930,000 | | 1.00 | |
| 1971S . . . . . . .(3,220,733) | | | 1.50 | 1977D . . . . . . .376,607,228 | | 1.00 | |
| 1972 . . . . . . . .431,540,000 | | 1.00 | | 1977S . . . . . . . .(3,251,152) | | | 1.75 |
| 1972D . . . . . . .330,290,000 | | 1.00 | | 1978 . . . . . . . .663,980,000 | | 1.00 | |

**a.** 1968, 1970, and 1975 Proof dimes without S mintmark were made in error. See page 20.

*Chart continued on next page.*

| | Mintage | MS-65 | PF-65 |
|---|---|---|---|
| 1978D | 282,847,540 | $1.00 | |
| 1978S | (3,127,781) | | $1.50 |
| 1979 | 315,440,000 | 1.00 | |
| 1979D | 390,921,184 | 1.00 | |
| 1979S, Filled S | (3,677,175) | | 1.50 |
| 1979S, Clear S | * | | 2.00 |
| 1980P | 735,170,000 | 1.00 | |
| 1980D | 719,354,321 | 1.00 | |
| 1980S | (3,554,806) | | 1.50 |
| 1981P | 676,650,000 | 1.00 | |
| 1981D | 712,284,143 | 1.00 | |
| 1981S | (4,063,083) | | 1.50 |
| 1982, No Mintmark (a) | | 225.00 | |
| 1982P | 519,475,000 | 5.00 | |
| 1982D | 542,713,584 | 1.50 | |
| 1982S | (3,857,479) | | 2.00 |
| 1983P | 647,025,000 | 5.00 | |
| 1983D | 730,129,224 | 1.50 | |
| 1983S (b) | (3,279,126) | | 1.50 |
| 1984P | 856,669,000 | 1.00 | |
| 1984D | 704,803,976 | 1.25 | |
| 1984S | (3,065,110) | | 2.00 |
| 1985P | 705,200,962 | 1.25 | |
| 1985D | 587,979,970 | 1.25 | |
| 1985S | (3,362,821) | | 1.50 |
| 1986P | 682,649,693 | 1.50 | |
| 1986D | 473,326,970 | 1.50 | |
| 1986S | (3,010,497) | | 3.00 |
| 1987P | 762,709,481 | 0.75 | |
| 1987D | 653,203,402 | 0.75 | |
| 1987S | (4,227,728) | | 3.00 |
| 1988P | 1,030,550,000 | 0.75 | |
| 1988D | 962,385,489 | 0.75 | |
| 1988S | (3,262,948) | | 3.00 |
| 1989P | 1,298,400,000 | 0.75 | |
| 1989D | 896,535,597 | 0.75 | |
| 1989S | (3,220,194) | | 4.00 |
| 1990P | 1,034,340,000 | 1.50 | |
| 1990D | 839,995,824 | 0.75 | |
| 1990S | (3,299,559) | | 2.00 |
| 1991P | 927,220,000 | 0.75 | |
| 1991D | 601,241,114 | 0.75 | |
| 1991S | (2,867,787) | | 3.00 |
| 1992P | 593,500,000 | 0.75 | |
| 1992D | 616,273,932 | 0.75 | |
| 1992S | (2,858,981) | | 4.00 |
| 1992S, Silver | (1,317,579) | | 6.00 |
| 1993P | 766,180,000 | 0.75 | |
| 1993D | 750,110,166 | 0.75 | |
| 1993S | (2,633,439) | | 5.00 |
| 1993S, Silver | (761,353) | | 7.00 |
| 1994P | 1,189,000,000 | 0.75 | |
| 1994D | 1,303,268,110 | $0.75 | |
| 1994S | (2,484,594) | | $5.00 |
| 1994S, Silver | (785,329) | | 8.00 |
| 1995P | 1,125,500,000 | 0.75 | |
| 1995D | 1,274,890,000 | 1.00 | |
| 1995S | (2,117,496) | | 15.00 |
| 1995S, Silver | (679,985) | | 20.00 |
| 1996P | 1,421,163,000 | 0.75 | |
| 1996D | 1,400,300,000 | 0.75 | |
| 1996W (c) | 1,457,000 | 20.00 | |
| 1996S | (1,750,244) | | 2.50 |
| 1996S, Silver | (775,021) | | 7.50 |
| 1997P | 991,640,000 | 0.75 | |
| 1997D | 979,810,000 | 0.75 | |
| 1997S | (2,055,000) | | 8.00 |
| 1997S, Silver | (741,678) | | 18.00 |
| 1998P | 1,163,000,000 | 0.75 | |
| 1998D | 1,172,250,000 | 0.75 | |
| 1998S | (2,086,507) | | 3.00 |
| 1998S, Silver | (878,792) | | 6.00 |
| 1999P | 2,164,000,000 | 0.75 | |
| 1999D | 1,397,750,000 | 0.75 | |
| 1999S | (2,543,401) | | 3.00 |
| 1999S, Silver | (804,565) | | 7.00 |
| 2000P | 1,842,500,000 | 0.75 | |
| 2000D | 1,818,700,000 | 0.75 | |
| 2000S | (3,082,483) | | 2.00 |
| 2000S, Silver | (965,421) | | 3.00 |
| 2001P | 1,369,590,000 | 0.75 | |
| 2001D | 1,412,800,000 | 0.75 | |
| 2001S | (2,294,043) | | 2.00 |
| 2001S, Silver | (889,697) | | 3.50 |
| 2002P | 1,187,500,000 | 0.75 | |
| 2002D | 1,379,500,000 | 0.75 | |
| 2002S | (2,319,766) | | 2.00 |
| 2002S, Silver | (892,229) | | 6.00 |
| 2003P | 1,085,500,000 | 0.75 | |
| 2003D | 986,500,000 | 0.75 | |
| 2003S | (2,172,684) | | 2.00 |
| 2003S, Silver | (1,125,755) | | 5.00 |
| 2004P | 1,328,000,000 | 0.75 | |
| 2004D | 1,159,500,000 | 0.75 | |
| 2004S | (1,804,396) | | 2.50 |
| 2004S, Silver | (1,187,673) | | 4.00 |
| 2005P | 1,412,000,000 | 0.75 | |
| 2005D | 1,423,500,000 | 0.75 | |
| 2005S | (2,275,000) | | 2.00 |
| 2005S, Silver | (998,000) | | 4.00 |
| 2006 | | 0.75 | |
| 2006D | | 0.75 | |
| 2006S | | | 2.00 |
| 2006S, Silver | | | 4.00 |

* Included in number above. **a.** Some of the 1982, circulation-strike dimes were also made without a mintmark. See page 20. **b.** 1983-S Proof dimes without S mintmark were made in error. See page 20. **c.** Issued in Mint sets only.

## LIBERTY SEATED (1875–1878)

This short-lived coin was authorized by the Act of March 3, 1875. Soon after the appearance of the first twenty-cent pieces, people complained about the similarity in design and size to the quarter dollar. The eagle is very similar to that used on the trade dollar, but the edge of this coin is plain. The mintmark is on the reverse below the eagle.

In the denomination's first year, more than one million pieces were struck at the San Francisco Mint; about 133,000 at the Carson City Mint; and roughly 37,000 at Philadelphia (not including about 2,800 Proofs struck there as well). These numbers dropped sharply in 1876. (Most of the Carson City coins of that year were melted at the mint and never released, a fate likely met by most of the Philadelphia twenty-cent pieces of 1876 as well.) In 1877 and 1878, only Proof examples were minted. None were struck for circulation.

Various factors caused the demise of the twenty-cent piece: the public was confused over the coin's similarity to the quarter dollar, which was better established as a foundation of American commerce; in the eastern United States, small-change transactions were largely satisfied by Fractional Currency notes; and the twenty-cent coin was essentially just a substitute for two dimes.

### TYPE COIN VALUES

|  | G-4 | F-12 | EF-40 | MS-60 | MS-63 | MS-65 | PF-63 | PF-65 |
|---|---|---|---|---|---|---|---|---|
| 1875–1878 | $120.+ | $185.+ | $200.+ | $575.+ | $1,200.+ | $6,000.+ | $2,250.+ | $11,000.+ |

+ or – indicates change from previous year

*Designer William Barber; weight 5 grams; composition .900 silver, .100 copper; diameter 22 mm; plain edge; mints: Philadelphia, Carson City, San Francisco.*

**G-4 GOOD**—LIBERTY on shield obliterated. Letters and date legible.
**VG-8 VERY GOOD**—One or two letters in LIBERTY barely visible. Other details bold.
**F-12 FINE**—Some letters of LIBERTY possibly visible.
**VF-20 VERY FINE**—LIBERTY readable, but partly weak.
**EF-40 EXTREMELY FINE**—LIBERTY mostly sharp. Only slight wear on high points of coin.
**AU-50 ABOUT UNCIRCULATED**—Slight trace of wear on breast, head, and knees.
**MS-60 UNCIRCULATED**—No trace of wear. Light blemishes.
**MS-63 CHOICE UNCIRCULATED**—Some distracting blemishes in prime focal areas. Some impairment of luster possible.

| | Mintage | G-4 | VG-8 | F-12 | VF-20 | EF-40 | AU-50 | MS-60 | MS-63 | PF-63 |
|---|---|---|---|---|---|---|---|---|---|---|
| 1875 (2,790) | 36,910 | $120. | $135. | $185. | $235. | $300. | $475. | $700. | $1,250. | $2,250. |
| 1875CC | 133,290 | 165. | 215. | 285. | 325. | 425. | 575. | 900. | 1,900. | |
| 1875S | 1,155,000 | 100. | 110. | 120. | 150. | 200. | 325. | 575. | 1,200. | |
| 1876 (1,260) | 14,640 | 160. | 185. | 275. | 350. | 425. | 550. | 800. | 1,400. | 2,400. |
| 1876CC | 10,000 | | | | | | | 125,000. | | |
| 1877 (350) | | | | | 2,400. | 2,750. | | | | 4,500. |
| 1878 (600) | | | | | 2,000. | 2,250. | | | | 3,650. |

Authorized in 1792, this denomination was not issued until four years later. The first coinage, dated 1796, follows the pattern of the early half dimes and dimes by the absence of a mark of value. In 1804 the value "25c" was added to the reverse. Figures were used until 1838, when the term QUAR. DOL. appeared. It was not until 1892 that the value was spelled out entirely.

The first type weighed 104 grains, which remained standard until modified to 103-1/8 grains by the Act of January 18, 1837. As with the dime and half dime, the weight was reduced and arrows placed at the date in 1853. Rays were placed in the field of the reverse during that year only.

The law of 1873 also affected the quarter, for the weight was slightly increased and arrows were again placed at the date.

Proofs of some dates prior to 1856 are known to exist, and all are rare.

## TYPE COIN VALUES

| | G-4 | F-12 | EF-40 | MS-60 | MS-63 | MS-65 | PF-63 | PF-65 |
|---|---|---|---|---|---|---|---|---|
| Drpd Bust, SE, 1796 | $11,000.00+ | $25,000.00+ | $37,500.+ | $67,500. | $90,000.+ | $225,000.+ | — | — |
| Drpd Bust, HE, 1804–1807 | 225.00+ | 550.00+ | 1,800. | 6,500.+ | 13,500.+ | 72,500.+ | — | — |
| Cap Bust, 1815–1828 | 80.00+ | 150.00+ | 1,000.+ | 2,650.+ | 5,000.+ | 24,000.+ | $30,000. | — |
| Cap Bust, 1831–1838 | 70.00+ | 95.00+ | 300. | 1,000.+ | 3,250.+ | 19,000.+ | 20,000. | $55,000.+ |
| Lib Std, NM, 1838–1853 | 19.00 | 35.00 | 80. | 475.- | 900. | 4,250.+ | 1,100.+ | 5,750.+ |
| Lib Std, A&R, 1853 | 20.00 | 35.00- | 150.+ | 950. | 2,150.+ | 22,500.+ | 45,000.+ | — |
| Lib Std, Arr, 1854–1855 | 20.00+ | 35.00+ | 85.+ | 500. | 1,300.+ | 10,000.+ | 14,000.+ | 32,500.+ |
| Lib Std, Motto, 1866–1891 | 20.00+ | 35.00+ | 65.+ | 250. | 500. | 1,950.+ | 650.+ | 2,400.+ |
| Lib Std, Arr, 1873–1874 | 20.00 | 40.00+ | 200. | 800. | 1,500. | 4,750.+ | 1,500. | 8,000.+ |
| Barber, 1892–1916 | 6.00+ | 18.00 | 65.- | 185.- | 325.+ | 1,450.+ | 650.+ | 2,000.+ |
| Standing Lib, 1916–1917 | 23.00+ | 50.00 | 90.+ | 225. | 300. | 800.+ | | |
| Standing Lib, 1917–1930 | 3.00 | 7.00 | 40.+ | 120. | 225.+ | 575.+ | | |
| Washington, 1932–1964 | 2.00+ | 2.25+ | 3. | 5. | 6. | 15.+ | 3. | 10.+ |

+ or – indicates change from previous year

## DRAPED BUST (1796–1807)

*Designer Robert Scot; weight 6.74 grams; composition .8924 silver, .1076 copper; approx. diameter 27.5 mm; reeded edge. All coined at Philadelphia.*

**AG-3 ABOUT GOOD**—Details clear enough to identify.
**G-4 GOOD**—Date readable. Bust outlined, but no detail.
**VG-8 VERY GOOD**—All but deepest drapery folds worn smooth. Hairlines nearly gone and curls lacking in detail.
**F-12 FINE**—All drapery lines visible. Hair partly worn.
**VF-20 VERY FINE**—Only left side of drapery indistinct.
**EF-40 EXTREMELY FINE**—Hair well outlined and detailed.
**AU-50 ABOUT UNCIRCULATED**—Slight trace of wear on shoulder and highest waves of hair.
**MS-60 UNCIRCULATED**—No trace of wear. Light blemishes.
**MS-63 CHOICE UNCIRCULATED**—Some distracting contact marks or blemishes in prime focal areas. Impaired luster possible.

## Small Eagle Reverse (1796)

| | Mintage | AG-3 | G-4 | VG-8 | F-12 | VF-20 | EF-40 | AU-50 | MS-60 | MS-63 |
|---|---|---|---|---|---|---|---|---|---|---|
| 1796 | 6,146 | $4,500. | $11,000. | $13,000. | $25,000. | $32,500. | $37,500. | $45,000. | $67,500. | $90,000. |

## Heraldic Eagle Reverse (1804–1807)

1805, 6 Over 5

| | Mintage | AG-3 | G-4 | VG-8 | F-12 | VF-20 | EF-40 | AU-50 | MS-60 | MS-63 |
|---|---|---|---|---|---|---|---|---|---|---|
| 1804 | .6,738 | $1,250. | $3,000. | $3,750. | $4,750. | $6,250. | $12,500. | $21,500. | $48,000. | $90,000. |
| 1805 | .121,394 | 115. | 225. | 325. | 550. | 950. | 1,800. | 3,250. | 6,500. | 13,500. |
| 1806, All kinds | ..206,124 | | | | | | | | | |
|    1806, 6 Over 5 | ...... | 125. | 250. | 350. | 600. | 1,150. | 2,350. | 3,750. | 7,500. | 20,000. |
|    1806 | .............. | 115. | 225. | 325. | 550. | 950. | 1,800. | 3,250. | 6,500. | 13,500. |
| 1807 | .220,643 | 115. | 225. | 325. | 550. | 950. | 1,800. | 3,250. | 6,500. | 13,500. |

## CAPPED BUST (1815–1838)
### Variety 1 – Large Diameter (1815–1828)

*Designer John Reich; weight 6.74 grams; composition .8924 silver, .1076 copper; approx. diameter 27 mm; reeded edge. All coined at Philadelphia.*

**AG-3 ABOUT GOOD**—Details clear enough to identify.
**G-4 GOOD**—Date, letters, stars legible. Hair under Liberty's headband smooth. Cap lines worn smooth.
**VG-8 VERY GOOD**—Rim well defined. Main details visible. Full LIBERTY on cap. Hair above eye nearly smooth.
**F-12 FINE**—All hair lines visible, but only partial detail visible in drapery. Shoulder clasp distinct.
**VF-20 VERY FINE**—All details visible, but some wear evident. Clasp and ear sharp.
**EF-40 EXTREMELY FINE**—All details distinct. Hair well outlined.
**AU-50 ABOUT UNCIRCULATED**—Slight trace of wear on tips of curls and above the eye, and on the wing and claw tips.
**MS-60 UNCIRCULATED**—No trace of wear. Light blemishes.
**MS-63 CHOICE UNCIRCULATED**—Some distracting contact marks or blemishes in prime focal areas. Impaired luster possible.

                                          1818, 8 Over 5            1823, 3 Over 2

1819, Small 9      1819, Large 9      1820, Small 0      1820, Large 0

1822, 25 Over 50c      1824, 4 Over 2      1825, 5 Over 2 (Wide Date)      1825, 5 Over 3 or 4 (Close Date)

*See next page for chart.*

| | Mintage | AG-3 | G-4 | VG-8 | F-12 | VF-20 | EF-40 | AU-50 | MS-60 | MS-63 |
|---|---|---|---|---|---|---|---|---|---|---|
| 1815 | .89,235 | $35. | $95. | $115. | $155. | $375. | $1,150. | $1,550. | $2,950. | $5,750. |
| 1818, 8 Over 5 | .361,174 | 35. | 85. | 105. | 160. | 385. | 1,150. | 1,550. | 2,950. | 5,500. |
| 1818, Nml Date | * | 35. | 85. | 100. | 150. | 375. | 1,100. | 1,500. | 2,850. | 5,250. |
| 1819, Small 9 | .144,000 | 35. | 85. | 100. | 150. | 375. | 1,100. | 1,500. | 2,850. | 5,250. |
| 1819, Large 9 | * | 35. | 85. | 100. | 150. | 375. | 1,100. | 1,500. | 2,850. | 5,250. |
| 1820, Small 0 | .127,444 | 35. | 85. | 100. | 150. | 375. | 1,100. | 1,500. | 2,850. | 5,250. |
| 1820, Large 0 | * | 35. | 85. | 100. | 150. | 375. | 1,100. | 1,500. | 2,850. | 5,250. |
| 1821 | .216,851 | 35. | 85. | 100. | 150. | 375. | 1,100. | 1,500. | 2,850. | 5,250. |
| 1822 | .604,080 | 35. | 95. | 115. | 160. | 400. | 1,150. | 2,350. | 3,500. | 7,000. |
| 1822, 25 Over 50c | * | 650. | 1,600. | 3,250. | 4,000. | 6,000. | 10,500. | 19,500. | 32,500. | — |
| 1823, 3 Over 2 | .17,800 | 6,500. | 14,500. | 18,500. | 28,500. | 36,500. | 47,500. | 72,500. | — | |
| 1824, 4 Over 2 | .168,000 | 40. | 150. | 225. | 300. | 750. | 2,350. | 4,250. | 8,500. | |
| 1825, 5 Over 2 | * | 40. | 110. | 125. | 165. | 450. | 1,200. | 1,750. | 3,500. | 6,000. |
| 1825, 5 Over 4 | * | 30. | 80. | 110. | 150. | 350. | 1,000. | 1,450. | 2,650. | 5,000. |
| 1827, Orig. (Curl Base 2 in 25c) | 4,000 | | | | | | | | | 175,000. |
| 1827, Restrike (Square Base 2 in 25c) | ..... | | | | | | | | | 75,000. |
| 1828 | .102,000 | 30. | 80. | 100. | 150. | 350. | 1,000. | 1,450. | 2,750. | 6,000. |
| 1828, 25 Over 50c | * | 75. | 135. | 250. | 500. | 1,000. | 1,700. | 3,500. | 8,500. | — |

\* Included in number above.

## Variety 2 – Reduced Diameter (1831–1838)

*Designer William Kneass; weight 6.74 grams; composition .8924 silver, .1076 copper; diameter 24.3 mm; reeded edge. All coined at Philadelphia.*

**G-4 GOOD**—Bust of Liberty well defined. Hair under headband smooth. Date, letters, stars legible. Scant rims.
**VG-8 VERY GOOD**—Details apparent but worn on high spots. Rims strong. Full LIBERTY.
**F-12 FINE**—All hair lines visible. Drapery partly worn. Shoulder clasp distinct.
**VF-20 VERY FINE**—Only top spots worn. Clasp sharp. Ear distinct.
**EF-40 EXTREMELY FINE**—Hair details and clasp bold and clear.
**AU-50 ABOUT UNCIRCULATED**—Slight trace of wear on hair around forehead, on cheek, and at top and bottom tips of eagle's wings and left claw.
**MS-60 UNCIRCULATED**—No trace of wear. Light blemishes.
**MS-63 CHOICE UNCIRCULATED**—Some distracting contact marks or blemishes in prime focal areas. Impaired luster possible.

| Small Letters (1831) | Large Letters | O Over F in OF |
|---|---|---|

| | Mintage | G-4 | VG-8 | F-12 | VF-20 | EF-40 | AU-50 | MS-60 | MS-63 |
|---|---|---|---|---|---|---|---|---|---|
| 1831, Small Letters | .398,000 | $70. | $80. | $95. | $130. | $300. | $675. | $1,000. | $3,250. |
| 1831, Large Letters | * | 70. | 80. | 95. | 130. | 300. | 675. | 1,000. | 3,250. |
| 1832 | .320,000 | 70. | 80. | 95. | 130. | 300. | 675. | 1,000. | 3,250. |
| 1833 | .156,000 | 70 | 80. | 100. | 155. | 375. | 800. | 1,400. | 4,000. |
| 1834 | .286,000 | 70. | 80. | 95. | 130. | 300. | 675. | 1,000. | 3,250. |
| 1834, O Over F in OF | * | 70. | 80. | 100. | 145. | 375. | 750. | 1,200. | 3,750. |
| 1835 | .1,952,000 | 70. | 80. | 95. | 130. | 300. | 675. | 1,000. | 3,250. |
| 1836 | .472,000 | 70. | 80. | 95. | 130. | 300. | 675. | 1,000. | 3,750. |
| 1837 | .252,400 | 70. | 80. | 95. | 130. | 300. | 675. | 1,000. | 3,500. |
| 1838 | .366,000 | 70. | 80. | 95. | 130. | 300. | 675. | 1,000. | 3,250. |

\* Included in number above.

# LIBERTY SEATED (1838-1891)

*Designer Christian Gobrecht.*

**G-4 GOOD**—Scant rim. LIBERTY on shield worn off. Date and letters legible.
**VG-8 VERY GOOD**—Rim fairly defined, at least three letters in LIBERTY evident.
**F-12 FINE**—LIBERTY complete, but partly weak.
**VF-20 VERY FINE**—LIBERTY strong.
**EF-40 EXTREMELY FINE**—Complete LIBERTY and edges of scroll. Clasp clear.
**AU-50 ABOUT UNCIRCULATED**—Slight wear on Liberty's knees and breast and on eagle's neck, wing tips, and claws.
**MS-60 UNCIRCULATED**—No trace of wear. Light blemishes.
**MS-63 CHOICE UNCIRCULATED**—Some distracting contact marks or blemishes in prime focal areas. Impaired luster possible.

## Variety 1 – No Motto Above Eagle (1838-1853)

*Weight 6.68 grams; composition .900 silver, .100 copper; diameter 24.3 mm; reeded edge; mints: Philadelphia, New Orleans.*

**No Drapery from Elbow**      **Drapery from Elbow**
*Mintmark location is on reverse, below eagle.*

**Small Date**      **Large Date**

| | Mintage | G-4 | VG-8 | F-12 | VF-20 | EF-40 | AU-50 | MS-60 | MS-63 |
|---|---|---|---|---|---|---|---|---|---|
| 1838, No Drapery | 466,000 | $25 | $37. | $55. | $95. | $325. | $550. | $1,200. | $4,000. |
| 1839, No Drapery | 491,146 | 25 | 37. | 55. | 95. | 325. | 550. | 1,200. | 4,000. |
| 1840O, No Drapery | 382,200 | 33. | 38. | 65. | 115. | 375. | 550. | 1,300. | 4,500. |
| 1840, Drapery | 188,127 | 22. | 30. | 50. | 90. | 175. | 265. | 900. | 3,000. |
| 1840O, Drapery | 43,000 | 28. | 38. | 70. | 105. | 225. | 425. | 1,150. | 2,750. |
| 1841 | 120,000 | 45. | 70. | 100. | 150. | 250. | 325. | 900. | 2,000. |
| 1841O | 452,000 | 25. | 30. | 45. | 80. | 165. | 300. | 750. | 1,500. |
| 1842, Small Date (Pf only) | | | | | | | | | 50,000. |
| 1842, Large Date | 88,000 | 75. | 100. | 160. | 250. | 350. | 650. | 1,750. | 3,250. |
| 1842O, All kinds | 769,000 | | | | | | | | |
|   1842O, Small Date | | 375. | 500. | 950. | 1,600. | 3,200. | 7,000. | — | |
|   1842O, Large Date | | 25. | 30. | 45. | 70. | 150. | 325. | 1,500. | 4,250. |
| 1843 | 645,600 | 19. | 24. | 35. | 45. | 85. | 150. | 475. | 900. |
| 1843O | 968,000 | 26. | 35. | 55. | 115. | 235. | 675. | 2,500. | 5,500. |
| 1844 | 421,200 | 20. | 25. | 35. | 45. | 85. | 150. | 475. | 900. |
| 1844O | 740,000 | 25. | 30. | 45. | 85. | 200. | 300. | 1,150. | 3,000. |
| 1845 | 922,000 | 20. | 25. | 35. | 45. | 80. | 150. | 550. | 1,000. |
| 1846 | 510,000 | 20. | 25. | 35. | 45. | 80. | 150. | 550. | 1,000. |
| 1847 | 734,000 | 20. | 25. | 35. | 45. | 80. | 150. | 550. | 1,000. |
| 1847O | 368,000 | 35. | 45. | 65. | 135. | 250. | 650. | 2,000. | 5,750. |
| 1848 | 146,000 | 25. | 38. | 75. | 100. | 175. | 300. | 1,100. | 2,800. |
| 1849 | 340,000 | 20. | 25. | 45. | 75. | 150. | 250. | 800. | 1,500. |
| 1849O **(a)** | | 375. | 550. | 850. | 1,650. | 3,200. | 5,500. | — | |
| 1850 | 190,800 | 25. | 45. | 65. | 95. | 175. | 225. | 800. | 1,850. |
| 1850O | 412,000 | 25. | 45. | 65. | 95. | 175. | 475. | 1,400. | 2,700. |

**a.** Mintage for 1849-O included with 1850-O.

*Chart continued on next page.*

| | Mintage | G-4 | VG-8 | F-12 | VF-20 | EF-40 | AU-50 | MS-60 | MS-63 |
|---|---|---|---|---|---|---|---|---|---|
| 1851 | 160,000 | $35. | $55. | $90. | $125. | $200. | $275. | $850. | $1,750. |
| 1851O | 88,000 | 150. | 250. | 400. | 650. | 1,250. | 2,850. | 6,500. | |
| 1852 | 177,060 | 45. | 60. | 95. | 135. | 225. | 300. | 675. | 1,000. |
| 1852O | 96,000 | 175. | 250. | 400. | 675. | 1,500. | 3,500. | 7,500. | 17,500. |
| 1853, Recut Dt, No Arrows or Rays **(b)** | 44,200 | 275. | 350. | 525. | 700. | 1,200. | 1,750. | 2,750. | 4,000. |

**b.** Beware of altered 1858, or removed arrows and rays.

## Variety 2 – Arrows at Date, Rays Around Eagle (1853)

The reduction in weight is indicated by the arrows at the date. Rays were added on the reverse side in the field around the eagle. The arrows were retained through 1855, but the rays were omitted after 1853.

*Weight 6.22 grams; composition .900 silver, .100 copper; diameter 24.3 mm; reeded edge; mints: Philadelphia, New Orleans, San Francisco, Carson City.*

1853, 3 Over 4    1854-O, Huge O

| | Mintage | G-4 | VG-8 | F-12 | VF-20 | EF-40 | AU-50 | MS-60 | MS-63 |
|---|---|---|---|---|---|---|---|---|---|
| 1853 | 15,210,020 | $20. | $25. | $35. | $55. | $150. | $300. | $950. | $2,150. |
| 1853, 3 Over 4 | * | 40. | 75. | 100. | 225. | 350. | 650. | 1,950. | 5,500. |
| 1853O | 1,332,000 | 20. | 25. | 40. | 75. | 250. | 1,000. | 2,750. | 8,000. |

* Included in number above.

## Variety 3 – Arrows at Date, No Rays (1854–1855)

| | Mintage | G-4 | VG-8 | F-12 | VF-20 | EF-40 | AU-50 | MS-60 | MS-63 |
|---|---|---|---|---|---|---|---|---|---|
| 1854 | 12,380,000 | $20. | $25. | $35. | $45. | $85. | $225. | $500. | $1,300. |
| 1854O | 1,484,000 | 20. | 25. | 40. | 55. | 115. | 250. | 800. | 1,800. |
| 1854O, Huge O | * | 900. | 1,350. | 2,650. | 4,500. | 8,000. | 12,500. | 17,500. | 23,500. |
| 1855 | 2,857,000 | 20. | 25. | 35. | 45. | 85. | 225. | 575. | 1,300. |
| 1855O | 176,000 | 45 | 60. | 100. | 250. | 375. | 850. | 2,750. | 7,500. |
| 1855S | 396,400 | 45. | 60. | 85. | 150. | 350. | 700. | 1,850. | 6,000. |

* Included in number above.

## Variety 1 Resumed (1856–1865; Weight Standard of 1853)

| | Mintage | G-4 | VG-8 | F-12 | VF-20 | EF-40 | AU-50 | MS-60 | MS-63 | PF-63 |
|---|---|---|---|---|---|---|---|---|---|---|
| 1856 | 7,264,000 | $20. | $25. | $35. | $45. | $75. | $150. | $325. | $600. | $5,000. |
| 1856O | 968,000 | 20. | 25. | 40. | 50. | 85. | 250. | 1,100. | 2,000. | |
| 1856S, All kinds | 286,000 | | | | | | | | | |
| 1856S | | 40. | 55. | 90. | 185. | 375. | 750. | 2,250. | 8,000. | |
| 1856S, S Over Small S | | 45. | 75. | 130. | 275. | 600. | 900. | 2,500. | — | |
| 1857 | 9,644,000 | 20. | 25. | 35. | 45. | 75. | 150. | 325. | 600. | 3,750. |
| 1857O | 1,180,000 | 20. | 25. | 35. | 45. | 95. | 250. | 1,000. | 2,500. | |
| 1857S | 82,000 | 60. | 100. | 200. | 350. | 600. | 950. | 2,500. | 6,500. | |
| 1858 *(300)* | 7,368,000 | 20. | 25. | 35. | 45. | 75. | 150. | 325. | 600. | 2,500. |
| 1858O | 520,000 | 20. | 25. | 35. | 65. | 125. | 350. | 1,400. | 5,000. | |
| 1858S | 121,000 | 50. | 75. | 145. | 275. | 525. | 1,250. | 7,500. | — | |

| | Mintage | G-4 | VG-8 | F-12 | VF-20 | EF-40 | AU-50 | MS-60 | MS-63 | PF-63 |
|---|---|---|---|---|---|---|---|---|---|---|
| 1859 . .(800) | 1,343,200 | $20. | $25. | $35. | $45. | $80. | $150. | $350. | $900. | $1,300. |
| 1859O . . . . . . . | 260,000 | 20. | 28. | 50. | 65. | 120. | 375. | 1,200. | 3,500. | |
| 1859S . . . . . . . . | 80,000 | 100. | 135. | 225. | 350. | 1,250. | 7,500. | — | — | |
| 1860 (1,000) . . . | 804,400 | 22. | 28. | 35. | 45. | 80. | 150. | 400. | 700. | 1,150. |
| 1860O . . . . . . . | 388,000 | 22. | 25. | 40. | 50. | 95. | 350. | 1,000. | 1,950. | |
| 1860S . . . . . . . . | 56,000 | 175. | 250. | 450. | 850. | 2,750. | 6,750. | — | — | |
| 1861 (1,000) | 4,853,600 | 17. | 28. | 35. | 45. | 80. | 150. | 400. | 825. | 1,100. |
| 1861S . . . . . . . . | 96,000 | 60. | 90. | 200. | 375. | 950. | 4,500. | — | — | |
| 1862 . .(550) . . . | 932,000 | 17. | 28. | 35. | 45. | 80. | 150. | 400. | 825. | 1,100. |
| 1862S . . . . . . . . | 67,000 | 55. | 70. | 135. | 235. | 550. | 900. | 2,500. | 7,500. | |
| 1863 . .(460) . . . | 191,600 | 35. | 45. | 75. | 125. | 175. | 300. | 625. | 950. | 1,100. |
| 1864 . .(470) . . . . | 93,600 | 75. | 85. | 115. | 155. | 250. | 400. | 625. | 1,300. | 1,100. |
| 1864S . . . . . . . . | 20,000 | 275. | 400. | 650. | 900. | 1,900. | 3,500. | — | — | |
| 1865 . .(500) . . . . | 58,800 | 75. | 85. | 125. | 175. | 250. | 350. | 700. | 1,200. | 1,100. |
| 1865S . . . . . . . . | 41,000 | 85. | 115. | 150. | 375. | 650. | 1,000. | 2,350. | 3,750. | |
| 1866 *(unique)* . . . . . . . . | | | | | | | | | | — |

*Note:* The 1866 Proof quarter, half, and dollar without motto are not mentioned in the Mint director's report, and were not issued for circulation.

## Variety 4 – Motto Above Eagle (1866–1873)

The motto IN GOD WE TRUST was added to the reverse side in 1866. As with the half dollar and silver dollar, the motto has been retained since that time.

| | Mintage | G-4 | VG-8 | F-12 | VF-20 | EF-40 | AU-50 | MS-60 | MS-63 | PF-63 |
|---|---|---|---|---|---|---|---|---|---|---|
| 1866 . . .(725) . . . | 16,800 | $325. | $475. | $550. | $800. | $1,250. | $1,450. | $1,850. | $2,500. | $900. |
| 1866S . . . . . . . . . | 28,000 | 185. | 285. | 525. | 900. | 1,350. | 2,000. | 3,500. | 5,000. | |
| 1867 . . .(625) . . . | 20,000 | 200. | 275. | 400. | 600. | 725. | 825. | 1,200. | 2,500. | 900. |
| 1867S . . . . . . . . . | 48,000 | 175. | 275. | 425. | 600. | 750. | 1,000. | 3,500. | — | |
| 1868 . .(600) . . . | 29,400 | 115. | 150. | 200. | 275. | 375. | 500. | 850. | 1,500. | 900. |
| 1868S . . . . . . . . . | 96,000 | 75. | 100. | 145. | 275. | 650. | 850. | 2,600. | 4,500. | |
| 1869 . . .(600) . . . | 16,000 | 250. | 300. | 400. | 550. | 700. | 900. | 1,400. | 2,500. | 900. |
| 1869S . . . . . . . . . | 76,000 | 80. | 120. | 185. | 300. | 600. | 1,150. | 2,400. | 4,250. | |
| 1870 . .(1,000) . . . | 86,400 | 50. | 60. | 105. | 160. | 275. | 400. | 800. | 1,200. | 900. |
| 1870CC . . . . . . . . . . | 8,340 | 2,500. | 4,000. | 7,500. | 13,500. | 22,500. | 35,000. | 55,000. | — | |
| 1871 . . .(960) . . | 118,200 | 30. | 40. | 60. | 115. | 150. | 300. | 550. | 900. | 800. |
| 1871CC . . . . . . . . . | 10,890 | 1,750. | 3,500. | 5,500. | 13,500. | 22,500. | 32,500. | — | — | |
| 1871S . . . . . . . . . | 30,900 | 250. | 350. | 475. | 675. | 1,000. | 1,850. | 3,000. | 4,250. | |
| 1872 . . .(950) . . | 182,000 | 30. | 40. | 60. | 115. | 155. | 225. | 600. | 1,650. | 800. |
| 1872CC . . . . . . . . . | 22,850 | 550. | 800. | 1,500. | 2,500. | 5,500. | 9,000. | 22,500. | | |
| 1872S . . . . . . . . . | 83,000 | 650. | 950. | 1,300. | 1,600. | 2,500. | 4,000. | 6,750. | | |
| 1873, | | | | | | | | | | |
|    Cl 3 (600) . . . | 40,000 | 100. | 200. | 300. | 450. | 675. | 1,250. | 2,500. | 3,500. | 800. |
| 1873, Open 3 . . . | 172,000 | 30. | 45. | 65. | 90. | 150. | 215. | 450. | 900. | |
| 1873CC *(5 known)* | 4,000 | | | — | — | — | 350,000. | | | |

## Variety 5 – Arrows at Date (1873–1874)

Arrows were placed at the date in the years 1873 and 1874 to denote the change of weight from 6.22 to 6.25 grams.

*Weight 6.25 grams; composition .900 silver, .100 copper; diameter 24.3 mm; reeded edge; mints: Philadelphia, San Francisco, Carson City, New Orleans.*

| | Mintage | G-4 | VG-8 | F-12 | VF-20 | EF-40 | AU-50 | MS-60 | MS-63 | PF-63 |
|---|---|---|---|---|---|---|---|---|---|---|
| 1873 . .(540) | 1,271,160 | $20. | $25. | $40. | $60. | $200. | $400. | $800. | $1,500. | $1,500. |
| 1873CC . . . . . . . . | 12,462 | 1,500. | 2,400. | 4,800. | 8,000. | 20,000. | 30,000. | 47,500. | 75,000. | |
| 1873S . . . . . . . | 156,000 | 35. | 40. | 65. | 115. | 250. | 500. | 1,100. | 2,250. | |
| 1874 . .(700) . . . | 471,200 | 20. | 25. | 40. | 65. | 200. | 450. | 900. | 1,600. | 1,500. |
| 1874S . . . . . . . . | 392,000 | 25. | 35. | 65. | 115. | 265. | 485. | 900. | 1,600. | |

## Variety 4 Resumed (1875–1891)

**1877-S, S Over Horizontal S**

| | Mintage | G-4 | VG-8 | F-12 | VF-20 | EF-40 | AU-50 | MS-60 | MS-63 | PF-63 |
|---|---|---|---|---|---|---|---|---|---|---|
| 1875 . .(700). . | 4,292,800 | $20. | $28. | $35. | $45. | $65. | $150. | $250. | $500. | $650. |
| 1875CC . . . . . . . | 140,000 | 75. | 115. | 175. | 300. | 525. | 700. | 1,700. | 2,500. | |
| 1875S . . . . . . . . | 680,000 | 35. | 45. | 70. | 115. | 200. | 275. | 600. | 1,150. | |
| 1876 (1,150) | 17,816,000 | 20. | 28. | 35. | 45. | 65. | 150. | 250. | 500. | 650. |
| 1876CC . . . . . . | 4,944,000 | 40. | 45. | 55. | 70. | 115. | 200. | 450. | 950. | |
| 1876S . . . . . . . | 8,596,000 | 20. | 28. | 35. | 45. | 65. | 150. | 250. | 500. | |
| 1877 . .(510) | 10,911,200 | 20. | 28. | 35. | 45. | 65. | 150. | 250. | 500. | 650. |
| 1877CC **(a)** . . . | 4,192,000 | 35. | 45. | 55. | 70. | 115. | 200. | 450. | 800. | |
| 1877S . . . . . . . | 8,996,000 | 20. | 28. | 35. | 45. | 65. | 150. | 250. | 500. | |
| 1877S, S/Horiz S . . . . . * | — | — | 85. | 150. | 250. | 400. | 800. | 1,850. | |
| 1878 . .(800). . | 2,260,000 | 20. | 28. | 35. | 45. | 65. | 150. | 250. | 500. | 650. |
| 1878CC . . . . . . . | 996,000 | 40. | 55. | 70. | 115. | 150. | 225. | 600. | 1,000. | |
| 1878S . . . . . . . . | 140,000 | 125. | 185. | 275. | 350. | 600. | 750. | 1,350. | 2,750. | |
| 1879 *(1,100)* . . . . | 13,600 | 120. | 140. | 200. | 250. | 325. | 400. | 575. | 800. | 650. |
| 1880 (1,355) . . . . | 13,600 | 120. | 140. | 200. | 250. | 325. | 400. | 575. | 800. | 650. |
| 1881 . .(975) . . . . | 12,000 | 150. | 175. | 235. | 300. | 375. | 475. | 625. | 850. | 650. |
| 1882 (1,100) . . . . | 15,200 | 130. | 160. | 210. | 265. | 325. | 400. | 600. | 800. | 650. |
| 1883 (1,039) . . . . | 14,400 | 130. | 160. | 210. | 265. | 325. | 400. | 600. | 800. | 650. |
| 1884 . .(875) . . . . . | 8,000 | 225. | 275. | 325. | 425. | 550. | 600. | 800. | 1,100. | 650. |
| 1885 . .(930) . . . . | 13,600 | 135. | 150. | 225. | 275. | 325. | 400. | 600. | 950. | 650. |
| 1886 . .(886) . . . . . | 5,000 | 300. | 375. | 475. | 575. | 675. | 750. | 900. | 1,250. | 750. |
| 1887 . .(710) . . . . | 10,000 | 225. | 250. | 325. | 385. | 475. | 525. | 750. | 1,100. | 650. |

* Included in number above. **a.** Variety with fine edge-reeding is scarcer than that with normally spaced reeding.

| | Mintage | G-4 | VG-8 | F-12 | VF-20 | EF-40 | AU-50 | MS-60 | MS-63 | PF-63 |
|---|---|---|---|---|---|---|---|---|---|---|
| 1888.. (832) .... | 10,001 | $200. | $245. | $325. | $425. | $500. | $650. | $700. | $1,000. | $650. |
| 1888S ....... | 1,216,000 | 25. | 30. | 35. | 45. | 70. | 150. | 275. | 850. | |
| 1889.. (711) .... | 12,000 | 150. | 175. | 225. | 275. | 325. | 450. | 650. | 850. | 700. |
| 1890.. (590) .... | 80,000 | 60. | 75. | 100. | 125. | 175. | 300. | 525. | 775. | 650. |
| 1891.. (600).. | 3,920,000 | 22. | 30. | 35. | 45. | 65. | 150. | 250. | 500. | 650. |
| 18910 .......... | 6,800 | 135. | 175. | 300. | 475. | 800. | 1,000. | 2,500. | 5,500. | |
| 1891S ....... | 2,216,000 | 22. | 30. | 35. | 45. | 70. | 150. | 250. | 500. | |

# BARBER OR LIBERTY HEAD (1892–1916)

Like other silver coins of this type, the quarter dollars minted from 1892 to 1916 were designed by Charles E. Barber. His initial B is found at the truncation of the neck of Liberty. There are two varieties of the 1892 reverse: (1) the eagle's wing covers only half of E in UNITED; (2) the eagle's wing covers most of E. Coins of the first variety reverse are somewhat scarcer than those of the second variety.

*Designer Charles E. Barber; weight 6.25 grams; composition .900 silver, .100 copper (net weight: .18084 oz. pure silver); diameter 24.3 mm; reeded edge; mints: Philadelphia, Denver, New Orleans, San Francisco.*

**G-4 GOOD**—Date and legends legible. LIBERTY worn off headband.
**VG-8 VERY GOOD**—Some letters in LIBERTY legible.
**F-12 FINE**—LIBERTY completely legible but not sharp.
**VF-20 VERY FINE**—All letters in LIBERTY evenly plain.
**EF-40 EXTREMELY FINE**—LIBERTY bold, and its ribbon distinct.
**AU-50 ABOUT UNCIRCULATED**—Slight trace of wear above forehead, on cheek, and on eagle's head, wings, and tail.
**MS-60 UNCIRCULATED**—No trace of wear. Light blemishes.
**MS-63 CHOICE UNCIRCULATED**—Some distracting contact marks or blemishes in prime focal areas. Impaired luster possible.
**PF-63 CHOICE PROOF**—Reflective surfaces with only a few blemishes in secondary focal places. No major flaws.

*Mintmark location is on reverse, below eagle.*

| | Mintage | G-4 | VG-8 | F-12 | VF-20 | EF-40 | AU-50 | MS-60 | MS-63 | PF-63 |
|---|---|---|---|---|---|---|---|---|---|---|
| 1892 (1,245).. | 8,236,000 | $6. | $9. | $24. | $45. | $75. | $125. | $200. | $325. | $650. |
| 18920 ....... | 2,460,000 | 12. | 18. | 35. | 50. | 95. | 150. | 300. | 450. | |
| 1892S ........ | 964,079 | 28. | 45. | 80. | 115. | 175. | 300. | 450. | 850. | |
| 1893.. (792).. | 5,444,023 | 7. | 9. | 27. | 35. | 75. | 125. | 200. | 375. | 650. |
| 18930 ....... | 3,396,000 | 8. | 12. | 30. | 55. | 95. | 155. | 275. | 500. | |
| 1893S ....... | 1,454,535 | 16. | 35. | 60. | 105. | 155. | 275. | 450. | 1,100. | |
| 1894.. (972).. | 3,432,000 | 6. | 9. | 35. | 45. | 85. | 150. | 230. | 475. | 650. |
| 18940 ....... | 2,852,000 | 9. | 15. | 45. | 70. | 115. | 215. | 325. | 700. | |
| 1894S ....... | 2,648,821 | 8. | 12. | 35. | 55. | 105. | 200. | 325. | 700. | |
| 1895.. (880).. | 4,440,000 | 6. | 9. | 30. | 45. | 80. | 135. | 225. | 500. | 650. |
| 18950 ....... | 2,816,000 | 10. | 17. | 45. | 70. | 125. | 200. | 350. | 900. | |
| 1895S ....... | 1,764,681 | 18. | 25. | 60. | 95. | 135. | 250. | 375. | 900. | |
| 1896.. (762).. | 3,874,000 | 6. | 8. | 25. | 40. | 80. | 135. | 225. | 450. | 650. |
| 18960 ....... | 1,484,000 | 25. | 45. | 115. | 235. | 375. | 650. | 850. | 1,800. | |
| 1896S ........ | 188,039 | 675. | 1,100. | 1,750. | 2,750. | 4,250. | 5,250. | 7,500. | 15,000. | |
| 1897.. (731).. | 8,140,000 | 6. | 8. | 22. | 35. | 70. | 105. | 200. | 325. | 650. |
| 18970 ....... | 1,414,800 | 16. | 35. | 115. | 225. | 350. | 550. | 775. | 1,500. | |

*Chart continued on next page.*

| | Mintage | G-4 | VG-8 | F-12 | VF-20 | EF-40 | AU-50 | MS-60 | MS-63 | PF-63 |
|---|---|---|---|---|---|---|---|---|---|---|
| 1897S | 542,229 | $40. | $70. | $200. | $250. | $400. | $600. | $900. | $1,600. | |
| 1898 ..(735) | 11,100,000 | 6. | 8. | 22. | 35. | 70. | 125. | 200. | 325. | $650. |
| 1898O | 1,868,000 | 12. | 25. | 65. | 135. | 255. | 385. | 600. | 1,500. | |
| 1898S | 1,020,592 | 10. | 18. | 45. | 60. | 90. | 200. | 375. | 1,200. | |
| 1899 ..(846) | 12,624,000 | 6. | 8. | 21. | 32. | 75. | 125. | 200. | 325. | 650. |
| 1899O | 2,644,000 | 10. | 17. | 35. | 60. | 115. | 250. | 375. | 750. | |
| 1899S | 708,000 | 15. | 28. | 65. | 85. | 130. | 245. | 385. | 1,050. | |
| 1900 ..(912) | 10,016,000 | 6. | 8. | 22. | 35. | 70. | 135. | 185. | 350. | 650. |
| 1900O | 3,416,000 | 10. | 24. | 65. | 95. | 140. | 300. | 550. | 800. | |
| 1900S | 1,858,585 | 8. | 15. | 35. | 55. | 80. | 130. | 350. | 900. | |
| 1901 ..(813) | 8,892,000 | 10. | 13. | 23. | 40. | 80. | 135. | 190. | 325. | 650. |
| 1901O | 1,612,000 | 40. | 60. | 125. | 245. | 400. | 600. | 850. | 1,850. | |
| 1901S | 72,664 | 5,500. | 11,000. | 16,000. | 17,500. | 22,500. | 24,500. | 32,500. | 42,500. | |
| 1902 ..(777) | 12,196,967 | 7. | 8. | 18. | 32. | 65. | 115. | 200. | 325. | 650. |
| 1902O | 4,748,000 | 9. | 15. | 45. | 85. | 135. | 215. | 450. | 1,400. | |
| 1902S | 1,524,612 | 12. | 20. | 55. | 80. | 150. | 235. | 475. | 1,000. | |
| 1903 ..(755) | 9,759,309 | 7. | 8. | 20. | 35. | 60. | 115. | 200. | 475. | 650. |
| 1903O | 3,500,000 | 8. | 11. | 40. | 58. | 115. | 250. | 400. | 1,300. | |
| 1903S | 1,036,000 | 15. | 22. | 40. | 80. | 135. | 250. | 425. | 850. | |
| 1904 ..(670) | 9,588,143 | 8. | 9. | 20. | 35. | 70. | 115. | 205. | 325. | 650. |
| 1904O | 2,456,000 | 10. | 18. | 60. | 95. | 225. | 400. | 800. | 1,350. | |
| 1905 ..(727) | 4,967,523 | 10. | 12. | 25. | 38. | 70. | 115. | 215. | 350. | 650. |
| 1905O | 1,230,000 | 15. | 30. | 80. | 150. | 240. | 350. | 475. | 1,250. | |
| 1905S | 1,884,000 | 9. | 15. | 45. | 60. | 105. | 200. | 350. | 1,000. | |
| 1906 ..(675) | 3,655,760 | 7. | 8. | 17. | 35. | 70. | 115. | 200. | 315. | 650. |
| 1906D | 3,280,000 | 7. | 8. | 25. | 40. | 70. | 145. | 225. | 450. | |
| 1906O | 2,056,000 | 7. | 9. | 40. | 60. | 95. | 175. | 265. | 550. | |
| 1907 ..(575) | 7,132,000 | 6. | 8. | 17. | 32. | 60. | 105. | 200. | 315. | 650. |
| 1907D | 2,484,000 | 6. | 8. | 25. | 48. | 70. | 175. | 235. | 750. | |
| 1907O | 4,560,000 | 6. | 9. | 18. | 38. | 70. | 135. | 225. | 475. | |
| 1907S | 1,360,000 | 10. | 18. | 45. | 70. | 135. | 245. | 450. | 900. | |
| 1908 ..(545) | 4,232,000 | 6. | 8. | 20. | 35. | 70. | 115. | 185. | 315. | 650. |
| 1908D | 5,788,000 | 6. | 8. | 20. | 35. | 70. | 115. | 225. | 400. | |
| 1908O | 6,244,000 | 6. | 9. | 18. | 35. | 65. | 115. | 185. | 325. | |
| 1908S | 784,000 | 18. | 38. | 85. | 155. | 285. | 465. | 750. | 1,250. | |
| 1909 ..(650) | 9,268,000 | 6. | 7. | 18. | 35. | 65. | 110. | 190. | 325. | 650. |
| 1909D | 5,114,000 | 7. | 8. | 20. | 40. | 85. | 150. | 185. | 325. | |
| 1909O | 712,000 | 15. | 35. | 80. | 165. | 300. | 450. | 800. | 1,500. | |
| 1909S | 1,348,000 | 8. | 10. | 35. | 55. | 90. | 185. | 285. | 750. | |
| 1910 ..(551) | 2,244,000 | 8. | 10. | 30. | 45. | 80. | 135. | 200. | 325. | 650. |
| 1910D | 1,500,000 | 8. | 11. | 45. | 70. | 125. | 235. | 350. | 950. | |
| 1911 ..(543) | 3,720,000 | 6. | 8. | 18. | 35. | 70. | 125. | 200. | 325. | 650. |
| 1911D | 933,600 | 8. | 18. | 90. | 200. | 300. | 475. | 675. | 1,250. | |
| 1911S | 988,000 | 7. | 9. | 45. | 75. | 155. | 275. | 350. | 750. | |
| 1912 ..(700) | 4,400,000 | 6. | 8. | 15. | 35. | 70. | 115. | 185. | 325. | 650. |
| 1912S | 708,000 | 8. | 10. | 45. | 70. | 115. | 215. | 350. | 900. | |
| 1913 ..(613) | 484,000 | 14. | 22. | 70. | 160. | 375. | 475. | 900. | 1,150. | 750. |
| 1913D | 1,450,800 | 11. | 13. | 35. | 60. | 85. | 175. | 275. | 425. | |
| 1913S | 40,000 | 1,000. | 1,750. | 3,750. | 5,500. | 6,750. | 7,250. | 8,500. | 11,000. | |
| 1914 ..(380) | 6,244,230 | 6. | 7. | 18. | 34. | 65. | 115. | 195. | 325. | 750. |
| 1914D | 3,046,000 | 6. | 7. | 18. | 34. | 65. | 115. | 195. | 325. | |
| 1914S | 264,000 | 70. | 95. | 185. | 275. | 450. | 625. | 800. | 1,350. | |
| 1915 ..(450) | 3,480,000 | 6. | 7. | 18. | 34. | 65. | 115. | 195. | 325. | 750. |
| 1915D | 3,694,000 | 6. | 7. | 18. | 32. | 70. | 115. | 195. | 325. | |
| 1915S | 704,000 | 9. | 13. | 38. | 55. | 115. | 195. | 285. | 415. | |
| 1916 | 1,788,000 | 6. | 7. | 18. | 32. | 70. | 115. | 195. | 325. | |
| 1916D | 6,540,800 | 6. | 7. | 18. | 32. | 70. | 115. | 195. | 325. | |

# STANDING LIBERTY (1916–1930)

This type quarter was designed by Hermon A. MacNeil. The left arm of Liberty is upraised, uncovering a shield in the attitude of protection. Her right hand bears the olive branch of peace. MacNeil's initial M is located above and to the right of the date.

There was a modification in 1917 to cover Liberty's exposed breast. The reverse has a new arrangement of the stars, and the eagle is higher.

In 1925 a depression was made in the pedestal on which Liberty stands and that bears the date. On the earlier issues the dates wore off easily because they were too high and were not protected by other features of the coin. The new "recessed" dates proved more durable as a result of this change.

No Proof coins of this type were officially issued, but specimen strikings of the first variety, dated 1917, are known to exist.

*Designer Hermon A. MacNeil; standards same as for previous issue; mints: Philadelphia, Denver, San Francisco.*

**G-4 GOOD**—Date and lettering legible. Top of date worn. Liberty's right leg and toes worn off. Much wear evident on left leg and drapery lines.

**VG-8 VERY GOOD**—Distinct date. Toes faintly visible. Drapery lines visible above Liberty's left leg.

**F-12 FINE**—High curve of right leg flat from thigh to ankle. Only slight wear evident on left leg. Drapery lines over right thigh seen only at sides of leg.

**VF-20 VERY FINE**—Garment line across right leg worn, but visible at sides.

**EF-40 EXTREMELY FINE**—Flattened only at high spots. Liberty's toes are sharp. Drapery lines across right leg evident.

**AU-50 ABOUT UNCIRCULATED**—Slight trace of wear on head, kneecap, shield's center, and highest point on eagle's body.

**MS-60 UNCIRCULATED**—No trace of wear, but contact marks, surface spots, or faded luster possible.

**MS-63 CHOICE UNCIRCULATED**—No trace of wear. Light blemishes. Attractive mint luster.

*Some modifications must be made for grading variety 2.*

## Variety 1 – No Stars Below Eagle (1916–1917)

*Mintmark location is on obverse, to left of date.*

*Uncirculated pieces with fully struck head of Liberty are worth more than double the prices listed below.*

| | Mintage | G-4 | VG-8 | F-12 | VF-20 | EF-40 | AU-50 | MS-60 | MS-63 |
|---|---|---|---|---|---|---|---|---|---|
| 1916 . . . . . . . . . . . . . .52,000 | | $3,000. | $5,500. | $8,500. | $11,000. | $12,000. | $13,500. | $16,000. | $20,000. |
| 1917, Variety 1 . . . .8,740,000 | | 23. | 35 | 50. | 75. | 90. | 165. | 225. | 300. |
| 1917D, Variety 1 . . .1,509,200 | | 25. | 35. | 50. | 80. | 120. | 175. | 225. | 350. |
| 1917S, Variety 1 . . .1,952,000 | | 30. | 40. | 50. | 85. | 155. | 200. | 300. | 400. |

## Variety 2 – Stars Below Eagle (1917–1930)
### *Pedestal Date (1917–1924)*

**1918-S, 8 Over 7**

*See next page for chart.*

| | Mintage | G-4 | VG-8 | F-12 | VF-20 | EF-40 | AU-50 | MS-60 | MS-63 |
|---|---|---|---|---|---|---|---|---|---|
| 1917, Variety 2 | 13,880,000 | $20. | $25. | $35. | $40. | $60. | $90. | $140. | $225. |
| 1917D, Variety 2 | 6,224,400 | 40. | 45. | 65. | 75. | 100. | 140. | 200. | 300. |
| 1917S, Variety 2 | 5,552,000 | 40. | 50. | 70. | 75. | 95. | 135. | 200. | 300. |
| 1918 | 14,240,000 | 15. | 18. | 30. | 35. | 50. | 90. | 135. | 225. |
| 1918D | 7,380,000 | 25. | 30. | 50. | 70. | 100. | 155. | 215. | 275. |
| 1918S, Normal Date | 11,072,000 | 18. | 22. | 35. | 40. | 50. | 100. | 185. | 300. |
| 1918S, 8 Over 7 | * | 1,500. | 2,000. | 3,500. | 4,500. | 7,500. | 13,000. | 18,000. | 30,000. |
| 1919 | 11,324,000 | 35. | 45. | 60. | 65. | 75. | 110. | 155. | 215. |
| 1919D | 1,944,000 | 80. | 110. | 175. | 290. | 475. | 600. | 700. | 1,400. |
| 1919S | 1,836,000 | 75. | 100. | 175. | 285. | 500. | 600. | 725. | 1,600. |
| 1920 | 27,860,000 | 15. | 20. | 30. | 35. | 45. | 85. | 150. | 225. |
| 1920D | 3,586,400 | 50. | 60. | 80. | 110. | 135. | 190. | 250. | 750. |
| 1920S | 6,380,000 | 20. | 25. | 35. | 45. | 60. | 105. | 225. | 750. |
| 1921 | 1,916,000 | 160. | 200. | 325. | 475. | 550. | 675. | 850. | 1,350. |
| 1923 | 9,716,000 | 15. | 20. | 30. | 38. | 50. | 85. | 145. | 235. |
| 1923S | 1,360,000 | 250. | 350. | 500. | 600. | 800. | 950. | 1,350. | 1,750. |
| 1924 | 10,920,000 | 17. | 20. | 25. | 35. | 40. | 90. | 135. | 225. |
| 1924D | 3,112,000 | 55. | 70. | 100. | 125. | 175. | 200. | 250. | 325. |
| 1924S | 2,860,000 | 26. | 33. | 40. | 50. | 100. | 200. | 275. | 950. |

* Included in number above.

## Recessed Date (1925–1930)

| | Mintage | G-4 | VG-8 | F-12 | VF-20 | EF-40 | AU-50 | MS-60 | MS-63 |
|---|---|---|---|---|---|---|---|---|---|
| 1925 | 12,280,000 | $3. | $5. | $7. | $15. | $40. | $80. | $130. | $235. |
| 1926 | 11,316,000 | 3. | 5. | 7. | 15. | 40. | 80. | 130. | 235. |
| 1926D | 1,716,000 | 7. | 10. | 18. | 35. | 60. | 100. | 150. | 235. |
| 1926S | 2,700,000 | 4. | 6. | 12. | 25. | 105. | 225. | 350. | 750. |
| 1927 | 11,912,000 | 3. | 5. | 7. | 15. | 40. | 70. | 120. | 225. |
| 1927D | 976,000 | 15. | 20. | 25. | 60. | 130. | 175. | 250. | 300. |
| 1927S | 396,000 | 30. | 50. | 90. | 275. | 1,100. | 2,800. | 4,500. | 7,000. |
| 1928 | 6,336,000 | 3. | 5. | 7. | 15. | 40. | 70. | 120. | 225. |
| 1928D | 1,627,600 | 4. | 7. | 8. | 20. | 45. | 90. | 125. | 225. |
| 1928S (a) | 2,644,000 | 4. | 7. | 8. | 20. | 45. | 90. | 125. | 225. |
| 1929 | 11,140,000 | 3. | 5. | 7. | 15. | 35. | 70. | 120. | 225. |
| 1929D | 1,358,000 | 5. | 8. | 10. | 16. | 38. | 85. | 135. | 225. |
| 1929S | 1,764,000 | 3. | 5. | 7. | 15. | 35. | 85. | 135. | 225. |
| 1930 | 5,632,000 | 3. | 5. | 7. | 15. | 35. | 80. | 135. | 225. |
| 1930S | 1,556,000 | 3. | 5. | 7. | 15. | 35. | 80. | 135. | 225. |

a. Large and small mintmark varieties; see page 20.

# WASHINGTON (1932 TO DATE)

This type was intended to be a commemorative issue marking the 200th anniversary of George Washington's birth. John Flanagan, a New York sculptor, was the designer; his initials, JF, can be found at the base of Washington's neck. The mintmark is on the reverse below the wreath (1932–1964).

*Weight 6.25 grams; composition .900 silver, .100 copper (net weight .18084 oz. pure silver); diameter 24.3 mm; reeded edge; mints: Philadelphia, Denver, San Francisco.*

# QUARTER DOLLARS

**F-12 FINE**—Hair lines about Washington's ear visible. Tiny feathers on eagle's breast faintly visible.
**VF-20 VERY FINE**—Most hair details visible. Wing feathers clear.
**EF-40 EXTREMELY FINE**—Hair lines sharp. Wear spots confined to top of eagle's legs and center of breast.
**MS-60 UNCIRCULATED**—No trace of wear, but many contact marks, surface spotting, or faded luster possible.
**MS-63 CHOICE UNCIRCULATED**—No trace of wear. Light blemishes. Attractive mint luster.
**MS-64 UNCIRCULATED**—A few scattered contact marks. Good eye appeal and attractive luster.
**MS-65 GEM UNCIRCULATED**—Only light, scattered contact marks that are not distracting. Strong luster, good eye appeal.
**PF-65 GEM PROOF**—Hardly any blemishes, and no flaws.

1934, Doubled Die

## Silver Coinage (1932–1964)

| | Mintage | VG-8 | F-12 | VF-20 | EF-40 | AU-50 | MS-60 | MS-63 | MS-65 |
|---|---|---|---|---|---|---|---|---|---|
| 1932 . . . . . . . . . . . . | 5,404,000 | $5.00 | $6.00 | $7. | $10. | $15. | $25. | $50. | $425. |
| 1932D . . . . . . . . . . . . | 436,800 | 145.00 | 185.00 | 215. | 285. | 500. | 1,100. | 3,200. | 24,000. |
| 1932S . . . . . . . . . . . . | 408,000 | 140.00 | 170.00 | 185. | 215. | 240. | 500. | 1,400. | 6,750. |
| 1934, All kinds . . . . . | 31,912,052 | | | | | | | | |
|    1934, Doubled Die . . . . . . . . . . | | 75.00 | 85.00 | 135. | 225. | 325. | 500. | 1,350. | 4,500. |
|    1934, Light Motto . . . . . . . . . . | | 4.00 | 5.00 | 7. | 10. | 24. | 50. | 75. | 250. |
|    1934, Heavy Motto . . . . . . . . . | | 4.00 | 5.00 | 6. | 8. | 12. | 30. | 50. | 125. |
| 1934D . . . . . . . . . . . . | 3,527,200 | 6.00 | 7.00 | 10. | 25. | 85. | 250. | 350. | 1,500. |
| 1935 . . . . . . . . . . . . | 32,484,000 | 3.00 | 3.50 | 4. | 7. | 9. | 22. | 35. | 120. |
| 1935D . . . . . . . . . . . . | 5,780,000 | 6.00 | 7.00 | 10. | 20. | 125. | 250. | 300. | 900. |
| 1935S . . . . . . . . . . . . | 5,660,000 | 5.00 | 6.00 | 7. | 15. | 38. | 100. | 135. | 350. |

| 1937, Doubled-<br>Die Obverse | 1942-D, Doubled-<br>Die Obverse | 1943, Doubled-<br>Die Obverse |
|---|---|---|

| | Mintage | EF-40 | AU-50 | MS-60 | MS-63 | MS-65 | PF-65 |
|---|---|---|---|---|---|---|---|
| 1936 . . . . . . . . . . . (3,837) . . | 41,300,000 | $5. | $10. | $21. | $32. | $100. | $1,800. |
| 1936D . . . . . . . . . . . . . . . . . . | 5,374,000 | 45. | 250. | 550. | 900. | 1,650. | |
| 1936S . . . . . . . . . . . . . . . . . . | 3,828,000 | 15. | 50. | 120. | 150. | 425. | |
| 1937 . . . . . . . . . . (5,542) . . | 19,696,000 | 5. | 18. | 25. | 35. | 90. | 750. |
| 1937, Doubled-Die Obv . . . . . . . . . . . . . * | | 100. | 300. | 500. | 850. | 2,500. | |
| 1937D . . . . . . . . . . . . . . . . . . | 7,189,600 | 15. | 30. | 70. | 85. | 155. | |
| 1937S . . . . . . . . . . . . . . . . . . | 1,652,000 | 35. | 95. | 150. | 205. | 350. | |
| 1938 . . . . . . . . . . . (8,045) . . | 9,472,000 | 15. | 45. | 95. | 105. | 215. | 450. |
| 1938S . . . . . . . . . . . . . . . . . . | 2,832,000 | 20. | 55. | 105. | 130. | 265. | |
| 1939 . . . . . . . . . . . (8,795) . . | 33,540,000 | 4. | 12. | 15. | 25. | 60. | 400. |
| 1939D . . . . . . . . . . . . . . . . . . | 7,092,000 | 11. | 20. | 40. | 50. | 115. | |

\* Included in number above.

*Chart continued on next page.*

# QUARTER DOLLARS

| | Mintage | EF-40 | AU-50 | MS-60 | MS-63 | MS-65 | PF-65 |
|---|---|---|---|---|---|---|---|
| 1939S | 2,628,000 | $20. | $60. | $95. | $135. | $325. | |
| 1940 . . . . . (11,246) | 35,704,000 | 4. | 6. | 17. | 35. | 60. | $350. |
| 1940D | 2,797,600 | 24. | 65. | 120. | 165. | 315. | |
| 1940S | 8,244,000 | 9. | 16. | 21. | 32. | 65. | |
| 1941 . . . . . (15,287) | 79,032,000 | 4. | 6. | 8. | 14. | 37. | 250. |
| 1941D | 16,714,800 | 7. | 13. | 32. | 58. | 68. | |
| 1941S (a) | 16,080,000 | 5. | 11. | 28. | 55. | 65. | |
| 1942 . . . . . (21,123) | 102,096,000 | 3. | 4. | 6. | 9. | 35. | 250. |
| 1942D | 17,487,200 | 5. | 10. | 17. | 20. | 38. | |
| 1942D, Doubled-Die Obverse | * | 400. | 600. | 1,000. | 1,800. | — | |
| 1942S | 19,384,000 | | 20. | 70. | 115. | 165. | |
| 1943 | 99,700,000 | 3. | 4. | 5. | 9. | 40. | |
| 1943, Doubled-Die Obverse | * | 225. | 350. | 500. | 800. | — | |
| 1943D | 16,095,600 | 8. | 15. | 28. | 39. | 50. | |
| 1943S | 21,700,000 | 9. | 13. | 26. | 42. | 50. | |
| 1943S, Doubled-Die Obverse | * | 125. | 250. | 500. | 1,000. | 3,000. | |
| 1944 | 104,956,000 | 3. | 4. | 5. | 9. | 35. | |
| 1944D | 14,600,800 | 7. | 10. | 17. | 19. | 38. | |
| 1944S | 12,560,000 | 7. | 10. | 14. | 20. | 35. | |
| 1945 | 74,372,000 | 3. | 4. | 5. | 8. | 38. | |
| 1945D | 12,341,600 | 8. | 12. | 18. | 25. | 42. | |
| 1945S | 17,004,001 | 5. | 7. | 9. | 13. | 35. | |
| 1946 | 53,436,000 | 3. | 4. | 5. | 9. | 42. | |
| 1946D | 9,072,800 | 3. | 5. | 6. | 9. | 43. | |
| 1946S | 4,204,000 | 3. | 4. | 5. | 9. | 47. | |
| 1947 | 22,556,000 | 3. | 5. | 11. | 19. | 45. | |
| 1947D | 15,338,400 | 3. | 5. | 11. | 17. | 40. | |
| 1947S | 5,532,000 | 3. | 4. | 9. | 15. | 35. | |
| 1948 | 35,196,000 | 3. | 4. | 5. | 9. | 40. | |
| 1948D | 16,766,800 | 4. | 7. | 13. | 18. | 65. | |
| 1948S | 15,960,000 | 3. | 5. | 7. | 13. | 45. | |
| 1949 | 9,312,000 | 10. | 14. | 35. | 47. | 60. | |
| 1949D | 10,068,400 | 4. | 9. | 16. | 38. | 50. | |
| 1950 . . . . . (51,386) | 24,920,126 | 4. | 5. | 7. | 8. | 35. | 70. |
| 1950D | 21,075,600 | 4. | 5. | 6. | 9. | 35. | |
| 1950D, D Over S | * | 135. | 185. | 265. | 400. | 3,000. | |
| 1950S | 10,284,004 | 4. | 8. | 12. | 16. | 45. | |
| 1950S, S Over D | * | 150. | 300. | 400. | 475. | 1,100. | |
| 1951 . . . . . (57,500) | 43,448,102 | 4. | 5. | 6. | 8. | 30. | 60. |
| 1951D | 35,354,800 | 4. | 5. | 6. | 7. | 35. | |
| 1951S | 9,048,000 | 5. | 7. | 14. | 27. | 40. | |
| 1952 . . . . . (81,980) | 38,780,093 | 3. | 7. | 10. | 12. | 21. | 50. |
| 1952D | 49,795,200 | 3. | 4. | 5. | 9. | 40. | |
| 1952S | 13,707,800 | 5. | 6. | 12. | 25. | 42. | |
| 1953 . . . . . (128,800) | 18,536,120 | 3. | 5. | 6. | 10. | 40. | 50. |
| 1953D | 56,112,400 | 3. | 4. | 5. | 7. | 40. | |
| 1953S | 14,016,000 | 3. | 4. | 5. | 7. | 34. | |
| 1954 . . . . . (233,300) | 54,412,203 | 3. | 4. | 5. | 12. | 32. | 25. |
| 1954D | 42,305,500 | 3. | 4. | 6. | 10. | 42. | |
| 1954S | 11,834,722 | 3. | 4. | 5. | 7. | 36. | |

* Included in number above. **a.** Large and small mintmark varieties; see page 20.

# QUARTER DOLLARS

| | Mintage | EF-40 | AU-50 | MS-60 | MS-63 | MS-65 | PF-65 |
|---|---|---|---|---|---|---|---|
| 1955 . . . . .(378,200) . . . . . . 18,180,181 | | $3. | $4. | $5. | $7. | $27. | $25. |
| 1955D. . . . . . . . . . . . . . . . . 3,182,400 | | 4. | 5. | 7. | 10. | 60. | |
| 1956 . . . . .(669,384) . . . . . . 44,144,000 | | 3. | 4. | 5. | 10. | 21. | 10. |
| 1956D. . . . . . . . . . . . . . . . 32,334,500 | | 3. | 4. | 5. | 7. | 27. | |
| 1957 . . . .(1,247,952) . . . . . . 46,532,000 | | 3. | 4. | 5. | 7. | 27. | 8. |
| 1957D. . . . . . . . . . . . . . . . 77,924,160 | | 3. | 4. | 5. | 8. | 25. | |
| 1958 . . . . .(875,652) . . . . . . . 6,360,000 | | 3. | 4. | 5. | 6. | 20. | |
| 1958D. . . . . . . . . . . . . . . . 78,124,900 | | 3. | 4. | 5. | 6. | 25. | |
| 1959 . . .(1,149,291) . . . . . . 24,384,000 | | 3. | 4. | 5. | 6. | 25. | 8. |
| 1959D. . . . . . . . . . . . . . . . 62,054,232 | | 3. | 4. | 5. | 6. | 35. | |
| 1960 . . . .(1,691,602) . . . . . . 29,164,000 | | 3. | 4. | 5. | 6. | 20. | 8. |
| 1960D. . . . . . . . . . . . . . . . 63,000,324 | | 3. | 4. | 5. | 6. | 20. | |
| 1961 . . . .(3,028,244) . . . . . 37,036,000 | | 3. | 4. | 5. | 6. | 15. | 8. |
| 1961D. . . . . . . . . . . . . . . . 83,656,928 | | 3. | 4. | 5. | 6. | 15. | |
| 1962 . . . .(3,218,019) . . . . . . 36,156,000 | | 3. | 4. | 5. | 6. | 15. | 8. |
| 1962D. . . . . . . . . . . . . . . 127,554,756 | | 3. | 4. | 5. | 6. | 15. | |
| 1963 . . . .(3,075,645) . . . . . . 74,316,000 | | 3. | 4. | 5. | 6. | 15. | 8. |
| 1963D. . . . . . . . . . . . . . . 135,288,184 | | 3. | 4. | 5. | 6. | 12. | |
| 1964 . . . .(3,950,762) . . . . . 560,390,585 | | 3. | 4. | 5. | 6. | 12. | 8. |
| 1964D. . . . . . . . . . . . . . . 704,135,528 | | 3. | 4. | 5. | 6. | 12. | |

## Clad Coinage and Silver Proofs (1965 to Date)

Proof coins from 1937 through 1972 were made from special dies with high relief and minor detail differences. Some of the circulation coins of 1956 through 1964 and 1969-D through 1972-D were also made from reverse dies with these same features. A variety of the 1964-D quarter occurs with the modified reverse normally found only on the clad coins.

*Weight 5.67 grams; composition, outer layers of copper-nickel (.750 copper, .250 nickel) bonded to inner core of pure copper; diameter 24.3 mm; reeded edge. Silver Proofs 1992–1998: same as pre-1965 standards.*

**◄—— Starting in 1968 mintmark is on obverse, to right of ribbon.**

| | Mintage | MS-63 | MS-65 | PF-65 |
|---|---|---|---|---|
| 1965 . . . . .1,819,717,540 | | $1. | $9. | |
| 1966 . . . . . .821,101,500 | | 1. | 6. | |
| 1967 . . . . .1,524,031,848 | | 1. | 5. | |
| 1968 . . . . . . .220,731,500 | | 1. | 5. | |
| 1968D . . . . .101,534,000 | | 1. | 5. | |
| 1968S . . . . .(3,041,506) | | | | $4. |
| 1969 . . . . . .176,212,000 | | 1. | 5. | |
| 1969D . . . .114,372,000 | | 1. | 5. | |
| 1969S . . . . .(2,934,631) | | | | 4. |
| 1970 . . . . . .136,420,000 | | 1. | 9. | |
| 1970D (a) . . .417,341,364 | | 1. | 6. | |
| 1970S . . . . . .(2,632,810) | | | | 4. |

| | Mintage | MS-63 | MS-65 | PF-65 |
|---|---|---|---|---|
| 1971 . . . . . . .109,284,000 | | $1. | $5. | |
| 1971D . . . .258,634,428 | | 1. | 2. | |
| 1971S . . . . . .(3,220,733) | | | | $4. |
| 1972 . . . . . .215,048,000 | | 1. | 4. | |
| 1972D . . . .311,067,732 | | 1. | 5. | |
| 1972S . . . . . .(3,260,996) | | | | 4. |
| 1973 . . . . . .346,924,000 | | 1. | 7. | |
| 1973D . . . .232,977,400 | | 1. | 9. | |
| 1973S . . . . . .(2,760,339) | | | | 4. |
| 1974 . . . . . .801,456,000 | | 1. | 5. | |
| 1974D . . . .353,160,300 | | 1. | 11. | |
| 1974S . . . . . .(2,612,568) | | | | 4. |

**a.** Lightweight, thin quarters of 1970-D are errors struck on metal intended for dimes.

## Bicentennial (1776–1976)

In October of 1973, the Treasury announced an open contest for the selection of suitable designs for the Bicentennial reverses of the quarter, half dollar, and dollar, with $5,000 to be awarded to each winner. Twelve semifinalists were chosen, and from these the symbolic entry of Jack L. Ahr was selected for the quarter reverse. It features a colonial drummer facing left, with a victory torch encircled by 13 stars at the upper left. Except for the dual dating, "1776–1976," the obverse remained unchanged. Pieces with this dual dating were coined during 1975 and 1976. They were struck for general circulation and included in all the Mint's offerings of Proof and Uncirculated sets.

*Designers John Flanagan and Jack L. Ahr; diameter 24.3 mm; reeded edge. Silver issue—Weight 5.75 grams; composition, outer layers of .800 silver, .200 copper bonded to inner core of .209 silver, .791 copper (net weight .0739 oz. pure silver). Copper-nickel issue—Weight 5.67 grams; composition, outer layers of .750 copper, .250 nickel bonded to inner core of pure copper.*

| | Mintage | MS-63 | MS-65 | PF-65 |
|---|---|---|---|---|
| 1776–1976, Copper-Nickel Clad | 809,784,016 | $1. | $6. | |
| 1776–1976D, Copper-Nickel Clad | 860,118,839 | 1. | 6. | |
| 1776–1976S, Copper-Nickel Clad | (7,059,099) | | | $3. |
| 1776–1976S, Silver Clad (a) | 7,000,000 | 3. | 5. | |
| 1776–1976S, Silver Clad (a) | (4,000,000) | | | 7. |

**a.** Mintages are approximate. Several million were melted in 1982.

## Eagle Reverse Resumed (1977–1998)
### (Dies Slightly Modified to Lower Relief)

| | Mintage | MS-63 | MS-65 | PF-65 |
|---|---|---|---|---|
| 1977 | 468,556,000 | $1.00 | $6. | |
| 1977D | 256,524,978 | 1.00 | 4. | |
| 1977S | (3,251,152) | | | $4. |
| 1978 | 521,452,000 | 1.00 | 6. | |
| 1978D | 287,373,152 | 1.00 | 6. | |
| 1978S | (3,127,781) | | | 4. |
| 1979 | 515,708,000 | 1.00 | 6. | |
| 1979D | 489,789,780 | 1.00 | 4. | |
| 1979S, All kinds | 3,677,175 | | | |
| 1979S, Filled S | | | | 4. |
| 1979S, Clear S | | | | 4. |
| 1980P | 635,832,000 | 1.00 | 7. | |
| 1980D | 518,327,487 | 1.00 | 5. | |
| 1980S | (3,554,806) | | | 3. |
| 1981P | 601,716,000 | 1.00 | 6. | |
| 1981D | 575,722,833 | 1.00 | 4. | |
| 1981S | (4,063,083) | | | 3. |
| 1982P | 500,931,000 | 3.00 | 15 | |
| 1982D | 480,042,788 | 1.50 | 10 | |
| 1982S | (3,857,479) | | | 3. |
| 1983P | 673,535,000 | 3.00 | 55. | |
| 1983D | 617,806,446 | 3.00 | 35. | |
| 1983S | (3,279,126) | | | $4. |
| 1984P | 676,545,000 | $1.00 | $8. | |
| 1984D | 546,483,064 | 1.00 | 8. | |
| 1984S | (3,065,110) | | | 4. |
| 1985P | 775,818,962 | 1.00 | 15. | |
| 1985D | 519,962,888 | 1.00 | 8. | |
| 1985S | (3,362,821) | | | 3. |
| 1986P | 551,199,333 | 1.00 | 3. | |
| 1986D | 504,298,660 | 2.00 | 10. | |
| 1986S | (3,010,497) | | | 4. |
| 1987P | 582,499,481 | 0.50 | 8. | |
| 1987D | 655,594,696 | 0.50 | 5. | |
| 1987S | (4,227,728) | | | 4. |
| 1988P | 562,052,000 | 1.00 | 14. | |
| 1988D | 596,810,688 | 0.50 | 10. | |
| 1988S | (3,262,948) | | | 3. |
| 1989P | 512,868,000 | 0.75 | 15. | |
| 1989D | 896,535,597 | 0.75 | 3. | |
| 1989S | (3,220,194) | | | 3. |
| 1990P | 613,792,000 | 0.75 | 10. | |
| 1990D | 927,638,181 | 0.75 | 3. | |
| 1990S | (3,299,559) | | | 4. |
| 1991P | 570,968,000 | 0.75 | 12. | |

| | Mintage | MS-63 | MS-65 | PF-65 |
|---|---|---|---|---|
| 1991D | .....630,966,693 | $0.75 | $8. | |
| 1991S | ......(2,867,787) | | | $3. |
| 1992P | .....384,764,000 | 0.75 | 15. | |
| 1992D | .....389,777,107 | 0.75 | 15. | |
| 1992S | ......(2,858,981) | | | 3. |
| 1992S, Silver | .(1,317,579) | | | 5. |
| 1993P | .....639,276,000 | 0.75 | 6. | |
| 1993D | .....645,476,128 | 0.75 | 6. | |
| 1993S | ......(2,633,439) | | | 6. |
| 1993S, Silver | ..(761,353) | | | 6. |
| 1994P | .....825,600,000 | 0.50 | 18. | |
| 1994D | .....880,034,110 | 0.50 | 8. | |
| 1994S | ......(2,484,594) | | | 4. |
| 1994S, Silver | ..(785,329) | | | 6. |
| 1995P | ....1,004,336,000 | 0.75 | 14. | |
| 1995D | ....1,103,216,000 | $0.75 | $12. | |
| 1995S | ......(2,117,496) | | | $8. |
| 1995S, Silver | ..(679,985) | | | 8. |
| 1996P | .....925,040,000 | 0.50 | 8. | |
| 1996D | .....906,868,000 | 0.50 | 8. | |
| 1996S | ......(1,750,244) | | | 5. |
| 1996S, Silver | ..(775,021) | | | 7. |
| 1997P | .....595,740,000 | 0.50 | 5. | |
| 1997D | .....599,680,000 | 0.50 | 5. | |
| 1997S | ......(2,055,000) | | | 7. |
| 1997S, Silver | ..(741,678) | | | 8. |
| 1998P | .....896,268,000 | 0.50 | 6. | |
| 1998D | .....821,000,000 | 0.50 | 6. | |
| 1998S | ......(2,086,507) | | | 6. |
| 1998S, Silver | ..(878,792) | | | 8. |

## State Quarters (1999–2008)

The United States Mint 50 State Quarters® Program begun in 1999 will produce a series of 50 quarter dollar coins with special designs honoring each state. Five different designs are being issued each year from 1999 through 2008. States are being commemorated in the order of their entrance into statehood.

These are all legal tender coins of standard weight and composition. The obverse side depicting President George Washington has been modified to include some of the wording previously used on the reverse. The modification was authorized by special legislation, and carried out by Mint sculptor-engraver William Cousins, whose initials have been added to the truncation of Washington's neck adjacent to those of the original designer, John Flanagan.

Each state theme is being proposed, and approved, by the governor of that state. Final designs will be created by Mint personnel.

Circulation coins are made at the Philadelphia and Denver mints. Proof coins are made in San Francisco.

*Weight 5.67 grams; composition, outer layers of copper-nickel (.750 copper, .250 nickel) bonded to inner core of pure copper; diameter 24.3 mm; reeded edge. Silver Proof—Pre-1965 standards.*

*See next page for chart.*

| | Mintage | AU-50 | MS-63 | MS-65 | PF-65 |
|---|---|---|---|---|---|
| 1999P, Delaware | 373,400,000 | $0.50 | $1.25 | $3.00 | |
| 1999D, Delaware | 401,424,000 | 0.50 | 1.25 | 3.00 | |
| 1999S, Delaware | (3,713,359) | | | | $8.00 |
| 1999S, Delaware, Silver | (804,565) | | | | 20.00 |
| 1999P, Pennsylvania | 349,000,000 | 0.50 | 1.25 | 3.00 | |
| 1999D, Pennsylvania | 358,332,000 | 0.50 | 1.25 | 3.00 | |
| 1999S, Pennsylvania | (3,713,359) | | | | 8.00 |
| 1999S, Pennsylvania, Silver | (804,565) | | | | 20.00 |
| 1999P, New Jersey | 363,200,000 | 0.50 | 1.25 | 3.00 | |
| 1999D, New Jersey | 299,028,000 | 0.50 | 1.25 | 3.00 | |
| 1999S, New Jersey | (3,713,359) | | | | 8.00 |
| 1999S, New Jersey, Silver | (804,565) | | | | 20.00 |
| 1999P, Georgia | 451,188,000 | 0.40 | 1.00 | 2.00 | |
| 1999D, Georgia | 488,744,000 | 0.40 | 1.00 | 2.00 | |
| 1999S, Georgia | (3,713,359) | | | | 8.00 |
| 1999S, Georgia, Silver | (804,565) | | | | 20.00 |
| 1999P, Connecticut | 688,744,000 | 0.35 | 1.00 | 2.00 | |
| 1999D, Connecticut | 657,880,000 | 0.35 | 1.00 | 2.00 | |
| 1999S, Connecticut | (3,713,359) | | | | 10.00 |
| 1999S, Connecticut, Silver | (804,565) | | | | 20.00 |

| | Mintage | AU-50 | MS-63 | MS-65 | PF-65 |
|---|---|---|---|---|---|
| 2000P, Massachusetts | 628,600,000 | $0.35 | $1.00 | $2.00 | |
| 2000D, Massachusetts | 535,184,000 | 0.35 | 1.00 | 2.00 | |
| 2000S, Massachusetts | (4,020,172) | | | | $5.00 |
| 2000S, Massachusetts, Silver | (965,421) | | | | 8.00 |
| 2000P, Maryland | 678,200,000 | 0.35 | 1.00 | 2.00 | |
| 2000D, Maryland | 556,532,000 | 0.35 | 1.00 | 2.00 | |
| 2000S, Maryland | (4,020,172) | | | | 5.00 |
| 2000S, Maryland, Silver | (965,421) | | | | 8.00 |
| 2000P, South Carolina | 742,576,000 | 0.35 | 1.25 | 2.50 | |
| 2000D, South Carolina | 566,208,000 | 0.35 | 1.25 | 2.50 | |
| 2000S, South Carolina | (4,020,172) | | | | 6.00 |
| 2000S, South Carolina, Silver | (965,421) | | | | 9.00 |
| 2000P, New Hampshire | 673,040,000 | 0.35 | 1.00 | 2.00 | |
| 2000D, New Hampshire | 495,976,000 | 0.40 | 1.00 | 2.00 | |
| 2000S, New Hampshire | (4,020,172) | | | | 5.00 |
| 2000S, New Hampshire, Silver | (965,421) | | | | 8.00 |
| 2000P, Virginia | 943,000,000 | 0.35 | 1.00 | 2.00 | |
| 2000D, Virginia | 651,616,000 | 0.35 | 1.00 | 2.00 | |
| 2000S, Virginia | (4,020,172) | | | | 5.00 |
| 2000S, Virginia, Silver | (965,421) | | | | 8.00 |

# QUARTER DOLLARS

| | Mintage | AU-50 | MS-63 | MS-65 | PF-65 |
|---|---|---|---|---|---|
| 2001P, New York | 655,400,000 | $0.35 | $1.00 | $1.25 | |
| 2001D, New York | 619,640,000 | 0.35 | 1.00 | 1.25 | |
| 2001S, New York | (3,094,140) | | | | $8.00 |
| 2001S, New York, Silver | (889,697) | | | | 10.00 |
| 2001P, North Carolina | 627,600,000 | 0.35 | 1.00 | 1.25 | |
| 2001D, North Carolina | 427,876,000 | 0.40 | 1.00 | 1.25 | |
| 2001S, North Carolina | (3,094,140) | | | | 8.00 |
| 2001S, North Carolina, Silver | (889,697) | | | | 10.00 |
| 2001P, Rhode Island | 423,000,000 | 0.40 | 1.00 | 1.25 | |
| 2001D, Rhode Island | 447,100,000 | 0.40 | 1.00 | 1.25 | |
| 2001S, Rhode Island | (3,094,140) | | | | 7.00 |
| 2001S, Rhode Island, Silver | (889,697) | | | | 9.00 |
| 2001P, Vermont | 423,400,000 | 0.50 | 1.25 | 1.50 | |
| 2001D, Vermont | 459,404,000 | 0.50 | 1.00 | 1.25 | |
| 2001S, Vermont | (3,094,140) | | | | 8.00 |
| 2001S, Vermont, Silver | (889,697) | | | | 10.00 |
| 2001P, Kentucky | 353,000,000 | 0.75 | 1.25 | 1.50 | |
| 2001D, Kentucky | 370,564,000 | 0.75 | 1.00 | 1.25 | |
| 2001S, Kentucky | (3,094,140) | | | | 8.00 |
| 2001S, Kentucky, Silver | (889,697) | | | | 10.00 |

| | Mintage | AU-50 | MS-63 | MS-65 | PF-65 |
|---|---|---|---|---|---|
| 2002P, Tennessee | 361,600,000 | $1.00 | $2.00 | $3.25 | |
| 2002D, Tennessee | 286,468,000 | 0.80 | 1.75 | 3.25 | |
| 2002S, Tennessee | (3,084,245) | | | | $8.00 |
| 2002S, Tennessee, Silver | (892,229) | | | | 10.00 |
| 2002P, Ohio | 217,200,000 | 0.40 | 1.10 | 2.25 | |
| 2002D, Ohio | 414,832,000 | 0.35 | 1.00 | 2.00 | |
| 2002S, Ohio | (3,084,245) | | | | 6.00 |
| 2002S, Ohio, Silver | (892,229) | | | | 9.00 |

*Chart continued on next page.*

| | Mintage | AU-50 | MS-63 | MS-65 | PF-65 |
|---|---|---|---|---|---|
| 2002P, Louisiana | .362,000,000 | $0.40 | $1.25 | $2.50 | |
| 2002D, Louisiana | .402,204,000 | 0.40 | 1.25 | 2.50 | |
| 2002S, Louisiana | .(3,084,245) | | | | $6.00 |
| 2002S, Louisiana, Silver | .(892,229) | | | | 9.00 |
| 2002P, Indiana | .362,600,000 | 0.40 | 1.25 | 2.50 | |
| 2002D, Indiana | .327,200,000 | 0.40 | 1.25 | 2.50 | |
| 2002S, Indiana | .(3,084,245) | | | | 5.00 |
| 2002S, Indiana, Silver | .(892,229) | | | | 8.00 |
| 2002P, Mississippi | .290,000,000 | 0.40 | 1.00 | 2.00 | |
| 2002D, Mississippi | .289,600,000 | 0.40 | 1.00 | 2.00 | |
| 2002S, Mississippi | .(3,084,245) | | | | 5.00 |
| 2002S, Mississippi, Silver | .(892,229) | | | | 8.00 |

| | Mintage | AU-50 | MS-63 | MS-65 | PF-65 |
|---|---|---|---|---|---|
| 2003P, Illinois | .225,800,000 | $0.50 | $1.25 | $2.00 | |
| 2003D, Illinois | .237,400,000 | 0.40 | 1.25 | 2.00 | |
| 2003S, Illinois | .(3,408,516) | | | | $5.00 |
| 2003S, Illinois, Silver | .(1,125,755) | | | | 8.00 |
| 2003P, Alabama | .225,000,000 | 0.45 | 1.00 | 2.10 | |
| 2003D, Alabama | .232,400,000 | 0.40 | 0.90 | 2.00 | |
| 2003S, Alabama | .(3,408,516) | | | | 5.00 |
| 2003S, Alabama, Silver | .(1,125,755) | | | | 8.00 |
| 2003P, Maine | .217,400,000 | 0.45 | 0.70 | 1.40 | |
| 2003D, Maine | .231,400,000 | 0.40 | 0.70 | 1.40 | |
| 2003S, Maine | .(3,408,516) | | | | 5.00 |
| 2003S, Maine, Silver | .(1,125,755) | | | | 8.00 |
| 2003P, Missouri | .225,000,000 | 0.40 | 0.65 | 1.40 | |
| 2003D, Missouri | .228,200,000 | 0.40 | 0.65 | 1.40 | |
| 2003S, Missouri | .(3,408,516) | | | | 5.00 |
| 2003S, Missouri, Silver | .(1,125,755) | | | | 8.00 |
| 2003P, Arkansas | .228,000,000 | 0.40 | 0.65 | 1.40 | |
| 2003D, Arkansas | .229,800,000 | 0.40 | 0.65 | 1.40 | |
| 2003S, Arkansas | .(3,408,516) | | | | 5.00 |
| 2003S, Arkansas, Silver | .(1,125,755) | | | | 8.00 |

*Some 2004-D Wisconsin quarters show one of two different die flaws on the reverse, in the shape of an extra leaf on the corn. On one (middle), the extra leaf extends upward; on the other (right), it bends low. The normal die is shown at left. Their status as die varieties or as production errors remains uncertain.*

| | Mintage | AU-50 | MS-63 | MS-65 | PF-65 |
|---|---|---|---|---|---|
| 2004P, Michigan | 233,800,000 | $0.40 | $0.65 | $1.30 | |
| 2004D, Michigan | 225,800,000 | 0.40 | 0.65 | 1.30 | |
| 2004S, Michigan | (2,761,163) | | | | $5.00 |
| 2004S, Michigan, Silver | (1,789,344) | | | | 8.00 |
| 2004P, Florida | 240,200,000 | 0.35 | 0.60 | 1.25 | |
| 2004D, Florida | 241,600,000 | 0.35 | 0.60 | 1.25 | |
| 2004S, Florida | (2,761,163) | | | | 5.00 |
| 2004S, Florida, Silver | (1,789,344) | | | | 8.00 |
| 2004P, Texas | 278,800,000 | 0.35 | 0.60 | 1.25 | |
| 2004D, Texas | 263,000,000 | 0.35 | 0.60 | 1.25 | |
| 2004S, Texas | (2,761,163) | | | | 5.00 |
| 2004S, Texas, Silver | (1,789,344) | | | | 8.00 |
| 2004P, Iowa | 213,800,000 | 0.40 | 0.65 | 1.30 | |
| 2004D, Iowa | 251,800,000 | 0.35 | 0.60 | 1.25 | |
| 2004S, Iowa | (2,761,163) | | | | 5.00 |
| 2004S, Iowa, Silver | (1,789,344) | | | | 8.00 |
| 2004P, Wisconsin | 226,400,000 | 0.35 | 0.60 | 1.25 | |
| 2004D, Wisconsin (a) | 226,800,000 | 0.35 | 0.60 | 1.25 | |
| 2004S, Wisconsin | (2,761,163) | | | | 5.00 |
| 2004S, Wisconsin, Silver | (1,789,344) | | | | 8.00 |

a. Extra Leaf High and Extra Leaf Low coins (see photos above) trade for premiums in Mint State.

| | Mintage | AU-50 | MS-63 | MS-65 | PF-65 |
|---|---|---|---|---|---|
| 2005P, California | 257,200,000 | $0.35 | $0.50 | $1.00 | |
| 2005D, California | 263,200,000 | 0.35 | 0.50 | 1.00 | |
| 2005S, California | (3,262,000) | | | | $5.00 |
| 2005S, California, Silver | (1,606,970) | | | | 8.00 |
| 2005P, Minnesota | 239,600,000 | 0.35 | 0.50 | 1.00 | |
| 2005D, Minnesota | 248,400,000 | 0.35 | 0.50 | 1.00 | |
| 2005S, Minnesota | (3,262,000) | | | | 5.00 |
| 2005S, Minnesota, Silver | (1,606,970) | | | | 8.00 |
| 2005P, Oregon | 316,200,000 | 0.35 | 0.50 | 1.00 | |
| 2005D, Oregon | 404,000,000 | 0.35 | 0.50 | 1.00 | |

*Chart continued on next page.*

| | Mintage | AU-50 | MS-63 | MS-65 | PF-65 |
|---|---|---|---|---|---|
| 2005S, Oregon | (3,262,000) | | | | $5.00 |
| 2005S, Oregon, Silver | (1,606,970) | | | | 8.00 |
| 2005P, Kansas | 263,400,000 | $0.35 | $0.50 | $1.00 | |
| 2005D, Kansas | 300,000,000 | 0.35 | 0.50 | 1.00 | |
| 2005S, Kansas | (3,262,000) | | | | 5.00 |
| 2005S, Kansas, Silver | (1,606,970) | | | | 8.00 |
| 2005P, West Virginia | 365,400,000 | 0.35 | 0.50 | 1.00 | |
| 2005D, West Virginia | 356,200,000 | 0.35 | 0.50 | 1.00 | |
| 2005S, West Virginia | (3,262,000) | | | | 5.00 |
| 2005S, West Virginia, Silver | (1,606,970) | | | | 8.00 |

| | Mintage | AU-50 | MS-63 | MS-65 | PF-65 |
|---|---|---|---|---|---|
| 2006P, Nevada | | $0.35 | $0.50 | $1.00 | |
| 2006D, Nevada | | 0.35 | 0.50 | 1.00 | |
| 2006S, Nevada | | | | | $5.00 |
| 2006S, Nevada, Silver | | | | | 8.00 |
| 2006P, Nebraska | | 0.35 | 0.50 | 1.00 | |
| 2006D, Nebraska | | 0.35 | 0.50 | 1.00 | |
| 2006S, Nebraska | | | | | 5.00 |
| 2006S, Nebraska, Silver | | | | | 8.00 |
| 2006P, Colorado | | 0.35 | 0.50 | 1.00 | |
| 2006D, Colorado | | 0.35 | 0.50 | 1.00 | |
| 2006S, Colorado | | | | | 5.00 |
| 2006S, Colorado, Silver | | | | | 8.00 |
| 2006P, North Dakota | | 0.35 | 0.50 | 1.00 | |
| 2006D, North Dakota | | 0.35 | 0.50 | 1.00 | |
| 2006S, North Dakota | | | | | 5.00 |
| 2006S, North Dakota, Silver | | | | | 8.00 |
| 2006P, South Dakota | | 0.35 | 0.50 | 1.00 | |
| 2006D, South Dakota | | 0.35 | 0.50 | 1.00 | |
| 2006S, South Dakota | | | | | 5.00 |
| 2006S, South Dakota, Silver | | | | | 8.00 |

Some statehood quarters were accidentally made with "dis-oriented" dies and are valued higher than ordinary pieces. Normal United States coins have dies oriented in "coin alignment," such that the reverse appears upside down when the coin is rotated from right to left. Values for the rotated-die quarters vary according to the amount of shifting. The most valuable are those that are shifted 180 degrees, so that both sides appear upright when the coin is turned over (called *medal alignment*).

In 2007, statehood quarters will be released for Montana, Washington, Idaho, Wyoming, and Utah; in 2008, for Oklahoma, New Mexico, Arizona, Alaska, and Hawaii.

The half dollar, authorized by the Act of April 2, 1792, was not minted until December 1794. The early types of this series have been extensively collected by die varieties, of which many exist for most dates. Valuations given below are in each case for the most common variety; scarcer ones as listed by Overton (see the Bibliography section at the end of the book) generally command higher prices.

When the half dollar was first issued, its weight was 208 grains and its fineness .8924. This standard was not changed until 1837, when the law of January 18, 1837, specified 206-1/4 grains, .900 fine. This fineness continued in use until 1965.

Arrows at the date in 1853 indicate the reduction of weight to 192 grains, in conformity with the Act of February 21, 1853. During that year only, rays were added to the field on the reverse side to identify the lighter coins. Arrows remained in 1854 and 1855.

The 1866 Proof quarter, half, and dollar without motto are not mentioned in the Mint director's report, and were not issued for circulation.

In 1873 the weight was raised by law to 192.9 grains and arrows were again placed at the date, to be removed in 1875.

## TYPE COIN VALUES

| | G-4 | F-12 | EF-40 | MS-60 | MS-63 | MS-65 | PF-63 | PF-65 |
|---|---|---|---|---|---|---|---|---|
| Flowing Hair, 1794–1795 | $750.00+ | $1,550.00+ | $9,500.00+ | $32,000.00+ | $70,000.+ | $175,000. | | |
| Drpd Bust, SE, 1796–1797 | 32,000.00+ | 42,500.00+ | 82,500.00+ | 180,000.00+ | 265,000.+ | 600,000.+ | | |
| Drpd Bust, HE, 1801–1807 | 165.00+ | 235.00+ | 1,000.00+ | 6,500.00+ | 17,500.+ | 50,000. | | |
| Cap Bust, 1807–1836 | 60.00+ | 85.00+ | 125.00+ | 575.00+ | 1,600.+ | 9,000.+ | $25,000. | $80,000. |
| Cap Bust, 1836–1839 | 65.00+ | 95.00+ | 175.00+ | 825.00+ | 2,250.+ | 20,000.+ | 38,500.+ | 85,000. |
| Lib Std, NM, 1839–1866 | 24.00+ | 50.00 | 100.00 | 450.00 | 950.+ | 6,500. | 1,200 | 7,250.+ |
| Lib Std, A&R, 1853 | 25.00+ | 50.00+ | 275.00+ | 1,500.00 | 3,500 | 26,000.+ | 77,500.+ | — |
| Lib Std, Arr, 1854–1855 | 25.00+ | 55.00+ | 115.00+ | 700.00 | 1,500. | 8,250.+ | 13,500.+ | 37,500.+ |
| Lib Std, Motto, 1866–1891 | 24.00+ | 50.00+ | 95.00+ | 500.00+ | 700. | 4,000.+ | 900.+ | 4,000. |
| Lib Std, Arr, 1873–1874 | 25.00 | 55.00 | 250.00 | 950.00 | 2,000. | 17,500.+ | 2,150.+ | 12,250.+ |
| Barber, 1892–1915 | 12.00 | 30.00+ | 150.00 | 475.00+ | 850.+ | 3,250.+ | 800.+ | 4,000.+ |
| Lib Walking, 1916–1947 | 4.00+ | 5.00+ | 7.00 | 40.00+ | 60.+ | 150.+ | 425.+ | 950.+ |
| Franklin, 1948–1963 | 3.50+ | 3.75+ | 4.50 | 5.00- | 10. | 80.+ | 17.+ | 25.+ |
| Kennedy, 1964 to Date | 3.50+ | 3.75+ | 4.00+ | 4.50+ | 5. | 12.+ | 5. | 9. |
| + or – indicates change from previous year | | | | | | | | |

## FLOWING HAIR (1794–1795)

*Designer Robert Scot; weight 13.48 grams; composition .8924 silver, .1076 copper; approx. diameter 32.5 mm; edge: FIFTY CENTS OR A HALF DOLLAR with decorations between words.*

**AG-3 ABOUT GOOD**—Clear enough to identify.

**G-4 GOOD**—Date and letters sufficient to be legible. Main devices outlined, but lacking in detail.

**VG-8 VERY GOOD**—Major details discernible. Letters well formed but worn.

**F-12 FINE**—Hair ends distinguishable. Top hair lines visible, but otherwise worn smooth.

**VF-20 VERY FINE**—Some detail visible in hair in center; other details more bold.

**EF-40 EXTREMELY FINE**—Hair above head and down neck detailed, with slight wear.

**AU-50 ABOUT UNCIRCULATED**—All hair visible; slight wear on bust of Liberty and on top edges of eagle's wings, head, and breast.

**Two Leaves Under Wings**

*See next page for chart.*

| | Mintage | AG-3 | G-4 | VG-8 | F-12 | VF-20 | EF-40 | AU-50 |
|---|---|---|---|---|---|---|---|---|
| 1794 | 23,464 | $1,750. | $2,500. | $5,500. | $7,500. | $16,500. | $32,500. | $67,500. |
| 1795, All kinds | 299,680 | 375. | 750. | 950. | 1,550. | 3,200. | 9,500. | 14,500. |
| 1795, Recut Date | | 375. | 750. | 950. | 1,500. | 3,250. | 10,000. | 15,000. |
| 1795, 3 Leaves Under Ea Wing | | 550. | 1,200. | 1,850. | 3,200. | 5,500. | 13,000. | 21,500. |

*Note:* Varieties of 1795 are known with final S in STATES over D, with A in STATES over E, and with Y in LIBERTY over a star. All are scarce. Some 1795 half dollars were weight-adjusted by insertion of a silver plug in the center of the blank planchet before the coin was struck.

## DRAPED BUST

*Designer Robert Scot; weight 13.48 grams; composition .8924 silver, .1076 copper; approx. diameter 32.5 mm; edge: FIFTY CENTS OR HALF A DOLLAR with decorations between words.*

**AG-3 ABOUT GOOD**—Clear enough to identify.

**G-4 GOOD**—Date and letters sufficiently clear to be legible. Main devices outlined, but lacking in detail.

**VG-8 VERY GOOD**—Major details discernible. Letters well formed but worn.

**F-12 FINE**—Hair ends distinguishable. Top hair lines visible, but otherwise worn smooth.

**VF-20 VERY FINE**—Right side of drapery slightly worn. Left side to curls smooth.

**EF-40 EXTREMELY FINE**—All lines in drapery on bust distinctly visible around to hair curls.

**AU-50 ABOUT UNCIRCULATED**—Slight trace of wear on cheek, hair, and shoulder.

### Small Eagle Reverse (1796–1797)

**1796, 16 Stars**                **1797, 15 Stars**

| | Mintage | AG-3 | G-4 | VG-8 | F-12 | VF-20 | EF-40 | AU-50 |
|---|---|---|---|---|---|---|---|---|
| 1796, 15 Stars | 3,918 | $18,500. | $32,000. | $35,000. | $42,500. | $62,000. | $82,500. | $115,000. |
| 1796, 16 Stars | * | 18,500. | 32,000. | 35,000. | 45,000. | 66,000. | 87,500. | 125,000. |
| *$460,000, MS-66, Stack's auction, May-99* | | | | | | | | |
| 1797, 15 Stars | * | 18,500. | 32,000. | 35,000. | 42,500. | 62,000. | 82,500. | 115,000. |
| *$966,000, MS-66, ANR auction, Mar-04* | | | | | | | | |

* Included in number above.

### Heraldic Eagle Reverse (1801–1807)

| | Mintage | G-4 | VG-8 | F-12 | VF-20 | EF-40 | AU-50 | MS-60 |
|---|---|---|---|---|---|---|---|---|
| 1801 | 30,289 | $300. | $500. | $800. | $2,000. | $5,000. | $13,000. | $34,000. |
| 1802 | 29,890 | 275. | 500. | 950. | 1,750. | 4,500. | 12,000. | 32,500. |
| 1803, All kinds | 188,234 | | | | | | | |
| 1803, Small 3 | | 160. | 225. | 325. | 550. | 1,300. | 3,800. | 8,750. |
| 1803, Large 3 | | 140. | 180. | 250. | 500. | 1,000. | 3,000. | 8,000. |

# HALF DOLLARS

**1805, 5 Over 4**

| | Mintage | G-4 | VG-8 | F-12 | VF-20 | EF-40 | AU-50 | MS-60 |
|---|---|---|---|---|---|---|---|---|
| 1805, All kinds . . . . .211,722 | | | | | | | | |
| 1805, 5 Over 4 . . . . . . . . . | | $200. | $300. | $600. | $800. | $2,100. | $5,500. | $24,500. |
| 1805, Normal Date . . . . . . | | 165. | 180. | 250. | 450. | 1,050. | 2,850. | 7,500. |

**1806, 6 Over 5**

**Knobbed-Top 6, Small Stars**

**Pointed-Top 6**

**Branch Stem Not Through Claw**     **Branch Stem Through Claw**

| | Mintage | G-4 | VG-8 | F-12 | VF-20 | EF-40 | AU-50 | MS-60 |
|---|---|---|---|---|---|---|---|---|
| 1806, All kinds . . . . .839,576 | | | | | | | | |
| 1806, 6 Over 5 . . . . . . . . . | | $165. | $185. | $250. | $450. | $1,050. | $2,850. | $7,200. |
| 1806, 6 Over Inv 6 . . . . . . . | | 175. | 275. | 650. | 1,000. | 2,300. | 5,500. | 12,500. |
| 1806, Knbd 6, Lg Stars | | | | | | | | |
| (Traces of Overdate) . . . . | | 165. | 175. | 250. | 450. | 1,000. | 2,850. | 6,500. |
| 1806, Knbd 6, Sm Stars . . | | 165. | 175. | 235. | 450. | 1,000. | 2,650. | 6,500. |
| 1806, Knobbed 6, Stem | | | | | | | | |
| Not Through Claw . . . . . | | 19,500. | 25,000. | 35,000. | 55,000. | 85,000. | | |
| 1806, Pointed 6, Stem | | | | | | | | |
| Through Claw **(a)** . . . . . . | | 165. | 175. | 235. | 450. | 1,000. | 2,650. | 6,500. |
| 1806, Pointed 6, Stem | | | | | | | | |
| Not Through Claw . . . . . | | 165. | 175. | 235. | 450. | 1,000. | 2,650. | 6,500. |
| 1807 . . . . . . . . . . . .301,076 | | 165. | 175. | 235. | 450. | 1,000. | 2,650. | 6,500. |

**a.** One variety shows E in STATES over A.

## CAPPED BUST, LETTERED EDGE (1807–1836)

John Reich designed this capped-head concept of Liberty. The Capped Bust style was used on most other silver coin denominations for the next 30 years. Reich was the first artist to consistently include the denomination on U.S. gold and silver coins. A German immigrant, John Reich became an engraver for the Mint, and served from 1807 to 1817, after having been freed from a bond of servitude by a Mint official.

*Designer John Reich; weight 13.48 grams; composition .8924 silver, .1076 copper; approx. diameter 32.5 mm. 1807–1814—Edge: FIFTY CENTS OR HALF A DOLLAR. 1814–1831—Edge: Star added between DOLLAR and FIFTY. 1832–1836—Edge: Vertical lines added between words.*

**G-4 GOOD**—Date and letters legible. Bust worn smooth with outline distinct.

**VG-8 VERY GOOD**—LIBERTY faint. Legends distinguishable. Clasp at shoulder visible; curl above it nearly smooth.

**F-12 FINE**—Clasp and adjacent curl clearly outlined with slight details.

**VF-20 VERY FINE**—Clasp at shoulder clear. Wear visible on highest point of curl. Hair over brow distinguishable.

**EF-40 EXTREMELY FINE**—Clasp and adjacent curl fairly sharp. Brow and hair above distinct. Curls well defined.

**AU-50 ABOUT UNCIRCULATED**—Trace of wear on hair over eye and over ear.

**MS-60 UNCIRCULATED**—No trace of wear. Light blemishes. Possible slide marks from storage handling.

**MS-63 CHOICE UNCIRCULATED**—Some distracting contact marks or blemishes in prime focal areas. Impaired luster possible.

## First Style (1807–1808)

**1807, Small Stars**     **1807, Large Stars**     **1807, 50 Over 20**

| | Mintage | G-4 | F-12 | VF-20 | EF-40 | AU-50 | MS-60 | MS-63 |
|---|---|---|---|---|---|---|---|---|
| 1807, All kinds . . . . .750,500 | | | | | | | | |
| 1807, Small Stars . . . . . . . | | $70. | $200. | $365. | $825. | $2,650. | $4,500. | $11,500. |
| 1807, Large Stars . . . . . . . | | 55. | 180. | 350. | 850. | 2,450. | 4,250. | 12,500. |
| 1807, Lg Stars, 50/20 . . . . | | 50. | 150. | 260. | 500. | 2,100. | 4,000. | 8,250. |
| 1807, "Bearded" Lib . . . . . . | | 350. | 750. | 1,250. | 2,600. | 8,000. | 16,000. | — |
| 1808, All kinds . . . .1,368,600 | | | | | | | | |
| 1808, 8 Over 7 . . . . . . . . . | | 50. | 100. | 175. | 425. | 1,000. | 2,200. | 6,000. |
| 1808 . . . . . . . . . . . . . . . . | | 45. | 75. | 120. | 290. | 650. | 1,600. | 3,750. |

## Remodeled Portrait and Eagle (1809–1836)

**1809, Experimental Edge,**     **1809, Experimental Edge,**
**xxxx Between Words**     **IIIIII Between Words**

| | Mintage | G-4 | F-12 | VF-20 | EF-40 | AU-50 | MS-60 | MS-63 |
|---|---|---|---|---|---|---|---|---|
| 1809, All kinds . . . .1,405,810 | | | | | | | | |
| 1809, Normal Edge . . . . . . | | $45. | $90. | $125. | $250. | $550. | $1,450. | $3,250. |
| 1809, xxxx Edge . . . . . . . . | | 45. | 90. | 150. | 275. | 850. | 1,850. | 4,800. |
| 1809, IIIIII Edge . . . . . . . . | | 45. | 90. | 150. | 275. | 850. | 1,850. | 6,500. |
| 1810 . . . . . . . . . . . .1,276,276 | | 45. | 90. | 125. | 225. | 550. | 1,300. | 3,850. |

| "Punctuated" Date 18.11 | 1811, Small 8 | 1811, Large 8 |

| 1812, 2 Over 1, Small 8 | 1812, 2 Over 1, Large 8 | Single Leaf Below Wing |

|  | Mintage | G-4 | F-12 | VF-20 | EF-40 | AU-50 | MS-60 | MS-63 |
|---|---|---|---|---|---|---|---|---|
| 1811, All kinds | 1,203,644 | | | | | | | |
| 1811, (18.11), 11/10 | | $55. | $100. | $175. | $400. | $700. | $1,600. | $7,500. |
| 1811, Small 8 | | 45. | 90. | 125. | 185. | 450. | 1,000. | 2,000. |
| 1811, Large 8 | | 45. | 90. | 125. | 185. | 450. | 1,000. | 2,000. |
| 1812, All kinds | 1,628,059 | | | | | | | |
| 1812, 2 /1, Small 8 | | 55. | 125. | 200. | 325. | 700. | 2,200. | 5,500. |
| 1812, 2/1, Large 8 | | 1,500. | 4,000. | 6,000. | 8,500. | 19,500. | 30,000. | — |
| 1812 | | 45. | 90. | 125. | 185. | 450. | 1,000. | 2,000. |
| 1812, Single Leaf Below Wing | | 700. | 1,150. | 2,250. | 3,600. | 6,250. | 11,000. | — |

| 1813, 50 C. Over UNI | 1814, 4 Over 3 | 1814, E Over A in STATES |

|  | Mintage | G-4 | F-12 | VF-20 | EF-40 | AU-50 | MS-60 | MS-63 |
|---|---|---|---|---|---|---|---|---|
| 1813, All kinds | 1,241,903 | | | | | | | |
| 1813 | | $55. | $90. | $115. | $175. | $400. | $1,000. | $2,500. |
| 1813, 50 C./UNI | | 65. | 100. | 170. | 325. | 800. | 1,800. | 5,500. |
| 1814, All kinds | 1,039,075 | | | | | | | |
| 1814, 4 Over 3 | | 85. | 145. | 215. | 350. | 1,100. | 2,000. | 5,750. |
| 1814, E/A IN STATES | | 65. | 100. | 120. | 250. | 750. | 1,350. | 4,350. |
| 1814 | | 60. | 90. | 115. | 200. | 425. | 900. | 2,500. |
| 1814, Single Leaf Below Wing | | 70. | 115. | 215. | 550. | 1,500. | 2,750. | 4,750. |

| 1817, 7 Over 3 | 1817, 7 Over 4 | 1817, Punctuated Date |

|  | Mintage | G-4 | F-12 | VF-20 | EF-40 | AU-50 | MS-60 | MS-63 |
|---|---|---|---|---|---|---|---|---|
| 1815, 5 Over 2 | 47,150 | $1,100. | $1,900. | $2,450. | $4,000. | $6,000. | $12,000. | $25,000. |
| 1817, All kinds | 1,215,567 | | | | | | | |
| 1817, 7 Over 3 | | 110. | 240. | 415. | 775. | 1,800. | 4,000. | 10,000. |
| 1817, 7 Over 4 (8 known) | 55,000. | 150,000. | 200,000. | | | 325,000. | | |
| 1817, Dated 181.7 | | 65. | 95. | 120. | 200. | 425. | 1,000. | 2,300. |

*Chart continued on next page.*

| | Mintage | G-4 | F-12 | VF-20 | EF-40 | AU-50 | MS-60 | MS-63 |
|---|---|---|---|---|---|---|---|---|
| 1817 | | $65. | $90. | $115. | $185. | $400. | $1,000. | $2,200. |
| 1817, Single Leaf | | | | | | | | |
| Below Wing | | 70. | 100. | 135. | 375. | 850. | 1,850. | 3,000. |

**1818, First 8 Small, Second 8 Over 7**

**1818, First 8 Large, Second 8 Over 7**

**1819, Small 9 Over 8**

**1819, Large 9 Over 8**

| | Mintage | G-4 | F-12 | VF-20 | EF-40 | AU-50 | MS-60 | MS-63 |
|---|---|---|---|---|---|---|---|---|
| 1818, All kinds | 2,208,000 | | | | | | | |
| 1818, 8/7, Sm 8 | | $85. | $120. | $150. | $205. | $775. | $1,350. | $5,000. |
| 1818, 8/7, Lg 8 | | 85. | 120. | 150. | 205. | 775. | 1,350. | 5,000. |
| 1818 | | 60. | 90. | 115. | 180. | 375. | 925. | 1,900. |
| 1819, All kinds | 2,208,000 | | | | | | | |
| 1819, Small 9/8 | | 70. | 100. | 120. | 215. | 500. | 1,200. | 3,250. |
| 1819, Large 9/8 | | 70. | 100. | 120. | 215. | 500. | 1,200. | 3,250. |
| 1819 | | 60. | 85. | 115. | 165. | 375. | 900. | 2,500. |

**1820, 20 Over 19, Square Base 2**

**1820, 20 Over 19, Curl Base 2**

**1820, Curl Base, No Knob 2, Small Date**

| | Mintage | G-4 | F-12 | VF-20 | EF-40 | AU-50 | MS-60 | MS-63 |
|---|---|---|---|---|---|---|---|---|
| 1820, All kinds | 751,122 | | | | | | | |
| 1820, 20/19, Sq 2 | | $70. | $95. | $175. | $375. | $850. | $1,550. | $4,250. |
| 1820, 20/19, Curl 2 | | 70. | 95. | 175. | 375. | 850. | 1,550. | 4,250. |
| 1820, Curl Base 2, | | | | | | | | |
| Small Date | | 65. | 90. | 145. | 275. | 625. | 1,100. | 3,000. |

**Square Base, Knob 2, Large Date**

**Square Base, No Knob 2, Large Date**

| | Mintage | G-4 | F-12 | VF-20 | EF-40 | AU-50 | MS-60 | MS-63 |
|---|---|---|---|---|---|---|---|---|
| 1820, Sq Base Knob 2, Lg Dt | | $65. | $90. | $145. | $275. | $625. | $1,100. | $3,000. |
| 1820, Sq Base No Knob 2, Lg Dt | | 65. | 90. | 145. | 275. | 625. | 1,100. | 3,000. |
| 1820, No Serifs on E's | | 275. | 400. | 625. | 850. | 2,250. | 5,000. | 8,500. |
| 1821 | 1,305,797 | 65. | 90. | 115. | 165. | 600. | 1,000. | 2,000. |

| | Mintage | G-4 | F-12 | VF-20 | EF-40 | AU-50 | MS-60 | MS-63 |
|---|---|---|---|---|---|---|---|---|
| 1822, All kinds | 1,559,573 | | | | | | | |
| 1822 | | $65. | $90. | $115. | $165. | $375. | $625. | $1,850. |
| 1822, 2 Over 1 | | 80. | 120. | 165. | 275. | 650. | 1,400. | 3,000. |

**1823, Broken 3**

**1823, Patched 3**

**1823, Ugly 3**

| | Mintage | G-4 | F-12 | VF-20 | EF-40 | AU-50 | MS-60 | MS-63 |
|---|---|---|---|---|---|---|---|---|
| 1823, All kinds | 1,694,200 | | | | | | | |
| 1823, Broken 3 | | $75. | $105. | $150. | $350. | $675. | $1,400. | $3,000. |
| 1823, Patched 3 | | 65. | 100. | 125. | 235. | 575. | 1,150. | 2,500. |
| 1823, Ugly 3 | | 60. | 90. | 110. | 185. | 425. | 875. | 2,200. |
| 1823, Normal | | 60. | 85. | 100. | 135. | 325. | 750. | 1,800. |

**"Various Dates"**
*Probably 4 over
2 over 0.*

**1824, 4 Over 1**

**1824, 4 Over 4**

**1824, 4 Over 4**

*4 Over 4 varieties are easily mistaken for scarcer 4 Over 1.
Note distance between 2's and 4's in each.*

**1827, 7 Over 6**

| | Mintage | G-4 | F-12 | VF-20 | EF-40 | AU-50 | MS-60 | MS-63 |
|---|---|---|---|---|---|---|---|---|
| 1824, All kinds | 3,504,954 | | | | | | | |
| 1824, 4/Various Dts | | $60. | $85. | $95. | $125. | $275. | $575. | $1,600. |
| 1824, 4 Over 1 | | 60. | 85. | 95. | 125. | 275. | 575. | 1,600. |
| 1824, 4/4 (2 var) | | 60. | 85. | 95. | 135. | 325. | 750. | 1,650. |
| 1824, Normal | | 60. | 85. | 95. | 125. | 275. | 575. | 1,600. |
| 1825 | 2,943,166 | 60. | 85. | 95. | 125. | 275. | 525. | 1,600. |
| 1826 | 4,004,180 | 60. | 85. | 95. | 125. | 275. | 525. | 1,600. |
| 1827, All kinds | 5,493,400 | | | | | | | |
| 1827, 7 Over 6 | | 60. | 85. | 115. | 175. | 400. | 1,000. | 1,950. |
| 1827, Sq Base 2 | | 60. | 85. | 95. | 125. | 275. | 525. | 1,600. |
| 1827, Curl Base 2 | | 60. | 85. | 95. | 125. | 300. | 575. | 1,600. |

**1828, Curl Base,
No Knob 2**

**1828, Curl Base,
Knob 2**

**1828, Square Base
2, Large 8's**

**1828, Square Base 2,
Small 8's**

**1828, Large
Letters**

**1828, Small
Letters**

*See next page for chart.*

| | Mintage | G-4 | F-12 | VF-20 | EF-40 | AU-50 | MS-60 | MS-63 |
|---|---|---|---|---|---|---|---|---|
| 1828, All kinds ........3,075,200 | | | | | | | | |
| 1828, Curl Base No Knob 2 ...... | | $60. | $85. | $95. | $125. | $275. | $575. | $1,600. |
| 1828, Curl Base Knob 2 ........ | | 65. | 90. | 100. | 150. | 315. | 700. | 1,650. |
| 1828, Sq Base 2, Lg 8's ........ | | 60. | 85. | 95. | 125. | 275. | 575. | 1,600. |
| 1828, Sq Base 2, Sm 8's, Large Letters .............. | | 60. | 85. | 95. | 125. | 275. | 575. | 1,600. |
| 1828, Sq Base 2, Sm 8's and Letters ................ | | 65. | 90. | 110. | 160. | 350. | 825. | 1,900. |
| 1829, All kinds ........3,712,156 | | | | | | | | |
| 1829, 9 Over 7 .............. | | 65. | 95. | 115. | 165. | 375. | 900. | 2,950. |
| 1829 ...................... | | 60. | 85. | 95. | 125. | 275. | 575. | 1,600. |
| 1829, Large Letters ....3,712,156 | | 65. | 90. | 110. | 135. | 350. | 900. | 1,850. |

**1830, Small 0**

**1832, Large Letters Reverse**

*Raised segment lines to right, 1830.*

*Raised segment lines to left, 1830–1831.*

*Adopted edge, 1830–1836.*

| | Mintage | G-4 | F-12 | VF-20 | EF-40 | AU-50 | MS-60 | MS-63 |
|---|---|---|---|---|---|---|---|---|
| 1830, All kinds.... 4,764,800 | | | | | | | | |
| 1830, Small 0.......... | | $60. | $85. | $95. | $125. | $275. | $575. | $1,600. |
| 1830, Large 0.......... | | 60. | 85. | 95. | 125. | 275. | 575. | 1,600. |
| 1830, Large Letters ...... | | 1,250. | 2,750. | 3,750. | 4,750. | 9,500. | — | |
| 1831............5,873,660 | | 60. | 85. | 95. | 125. | 275. | 575. | 1,600. |
| 1832, All kinds.... 4,797,000 | | | | | | | | |
| 1832.............. | | 60. | 85. | 95. | 125. | 275. | 575. | 1,600. |
| 1832, Large Letters ...... | | 60. | 85. | 95. | 125. | 275. | 575. | 1,700. |
| 1833............5,206,000 | | 60. | 85. | 95. | 125. | 275. | 575. | 1,600. |

## Slightly Modified Portrait (1834–1836)

**1834, Large Date**

**1834, Small Date**

**1834, Large Letters Reverse**

**1834, Small Letters Reverse**

**1836, 50 Over 00**

*Proofs of 1833, 1834, and 1835 with crushed edge-lettering use the same reverse die as the 1836 with beaded border reverse. All are very rare.*

# HALF DOLLARS

| | Mintage | G-4 | F-12 | VF-20 | EF-40 | AU-50 | MS-60 | MS-63 |
|---|---|---|---|---|---|---|---|---|
| 1834, All kinds ........6,412,004 | | | | | | | | |
| 1834, Lg Dt and Ltrs ........... | | $60. | $85. | $95. | $125. | $275. | $575. | $1,600. |
| 1834, Lg Dt, Sm Ltrs ........... | | 60. | 85. | 95. | 125. | 275. | 575. | 1,600. |
| 1834, Sm Dt, Stars, Ltrs ........ | | 60. | 85. | 95. | 125. | 275. | 575. | 1,600. |
| 1835 ...............5,352,006 | | 60. | 85. | 95. | 125. | 275. | 575. | 1,600. |
| 1836, All kinds ........6,545,000 | | | | | | | | |
| 1836 ........................ | | 60. | 85. | 95. | 125. | 275. | 575. | 1,600. |
| 1836 Over 1336 .............. | | 75. | 95. | 115. | 140. | 325. | 700. | 1,750. |
| 1836, 50 Over 00 ............. | | 85. | 115. | 140. | 275. | 750. | 1,500. | 4,000. |
| 1836, Beaded Border on Rev .... | | 75. | 100. | 120. | 225. | 475. | 950. | 1,850. |

## CAPPED BUST, REEDED EDGE

*Designer Christian Gobrecht; weight 13.36 grams; composition .900 silver, .100 copper; diameter 30 mm; reeded edge. All coined at Philadelphia.*

**G-4 GOOD**—LIBERTY barely discernible on headband.
**VG-8 VERY GOOD**—Some letters in LIBERTY clear.
**F-12 FINE**—LIBERTY complete but faint.
**VF-20 VERY FINE**—LIBERTY sharp. Shoulder clasp clear.
**EF-40 EXTREMELY FINE**—LIBERTY sharp and strong. Hair details visible.
**AU-50 ABOUT UNCIRCULATED**—Slight trace of wear on cap, cheek, and hair above forehead, and on eagle's claws, wing tops, and head.
**MS-60 UNCIRCULATED**—No trace of wear. Light blemishes.
**MS-63 CHOICE UNCIRCULATED**—Some distracting contact marks or blemishes in prime focal areas. Impaired luster possible.

## Reverse 50 CENTS (1836–1837)

| | Mintage | G-4 | VG-8 | F-12 | VF-20 | EF-40 | AU-50 | MS-60 | MS-63 |
|---|---|---|---|---|---|---|---|---|---|
| 1836 .................1,200 | | $850. | $1,100. | $1,650. | $1,950. | $2,750. | $4,000. | $8,500. | $17,500. |
| 1837 .............3,629,820 | | 65. | 75. | 95. | 120. | 175. | 375. | 825. | 2,250. |

## Reverse HALF DOL. (1838–1839)

The 1838-O was the first branch mint half dollar, though not mentioned in the Mint director's report. The New Orleans chief coiner stated that only 20 were struck. In 1838 and 1839 the mintmark appears on the obverse; thereafter, through 1915, all mintmarks are on the reverse.

*See next page for chart.*

| | Mintage | G-4 | VG-8 | F-12 | VF-20 | EF-40 | AU-50 | MS-60 | MS-63 |
|---|---|---|---|---|---|---|---|---|---|
| 1838 | 3,546,000 | $70. | $80. | $95. | $115. | $190. | $375. | $850. | $2,250. |
| 1838O | 20 | | | | | 150,000. | 200,000. | 375,000. | 675,000. |
| *$632,500, PF-64 BM, Heritage auction, Jun-05* | | | | | | | | | |
| 1839 | 1,392,976 | 70. | 80. | 95. | 115. | 190. | 375. | 950. | 2,350. |
| 1839, Sm Ltr Rev *(ex. rare)* | | | | | — | — | | | |
| 1839O | 178,976 | 170. | 245. | 325. | 450. | 775. | 1,200. | 3,000. | 6,250. |

## LIBERTY SEATED (1839–1891)

**G-4 GOOD**—Scant rim. LIBERTY on shield worn off. Date and letters legible.
**VG-8 VERY GOOD**—Rim fairly defined. Some letters in LIBERTY evident.
**F-12 FINE**—LIBERTY complete, but weak.
**VF-20 VERY FINE**—LIBERTY mostly sharp.
**EF-40 EXTREMELY FINE**—LIBERTY entirely sharp. Scroll edges and clasp distinct.
**AU-50 ABOUT UNCIRCULATED**—Slight trace of wear on Liberty's breast and knees, and on eagle's head, claws, and wing tops.
**MS-60 UNCIRCULATED**—No trace of wear. Light blemishes.
**MS-63 CHOICE UNCIRCULATED**—Some distracting contact marks or blemishes in prime focal areas. Impaired luster possible.

## Variety 1 – No Motto Above Eagle (1839–1853)

*Designer Christian Gobrecht; weight 13.36 grams; composition .900 silver, .100 copper; diameter 30.6 mm; reeded edge; mints: Philadelphia, New Orleans.*

**No Drapery From Elbow**

| | G-4 | VG-8 | F-12 | VF-20 | EF-40 | AU-50 | MS-60 |
|---|---|---|---|---|---|---|---|
| 1839, No Drapery From Elbow | $45. | $85. | $135. | $340. | $850. | $1,750. | $6,000. |

**Drapery From Elbow (Starting 1839)** | **Small Letters in Legend (1839–1841)** | **1840 (Only), Medium Letters, Large Eagle**

| | Mintage | G-4 | VG-8 | F-12 | VF-20 | EF-40 | AU-50 | MS-60 | MS-63 |
|---|---|---|---|---|---|---|---|---|---|
| 1839, Drap From Elbow | 1,972,400 | $27. | $35. | $60. | $90. | $140. | $250. | $500. | $2,350. |
| 1840, Sm Letters | 1,435,008 | 30. | 40. | 60. | 85. | 145. | 245. | 550. | 1,000. |
| 1840, Med Letters **(a)** | * | 125. | 175. | 225. | 300. | 575. | 1,200. | 3,000. | 6,500. |
| 1840O | 855,100 | 27. | 35. | 60. | 90. | 115. | 225. | 700. | 2,250. |
| 1841 | 310,000 | 45. | 60. | 95. | 145. | 250. | 350. | 1,300. | 2,250. |
| 1841O | 401,000 | 25. | 35. | 55. | 85. | 180. | 215. | 700. | 2,000. |

* Included in number below. **a.** Struck at the New Orleans Mint from a reverse die of the previous style without mintmark.

| | Mintage | G-4 | VG-8 | F-12 | VF-20 | EF-40 | AU-50 | MS-60 | MS-63 |
|---|---|---|---|---|---|---|---|---|---|
| 1842, Sm Dt, Sm Ltrs ........ | | | | | — | — | — | |
| 1842O, Sm Dt, Sm Ltrs | .203,000 | 550. | 825. | 1,350. | 2,200. | 4,500. | 7,500. | 15,000. | 27,500. |

## *Modified Reverse With Large Letters in Legend (1842–1853)*

**Small Date**

**Medium Date**

**1844-O, Doubled Date**

### Large Letters in Legend (1842–1853)

| | Mintage | G-4 | VG-8 | F-12 | VF-20 | EF-40 | AU-50 | MS-60 | MS-63 |
|---|---|---|---|---|---|---|---|---|---|
| 1842, Medium Date | .2,012,764 | $25. | $35. | $55. | $65. | $115. | $245. | $675. | $1,400. |
| 1842, Small Date | .........* | 25. | 40. | 55. | 80. | 150. | 250. | 1,000. | 2,500. |
| 1842O, Medium Date | .754,000 | 25. | 35. | 55. | 65. | 115. | 315. | 950. | 4,000. |
| 1843 | .3,844,000 | 25. | 35. | 50. | 60. | 105. | 200. | 500. | 1,050. |
| 1843O | .2,268,000 | 25. | 35. | 50. | 60. | 105. | 200. | 700. | 1,250. |
| 1844 | .1,766,000 | 25. | 35. | 50. | 60. | 105. | 200. | 500. | 1,050. |
| 1844O | .2,005,000 | 25. | 35. | 50. | 60. | 105. | 200. | 800. | 2,000. |
| 1844O, Double Date | .........* | 550. | 750. | 1,100. | 1,500. | 2,500. | 6,000. | 9,000. | — |
| 1845 | .589,000 | 30. | 45. | 65. | 115. | 185. | 325. | 850. | 3,000. |
| 1845O | .2,094,000 | 25. | 35. | 50. | 60. | 105. | 200. | 675. | 1,050. |
| 1845O, No Drapery (b) | .......* | 35. | 55. | 75. | 115. | 185. | 300. | 1,250. | 4,500. |

* Included in number above. **b.** Drapery missing because of excessive die polishing.

In 1846 the date size was again enlarged. The 1846 Medium Date is approximately the size of the 1842 Medium Date shown. Tall Date is similar to 1853. See illustrations of cents on page 107.

| | Mintage | G-4 | VG-8 | F-12 | VF-20 | EF-40 | AU-50 | MS-60 | MS-63 |
|---|---|---|---|---|---|---|---|---|---|
| 1846, All kinds | .2,210,000 | | | | | | | | |
| 1846, Medium Date | ......... | $25. | $35. | $50. | $70. | $115. | $225. | $575. | $1,350. |
| 1846, Tall Date | ............. | 30. | 40. | 55. | 75. | 130. | 275. | 800. | 1,500. |
| 1846, 6 Over Horiz 6 | ........ | 135. | 200. | 275. | 425. | 575. | 1,250. | 3,250. | 10,000. |
| 1846O, Medium Date | .2,304,000 | 30. | 40. | 55. | 75. | 115. | 250. | 950. | 1,950. |
| 1846O, Tall Date | .............* | 135. | 265. | 350. | 550. | 1,000. | 1,850. | 6,500. | |
| 1847, 7 Over 6 | .............* | 1,800. | 2,500. | 3,250. | 4,500. | 6,500. | 10,000. | 20,000. | |
| 1847 | .1,156,000 | 25. | 35. | 50. | 70. | 115. | 225. | 575. | 1,000. |
| 1847O | .2,584,000 | 25. | 35. | 50. | 70. | 120. | 250. | 650. | 2,250. |
| 1848 | .580,000 | 45. | 65. | 90. | 150. | 225. | 475. | 1,000. | 1,650. |
| 1848O | .3,180,000 | 25. | 35. | 55. | 75. | 115. | 250. | 750. | 1,950. |
| 1849 | .1,252,000 | 25. | 35. | 55. | 75. | 140. | 350. | 850. | 1,950. |
| 1849O | .2,310,000 | 25. | 35. | 55. | 75. | 115. | 250. | 750. | 2,250. |
| 1850 | .227,000 | 225. | 275. | 425. | 550. | 750. | 800. | 1,600. | 4,000. |
| 1850O | .2,456,000 | 25. | 35. | 55. | 75. | 115. | 250. | 600. | 1,200. |
| 1851 | .200,750 | 275. | 375. | 475. | 575. | 750. | 1,000. | 1,750. | 3,250. |
| 1851O | .402,000 | 25. | 35. | 55. | 75. | 165. | 250. | 675. | 1,250. |

* Included in regular mintage.

*Chart continued on next page.*

| | Mintage | G-4 | VG-8 | F-12 | VF-20 | EF-40 | AU-50 | MS-60 | MS-63 |
|---|---|---|---|---|---|---|---|---|---|
| 1852 | 77,130 | $350. | $475. | $600. | $850. | $950. | $1,250. | $1,850. | $2,250. |
| 1852O | 144,000 | 65. | 115. | 175. | 300. | 550. | 1,100. | 2,500. | 7,500. |
| 1853O *(3 known)* | | | 225,000. | 275,000. | 350,000. | | | | |

## Variety 2 – Arrows at Date, Rays Around Eagle (1853)

*Weight 12.44 grams; composition .900 silver, .100 copper; diameter 30.6 mm; reeded edge; mints: Philadelphia, New Orleans, San Francisco, Carson City.*

| | Mintage | G-4 | VG-8 | F-12 | VF-20 | EF-40 | AU-50 | MS-60 | MS-63 |
|---|---|---|---|---|---|---|---|---|---|
| 1853 | 3,532,708 | $25. | $35. | $50. | $105. | $275. | $625. | $1,500. | $3,500. |
| 1853O | 1,328,000 | 30. | 40. | 60. | 120. | 300. | 725. | 2,500. | 4,750. |

## Variety 3 – Arrows at Date, No Rays (1854–1855)

| | Mintage | G-4 | VG-8 | F-12 | VF-20 | EF-40 | AU-50 | MS-60 | MS-63 |
|---|---|---|---|---|---|---|---|---|---|
| 1854 | 2,982,000 | $25. | $35. | $55. | $75. | $115. | $285. | $700. | $1,500. |
| 1854O | 5,240,000 | 25. | 35. | 55. | 75. | 115. | 285. | 700. | 1,500. |
| 1855, All kinds | 759,500 | | | | | | | | |
| 1855 Over 1854 | | 65. | 85. | 175. | 265. | 400. | 600. | 2,150. | 3,500. |
| 1855, Normal Date | | 25. | 35. | 55. | 75. | 115. | 285. | 700. | 1,750. |
| 1855O | 3,688,000 | 25. | 35. | 55. | 75. | 115. | 285. | 700. | 1,650. |
| 1855S | 129,950 | 325. | 500. | 800. | 1,400. | 3,250. | 6,500. | 16,500. | — |

## Variety 1 Resumed (1856–1866; Weight Standard of 1853)

| | Mintage | G-4 | VG-8 | F-12 | VF-20 | EF-40 | AU-50 | MS-60 | MS-63 | PF-63 |
|---|---|---|---|---|---|---|---|---|---|---|
| 1856 | 938,000 | $24. | $32. | $50. | $65. | $100. | $225. | $500. | $950. | |
| 1856O | 2,658,000 | 24. | 32. | 50. | 65. | 100. | 200. | 500. | 950. | |
| 1856S | 211,000 | 45. | 70. | 115. | 235. | 500. | 950. | 3,500. | — | |
| 1857 | 1,988,000 | 24. | 32. | 50. | 65. | 100. | 200. | 500. | 950. | |
| 1857O | 818,000 | 24. | 32. | 50. | 65. | 135. | 250. | 950. | 3,000. | |
| 1857S | 158,000 | 60. | 90. | 165. | 250. | 500. | 1,050. | 3,750. | — | |
| 1858 *(300+)* | 4,225,700 | 24. | 32. | 50. | 65. | 100. | 200. | 450. | 950. | $2,500. |
| 1858O | 7,294,000 | 24. | 32. | 50. | 65. | 100. | 200. | 450. | 950. | |
| 1858S | 476,000 | 35. | 48. | 65. | 115. | 225. | 400. | 950. | 3,750. | |
| 1859 *(800)* | 747,200 | 24. | 32. | 50. | 65. | 100. | 250. | 500. | 1,100. | 1,300. |
| 1859O | 2,834,000 | 24. | 32. | 50. | 65. | 100. | 225. | 450. | 1,000. | |
| 1859S | 566,000 | 35. | 40. | 60. | 85. | 175. | 300. | 950. | 3,000. | |
| 1860 *(1,000)* | 302,700 | 30. | 35. | 55. | 65. | 115. | 275. | 600. | 1,000. | 1,200. |
| 1860O | 1,290,000 | 25. | 35. | 50. | 65. | 100. | 200. | 450. | 1,000. | |
| 1860S | 472,000 | 30. | 35. | 55. | 65. | 115. | 215. | 700. | 3,000. | |

The 1861-O quantity includes 330,000 struck under the United States government, 1,240,000 for the State of Louisiana after it seceded from the Union, and 962,633 after Louisiana joined the Confederate States of America. As all these 1861-O coins were struck from U.S. dies, it is impossible to distinguish one from another. They should not be confused with the very rare Confederate half dollar of 1861, which has a distinctive reverse (see page 375).

| | Mintage | G-4 | VG-8 | F-12 | VF-20 | EF-40 | AU-50 | MS-60 | MS-63 | PF-63 |
|---|---|---|---|---|---|---|---|---|---|---|
| 1861 (1,000) | 2,887,400 | $24. | $32. | $50. | $65. | $115. | $200. | $500. | $950. | $1,200. |
| 1861O | 2,532,633 | 24. | 32. | 50. | 65. | 115. | 215. | 500. | 950. | |
| 1861O, Cracked Obv **(a)** | | 75. | 100. | 175. | 275. | 350. | 550. | 1,250. | 2,250. | |
| 1861S | 939,500 | 24. | 32. | 50. | 65. | 115. | 225. | 625. | 2,150. | |
| 1862 ...(550) | 253,000 | 35. | 50. | 75. | 115. | 225. | 275. | 650. | 1,000. | 1,200. |
| 1862S | 1,352,000 | 24. | 32. | 50. | 65. | 115. | 215. | 600. | 1,650. | |
| 1863 ...(460) | 503,200 | 35. | 45. | 75. | 90. | 135. | 275. | 525. | 1,150. | 1,200. |
| 1863S | 916,000 | 35. | 45. | 75. | 90. | 135. | 275. | 600. | 1,450. | |
| 1864 ...(470) | 379,100 | 35. | 45. | 65. | 100. | 155. | 300. | 500. | 1,150. | 1,200. |
| 1864S | 658,000 | 28. | 35. | 55. | 65. | 115. | 250. | 675. | 2,800. | |
| 1865 ...(500) | 511,400 | 30. | 40. | 60. | 80. | 150. | 300. | 700. | 1,150. | 1,200. |
| 1865S | 675,000 | 28. | 35. | 55. | 65. | 115. | 250. | 650. | 1,750. | |
| 1866S, No Motto | 60,000 | 225. | 325. | 450. | 800. | 1,500. | 2,000. | 4,750. | 9,500. | |
| 1866 *(unique)* | | | | | | | | | | |

a. Crack from nose to border; same obverse die used to coin pattern Confederate half dollars (see page 375).

# Variety 4 – Motto Above Eagle (1866–1873, 1875–1891)

| | Mintage | G-4 | VG-8 | F-12 | VF-20 | EF-40 | AU-50 | MS-60 | MS-63 | PF-63 |
|---|---|---|---|---|---|---|---|---|---|---|
| 1866 .... (725) | 744,900 | $25. | $35. | $55. | $65. | $115. | $185. | $475. | $1,250. | $900. |
| 1866S | 994,000 | 25. | 35. | 55. | 65. | 115. | 200. | 600. | 2,000. | |
| 1867 .... (625) | 449,300 | 30. | 40. | 70. | 115. | 175. | 250. | 525. | 1,350. | 900. |
| 1867S | 1,196,000 | 25. | 35. | 55. | 65. | 115. | 185. | 575. | 1,900. | |
| 1868 .... (600) | 417,600 | 45. | 55. | 90. | 165. | 250. | 285. | 600. | 1,200. | 900. |
| 1868S | 1,160,000 | 25. | 35. | 55. | 65. | 100. | 225. | 600. | 1,750. | |
| 1869 .... (600) | 795,300 | 25. | 35. | 55. | 70. | 125. | 200. | 525. | 1,150. | 900. |
| 1869S | 656,000 | 25. | 35. | 55. | 70. | 125. | 200. | 825. | 2,600. | |
| 1870... (1,000) | 633,900 | 25. | 35. | 55. | 65. | 115. | 190. | 475. | 1,100. | 900. |
| 1870CC | 54,617 | 850. | 1,250. | 2,500. | 5,500. | 13,500. | 24,000. | — | — | |
| 1870S | 1,004,000 | 24. | 32. | 50. | 65. | 120. | 250. | 850. | 2,850. | |
| 1871 .... (960) | 1,203,600 | 24. | 32. | 50. | 65. | 100. | 200. | 475. | 1,100. | 900. |
| 1871CC | 153,950 | 175. | 275. | 475. | 850. | 1,800. | 3,250. | 13,500. | 42,500. | |
| 1871S | 2,178,000 | 24. | 32. | 50. | 65. | 105. | 200. | 600. | 1,400. | |
| 1872 .... (950) | 880,600 | 24. | 32. | 50. | 65. | 115. | 215. | 500. | 1,400. | 900. |
| 1872CC | 257,000 | 75. | 115. | 225. | 450. | 900. | 1,750. | 5,500. | 35,000. | |
| 1872S | 580,000 | 28. | 48. | 65. | 115. | 200. | 350. | 1,200. | 2,750. | |
| 1873, Cl 3 (600) | 587,000 | 28. | 48. | 65. | 105. | 155. | 235. | 600. | 1,100. | 900. |

*Chart continued on next page.*

| | Mintage | G-4 | VG-8 | F-12 | VF-20 | EF-40 | AU-50 | MS-60 | MS-63 | PF-63 |
|---|---|---|---|---|---|---|---|---|---|---|
| 1873, Open 3 | ...214,200 | $2,750. | $3,500. | $4,500. | $6,000. | $7,000. | $8,500. | $17,500. | | |
| 1873CC | ......122,500 | 150. | 250. | 350. | 625. | 1,350. | 3,500. | 9,000. | $50,000. | |
| 1873S, No Arr | .....5,000 | *Unknown in any collection.* | | | | | | | | |

## Variety 5 – Arrows at Date (1873–1874)

*Weight 12.50 grams; composition .900 silver, .100 copper; diameter 30.6 mm; reeded edge; mints: Philadelphia, Carson City, San Francisco.*

*Arrows placed at date to show change in weight from 12.44 to 12.50 grams.*

| | Mintage | G-4 | VG-8 | F-12 | VF-20 | EF-40 | AU-50 | MS-60 | MS-63 | PF-63 |
|---|---|---|---|---|---|---|---|---|---|---|
| 1873 | ...(550) 1,815,150 | $35. | $45. | $60. | $100. | $250. | $375. | $950. | $2,000. | $2,150. |
| 1873CC | .......214,560 | 140. | 235. | 375. | 950. | 1,850. | 3,000. | 6,500. | 17,500. | |
| 1873S | .......228,000 | 55. | 80. | 125. | 250. | 450. | 700. | 2,500. | 6,000. | |
| 1874 | ...(700) 2,359,600 | 35. | 45. | 60. | 100. | 250. | 375. | 950. | 2,000. | 2,150. |
| 1874CC | ........59,000 | 350. | 550. | 950. | 1,650. | 3,000. | 5,000. | 10,500. | 20,000. | |
| 1874S | .......394,000 | 40. | 50. | 90. | 200. | 350. | 700. | 1,800. | 4,000. | |

## Variety 4 Resumed (1875–1891)

| | Mintage | G-4 | VG-8 | F-12 | VF-20 | EF-40 | AU-50 | MS-60 | MS-63 | PF-63 |
|---|---|---|---|---|---|---|---|---|---|---|
| 1875 | ... (700) 6,026,800 | $24. | $30. | $50. | $65. | $95. | $185. | $500. | $700. | $900. |
| 1875CC | .....1,008,000 | 35. | 45. | 65. | 95. | 175. | 275. | 650. | 1,500. | |
| 1875S | .........3,200,000 | 24. | 30. | 50. | 65. | 95. | 185. | 500. | 700. | |
| 1876 | (1,150) 8,418,000 | 24. | 30. | 50. | 65. | 95. | 185. | 500. | 700. | 900. |
| 1876CC | .....1,956,000 | 25. | 35. | 55. | 85. | 150. | 250. | 675. | 1,350. | |
| 1876S | .......4,528,000 | 24. | 30. | 50. | 65. | 95. | 185. | 500. | 700. | |
| 1877 | ... (510) 8,304,000 | 24. | 30. | 50. | 65. | 95. | 185. | 500. | 700. | |
| 1877, 7/6 | ...........* | | 115. | 350. | 700. | 1,100. | | | | |
| 1877CC | .....1,420,000 | 35. | 45. | 65. | 95. | 165. | 275. | 700. | 1,000. | |
| 1877S | .......5,356,000 | 24. | 30. | 50. | 65. | 95. | 185. | 500. | 700. | |
| 1878 | ... (800) 1,377,600 | 24. | 30. | 50. | 65. | 95. | 185. | 500. | 700. | 900. |
| 1878CC | ........62,000 | 350. | 500. | 950. | 1,500. | 3,000. | 4,000. | 6,750. | 20,000. | |
| 1878S | .........12,000 | 15,000. | 25,000. | 30,000. | 35,000. | 40,000. | 45,000. | 55,000. | 95,000. | |
| 1879 | (1,100) ...4,800 | 250. | 300. | 350. | 400. | 500. | 600. | 800. | 1,000. | 900. |
| 1880 | (1,355) ....8,400 | 250. | 300. | 350. | 400. | 500. | 600. | 800. | 1,000. | 900. |
| 1881 | ... (975) ...10,000 | 250. | 300. | 350. | 400. | 500. | 600. | 800. | 1,000. | 900. |
| 1882 | (1,100) ...4,400 | 250. | 300. | 350. | 400. | 500. | 600. | 800. | 1,000. | 900. |
| 1883 | (1,039) ....8,000 | 250. | 300. | 350. | 400. | 500. | 600. | 800. | 1,000. | 900. |
| 1884 | ... (875) ....4,400 | 300. | 350. | 400. | 500. | 600. | 800. | 900. | 1,100. | 900. |
| 1885 | ... (930) ....5,200 | 300. | 350. | 400. | 500. | 600. | 800. | 900. | 1,100. | 900. |
| 1886 | ... (886) ....5,000 | 350. | 450. | 550. | 650. | 750. | 800. | 900. | 1,200. | 900. |
| 1887 | ... (710) ....5,000 | 450. | 500. | 550. | 650. | 750. | 800. | 1,000. | 1,300. | 900. |
| 1888 | ... (832) ...12,001 | 250. | 300. | 350. | 400. | 450. | 550. | 750. | 1,000. | 900. |
| 1889 | ... (711) ...12,000 | 250. | 300. | 350. | 400. | 450. | 550. | 750. | 1,000. | 900. |
| 1890 | ... (590) ...12,000 | 250. | 300. | 350. | 400. | 450. | 550. | 750. | 1,000. | 900. |
| 1891 | ... (600) ..200,000 | 50. | 65. | 100. | 125. | 150. | 225. | 450. | 750. | 900. |

* Included in number above.

# BARBER OR LIBERTY HEAD (1892–1915)

Like the dime and quarter dollar, this type was designed by Charles E. Barber, whose initial B is at the truncation of the neck.

*Designer Charles E. Barber; weight 12.50 grams; composition .900 silver, .100 copper; diameter 30.6 mm; reeded edge; mints: Philadelphia, Denver, New Orleans, San Francisco.*

**G-4 GOOD**—Date and legends legible. LIBERTY worn off headband.
**VG-8 VERY GOOD**—Some letters legible in LIBERTY.
**F-12 FINE**—LIBERTY nearly completely legible, but worn.
**VF-20 VERY FINE**—All letters in LIBERTY evenly plain.
**EF-40 EXTREMELY FINE**—LIBERTY bold, and its ribbon distinct.
**AU-50 ABOUT UNCIRCULATED**—Slight trace of wear above forehead, leaf tips, and cheek, and on eagle's head, tail, and wing tips.
**MS-60 UNCIRCULATED**—No trace of wear. Light blemishes.
**MS-63 CHOICE UNCIRCULATED**—Some distracting contact marks or blemishes in prime focal areas. Impaired luster possible.
**PF-63 CHOICE PROOF**—Reflective surfaces with only a few blemishes in secondary focal places. No major flaws.

*Mintmark location on reverse, below eagle.*

| Mintage | G-4 | VG-8 | F-12 | VF-20 | EF-40 | AU-50 | MS-60 | MS-63 | PF-63 |
|---|---|---|---|---|---|---|---|---|---|
| 1892 . .(1,245) . .934,000 | $27. | $40. | $70. | $115. | $200. | $300. | $500. | $850. | $900. |
| 1892O . . . . . . . .390,000 | 275. | 350. | 450. | 500. | 550. | 675. | 850. | 1,700. | |
| 1892O, Micro O (a) . . . .* | 1,500. | 2,500. | 4,000. | 6,000. | 10,000. | 13,500. | 20,000. | | |
| 1892S . . . . . . .1,029,028 | 225. | 300. | 400. | 500. | 550. | 700. | 950. | 2,250. | |
| 1893 . . .(792) 1,826,000 | 20. | 30. | 75. | 125. | 200. | 325. | 550. | 1,350. | 900. |
| 1893O . . . . . . .1,389,000 | 35. | 55. | 115. | 185. | 350. | 400. | 650. | 1,750. | |
| 1893S . . . . . . . .740,000 | 155. | 215. | 275. | 425. | 525. | 650. | 1,250. | 3,500. | |
| 1894 . . .(972) 1,148,000 | 30. | 45. | 110. | 185. | 275. | 375. | 525. | 1,050. | 900. |
| 1894O . . . . . . .2,138,000 | 25. | 35. | 90. | 160. | 275. | 325. | 500. | 1,050. | |
| 1894S . . . . . . .4,048,690 | 20. | 30. | 75. | 135. | 235. | 350. | 500. | 1,500. | |
| 1895 . . .(880) 1,834,338 | 18. | 25. | 70. | 140. | 200. | 300. | 550. | 1,000. | 900. |
| 1895O . . . . . . .1,766,000 | 25. | 35. | 100. | 175. | 250. | 350. | 575. | 1,500. | |
| 1895S . . . . . . .1,108,086 | 28. | 50. | 125. | 225. | 275. | 375. | 550. | 1,400. | |
| 1896 . . .(762) . .950,000 | 20. | 25. | 85. | 140. | 235. | 325. | 550. | 950. | 900. |
| 1896O . . . . . . . .924,000 | 40. | 55. | 175. | 250. | 425. | 700. | 1,400. | 5,750. | |
| 1896S . . . . . . .1,140,948 | 90. | 125. | 200. | 300. | 475. | 700. | 1,300. | 3,500. | |
| 1897 . . .(731) 2,480,000 | 13. | 14. | 45. | 95. | 165. | 300. | 475. | 900. | 900. |
| 1897O . . . . . . . .632,000 | 150. | 225. | 475. | 750. | 975. | 1,200. | 1,700. | 3,750. | |
| 1897S . . . . . . . .933,900 | 150. | 185. | 350. | 500. | 800. | 950. | 1,400. | 3,750. | |
| 1898 . . .(735) 2,956,000 | 12. | 15. | 38. | 95. | 150. | 300. | 475. | 900. | 900. |
| 1898O . . . . . . . .874,000 | 35. | 70. | 225. | 325. | 425. | 600. | 1,150. | 3,250. | |
| 1898S . . . . . . .2,358,550 | 28. | 45. | 85. | 150. | 275. | 375. | 900. | 3,600. | |
| 1899 . . .(846) 5,538,000 | 14. | 19. | 35. | 95. | 150. | 300. | 475. | 900. | 900. |
| 1899O . . . . . . .1,724,000 | 24. | 35. | 75. | 150. | 250. | 350. | 600. | 1,500. | |
| 1899S . . . . . . .1,686,411 | 24. | 35. | 70. | 135. | 225. | 325. | 600. | 2,250. | |

* Included in number above. **a.** Normal and "microscopic" mintmarks; see page 20.

*Chart continued on next page.*     

| | Mintage | G-4 | VG-8 | F-12 | VF-20 | EF-40 | AU-50 | MS-60 | MS-63 | PF-63 |
|---|---|---|---|---|---|---|---|---|---|---|
| 1900 ..(912) | 4,762,000 | $13. | $16. | $38. | $90. | $150. | $300. | $475. | $900. | $800. |
| 1900O | 2,744,000 | 16. | 25. | 55. | 165. | 250. | 350. | 750. | 3,250. | |
| 1900S | 2,560,322 | 15. | 19. | 45. | 100. | 200. | 300. | 600. | 2,400. | |
| 1901 ..(813) | 4,268,000 | 13. | 16. | 38. | 90. | 150. | 300. | 475. | 900. | 800. |
| 1901O | 1,124,000 | 16. | 25. | 75. | 190. | 325. | 450. | 1,300. | 5,250. | |
| 1901S | 847,044 | 30. | 55. | 165. | 325. | 650. | 1,000. | 1,800. | 5,500. | |
| 1902 ..(777) | 4,922,000 | 12. | 14. | 30. | 90. | 155. | 300. | 475. | 900. | 800. |
| 1902O | 2,526,000 | 14. | 18. | 55. | 100. | 200. | 350. | 750. | 3,500. | |
| 1902S | 1,460,670 | 16. | 25. | 60. | 145. | 250. | 365. | 750. | 2,500. | |
| 1903 ..(755) | 2,278,000 | 12. | 14. | 30. | 90. | 160. | 300. | 500. | 1,600. | 800. |
| 1903O | 2,100,000 | 14. | 18. | 55. | 115. | 225. | 350. | 600. | 1,900. | |
| 1903S | 1,920,772 | 15. | 18. | 58. | 115. | 225. | 350. | 600. | 2,000. | |
| 1904 ..(670) | 2,992,000 | 13. | 14. | 35. | 85. | 155. | 300. | 450. | 1,250. | 800. |
| 1904O | 1,117,600 | 20. | 30. | 80. | 200. | 375. | 600. | 1,200. | 3,500. | |
| 1904S | 553,038 | 38. | 70. | 250. | 525. | 1,000. | 1,500. | 6,000. | 13,500. | |
| 1905 ..(727) | 662,000 | 24. | 28. | 85. | 165. | 250. | 325. | 550. | 1,500. | 800. |
| 1905O | 505,000 | 30. | 45. | 115. | 225. | 325. | 400. | 750. | 1,750. | |
| 1905S | 2,494,000 | 15. | 18. | 50. | 120. | 225. | 350. | 650. | 2,000. | |
| 1906 ..(675) | 2,638,000 | 12. | 14. | 30. | 85. | 165. | 300. | 475. | 850. | 800. |
| 1906D | 4,028,000 | 12. | 14. | 35. | 85. | 160. | 300. | 450. | 850. | |
| 1906O | 2,446,000 | 12. | 14. | 40. | 95. | 180. | 300. | 600. | 1,500. | |
| 1906S | 1,740,154 | 12. | 16. | 55. | 110. | 220. | 300. | 600. | 1,300. | |
| 1907 ..(575) | 2,598,000 | 12. | 14. | 30. | 85. | 150. | 300. | 475. | 850. | 800. |
| 1907D | 3,856,000 | 12. | 14. | 35. | 80. | 150. | 300. | 475. | 850. | |
| 1907O | 3,946,600 | 12. | 14. | 35. | 80. | 150. | 300. | 475. | 850. | |
| 1907S | 1,250,000 | 16. | 25. | 80. | 155. | 300. | 600. | 1,200. | 6,500. | |
| 1908 ..(545) | 1,354,000 | 12. | 14. | 30. | 80. | 150. | 300. | 475. | 850. | 800. |
| 1908D | 3,280,000 | 12. | 14. | 30. | 80. | 150. | 300. | 475. | 850. | |
| 1908O | 5,360,000 | 12. | 14. | 30. | 85. | 150. | 300. | 475. | 950. | |
| 1908S | 1,644,828 | 12. | 25. | 70. | 150. | 250. | 380. | 850. | 2,400. | |
| 1909 ..(650) | 2,368,000 | 12. | 14. | 30. | 80. | 150. | 300. | 475. | 850. | 800. |
| 1909O | 925,400 | 17. | 22. | 55. | 135. | 300. | 475. | 800. | 1,750. | |
| 1909S | 1,764,000 | 12. | 14. | 38. | 95. | 200. | 315. | 600. | 1,250. | |
| 1910 ..(551) | 418,000 | 20. | 28. | 85. | 160. | 300. | 400. | 600. | 1,150. | 800. |
| 1910S | 1,948,000 | 14. | 18. | 35. | 95. | 180. | 325. | 600. | 1,850. | |
| 1911 ..(543) | 1,406,000 | 12. | 14. | 30. | 85. | 150. | 300. | 450. | 850. | 800. |
| 1911D | 695,080 | 12. | 17. | 40. | 95. | 185. | 275. | 525. | 900. | |
| 1911S | 1,272,000 | 12. | 16. | 40. | 90. | 175. | 300. | 600. | 1,350. | |
| 1912 ..(700) | 1,550,000 | 12. | 14. | 30. | 85. | 150. | 300. | 475. | 850. | 800. |
| 1912D | 2,300,800 | 12. | 14. | 30. | 85. | 150. | 300. | 475. | 850. | |
| 1912S | 1,370,000 | 12. | 14. | 30. | 85. | 185. | 300. | 525. | 1,100. | |
| 1913 ..(627) | 188,000 | 70. | 85. | 200. | 375. | 550. | 800. | 1,100. | 1,500. | 1,000. |
| 1913D | 534,000 | 12. | 15. | 40. | 100. | 200. | 300. | 475. | 950. | |
| 1913S | 604,000 | 18. | 25. | 50. | 100. | 225. | 325. | 600. | 1,250. | |
| 1914 ..(380) | 124,230 | 130. | 155. | 300. | 500. | 750. | 950. | 1,250. | 1,800. | 1,300. |
| 1914S | 992,000 | 15. | 18. | 40. | 95. | 200. | 300. | 550. | 1,150. | |
| 1915 ..(450) | 138,000 | 85. | 115. | 230. | 350. | 550. | 800. | 1,200. | 2,200. | 1,200. |
| 1915D | 1,170,400 | 12. | 14. | 30. | 80. | 150. | 300. | 475. | 850. | |
| 1915S | 1,604,000 | 12. | 14. | 30. | 80. | 150. | 300. | 475. | 850. | |

## LIBERTY WALKING (1916–1947)

This type was designed by Adolph A. Weinman, whose monogram, AW, appears under the tips of the wing feathers. On the 1916 coins and some of the 1917 coins the mintmark is located on the obverse below the motto.

*Designer Adolph A. Weinman; weight 12.50 grams; composition .900 silver, .100 copper (net weight: .36169 oz. pure silver); diameter 30.6 mm; reeded edge; mints: Philadelphia, Denver, San Francisco.*

**G-4 GOOD**—Rims defined. Motto IN GOD WE TRUST legible.
**VG-8 VERY GOOD**—Motto distinct. About half of skirt lines at left clear.
**F-12 FINE**—All skirt lines evident, but worn in spots. Clear details in sandal below motto.
**VF-20 VERY FINE**—Skirt lines sharp, including leg area. Little wear on breast and right arm.
**EF-40 EXTREMELY FINE**—All skirt lines bold.
**AU-50 ABOUT UNCIRCULATED**—Slight trace of wear on Liberty's head, knee, and breasts, and on eagle's claws and head.
**MS-60 UNCIRCULATED**—No trace of wear. Light blemishes.
**MS-63 CHOICE UNCIRCULATED**—Some distracting contact marks or blemishes in prime focal areas. Impaired luster possible.
**PF-65 GEM PROOF**—Brilliant surfaces with no noticeable blemishes or flaws. A few scattered, barely noticeable marks or hairlines possible.

**Mintmark Locations**

*Choice Uncirculated, well-struck specimens are worth more than values listed.*

| | Mintage | G-4 | VG-8 | F-12 | VF-20 | EF-40 | AU-50 | MS-60 | MS-63 | PF-65 |
|---|---|---|---|---|---|---|---|---|---|---|
| 1916 | 608,000 | $40. | $45. | $95. | $165. | $225. | $260. | $350. | $450. | |
| 1916D, Obv | 1,014,400 | 35. | 45. | 80. | 135. | 200. | 250. | 350. | 600. | |
| 1916S, Obv | 508,000 | 120. | 135. | 250. | 400. | 650. | 800. | 1,200. | 2,100. | |
| 1917 | 12,292,000 | 5. | 7. | 10. | 20. | 40. | 65. | 150. | 200. | |
| 1917D, Obv | 765,400 | 20. | 30. | 80. | 150. | 225. | 300. | 550. | 1,250. | |
| 1917D, Rev | 1,940,000 | 12. | 18. | 45. | 150. | 275. | 525. | 900. | 2,000. | |
| 1917S, Obv | 952,000 | 25. | 40. | 125. | 325. | 750. | 1,300. | 2,400. | 5,000. | |
| 1917S, Rev | 5,554,000 | 6. | 9. | 16. | 35. | 65. | 160. | 350. | 2,000. | |
| 1918 | 6,634,000 | 6. | 9. | 18. | 70. | 160. | 250. | 650. | 1,000. | |
| 1918D | 3,853,040 | 9. | 14. | 35. | 90. | 225. | 475. | 1,250. | 2,800. | |
| 1918S | 10,282,000 | 6. | 7. | 15. | 35. | 60. | 195. | 500. | 2,250. | |
| 1919 | 962,000 | 20. | 30. | 75. | 275. | 500. | 800. | 1,250. | 3,500. | |
| 1919D | 1,165,000 | 18. | 35. | 95. | 300. | 750. | 1,750. | 6,000. | 17,500. | |
| 1919S | 1,552,000 | 20. | 30. | 70. | 300. | 850. | 1,700. | 3,000. | 9,500. | |
| 1920 | 6,372,000 | 6. | 7. | 15. | 40. | 80. | 165. | 325. | 650. | |
| 1920D | 1,551,000 | 10. | 20. | 75. | 245. | 450. | 900. | 1,400. | 3,750. | |
| 1920S | 4,624,000 | 6. | 8. | 20. | 80. | 225. | 475. | 850. | 2,800. | |
| 1921 | 246,000 | 165. | 220. | 325. | 750. | 1,800. | 2,850. | 4,250. | 8,500. | |
| 1921D | 208,000 | 265. | 350. | 500. | 875. | 2,500. | 3,500. | 4,750. | 13,500. | |
| 1921S | 548,000 | 50. | 80. | 250. | 900. | 5,500. | 9,000. | 14,000. | 27,500. | |
| 1923S | 2,178,000 | 10. | 14. | 25. | 115. | 275. | 800. | 1,500. | 3,800. | |
| 1927S | 2,392,000 | 7. | 9. | 14. | 50. | 150. | 350. | 950. | 2,000. | |
| 1928S (a, b) | 1,940,000 | 7. | 9. | 16. | 75. | 175. | 425. | 950. | 2,750. | |
| 1929D | 1,001,200 | 8. | 10. | 14. | 28. | 95. | 225. | 375. | 700. | |
| 1929S | 1,902,000 | 7. | 9. | 13. | 26. | 115. | 225. | 385. | 850. | |

**a.** Pieces dated 1928-D are counterfeit. **b.** Large and small mintmark varieties; see page 20.

*Chart continued on next page.*

| | Mintage | G-4 | VG-8 | F-12 | VF-20 | EF-40 | AU-50 | MS-60 | MS-63 | PF-65 |
|---|---|---|---|---|---|---|---|---|---|---|
| 1933S | .......1,786,000 | $8. | $10. | $13. | $18. | $60. | $225. | $600. | $1,200. | |
| 1934 | .......6,964,000 | 4. | 5. | 6. | 7. | 12. | 25. | 85. | 110. | |
| 1934D (b) | ....2,361,000 | 4. | 5. | 7. | 11. | 35. | 85. | 150. | 225. | |
| 1934S | .......3,652,000 | 4. | 5. | 6. | 7. | 30. | 100. | 350. | 800. | |
| 1935 | .......9,162,000 | 4. | 5. | 6. | 7. | 10. | 25. | 45. | 75. | |
| 1935D | .......3,003,800 | 4. | 6. | 7. | 10. | 30. | 70. | 135. | 225. | |
| 1935S | .......3,854,000 | 4. | 5. | 6. | 8. | 28. | 100. | 275. | 425. | |
| 1936 (3,901) | 12,614,000 | 4. | 5. | 6. | 7. | 9. | 25. | 45. | 75. | $6,500. |
| 1936D | .......4,252,400 | 4. | 5. | 6. | 7. | 20. | 55. | 80. | 115. | |
| 1936S | .......3,884,000 | 4. | 5. | 6. | 7. | 20. | 60. | 130. | 185. | |
| 1937 (5,728) | 9,522,000 | 4. | 5. | 6. | 7. | 10. | 25. | 40. | 65. | 1,750. |
| 1937D | .......1,676,000 | 6. | 8. | 9. | 14. | 32. | 110. | 225. | 275. | |
| 1937S | .......2,090,000 | 6. | 7. | 8. | 10. | 20. | 60. | 150. | 185. | |
| 1938 (8,152) | 4,110,000 | 4. | 5. | 6. | 8. | 12. | 45. | 70. | 135. | 1,250. |
| 1938D | ........491,600 | 95. | 105. | 115. | 130. | 165. | 250. | 500. | 650. | |
| 1939 (8,808) | 6,812,000 | | | 5. | 6. | 8. | 25. | 45. | 70. | 1,150. |
| 1939D | .......4,267,800 | | | 6. | 7. | 10. | 25. | 45. | 80. | |
| 1939S | .......2,552,000 | | | 7. | 9. | 16. | 75. | 140. | 165. | |
| 1940 (11,279) | 9,156,000 | | | 5. | 6. | 7. | 15. | 30. | 55. | 1,100. |
| 1940S | .......4,550,000 | | | 5. | 6. | 7. | 20. | 45. | 70. | |
| 1941 (15,412) | 24,192,000 | | | 5. | 6. | 7. | 12. | 35. | 50. | (c) 950. |
| 1941D | .....11,248,400 | | | 5. | 6. | 9. | 18. | 40. | 65. | |
| 1941S | .......8,098,000 | | | 5. | 6. | 8. | 30. | 75. | 100. | |
| 1942 (21,120) | 47,818,000 | | | 5. | 6. | 7. | 12. | 40. | 60. | 950. |
| 1942D | .....10,973,800 | | | 5. | 6. | 7. | 18. | 35. | 75. | |
| 1942S (b) | ...12,708,000 | | | 5. | 6. | 7. | 18. | 40. | 60. | |
| 1943 | .......53,190,000 | | | 5. | 6. | 7. | 12. | 35. | 45. | |
| 1943D | .....11,346,000 | | | 5. | 6. | 7. | 20. | 50. | 75. | |
| 1943S | .....13,450,000 | | | 5. | 6. | 7. | 20. | 45. | 55. | |
| 1944 | .......28,206,000 | | | 5. | 6. | 7. | 12. | 35. | 45. | |
| 1944D | .......9,769,000 | | | 5. | 6. | 7. | 18. | 35. | 55. | |
| 1944S | .......8,904,000 | | | 5. | 6. | 7. | 18. | 45. | 65. | |
| 1945 | .......31,502,000 | | | 5. | 6. | 7. | 12. | 35. | 45. | |
| 1945D | .......9,966,800 | | | 5. | 6. | 7. | 15. | 35. | 55. | |
| 1945S | ......10,156,000 | | | 5. | 6. | 7. | 15. | 40. | 50. | |
| 1946 | .......12,118,000 | | | 5. | 6. | 7. | 12. | 40. | 50. | |
| 1946, DblDie Rev | .....* | | | 15. | 35. | 55. | 100. | 250. | 400. | |
| 1946D | .......2,151,000 | | | 7. | 10. | 14. | 20. | 40. | 60. | |
| 1946S | .......3,724,000 | | | 5. | 6. | 7. | 18. | 40. | 55. | |
| 1947 | ........4,094,000 | | | 5. | 6. | 7. | 18. | 40. | 55. | |
| 1947D | .......3,900,600 | | | 5. | 6. | 7. | 22. | 45. | 60. | |

* Included in number above. **b.** Large and small mintmark varieties; see page 20. **c.** Proofs struck with and without designer's initials.

## FRANKLIN (1948–1963)

The Benjamin Franklin half dollar and the Roosevelt dime were both designed by John R. Sinnock, whose initials appear below the shoulder. The Liberty Bell is similar to that used by Sinnock on the 1926 Sesquicentennial of American Independence commemorative half dollar modeled from a sketch by John Frederick Lewis (see page 272).

# HALF DOLLARS

*Designer John R. Sinnock; weight 12.50 grams; composition .900 silver, .100 copper (net weight .36169 oz. pure silver); diameter 30.6 mm; reeded edge; mints: Philadelphia, Denver, San Francisco.*

**VF-20 VERY FINE**—At least half of the lower and upper incused lines on rim of Liberty Bell on reverse visible.
**EF-40 EXTREMELY FINE**—Wear spots at top of end of Franklin's curls and hair at back of ears. Wear evident at top and on lettering of Liberty Bell.
**MS-63 CHOICE UNCIRCULATED**—Some distracting contact marks or blemishes in prime focal areas. Impaired luster possible.
**MS-65 GEM UNCIRCULATED**—Only light, scattered contact marks that are not distracting. Strong luster, good eye appeal.
**PF-65 GEM PROOF**—Brilliant surfaces with no noticeable blemishes or flaws. A few scattered, barely noticeable marks or hairlines possible.

**Mintmark Location**

*Choice, well-struck Uncirculated halves, and those with full bell lines, command higher prices.*

| | Mintage | VF-20 | EF-40 | MS-60 | MS-63 | MS-65 | PF-65 |
|---|---|---|---|---|---|---|---|
| 1948 | 3,006,814 | $5.00 | $7.00 | $18. | $22. | $85. | |
| 1948D | 4,028,600 | 4.00 | 5.00 | 12. | 20. | 160. | |
| 1949 | 5,614,000 | 5.00 | 8.00 | 40. | 60. | 175. | |
| 1949D | 4,120,600 | 5.00 | 10.00 | 40. | 65. | 850. | |
| 1949S | 3,744,000 | 5.00 | 18.00 | 65. | 95. | 150. | |
| 1950 ......(51,386) | 7,742,123 | 4.00 | 5.00 | 30. | 40. | 125. | $500. |
| 1950D | 8,031,600 | 4.00 | 4.50 | 25. | 35. | 500. | |
| 1951 ......(57,500) | 16,802,102 | 4.00 | 4.50 | 14. | 20. | 75. | 380. |
| 1951D | 9,475,200 | 4.00 | 6.00 | 27. | 40. | 200. | |
| 1951S | 13,696,000 | 4.00 | 5.00 | 25. | 35. | 110. | |
| 1952 ......(81,980) | 21,192,093 | 4.00 | 4.50 | 12. | 20. | 85. | 225. |
| 1952D | 25,395,600 | 4.00 | 4.50 | 9. | 15. | 175. | |
| 1952S | 5,526,000 | 5.00 | 8.00 | 40. | 50. | 110. | |
| 1953 .....(128,800) | 2,668,120 | 4.00 | 7.00 | 15. | 30. | 175. | 150. |
| 1953D | 20,900,400 | 4.00 | 6.00 | 12. | 15. | 120. | |
| 1953S | 4,148,000 | 4.00 | 6.00 | 25. | 30. | 90. | |
| 1954 .....(233,300) | 13,188,202 | 4.00 | 4.50 | 8. | 12. | 85. | 100. |
| 1954D | 25,445,580 | 4.00 | 4.50 | 8. | 15. | 150. | |
| 1954S | 4,993,400 | 4.00 | 4.50 | 8. | 15. | 60. | |
| 1955 .....(378,200) | 2,498,181 | 7.00 | 8.00 | 20. | 30. | 60. | 90. |
| 1956 .....(669,384) | 4,032,000 | 4.00 | 5.00 | 8. | 15. | 50. | 45. |
| 1957 ....(1,247,952) | 5,114,000 | 4.00 | 5.00 | 7. | 12. | 50. | 30. |
| 1957D | 19,966,850 | 4.00 | 4.50 | 8. | 12. | 50. | |
| 1958 .....(875,652) | 4,042,000 | 4.00 | 5.00 | 8. | 15. | 65. | 35. |
| 1958D | 23,962,412 | 4.00 | 4.50 | 6. | 10. | 55. | |
| 1959 ....(1,149,291) | 6,200,000 | 4.00 | 5.00 | 6. | 12. | 125. | 30. |
| 1959D | 13,053,750 | 4.00 | 4.50 | 6. | 12. | 150. | |
| 1960 ....(1,691,602) | 6,024,000 | 4.00 | 4.50 | 6. | 12. | 160. | 30. |
| 1960D | 18,215,812 | 4.00 | 4.50 | 6. | 10. | 500. | |

**1961, Proof Doubled Die**

| | Mintage | VF-20 | EF-40 | MS-60 | MS-63 | MS-65 | PF-65 |
|---|---|---|---|---|---|---|---|
| 1961 . .(3,028,244) . . . 8,290,000 | | $4.00 | $4.50 | $6. | $10. | $175. | $30. |
| 1961, DblDie Pf . . . . . . . . . . . . . . | | | | | | | 1,250. |
| 1961D . . . . . . . . . . . . . 20,276,442 | | 4.00 | 4.50 | 5. | 10. | 250. | |
| 1962 . .(3,218,019) . . . 9,714,000 | | 4.00 | 4.50 | 5. | 10. | 200. | 25. |
| 1962D . . . . . . . . . . . . 35,473,281 | | 4.00 | 4.50 | 5. | 9. | 275. | |
| 1963 . .(3,075,645) . . 22,164,000 | | 4.00 | 4.50 | 5. | 10. | 80. | 30. |
| 1963D . . . . . . . . . . . . 67,069,292 | | 4.00 | 4.50 | 5. | 9. | 80. | |

## KENNEDY (1964 TO DATE)

Gilroy Roberts, chief engraver of the Mint in 1963, designed the obverse of this coin. His stylized initials are on the truncation of the forceful bust of President John F. Kennedy. The reverse, which uses the presidential coat of arms for the motif, is the work of Frank Gasparro, who was appointed chief engraver in February 1965. A few of the pieces dated 1971-D and 1977-D were struck in silver clad composition by error.

*Designers Gilroy Roberts and Frank Gasparro. 1964—Standards same as for previous issue (net weight .36169 oz. pure silver). 1965–1970—Weight 11.50 grams; composition, outer layers of .800 silver and .200 copper bonded to inner core of .209 silver, .791 copper (net weight .1479 oz. pure silver net composition .400 silver, .600 copper). 1971—Weight 11.34 grams; composition, outer layers of copper-nickel (.750 copper, .250 nickel) bonded to inner core of pure copper; diameter 30.6 mm; reeded edge. Mints: Philadelphia, Denver, San Francisco.*

**Mintmark Location (1964)**

**Mintmark Location (1968 to Date)**

**1964, Heavily Accented Hair**

### Silver Coinage (1964)

| | Mintage | MS-63 | PF-65 | | Mintage | MS-63 | PF-65 |
|---|---|---|---|---|---|---|---|
| 1964 . . . . . . . . 273,304,004 | | $5. | | 1964, Heavily Accented Hair * | | | $20. |
| 1964 . . . . . . . . (3,950,762) | | | $9. | 1964D . . . . . . . 156,205,446 | | $5. | |

\* Included in number at left.

### Silver Clad Coinage (1965–1970)

| | Mintage | MS-63 | PF-65 | | Mintage | MS-63 | PF-65 |
|---|---|---|---|---|---|---|---|
| 1965 . . . . . . . . . .65,879,366 | | $3. | | 1969D . . . . . . .129,881,800 | | $3. | |
| 1966 . . . . . . . .108,984,932 | | 3. | | 1969S . . . . . . . .(2,934,631) | | | $8. |
| 1967 . . . . . . . .295,046,978 | | 3. | | 1970D (a) . . . . . .2,150,000 | | 13. | |
| 1968D . . . . . . .246,951,930 | | 3. | | 1970S . . . . . . . .(2,632,810) | | | 20. |
| 1968S . . . . . . . .(3,041,506) | | | $8. | | | | |

**a.** Issued only in Mint sets.

# Clad Coinage and Silver Proofs (1971 to Date)

The design was slightly modified several times between 1971 and the present.

**1974-D, Doubled-Die Obverse**
*Note prominent doubling of RUS.*

| | Mintage | MS-63 | PF-65 |
|---|---|---|---|
| 1971 | 155,164,000 | $1.50 | |
| 1971D | 302,097,424 | 1.50 | |
| 1971S | (3,220,733) | | $7.00 |
| 1972 | 153,180,000 | 2.00 | |
| 1972D | 141,890,000 | 2.00 | |
| 1972S | (3,260,996) | | 7.00 |
| 1973 | 64,964,000 | 2.00 | |

| | Mintage | MS-63 | PF-65 |
|---|---|---|---|
| 1973D | 83,171,400 | $1.50 | |
| 1973S | (2,760,339) | | $7.00 |
| 1974 | 201,596,000 | 1.50 | |
| 1974D | 79,066,300 | 1.50 | |
| 1974D, DblDie Obv | * | 150.00 | |
| 1974S | (2,612,568) | | 5.00 |
| * Included in number above. | | | |

## Bicentennial (1976)

In an open contest for the selection of suitable designs for the special Bicentennial reverses of the quarter, half dollar, and dollar, Seth G. Huntington's winning entry was featured on the half dollar. It shows Independence Hall in Philadelphia as the center device. The obverse was unchanged except for the dual dating 1776–1976. They were struck during 1975 and 1976 and were used for general circulation as well as being included in Proof and Uncirculated sets for 1975 and 1976.

*Designers Gilroy Roberts and Seth Huntington; diameter 30.6 mm; reeded edge. Silver clad—Weight 11.50 grams; composition, outer layers of .800 silver, .200 copper bonded to inner core of .209 silver, .791 copper (net weight .14792 oz. pure silver). Copper-nickel clad—Weight 11.34 grams; composition, outer layers of copper-nickel (.750 copper, .250 nickel) bonded to inner core of pure copper.*

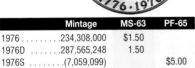

| | Mintage | MS-63 | PF-65 |
|---|---|---|---|
| 1976 | 234,308,000 | $1.50 | |
| 1976D | 287,565,248 | 1.50 | |
| 1976S | (7,059,099) | | $5.00 |

| | Mintage | MS-63 | PF-65 |
|---|---|---|---|
| 1976S, Silver Clad | *11,000,000* | $4.00 | |
| 1976S, Silver Clad | *(4,000,000)* | | $7.00 |

*Note:* Mintage figures for 1976-S silver coins are approximate; many were melted in 1982.

## Eagle Reverse Resumed (1977)

*Copper-nickel clad coinage. Silver Proofs are of pre-1965 standards.*

| | Mintage | MS-63 | PF-65 |
|---|---|---|---|
| 1977 | 43,598,000 | $1.50 | |
| 1977D | 31,449,106 | 1.50 | |
| 1977S | (3,251,152) | | $5.00 |
| 1978 | 14,350,000 | 1.75 | |

| | Mintage | MS-63 | PF-65 |
|---|---|---|---|
| 1978D | 13,765,799 | $3.00 | |
| 1978S | (3,127,781) | | $5.00 |
| 1979 | 68,312,000 | 1.50 | |
| 1979D | 15,815,422 | 1.50 | |

*Chart continued on next page.*

# HALF DOLLARS

| | Mintage | MS-65 | PF-65 |
|---|---|---|---|
| 1979S | (3,677,175) | | |
| 1979S, Filled S | | | $5.00 |
| 1979S, Clear S | | | 23.00 |
| 1980P | 44,134,000 | $1.75 | |
| 1980D | 33,456,449 | 1.75 | |
| 1980S | (3,554,806) | | 6.00 |
| 1981P | 29,544,000 | 2.00 | |
| 1981D | 27,839,533 | 1.75 | |
| 1981S | (4,063,083) | | 15.00 |
| 1982P | 10,819,000 | 4.00 | |
| 1982D | 13,140,102 | 4.00 | |
| 1982S | (3,857,479) | | 6.00 |
| 1983P | 34,139,000 | 4.50 | |
| 1983D | 32,472,244 | 4.50 | |
| 1983S | (3,279,126) | | 6.00 |
| 1984P | 26,029,000 | 2.00 | |
| 1984D | 26,262,158 | 2.00 | |
| 1984S | (3,065,110) | | 6.00 |
| 1985P | 18,706,962 | 5.00 | |
| 1985D | 19,814,034 | 4.00 | |
| 1985S | (3,362,821) | | 6.00 |
| 1986P | 13,107,633 | 7.00 | |
| 1986D | 15,336,145 | 6.00 | |
| 1986S | (3,010,497) | | 10.00 |
| 1987P (a) | 2,890,758 | 5.00 | |
| 1987D (a) | 2,890,758 | 5.00 | |
| 1987S | (4,227,728) | | 7.00 |
| 1988P | 13,626,000 | 5.00 | |
| 1988D | 12,000,096 | 4.00 | |
| 1988S | (3,262,948) | | 7.00 |
| 1989P | 24,542,000 | 4.00 | |
| 1989D | 23,000,216 | 3.00 | |
| 1989S | (3,220,194) | | 9.00 |
| 1990P | 22,278,000 | 2.50 | |
| 1990D | 20,096,242 | 3.00 | |
| 1990S | (3,299,559) | | 7.00 |
| 1991P | 14,874,000 | 4.00 | |
| 1991D | 15,054,678 | 5.00 | |
| 1991S | (2,867,787) | | 15.00 |
| 1992P | 17,628,000 | 2.00 | |
| 1992D | 17,000,106 | 3.00 | |
| 1992S | (2,858,981) | | 9.00 |
| 1992S, Silver | (1,317,579) | | 15.00 |
| 1993P | 15,510,000 | 3.00 | |
| 1993D | 15,000,006 | 3.00 | |
| 1993S | (2,633,439) | | 14.00 |
| 1993S, Silver | (761,353) | | 35.00 |
| 1994P | 23,718,000 | 2.00 | |
| 1994D | 23,828,110 | 2.00 | |
| 1994S | (2,484,594) | | 10.00 |
| 1994S, Silver | (785,329) | | 40.00 |
| 1995P | 26,496,000 | $2.00 | |
| 1995D | 26,288,000 | 2.00 | |
| 1995S | (2,117,496) | | $35.00 |
| 1995S, Silver | (679,985) | | 100.00 |
| 1996P | 24,442,000 | 2.00 | |
| 1996D | 24,744,000 | 2.00 | |
| 1996S | (1,750,244) | | 15.00 |
| 1996S, Silver | (775,021) | | 45.00 |
| 1997P | 20,882,000 | 2.00 | |
| 1997D | 19,876,000 | 2.00 | |
| 1997S | (2,055,000) | | 35.00 |
| 1997S, Silver | (741,678) | | 90.00 |
| 1998P | 15,646,000 | 1.75 | |
| 1998D | 15,064,000 | 1.75 | |
| 1998S | (2,086,507) | | 18.00 |
| 1998S, Silver | (878,792) | | 30.00 |
| 1998S, Silver, Matte Finish (b) | | | 275.00 |
| 1999P | 8,900,000 | 1.50 | |
| 1999D | 10,682,000 | 1.50 | |
| 1999S | (2,543,401) | | 18.00 |
| 1999S, Silver | (804,565) | | 35.00 |
| 2000P | 22,600,000 | 1.50 | |
| 2000D | 19,466,000 | 1.50 | |
| 2000S | (3,082,483) | | 7.00 |
| 2000S, Silver | (965,421) | | 22.00 |
| 2001P (c) | 21,200,000 | 2.00 | |
| 2001D (c) | 19,504,000 | 2.00 | |
| 2001S | (2,294,043) | | 10.00 |
| 2001S, Silver | (889,697) | | 20.00 |
| 2002P (c) | 3,100,000 | 2.00 | |
| 2002D (c) | 2,500,000 | 2.00 | |
| 2002S | (2,319,766) | | 7.00 |
| 2002S, Silver | (892,229) | | 20.00 |
| 2003P (c) | 2,500,000 | 2.50 | |
| 2003D (c) | 2,500,000 | 2.50 | |
| 2003S | (2,172,684) | | 7.00 |
| 2003S, Silver | (1,125,755) | | 12.00 |
| 2004P (c) | 2,900,000 | 2.00 | |
| 2004D (c) | 2,900,000 | 2.00 | |
| 2004S | (1,804,396) | | 15.00 |
| 2004S, Silver | (1,187,673) | | 12.00 |
| 2005P (c) | 3,800,000 | 2.00 | |
| 2005D (c) | 3,500,000 | 2.00 | |
| 2005S | (2,275,000) | | 7.00 |
| 2005S, Silver | (998,000) | | 12.00 |
| 2006P (c) | | 2.00 | |
| 2006D (c) | | 2.00 | |
| 2006S | | | 7.00 |
| 2006S, Silver | | | 12.00 |

a. Not issued for circulation; included with Uncirculated and Souvenir sets. b. Included in commemorative set (see page 317). c. Not issued for circulation.

The silver dollar was authorized by Congress on April 2, 1792. Weight and fineness were specified at 416 grains and .8924 fine. The first issues appeared in 1794, and until 1804 all silver dollars had the value stamped on the edge: HUNDRED CENTS, ONE DOLLAR OR UNIT. After a lapse in coinage of the silver dollar during the period 1804 through 1835, coins were made with either plain or reeded edges and the value was placed on the reverse.

The weight was changed by the law of January 18, 1837, to 412-1/2 grains, .900 fineness. The coinage was discontinued by the Act of February 12, 1873, and reauthorized by the Act of February 28, 1878. The dollar was again discontinued after 1935, and since then only base-metal pieces have been coined for circulation (also see Silver Bullion on page 326).

## ORIGIN OF THE DOLLAR

The word *dollar* evolves from the German *thaler*, the name given to the first large-sized European silver coin. Designed as a substitute for the gold florin, the coin originated in the Tyrol in 1484. So popular did these large silver coins become during the 16th century that many other countries struck similar pieces, giving them names derived from *thaler*. In the Netherlands the coin was called *rijksdaalder*, in Denmark *rigsdaler*, in Italy *tallero*, in Poland *talar*, in France *jocandale*, in Russia *jefimok*. All these names are abbreviations of *joachimsthaler*. Until the discovery of the great silver deposits in Mexican and South American mines, the mint with the greatest output of large silver coins was that of Joachimsthal in the Bohemian Erzgebirge.

The Spanish dollar, or *piece of eight*, was widely used and familiar to everyone in the British American colonies. It was only natural, therefore, that the word *dollar* was adopted officially as the standard monetary unit of the United States by Congress on July 6, 1785. The Continental Dollar of 1776 is described on page 81.

## TYPE COIN VALUES

| | G-4 | F-12 | EF-40 | MS-60 | MS-63 | MS-65 | PF-63 | PF-65 |
|---|---|---|---|---|---|---|---|---|
| Flowing Hair, 1794–1795 | $1,300.00+ | $3,500.+ | $13,000.+ | $45,000.+ | $95,000.+ | $325,000.+ | | |
| Drpd Bust, SE, 1795–1798 | 1,125.00+ | 2,750.+ | 9,000.+ | 45,000.+ | 85,000.+ | 275,000.+ | | |
| Drpd Bust, HE, 1798–1804 | 800.00+ | 1,450.+ | 4,200.+ | 19,000.+ | 45,000.+ | 150,000.+ | $225,000.+ | |
| Lib Std, NM, 1840–1866 | 170.00+ | 250.+ | 400. | 1,100. | 3,000. | 27,500.+ | 4,500.+ | $20,000.+ |
| Lib Std, Motto, 1866–1873 | 170.00+ | 260.+ | 450.+ | 1,400.+ | 3,500.+ | 32,000.+ | 3,750.+ | 18,000.+ |
| Trade Dollar, 1873–1883 | 75.00 | 140. | 220.+ | 500.+ | 1,500.+ | 11,250.+ | 2,800.+ | 11,000.+ |
| Morgan, 1878–1921 | 10.50+ | 14.+ | 17.+ | 24.+ | 38.+ | 180.+ | 2,200.+ | 7,000.+ |
| Peace, 1921–1935 | 9.50+ | 11. | 13. | 20.+ | 32.+ | 165.+ | 22,500.+ | 47,000. |

+ or – indicates change from previous year

## FLOWING HAIR (1794–1795)

Varieties listed are those most significant to collectors, but numerous minor variations may be found because each of the early dies was individually made. Blanks were weighed before the dollars were struck and overweight pieces were filed to remove excess silver. Coins with old adjustment marks may be worth less than values shown here. Some Flowing Hair type dollars of 1794 and 1795 were weight-adjusted through insertion of a small (8 mm) silver plug in the center of the blank planchet before the coin was struck. Values of varieties not listed in this guide depend on collector interest and demand.

*Designer Robert Scot; weight 26.96 grams; composition .8924 silver, .1076 copper; approx. diameter 39–40 mm; edge: HUNDRED CENTS ONE DOLLAR OR UNIT with decorations between words.*

**AG-3 ABOUT GOOD**—Clear enough to identify.
**G-4 GOOD**—Date and letters legible. Main devices outlined, but lacking in detail.
**VG-8 VERY GOOD**—Major details discernible. Letters well formed but worn.
**F-12 FINE**—Hair ends distinguishable. Top hair lines visible, but otherwise worn smooth.
**VF-20 VERY FINE**—Some detail visible in hair in center. Other details more bold.
**EF-40 EXTREMELY FINE**—Hair well defined but with some wear.
**AU-50 ABOUT UNCIRCULATED**—Slight trace of wear on tips of highest curls; feathers on eagles's breast usually weak.
**MS-60 UNCIRCULATED**—No trace of wear. Light blemishes.

*Values shown for Uncirculated pieces of this type are for well-struck, attractive coins with minimal surface marks.*

| | Mintage | AG-3 | G-4 | VG-8 | F-12 | VF-20 | EF-40 | AU-50 | MS-60 |
|---|---|---|---|---|---|---|---|---|---|
| 1794 | 1,758 | $22,500. | $35,000. | $50,000. | $70,000. | $110,000. | $200,000. | $300,000. | $475,000. |
| $1,150,000, MS-64, ANR auction, Jun-05 | | | | | | | | | |
| 1794, Silver Plug | * (unique) | | | | | | | | |

\* Included in number above.

**Two Leaves Beneath**
**Each Wing**

**Three Leaves Beneath**
**Each Wing**

**Silver Plug**
**(1795)**

| | Mintage | AG-3 | G-4 | VG-8 | F-12 | VF-20 | EF-40 | AU-50 | MS-60 |
|---|---|---|---|---|---|---|---|---|---|
| 1795, All kinds | 160,295 | | | | | | | | |
| 1795, Two Leaves | | $800. | $1,350. | $2,000. | $3,700. | $6,200. | $14,000. | $20,000. | $50,000. |
| 1795, Three Leaves | | 750. | 1,300. | 1,750. | 3,500. | 5,500. | 13,000. | 18,500. | 45,000. |
| 1795, Silver Plug | | 1,050. | 2,000. | 3,250. | 6,000. | 10,000. | 30,000. | 30,000. | 100,000. |

# DRAPED BUST (1795–1804)
## Small Eagle Reverse (1795–1798)

**AG-3 ABOUT GOOD**—Clear enough to identify.
**G-4 GOOD**—Bust outlined, no detail. Date legible, some leaves evident.
**VG-8 VERY GOOD**—Drapery worn except deepest folds. Hair lines smooth.
**F-12 FINE**—All drapery lines distinguishable. Some detail visible in hair lines near cheek and neck.
**VF-20 VERY FINE**—Left side of drapery worn smooth.
**EF-40 EXTREMELY FINE**—Drapery distinctly visible. Hair well outlined and detailed.
**AU-50 ABOUT UNCIRCULATED**—Slight trace of wear on the bust shoulder and hair to left of forehead, as well as on eagle's breast and top edges of wings.
**MS-60 UNCIRCULATED**—No trace of wear. Light blemishes.

*See next page for chart.*

| | Mintage | AG-3 | G-4 | VG-8 | F-12 | VF-20 | EF-40 | AU-50 | MS-60 |
|---|---|---|---|---|---|---|---|---|---|
| 1795, All kinds ........*42,738* | | | | | | | | | |
| 1795, Off-Center Bust ....... | | $800. | $1,250. | $1,550. | $2,600. | $4,500. | $9,000. | $14,500. | $35,000. |
| 1795, Centered Bust ........ | | 825. | 1,250. | 1,575. | 2,600. | 4,500. | 9,000. | 14,500. | 35,000. |

**Small Date**      **Large Date**

**Small Letters**      **Large Letters**

| | Mintage | AG-3 | G-4 | VG-8 | F-12 | VF-20 | EF-40 | AU-50 | MS-60 |
|---|---|---|---|---|---|---|---|---|---|
| 1796, All kinds ........*79,920* | | | | | | | | | |
| 1796, Small Date, Small Letters *(3 varieties)* ...... | | $750. | $1,250. | $1,600. | $2,750. | $4,500. | $9,250. | $14,500. | $45,000. |
| 1796, Small Date, Lg Ltrs .... | | 675. | 1,150. | 1,500. | 6,000. | 8,500. | 11,000. | 12,500. | 40,000. |
| 1796, Large Date, Sm Ltrs ... | | 675. | 1,100. | 1,500. | 7,000. | 8,500. | 11,000. | 12,500. | 40,000. |
| 1797, All kinds ..........*7,776* | | | | | | | | | |
| 1797, 10 Stars Left, 6 Rt .... | | 700. | 1,100. | 1,500. | 2,700. | 4,250. | 9,000. | 13,000. | 42,500. |
| 1797, 9 Stars Left, 7 Right, Large Letters ...... | | 700. | 1,125. | 1,500. | 2,750. | 3,500. | 9,000. | 13,000. | 45,000. |
| 1797, 9 Stars Left, 7 Right, Small Letters ...... | | 900. | 1,500. | 2,600. | 3,500. | 7,000. | 13,500. | 30,000. | 82,500. |
| 1798, All kinds ........*327,536* | | | | | | | | | |
| 1798, 15 Stars on Obv ........ | | 1,000. | 1,500. | 2,100. | 3,200. | 5,250. | 11,000. | 20,000. | 60,000. |
| 1798, 13 Stars on Obv ........ | | 775. | 1,250. | 1,700. | 2,700. | 4,500. | 9,000. | 15,000. | 55,000. |

## Heraldic Eagle Reverse (1798–1804)

**G-4 GOOD**—Letters and date legible. E PLURIBUS UNUM illegible.
**VG-8 VERY GOOD**—Motto partially legible. Only deepest drapery details visible. All other lines smooth.
**F-12 FINE**—All drapery lines distinguishable. Some detail visible in hair lines near cheek and neck.
**VF-20 VERY FINE**—Left side of drapery worn smooth.
**EF-40 EXTREMELY FINE**—Drapery distinct. Hair well detailed.
**AU-50 ABOUT UNCIRCULATED**—Slight trace of wear on the bust shoulder and hair to left of forehead, as well as on eagle's breast and top edges of wings.
**MS-60 UNCIRCULATED**—No trace of wear. Light blemishes.

The two earliest reverse dies of 1798 have five vertical lines in the stripes in the shield. All dollar dies thereafter have four vertical lines.

**Four Vertical Lines in Shield**

# SILVER AND RELATED DOLLARS

| | G-4 | VG-8 | F-12 | VF-20 | EF-40 | AU-50 | MS-60 |
|---|---|---|---|---|---|---|---|
| 1798, Knob 9, 5 Vertical Lines **(a)** | $800. | $950. | $1,425. | $2,400. | $4,000. | $8,000. | $18,000. |
| 1798, Knob 9, 4 Vertical Lines .. | 825. | 950. | 1,450. | 2,450. | 4,250. | 9,000. | — |
| 1798, Knob 9, 10 Arrows ...... | 825. | 950. | 1,550. | 2,500. | 4,250. | 9,000. | — |
| 1798, Pointed 9, Close Date .... | 825. | 950. | 1,450. | 2,500. | 4,250. | 8,500. | 18,000. |
| 1798, Pointed 9, Wide Date .... | 825. | 850. | 1,450. | 2,500. | 4,250. | 8,500. | 18,000. |

**a.** 327,536 silver dollars were minted in 1798, but the Mint did not break this figure down by type.

1799 Over 98, Stars 7 and 6

Stars 8 and 5

| | Mintage | G-4 | VG-8 | F-12 | VF-20 | EF-40 | AU-50 | MS-60 |
|---|---|---|---|---|---|---|---|---|
| 1798, Pointed 9,<br>5 Vertical Lines ....... | | $825. | $950. | $1,450. | $2,500. | $4,250. | $8,500. | $21,000. |
| 1798, Pointed 9,<br>10 Arrows ........... | | 825. | 950. | 1,450. | 2,400. | 4,000. | 8,000. | 18,000. |
| 1798, Pointed 9,<br>4 Berries ............ | | 825. | 975. | 1,400. | 2,400. | 4,200. | 8,250. | — |
| 1799, All kinds .....423,515 | | | | | | | | |
| 1799, 99 Over 98,<br>15-Star Reverse ....... | | 850. | 1,100. | 1,550. | 2,600. | 4,500. | 8,250. | 18,500. |
| 1799, 99 Over 98,<br>13-Star Reverse ....... | | 850. | 1,050. | 1,400. | 2,400. | 4,250. | 8,500. | 18,500. |
| 1799, Irregular Date,<br>15-Star Reverse ....... | | 825. | 1,000. | 1,350. | 2,400. | 4,200. | 7,750. | — |
| 1799, Irregular Date,<br>13-Star Reverse ....... | | 825. | 1,000. | 1,350. | 2,400. | 4,250. | 7,750. | — |
| 1799, Normal Date ....... | | 825. | 1,000. | 1,350. | 2,450. | 4,000. | 7,750. | 18,000. |
| 1799, 8 Stars Left,<br>5 Right .............. | | 900. | 1,200. | 1,750. | 3,000. | 5,250. | 10,000. | 24,500. |
| 1800, All kinds .....220,920 | | | | | | | | |
| 1800, Very Wide Date,<br>Low 8 .............. | | 800. | 850. | 1,450. | 2,450. | 4,250. | 8,000. | 19,000. |
| 1800, "Dotted Date"<br>(from die breaks) ...... | | 850. | 1,100. | 1,500. | 2,500. | 5,250. | 8,000. | — |
| 1800, Only 12 Arrows .... | | 800. | 1,000. | 1,450. | 2,400. | 4,200. | 8,000. | 19,000. |
| 1800, Normal Dies ....... | | 800. | 1,000. | 1,450. | 2,400. | 4,000. | 8,000. | 18,000. |
| 1800, AMERICAI ........ | | 800. | 1,000. | 1,500. | 2,500. | 4,000. | 8,000. | 20,000. |
| 1801 .............54,454 | | 800. | 1,000. | 1,500. | 2,500. | 5,000. | 8,200. | 25,000. |
| 1801, Proof Restrike *(rev struck from first die of 1804 dollar) (2 known)* | | | | | | | | 220,000. |

| 1802, 2 Over 1, Narrow Date | 1802, 2 Over 1, Wide Date | 1803, Small 3 | 1803, Large 3 |

| | Mintage | G-4 | VG-8 | F-12 | VF-20 | EF-40 | AU-50 | MS-60 |
|---|---|---|---|---|---|---|---|---|
| 1802, All kinds . . . . . . . . | .41,650 | | | | | | | |
| 1802, 2/1, Narrow Date . . . . . . | | $900. | $1,100. | $1,600. | $2,700. | $5,000. | $9,000. | $23,000. |
| 1802, 2/1, Wide Date . . . . . . . | | 900. | 1,100. | 1,600. | 2,700. | 5,000. | 11,000. | 25,000. |
| 1802, Narrow Nml Date . . . . . | | 800. | 1,000. | 1,500. | 2,600. | 4,800. | 8,200. | 18,000. |
| 1802, Wide Nml Date . . . . . . . | | 900. | 1,100. | 1,700. | 2,900. | 5,000. | 10,000. | 30,000. |
| 1802, Proof Restrike *(4 known)* | | | | | | | | 200,000. |
| 1803, All kinds . . . . . . . . | .85,634 | | | | | | | |
| 1803, Small 3 . . . . . . . . . . . . | | 850. | 1,100. | 1,600. | 2,700. | 4,800. | 9,000. | 20,000. |
| 1803, Large 3 . . . . . . . . . . . . | | 900. | 1,000. | 1,600. | 2,700. | 4,800. | 8,800. | 20,000. |
| 1803, Proof Restrike *(4 known)* | | | | | | | | 200,000. |

## 1804 DOLLAR

First Reverse                    Second Reverse

*Note position of words STATES OF with relation to clouds.*

1804 First Reverse, Original  *$4,140,000, PF-68, B&M auction, Aug-99* . . . . . . . . . . . . . . . . . . . . .*(8 known)*
1804 Second Reverse, Restrike  *$1,207,500, PF-58, B&M auction, Jul-03* . . . . . . . . . . . . . . . . . . .*(6 known)*
1804 Second Reverse, Restrike With Plain Edge  *(Smithsonian Collection)* . . . . . . . . . . . . . . . . . . . .*(unique)*

The 1804 dollar is one of the most publicized rarities in the entire series of United States coins. There are specimens known as *originals* (first reverse), of which eight are known; and *restrikes* (second reverse), of which seven are known, one of which has a plain edge.

Numismatists have found that the 1804 original dollars were struck at the Mint in the 1834 through 1835 period, for use in presentation Proof sets. The first known coin, a Proof, was obtained from a Mint officer by a Mr. Stickney on May 9, 1843, in exchange for an Immune Columbia piece in gold. Later, in 1859, the pieces known as *restrikes* and *electrotypes* were made at the Mint to supply the needs of collectors who wanted examples of these dollars.

Evidence that these pieces were struck during the later period is based on the fact that the 1804 dollars differ from issues of 1803 or earlier and conform more closely to those struck after 1836, their edges or borders having beaded segments and raised rims, not elongated denticles such as are found on the earlier dates.

Although the Mint record states that 19,570 dollars were coined in 1804, in no place does it mention that they were dated 1804. It was the practice in those days to use old dies as long as they were serviceable with no regard in the annual reports for the dating of the coins. It is probable that the 1804 total for dollars actually covered coins that were dated 1803.

## GOBRECHT DOLLARS (1836–1839)

Suspension of silver dollar coinage was lifted in 1831, but it was not until 1835 that steps were taken to resume coinage. Late in that year the Mint director, R.M. Patterson, ordered engraver Christian Gobrecht to prepare a pair of dies based on designs by Thomas Sully and Titian Peale. The first obverse die, dated 1836, bore the seated figure of Liberty on the obverse with the inscription C. GOBRECHT F. ("F." is an abbreviation for the Latin word *Fecit*, or "made it") in the field above the date. On the reverse was a large eagle flying left, surrounded by 26 stars and the legend UNITED STATES OF AMERICA • ONE DOLLAR •. It is not known whether coins from these dies were struck at that time. A new obverse die with Gobrecht's name on the base of Liberty was prepared, and in December 1836, 1,000 coins were struck for circulation. These coins weighed 416 grains, which was the standard enacted in 1792.

In January 1837 the standard weight the dollar was lowered to 412-1/2 grains, and pieces were struck in March 1837 using the dies of 1836. Dies were oriented in a "medal" fashion (top to top when rotated) to distinguish them from those struck in December 1836. Dollars issued for circulation in 1836, 1837, and 1839 are found with different die alignments. The "original" issue of December 1836 has the normal "coin" orientation (reverse upright when coin is turned on a horizontal axis) with the eagle flying upward.

From the late 1850s to the 1870s, the Mint continued to strike Gobrecht dollars to satisfy collector demands. Mules, which had mismatched designs or edge devices, were made in that period and are very rare. Restrikes and mules are seldom seen in worn condition.

*Original 1836 die orientation using either "coin" or "medal" turn.*

*Die alignment of original issues dated 1838 and 1839.*

*See next page for chart.*

Gobrecht dollars, both original issues and restrikes, were made in either coin-turn orientation ↑↓ (I and III) or medal-turn orientation ↑↑ (II and IV), and were struck in four basic die alignments.

- Die alignment I: ↑↓, head of Liberty opposite DO of DOLLAR, eagle flying upward.
- Die alignment II: ↑↑, head of Liberty opposite ES of STATES, eagle flying upward.
- Die alignment III: ↑↓, head of Liberty opposite N of ONE, eagle flying level.
- Die alignment IV: ↑↑, head of Liberty opposite F of OF, eagle flying level.

Rotated dies are common for original issue and restrike Gobrecht dollars. The 600 coins produced for circulation in March 1837 had dies that rotated from die alignment II to die alignment IV during the striking.

## Circulation Issues and Patterns

| | VF-20 | EF-40 | AU-50 | PF-60 |
|---|---|---|---|---|
| 1836, C. GOBRECHT F. in field above date; eagle flying left amid stars. Plain edge. Die alignment I, ↑↓. Pattern | | | | $33,000. |
| 1836, C. GOBRECHT F. on base. Rev as above. Plain edge. Die alignment I, ↑↓. Circulation issue. 1,000 struck | $8,750. | $13,000. | $16,000. | 20,000. |
| 1836, As above. Plain edge. Die alignment II–die alignment IV, ↑↑. Circulation issue struck in 1837. 600 struck | 8,750. | 13,000. | 17,000. | 22,000. |

| | VF-20 | EF-40 | AU-50 | PF-60 |
|---|---|---|---|---|
| 1838, Similar obv, designer's name omitted, stars added around border. Rev eagle flying in plain field. Reeded edge. Die alignment IV, ↑↑. Pattern | $14,000. | $20,000. | $23,000. | $34,000. |
| 1839, As above. Reeded edge. Die alignment IV, ↑↑. Circulation issue. 300 struck . . . . . . . . . . . . | 13,000. | 18,000. | 20,000. | 28,000. |

## Restrikes

Restrikes were produced from the late 1850s to the 1870s, and are not official coins. They were all oriented in either die alignment III (coin turn) or die alignment IV (medal turn), with eagle flying level, and almost all were struck from a cracked reverse die.

| | PF-60 |
|---|---|
| 1836, Name below base; eagle in starry field; plain edge | $60,000. |
| 1836, Name on base; plain edge | 13,000. |
| 1838, Designer's name omitted; reeded edge | 60,000. |
| 1839, Designer's name omitted; eagle in plain field; reeded edge | 40,000. |

# LIBERTY SEATED (1840–1873)

Starting in 1840, silver dollars were issued for general circulation; by spring 1853 the silver content of such pieces was worth more than their face value, and later issues were not seen in circulation but were used mainly in export trade. This situation continued through the late 1860s. The seated figure of Liberty was adopted for the obverse, but the flying eagle design was rejected in favor of the more familiar form with olive branch and arrows used for the other silver denominations.

The 1866 Proof quarter, half, and dollar without motto are not mentioned in the Mint director's report, and were not issued for circulation.

*Designer Christian Gobrecht; weight 26.73 grams; composition .900 silver, .100 copper (net weight .77344 oz. pure silver); diameter 38.1 mm; reeded edge; mints: Philadelphia, New Orleans, Carson City, San Francisco.*

**VG-8 VERY GOOD**—Any three letters of LIBERTY at least two-thirds complete.
**F-12 FINE**—All seven letters of LIBERTY visible, though weak.
**VF-20 VERY FINE**—LIBERTY strong, but slight wear visible on its ribbon.
**EF-40 EXTREMELY FINE**—Horizontal lines of shield complete. Eagle's eye plain.
**AU-50 ABOUT UNCIRCULATED**—Traces of light wear on only the high points of the design. Half of mint luster present.
**MS-60 UNCIRCULATED**—No trace of wear. Light marks or blemishes.
**PF-60 PROOF**—Several contact marks, hairlines, or light rubs possible on surface. Luster possibly dull and eye appeal lacking.
**PF-63 CHOICE PROOF**—Reflective surfaces with only a few blemishes in secondary focal places. No major flaws.

## No Motto (1840–1865)

*Mintmark location is on reverse, below eagle.*

| | Mintage | VG-8 | F-12 | VF-20 | EF-40 | AU-50 | MS-60 | PF-60 | PF-63 |
|---|---|---|---|---|---|---|---|---|---|
| 1840 | 61,005 | $250. | $300. | $350. | $500. | $800. | $3,000. | $15,000. | $35,000. |
| 1841 | 173,000 | 200. | 250. | 300. | 450. | 700. | 1,800. | 15,000. | 40,000. |
| 1842 | 184,618 | 200. | 250. | 300. | 450. | 700. | 1,500. | 15,000. | 35,000. |

*Chart continued on next page.*

| | Mintage | VG-8 | F-12 | VF-20 | EF-40 | AU-50 | MS-60 | PF-60 | PF-63 |
|---|---|---|---|---|---|---|---|---|---|
| 1843 | 165,100 | $200. | $250. | $300. | $450. | $700. | $1,500. | $15,000. | $35,000. |
| 1844 | 20,000 | 220. | 300. | 400. | 550. | 1,200. | 3,200. | 11,000. | 40,000. |
| 1845 | 24,500 | 250. | 300. | 400. | 600. | 1,200. | 9,000. | 20,000. | 35,000. |
| 1846 | 110,600 | 230. | 260. | 320. | 460. | 660. | 1,700. | 11,000. | 30,000. |
| 1846O | 59,000 | 250. | 300. | 400. | 600. | 1,200. | 4,000. | | |
| 1847 | 140,750 | 200. | 250. | 300. | 450. | 700. | 1,200. | 15,000. | 27,000. |
| 1848 | 15,000 | 350. | 450. | 650. | 850. | 1,500. | 3,500. | 15,000. | 35,000. |
| 1849 | 62,600 | 200. | 250. | 300. | 450. | 800. | 2,000. | 20,000. | 45,000. |
| 1850 | 7,500 | 500. | 600. | 900. | 1,400. | 2,200. | 5,500. | 15,000. | 35,000. |
| 1850O | 40,000 | 260. | 400. | 700. | 1,400. | 3,300. | 13,000. | | |
| 1851, Orig, High Date | 1,300 | 5,000. | 8,500. | 11,000. | 14,000. | 20,000. | 33,000. | 25,000. | |
| 1851, Restrike, Dt Cntrd | | | | | | | | 22,000. | 35,000. |
| 1852, Original | 1,100 | 4,400. | 8,800. | 11,000. | 14,000. | 20,000. | 28,000. | 32,000. | 50,000. |
| 1852, Restrike | | | | | | | | 14,000. | 35,000. |
| 1853 | 46,110 | 240. | 330. | 440. | 650. | 1,300. | 2,600. | 20,000. | 50,000. |
| 1854 | 33,140 | 1,300. | 2,000. | 2,800. | 4,000. | 6,000. | 8,500. | 12,000. | 20,000. |
| 1855 | 26,000 | 1,100. | 1,400. | 2,200. | 3,500. | 5,000. | 8,000. | 12,500. | 22,000. |
| 1856 | 63,500 | 400. | 500. | 650. | 1,200. | 2,000. | 4,000. | 6,000. | 16,000. |
| 1857 | 94,000 | 400. | 450. | 650. | 1,300. | 1,700. | 3,000. | 5,500. | 10,000. |
| 1858 | (300+) | 3,400. | 3,900. | 5,000. | 6,000. | 7,000. | | 8,000. | 13,000. |

| | Mintage | VG-8 | F-12 | VF-20 | EF-40 | AU-50 | MS-60 | MS-63 | PF-63 |
|---|---|---|---|---|---|---|---|---|---|
| 1859 ......(800) | 255,700 | $250. | $350. | $460. | $600. | $800. | $2,000. | $5,500. | $5,000. |
| 1859O | 360,000 | 200. | 250. | 300. | 450. | 650. | 1,000. | 3,300. | |
| 1859S | 20,000 | 330. | 460. | 600. | 1,700. | 3,700. | 13,000. | — | |
| 1860 ....(1,330) | 217,600 | 260. | 330. | 460. | 550. | 650. | 1,200. | 3,300. | 4,000. |
| 1860O | 515,000 | 230. | 250. | 300. | 400. | 650. | 1,100. | 3,000. | |
| 1861 ....(1,000) | 77,500 | 650. | 800. | 950. | 1,200. | 2,200. | 3,300. | 5,250. | 4,000. |
| 1862 ......(550) | 11,540 | 600. | 750. | 900. | 1,200. | 2,200. | 3,300. | 5,250. | 4,500. |
| 1863 ......(460) | 27,200 | 400. | 450. | 500. | 700. | 1,400. | 3,000. | 5,000. | 4,500. |
| 1864 ......(470) | 30,700 | 250. | 340. | 500. | 700. | 1,300. | 3,700. | 5,400. | 4,500. |
| 1865 ......(500) | 46,500 | 250. | 300. | 500. | 600. | 1,300. | 2,700. | 5,400. | 4,500. |

1866, No Motto *(2 known)* $1,207,500, PF-63, ANR auction, Jan-05 — —

## With Motto (1866–1873)

**Motto IN GOD WE TRUST on Reverse (1866–1873)**

| | Mintage | VG-8 | F-12 | VF-20 | EF-40 | AU-50 | MS-60 | MS-63 | PF-63 |
|---|---|---|---|---|---|---|---|---|---|
| 1866 .... (725) .... 48,900 | | $250. | $330. | $480. | $600. | $1,000. | $1,900. | $3,500. | $3,750. |
| 1867 .... (625) .... 46,900 | | 230. | 300. | 450. | 550. | 1,000. | 1,900. | 3,750. | 3,750. |
| 1868 .... (600) ... 162,100 | | 220. | 275. | 400. | 500. | 1,000. | 1,800. | 6,500. | 3,750. |
| 1869 .... (600) ... 423,700 | | 220. | 250. | 330. | 460. | 800. | 1,800. | 4,200. | 3,750. |
| 1870.... (1,000) ... 415,000 | | 220. | 260. | 320. | 450. | 700. | 1,400. | 3,300. | 3,750. |
| 1870CC ........... 11,758 | | 500. | 1,000. | 1,600. | 3,800. | 11,000. | 25,000. | | |
| 1870S ............ | | 100,000. | 130,000. | 230,000. | 400,000. | 650,000. | 1,000,000. | | |
| *$1,092,500, BU PL, Stack's auction, May-03* | | | | | | | | | |
| 1871 .... (960).. 1,073,800 | | 220. | 260. | 310. | 440. | 650. | 1,200. | 3,300. | 3,750. |
| 1871CC ............ 1,376 | | 2,400. | 3,500. | 5,500. | 10,000. | 25,000. | 65,000. | | |
| 1872 .... (950).. 1,105,500 | | 220. | 250. | 320. | 450. | 700. | 1,200. | 3,300. | 3,750. |
| 1872CC ............ 3,150 | | 1,300. | 2,000. | 3,200. | 5,000. | 11,000. | 26,000. | 50,000. | |
| 1872S ............. 9,000 | | 300. | 450. | 600. | 1,400. | 3,000. | 9,000. | 33,000. | |
| 1873 .... (600) ... 293,000 | | 240. | 250. | 330. | 450. | 750. | 1,400. | 3,300. | 3,750. |
| 1873CC ............ 2,300 | | 5,000. | 6,600. | 10,000. | 18,000. | 32,000. | 80,000. | 130,000. | |
| 1873S ............. 700 | | *(unknown in any collection)* | | | | | | | |

# TRADE DOLLARS (1873–1885)

This coin was issued for circulation in the Orient to compete with dollar-sized coins of other countries. Many pieces that circulated in the Orient were counterstamped with Oriental characters, known as *chop marks*. They were legal tender in the United States, but when silver prices declined, Congress repealed the provision and authorized the Treasury to limit coinage to export demand. In 1887, the Treasury redeemed all trade dollars that were not mutilated. The law authorizing trade dollars was repealed in February 1887. Modifications to the trade dollar design are distinguished as follows:

- **Reverse 1:** Berry under eagle's left talon; arrowhead ends over 0. Used on all coins from all mints in 1873 and 1874, and occasionally in 1875 and 1876.
- **Reverse 2:** Without extra berry under talon; arrowhead ends over 2. Used occasionally at all mints from 1875 through 1876, and on all coins from all mints 1877 through 1885.
- **Obverse 1:** Ends of scroll point to left; extended hand has only three fingers. Used on all coins at all mints 1873 through 1876.
- **Obverse 2:** Ends of scroll point downward; hand has four fingers. Used in combination with Reverse 2 on varieties of 1876 and 1876S, and on all coins at all mints from 1877 through 1885.

*Designer William Barber; weight 27.22 grams; composition .900 silver, .100 copper (net weight .7874 oz. pure silver); diameter 38.1 mm; reeded edge; mints: Philadelphia, Carson City, San Francisco.*

**VG-8 VERY GOOD**—About half of mottoes IN GOD WE TRUST (on Liberty's pedestal) and E PLURIBUS UNUM (on reverse ribbon) visible. Rim on both sides well defined.

**F-12 FINE**—Mottoes and LIBERTY legible but worn.

**EF-40 EXTREMELY FINE**—Mottoes and LIBERTY sharp. Only slight wear on rims.

**AU-50 ABOUT UNCIRCULATED**—Slight trace of wear on Liberty's left breast and left knee and on hair above ear, as well as on eagle's head, knee, and wing tips.

**MS-60 UNCIRCULATED**—No trace of wear. Light blemishes.

**MS-63 CHOICE UNCIRCULATED**—Some distracting contact marks or blemishes in prime focal areas. Impaired luster possible.

**PF-63 CHOICE PROOF**—Reflective surfaces with only a few blemishes in secondary focal places. No major flaws.

**1875-S,
S Over CC**

*Mintmark location on reverse, above D in DOLLAR.*

*See next page for chart.*

| | Mintage | VG-8 | F-12 | EF-40 | AU-50 | MS-60 | MS-63 | PF-63 |
|---|---|---|---|---|---|---|---|---|
| 1873 ......(865)...396,635 | | $110. | $180. | $220. | $330. | $750. | $1,600. | $2,800. |
| 1873CC ...........124,500 | | 200. | 260. | 600. | 1,300. | 4,000. | 20,000. | |
| 1873S .............703,000 | | 110. | 140. | 240. | 350. | 1,000. | 2,200. | |
| 1874 ......(700)...987,100 | | 110. | 140. | 220. | 330. | 500. | 1,500. | 2,800. |
| 1874CC ..........1,373,200 | | 200. | 250. | 400. | 550. | 1,300. | 5,000. | |
| 1874S ..........2,549,000 | | 110. | 140. | 160. | 270. | 500. | 1,500. | |
| 1875 ......(700)...218,200 | | 160. | 330. | 550. | 900. | 1,900. | 3,000. | 3,300. |
| 1875, Rev 2 ..............* | | 160. | 330. | 500. | 800. | 1,800. | 2,700. | |
| 1875CC, All kinds ..1,573,700 | | | | | | | | |
| 1875CC ............... | | 180. | 240. | 340. | 400. | 900. | 3,000. | |
| 1875CC, Rev 2 .......... | | 200. | 270. | 350. | 450. | 1,100. | 3,300. | |
| 1875S, All kinds ...4,487,000 | | | | | | | | |
| 1875S ................ | | 110. | 140. | 160. | 270. | 500. | 1,600. | |
| 1875S, Rev 2 ........... | | 110. | 140. | 190. | 300. | 650. | 1,800. | |
| 1875S, S Over CC ....... | | 220. | 330. | 800. | 1,200. | 2,700. | 9,000. | |
| 1876 .....(1,150)...455,000 | | 110. | 140. | 190. | 300. | 550. | 1,600. | 2,800. |
| 1876, Obv 2, Rev 2 (ex. rare) * | | | | — | | | | |
| 1876, Rev 2 ..............* | | 110. | 140. | 160. | 270. | 500. | 1,500. | |
| 1876CC, All kinds ....509,000 | | | | | | | | |
| 1876CC ............... | | 160. | 220. | 400. | 1,000. | 3,000. | 19,000. | |
| 1876CC, Rev 1 .......... | | 190. | 250. | 450. | 1,100. | 3,600. | 20,000. | |
| 1876CC, DblDie Rev ...... | | | | — | — | | — | |
| 1876S, All kinds ...5,227,000 | | | | | | | | |
| 1876S ................. | | 110. | 140. | 180. | 300. | 500. | 1,700. | |
| 1876S, Rev 2 .......... | | 110. | 140. | 160. | 270. | 480. | 1,500. | |
| 1876S, Obv 2/Rev 2 ...... | | 140. | 160. | 220. | 330. | 650. | 1,900. | |
| 1877 ......(510) .3,039,200 | | 110. | 140. | 160. | 270. | 550. | 1,600. | 2,800. |
| 1877CC ...........534,000 | | 190. | 270. | 550. | 650. | 1,200. | 6,500. | |
| 1877S ..........9,519,000 | | 110. | 140. | 160. | 270. | 550. | 1,500. | |
| 1878 ......(900) ......... | | | | 1,200. | | | | 2,800. |
| 1878CC (a) .........97,000 | | 450. | 700. | 2,000. | 3,600. | 10,000. | 20,000. | |
| 1878S ..........4,162,000 | | 110. | 140. | 160. | 270. | 550. | 1,600. | |
| 1879 ....(1,541) ........ | | | | 1,200. | | | | 2,800. |
| 1880 ....(1,987) ........ | | | | 1,200. | | | | 2,800. |
| 1881 ......(960) ........ | | | | 1,300. | | | | 2,800. |
| 1882 ....(1,097) ........ | | | | 1,300. | | | | 2,800. |
| 1883 ......(979) ........ | | | | 1,300. | | | | 2,800. |
| 1884 (b) ....(10) ........ | | $603,750, PF-65, Heritage auction, Nov-05 | | | | | | 400,000. |
| 1885 (b) .....(5) ........ | | $1,006,250, PF-62, DLRC auction, Nov-04 | | | | | | 1,500,000. |

* Included in number above. **a.** 44,148 trade dollars were melted on July 19, 1878. Many of these may have been 1878-CC. **b.** The trade dollars of 1884 and 1885 were unknown to collectors until 1908. None are listed in the Mint director's report, and numismatists believe that they are not a part of the regular Mint issue.

## MORGAN (1878–1921)

The coinage law of 1873 made no provision for the standard silver dollar. During the lapse in coinage of this denomination, the gold dollar became the unit coin, and the trade dollar was used for commercial transactions with the Orient.

Resumption of coinage of the silver dollar was authorized by the Act of February 28, 1878, known as the Bland-Allison Act. The weight (412-1/2 grains) and fineness (.900) were to conform with the Act of January 18, 1837.

# SILVER AND RELATED DOLLARS

George T. Morgan, formerly a pupil of William Wyon in the Royal Mint in London, designed the new dollar. His initial M is found at the truncation of the neck, at the last tress. It also appears on the reverse on the left-hand loop of the ribbon.

Coinage of the silver dollar was suspended after 1904, when demand was low and the bullion supply became exhausted. Under provisions of the Pittman Act of 1918, 270,232,722 silver dollars were melted, and later, in 1921, coinage of the silver dollar was resumed. The Morgan design, with some slight refinements, was employed until the new Peace design was adopted later in that year.

Varieties listed are those most significant to collectors. Numerous other variations exist. Values are shown for the most common pieces. Prices of variations not listed in this guide depend on collector interest and demand.

Sharply struck, prooflike coins have highly reflective surfaces and are very scarce, usually commanding substantial premiums.

*Designer George T. Morgan; weight 26.73 grams; composition .900 silver, .100 copper (net weight .77344 oz. pure silver); diameter 38.1 mm; reeded edge; mints: Philadelphia, New Orleans, Carson City, Denver, San Francisco.*

**VF-20 VERY FINE**—Two thirds of hair lines from top of forehead to ear visible. Ear well defined. Feathers on eagle's breast worn.

**EF-40 EXTREMELY FINE**—All hair lines strong and ear bold. Eagle's feathers all plain but with slight wear on breast and wing tips.

**AU-50 ABOUT UNCIRCULATED**—Slight trace of wear on the bust shoulder and hair left of forehead, and on eagle's breast and top edges of wings.

**MS-60 UNCIRCULATED**—No trace of wear. Full mint luster present, but may be noticeably marred by scuff marks or bag abrasions.

**MS-63 CHOICE UNCIRCULATED**—No trace of wear; full mint luster; few noticeable surface marks.

**MS-64 UNCIRCULATED**—A few scattered contact marks. Good eye appeal and attractive luster.

**MS-65 GEM UNCIRCULATED**—Only light, scattered contact marks that are not distracting. Strong luster, good eye appeal.

**PF-63 CHOICE PROOF**—Reflective surfaces with only a few blemishes in secondary focal places. No major flaws.

### 8 Tail Feathers, 1878, Philadelphia Only

**First Reverse**

*Mintmark location on reverse, below wreath.*

| **Second Reverse** | **Third Reverse** | **1878, Doubled Tail Feathers** |
|---|---|---|
| *Parallel top arrow feather, concave breast.* | *Slanted top arrow feather, convex breast.* | |

*See next page for chart.*

| | Mintage | VF-20 | EF-40 | AU-50 | MS-60 | MS-63 | MS-64 | MS-65 | PF-63 |
|---|---|---|---|---|---|---|---|---|---|
| 1878, 8 Feathers (500) | *749,500* | $35. | $40. | $65. | $140. | $175. | $450. | $1,300. | $2,750. |
| 1878, 7 Feathers (250) | *9,759,300* | | | | | | | | |
| 1878, 7 Over 8 Clear Double Feathers . . . . . . . . . . . * | | 25. | 35. | 60. | 130. | 350. | 500. | 3,200. | |
| 1878, 7 Feathers, 2nd Rev . . . . . * | | 22. | 30. | 45. | 70. | 140. | 360. | 1,700. | |
| 1878, 7 Feathers, 3rd Rev . . . . . * | | 25. | 30. | 42. | 75. | 140. | 450. | 2,700. | 7,600. |
| 1878CC . . . . . . . . . . . . . . | 2,212,000 | 100. | 120. | 140. | 240. | 400. | 600. | 2,200. | |
| 1878S . . . . . . . . . . . . . . | 9,774,000 | 25. | 30. | 40. | 55. | 65. | 110. | 300. | |
| 1879 . . . . . . . . . (1,100) | 14,806,000 | 18. | 20. | 25. | 35. | 65. | 150. | 1,200. | 2,400. |
| 1879CC, CC Over CC . . . . . . | 756,000 | 170. | 560. | 1,300. | 3,000. | 6,500. | 9,000. | 22,000. | |
| 1879CC, Clear CC . . . . . . . . . . . . . * | | 200. | 650. | 1,350. | 3,200. | 7,500. | 10,000. | 32,000. | |
| 1879O . . . . . . . . . . . . . . | 2,887,000 | 22. | 25. | 30. | 90. | 200. | 500. | 3,300. | |
| 1879S, 2nd Rev . . . . . . . . | 9,110,000 | 22. | 25. | 45. | 110. | 380. | 1,350. | 7,500. | |
| 1879S, 3rd Rev . . . . . . . . . . . . . * | | 20. | 23. | 25. | 43. | 55. | 65. | 170. | |
| 1880 . . . . . . . . . (1,355) | 12,600,000 | 19. | 22. | 25. | 38. | 60. | 140. | 800. | 3,000. |
| 1880, 80 Over 79 (a) . . . . . . . . . . * | | 20. | 25. | 45. | 90. | 330. | 600. | 3,300. | |

* Included in number above. **a.** Several die varieties. Values shown are for the most common.

**1880-CC, 80 Over 79 (b)**     **1880-CC, 8 Over High 7 (a)**     **1880-CC, 8 Over Low 7**

| | Mintage | VF-20 | EF-40 | AU-50 | MS-60 | MS-63 | MS-64 | MS-65 | PF-63 |
|---|---|---|---|---|---|---|---|---|---|
| 1880CC, All kinds . . . . . . . . | 591,000 | | | | | | | | |
| 1880CC, 80/79, 2nd Rev (b) . . . . . | | $160. | $210. | $280. | $460. | $580. | $1,500. | $2,750. | |
| 1880CC, 8 Over 7, 2nd Rev (a) . . | | 170. | 220. | 300. | 475. | 550. | 1,000. | 2,600. | |
| 1880CC, 8 Over High 7, 3rd Rev (a) . . . . . . . . . . . . | | 170. | 220. | 290. | 420. | 500. | 675. | 1,500. | |
| 1880CC, 8 Over Low 7, 3rd Rev (a) . . . . . . . . . . . . | | 170. | 220. | 310. | 460. | 520. | 680. | 1,500. | |
| 1880CC, 3rd Rev | | 160. | 220. | 300. | 450. | 500. | 750. | 1,600. | |
| 1880O, All kinds . . . . . . . . | 5,305,000 | | | | | | | | |
| 1880O, 80 Over 79 (a) . . . . . . . . . | | 20. | 25. | 30. | 80. | 500. | 2,500. | — | |
| 1880O . . . . . . . . . . . . . . . . . . . . . | | 18. | 20. | 25. | 75. | 350. | 1,750. | 22,000. | |
| 1880S, All kinds . . . . . . . . | 8,900,000 | | | | | | | | |
| 1880S, 80 Over 79 . . . . . . . . . . . | | 20. | 25. | 30. | 45. | 55. | 100. | 275. | |
| 1880S, 0 Over 9 . . . . . . . . . . . . . | | 20. | 25. | 30. | 50. | 55. | 100. | 275. | |
| 1880S . . . . . . . . . . . . . . . . . . . . . | | 17. | 20. | 25. | 35. | 45. | 57. | 175. | |
| 1881 . . . . . . . (984) . . . . . | 9,163,000 | 18. | 20. | 25. | 35. | 60. | 155. | 900. | $2,200. |
| 1881CC . . . . . . . . . . . . . . | 296,000 | 330. | 375. | 425. | 520. | 550. | 600. | 920. | |
| 1881O . . . . . . . . . . . . . . | 5,708,000 | 18. | 20. | 25. | 35. | 50. | 155. | 1,600. | |
| 1881S . . . . . . . . . . . . . . | 12,760,000 | 18. | 20. | 25. | 35. | 50. | 70. | 175. | |
| 1882 . . . . . (1,100) . . . . | 11,100,000 | 18. | 20. | 25. | 35. | 50. | 70. | 475. | 2,200. |
| 1882CC . . . . . . . . . . . . . . | 1,133,000 | 120. | 130. | 140. | 240. | 270. | 320. | 590. | |
| 1882O . . . . . . . . . . . . . . | 6,090,000 | 18. | 20. | 25. | 35. | 50. | 75. | 800. | |
| 1882O, O Over S . . . . . . . . . . . . * | | 35. | 40. | 65. | 200. | 1,200. | 3,500. | 28,000. | |
| 1882S . . . . . . . . . . . . . . | 9,250,000 | 18. | 20. | 25. | 37. | 50. | 70. | 175. | |
| 1883 . . . . . (1,039) . . . . | 12,290,000 | 18. | 20. | 25. | 37. | 50. | 70. | 200. | 2,300. |
| 1883CC . . . . . . . . . . . . . . | 1,204,000 | 120. | 130. | 140. | 225. | 250. | 300. | 480. | |
| 1883O . . . . . . . . . . . . . . | 8,725,000 | 18. | 20. | 25. | 35. | 50. | 65. | 170. | |
| 1883S . . . . . . . . . . . . . . | 6,250,000 | 20. | 40. | 190. | 560. | 2,800. | 4,600. | 23,000. | |

* Included in number above. **a.** Several die varieties. Values shown are for the most common. **b.** The 7 and 9 show within the 80; no tip below second 8.

| | Mintage | VF-20 | EF-40 | AU-50 | MS-60 | MS-63 | MS-64 | MS-65 | PF-63 |
|---|---|---|---|---|---|---|---|---|---|
| 1884 ......(875) | 14,070,000 | $18. | $20. | $25. | $35. | $50. | $65. | $250. | $2,000. |
| 1884CC | 1,136,000 | 140. | 160. | 190. | 220. | 260. | 300. | 500. | |
| 1884O | 9,730,000 | 18. | 20. | 25. | 35. | 50. | 65. | 170. | |
| 1884S | 3,200,000 | 20. | 45. | 300. | 5,500. | 28,000. | 120,000. | 200,000. | |
| 1885 ......(930) | 17,787,000 | 18. | 20. | 25. | 35. | 50. | 65. | 170. | 2,200. |
| 1885CC | 228,000 | 475. | 500. | 525. | 600. | 650. | 750. | 1,600. | |
| 1885O | 9,185,000 | 18. | 20. | 25. | 35. | 50. | 65. | 170. | |
| 1885S | 1,497,000 | 35. | 60. | 130. | 250. | 300. | 600. | 2,000. | |
| 1886 ......(886) | 19,963,000 | 18. | 20. | 25. | 35. | 50. | 65. | 170. | 2,200. |
| 1886O | 10,710,000 | 20. | 25. | 100. | 600. | 4,100. | 9,500. | 205,000. | |
| 1886S | 750,000 | 70. | 90. | 160. | 300. | 440. | 700. | 3,200. | |
| 1887, 7 Over 6 (710) | * | 40. | 65. | 125. | 300. | 730. | 1,200. | 4,750. | |
| 1887 | 20,290,000 | 18. | 20. | 25. | 35. | 50. | 65. | 170. | 2,200. |
| 1887O, 7 Over 6 | * | 35. | 70. | 160. | 400. | 2,700. | 10,000. | 30,000. | |
| 1887O | 11,550,000 | 22. | 25. | 35. | 65. | 135. | 400. | 3,500. | |
| 1887S | 1,771,000 | 25. | 30. | 55. | 110. | 300. | 660. | 3,600. | |

* Included in number below.

**1888-O,**
**Doubled-Die**
**Obverse**
*Lips especially
prominent
("hot lips"
variety).*

| | Mintage | VF-20 | EF-40 | AU-50 | MS-60 | MS-63 | MS-64 | MS-65 | PF-63 |
|---|---|---|---|---|---|---|---|---|---|
| 1888 ......(832) | 19,183,100 | $18. | $20. | $25. | $35. | $50. | $65. | $210. | $2,200. |
| 1888O | 12,150,000 | 18. | 20. | 25. | 35. | 50. | 65. | 450. | |
| 1888O, DblDie Obv | * | 30. | 100. | 150. | 350. | 1,600. | — | | |
| 1888S | 657,000 | 175. | 200. | 215. | 290. | 450. | 800. | 3,700. | |
| 1889 ......(811) | 21,726,000 | 18. | 20. | 25. | 35. | 50. | 65. | 175. | 2,200. |
| 1889CC | 350,000 | 2,100. | 4,000. | 7,000. | 20,000. | 33,000. | 55,000. | 300,000. | |
| 1889O | 11,875,000 | 20. | 23. | 40. | 160. | 440. | 750. | 5,000. | |
| 1889S | 700,000 | 60. | 80. | 110. | 260. | 440. | 540. | 2,000. | |
| 1890 ......(590) | 16,802,000 | 18. | 20. | 30. | 35. | 60. | 150. | 2,200. | 2,300. |
| 1890CC | 2,309,041 | 110. | 165. | 200. | 375. | 975. | 2,650. | 6,600. | |
| 1890O | 10,701,000 | 22. | 26. | 35. | 70. | 120. | 320. | 1,600. | |
| 1890S | 8,230,373 | 18. | 20. | 30. | 65. | 120. | 250. | 900. | |
| 1891 ......(650) | 8,693,556 | 18. | 20. | 30. | 65. | 190. | 500. | 6,700. | 2,200. |
| 1891CC | 1,618,000 | 110. | 170. | 220. | 375. | 850. | 1,500. | 4,800. | |
| 1891O | 7,954,529 | 20. | 25. | 45. | 150. | 350. | 720. | 7,500. | |
| 1891S | 5,296,000 | 20. | 25. | 30. | 70. | 140. | 280. | 1,200. | |
| 1892 ....(1,245) | 1,036,000 | 30. | 40. | 90. | 175. | 430. | 930. | 4,100. | 2,250. |
| 1892CC | 1,352,000 | 240. | 440. | 630. | 1,100. | 2,500. | 3,500. | 10,000. | |
| 1892O | 2,744,000 | 25. | 35. | 70. | 190. | 320. | 650. | 5,000. | |
| 1892S | 1,200,000 | 75. | 210. | 1,900. | 3,300. | 60,000. | 90,000. | 160,000. | |
| 1893 ......(792) | 378,000 | 220. | 250. | 350. | 650. | 1,300. | 2,350. | 7,000. | 2,500. |

* Included in number above.

*Chart continued on next page.*

**1901, Doubled-Die Reverse**
*Note tail feathers.*

| | Mintage | VF-20 | EF-40 | AU-50 | MS-60 | MS-63 | MS-64 | MS-65 | PF-63 |
|---|---|---|---|---|---|---|---|---|---|
| 1893CC . . . . . . . . . . . 677,000 | | $550. | $1,600. | $2,100. | $3,400. | $7,300. | $13,000. | $51,500. | |
| 1893O . . . . . . . . . . . . 300,000 | | 350. | 575. | 1,000. | 1,750. | 7,000. | 22,000. | 200,000. | |
| 1893S **(c)** . . . . . . . . . . 100,000 | | 6,000. | 10,000. | 25,000. | 80,000. | 120,000. | 300,000. | 450,000. | |
| *$414,000. Superb Gem BU, Stack's auction, Nov-01* | | | | | | | | | |
| 1894 . . . . . . . . (972). . 110,000 | | 1,600. | 2,300. | 2,750. | 4,500. | 6,000. | 10,000. | 34,000. | $3,500. |
| 1894O . . . . . . . . . . . 1,723,000 | | 60. | 120. | 300. | 625. | 3,750. | 9,500. | 50,000. | |
| 1894S . . . . . . . . . . . 1,260,000 | | 85. | 140. | 500. | 680. | 1,100. | 1,900. | 5,500. | |
| 1895, Proof **(d)** (880). . . 12,000 | | | 30,000. | 35,000. | 40,000. | 47,500. | 55,000. | 66,000. | 47,500. |
| 1895O . . . . . . . . . . . . 450,000 | | 550. | 825. | 1,750. | 16,500. | 50,000. | 100,000. | 200,000. | |
| *$575,000, MS-67, Heritage auction, Nov-05* | | | | | | | | | |
| 1895S . . . . . . . . . . . . 400,000 | | 400. | 700. | 1,600. | 3,500. | 5,500. | 7,800. | 20,000. | |
| 1896 . . . . . . . . (762) 9,976,000 | | 18. | 20. | 25. | 32. | 50. | 65. | 175. | 2,200. |
| 1896O . . . . . . . . . . . 4,900,000 | | 20. | 23. | 190. | 1,000. | 7,750. | 44,000. | 170,000. | |
| 1896S . . . . . . . . . . . 5,000,000 | | 60. | 200. | 750. | 1,350. | 3,000. | 4,250. | 16,000. | |
| *$402,500, MS-69, Heritage auction, Nov-05* | | | | | | | | | |
| 1897 . . . . . . . . (731) 2,822,000 | | 18. | 20. | 25. | 35. | 50. | 65. | 200. | 2,200. |
| 1897O . . . . . . . . . . . 4,004,000 | | 20. | 25. | 130. | 675. | 5,000. | 15,000. | 47,000. | |
| 1897S . . . . . . . . . . . 5,825,000 | | 18. | 20. | 30. | 65. | 110. | 165. | 600. | |
| 1898 . . . . . . . . (735) 5,884,000 | | 18. | 20. | 25. | 35. | 50. | 65. | 275. | 2,300. |
| 1898O . . . . . . . . . . . 4,440,000 | | 18. | 20. | 25. | 35. | 50. | 65. | 175. | |
| 1898S . . . . . . . . . . . 4,102,000 | | 30. | 40. | 100. | 250. | 500. | 900. | 2,300. | |
| 1899 . . . . . . . . (846). . 330,000 | | 100. | 125. | 160. | 210. | 320. | 450. | 850. | 2,300. |
| 1899O . . . . . . . . . . . 12,290,000 | | 18. | 20. | 25. | 35. | 50. | 65. | 175. | |
| 1899S . . . . . . . . . . . 2,562,000 | | 35. | 55. | 120. | 350. | 450. | 750. | 2,000. | |
| 1900 . . . . . . . . (912) 8,830,000 | | 18. | 20. | 25. | 35. | 50. | 65. | 210. | 2,200. |
| 1900O . . . . . . . . . . . 12,590,000 | | 18. | 20. | 25. | 35. | 50. | 65. | 225. | |
| 1900O, O Over CC **(e)** . . . . . . . * | | 50. | 80. | 165. | 300. | 900. | 1,500. | 3,300. | |
| 1900S . . . . . . . . . . . 3,540,000 | | 25. | 40. | 90. | 275. | 400. | 535. | 1,550. | |
| 1901 **(c)** . . . . . (813) 6,962,000 | | 45. | 100. | 420. | 2,100. | 16,500. | 55,000. | 225,000. | 3,000. |
| 1901, DblDie Rev . . . . . . . . . * | | 245. | 680. | 2,200. | 4,500. | — | | | |
| 1901O . . . . . . . . . . . 13,320,000 | | 18. | 20. | 25. | 35. | 50. | 65. | 220. | |
| 1901S . . . . . . . . . . . 2,284,000 | | 38. | 55. | 230. | 380. | 700. | 900. | 4,000. | |
| 1902 . . . . . . . . (777) 7,994,000 | | 18. | 22. | 28. | 50. | 110. | 170. | 525. | 2,200. |
| 1902O . . . . . . . . . . . 8,636,000 | | 18. | 20. | 25. | 35. | 50. | 65. | 175. | |
| 1902S . . . . . . . . . . . 1,530,000 | | 130. | 190. | 280. | 420. | 650. | 1,000. | 3,200. | |
| 1903 . . . . . . . . (755) 4,652,000 | | 50. | 57. | 70. | 85. | 100. | 125. | 300. | 2,200. |
| 1903O . . . . . . . . . . . 4,450,000 | | 340. | 370. | 425. | 475. | 500. | 550. | 760. | |
| 1903S . . . . . . . . . . . 1,241,000 | | 140. | 300. | 1,600. | 3,600. | 6,000. | 7,500. | 9,000. | |
| 1904 . . . . . . . . (650) 2,788,000 | | 25. | 37. | 45. | 85. | 300. | 600. | 4,200. | 2,200. |
| 1904O . . . . . . . . . . . 3,720,000 | | 18. | 20. | 25. | 35. | 50. | 65. | 170. | |
| 1904S . . . . . . . . . . . 2,304,000 | | 85. | 240. | 620. | 1,100. | 3,300. | 4,800. | 7,500. | |
| 1921 . . . . . . . . . . . 44,690,000 | | 16. | 17. | 19. | 24. | 38. | 50. | 180. | — |
| 1921D . . . . . . . . . . . 20,345,000 | | 17. | 18. | 20. | 40. | 65. | 140. | 310. | |
| 1921S . . . . . . . . . . . 21,695,000 | | 17. | 18. | 20. | 35. | 70. | 180. | 1,200. | |

* Included in number above. **c.** Authentication is recommended. Beware of altered mintmark. **d.** Beware of removed mintmark. Values are for Proofs; business strikes are not known to exist. **e.** Several die varieties.

# SILVER AND RELATED DOLLARS

## Peace (1921–1935)

The dollar issued from 1921 through 1935 was a commemorative peace coin, which might easily have been a half dollar. The Peace dollar, in fact, was issued without congressional sanction, under the terms of the Pittman Act, which referred to the bullion and in no way affected the design. Anthony de Francisci, a medalist, designed this dollar. His monogram is located in the field of the coin under the neck of Liberty.

The new Peace dollar was placed in circulation on January 3, 1922; 1,006,473 pieces had been struck in December 1921.

The high relief of the 1921 design was found impractical for coinage and was slightly modified in 1922, after 35,401 coins had been made and most of them melted at the mint. The rare Matte and Satin Finish Proofs of 1922 are of both the high-relief style of 1921 and the normal-relief style.

Legislation dated August 3, 1964, authorized the coinage of 45 million silver dollars, and 316,076 dollars of the Peace design dated 1964 were struck at the Denver Mint in 1965. Plans for completing this coinage were subsequently abandoned and all of these coins were melted. None were preserved or released for circulation.

*Designer Anthony de Francisci; weight 26.73 grams; composition .900 silver, .100 copper (net weight .77344 oz. pure silver); diameter 38.1 mm; reeded edge; mints: Philadelphia, Denver, San Francisco.*

**VF-20 VERY FINE**—Hair over eye well worn. Some strands over ear well defined. Some eagle feathers on top and outside edge of right wing visible.

**EF-40 EXTREMELY FINE**—Hair lines over brow and ear are strong, though slightly worn. Outside wing feathers at right and those at top visible but faint.

**AU-50 ABOUT UNCIRCULATED**—Slight trace of wear. Most of mint luster present, although marred by contact marks.

**MS-60 UNCIRCULATED**—No trace of wear. Full mint luster, but possibly noticeably marred by stains, surface marks, or bag abrasions.

**MS-63 CHOICE UNCIRCULATED**—Some distracting contact marks or blemishes in prime focal areas. Impaired luster possible.

**MS-64 UNCIRCULATED**—A few scattered contact marks. Good eye appeal and attractive luster.

**MS-65 GEM UNCIRCULATED**—Only light, scattered contact marks that are not distracting. Strong luster, good eye appeal.

*Mintmark location on reverse, below ONE.*

| | Mintage | VF-20 | EF-40 | AU-50 | MS-60 | MS-63 | MS-64 | MS-65 | MATTE PF-65 |
|---|---|---|---|---|---|---|---|---|---|
| 1921, High Relief | . . . .1,006,473 | $110. | $120. | $160. | $260. | $450. | $700. | $2,700. | $47,000. |
| 1922, High Relief | . . . . . . .35,401 | | | — | | | | | 70,000. |
| 1922, Nml Relief | . . . .51,737,000 | 12. | 13. | 14. | 20. | 32. | 50. | 165. | 55,000. |
| 1922D | . . . . . . . . . . .15,063,000 | 12. | 13. | 16. | 30. | 50. | 90. | 400. | |
| 1922S | . . . . . . . . . . .17,475,000 | 13. | 14. | 17. | 30. | 65. | 220. | 2,250. | |
| 1923 | . . . . . . . . . . . .30,800,000 | 12. | 13. | 15. | 20. | 32. | 50. | 160. | |
| 1923D | . . . . . . . . . . . .6,811,000 | 12. | 13. | 20. | 60. | 130. | 275. | 1,200. | |
| 1923S | . . . . . . . . . . .19,020,000 | 13. | 14. | 16. | 30. | 75. | 300. | 6,000. | |
| 1924 | . . . . . . . . . . .11,811,000 | 13. | 14. | 16. | 21. | 35. | 55. | 175. | |

*Chart continued on next page.*

| | Mintage | VF-20 | EF-40 | AU-50 | MS-60 | MS-63 | MS-64 | MS-65 | MATTE PF-65 |
|---|---|---|---|---|---|---|---|---|---|
| 1924S | 1,728,000 | $30. | $40. | $70. | $225. | $500. | $1,150. | $8,000. | |
| 1925 | 10,198,000 | 12. | 14. | 15. | 20. | 35. | 60. | 165. | |
| 1925S | 1,610,000 | 22. | 26. | 42. | 78. | 170. | 700. | 2,500. | |
| 1926 | 1,939,000 | 15. | 17. | 22. | 40. | 80. | 110. | 380. | |
| 1926D | 2,348,700 | 16. | 20. | 34. | 70. | 150. | 300. | 600. | |
| 1926S | 6,980,000 | 13. | 16. | 22. | 45. | 95. | 260. | 850. | |
| 1927 | 848,000 | 28. | 35. | 57. | 75. | 160. | 340. | 2,350. | |
| 1927D | 1,268,900 | 27. | 35. | 85. | 160. | 350. | 880. | 5,200. | |
| 1927S | 866,000 | 28. | 32. | 80. | 160. | 370. | 850. | 11,500. | |
| 1928 | 360,649 | 430. | 460. | 500. | 530. | 750. | 1,000. | 5,000. | |
| 1928S | 1,632,000 | 30. | 40. | 65. | 180. | 600. | 2,000. | 21,000. | |
| 1934 | 954,057 | 22. | 28. | 52. | 110. | 240. | 400. | 1,000. | |
| 1934D (a) | 1,569,500 | 24. | 28. | 53. | 110. | 375. | 600. | 1,750. | |
| 1934S | 1,011,000 | 75. | 200. | 570. | 1,900. | 4,100. | 5,300. | 7,700. | |
| 1935 | 1,576,000 | 22. | 24. | 35. | 80. | 125. | 220. | 650. | |
| 1935S (b) | 1,964,000 | 20. | 30. | 110. | 250. | 400. | 600. | 1,300. | |

a. Large and small mintmark varieties; see page 20. b. Varieties exist with either three or four rays below ONE, and are of equal value.

## EISENHOWER (1971–1978)
### Eagle Reverse (1971–1974)

Honoring both President Dwight D. Eisenhower and the first landing of man on the moon, this design is the work of Chief Engraver Frank Gasparro, whose initials are on the truncation and below the eagle. The reverse is an adaptation of the official Apollo 11 insignia. Collectors' coins were struck in 40% silver composition, and the circulation issue in copper-nickel.

Since 1971, the dies for the Eisenhower dollar have been modified several times by changing the relief, strengthening the design, and making Earth above the eagle more clearly defined. Low-relief (Variety I) dies, with flattened Earth and three islands off Florida, were used for all copper-nickel issues of 1971, uncirculated silver coins of 1971, and most copper-nickel coins of 1972. High-relief (Variety II) dies, with round Earth and weak or indistinct islands, were used for all Proofs of 1971, all silver issues of 1972, and the reverse of some exceptional and scarce Philadelphia copper-nickel coins of 1972. Improved high-relief reverse dies (Variety III) were used for late 1972 Philadelphia copper-nickel coins and for all subsequent issues. Modified high-relief dies were also used on all issues beginning in 1973.

A few 1974-D and 1977-D dollars in silver clad composition were made in error.

*Designer Frank Gasparro; diameter 38.1 mm; reeded edge; mints: Philadelphia, Denver, San Francisco. Silver issue: weight 24.59 grams; composition, outer layers of .800 silver, .200 copper bonded to inner core of .209 silver, .791 copper (net weight.3161 oz. pure silver). Copper-nickel issue: weight 22.68 grams; composition, outer layers of .750 copper, .250 nickel bonded to inner core of pure copper.*

Mintmark location is above date.

| | Mintage | EF-40 | MS-63 | PF-65 |
|---|---|---|---|---|
| 1971, Copper-Nickel Clad | 47,799,000 | $2.00 | $6.00 | |
| 1971D, Copper-Nickel Clad | 68,587,424 | 2.00 | 4.50 | |
| 1971S, Silver Clad | (4,265,234) . . . . 6,868,530 | | 8.00 | $8.50 |
| 1972, Copper-Nickel Clad, Variety I | 75,890,000 | 2.00 | 5.00 | |
| 1972 , Copper-Nickel Clad, Variety II | * | 6.00 | 60.00 | |
| 1972, Copper-Nickel Clad, Variety III | * | 2.50 | 5.00 | |
| 1972D, Copper-Nickel Clad | 92,548,511 | 2.00 | 4.00 | |
| 1972S, Silver Clad | (1,811,631) . . . . 2,193,056 | | 8.50 | 9.00 |
| 1973, Copper-Nickel Clad **(a)** | 2,000,056 | | 13.00 | |
| 1973D, Copper-Nickel Clad **(a)** | 2,000,000 | | 13.00 | |
| 1973S, Copper-Nickel Clad | (2,760,339) . . . . . . . . . . . . | | | 11.00 |
| 1973S, Silver Clad | (1,013,646) . . . . 1,883,140 | | 11.00 | 32.00 |
| 1974, Copper-Nickel Clad | 27,366,000 | 2.00 | 6.00 | |
| 1974D, Copper-Nickel Clad | 45,517,000 | 2.00 | 6.00 | |
| 1974S, Copper-Nickel Clad | (2,612,568) . . . . . . . . . . . | | | 9.00 |
| 1974S, Silver Clad | (1,306,579) . . . . 1,900,156 | | 9.00 | 12.00 |

* Included in number above. **a.** 1,769,258 of each sold only in sets and not released for circulation. Unissued coins destroyed at mint.

## Bicentennial Coinage Dated 1776–1976

The national significance of the Bicentennial of the United States was highlighted with the adoption of new reverse designs for the quarter, half dollar, and dollar. Nearly a thousand entries were submitted after the Treasury announced in October 1973 that an open contest was to be held for the selection of the new designs. After the field was narrowed down to 12 semifinalists, the judges chose the rendition of the Liberty Bell superimposed on the moon to appear on the dollar coins. This design is the work of Dennis R. Williams.

The obverse remained unchanged except for the dual date "1776–1976," which appeared on these dollars made during 1975 and 1976. These dual-dated coins were included in the various offerings of Proof and uncirculated coins made by the Mint. They were also struck for general circulation. The lettering was modified early in 1975 to produce a more attractive design.

*Designers Frank Gasparro and Dennis R. Williams; diameter 38.1 mm; reeded edge; mints: Philadelphia, Denver, San Francisco. Silver issue—Weight 24.59 grams; composition, outer layers of .800 silver, .200 copper bonded to inner core of .209 silver, .791 copper (net weight .3161 oz. pure silver). Copper-nickel issue—Weight 22.68 grams; composition, outer layers of .750 copper, .250 nickel bonded to inner core of pure copper.*

**Variety 1**
*Design in low relief, bold lettering on reverse.*

**Variety 2**
*Sharp design, delicate lettering on reverse.*

*See next page for chart.*

| | Mintage | EF-40 | MS-63 | PF-65 |
|---|---|---|---|---|
| 1776–1976, Copper-Nickel Clad, Variety 1 . . . . . . . . . .4,019,000 | | $2. | $8. | |
| 1776–1976, Copper-Nickel Clad, Variety 2 . . . . . . . . .113,318,000 | | 2. | 5. | |
| 1776–1976D, Copper-Nickel Clad, Variety 1 . . . . . . . .21,048,710 | | 2. | 6. | |
| 1776–1976D, Copper-Nickel Clad, Variety 2 . . . . . . . .82,179,564 | | 2. | 5. | |
| 1776–1976S, Copper-Nickel Clad, Variety 1 . . . . . . . .(2,845,450) | | | | $13. |
| 1776–1976S, Copper-Nickel Clad, Variety 2 . . . . . . . .(4,149,730) | | | | 10. |
| 1776–1976, Silver Clad, Variety 2 . . . . . . . . . . . . . . . . . . . . . . . . . . | | | | — |
| 1776–1976S, Silver Clad, Variety 1 **(a)** . . . . . . . . . . . .11,000,000 | | | 16. | |
| 1776–1976S, Silver Clad, Variety 1 **(a)** . . . . . . . . . . .(4,000,000) | | | | 19. |

**a.** Mintage is approximate.

## Eagle Reverse Resumed (1977–1978)

| | Mintage | EF-40 | MS-63 | PF-65 |
|---|---|---|---|---|
| 1977, Copper-Nickel Clad . . . . . . . . . . . . . . . . . . . . . . .12,596,000 | | $2.00 | $6.50 | |
| 1977D, Copper-Nickel Clad . . . . . . . . . . . . . . . . . . . . . .32,983,006 | | 2.00 | 5.50 | |
| 1977S, Copper-Nickel Clad . . . . . . . . . . . . . . . . . . . . . .(3,251,152) | | | | $8.50 |
| 1978, Copper-Nickel Clad . . . . . . . . . . . . . . . . . . . . . . .25,702,000 | | 2.00 | 4.50 | |
| 1978D, Copper-Nickel Clad . . . . . . . . . . . . . . . . . . . . . .33,012,890 | | 2.00 | 5.50 | |
| 1978S, Copper-Nickel Clad . . . . . . . . . . . . . . . . . . . . . .(3,127,781) | | | | 11.00 |

## SUSAN B. ANTHONY (1979–1999)

Intended to honor this pioneer in women's rights, legislation dated October 10, 1978, provided for the issuance of the Susan B. Anthony dollar coin. Both obverse and reverse designs were the work of Chief Engraver of the U.S. Mint, Frank Gasparro, whose initials FG are located below the portrait and the eagle.

Placement of Susan B. Anthony's likeness on the dollar represented the first time that a woman other than a model or mythical figure has appeared on a circulating U.S. coin. The reverse design is the same as that used on the Eisenhower dollar. Mintmarks P, D, or S appear on the obverse, slightly above Anthony's right shoulder.

The size of this coin caused it to be confused with the quarter, and it failed to gain widespread public acceptance. No coins were made for circulation from 1981 to 1998. In 1999 additional pieces were made to meet the needs of vending machines.

*Designer Frank Gasparro; weight 8.1 grams; composition, outer layers of copper-nickel (.750 copper, .250 nickel) bonded to inner core of pure copper; diameter 26.5 mm; reeded edge; mints: Philadelphia, Denver, San Francisco.*

| 1979-S, Filled S (Type I) | 1979-S, Clear S (Type II, Rounded)<br>1981-S, First S (Type I, Rounded) | 1981-S, Clear S<br>(Type II, Flat) |

| 1979, Narrow Rim<br>(Far Date) | 1979, Wide Rim<br>(Near Date) |

|  | Mintage | MS-63 | PF-65 |
|---|---|---|---|
| 1979P, Narrow Rim **(a)** . . . . . . . . . . . . . . . . . . . . . . . . . . . . . . . . . . . . |  | $3. |  |
| 1979P, Wide Rim **(a)** . . . . . . . . . . . . . . . . . . . . . . . . . . . . . . . . . . . . . . |  | 20. |  |
| 1979D . . . . . . . . . . . . . . . . . . . . . . . . . . . . . . . . . . . . | 288,015,744 | 3. |  |
| 1979S . . . . . . . . . . . . . . . . . . . . . . . . . . . . . . . . . . . . | 109,576,000 | 3. |  |
| 1979S, Proof, Filled S . . . . . . . . . . . . . . . . . . . . . . . . . . . . . |  |  | $10. |
| 1979S, Proof, Clear S . . . . . . . . . . . . . . . . . . . . . . . . . . . . . |  |  | 125. |
| 1980P . . . . . . . . . . . . . . . . . . . . . . . . . . . . . . . . . . . . | 27,610,000 | 3. |  |
| 1980D . . . . . . . . . . . . . . . . . . . . . . . . . . . . . . . . . . . . | 41,628,708 | 3. |  |
| 1980S . . . . . . . . . . . . . . . . . . . . . . . . . . . . . . . . . . . . | 20,422,000 | 3. |  |
| 1980S, Proof . . . . . . . . . . . . . . . . . . . . . . . . . . . . . . . . | (3,554,806) |  | 10. |
| 1981P **(b)** . . . . . . . . . . . . . . . . . . . . . . . . . . . . . . . . . . . . | 3,000,000 | 7. |  |
| 1981D **(b)** . . . . . . . . . . . . . . . . . . . . . . . . . . . . . . . . . . . . | 3,250,000 | 7. |  |
| 1981S **(b)** . . . . . . . . . . . . . . . . . . . . . . . . . . . . . . . . . . . . | 3,492,000 | 7. |  |
| 1981S, Proof, First S . . . . . . . . . . . . . . . . . . . . . . . . . . | (4,063,083) |  | 10. |
| 1981S, Proof, Clear S . . . . . . . . . . . . . . . . . . . . . . . . . . . . . . * |  |  | 250. |
| 1999P . . . . . . . . . . . . . . . . . . . . . . . . . . . . . . . . . . . . | 29,592,000 | 3. |  |
| 1999P, Proof . . . . . . . . . . . . . . . . . . . . . . . . . . . . . . . . . . . . |  |  | 30. |
| 1999D . . . . . . . . . . . . . . . . . . . . . . . . . . . . . . . . . . . . | 11,776,000 | 3. |  |

* Included in number above. **a.** The obverse design was modified in 1979 to widen the border rim. Late issues of 1979-P and subsequent issues have the wide rim. Dies for the 1999 coins were further modified to strengthen details on the reverse. **b.** Issued only in Mint Sets.

# SACAGAWEA (2000 TO DATE)

The design of this coin was selected in national competition from among 120 submissions that were considered by a panel appointed by Treasury Secretary Robert Rubin. The adopted motif depicts Sacagawea, a young Native American Shoshone, as conceived by artist Glenna Goodacre. On her back she carries Jean Baptiste, her infant son. The reverse shows an eagle in flight designed by mint engraver Thomas D. Rogers Sr.

The composition exemplifies the spirit of liberty, peace, and freedom shown by Sacagawea in her conduct as interpreter and guide to explorers Meriwether Lewis and William Clark during their famed journey westward from the great northern plains to the Pacific.

These coins have a distinctive golden color and a plain edge to distinguish them from other denominations or coins of a similar size. The change in composition and appearance was mandated under the United States Dollar Coin Act of 1997.

Several distinctive finishes can be identified on the Sacagawea dollars as a result of the Mint's attempts to adjust the dies, blanks, strikes, or finishing to produce coins with minimum spotting and better surface color. One group of 5,000 pieces, dated 2000 and with a special finish, were presented to sculptor Glenna Goodacre in payment for the obverse design. Unexplained error coins made from mismatched dies (a state quarter obverse combined with a Sacagawea dollar reverse) are extremely rare.

*Designers: obv. Glenna Goodacre; rev. Thomas D. Rogers Sr.; weight 8.1 grams; composition, pure copper core with outer layers of manganese brass (.770 copper, .120 zinc, .070 manganese, and .040 nickel; diameter 26.5 mm; plain edge; mints: Philadelphia, Denver, San Francisco; 22-karat gold numismatic specimens dated 2000-W were struck at West Point in 1999 using a prototype reverse design with boldly detailed tail feathers. Some of the early 2000-P circulation strikes were also made using that same prototype design.*

| | Mintage | MS-65 | PF-65 |
|---|---|---|---|
| 2000P | 767,140,000 | $3. | |
| 2000P, Goodacre Presentation Finish | 5,000 | 500. | |
| 2000P, Boldly Detailed Tail Feathers | *5,500* | — | |
| 2000D | 518,916,000 | 3. | |
| 2000S | (4,047,993) | | $15. |
| 2001P | 62,468,000 | 6. | |
| 2001D | 70,939,500 | 6. | |
| 2001S | (3,184,606) | | 100. |
| 2002P | 3,865,610 | 4. | |
| 2002D | 3,732,000 | 4. | |
| 2002S | (3,211,995) | | 30. |
| 2003P | 3,080,000 | 4. | |
| 2003D | 3,080,000 | 4. | |
| 2003S | (3,298,439) | | 20. |
| 2004P | 2,660,000 | 4. | |
| 2004D | 2,660,000 | 4. | |
| 2004S | (2,992,069) | | 20. |
| 2005P | 2,520,000 | 4. | |
| 2005D | 2,520,000 | 4. | |
| 2005S | (3,273,000) | | 15. |
| 2006P | | 4. | |
| 2006D | | 4. | |
| 2006S | | | 15. |

## Special Millennium Set

| | Unc. |
|---|---|
| 2000D Sacagawea dollar, 2000(W) Silver Eagle dollar, Series 1999 $1 Federal Reserve Note . . . | $125. |

Gold has served as money or established the monetary value of currencies longer than any other material. The use of gold coins was widespread in Europe by the fourth century B.C.

The earliest coins circulated in the United States were foreign coins, mostly silver and gold, brought from Europe. The Coinage Act in 1792 established an independent monetary system with the dollar as the basic United States monetary unit containing 24-3/4 grains of fine gold, based on the world price of $19.39 a troy ounce (480 grains). Congress changed the gold specification in 1834 and again in 1837, when it set the dollar price of gold at $20.67 an ounce.

In 1934, U.S. citizens were prohibited from holding monetary gold in the United States; this was extended in 1961 to gold held abroad as well. The dollar price was set at $35 per ounce in 1934. Use of gold in international trade was further restricted as the price rose. The government revalued it at $38 per ounce in 1972, then $42.22 in 1973. It has fluctuated widely over the past few years. All restrictions on holding gold were removed on December 31, 1974.

Coinage of the gold dollar was authorized by the Act of March 3, 1849. The weight was 25.8 grains, .900 fineness. The first type, struck until 1854, is known as the Liberty Head or small-sized type (Type 1).

In 1854, the dollar coins were made larger in diameter and thinner. The design was changed to a feather headdress on a female, generally referred to as the Indian Princess Head or large-sized type (Type 2). In 1856, the type was changed slightly by enlarging the size of the head (Type 3).

*Note: Values of common gold coins have been based on the current bullion price of gold, $550 per ounce, and may vary with the prevailing spot price. The net weight and content listed may be used to recalculate bullion value.*

## TYPE COIN VALUES

| | F-12 | VF-20 | EF-40 | MS-60 | MS-63 | MS-65 | PF-63 | PF-65 |
|---|---|---|---|---|---|---|---|---|
| Liberty, Type I, 1849–1854 | $120.+ | $145. | $195. | $325.+ | $1,250.+ | $5,750.+ | $145,000.+ | $250,000.+ |
| Princess, Type 2, 1854–1856 | 185.+ | 350.+ | 450.+ | 3,500.- | 13,500.- | 38,000.+ | 185,000. | 275,000.+ |
| Princess, Type 3, 1856–1889 | 120.+ | 140.+ | 175. | 325.+ | 1,150.+ | 2,500.+ | 5,000. | 10,000.+ |

+ or – indicates change from previous year

## LIBERTY HEAD (1849–1854)

*Designer James B. Longacre; weight 1.672 grams; composition .900 gold, .100 copper (net weight .04837 oz. pure gold); diameter 13 mm; reeded edge; mints: Philadelphia, Charlotte, Dahlonega, New Orleans, San Francisco.*

**VF-20 VERY FINE**—LIBERTY on headband complete and legible. Knobs on coronet defined.
**EF-40 EXTREMELY FINE**—Slight wear on Liberty's hair. Knobs on coronet sharp.
**AU-50 ABOUT UNCIRCULATED**—Trace of wear on headband. Nearly full luster.
**AU-55 CHOICE ABOUT UNCIRCULATED**—Evidence of friction on design high points.
**MS-60 UNCIRCULATED**—No trace of wear. Light marks and blemishes.
**MS-63 CHOICE UNCIRCULATED**—Some distracting contact marks or blemishes in prime focal areas. Impaired luster possible.

### Liberty Head (Type 1)
*Mintmark is below wreath.*

**Obverse**  **Close Wreath Reverse**  **Open Wreath Reverse**

*See next page for chart.*

| | Mintage | VF-20 | EF-40 | AU-50 | AU-55 | MS-60 | MS-63 |
|---|---|---|---|---|---|---|---|
| 1849, Open Wreath, With L **(a)** ....688,567 | | $150. | $200. | $245. | $265. | $400. | $1,750. |
| 1849, Small Head, No L ...............* | | 175. | 275. | 300. | 325. | 650. | 2,400. |
| 1849, Close Wreath (Ends Closer to Numeral) | | 150. | 200. | 245. | 265. | 400. | 1,600. |
| 1849C, Close Wreath ............11,634 | | 1,350. | 1,800. | 2,600. | 4,300. | 9,500. | 18,500. |
| 1849C, Open Wreath *(ex. rare)* ..........* | | 245,000. | 345,000. | 400,000. | 475,000. | 600,000. | 750,000. |
| $690,000, MS-63, DLRC auction, Jul-04 | | | | | | | |
| 1849D, Open Wreath ............21,588 | | 1,350. | 1,800. | 2,350. | 3,400. | 5,500. | 14,000. |
| 1849O, Open Wreath ...........215,000 | | 185. | 300. | 425. | 650. | 1,150. | 3,750. |
| 1850 .......................481,953 | | 145. | 200. | 225. | 245. | 345. | 1,250. |
| 1850C ........................6,966 | | 1,350. | 1,600. | 2,750. | 5,000. | 9,000. | 26,000. |
| 1850D ........................8,382 | | 1,400. | 1,850. | 3,250. | 5,500. | 10,000. | 27,500. |
| 1850O .......................14,000 | | 275. | 425. | 875. | 1,450. | 3,250. | 7,500. |
| 1851 ......................3,317,671 | | 145. | 195. | 230. | 250. | 325. | 1,250. |
| 1851C .......................41,267 | | 1,300. | 1,650. | 2,000. | 2,500. | 3,600. | 7,750. |
| 1851D ........................9,882 | | 1,400. | 1,800. | 2,350. | 3,000. | 6,250. | 15,000. |
| 1851O ......................290,000 | | 175. | 215. | 300. | 400. | 900. | 2,750. |
| 1852 ......................2,045,351 | | 145. | 195. | 230. | 250. | 325. | 1,250. |
| 1852C ........................9,434 | | 1,300. | 1,600. | 2,000. | 2,600. | 4,750. | 12,500. |
| 1852D ........................6,360 | | 1,350. | 1,800. | 2,750. | 3,750. | 9,000. | 27,500. |
| 1852O ......................140,000 | | 165. | 235. | 400. | 800. | 1,650. | 6,250. |
| 1853 ......................4,076,051 | | 145. | 195. | 230. | 250. | 325. | 1,250. |
| 1853C .......................11,515 | | 1,350. | 1,600. | 2,350. | 2,850. | 6,000. | 13,500. |
| 1853D ........................6,583 | | 1,400. | 1,850. | 2,850. | 4,250. | 9,500. | 30,000. |
| 1853O ......................290,000 | | 175. | 215. | 285. | 400. | 750. | 2,800. |
| 1854 .......................855,502 | | 145. | 195. | 230. | 250. | 325. | 1,250. |
| 1854D ........................2,935 | | 1,750. | 2,400. | 5,750. | 7,500. | 12,000. | 35,000. |
| 1854S .......................14,632 | | 350. | 475. | 850. | 1,200. | 2,500. | 6,500. |

\* Included in number above. **a.** Small and Large Head varieties exist.

## INDIAN PRINCESS HEAD, SMALL HEAD (1854–1856)

*Standards same as for previous issue, except diameter changed to 15 mm.*

**VF-20 VERY FINE**—Feather-curl tips on headdress outlined but details worn.
**EF-40 EXTREMELY FINE**—Slight wear on tips of feather curls on headdress.
**AU-50 ABOUT UNCIRCULATED**—Trace of wear on feathers, nearly full luster.
**AU-55 CHOICE ABOUT UNCIRCULATED**—Evidence of friction on design high points. Most of original mint luster present.
**MS-60 UNCIRCULATED**—No trace of wear. Light marks and blemishes.
**MS-63 CHOICE UNCIRCULATED**—Some distracting contact marks or blemishes in prime focal areas. Impaired luster possible.
**PF-63 CHOICE PROOF**—Reflective surfaces with only a few blemishes in secondary focal areas. No major flaws.

**Indian Princess Head, Small Head (Type 2)**

| | Mintage | VF-20 | EF-40 | AU-50 | AU-55 | MS-60 | MS-63 | PF-63 |
|---|---|---|---|---|---|---|---|---|
| 1854 .............783,943 | | $350. | $450. | $675. | $1,100. | $3,500. | $13,500. | $225,000. |
| 1855 .............758,269 | | 350. | 450. | 675. | 1,100. | 3,500. | 13,500. | 185,000. |
| 1855C .............9,803 | | 1,650. | 3,500. | 6,500. | 12,000. | 22,500. | | |
| 1855D .............1,811 | | 5,000. | 9,500. | 22,500. | 27,500. | 48,500. | 95,000. | |
| 1855O ............55,000 | | 550. | 775. | 1,650. | 2,600. | 6,500. | 22,500. | |
| 1856S ............24,600 | | 950. | 1,350. | 2,250. | 3,000. | 8,000. | 32,500. | |

# INDIAN PRINCESS HEAD, LARGE HEAD (1856–1889)

**VF-20 VERY FINE**—Slight detail in curled feathers in headdress. Details worn smooth at eyebrow, hair below headdress, and behind ear and bottom curl.

**EF-40 EXTREMELY FINE**—Slight wear above and to right of eye and on top of curled feathers.

**AU-50 ABOUT UNCIRCULATED**—Trace of wear on feathers, nearly full luster.

**AU-55 CHOICE ABOUT UNCIRCULATED**—Evidence of friction on design high points. Most of original mint luster present.

**MS-60 UNCIRCULATED**—No trace of wear. Light marks and blemishes.

**MS-63 CHOICE UNCIRCULATED**—Some distracting contact marks or blemishes in prime focal areas. Impaired luster possible.

**PF-63 CHOICE PROOF**—Reflective surfaces with only a few blemishes in secondary focal places. No major flaws.

**Indian Princess Head,
Large Head (Type 3)**

| | Mintage | VF-20 | EF-40 | AU-50 | AU-55 | MS-60 | MS-63 | PF-63 |
|---|---|---|---|---|---|---|---|---|
| 1856, All kinds | 1,762,936 | | | | | | | |
| 1856, Upright 5 | | $150. | $195. | $235. | $300. | $525. | $1,150. | |
| 1856, Slant 5 | | 140. | 175. | 215. | 235. | 325. | 1,150. | $25,000. |
| 1856D | 1,460 | 4,000. | 6,250. | 9,500. | 12,000. | 32,500. | 75,000. | |
| 1857 | 774,789 | 140. | 175. | 215. | 235. | 325. | 1,150. | 15,000. |
| 1857C | 13,280 | 1,100. | 1,650. | 3,500. | 5,500. | 12,500. | 30,000. | |
| 1857D | 3,533 | 1,200. | 2,150. | 4,250. | 5,500. | 11,000. | 35,000. | |
| 1857S | 10,000 | 500. | 625. | 1,100. | 1,850. | 6,500. | 21,000. | |
| 1858 | 117,995 | 140. | 175. | 215. | 235. | 325. | 1,150. | 11,000. |
| 1858D | 3,477 | 1,250. | 1,750. | 3,000. | 4,750. | 11,000. | 27,500. | |
| 1858S | 10,000 | 350. | 550. | 1,400. | 1,800. | 6,250. | 16,500. | |
| 1859 | (80) 168,244 | 140. | 175. | 215. | 235. | 325. | 1,150. | 9,000. |
| 1859C | 5,235 | 1,300. | 1,850. | 3,750. | 7,000. | 16,000. | 34,500. | |
| 1859D | 4,952 | 1,300. | 1,850. | 3,200. | 5,500. | 11,500. | 26,500. | |
| 1859S | 15,000 | 250. | 615. | 1,650. | 2,250. | 5,800. | 16,500. | |
| 1860 | (154) 36,514 | 150. | 215. | 235. | 265. | 475. | 1,150. | 7,500. |
| 1860D | 1,566 | 3,000. | 4,350. | 7,750. | 12,000. | 22,500. | 55,000. | |
| 1860S | 13,000 | 300. | 450. | 775. | 1,100. | 2,500. | 7,000. | |
| 1861 | (349) 527,150 | 145. | 200. | 225. | 250. | 425. | 1,150. | 6,500. |
| 1861D | | 8,000. | 12,500. | 22,000. | 27,500. | 42,000. | 85,000. | |
| 1862 | (35) 1,361,355 | 145. | 200. | 225. | 250. | 425. | 1,150. | 6,500. |
| 1863 | (50) 6,200 | 600. | 1,150. | 2,300. | 3,250. | 4,500. | 8,500. | 7,500. |
| 1864 | (50) 5,900 | 375. | 500. | 750. | 950. | 1,250. | 3,000. | 8,500. |
| 1865 | 3,725 | 400. | 650. | 850. | 1,100. | 1,800. | 3,750. | 8,500. |
| 1866 | (30) 7,100 | 375. | 525. | 750. | 900. | 1,200. | 2,300. | 8,500. |
| 1867 | (50) 5,200 | 425. | 550. | 750. | 900. | 1,250. | 2,300. | 7,000. |
| 1868 | (25) 10,500 | 275. | 400. | 550. | 625. | 1,150. | 2,250. | 7,500. |
| 1869 | (25) 5,900 | 350. | 475. | 750. | 875. | 1,300. | 2,350. | 7,500. |
| 1870 | (35) 6,300 | 300. | 425. | 675. | 775. | 1,200. | 2,350. | 7,250. |
| 1870S | 3,000 | 500. | 825. | 1,300. | 1,650. | 2,850. | 7,500. | |
| 1871 | (30) 3,900 | 300. | 425. | 650. | 750. | 1,150. | 2,250. | 7,250. |
| 1872 | (30) 3,500 | 300. | 400. | 650. | 775. | 1,150. | 2,350. | 7,500. |
| 1873, Cl 3 | (25) 1,800 | 425. | 775. | 1,150. | 1,400. | 1,900. | 4,500. | 15,000. |
| 1873, Open 3 | 123,300 | 145. | 200. | 225. | 250. | 450. | 1,150. | |
| 1874 | (20) 198,800 | 145. | 200. | 225. | 250. | 450. | 1,150. | 10,000. |
| 1875 | (20) 400 | 2,350. | 3,900. | 5,250. | 5,750. | 7,500. | 10,000. | 16,500. |
| 1876 | (45) 3,200 | 275. | 325. | 525. | 600. | 775. | 1,350. | 5,500. |
| 1877 | (20) 3,900 | 275. | 325. | 525. | 600. | 775. | 1,350. | 7,000. |
| 1878 | (20) 3,000 | 275. | 325. | 525. | 600. | 775. | 1,350. | 6,500. |
| 1879 | (30) 3,000 | 175. | 275. | 375. | 500. | 650. | 1,300. | 5,500. |
| 1880 | (36) 1,600 | 175. | 275. | 375. | 500. | 650. | 1,300. | 5,500. |
| 1881 | (87) 7,620 | 175. | 275. | 375. | 425. | 600. | 1,250. | 5,500. |
| 1882 | (125) 5,000 | 175. | 275. | 375. | 425. | 600. | 1,250. | 5,000. |
| 1883 | (207) 10,800 | 175. | 275. | 375. | 425. | 600. | 1,250. | 5,000. |
| 1884 | (1,006) 5,230 | 175. | 275. | 375. | 425. | 600. | 1,250. | 5,000. |
| 1885 | (1,105) 11,156 | 175. | 275. | 375. | 425. | 600. | 1,250. | 5,000. |
| 1886 | (1,016) 5,000 | 175. | 275. | 375. | 425. | 600. | 1,250. | 5,000. |
| 1887 | (1,043) 7,500 | 175. | 275. | 375. | 425. | 600. | 1,250. | 5,000. |
| 1888 | (1,079) 15,501 | 175. | 275. | 375. | 425. | 600. | 1,250. | 5,000. |
| 1889 | (1,779) 28,950 | 165. | 265. | 350. | 400. | 575. | 1,200. | 5,000. |

Authorized by the Act of April 2, 1792, quarter eagles weighed 67.5 grains, .9167 fineness until the weight was changed to 64.5 grains, .8992 fineness, by the Act of June 28, 1834. The Act of January 18, 1837, established fineness at .900. Most dates before 1834 are rare. The first issue was struck in 1796; most of these had no stars on the obverse.

Proofs of some dates prior to 1855 are known to exist, and all are rare.

*Note: Values of common gold coins have been based on the current bullion price of gold, $550 per ounce, and may vary with the prevailing spot price. The net weight and content listed may be used to recalculate bullion value.*

## TYPE COIN VALUES

| | F-12 | VF-20 | EF-40 | MS-60 | MS-63 | MS-65 | PF-63 | PF-65 |
|---|---|---|---|---|---|---|---|---|
| Cap Bust Rt, NS, 1796 | $35,000.+ | $47,500.+ | $75,000.+ | $185,000.+ | $320,000.+ | $775,000.+ | | |
| Cap Bust Rt, 1796–1807 | 5,500.+ | 7,500.+ | 9,000.+ | 24,500.+ | 60,000.+ | 175,000.+ | | |
| Cap Bust Left, Lg, 1808 | 28,500.+ | 37,500.+ | 47,500.+ | 135,000.+ | 350,000.+ | 875,000.+ | | |
| Cap Head Left, Lg, 1821–1827 | 5,750. | 7,500. | 9,250.+ | 24,500.+ | 39,000.+ | 135,000. | $100,000. | $325,000. |
| Cap Head Left, Sm, 1829–1834 | 4,850. | 6,250. | 8,500.+ | 17,500.+ | 30,000.+ | 60,000.+ | 125,000. | 225,000. |
| Classic Head, 1834–1839 | 275.+ | 450.+ | 650.+ | 3,000.+ | 7,500.+ | 35,000.+ | 65,000. | 140,000. |
| Liberty Head, 1840–1907 | 165.+ | 200.+ | 225.+ | 1,050.+ | 5,500.+ | 6,000.+ | 5,500.+ | 15,000.+ |
| Indian Head, 1908–1929 | 130.+ | 165.+ | 180.+ | 305.+ | 1,350. | 6,000.+ | 8,000.+ | 20,000.+ |
| + or – indicates change from previous year | | | | | | | | |

## CAPPED BUST TO RIGHT (1796–1807)

*Designer Robert Scot; weight 4.37 grams; composition .9167 gold, .0833 silver and copper; approx. diameter 20 mm; reeded edge.*

**F-12 FINE**—Hair worn smooth on high spots. E PLURIBUS UNUM on ribbon weak but legible.
**VF-20 VERY FINE**—Some wear on high spots.
**EF-40 EXTREMELY FINE**—Only slight wear on Liberty's hair and cheek.
**AU-50 ABOUT UNCIRCULATED**—Trace of wear on cap, hair, cheek, and drapery.
**AU-55 CHOICE ABOUT UNCIRCULATED**—Evidence of friction on design high points. Some original mint luster present.
**MS-60 UNCIRCULATED**—No trace of wear. Light blemishes.

**No Stars on Obverse (1796)**          **Stars on Obverse (1796–1807)**

| | Mintage | F-12 | VF-20 | EF-40 | AU-50 | AU-55 | MS-60 |
|---|---|---|---|---|---|---|---|
| 1796, No Stars on Obverse . . . . . . . .963 | | $35,000. | $47,500. | $75,000. | $95,000. | $115,000. | $185,000. |
| *$1,380,000, MS-65, ANR, Jun-05* | | | | | | | |
| 1796, Stars on Obverse . . . . . . . . . .432 | | 28,500. | 39,500. | 65,000. | 87,500. | 110,000. | 165,000. |
| 1797 . . . . . . . . . . . . . . . . . . . . . . . . .427 | | 18,500. | 24,500. | 37,500. | 60,000. | 77,500. | 130,000. |
| 1798 . . . . . . . . . . . . . . . . . . . . . . . .1,094 | | 8,500. | 11,500. | 15,000. | 30,000. | 37,500. | 65,000. |
| 1802, 2 Over 1 . . . . . . . . . . . . . . . .3,035 | | 6,500. | 8,500. | 11,500. | 14,500. | 18,250. | 30,000. |
| 1804, 13-Star Reverse . . . . . . . . . . . .* | | 30,000. | 40,000. | 77,500. | 150,000. | 185,000. | |
| 1804, 14-Star Reverse . . . . . . . . . .3,327 | | 5,500. | 7,750. | 9,500. | 13,000. | 17,000. | 30,000. |
| 1805 . . . . . . . . . . . . . . . . . . . . . . . .1,781 | | 5,500. | 7,750. | 9,250. | 13,000. | 17,000. | 30,000. |
| 1806, 6/4, 8 Stars Left, 5 Right . . .1,136 | | 5,500. | 7,750. | 9,250. | 13,000. | 17,000. | 30,000. |
| 1806, 6/5, 7 Stars Left, 6 Right . . . .480 | | 9,250. | 14,000. | 19,000. | 39,500. | 55,000. | 95,000. |
| 1807 . . . . . . . . . . . . . . . . . . . . . . . .6,812 | | 5,500. | 7,500. | 9,000. | 13,000. | 15,000. | 24,500. |

* Included in number below.

# CAPPED BUST TO LEFT, LARGE SIZE (1808)

*Designer John Reich; standards same as for previous issue.*

**F-12 FINE**—E PLURIBUS UNUM on reverse, and LIBERTY on headband, legible but weak.
**VF-20 VERY FINE**—Motto and LIBERTY clear.
**EF-40 EXTREMELY FINE**—All details of hair plain.
**AU-50 ABOUT UNCIRCULATED**—Trace of wear above eye, on top of cap, and on cheek, and hair.
**AU-55 CHOICE ABOUT UNCIRCULATED**—Evidence of friction on design high points. Some original mint luster present.
**MS-60 UNCIRCULATED**—No trace of wear. Light blemishes.

| | Mintage | F-12 | VF-20 | EF-40 | AU-50 | AU-55 | MS-60 |
|---|---|---|---|---|---|---|---|
| 1808 . . . . . . . . . . . . . . . . . . . . . .2,710 | | $28,500. | $37,500. | $47,500. | $87,500. | $100,000. | $135,000. |

# CAPPED HEAD TO LEFT (1821–1834)
## Large Diameter (1821–1827)

*Standards same as for previous issue, except diameter changed to approximately 18.5 mm in 1829.*

| | Mintage | F-12 | VF-20 | EF-40 | AU-50 | AU-55 | MS-60 |
|---|---|---|---|---|---|---|---|
| 1821 . . . . . . . . . . . . . . . . . . . . . .6,448 | | $5,750. | $7,500. | $9,000. | $12,500. | $15,000. | $28,500. |
| 1824, 4 Over 1 . . . . . . . . . . . . . .2,600 | | 5,750. | 7,500. | 9,000. | 12,500. | 15,000. | 26,500. |
| 1825 . . . . . . . . . . . . . . . . . . . . . .4,434 | | 5,750. | 7,500. | 9,000. | 12,500. | 15,000. | 26,500. |
| 1826, 6 Over 5 . . . . . . . . . . . . . . .760 | | 8,250. | 9,750. | 13,500. | 15,000. | 22,500. | 41,500. |
| 1827 . . . . . . . . . . . . . . . . . . . . . .2,800 | | 5,750. | 7,500. | 9,250. | 12,500. | 14,000. | 24,500. |

## Reduced Diameter (1829–1834)

Those dated 1829 through 1834 are smaller in diameter (18.2 mm) than the 1821 through 1827 pieces. They also have smaller letters, dates, and stars.

| | Mintage | F-12 | VF-20 | EF-40 | AU-50 | AU-55 | MS-65 |
|---|---|---|---|---|---|---|---|
| 1829 . . . . . . . . . . . . . . . . . . . . . .3,403 | | $4,850. | $6,250. | $8,500. | $11,500. | $13,500. | $17,500. |
| 1830 . . . . . . . . . . . . . . . . . . . . . .4,540 | | 4,850. | 6,250. | 8,500. | 11,500. | 13,500. | 17,500. |
| 1831 . . . . . . . . . . . . . . . . . . . . . .4,520 | | 4,850. | 6,250. | 8,500. | 11,500. | 13,500. | 17,500. |
| 1832 . . . . . . . . . . . . . . . . . . . . . .4,400 | | 4,850. | 6,250. | 8,500. | 11,500. | 13,500. | 17,500. |
| 1833 . . . . . . . . . . . . . . . . . . . . . .4,160 | | 4,850. | 6,250. | 8,500. | 11,500. | 13,500. | 17,500. |
| 1834, With Motto . . . . . . . . . . . .4,000 | | 9,250. | 14,500. | 20,000. | 32,500. | 38,500. | 52,500. |

# CLASSIC HEAD, NO MOTTO ON REVERSE (1834–1839)

In 1834, a ribbon binding Liberty's hair, bearing the word LIBERTY, replaced the liberty cap. The motto was omitted from the reverse. In 1840 a coronet and smaller head were designed to conform with the appearance of the larger gold coins.

*Designer William Kneass; weight 4.18 grams; composition .8992 gold, .1008 silver and copper (changed to .900 gold in 1837); diameter 18.2 mm; reeded edge; mints: Philadelphia, Charlotte, Dahlonega, New Orleans.*

**F-12 FINE**—LIBERTY on headband legible and complete. Curl under ear outlined but no detail.
**VF-20 VERY FINE**—LIBERTY plain; detail in hair curl.
**EF-40 EXTREMELY FINE**—Small amount of wear on top of hair and below L in LIBERTY. Wear evident on wing.
**AU-50 ABOUT UNCIRCULATED**—Trace of wear on coronet and hair above ear.
**AU-55 CHOICE ABOUT UNCIRCULATED**—Evidence of friction on design high points. Some of original mint luster present.
**MS-60 UNCIRCULATED**—No trace of wear. Light blemishes.
**MS-63 CHOICE UNCIRCULATED**—Some distracting contact marks or blemishes in prime focal areas. Impaired luster possible.

**Mintmark Location**

| Mintage | F-12 | VF-20 | EF-40 | AU-50 | AU-55 | MS-60 | MS-63 |
|---|---|---|---|---|---|---|---|
| 1834, No Motto . . . . .112,234 | $275. | $450. | $650. | $1,050. | $1,350. | $3,000. | $7,500. |
| 1835 . . . . . . . . . . .131,402 | 275. | 450. | 650. | 1,050. | 1,350. | 3,150. | 7,750. |
| 1836, All kinds . . . . .547,986 | | | | | | | |
|    1836, Script 8 . . . . . . . . | 275. | 450. | 650. | 1,050. | 1,350. | 3,000. | 7,500. |
|    1836, Block 8 . . . . . . . . . | 275. | 450. | 650. | 1,050. | 1,350. | 3,000. | 7,500. |
| 1837 . . . . . . . . . . . .45,080 | 275. | 450. | 675. | 1,150. | 1,450. | 4,250. | 12,500. |
| 1838 . . . . . . . . . . . .47,030 | 275. | 450. | 675. | 1,100. | 1,450. | 3,100. | 8,000. |
| 1838C . . . . . . . . . . . .7,880 | 1,350. | 2,000. | 3,250. | 7,500. | 11,500. | 27,500. | 42,500. |
| 1839 . . . . . . . . . . . .27,021 | 300. | 550. | 950. | 2,150. | 3,500. | 6,500. | 19,500. |
| 1839C . . . . . . . . . . .18,140 | 1,300. | 2,000. | 2,850. | 4,500. | 8,250. | 25,000. | 42,500. |
| 1839D . . . . . . . . . . .13,674 | 1,300. | 1,850. | 3,600. | 7,250. | 9,750. | 27,500. | 47,500. |
| 1839O . . . . . . . . . . .17,781 | 500. | 700. | 1,250. | 2,200. | 3,500. | 6,750. | 23,000. |

*Note: So-called 9 Over 8 varieties for P, C, and D mints are made from defective punches.*

# LIBERTY HEAD (1840–1907)

*Designer Christian Gobrecht; weight 4.18 grams; composition .900 gold, .100 copper (net weight .12094 oz. pure gold); diameter 18 mm; reeded edge; mints: Philadelphia, Charlotte, Dahlonega, New Orleans, San Francisco.*
See previous type for grading standards.

**Mintmark Location**

| Mintage | VF-20 | EF-40 | AU-50 | AU-55 | MS-60 | MS-63 |
|---|---|---|---|---|---|---|
| 1840 . . . . . . . . . . . . . . . . . . . .18,859 | $300. | $875. | $3,250. | $4,000. | $7,500. | $16,000. |
| 1840C . . . . . . . . . . . . . . . . . . .12,822 | 1,600. | 2,200. | 5,250. | 7,750. | 15,000. | 32,000. |
| 1840D . . . . . . . . . . . . . . . . . . . .3,532 | 3,250. | 8,500. | 15,500. | 23,000. | 35,000. | |
| 1840O . . . . . . . . . . . . . . . . . . .33,580 | 375. | 875. | 2,150. | 2,900. | 10,500. | 27,500. |
| 1841 . . . . . . . . . . . . . . . .*(unknown)* | 60,000. | 90,000. | 115,000. | 135,000. | 165,000. | |
| 1841C . . . . . . . . . . . . . . . . . . .10,281 | 1,300. | 2,100. | 3,600. | 6,250. | 19,000. | |

| | Mintage | VF-20 | EF-40 | AU-50 | AU-55 | MS-60 | MS-63 |
|---|---|---|---|---|---|---|---|
| 1841D | 4,164 | $2,250. | $3,950. | $9,750. | $15,000. | $28,500. | $52,500. |
| 1842 | 2,823 | 1,100. | 3,000. | 7,000. | 13,500. | 23,500. | |
| 1842C | 6,729 | 1,600. | 3,250. | 8,500. | 11,500. | 26,500. | |
| 1842D | 4,643 | 2,000. | 3,750. | 11,000. | 17,500. | 34,500. | |
| 1842O | 19,800 | 575. | 1,400. | 2,850. | 5,000. | 14,500. | 32,500. |
| 1843 | 100,546 | 225. | 450. | 850. | 1,200. | 2,500. | 6,500. |
| 1843C, Sm Dt, Crosslet 4 | 2,988 | 2,600. | 5,000. | 8,750. | 12,000. | 27,000. | |
| 1843C, Lg Dt, Plain 4 | 23,076 | 1,300. | 1,950. | 3,500. | 5,750. | 9,000. | 22,500. |
| 1843D, Sm Dt, Crosslet 4 | 36,209 | 1,400. | 2,250. | 3,150. | 4,750. | 9,500. | 35,000. |
| 1843O, Sm Dt, Crosslet 4 | 288,002 | 225. | 300. | 550. | 825. | 2,350. | 9,000. |
| 1843O, Lg Dt, Plain 4 | 76,000 | 325. | 775. | 1,750. | 3,250. | 8,000. | |
| 1844 | 6,784 | 475. | 850. | 2,100. | 4,000. | 8,250. | |
| 1844C | 11,622 | 1,300. | 2,250. | 6,250. | 9,500. | 20,000. | 47,000. |
| 1844D | 17,332 | 1,300. | 2,250. | 3,150. | 4,500. | 9,250. | 28,000. |
| 1845 | 91,051 | 250. | 325. | 550. | 750. | 1,400. | 4,600. |
| 1845D | 19,460 | 1,300. | 2,200. | 3,400. | 5,500. | 13,500. | 35,000. |
| 1845O | 4,000 | 1,225. | 2,450. | 6,000. | 8,000. | 18,500. | 52,500. |
| 1846 | 21,598 | 300. | 700. | 1,350. | 2,000. | 6,500. | 22,000. |
| 1846C | 4,808 | 1,600. | 2,600. | 9,250. | 12,000. | 19,000. | 37,500. |
| 1846D | 19,303 | 1,300. | 2,200. | 3,350. | 5,750. | 12,500. | 27,500. |
| 1846O | 62,000 | 300. | 525. | 1,150. | 1,850. | 5,500. | 20,000. |
| 1847 | 29,814 | 240. | 375. | 850. | 1,400. | 4,000. | 10,000. |
| 1847C | 23,226 | 1,300. | 2,200. | 2,750. | 4,250. | 7,000. | 17,500. |
| 1847D | 15,784 | 1,300. | 2,200. | 2,750. | 5,500. | 10,000. | 24,000. |
| 1847O | 124,000 | 300. | 465. | 1,100. | 2,200. | 5,000. | 17,500. |

## CAL. Gold Quarter Eagle (1848)

In 1848, about 230 ounces of gold were sent to Secretary of War Marcy by Colonel R.B. Mason, military governor of California. The gold was turned over to the Mint and made into quarter eagles. The distinguishing mark CAL. was punched above the eagle on the reverse side, while the coins were in the die. Several specimens with prooflike surfaces are known.

**CAL. Above Eagle on Reverse (1848)**

| | Mintage | VF-20 | EF-40 | AU-50 | AU-55 | MS-60 | MS-63 |
|---|---|---|---|---|---|---|---|
| 1848 | 6,500 | $575. | $1,150. | $2,000. | $2,750. | $6,500. | $16,500. |
| 1848, CAL. Above Eagle | 1,389 | 20,000. | 35,000. | 42,500. | 47,500. | 62,500. | 90,000. |
| *$402,500, MS-68, Heritage auction, Jan-06* | | | | | | | |
| 1848C | 16,788 | 1,300. | 2,200. | 3,000. | 4,850. | 14,000. | 32,500. |
| 1848D | 13,771 | 1,300. | 2,200. | 3,000. | 5,000. | 11,500. | 34,000. |
| 1849 | 23,294 | 265. | 500. | 1,000. | 1,550. | 2,900. | 7,250. |
| 1849C | 10,220 | 1,300. | 2,200. | 5,000. | 9,000. | 22,500. | 52,500. |
| 1849D | 10,945 | 1,300. | 2,200. | 4,200. | 8,000. | 18,000. | |
| 1850 | 252,923 | 175. | 200. | 325. | 550. | 1,200. | 3,500. |
| 1850C | 9,148 | 1,300. | 2,200. | 3,500. | 6,500. | 19,000. | 32,500. |
| 1850D | 12,148 | 1,300. | 2,200. | 3,500. | 6,750. | 16,500. | 47,500. |
| 1850O | 84,000 | 275. | 500. | 1,500. | 2,250. | 5,000. | 15,000. |
| 1851 | 1,372,748 | 180. | 205. | 240. | 300. | 375. | 1,800. |

*Chart continued on next page.*

| | Mintage | VF-20 | EF-40 | AU-50 | AU-55 | MS-60 | MS-63 | PF-63 |
|---|---|---|---|---|---|---|---|---|
| 1851C | 14,923 | $1,300. | $2,200. | $4,500. | $7,000. | $14,000. | $35,000. | |
| 1851D | 11,264 | 1,300. | 2,200. | 3,850. | 6,750. | 13,500. | 35,000. | |
| 1851O | 148,000 | 235. | 450. | 1,000. | 2,250. | 5,000. | 13,500. | |
| 1852 | 1,159,681 | 180. | 205. | 240. | 300. | 375. | 1,800. | |
| 1852C | 9,772 | 1,300. | 2,200. | 4,000. | 8,000. | 18,000. | 35,000. | |
| 1852D | 4,078 | 1,750. | 3,000. | 7,500. | 11,000. | 21,500. | 42,500. | |
| 1852O | 140,000 | 240. | 340. | 1,000. | 1,450. | 5,250. | 13,750. | |
| 1853 | 1,404,668 | 180. | 205. | 240. | 300. | 375. | 1,800. | |
| 1853D | 3,178 | 1,700. | 3,200. | 5,500. | 7,500. | 18,500. | 45,000. | |
| 1854 | 596,258 | 180. | 205. | 240. | 300. | 375. | 1,800. | |
| 1854C | 7,295 | 1,450. | 2,600. | 5,500. | 8,500. | 18,500. | | |
| 1854D | 1,760 | 3,500. | 7,700. | 14,000. | 19,000. | 34,000. | 85,000. | |
| 1854O | 153,000 | 235. | 330. | 625. | 850. | 1,850. | 8,750. | |
| 1854S | 246 | 100,000. | 150,000. | 250,000. | | | | |
| 1855 | 235,480 | 180. | 205. | 240. | 300. | 375. | 2,350. | |
| 1855C | 3,677 | 1,850. | 3,600. | 7,250. | 12,500. | 30,000. | 47,500. | |
| 1855D | 1,123 | 4,750. | 8,750. | 17,500. | 25,000. | 48,500. | | |
| 1856 | 384,240 | 175. | 205. | 240. | 275. | 350. | 2,000. | $60,000. |
| 1856C | 7,913 | 1,350. | 2,600. | 4,750. | 7,500. | 16,000. | 35,000. | |
| 1856D | 874 | 7,750. | 13,500. | 28,500. | 35,000. | 67,500. | | |
| 1856O | 21,100 | 290. | 775. | 1,600. | 2,800. | 8,250. | | |
| 1856S | 72,120 | 240. | 440. | 1,300. | 1,900. | 6,000. | 12,500. | |
| 1857 | 214,130 | 175. | 205. | 240. | 275. | 350. | 2,000. | 45,000. |
| 1857D | 2,364 | 1,600. | 3,200. | 4,400. | 7,250. | 15,500. | 32,500. | |
| 1857O | 34,000 | 230. | 380. | 1,550. | 2,250. | 5,500. | 14,500. | |
| 1857S | 69,200 | 230. | 440. | 1,400. | 2,350. | 6,500. | 15,000. | |
| 1858 | 47,377 | 180. | 240. | 450. | 600. | 1,400. | 3,250. | 35,000. |
| 1858C | 9,056 | 1,300. | 2,200. | 3,250. | 4,500. | 9,500. | 35,000. | |

A modified reverse design (smaller letters and arrowheads) was used on Philadelphia issues from 1859 through 1907, and on San Francisco issues of 1877 through 1879. A few Philadelphia Mint pieces were made in 1859, 1860, and 1861 with the old Large Letters reverse design.

**Old Reverse**     **New Reverse**

| | Mintage | VF-20 | EF-40 | AU-50 | AU-55 | MS-60 | MS-63 | PF-63 |
|---|---|---|---|---|---|---|---|---|
| 1859, Old Rev ..(80)... | 39,364 | $225. | $450. | $900. | $1,250. | $3,750. | $8,500. | $25,000. |
| 1859, New Reverse | * | 185. | 250. | 500. | 750. | 1,300. | 3,250. | |
| 1859D | 2,244 | 2,200. | 3,400. | 5,500. | 8,750. | 25,000. | | |
| 1859S | 15,200 | 450. | 1,125. | 2,500. | 3,600. | 8,000. | 17,500. | |
| 1860, Old Rev (112) | 22,563 | 2,000. | 3,500. | 5,500. | 7,500. | 11,000. | 18,000. | 19,000. |
| 1860, New Reverse | * | 180. | 240. | 450. | 575. | 1,100. | 2,500. | |
| 1860C | 7,469 | 1,450. | 2,350. | 4,250. | 7,500. | 22,500. | 47,500. | |
| 1860S | 35,600 | 275. | 650. | 1,400. | 2,100. | 4,250. | 13,500. | |
| 1861, Old Rev ..(90) | 1,283,788 | 500. | 1,000. | 2,000. | 3,000. | 5,000. | 10,000. | 17,500. |
| 1861, New Reverse | * | 165. | 195. | 210. | 225. | 400. | 10,000. | |
| 1861S | 24,000 | 400. | 1,000. | 3,500. | 5,000. | 8,500. | | |
| 1862, 2 Over 1 | ** | 1,000. | 1,950. | 4,000. | 5,750. | 9,000. | | |
| 1862 | (35)... 98,508 | 185. | 275. | 500. | 750. | 1,500. | 3,750. | 17,000. |
| 1862S | 8,000 | 1,100. | 2,200. | 4,500. | 7,500. | 18,500. | | |

* Included in number above.  ** Included in number below.

| | Mintage | VF-20 | EF-40 | AU-50 | AU-55 | MS-60 | MS-63 | PF-63 |
|---|---|---|---|---|---|---|---|---|
| 1863, Pf only (30) . . . . . . . . . | | | | | | | | $60,000. |
| 1863S . . . . . . . . . . . . 10,800 | | $750. | $1,650. | $4,500. | $7,500. | $18,000. | $34,500. | |
| 1864 . . . . . . .(50) . . . . 2,824 | | 6,000. | 12,500. | 24,000. | 30,000. | 42,500. | | 17,000. |
| 1865 . . . . . . .(25) . . . . 1,520 | | 4,350. | 10,000. | 22,500. | 28,000. | 37,500. | 45,000. | 17,000. |
| 1865S . . . . . . . . . . . . 23,376 | | 300. | 700. | 1,400. | 2,250. | 5,500. | 13,500. | |
| 1866 . . . . . . .(30) . . . . 3,080 | | 1,250. | 3,550. | 6,250. | 9,750. | 17,000. | 28,000. | 14,000. |
| 1866S . . . . . . . . . . . . 38,960 | | 375. | 850. | 1,850. | 3,500. | 8,750. | 22,000. | |
| 1867 . . . . . . .(50) . . . . 3,200 | | 375. | 750. | 1,500. | 2,200. | 4,550. | 8,750. | 14,000. |
| 1867S . . . . . . . . . . . . 28,000 | | 375. | 800. | 1,750. | 2,650. | 5,500. | 16,750. | |
| 1868 . . . . . . .(25) . . . . 3,600 | | 225. | 450. | 750. | 925. | 3,000. | 8,750. | 15,500. |
| 1868S . . . . . . . . . . . . 34,000 | | 225. | 500. | 1,100. | 1,750. | 5,000. | 12,500. | |
| 1869 . . . . . . .(25) . . . . 4,320 | | 225. | 375. | 800. | 1,200. | 3,200. | 8,750. | 12,500. |
| 1869S . . . . . . . . . . . . 29,500 | | 300. | 550. | 1,200. | 1,750. | 4,750. | 12,000. | |
| 1870 . . . . . . .(35) . . . . 4,520 | | 235. | 375. | 750. | 1,200. | 3,450. | 9,250. | 12,500. |
| 1870S . . . . . . . . . . . . 16,000 | | 235. | 450. | 1,000. | 1,850. | 5,250. | 15,000. | |
| 1871 . . . . . . .(30) . . . . 5,320 | | 225. | 435. | 650. | 1,050. | 2,450. | 4,500. | 12,500. |
| 1871S . . . . . . . . . . . . 22,000 | | 200. | 325. | 650. | 1,000. | 2,500. | 4,750. | |
| 1872 . . . . . . .(30) . . . . 3,000 | | 400. | 800. | 1,500. | 2,500. | 5,750. | 13,500. | 12,500. |
| 1872S . . . . . . . . . . . . 18,000 | | 225. | 400. | 1,000. | 1,800. | 4,750. | 13,000. | |
| 1873, Cl 3 . . .(25) . . . . 55,200 | | 180. | 205. | 300. | 375. | 750. | 1,500. | 12,500. |
| 1873, Open 3. . . . . . . 122,800 | | 165. | 195. | 205. | 230. | 285. | 1,250. | |
| 1873S . . . . . . . . . . . . 27,000 | | 230. | 450. | 1,100. | 1,450. | 2,750. | 7,500. | |
| 1874 . . . . . . .(20) . . . . 3,920 | | 275. | 400. | 800. | 1,100. | 3,500. | 7,000. | 14,500. |
| 1875 . . . . . . .(20) . . . . . 400 | | 4,000. | 5,750. | 10,000. | 12,000. | 21,500. | 37,500. | 30,000. |
| 1875S . . . . . . . . . . . . 11,600 | | 200. | 400. | 750. | 1,100. | 4,250. | 9,750. | |
| 1876 . . . . . . .(45) . . . . 4,176 | | 250. | 650. | 1,100. | 2,100. | 3,600. | 8,500. | 11,500. |
| 1876S . . . . . . . . . . . . 5,000 | | 250. | 600. | 1,100. | 1,750. | 4,000. | 9,500. | |
| 1877 . . . . . . .(20) . . . . 1,632 | | 375. | 700. | 1,000. | 1,350. | 3,500. | 9,000. | 11,500. |
| 1877S . . . . . . . . . . . . 35,400 | | 175. | 200. | 225. | 300. | 700. | 2,750. | |
| 1878 . . . . . . .(20) . . . 286,240 | | 175. | 195. | 215. | 255. | 375. | 850. | 11,500. |
| 1878S . . . . . . . . . . . 178,000 | | 175. | 195. | 215. | 255. | 475. | 2,250. | |
| 1879 . . . . . . .(30) . . . 88,960 | | 175. | 195. | 215. | 255. | 375. | 1,500. | 11,500. |
| 1879S . . . . . . . . . . . . 43,500 | | 185. | 275. | 600. | 1,150. | 2,100. | 5,500. | |
| 1880 . . . . . . .(36) . . . . 2,960 | | 250. | 375. | 650. | 875. | 1,450. | 3,250. | 11,500. |
| 1881 . . . . . . .(51) . . . . . 640 | | 1,900. | 3,250. | 4,500. | 5,500. | 10,000. | 24,500. | 12,500. |
| 1882 . . . . . . .(67) . . . . 4,000 | | 250. | 350. | 525. | 650. | 875. | 2,850. | 7,000. |
| 1883 . . . . . . .(82) . . . . 1,920 | | 250. | 375. | 850. | 1,250. | 2,400. | 6,500. | 7,000. |
| 1884 . . . . . . .(73) . . . . 1,950 | | 250. | 375. | 775. | 825. | 1,800. | 3,250. | 7,000. |
| 1885 . . . . . . .(87) . . . . . 800 | | 1,000. | 1,800. | 2,800. | 3,250. | 4,750. | 8,500. | 7,000. |
| 1886 . . . . . . .(88) . . . . 4,000 | | 240. | 300. | 525. | 750. | 1,300. | 2,800. | 7,000. |
| 1887 . . . . . .(122) . . . . 6,160 | | 235. | 275. | 400. | 450. | 1,050. | 2,600. | 7,000. |
| 1888 . . . . . . .(97) . . . 16,001 | | 175. | 225. | 275. | 325. | 500. | 925. | 7,000. |
| 1889 . . . . . . .(48) . . . 17,600 | | 175. | 225. | 275. | 325. | 500. | 925. | 7,000. |
| 1890 . . . . . . .(93) . . . . 8,720 | | 185. | 235. | 305. | 360. | 625. | 1,000. | 7,000. |
| 1891 . . . . . . .(80) . . . 10,960 | | 180. | 250. | 300. | 350. | 475. | 1,050. | 7,000. |
| 1892 . . . . . .(105) . . . . 2,440 | | 205. | 300. | 420. | 450. | 900. | 2,750. | 6,000. |
| 1893 . . . . . .(106) . . . 30,000 | | 170. | 205. | 250. | 300. | 425. | 975. | 6,000. |
| 1894 . . . . . .(122) . . . . 4,000 | | 190. | 250. | 375. | 450. | 750. | 1,850. | 6,000. |
| 1895 . . . . . .(119) . . . . 6,000 | | 165. | 205. | 250. | 300. | 375. | 1,200. | 6,000. |
| 1896 . . . . . .(132) . . . 19,070 | | 165. | 200. | 225. | 300. | 345. | 1,050. | 6,000. |
| 1897 . . . . . .(136) . . . 29,768 | | 165. | 200. | 225. | 300. | 345. | 1,050. | 6,000. |
| 1898 . . . . . .(165) . . . 24,000 | | 165. | 200. | 225. | 300. | 345. | 1,050. | 6,000. |
| 1899 . . . . . .(150) . . . 27,200 | | 165. | 200. | 225. | 300. | 345. | 1,050. | 6,000. |
| 1900 . . . . . .(205) . . . 67,000 | | 165. | 200. | 225. | 300. | 345. | 1,050. | 6,000. |
| 1901 . . . . . .(223) . . . 91,100 | | 165. | 200. | 225. | 300. | 345. | 1,050. | 6,000. |
| 1902 . . . . . .(193) . . . 133,540 | | 165. | 200. | 225. | 300. | 345. | 1,050. | 5,500. |
| 1903 . . . . . .(197) . . . 201,060 | | 165. | 200. | 225. | 300. | 345. | 1,050. | 5,500. |
| 1904 . . . . . .(170) . . . 160,790 | | 165. | 200. | 225. | 300. | 345. | 1,050. | 5,500. |
| 1905 (a) . . . .(144) . . . 217,800 | | 165. | 200. | 225. | 300. | 345. | 1,050. | 5,500. |
| 1906 . . . . . .(160) . . . 176,330 | | 165. | 200. | 225. | 300. | 345. | 1,050. | 5,500. |
| 1907 . . . . . .(154) . . . 336,294 | | 165. | 200. | 225. | 300. | 345. | 1,050. | 5,500. |

a. Pieces dated 1905-S are counterfeit.

# INDIAN HEAD (1908–1929)

This new type represents a departure from all precedents in United States coinage. Its design features no raised edge, and the main devices and legends are incuse—sunk below the surface of the coin.

Boston sculptor Bela Lyon Pratt was the designer of this and the similar half eagle piece. A pupil of the famous Augustus Saint-Gaudens, Pratt based his "standing eagle" motif on the reverse of his teacher's gold ten-dollar coin of 1907. (That eagle was itself derived from the reverse of Theodore Roosevelt's 1905 unofficial inaugural medal, designed by Saint-Gaudens and engraved by Adolph A. Weinman, who would later create the Liberty Walking half dollar. The general style had antecedents in coins of the ancient world.)

Among the public, there was some concern that the recessed design of Pratt's quarter eagle would collect germs—an unfounded fear. The artistry of the design was condemned loudly by some numismatists. Few people were interested in saving the coin for their collections. The result is a series with relatively few examples surviving in higher grades. Any initial disfavor has mellowed with time; today Pratt's design is recognized as part of the early 20th-century renaissance of American coinage.

*Designer Bela Lyon Pratt; weight 4.18 grams; composition .900 gold, .100 copper (net weight .12094 oz. pure gold); diameter 18 mm; reeded edge; mints: Philadelphia, Denver.*

**VF-20 VERY FINE**—Hair-cord knot distinct. Feathers at top of head clear. Cheekbone worn.
**EF-40 EXTREMELY FINE**—Cheekbone, war bonnet, and headband feathers slightly worn.
**AU-50 ABOUT UNCIRCULATED**—Trace of wear on cheekbone and headdress.
**MS-60 UNCIRCULATED**—No trace of wear. Light blemishes.
**MS-63 CHOICE UNCIRCULATED**—Some distracting contact marks or blemishes in prime focal areas. Impaired luster possible.
**MS-64 UNCIRCULATED**—A few scattered contact marks visible. Good eye appeal and attractive luster.
**MATTE PF-63 CHOICE MATTE PROOF**—Few blemishes in secondary focal areas. No major flaws.

*Mintmark location is on reverse, to left of arrows.*

| | Mintage | VF-20 | EF-40 | AU-50 | MS-60 | MS-63 | MS-64 | MATTE PF-63 |
|---|---|---|---|---|---|---|---|---|
| 1908 . . . . . . . .(236) . . . . 564,821 | | $165. | $180. | $205. | $345. | $1,850. | $2,750. | $7,500. |
| 1909 . . . . . . . .(139) . . . . 441,760 | | 165. | 180. | 205. | 345. | 2,350. | 2,950. | 8,000. |
| 1910 . . . . . . . .(682) . . . . 492,000 | | 165. | 180. | 205. | 345. | 2,450. | 3,450. | 8,000. |
| 1911 . . . . . . . .(191) . . . . 704,000 | | 165. | 180. | 205. | 345. | 2,250. | 3,250. | 7,500. |
| 1911D **(a)** . . . . . . . . . . . . .55,680 | | 2,600. | 3,750. | 5,000. | 8,500. | 25,000. | 34,500. | |
| 1912 . . . . . . . .(197) . . . . 616,000 | | 165. | 180. | 205. | 345. | 2,750. | 3,950. | 7,500. |
| 1913 . . . . . . . .(165) . . . . 722,000 | | 165. | 180. | 205. | 325. | 1,750. | 2,850. | 7,500. |
| 1914 . . . . . . . .(117) . . . . 240,000 | | 165. | 225. | 300. | 550. | 8,000. | 11,500. | 7,500. |
| 1914D . . . . . . . . . . . . . .448,000 | | 165. | 180. | 215. | 345. | 2,650. | 6,500. | |
| 1915 . . . . . . . .(100) . . . . 606,000 | | 165. | 180. | 205. | 325. | 1,750. | 2,750. | 8,000. |
| 1925D . . . . . . . . . . . . . .578,000 | | 165. | 180. | 205. | 305. | 1,350. | 2,150. | |
| 1926 . . . . . . . . . . . . . . .446,000 | | 165. | 180. | 205. | 305. | 1,350. | 2,150. | |
| 1927 . . . . . . . . . . . . . . .388,000 | | 165. | 180. | 205. | 305. | 1,350. | 2,150. | |
| 1928 . . . . . . . . . . . . . . .416,000 | | 165. | 180. | 205. | 305. | 1,350. | 2,150. | |
| 1929 . . . . . . . . . . . . . . .532,000 | | 165. | 180. | 205. | 305. | 1,350. | 2,150. | |

**a.** Values are for coins with bold mintmark; weak D pieces are worth less. Beware of counterfeits.

# INDIAN PRINCESS HEAD (1854–1889)

The three-dollar gold piece was authorized by the Act of February 21, 1853. First struck in 1854, the coin was never popular with the general public and saw very little circulation. Today, some numismatists theorize that the $3 denomination would have been useful for purchasing postage stamps of the day (with their face value of 3¢) or for acquiring 100 silver three-cent pieces ("trimes"), which were also in circulation at the time.

These gold coins changed hands in the East and Midwest until 1861, after which they disappeared from circulation; through the 1860s, fewer than 10,000 were struck annually. In 1874 and 1878, mintages were increased significantly in anticipation of the coins going into broader circulation. On the West Coast, the three-dollar gold piece did see circulation throughout the series' minting, though they probably weren't seen in change very often after the 1860s.

The head on the obverse represents an Indian princess with hair tightly curling over the neck, her head crowned with a circle of feathers (the band of which is inscribed LIBERTY). A wreath of tobacco, wheat, corn, and cotton occupies the field of the reverse, with the denomination and date within it. The coin weighs 77.4 grains, and was struck in .900 fine gold.

In the year 1854 only, the word DOLLARS is in much smaller letters than in later years. The 1856 Proof has DOLLARS in large letters cut over the same word in small letters. Restrikes of some years were made, particularly Proofs of 1865 and 1873.

Although these coins did not see extensive day-to-day circulation, collector interest was high, and many three-dollar gold pieces were saved by speculators beginning about 1879. As a result, Mint State examples are fairly numerous today. The 1870-S coin is unique, currently residing in the Harry W. Bass Jr. Collection on loan to the American Numismatic Association.

## TYPE COIN VALUES

| | F-12 | VF-20 | EF-40 | MS-60 | MS-63 | MS-65 | PF-63 | PF-65 |
|---|---|---|---|---|---|---|---|---|
| Indian Head, 1854–1889 | $525.+ | $800.+ | $1,150.+ | $3,250.+ | $9,500.+ | $22,000.+ | $12,500.+ | $32,500.+ |

+ or – indicates change from previous year

*Designer James B. Longacre; weight 5.015 grams; composition .900 gold, .100 copper (net weight .14512 oz. pure gold); diameter 20.5 mm; reeded edge; mints: Philadelphia, Dahlonega, New Orleans, San Francisco.*

**VF-20 VERY FINE**—Eyebrow, hair about forehead and ear, and bottom curl all worn smooth. Faint details visible on curled feather-ends of headdress.

**EF-40 EXTREMELY FINE**—Light wear above and to right of eye, and on top of curled feathers.

**AU-50 ABOUT UNCIRCULATED**—Trace of wear on top of curled feathers and in hair above and to right of eye.

**AU-55 CHOICE ABOUT UNCIRCULATED**—Evidence of friction on design high points. Much of original mint luster present.

**MS-60 UNCIRCULATED**—No trace of wear. Light blemishes.

**MS-63 CHOICE UNCIRCULATED**—Some distracting contact marks or blemishes in prime focal areas. Impaired luster possible.

**PF-63 CHOICE PROOF**—Reflective surfaces with only a few blemishes in secondary focal places. No major flaws.

*Mintmark location is on reverse, below wreath.*

*See next page for chart.*

| | Mintage | VF-20 | EF-40 | AU-50 | AU-55 | MS-60 | MS-63 | PF-63 |
|---|---|---|---|---|---|---|---|---|
| 1854 | 138,618 | $800. | $1,150. | $1,750. | $2,250. | $3,250. | $9,500. | $72,500. |
| 1854D | 1,120 | 11,500. | 20,000. | 34,500. | 47,500. | 95,000. | | |
| 1854O | 24,000 | 1,500. | 2,750. | 5,750. | 12,500. | 23,500. | | |
| 1855 | 50,555 | 850. | 1,150. | 1,950. | 2,400. | 3,750. | 11,500. | 50,000. |
| 1855S | 6,600 | 1,400. | 3,250. | 9,500. | 16,500. | 27,500. | 95,000. | |
| 1856 | 26,010 | 850. | 1,200. | 1,850. | 2,350. | 3,750. | 10,500. | 40,000. |
| 1856S (a) | 34,500 | 900. | 1,450. | 3,000. | 4,750. | 11,500. | 26,500. | |
| 1857 | 20,891 | 850. | 1,250. | 1,950. | 2,400. | 3,850. | 11,500. | 25,000. |
| 1857S | 14,000 | 1,250. | 3,250. | 6,250. | 13,500. | 19,500. | 40,000. | |
| 1858 | 2,133 | 950. | 1,750. | 3,850. | 5,500. | 9,500. | 24,000. | 23,500. |
| 1859 (80) | 15,558 | 850. | 1,350. | 1,900. | 2,350. | 3,750. | 9,500. | 18,500. |
| 1860 (b) (119) | 7,036 | 875. | 1,350. | 1,900. | 2,350. | 4,250. | 11,500. | 14,500. |
| 1860S | 7,000 | 1,150. | 2,250. | 7,500. | 10,000. | 19,500. | 42,500. | |
| 1861 (113) | 5,959 | 900. | 1,300. | 2,100. | 2,750. | 4,750. | 12,500. | 14,500. |
| 1862 (35) | 5,750 | 900. | 1,300. | 2,100. | 2,750. | 4,750. | 12,500. | 14,500. |
| 1863 (39) | 5,000 | 900. | 1,300. | 2,100. | 2,750. | 4,750. | 12,500. | 14,500. |
| 1864 (50) | 2,630 | 950. | 1,300. | 2,100. | 2,750. | 4,750. | 12,500. | 14,500. |
| 1865 (25) | 1,140 | 1,550. | 3,000. | 6,250. | 7,500. | 11,500. | 24,500. | 18,500. |
| 1866 (30) | 4,000 | 1,000. | 1,250. | 1,900. | 2,450. | 4,000. | 11,500. | 16,000. |
| 1867 (50) | 2,600 | 1,000. | 1,250. | 1,900. | 2,450. | 4,000. | 11,500. | 16,000. |
| 1868 (c) (25) | 4,850 | 925. | 1,250. | 1,950. | 2,500. | 4,000. | 9,500. | 16,000. |
| 1869 (c) (25) | 2,500 | 950. | 1,250. | 2,000. | 2,450. | 4,250. | 12,500. | 16,000. |
| 1870 (35) | 3,500 | 950. | 1,450. | 2,350. | 2,950. | 4,750. | 14,000. | 16,000. |
| 1870S | | 4,000,000. | | *(unique; Bass Foundation Collection)* | | | | |
| 1871 (30) | 1,300 | 1,050. | 1,250. | 2,450. | 2,950. | 4,750. | 14,000. | 16,000. |
| 1872 (30) | 2,000 | 1,050. | 1,200. | 1,950. | 2,450. | 4,250. | 13,500. | 16,000. |
| 1873, Open 3 (Orig) (25) | | 7,500. | 11,000. | | | | | 30,000. |
| 1873, Close 3 | | 3,750. | 7,500. | 10,500. | 15,000. | 27,500. | 45,000. | 34,500. |
| 1874 (20) | 41,800 | 850. | 1,150. | 1,750. | 1,950. | 3,250. | 10,500. | 23,500. |
| 1875, Pf only (20) | | | | 50,000. | | | | 110,000. |
| 1876, Pf only (45) | | | | 18,500. | | | | 32,500. |
| 1877 (20) | 1,468 | 1,750. | 3,250. | 8,000. | 10,500. | 16,500. | 35,000. | 22,000. |
| 1878 (c) (20) | 82,304 | 850. | 1,150. | 1,750. | 1,950. | 3,250. | 10,500. | 22,000. |
| 1879 (30) | 3,000 | 950. | 1,200. | 2,000. | 2,600. | 3,800. | 11,000. | 16,500. |
| 1880 (36) | 1,000 | 1,100. | 1,950. | 3,250. | 3,750. | 4,750. | 11,000. | 16,000. |
| 1881 (54) | 500 | 1,750. | 3,400. | 6,250. | 7,500. | 9,500. | 18,500. | 16,000. |
| 1882 (76) | 1,500 | 1,150. | 1,350. | 2,100. | 2,600. | 4,000. | 11,000. | 12,500. |
| 1883 (89) | 900 | 1,200. | 1,450. | 2,350. | 2,900. | 4,000. | 11,000. | 12,500. |
| 1884 (106) | 1,000 | 1,250. | 1,500. | 2,400. | 3,000. | 4,250. | 11,000. | 12,500. |
| 1885 (109) | 801 | 1,500. | 1,850. | 2,750. | 3,500. | 4,750. | 12,500. | 13,500. |
| 1886 (142) | 1,000 | 1,350. | 1,900. | 2,750. | 3,450. | 4,750. | 12,500. | 12,500. |
| 1887 (160) | 6,000 | 850. | 1,150. | 2,150. | 2,600. | 4,250. | 10,500. | 12,500. |
| 1888 (291) | 5,000 | 850. | 1,150. | 2,150. | 2,600. | 4,250. | 10,500. | 12,500. |
| 1889 (129) | 2,300 | 850. | 1,150. | 2,150. | 2,600. | 4,250. | 10,500. | 12,500. |

**a.** Small S and Medium S varieties exist. **b.** 2,592 melted at mint. **c.** Varieties showing traces of possible over-dating include 1868/7, 1869/8, and 1878/7.

# STELLA (1879–1880)

These pattern coins were first suggested by John A. Kasson, then U.S. envoy extraordinary and minister plenipotentiary to Austria-Hungary. It was through the efforts of W.W. Hubbell, who patented the alloy *goloid* (used in making another pattern piece, the goloid metric dollar), that we have these beautiful and interesting coins.

The four-dollar Stella—so called because of the five-pointed star on the reverse— was envisioned by Kasson as America's answer to various foreign gold coins popular in the international market. The British sovereign, Italy's 20 lire, and the 20 pesetas of Spain were three such coins: each smaller than a U.S. five-dollar gold piece, they were used widely in international trade.

The Stella was one of many proposals made to Congress for an international trade coin, and one of only several that made it to pattern-coin form (others include the 1868 five-dollar piece and 1874 Bickford ten-dollar piece).

Odds were stacked against the Stella from the start. The denomination of four U.S. dollars didn't match any of the coin's European counterparts, and at any rate the U.S. double eagle (twenty-dollar coin)—already used in international commerce— was a more convenient medium of exchange. The Stella was never minted in quantities for circulation. Those dated 1879 were struck for congressmen to examine. The 1880 coins were secretly made by Mint officials for sale to private collectors.

There are two distinct types in both years of issue. Charles E. Barber designed the Flowing Hair type, and George T. Morgan the Coiled Hair. They were struck as patterns in gold, aluminum, copper, and white metal. (Only those struck in gold are listed here.) It is likely that of the 1879-dated Flowing Hair Stellas, about 15 were struck in 1879, and the rest in 1880.

Precise mintage numbers are unknown. The estimates given below are based on surviving pieces, certified population reports, and auction records.

Some of the finest Stella specimens are housed in the National Numismatic Collection in the Smithsonian Institution. Others are in private collections, and cross the auction block from time to time.

Recent auction activity for Stellas certified PF-60 and higher:

- 1879 Flowing Hair: $120,750 (PF-61 Cameo) ANR     December 2005
- 1879 Coiled Hair: $655,500 (PF-67 Cameo) Heritage   January 2005
- 1880 Flowing Hair: $264,500 (PF-65)     Heritage   January 2005
- 1880 Coiled Hair: $618,125 (PF-63)     Superior   July 2005

**Flowing Hair Obverse**          **Reverse**          **Coiled Hair Obverse**

| | Mintage | EF-40 | AU-50 | PF-60 | PF-63 | PF-65 | PF-66 | PF-67 |
|---|---|---|---|---|---|---|---|---|
| 1879, Flowing Hair ...*(700+)* | | $70,000. | $75,000. | $100,000. | $145,000. | $215,000. | $250,000. | $400,000. |
| 1879, Coiled Hair *(12 known)* .......... | | | | 275,000. | 350,000. | 530,000. | 650,000. | 800,000. |
| 1880, Flowing Hair *(17 known)* .......... | | | | 145,000. | 215,000. | 300,000. | 350,000. | 575,000. |
| 1880, Coiled Hair *(8 known)* .......... | | | | 475,000. | 625,000. | 800,000. | 1,000,000. | 1,400,000. |

The half eagle was the first gold coin actually struck for the United States. The five-dollar piece was authorized to be coined by the Act of April 2, 1792, and the first type weighed 135 grains, .9167 fineness. The Act of June 28, 1834, changed the weight to 129 grains, .8992 fineness. Fineness became .900 by the Act of January 18, 1837.

There are many varieties among the early dates, caused by changes in the number of stars and style of eagle, by overdates, and by differences in the size of figures in the dates. Those dated prior to 1807 do not bear any mark of value. The 1822 half eagle is considered one of the most valuable regular-issue coins of the entire United States series. Proofs of some dates prior to 1855 are known to exist, and all are rare. Commemorative and bullion $5 coins have been made at West Point since 1986 and 1994, respectively; thus this is the only U.S. denomination made at each of the eight mints.

*Note: Values of common gold coins have been based on the current bullion price of gold, $550 per ounce, and may vary with the prevailing spot price. The net weight and content listed may be used to recalculate bullion value.*

## TYPE COIN VALUES

| | F-12 | VF-20 | EF-40 | MS-60 | MS-63 | MS-65 | PF-63 | PF-65 |
|---|---|---|---|---|---|---|---|---|
| Cap Bust, Small Eagle, 1795–1798 | $13,500.+ | $19,500.+ | $24,000.+ | $52,500.+ | $150,000.+ | $330,000.+ | | |
| Cap Bust, Large Eagle, 1795–1807 | 3,500.+ | 4,250.+ | 5,250.+ | 12,500.+ | 21,500.+ | 82,500.+ | | |
| Cap Bust Left, Large, 1807–1812 | 2,750.+ | 3,750.+ | 4,750.- | 8,500.+ | 16,500.+ | 53,000.+ | | |
| Cap Head, 1813–1834 | 2,500. | 3,800.+ | 4,800. | 8,750.+ | 16,500.+ | 67,500. | | $500,000. |
| Classic Head, 1834–1838 | 250.+ | 450.+ | 750.+ | 4,000.+ | 9,500.+ | 55,000.+ | $85,000.+ | 210,000.+ |
| Liberty Head, NM, 1839–1866 | 170.+ | 200. | 250. | 1,250.+ | 7,250. | 35,000.+ | 24,000.+. | 52,000.+ |
| Liberty Head, 1866–1908 | 145.+ | 185.+ | 195.+ | 250.+ | 950.+ | 4,250.+ | 11,000+ | 32,500.+ |
| Indian Head, 1908–1929 | 170.+ | 295.+ | 325.+ | 425.+ | 2,950.+ | 20,000.+ | 11,000. | 30,000.+ |

+ or − indicates change from previous year

## CAPPED BUST TO RIGHT (1795–1807)

This type was struck from mid-1795 through early 1798, when the Small Eagle reverse was changed to the Large or "Heraldic" Eagle. Note that the 1795 and 1797 dates exist for both types, but that the Heraldic Eagle reverses of these dates were probably struck in 1798 using serviceable 1795 and 1797 dies.

*Designer Robert Scot; weight 8.75 grams; composition .9167 gold, .0833 silver and copper; approx. diameter 25 mm; reeded edge.*

**F-12 FINE**—Liberty's hair worn smooth but with distinct outline. For heraldic type, E PLURIBUS UNUM faint but legible.
**VF-20 VERY FINE**—Slight to noticeable wear on high spots such as hair, turban, and eagle's head and wings.
**EF-40 EXTREMELY FINE**—Slight wear on hair and highest part of cheek.
**AU-50 ABOUT UNCIRCULATED**—Trace of wear on cap, hair, cheek, and drapery.
**MS-60 UNCIRCULATED**—No trace of wear. Light blemishes.
**MS-63 CHOICE UNCIRCULATED**—Some distracting contact marks or blemishes in prime focal areas. Impaired luster possible.

## Small Eagle (1795–1798)

| | Mintage | F-12 | VF-20 | EF-40 | AU-50 | AU-55 | MS-60 | MS-63 |
|---|---|---|---|---|---|---|---|---|
| 1795, Small Eagle | 8,707 | $13,500. | $19,500. | $24,000. | $32,500. | $36,500. | $52,500. | $150,000. |

*Note: One variety has the final S in STATES punched over an erroneous D.*

| | | | | | | | |
|---|---|---|---|---|---|---|---|
| **1796, 6 Over 5** | | **1797, 15 Stars** | | **1797, 16 Stars** | | | |

| | Mintage | F-12 | VF-20 | EF-40 | AU-50 | AU-55 | MS-60 | MS-63 |
|---|---|---|---|---|---|---|---|---|
| 1796, 6 Over 5 . . . . . . . .6,196 | | $13,500. | $19,000. | $27,500. | $37,500. | $44,500. | $85,000. | $185,000. |
| 1797, All kinds . . . . . . .3,609 | | | | | | | | |
| 1797, 15 Stars . . . . . . . . . . | | 16,500. | 24,500. | 37,500. | 62,500. | 95,000. | 155,000. | |
| 1797, 16 Stars . . . . . . . . . . | | 16,000. | 21,500. | 32,500. | 67,500. | 100,000. | 155,000. | |
| 1798, Small Eagle *(7 known)* . . | | | 185,000. | 300,000. | 400,000. | 500,000. | — | |

## Heraldic Eagle (1795–1807)

| | Mintage | F-12 | VF-20 | EF-40 | AU-50 | AU-55 | MS-60 | MS-63 |
|---|---|---|---|---|---|---|---|---|
| 1795, Heraldic Eagle **(a)** . . . . | | $10,000. | $17,500. | $27,500. | $52,500. | $62,500. | $95,000. | $200,000. |
| 1797, 7 Over 5 **(a)** . . . . . . . . | | 10,000. | 16,500. | 28,500. | 60,000. | 77,500. | 125,000. | |
| 1797, 16-Star Obv **(a)** *(unique)* | | | | — | | | | |
| 1797, 15-Star Obv **(a)** *(unique)* | | | | — | | | | |
| 1798, All kinds . . . . . .24,867 | | | | | | | | |
| 1798, Small 8 . . . . . . . . . . | | 3,750. | 4,750. | 6,500. | 13,500. | 16,500. | 25,000. | |
| 1798, Lg 8, 13-Star Rev . . | | 3,500. | 4,750. | 6,500. | 11,000. | 15,000. | | |
| 1798, Lg 8, 14-Star Rev . . | | 3,750. | 5,000. | 8,250. | 19,500. | 24,500. | 34,500. | |
| 1799 . . . . . . . . . . . . . . .7,451 | | 3,500. | 4,250. | 5,250. | 9,500. | 14,500. | 21,500. | 50,000. |

**a.** Thought to have been struck in 1798 and included in the mintage figure for that year.

| | | | | | | | |
|---|---|---|---|---|---|---|---|
| **1802 Over 1** | | **1803 Over 2** | | **Small 8 Over Large 8** | | | |

| | Mintage | F-12 | VF-20 | EF-40 | AU-50 | AU-55 | MS-60 | MS-63 |
|---|---|---|---|---|---|---|---|---|
| 1800 . . . . . . . . . . . . .37,628 | | $3,500. | $4,250. | $5,250. | $6,750. | $7,500. | $12,000. | $24,500. |
| 1802, 2 Over 1 . . . . . .53,176 | | 3,500. | 4,250. | 5,250. | 6,750. | 7,500. | 12,000. | 22,500. |
| 1803, 3 Over 2 . . . . . .33,506 | | 3,500. | 4,250. | 5,250. | 6,750. | 7,500. | 12,500. | 21,500. |
| 1804, All kinds . . . . . .30,475 | | | | | | | | |
| 1804, Small 8 . . . . . . . . . . | | 3,500. | 4,250. | 5,250. | 6,750. | 7,500. | 12,000. | 21,500. |
| 1804, Sm 8 Over Lg 8 . . . . | | 3,500. | 4,250. | 5,250. | 6,750. | 7,500. | 12,000. | 21,500. |
| 1805 . . . . . . . . . . . . .33,183 | | 3,500. | 4,250. | 5,250. | 6,750. | 7,500. | 12,500. | 21,500. |

**Pointed 6, Stars 8 and 5**  **Round-Top 6, Stars 7 and 6**

| | Mintage | F-12 | VF-20 | EF-40 | AU-50 | AU-55 | MS-60 | MS-63 |
|---|---|---|---|---|---|---|---|---|
| 1806, Pointed Top 6 . . .9,676 | | $3,750. | $4,500. | $5,500. | $7,000. | $7,750. | $11,500. | $22,500. |
| 1806, Round Top 6 . . .54,417 | | 3,500. | 4,250. | 5,250. | 6,750. | 7,500. | 12,500. | 21,500. |
| 1807 . . . . . . . . . . . . .32,488 | | 3,500. | 4,250. | 5,250. | 6,750. | 7,500. | 12,500. | 21,500. |

## CAPPED BUST TO LEFT (1807–1812)

*Designer John Reich; standards same as for previous issue.*

**F-12 FINE**—LIBERTY on cap legible but partly weak.
**VF-20 VERY FINE**—Headband edges slightly worn. LIBERTY bold.
**EF-40 EXTREMELY FINE**—Slight wear on highest portions of hair; 80% of major curls plain.
**AU-50 ABOUT UNCIRCULATED**—Trace of wear above eye and on top of cap, cheek, and hair.
**AU-55 CHOICE ABOUT UNCIRCULATED**—Evidence of friction on design high points. Some mint luster present.
**MS-60 UNCIRCULATED**—No trace of wear. Light blemishes.
**MS-63 CHOICE UNCIRCULATED**—Some distracting contact marks or blemishes in prime focal areas. Impaired luster possible.

| | Mintage | F-12 | VF-20 | EF-40 | AU-50 | AU-55 | MS-60 | MS-63 |
|---|---|---|---|---|---|---|---|---|
| 1807 . . . . . . . . . . . . .51,605 | | $2,750. | $3,750. | $4,750. | $5,750. | $6,250. | $8,500. | $16,500. |

**1808, 8 Over 7**  **Normal Date**  **1809, 9 Over 8**

| | Mintage | F-12 | VF-20 | EF-40 | AU-50 | AU-55 | MS-60 | MS-63 |
|---|---|---|---|---|---|---|---|---|
| 1808, All kinds . . . . . .55,578 | | | | | | | | |
| 1808, 8 Over 7 . . . . . . . . . . | | $2,850. | $4,000. | $5,000. | $6,750. | $8,500. | $13,500. | $27,500. |
| 1808 . . . . . . . . . . . . . . . . | | 2,750. | 3,750. | 4,750. | 5,750. | 6,250. | 8,500. | 16,500. |
| 1809, 9 Over 8 . . . . . .33,875 | | 2,750. | 3,750. | 4,750. | 5,750. | 6,250. | 8,500. | 16,500. |

# HALF EAGLES

| Small Date | Large Date | Large 5 | Tall 5 |
|:---:|:---:|:---:|:---:|

| | Mintage | F-12 | VF-20 | EF-40 | AU-50 | AU-55 | MS-60 | MS-63 |
|---|---|---|---|---|---|---|---|---|
| 1810, All kinds . . . . .100,287 | | | | | | | | |
| 1810, Sm Date, Sm 5 . . . . | | $9,000. | $23,500. | $37,000. | $55,000. | $67,500. | | |
| 1810, Sm Date, Tall 5 . . . . . | | 2,750. | 4,000. | 5,000. | 6,500. | 6,750. | $9,500. | $21,500. |
| 1810, Lg Date, Sm 5 . . . . . | | 13,500. | 23,000. | 37,500. | 60,000. | 65,000. | 95,000. | |
| 1810, Lg Date, Lg 5 . . . . . . | | 2,750. | 3,750. | 4,750. | 5,750. | 6,250. | 8,500. | 16,500. |
| 1811, All kinds . . . . . .99,581 | | | | | | | | |
| 1811, Small 5 . . . . . . . . . . . | | 2,750. | 3,750. | 4,750. | 5,750. | 6,250. | 8,500. | 16,500. |
| 1811, Tall 5 . . . . . . . . . . . . | | 2,750. | 3,750. | 4,750. | 5,750. | 6,250. | 8,500. | 16,500. |
| 1812 . . . . . . . . . . . . .58,087 | | 2,750. | 3,750. | 4,750. | 5,750. | 6,250. | 8,500. | 16,500. |

## CAPPED HEAD TO LEFT (1813–1834)
### Large Diameter (1813–1829)

| | Mintage | F-12 | VF-20 | EF-40 | AU-50 | AU-55 | MS-60 | MS-63 |
|---|---|---|---|---|---|---|---|---|
| 1813 . . . . . . . . . . . . .95,428 | | $2,750. | $4,000. | $5,000. | $6,500. | $7,000. | $9,000. | $18,500. |
| 1814, 4 Over 3 . . . . . .15,454 | | 3,250. | 4,500. | 5,500. | 6,500. | 7,500. | 11,000. | 30,000. |
| 1815 *(11 known)* . . . . . . .635 | | | | 85,000. | 115,000. | 135,000. | 165,000. | 225,000. |
| 1818, All kinds . . . . . .48,588 | | | | | | | | |
| 1818 . . . . . . . . . . . . . . . . . | | 3,500. | 4,500. | 5,500. | 6,500. | 7,500. | 9,500. | 27,500. |
| 1818, STATESOF one word | | 3,750. | 4,750. | 5,750. | 6,750. | 7,500. | 14,500. | 35,000. |
| 1818, 5D Over 50 . . . . . . . | | | 5,000. | 6,500. | 9,000. | 12,000. | 23,000. | 35,000. |
| 1819, All kinds . . . . . .51,723 | | | | | | | | |
| 1819 . . . . . . . . . . . . . . . . . | | | | 35,000. | 45,000. | 55,000. | 65,000. | |
| 1819, 5D Over 50 . . . . . . . . | | | | 27,500. | 40,000. | 45,000. | 55,000. | 95,000. |

| Curved Base 2 | Square Base 2 | Small Letters | Large Letters |
|:---:|:---:|:---:|:---:|

| | Mintage | F-12 | VF-20 | EF-40 | AU-50 | AU-55 | MS-60 | MS-63 |
|---|---|---|---|---|---|---|---|---|
| 1820, All kinds . . . . .263,806 | | | | | | | | |
| 1820, Curved-Base 2, | | | | | | | | |
| Small Letters . . . . . . . . | | $4,000. | $5,500. | $7,000. | $8,000. | $9,500. | $15,000. | $30,000. |
| 1820, Curved-Base 2, | | | | | | | | |
| Large Letters . . . . . . . . . | | 4,000. | 5,500. | 7,000. | 8,000. | 9,500. | 15,000. | 30,000. |
| 1820, Square-Base 2 . . . . . | | 4,000. | 5,500. | 7,000. | 8,000. | 8,750. | 12,500. | 25,000. |
| 1821 . . . . . . . . . . . . .34,641 | | 12,500. | 20,000. | 30,000. | 35,000. | 40,000. | 75,000. | 145,000. |

1825, 5 Over 1

1825, 5 Over 4

| | Mintage | F-12 | VF-20 | EF-40 | AU-50 | AU-55 | MS-60 | MS-63 |
|---|---|---|---|---|---|---|---|---|
| 1822 (3 known) . . . . .17,796 | | | | *$5,000,000.* | | | | |
| 1823 . . . . . . . . . . . . .14,485 | $3,000. | $3,750. | 5,500. | $8,000. | $11,000. | $18,500. | $35,000. |
| 1824 . . . . . . . . . . . . .17,340 | 6,000. | 12,000. | 19,500. | 30,000. | 34,500. | 40,000. | 65,000. |
| 1825, 5 Over 1 . . . . . .29,060 | 7,500. | 11,500. | 15,000. | 22,500. | 35,000. | 40,000. | 65,000. |
| 1825, 5/4 (2 known) . . . . . .* | | | 350,000. | | | | |
| 1826 . . . . . . . . . . . . .18,069 | 5,000. | 9,000. | 13,000. | 19,500. | 28,500. | 37,500. | 55,000. |
| 1827 . . . . . . . . . . . . .24,913 | 8,000. | 12,500. | 20,000. | 25,000. | 32,500. | 40,000. | 67,500. |

* Included in number above.

Large Date

| | Mintage | F-12 | VF-20 | EF-40 | AU-50 | AU-55 | MS-60 | MS-63 |
|---|---|---|---|---|---|---|---|---|
| 1828, 8/7 (5 known) . . . . . .* | $17,500. | $27,500. | $45,000. | $55,000. | $60,000. | $135,000. | $250,000. |
| 1828 . . . . . . . . . . . . .28,029 | 10,000. | 16,500. | 25,000. | 37,500. | 55,000. | 85,000. | 135,000. |
| 1829, Large Date . . . .57,442 | | | | — | — | | 250,000. |

* Included in number below.

## Reduced Diameter (1829–1834)

The half eagles dated 1829 (small date) through 1834 are smaller in diameter than the earlier pieces. They also have smaller letters, dates, and stars.

*Design modified by William Kneass; standards same as before; diameter 23.8 mm.*

1829, Small Date

1830, Large 5D

1830, Small 5D

1832, 13 Stars,
Square Base 2

| | Mintage | F-12 | VF-20 | EF-40 | AU-50 | AU-55 | MS-60 | MS-63 |
|---|---|---|---|---|---|---|---|---|
| 1829, Small Date . . . . . . . . . . . .* | | $55,000. | $100,000. | $150,000. | $200,000. | $250,000. | $300,000. |
| 1830, Sm or Lg 5D . . . .126,351 | $16,000. | 19,000. | 27,500. | 32,500. | 37,500. | 50,000. | 65,000. |
| 1831, Sm or Lg 5D . . . .140,594 | 16,000. | 19,000. | 27,500. | 32,500. | 37,500. | 50,000. | 65,000. |
| 1832, Curved-Base 2, 12 Stars (5 known) 157,487 | | 120,000. | 175,000. | — | | | |
| 1832, Sq-Base 2, 13 Stars . . . . . . . . . . . . . . .* | 16,000. | 19,000. | 27,500. | 32,500. | 37,500. | 50,000. | 65,000. |
| 1833, Large Date . . . . . .193,630 | 16,000. | 19,000. | 27,500. | 32,500. | 37,500. | 50,000. | 65,000. |
| $977,500, PF-67, Heritage auction, Jan-05 | | | | | | | |
| 1833, Small Date . . . . . . . . . . .* | 16,000. | 19,000. | 27,500. | 32,500. | 37,500. | 50,000. | 65,000. |

* Included in number above.

| | Plain 4 | | | Crosslet 4 | | | | |
|---|---|---|---|---|---|---|---|---|
| | **Mintage** | **F-12** | **VF-20** | **EF-40** | **AU-50** | **AU-55** | **MS-60** | **MS-63** |
| 1834, All kinds . . . . . .50,141 | | | | | | | | |
| 1834, Plain 4 . . . . . . . . . . | $16,000. | $19,000. | $27,500. | $32,500. | $37,500. | $50,000. | $65,000. |
| 1834, Crosslet 4 . . . . . . . . | 18,500. | 22,000. | 28,000. | 35,000. | 42,000. | 60,000. | |

# CLASSIC HEAD (1834–1838)

As on the quarter eagle of 1834, the motto E PLURIBUS UNUM was omitted from the new, reduced-size half eagle in 1834, to distinguish the old coins that had become worth more than face value.

*Designer William Kneass; weight 8.36 grams; composition (1834–1836) .8992 gold, .1008 silver and copper, (1837–1838) .900 gold; diameter 22.5 mm; reeded edge; mints: Philadelphia, Charlotte, Dahlonega.*

*Mintmark is above date (see page 226).*

| | **Mintage** | **VF-20** | **EF-40** | **AU-50** | **AU-55** | **MS-60** | **MS-63** |
|---|---|---|---|---|---|---|---|
| 1834, Plain 4 **(a)** . . . . .657,460 | | $450. | $750. | $1,500. | $1,850. | $4,000. | $9,500. |
| 1834, Crosslet 4 . . . . . . . . . . .* | | 1,750. | 3,500. | 6,000. | 9,000. | 18,500. | 50,000. |
| 1835 **(a)** . . . . . . . . . . . .371,534 | | 450. | 750. | 1,500. | 1,850. | 4,000. | 10,000. |
| 1836 . . . . . . . . . . . . . . .553,147 | | 450. | 750. | 1,500. | 1,850. | 4,000. | 10,000. |
| 1837 **(a)** . . . . . . . . . .207,121 | | 450. | 775. | 1,650. | 2,000. | 4,500. | 16,500. |
| 1838 . . . . . . . . . . . . . . .286,588 | | 450. | 750. | 1,500. | 1,850. | 4,250. | 12,500. |
| 1838C . . . . . . . . . . . . . .17,179 | | 2,750. | 4,750. | 11,500. | 18,500. | 36,000. | 90,000. |
| 1838D . . . . . . . . . . . . . .20,583 | | 2,500. | 4,750. | 9,000. | 12,000. | 25,000. | 50,000. |

* Included in number above. **a.** Varieties have either script 8 or block-style 8 in date.

# LIBERTY HEAD (1839–1908)
## Variety 1 – No Motto Above Eagle (1839–1866)

*Designer Christian Gobrecht; weight 8.359 grams; composition .900 gold, .100 copper (net weight .24187 oz. pure gold); diameter (1839–1840) 22.5 mm, (1840–1866) 21.6 mm; reeded edge; mints: Philadelphia, Charlotte, Dahlonega, New Orleans, San Francisco.*

**VF-20 VERY FINE**—LIBERTY on coronet bold. Major lines show in curls on neck.
**EF-40 EXTREMELY FINE**—Details clear in curls on neck. Slight wear on top and lower part of coronet and on hair.
**AU-50 ABOUT UNCIRCULATED**—Trace of wear on coronet and hair above eye.
**AU-55 CHOICE ABOUT UNCIRCULATED**—Evidence of friction on design high points. Some original mint luster.
**MS-60 UNCIRCULATED**—No trace of wear. Light blemishes.
**MS-63 CHOICE UNCIRCULATED**—Some distracting contact marks or blemishes in prime focal areas. Impaired luster possible.
**PF-63 CHOICE PROOF**—Attractive reflective surfaces with only a few blemishes in secondary focal places. No major flaws.

*Mintmark: 1839, above date; 1840–1908, below eagle.*

*See next page for chart.*

|  | Mintage | VF-20 | EF-40 | AU-50 | AU-55 | MS-60 | MS-63 |
|---|---|---|---|---|---|---|---|
| 1839 | 118,143 | $275. | $475. | $1,250. | $1,750. | $4,000. | $18,500. |
| 1839C | 17,205 | 2,400. | 3,500. | 6,750. | 11,000. | 23,500. | 55,000. |
| 1839D | 18,939 | 2,450. | 3,500. | 6,500. | 10,500. | 21,500. | |
| 1840 (a) | 137,382 | 250. | 400. | 1,300. | 2,000. | 3,750. | 12,000. |
| 1840C (a) | 18,992 | 2,350. | 3,600. | 7,750. | 12,500. | 27,500. | 57,500. |
| 1840D (a) | 22,896 | 2,350. | 3,750. | 8,000. | 10,500. | 17,500. | 47,500. |
| 1840O (a) | 40,120 | 475. | 1,000. | 1,750. | 2,850. | 8,000. | 27,500. |
| 1841 | 15,833 | 400. | 975. | 1,500. | 2,250. | 5,250. | 11,500. |
| 1841C | 21,467 | 1,750. | 2,300. | 3,750. | 7,500. | 20,000. | 45,000. |
| 1841D | 29,392 | 1,750. | 2,250. | 4,750. | 7,500. | 15,000. | 32,000. |
| 1841O (not known to exist) | .50 | | | | | | |

a. Scarce varieties of the 1840 coins have the fine edge-reeding and wide rims of the 1839 issues.

**1842, Large Date** — **Large Letters** — **Small Letters** — **1847, Extra 7 at Border**

|  | Mintage | VF-20 | EF-40 | AU-50 | AU-55 | MS-60 | MS-63 | PF-63 |
|---|---|---|---|---|---|---|---|---|
| 1842, All kinds | 27,578 | | | | | | | |
| 1842, Small Letters | | $375. | $1,200. | $3,500. | $6,000. | $12,000. | | |
| 1842, Large Letters | | 750. | 1,850. | 6,000. | 8,000. | 15,000. | | |
| 1842C, All kinds | 27,432 | | | | | | | |
| 1842C, Small Date | | 9,000. | 21,000. | 42,000. | 67,500. | 100,000. | | |
| 1842C, Large Date | | 1,750. | 2,400. | 3,950. | 6,500. | 18,500. | $37,500. | |
| 1842D, All kinds | 59,608 | | | | | | | |
| 1842D, Small Date | | 1,850. | 2,500. | 3,750. | 5,500. | 15,000. | 35,000. | |
| 1842D, Large Date | | 3,000. | 6,500. | 14,000. | 23,500. | 45,000. | | |
| 1842O | 16,400 | 1,050. | 3,500. | 12,000. | 16,500. | 24,500. | | |
| 1843 | 611,205 | 200. | 250. | 350. | 500. | 1,600. | 9,250. | |
| 1843C | 44,277 | 1,850. | 2,450. | 5,000. | 7,250. | 16,000. | 37,500. | |
| 1843D | 98,452 | 1,800. | 2,450. | 3,750. | 5,500. | 12,500. | 28,000. | |
| 1843O, Small Letters | 19,075 | 750. | 1,800. | 3,000. | 5,500. | 22,000. | 35,000. | |
| 1843O, Large Letters | 82,000 | 300. | 1,400. | 2,600. | 4,500. | 12,500. | 28,500. | |
| 1844 | 340,330 | 200. | 250. | 375. | 550. | 1,750. | 8,250. | |
| 1844C | 23,631 | 2,000. | 3,000. | 7,250. | 11,500. | 24,500. | 40,000. | |
| 1844D | 88,982 | 2,000. | 2,750. | 3,750. | 5,500. | 11,000. | 32,000. | |
| 1844O | 364,600 | 275. | 425. | 825. | 1,450. | 4,500. | 14,000. | |
| 1845 | 417,099 | 200. | 250. | 375. | 550. | 1,750. | 11,000. | |
| 1845D | 90,629 | 2,000. | 2,750. | 3,750. | 5,500. | 11,000. | 27,000. | |
| 1845O | 41,000 | 475. | 925. | 3,500. | 6,500. | 13,500. | 26,500. | |
| 1846, All kinds | 395,942 | | | | | | | |
| 1846, Large Date | | 200. | 275. | 650. | 1,400. | 3,500. | | |
| 1846, Small Date | | 200. | 275. | 400. | 650. | 2,750. | | |
| 1846C | 12,995 | 1,850. | 3,250. | 7,000. | 10,500. | 22,000. | 75,000. | |
| 1846D, All kinds | 80,294 | | | | | | | |
| 1846D | | 2,000. | 2,500. | 4,000. | 5,500. | 13,500. | | |
| 1846D, High 2nd D/D | | 2,200. | 2,750. | 4,500. | 6,000. | 14,500. | 28,000. | |

# HALF EAGLES

| | Mintage | VF-20 | EF-40 | AU-50 | AU-55 | MS-60 | MS-63 | PF-63 |
|---|---|---|---|---|---|---|---|---|
| 1846O | .58,000 | $425. | $1,100. | $4,000. | $6,500. | $12,000. | $25,000. | |
| 1847, All kinds | .915,981 | | | | | | | |
| 1847 | | 200. | 250. | 375. | 475. | 1,500. | 8,000. | |
| 1847, Top of Extra 7 | | | | | | | | |
| Very Low at Border | .... | 240. | 300. | 600. | 1,150. | 2,500. | 9,750. | |
| 1847C | .84,151 | 1,850. | 2,500. | 3,750. | 5,500. | 13,000. | 30,000. | |
| 1847D | .64,405 | 2,000. | 2,500. | 3,750. | 5,000. | 10,000. | 18,500. | |
| 1847O | .12,000 | 2,400. | 6,500. | 12,000. | 19,000. | 30,000. | | |
| 1848 | .260,775 | 225. | 285. | 450. | 650. | 1,600. | 10,000. | |
| 1848C | .64,472 | 1,950. | 2,500. | 3,750. | 7,250. | 18,500. | 50,000. | |
| 1848D | .47,465 | 1,950. | 2,500. | 3,750. | 7,000. | 14,000. | 37,500. | |
| 1849 | .133,070 | 200. | 250. | 700. | 1,200. | 2,800. | | |
| 1849C | .64,823 | 2,000. | 2,500. | 3,500. | 5,750. | 14,000. | 32,500. | |
| 1849D | .39,036 | 200. | 2,500. | 3,500. | 6,750. | 15,500. | 38,500. | |
| 1850 | .64,491 | 300. | 650. | 1,250. | 1,800. | 3,650. | 15,000. | |
| 1850C | .63,591 | 2,000. | 2,500. | 3,500. | 6,500. | 14,000. | 27,500. | |
| 1850D | .43,984 | 2,000. | 2,500. | 3,500. | 6,500. | 32,500. | | |
| 1851 | .377,505 | 200. | 250. | 350. | 550. | 2,800. | 10,000. | |
| 1851C | .49,176 | 2,000. | 2,500. | 3,750. | 6,500. | 16,000. | 48,000. | |
| 1851D | .62,710 | 2,000. | 2,500. | 4,000. | 7,000. | 14,000. | 32,500. | |
| 1851O | .41,000 | 600. | 1,350. | 3,750. | 6,500. | 13,000. | 22,000. | |
| 1852 | .573,901 | 200. | 250. | 350. | 450. | 1,400. | 8,500. | |
| 1852C | .72,574 | 2,000. | 2,500. | 3,500. | 5,000. | 7,750. | 24,500. | |
| 1852D | .91,584 | 2,000. | 2,500. | 3,750. | 5,500. | 12,500. | 28,500. | |
| 1853 | .305,770 | 200. | 250. | 350. | 475. | 1,500. | 8,500. | |
| 1853C | .65,571 | 2,000. | 2,500. | 3,500. | 4,850. | 8,500. | 27,500. | |
| 1853D | .89,678 | 2,000. | 2,500. | 3,500. | 4,500. | 8,750. | 24,000. | |
| 1854 | .160,675 | 200. | 250. | 525. | 1,100. | 2,000. | 9,000. | |
| 1854C | .39,283 | 2,000. | 2,500. | 4,000. | 6,500. | 14,000. | 42,500. | |
| 1854D | .56,413 | 2,000. | 2,500. | 3,500. | 5,500. | 11,000. | 30,000. | |
| 1854O | .46,000 | 325. | 600. | 1,500. | 2,500. | 7,500. | 23,500. | |
| 1854S | .268 | | | — | 1,000,000. | — | | |
| 1855 | .117,098 | 200. | 250. | 350. | 600. | 1,600. | 8,500. | — |
| 1855C | .39,788 | 2,000. | 2,500. | 4,000. | 6,000. | 16,000. | 37,000. | |
| 1855D | .22,432 | 2,000. | 2,500. | 4,000. | 6,000. | 17,500. | 42,000. | |
| 1855O | .11,100 | 800. | 2,100. | 4,500. | 6,500. | 20,000. | | |
| 1855S | .61,000 | 400. | 1,400. | 3,000. | 5,250. | 13,500. | | |
| 1856 | .197,990 | 200. | 250. | 350. | 600. | 2,100. | 12,500. | — |
| 1856C | .28,457 | 2,000. | 2,500. | 4,000. | 6,500. | 19,000. | | |
| 1856D | .19,786 | 2,000. | 2,500. | 4,000. | 6,500. | 12,000. | 37,500. | |
| 1856O | .10,000 | 750. | 1,850. | 5,000. | 7,500. | 16,000. | | |
| 1856S | .105,100 | 325. | 750. | 1,350. | 2,450. | 7,250. | 28,500. | |
| 1857 | .98,188 | 200. | 250. | 350. | 475. | 1,600. | 8,500. | — |
| 1857C | .31,360 | 1,950. | 2,500. | 4,000. | 5,250. | 9,500. | 32,000. | |
| 1857D | .17,046 | 2,000. | 2,500. | 4,000. | 6,500. | 13,000. | 36,500. | |
| 1857O | .13,000 | 800. | 1,650. | 4,500. | 7,000. | 13,500. | 48,500. | |
| 1857S | .87,000 | 325. | 750. | 1,500. | 2,750. | 11,000. | 19,000. | |
| 1858 | .15,136 | 250. | 500. | 800. | 1,550. | 3,650. | 11,000. | — |
| 1858C | .38,856 | 2,000. | 2,500. | 4,000. | 6,000. | 12,500. | 37,500. | |
| 1858D | .15,362 | 2,000. | 2,500. | 4,000. | 6,000. | 13,500. | 40,000. | |
| 1858S | .18,600 | 950. | 2,750. | 7,500. | 11,500. | 30,000. | | |

*Chart continued on next page.*

| | Mintage | VF-20 | EF-40 | AU-50 | AU-55 | MS-60 | MS-63 | PF-63 |
|---|---|---|---|---|---|---|---|---|
| 1859 . . . . . . . .(80). . . 16,734 | | $325. | $550. | $850. | $1,650. | $6,000. | $12,000. | $40,000. |
| 1859C . . . . . . . . . . . .31,847 | | 2,000. | 2,500. | 4,000. | 6,500. | 16,500. | 43,500. | |
| 1859D . . . . . . . . . . . .10,366 | | 2,000. | 2,500. | 4,000. | 6,250. | 15,000. | 39,000. | |
| 1859S . . . . . . . . . . . .13,220 | | 1,600. | 3,750. | 6,500. | 10,500. | 27,500. | | |
| 1860 . . . . . . . .(62). . . 19,763 | | 250. | 550. | 1,050. | 1,650. | 3,500. | 15,000. | 35,000. |
| 1860C . . . . . . . . . . . .14,813 | | 2,000. | 2,850. | 4,500. | 8,250. | 13,000. | 30,000. | |
| 1860D . . . . . . . . . . . .14,635 | | 2,000. | 3,000. | 4,500. | 8,500. | 17,000. | 47,500. | |
| 1860S . . . . . . . . . . . .21,200 | | 1,200. | 2,400. | 6,000. | 8,500. | 25,000. | | |
| 1861 . . . . . . . .(66). . 688,084 | | 200. | 250. | 375. | 450. | 1,250. | 7,250. | 32,500. |
| 1861C . . . . . . . . . . . . .6,879 | | 2,500. | 4,750. | 8,750. | 13,000. | 28,000. | 95,000. | |
| 1861D . . . . . . . . . . . . .1,597 | | 6,500. | 10,500. | 21,000. | 28,500. | 50,000. | 135,000. | |
| 1861S . . . . . . . . . . . .18,000 | | 1,250. | 4,000. | 7,500. | 11,500. | | | |
| 1862 . . . . . . . .(35). . . .4,430 | | 800. | 1,750. | 3,500. | 5,500. | 18,000. | | 32,500. |
| 1862S . . . . . . . . . . . . .9,500 | | 3,000. | 6,000. | 16,000. | 25,000. | 50,000. | | |
| 1863 . . . . . . . .(30). . . .2,442 | | 1,200. | 3,600. | 7,500. | 12,500. | 25,000. | | 32,500. |
| 1863S . . . . . . . . . . . .17,000 | | 1,500. | 4,500. | 12,500. | 17,500. | 32,500. | | |
| 1864 . . . . . . . .(50). . . .4,170 | | 700. | 1,800. | 3,500. | 7,500. | 13,500. | | 24,000. |
| 1864S . . . . . . . . . . . . .3,888 | | 6,500. | 12,500. | 32,500. | | | | |
| 1865 . . . . . . . .(25). . . .1,270 | | 1,500. | 3,750. | 11,000. | 14,500. | 21,000. | | 26,500. |
| 1865S . . . . . . . . . . . .27,612 | | 1,500. | 2,750. | 6,000. | 9,000. | 20,000. | | |
| 1866S . . . . . . . . . . . . .9,000 | | 1,750. | 4,000. | 12,500. | 17,500. | 35,000. | | |

## Variety 2 – Motto Above Eagle (1866–1908)

*Designer Christian Gobrecht; weight 8.359 grams; composition .900 gold, .100 copper (net weight .24187 oz. pure gold); diameter 21.6 mm; reeded edge; mints: Philadelphia, Carson City, Denver, New Orleans, San Francisco.*

**VF-20 VERY FINE**—Half of hair lines above coronet missing. Hair curls under ear evident, but worn. Motto and its ribbon sharp.

**EF-40 EXTREMELY FINE**—Small amount of wear on top of hair and below L in LIBERTY. Wear evident on wing tips and neck of eagle.

**AU-50 ABOUT UNCIRCULATED**—Trace of wear on tip of coronet and hair above eye.

**AU-55 CHOICE ABOUT UNCIRCULATED**—Evidence of friction on design high points. Some original mint luster present.

**MS-60 UNCIRCULATED**—No trace of wear. Light blemishes.

**MS-63 CHOICE UNCIRCULATED**—Some distracting contact marks or blemishes in prime focal areas. Impaired luster possible.

**PF-63 CHOICE PROOF**—Reflective surfaces with only a few blemishes in secondary focal places. No major flaws.

| | Mintage | VF-20 | EF-40 | AU-50 | AU-55 | MS-60 | MS-63 | PF-63 |
|---|---|---|---|---|---|---|---|---|
| 1866 . . . . . . . .(30). . . .6,700 | | $800. | $1,350. | $3,250. | $5,250. | $14,000. | | $21,500. |
| 1866S . . . . . . . . . . . .34,920 | | 950. | 2,750. | 8,500. | 12,000. | | | |
| 1867 . . . . . . . .(50). . . .6,870 | | 450. | 1,300. | 3,250. | 5,250. | 12,000. | | 18,500. |
| 1867S . . . . . . . . . . . .29,000 | | 1,250. | 3,000. | 13,000. | 17,000. | | | |
| 1868 . . . . . . . .(25). . . .5,700 | | 550. | 1,000. | 3,250. | 6,000. | 12,500. | | 22,500. |
| 1868S . . . . . . . . . . . .52,000 | | 425. | 1,500. | 3,750. | 6,000. | 17,500. | | |
| 1869 . . . . . . . .(25). . . .1,760 | | 850. | 1,850. | 4,000. | 6,000. | 14,000. | | 22,500. |
| 1869S . . . . . . . . . . . .31,000 | | 600. | 1,800. | 4,500. | 8,000. | 22,500. | | |

| | Mintage | VF-20 | EF-40 | AU-50 | AU-55 | MS-60 | MS-63 | PF-63 |
|---|---|---|---|---|---|---|---|---|
| 1870 . . . . . . .(35). . . . 4,000 | | $750. | $1,800. | $3,250. | $5,750. | $15,000. | | $22,500. |
| 1870CC . . . . . . . . . . .7,675 | | 6,000. | 16,500. | 32,000. | 40,000. | 105,000. | | |
| 1870S . . . . . . . . . . . .17,000 | | 1,000. | 2,300. | 8,000. | 12,500. | 25,000. | | |
| 1871 . . . . . . .(30). . . . 3,200 | | 750. | 1,500. | 3,250. | 6,000. | 12,500. | | 22,500. |
| 1871CC . . . . . . . . . . .20,770 | | 1,500. | 4,500. | 14,000. | 20,000. | 55,000. | $95,000. | |
| 1871S . . . . . . . . . . . .25,000 | | 400. | 1,100. | 3,750. | 7,500. | 14,500. | | |
| 1872 . . . . . . .(30). . . . 1,660 | | 750. | 1,650. | 3,000. | 5,000. | 12,500. | 19,500. | 22,500. |
| 1872CC . . . . . . . . . . .16,980 | | 1,350. | 6,000. | 21,500. | 30,000. | | | |
| 1872S . . . . . . . . . . . .36,400 | | 500. | 800. | 3,000. | 7,000. | 14,000. | | |
| 1873, Cl 3 . . .(25). . 112,480 | | 185. | 210. | 425. | 550. | 1,200. | 6,500. | 22,500. |
| 1873, Open 3 . . . . . .112,505 | | 185. | 210. | 300. | 350. | 750. | 4,250. | |
| 1873CC . . . . . . . . . . .7,416 | | 3,000. | 13,500. | 28,500. | 38,000. | 60,000. | | |
| 1873S . . . . . . . . . . . .31,000 | | 650. | 950. | 3,750. | 6,250. | 20,000. | | |
| 1874 . . . . . . .(20). . . . 3,488 | | 500. | 1,150. | 2,250. | 3,750. | 12,500. | 24,000. | 25,000. |
| 1874CC . . . . . . . . . . .21,198 | | 1,100. | 2,600. | 11,000. | 16,500. | 35,000. | | |
| 1874S . . . . . . . . . . . .16,000 | | 850. | 1,750. | 4,750. | 7,500. | | | |
| 1875 . . . . . . .(20) . . . . . 200 | | 38,500. | 50,000. | 70,000. | 82,000. | | | 80,000. |
| 1875CC . . . . . . . . . . .11,828 | | 1,750. | 4,250. | 12,000. | 22,000. | 45,000. | | |
| 1875S . . . . . . . . . . . .9,000 | | 800. | 2,200. | 6,250. | 9,250. | 22,500. | | |
| 1876 . . . . . . .(45). . . . 1,432 | | 800. | 2,000. | 3,500. | 6,500. | 10,000. | 18,000. | 16,000. |
| 1876CC . . . . . . . . . . .6,887 | | 1,600. | 4,500. | 13,500. | 18,000. | 38,500. | | |
| 1876S . . . . . . . . . . . .4,000 | | 1,300. | 3,500. | 8,500. | 11,000. | | | |
| 1877 . . . . . . .(20). . . . 1,132 | | 800. | 2,000. | 3,500. | 5,250. | 14,000. | | 20,000. |
| 1877CC . . . . . . . . . . .8,680 | | 1,200. | 3,500. | 11,500. | 14,500. | 45,000. | | |
| 1877S . . . . . . . . . . . .26,700 | | 300. | 600. | 1,750. | 4,500. | 8,750. | | |
| 1878 . . . . . . .(20). . 131,720 | | 185. | 190. | 210. | 235. | 425. | 2,000. | 20,000. |
| 1878CC . . . . . . . . . . .9,054 | | 3,750. | 10,000. | 20,000. | 28,500. | | | |
| 1878S . . . . . . . . . . . .144,700 | | 185. | 205. | 225. | 450. | 925. | 4,500. | |
| 1879 . . . . . . .(30). . 301,920 | | 185. | 205. | 225. | 260. | 400. | 1,750. | 19,000. |
| 1879CC . . . . . . . . . . .17,281 | | 700. | 1,600. | 3,250. | 6,500. | 20,000. | | |
| 1879S . . . . . . . . . . . .426,200 | | 185. | 200. | 225. | 275. | 950. | 3,500. | |
| 1880 . . . . . . .(36) 3,166,400 | | 185. | 195. | 205. | 215. | 250. | 1,100. | 15,000. |
| 1880CC . . . . . . . . . . .51,017 | | 425. | 875. | 1,650. | 4,500. | 10,500. | | |
| 1880S . . . . . . . . . . .1,348,900 | | 185. | 195. | 205. | 215. | 250. | 1,000. | |
| 1881, Final 1 Over 0 . . . . . . .* | | 300. | 625. | 775. | 975. | 1,250. | 5,000. | |
| 1881 . . . . . . .(42) 5,708,760 | | 185. | 195. | 205. | 215. | 250. | 950. | 14,500. |
| 1881CC . . . . . . . . . . .13,886 | | 650. | 1,850. | 8,500. | 11,500. | 21,500. | 57,500. | |
| 1881S . . . . . . . . . . .969,000 | | 185. | 195. | 205. | 215. | 250. | 950. | |
| 1882 . . . . . . .(48) 2,514,520 | | 185. | 195. | 205. | 215. | 250. | 950. | 14,500. |
| 1882CC . . . . . . . . . . .82,817 | | 425. | 725. | 950. | 2,250. | 8,500. | | |
| 1882S . . . . . . . . . . .969,000 | | 185. | 195. | 205. | 215. | 250. | 1,000. | |
| 1883 . . . . . . .(61). . 233,400 | | 185. | 195. | 205. | 215. | 305. | 1,500. | 14,500. |
| 1883CC . . . . . . . . . . .12,598 | | 550. | 1,250. | 3,250. | 6,750. | 18,500. | | |
| 1883S . . . . . . . . . . . .83,200 | | 185. | 195. | 205. | 215. | 800. | 3,500. | |
| 1884 . . . . . . .(48). . 191,030 | | 185. | 195. | 205. | 215. | 825. | 3,500. | 14,500. |
| 1884CC . . . . . . . . . . .16,402 | | 625. | 1,250. | 3,400. | 6,250. | 18,500. | | |
| 1884S . . . . . . . . . . . .177,000 | | 185. | 195. | 205. | 215. | 300. | 1,100. | |
| 1885 . . . . . . .(66). . 601,440 | | 185. | 195. | 205. | 215. | 250. | 950. | 14,500. |
| 1885S . . . . . . . . . . .1,211,500 | | 185. | 195. | 205. | 215. | 250. | 950. | |
| 1886 . . . . . . .(72). . 388,360 | | 185. | 195. | 205. | 215. | 250. | 1,100. | 14,500. |

* Included in number below.

*Chart continued on next page.*

| | Mintage | VF-20 | EF-40 | AU-50 | AU-55 | MS-60 | MS-63 | PF-63 |
|---|---|---|---|---|---|---|---|---|
| 1886S | 3,268,000 | $185. | $195. | $205. | $215. | $250. | $950. | |
| 1887, Pf Only (87) | | | | | | | | $55,000. |
| 1887S | 1,912,000 | 185. | 195. | 205. | 215. | 250. | 950. | |
| 1888 (95) | 18,201 | 185. | 235. | 285. | 350. | 525. | 1,850. | 11,500. |
| 1888S | 293,900 | 185. | 235. | 375. | 700. | 1,150. | 5,000. | |
| 1889 (45) | 7,520 | 245. | 325. | 525. | 675. | 1,000. | 3,000. | 14,500. |
| 1890 (88) | 4,240 | 305. | 500. | 700. | 950. | 1,850. | 7,250. | 14,500. |
| 1890CC | 53,800 | 350. | 475. | 675. | 800. | 1,400. | 7,750. | |
| 1891 (53) | 61,360 | 185. | 195. | 220. | 285. | 500. | 1,850. | 12,500. |
| 1891CC | 208,000 | 350. | 525. | 650. | 750. | 950. | 4,000. | |
| 1892 (92) | 753,480 | 185. | 195. | 205. | 215. | 250. | 1,200. | 12,500. |
| 1892CC | 82,968 | 350. | 475. | 675. | 900. | 1,650. | 8,500. | |
| 1892O | 10,000 | 475. | 850. | 1,300. | 1,800. | 3,000. | 11,500. | |
| 1892S | 298,400 | 185. | 195. | 225. | 375. | 600. | 3,500. | |
| 1893 (77) | 1,528,120 | 185. | 195. | 205. | 215. | 250. | 950. | 12,500. |
| 1893CC | 60,000 | 350. | 475. | 875. | 950. | 1,750. | 7,750. | |
| 1893O | 110,000 | 205. | 265. | 385. | 500. | 1,100. | 6,500. | |
| 1893S | 224,000 | 185. | 195. | 225. | 250. | 325. | 1,150. | |
| 1894 (75) | 957,880 | 185. | 195. | 205. | 215. | 250. | 950. | 12,500. |
| 1894O | 16,600 | 205. | 285. | 450. | 725. | 1,350. | 6,500. | |
| 1894S | 55,900 | 225. | 300. | 550. | 950. | 2,600. | 8,750. | |
| 1895 (81) | 1,345,855 | 185. | 195. | 205. | 215. | 250. | 950. | 11,000. |
| 1895S | 112,000 | 205. | 300. | 500. | 875. | 2,850. | 6,750. | |
| 1896 (103) | 58,960 | 185. | 195. | 205. | 215. | 250. | 1,100. | 11,000. |
| 1896S | 155,400 | 205. | 255. | 410. | 600. | 1,350. | 6,750. | |
| 1897 (83) | 867,800 | 185. | 195. | 205. | 215. | 250. | 950. | 11,000. |
| 1897S | 354,000 | 195. | 205. | 300. | 475. | 875. | 5,500. | |
| 1898 (75) | 633,420 | 185. | 195. | 205. | 215. | 250. | 950. | 11,000. |
| 1898S | 1,397,400 | 185. | 195. | 205. | 215. | 275. | 1,100. | |
| 1899 (99) | 1,710,630 | 185. | 195. | 205. | 215. | 250. | 950. | 11,000. |
| 1899S | 1,545,000 | 185. | 195. | 205. | 215. | 250. | 1,100. | |
| 1900 (230) | 1,405,500 | 185. | 195. | 205. | 215. | 250. | 950. | 11,000. |
| 1900S | 329,000 | 185. | 195. | 205. | 215. | 265. | 1,100. | |
| 1901 (140) | 615,900 | 185. | 195. | 205. | 215. | 250. | 950. | 11,000. |
| 1901S, All kinds | 3,648,000 | | | | | | | |
| 1901S, Final 1 Over 0 | | 195. | 200. | 250. | 300. | 350. | 1,100. | |
| 1901S | | 185. | 195. | 205. | 215. | 250. | 950. | |
| 1902 (162) | 172,400 | 185. | 195. | 205. | 215. | 250. | 950. | 11,000. |
| 1902S | 939,000 | 185. | 195. | 205. | 215. | 250. | 950. | |
| 1903 (154) | 226,870 | 185. | 195. | 205. | 215. | 250. | 950. | 11,000. |
| 1903S | 1,855,000 | 185. | 195. | 205. | 215. | 250. | 950. | |
| 1904 (136) | 392,000 | 185. | 195. | 205. | 215. | 250. | 950. | 11,000. |
| 1904S | 97,000 | 195. | 215. | 325. | 475. | 1,000. | 3,500. | |
| 1905 (108) | 302,200 | 185. | 195. | 205. | 215. | 250. | 950. | 11,000. |
| 1905S | 880,700 | 185. | 195. | 235. | 325. | 550. | 1,950. | |
| 1906 (85) | 348,735 | 185. | 195. | 205. | 215. | 250. | 950. | 11,000. |
| 1906D | 320,000 | 185. | 195. | 205. | 215. | 250. | 950. | |
| 1906S | 598,000 | 185. | 195. | 205. | 215. | 300. | 1,300. | |
| 1907 (92) | 626,100 | 185. | 195. | 205. | 215. | 250. | 950. | 11,000. |
| 1907D | 888,000 | 185. | 195. | 205. | 215. | 250. | 950. | |
| 1908 | 421,874 | 185. | 195. | 205. | 215. | 250. | 950. | |

# INDIAN HEAD (1908–1929)

This type conforms to the quarter eagle of the same date. The sunken (incuse) designs and lettering make these two series unique in United States coinage.

*Designer Bela Lyon Pratt; weight 8.359 grams; composition .900 gold, .100 copper (net weight .24187 oz. pure gold); diameter 21.6 mm; reeded edge; mints: Philadelphia, Denver, New Orleans, San Francisco.*

**VF-20 VERY FINE**—Noticeable wear on large middle feathers and tip of eagle's wing.
**EF-40 EXTREMELY FINE**—Cheekbone, war bonnet, and headband feathers slightly worn. Feathers on eagle's upper wing show considerable wear.
**AU-50 ABOUT UNCIRCULATED**—Trace of wear on cheekbone and headdress.
**AU-55 CHOICE ABOUT UNCIRCULATED**—Evidence of friction on design high points. Much of original mint luster present.
**MS-60 UNCIRCULATED**—No trace of wear. Light blemishes.
**MS-63 CHOICE UNCIRCULATED**—Some distracting contact marks or blemishes in prime focal areas. Impaired luster possible.

**Mintmark Location**

*Scarcer coins with well-struck mintmarks command higher prices.*

| | Mintage | VF-20 | EF-40 | AU-50 | AU-55 | MS-60 | MS-63 | MATTE PF-63 |
|---|---|---|---|---|---|---|---|---|
| 1908 . . . . . . (167) | . . 577,845 | $295. | $325. | $365. | $395. | $425. | $2,950. | $11,000. |
| 1908D . . . . . . . . . . . | 148,000 | 295. | 325. | 365. | 395. | 425. | 2,950. | |
| 1908S . . . . . . . . . . . | 82,000 | 350. | 450. | 600. | 800. | 1,350. | 3,750. | |
| 1909 . . . . . . (78) | . . 627,060 | 295. | 325. | 365. | 395. | 425. | 2,950. | 12,500. |
| 1909D . . . . . . . . . | 3,423,560 | 295. | 325. | 365. | 395. | 425. | 2,950. | |
| 1909O (a) . . . . . . . . . | 34,200 | 2,750. | 3,750. | 6,000. | 8,500. | 19,500. | 62,500. | |
| 1909S . . . . . . . . . . . | 297,200 | 300. | 345. | 385. | 450. | 1,500. | 11,500. | |
| 1910 . . . . . . (250) | . . 604,000 | 295. | 325. | 365. | 395. | 425. | 2,950. | 12,500. |
| 1910D . . . . . . . . . . . | 193,600 | 295. | 325. | 365. | 395. | 450. | 3,000. | |
| 1910S . . . . . . . . . . . | 770,200 | 300. | 345. | 385. | 600. | 1,300. | 6,750. | |
| 1911 . . . . . . (139) | . . 915,000 | 295. | 325. | 365. | 395. | 425. | 2,950. | 11,500. |
| 1911D . . . . . . . . . . . | 72,500 | 425. | 550. | 750. | 1,250. | 4,750. | 36,000. | |
| 1911S . . . . . . . . . | 1,416,000 | 300. | 350. | 400. | 550. | 750. | 3,250. | |
| 1912 . . . . . . (144) | . . 790,000 | 295. | 325. | 365. | 395. | 425. | 2,950. | 11,500. |
| 1912S . . . . . . . . . . . | 392,000 | 315. | 330. | 425. | 575. | 1,750. | 14,500. | |
| 1913 . . . . . . . (99) | . . 915,901 | 295. | 325. | 365. | 395. | 425. | 2,950. | 11,500. |
| 1913S . . . . . . . . . . . | 408,000 | 315. | 335. | 425. | 675. | 1,550. | 13,500. | |
| 1914 . . . . . . (125) | . . 247,000 | 295. | 325. | 365. | 395. | 425. | 2,950. | 11,500. |
| 1914D . . . . . . . . . . . | 247,000 | 295. | 325. | 365. | 395. | 425. | 3,000. | |
| 1914S . . . . . . . . . . . | 263,000 | 315. | 335. | 375. | 575. | 1,450. | 13,500. | |
| 1915 (b) . . . . (75) | . . 588,000 | 295. | 325. | 365. | 395. | 425. | 2,950. | 15,000. |
| 1915S . . . . . . . . . . . | 164,000 | 315. | 335. | 500. | 725. | 2,100. | 16,500. | |
| 1916S . . . . . . . . . . . | 240,000 | 305. | 340. | 400. | 450. | 625. | 3,250. | |
| 1929 . . . . . . . . . . . . | 662,000 | 6,750. | 8,500. | 9,750. | 10,500. | 12,000. | 17,500. | |

**a.** Beware spurious "O" mintmark.  **b.** Pieces dated 1915-D are counterfeit.

Coinage authority including specified weights and fineness of the eagle conforms to that of the half eagle. The Small Eagle reverse was used until 1797, when the large Heraldic Eagle replaced it. The early dates have variations in the number of stars, the rarest date being 1798. Many of these early pieces show file scratches from the Mint's practice of adjusting planchet weight before coining. No eagles were struck dated 1805 to 1837. Proofs of some dates prior to 1855 are known to exist, and all are rare.

*Note: Values of common gold coins have been based on the current bullion price of gold, $550 per ounce, and may vary with the prevailing spot price. The net weight and content listed may be used to recalculate bullion value.*

## TYPE COIN VALUES

| | F-12 | VF-20 | EF-40 | MS-60 | MS-63 | MS-65 | PF-63 | PF-65 |
|---|---|---|---|---|---|---|---|---|
| Cap Bust, Small Eagle, 1795–1797 | $23,500.+ | $29,500.+ | $41,500.+ | $87,500.+ | $250,000.+ | $550,000. | | |
| Cap Bust, Large Eagle, 1797–1804 | 8,250.+ | 10,500.+ | 13,500.+ | 21,500.+ | 32,500.+ | 200,000.+ | | |
| Liberty Head, NM, 1838–1866 | 300. | 350.- | 385.- | 3,750.- | 15,000.- | 72,500.+ | $37,500.+ | $120,000.+ |
| Liberty Head, 1866–1907 | 270.+ | 325.+ | 335.+ | 400.+ | 1,250.+ | 5,500.+ | 12,500.+ | 40,000.+ |
| Indian Head, NM, 1907–1908 | 300.+ | 425.+ | 500.+ | 1,050.+ | 4,000. | 8,500.+ | | |
| Indian Head, 1908–1933 | 300.+ | 400.+ | 450.+ | 600.+ | 1,450.+ | 4,750.+ | 15,500.+ | 45,000.+ |
| + or – indicates change from previous year | | | | | | | | |

## CAPPED BUST TO RIGHT (1795–1804)
### Small Eagle (1795–1797)

*Designer Robert Scot; weight 17.50 grams; composition .9167 gold, .0833 silver and copper; approx. diameter 33 mm; reeded edge.*

**F-12 FINE**—Details on turban and head obliterated.

**VF-20 VERY FINE**—Hair lines in curls on neck and details under turban and over forehead worn but distinguishable.

**EF-40 EXTREMELY FINE**—Definite wear on hair to left of eye and strand of hair across and around turban, as well as on eagle's wing tips.

**AU-50 ABOUT UNCIRCULATED**—Trace of wear on cap, hair, cheek, and drapery

**AU-55 CHOICE ABOUT UNCIRCULATED**—Evidence of friction on design high points. Most of original mint luster present.

**MS-60 UNCIRCULATED**—No trace of wear. Light blemishes.

**MS-63 CHOICE UNCIRCULATED**—Some distracting contact marks or blemishes in prime focal areas. Impaired luster possible.

13 Leaves     9 Leaves

| | Mintage | F-12 | VF-20 | EF-40 | AU-50 | AU-55 | MS-60 | MS-63 |
|---|---|---|---|---|---|---|---|---|
| 1795, 13 Leaves Below Eagle | 5,583 | $19,500. | $27,500. | $37,500. | $47,500. | $52,500. | $77,500. | $220,000. |
| *$506,000, MS-65, B&M auction, Jul-03* | | | | | | | | |
| 1795, 9 Leaves Below Eagle | * | 34,500. | 47,500. | 75,000. | 115,000. | 145,000. | 225,000. | |
| 1796 | 4,146 | 23,500. | 29,500. | 41,500. | 50,000. | 57,500. | 87,500. | 250,000. |
| 1797, Small Eagle | 3,615 | 27,500. | 37,500. | 45,000. | 85,000. | 100,000. | 185,000. | |

\* Included in number above.

## Heraldic Eagle (1797–1804)

| | Mintage | F-12 | VF-20 | EF-40 | AU-50 | AU-55 | MS-60 | MS-63 |
|---|---|---|---|---|---|---|---|---|
| 1797, Large Eagle . . . . .10,940 | | $8,250. | $11,500. | $14,500. | $23,500. | $27,500. | $38,500. | $75,000. |
| 1798, 8 Over 7, 9 Stars | | | | | | | | |
| Left, 4 Right . . . . . . . .900 | | 14,000. | 23,500. | 32,500. | 47,500. | 70,000. | 110,000. | 250,000. |
| 1798, 8 Over 7, 7 Stars | | | | | | | | |
| Left, 6 Right . . . . . . . .842 | | 27,500. | 45,000. | 75,000. | 145,000. | 165,000. | 235,000. | |
| 1799, Sm Obv Stars . . .37,449 | | 8,250. | 10,500. | 13,500. | 16,500. | 21,500. | 32,500. | 42,500. |
| 1799, Lg Obv Stars . . . . . . .* | | 8,250. | 10,500. | 13,500. | 16,500. | 21,500. | 32,500. | 42,500. |
| 1800 . . . . . . . . . . . . . . .5,999 | | 8,500. | 11,000. | 14,000. | 17,000. | 22,000. | 35,000. | 65,000. |

\* Included in number above.

| | Mintage | F-12 | VF-20 | EF-40 | AU-50 | AU-55 | MS-60 | MS-63 |
|---|---|---|---|---|---|---|---|---|
| 1801 . . . . . . . . . . . . . .44,344 | | $8,250. | $10,500. | $13,500. | $16,500. | $21,500. | $32,500. | $42,500. |
| 1803, Sm Rev Stars . . .15,017 | | 8,500. | 11,000. | 14,000. | 17,000. | 22,000. | 35,000. | 62,500. |
| 1803, Lg Rev Stars . . . . . . .* | | 8,500. | 11,000. | 14,000. | 17,000. | 22,000. | 35,000. | 62,500. |
| 1804 . . . . . . . . . . . . . . .3,757 | | 11,000. | 13,500. | 16,500. | 26,000. | 29,500. | 42,000. | 150,000. |
| 1804, Pl 4, Pf, Restrike *(4 known)* | | | | | | | | 1,500,000. |

\* Included in number above.

# LIBERTY HEAD, NO MOTTO ABOVE EAGLE (1838–1866)

In 1838, the weight and diameter of the eagle were reduced and the obverse and reverse were redesigned. Liberty now faces left and the word LIBERTY is placed on the coronet. A more natural-appearing eagle is used on the reverse. The value, TEN D., is shown for the first time on this denomination.

*Designer Christian Gobrecht; weight 16.718 grams; composition .900 gold, .100 copper (net weight: .48375 oz. pure gold); diameter 27 mm; reeded edge; mints: Philadelphia, New Orleans, San Francisco.*

**VF-20 VERY FINE**—Hair lines above coronet partly worn. Curls under ear worn but defined.

**EF-40 EXTREMELY FINE**—Small amount of wear on top of hair and below L in LIBERTY. Wear evident on wing tips and neck of eagle.

**AU-50 ABOUT UNCIRCULATED**—Trace of wear on tip of coronet and hair above eye.

**AU-55 CHOICE ABOUT UNCIRCULATED**—Evidence of friction on design high points. Some of original mint luster present.

**MS-60 UNCIRCULATED**—No trace of wear. Light blemishes.

**MS-63 CHOICE UNCIRCULATED**—Some distracting contact marks or blemishes in prime focal areas. Impaired luster possible.

**PF-63 CHOICE PROOF**—Attractive reflective surfaces with only a few blemishes in secondary focal places. No major flaws.

1853, 3 Over 2

*Mintmark is on reverse, below eagle.*

| | Mintage | VF-20 | EF-40 | AU-50 | AU-55 | MS-60 | MS-63 |
|---|---|---|---|---|---|---|---|
| 1838 **(a)** . . . . . . . . . . . . . .7,200 | | $1,200. | $3,000. | $6,000. | $10,000. | $36,000. | $85,000. |
| *$550,000, Ch Proof, Akers auction, May-98* | | | | | | | |
| 1839, Large Letters **(a)** . . .25,801 | | 1,000. | 2,000. | 5,000. | 9,000. | 30,000. | 57,500. |
| 9 Over 8, Type of 1838 *$402,500, MS-66, Heritage auction, Jan-05* | | | | | | | |
| 1839, Small Letters . . . . . .12,447 | | 1,600. | 3,500. | 6,500. | 9,500. | 35,000. | 90,000. |
| 1840 . . . . . . . . . . . . . . .47,338 | | 395. | 625. | 1,500. | 2,800. | 10,000. | |
| 1841 . . . . . . . . . . . . . . .63,131 | | 350. | 575. | 1,300. | 2,500. | 8,000. | 30,000. |
| 18410 . . . . . . . . . . . . . . .2,500 | | 2,600. | 5,500. | 12,500. | 27,500. | | |
| 1842, Small Date . . . . . . . .18,623 | | 350. | 525. | 1,850. | 3,250. | 13,500. | 27,500. |
| 1842, Large Date . . . . . . . .62,884 | | 350. | 575. | 1,600. | 3,000. | 13,000. | 23,500. |
| 18420 . . . . . . . . . . . . . .27,400 | | 475. | 750. | 2,800. | 7,500. | 27,500. | 45,000. |
| 1843 . . . . . . . . . . . . . . .75,462 | | 350. | 525. | 1,850. | 3,500. | 16,500. | |
| 18430 . . . . . . . . . . . . . .175,162 | | 450. | 600. | 1,500. | 3,750. | 13,000. | |
| 1844 . . . . . . . . . . . . . . .6,361 | | 1,350. | 2,500. | 5,500. | 8,000. | 17,000. | 38,000. |
| 18440 . . . . . . . . . . . . . .118,700 | | 425. | 600. | 1,800. | 3,500. | 16,000. | |
| 1845 . . . . . . . . . . . . . . .26,153 | | 500. | 900. | 2,250. | 3,250. | 14,500. | |
| 18450 . . . . . . . . . . . . . .47,500 | | 450. | 850. | 2,250. | 6,000. | 16,000. | |
| 1846 . . . . . . . . . . . . . . .20,095 | | 700. | 1,150. | 5,000. | 9,500. | 22,000. | |
| 18460, All kinds . . . . . . . .81,780 | | | | | | | |
| 18460 . . . . . . . . . . . . . . . . . | | 450. | 850. | 4,000. | 6,500. | 16,500. | |
| 18460, 6 Over 5 . . . . . . . . . . . | | 600. | 1,000. | 4,000. | 7,000. | 18,500. | |
| 1847 . . . . . . . . . . . . . .862,258 | | 350. | 400. | 575. | 1,000. | 3,500. | 22,500. |
| 18470 . . . . . . . . . . . . . .571,500 | | 375. | 450. | 675. | 1,200. | 5,500. | 18,000. |
| 1848 . . . . . . . . . . . . . .145,484 | | 350. | 450. | 750. | 1,300. | 5,000. | 24,500. |
| 18480 . . . . . . . . . . . . . .35,850 | | 575. | 1,200. | 3,600. | 7,500. | 17,500. | 30,000. |
| 1849 . . . . . . . . . . . . . .653,618 | | 350. | 400. | 675. | 1,000. | 3,750. | 13,000. |
| 18490 . . . . . . . . . . . . . .23,900 | | 850. | 1,850. | 5,250. | 8,000. | 23,000. | |
| 1850, All kinds . . . . . . . .291,451 | | | | | | | |
| 1850, Large Date . . . . . . . . . . | | 350. | 400. | 625. | 1,000. | 4,000. | 16,500. |
| 1850, Small Date . . . . . . . . . . | | 475. | 950. | 2,200. | 3,800. | 9,000. | 28,000. |
| 18500 . . . . . . . . . . . . . .57,500 | | 525. | 1,050. | 3,250. | 5,500. | 16,000. | |
| 1851 . . . . . . . . . . . . . .176,328 | | 350. | 425. | 950. | 1,300. | 4,500. | 27,500. |
| 18510 . . . . . . . . . . . . . .263,000 | | 450. | 650. | 1,350. | 3,250. | 6,750. | 27,500. |
| 1852 . . . . . . . . . . . . . .263,106 | | 350. | 405. | 575. | 1,100. | 4,500. | |
| 18520 . . . . . . . . . . . . . .18,000 | | 750. | 1,200. | 3,750. | 8,000. | 24,000. | |
| 1853, All kinds . . . . . . . .201,253 | | | | | | | |
| 1853, 3 Over 2 . . . . . . . . . . . | | 550. | 750. | 1,700. | 3,500. | | |
| 1853 . . . . . . . . . . . . . . . . . | | 350. | 405. | 575. | 1,000. | 3,800. | 18,500. |
| 18530 . . . . . . . . . . . . . .51,000 | | 425. | 525. | 1,050. | 2,500. | 14,500. | |
| 1854 . . . . . . . . . . . . . . .54,250 | | 350. | 425. | 750. | 1,350. | 6,000. | 23,000. |

**a.** The Liberty Head style of 1838 and 1839 (large letters) differs from that used for subsequent issues.

# EAGLES

| | Mintage | VF-20 | EF-40 | AU-50 | AU-55 | MS-60 | MS-63 | PF-63 |
|---|---|---|---|---|---|---|---|---|
| 1854O, Lg or Sm Dt | .52,500 | $425. | $750. | $1,500. | $3,000. | $10,500. | | |
| 1854S | 123,826 | 350. | 550. | 1,250. | 2,000. | 10,000. | | |
| 1855 | 121,701 | 350. | 400. | 625. | 1,000. | 4,500. | $18,500. | — |
| 1855O | 18,000 | 650. | 1,500. | 5,500. | 8,500. | 25,000. | | |
| 1855S | 9,000 | 1,450. | 2,500. | 6,500. | 9,500. | | | |
| 1856 | 60,490 | 350. | 400. | 650. | 1,050. | 4,500. | 13,000. | — |
| 1856O | 14,500 | 775. | 1,350. | 4,000. | 7,000. | 17,500. | | |
| 1856S | 68,000 | 350. | 625. | 1,250. | 2,600. | 9,500. | 25,000. | |
| 1857 | 16,606 | 450. | 850. | 2,000. | 3,800. | 12,500. | | — |
| 1857O | 5,500 | 1,200. | 2,000. | 3,750. | 6,250. | 27,500. | | |
| 1857S | 26,000 | 475. | 1,150. | 2,500. | 4,500. | 11,500. | 17,500. | |
| 1858 (b) | 2,521 | 5,250. | 8,500. | 13,500. | 17,500. | 38,000. | | — |
| 1858O | 20,000 | 425. | 775. | 1,850. | 3,500. | 10,000. | 28,500. | |
| 1858S | 11,800 | 1,800. | 3,500. | 6,000. | 13,500. | | | |
| 1859 (80) | 16,013 | 385. | 725. | 1,250. | 2,600. | 9,500. | 15,000. | $60,000. |
| 1859O | 2,300 | 4,250. | 9,500. | 20,000. | 25,000. | | | |
| 1859S | 7,000 | 2,200. | 5,000. | 13,500. | 19,500. | | | |
| 1860 (50) | 15,055 | 405. | 800. | 1,600. | 2,750. | 8,500. | 20,000. | 42,500. |
| 1860O | 11,100 | 600. | 1,200. | 2,250. | 4,250. | 14,500. | | |
| 1860S | 5,000 | 3,250. | 6,000. | 15,000. | 26,000. | | | |
| 1861 (69) | 113,164 | 350. | 385. | 600. | 1,000. | 3,750. | 15,000. | 37,500. |
| 1861S | 15,500 | 1,600. | 3,250. | 7,000. | 12,000. | 30,000. | | |
| 1862 (35) | 10,960 | 550. | 1,050. | 2,250. | 3,250. | 12,500. | | 37,500. |
| 1862S | 12,500 | 1,750. | 3,250. | 6,000. | 10,000. | | | |
| 1863 (30) | 1,218 | 4,250. | 8,500. | 17,000. | 24,000. | 42,500. | 75,000. | 39,500. |
| 1863S | 10,000 | 1,850. | 3,750. | 9,500. | 13,500. | 27,500. | | |
| 1864 (50) | 3,530 | 1,850. | 4,000. | 7,500. | 10,000. | 18,500. | | 38,500. |
| 1864S | 2,500 | 5,000. | 13,500. | 27,500. | 35,000. | | | |
| 1865 (25) | 3,980 | 1,850. | 4,000. | 6,750. | 9,500. | 37,500. | 65,000. | 38,500. |
| 1865S, All kinds | 16,700 | | | | | | | |
| 1865S | | 4,000. | 8,750. | 17,500. | 22,500. | 47,500. | | |
| 1865S, 865/Inverted 186 | | 3,000. | 7,000. | 12,500. | 18,500. | | | |
| 1866S | 8,500 | 2,850. | 3,750. | 12,000. | 17,500. | 45,000. | | |

b. Beware removed mintmark.

## LIBERTY HEAD, MOTTO ABOVE EAGLE (1866–1907)

*Standards as for No Motto variety; mints: Philadelphia, Carson City, Denver, New Orleans, San Francisco.*

**VF-20 VERY FINE**—Half of hair lines over coronet visible. Curls under ear worn but defined. IN GOD WE TRUST and its ribbon sharp.

**EF-40 EXTREMELY FINE**—Small amount of wear on top of hair and below L in LIBERTY. Wear evident on wing tips and neck of eagle.

**AU-50 ABOUT UNCIRCULATED**—Trace of wear on hair above eye and on coronet.

**AU-55 CHOICE ABOUT UNCIRCULATED**—Evidence of friction on design high points. Some of original mint luster present.

**MS-60 UNCIRCULATED**—No trace of wear. Light blemishes.

**MS-63 CHOICE UNCIRCULATED**—Some distracting contact marks or blemishes in prime focal areas. Impaired luster possible.

**PF-63 CHOICE PROOF**—Reflective surfaces with only a few blemishes in secondary focal areas. No major flaws.

**Mintmark is on reverse, below eagle.**

*See next page for chart.*

| | Mintage | VF-20 | EF-40 | AU-50 | AU-55 | MS-60 | MS-63 | PF-63 |
|---|---|---|---|---|---|---|---|---|
| 1866 . . . . .(30) . . . . . .3,750 | | $900. | $1,900. | $4,500. | $9,000. | $21,500. | | $30,000. |
| 1866S . . . . . . . . . . . .11,500 | | 1,500. | 3,750. | 8,000. | 11,000. | | | |
| 1867 . . . . .(50) . . . . . .3,090 | | 1,500. | 3,000. | 5,000. | 8,500. | 27,500. | | 30,000. |
| 1867S . . . . . . . . . . . . .9,000 | | 2,500. | 6,000. | 10,000. | 17,500. | | | |
| 1868 . . . . .(25) . . . . .10,630 | | 575. | 800. | 2,000. | 3,500. | | | 30,000. |
| 1868S . . . . . . . . . . . .13,500 | | 1,250. | 2,350. | 4,500. | 6,250. | | | |
| 1869 . . . .(25) . . . . . .1,830 | | 1,500. | 2,850. | 6,000. | 14,000. | 30,000. | | 30,000. |
| 1869S . . . . . . . . . . . . .6,430 | | 1,600. | 2,600. | 6,500. | 14,500. | 27,500. | | |
| 1870 . . . . .(35) . . . . . .3,990 | | 850. | 1,500. | 2,750. | 6,500. | 16,500. | | 30,000. |
| 1870CC . . . . . . . . . . . .5,908 | | 13,500. | 32,500. | 52,500. | 77,500. | | | |
| 1870S . . . . . . . . . . . . .8,000 | | 1,250. | 2,500. | 6,500. | 13,500. | 28,000. | | |
| 1871 . . . .(30) . . . . . .1,790 | | 1,450. | 2,600. | 4,250. | 9,500. | 21,000. | | 32,500. |
| 1871CC . . . . . . . . . . . .8,085 | | 3,000. | 6,000. | 20,000. | 25,000. | 67,500. | | |
| 1871S . . . . . . . . . . . .16,500 | | 1,200. | 2,000. | 6,000. | 11,000. | | | |
| 1872 . . . . .(30) . . . . . .1,620 | | 2,250. | 3,750. | 10,000. | 13,500. | 18,500. | | 30,000. |
| 1872CC . . . . . . . . . . . .4,600 | | 3,500. | 11,000. | 22,500. | 35,000. | | | |
| 1872S . . . . . . . . . . . .17,300 | | 600. | 1,100. | 2,000. | 4,750. | 18,000. | | |
| 1873 . . . . .(25) . . . . . . .800 | | 4,500. | 9,500. | 16,500. | 20,000. | 40,000. | | 35,000. |
| 1873CC . . . . . . . . . . . .4,543 | | 7,500. | 14,500. | 30,000. | 45,000. | | | |
| 1873S . . . . . . . . . . . .12,000 | | 1,000. | 2,500. | 4,750. | 8,000. | 22,000. | | |
| 1874 . . . . .(20) . . . . .53,140 | | 335. | 360. | 425. | 500. | 2,000. | $8,500. | 32,500. |
| 1874CC . . . . . . . . . . . .16,767 | | 1,000. | 2,850. | 8,750. | 13,500. | | | |
| 1874S . . . . . . . . . . . .10,000 | | 1,100. | 3,250. | 7,500. | 12,000. | | | |
| 1875 . . . . .(20) . . . . . . .100 | | 42,500. | 60,000. | 85,000. | 100,000. | | | 120,000. |
| 1875CC . . . . . . . . . . . .7,715 | | 4,800. | 10,000. | 22,500. | 32,500. | 75,000. | 100,000. | |
| 1876 . . . . .(45) . . . . . . .687 | | 3,250. | 7,500. | 16,500. | 20,000. | | | 30,000. |
| 1876CC . . . . . . . . . . . .4,696 | | 3,250. | 8,000. | 20,000. | 28,000. | | | |
| 1876S . . . . . . . . . . . . .5,000 | | 1,250. | 2,000. | 5,500. | 9,000. | | | |
| 1877 . . . . .(20) . . . . . . .797 | | 2,500. | 5,250. | 9,250. | 11,000. | 25,000. | | 32,500. |
| 1877CC . . . . . . . . . . . .3,332 | | 2,500. | 6,000. | 16,000. | 20,000. | | | |
| 1877S . . . . . . . . . . . .17,000 | | 500. | 750. | 2,000. | 4,000. | 20,000. | | |
| 1878 . . . . .(20) . . . . .73,780 | | 335. | 365. | 395. | 450. | 1,000. | 4,750. | 27,500. |
| 1878CC . . . . . . . . . . . .3,244 | | 4,500. | 9,750. | 20,000. | 28,000. | | | |
| 1878S . . . . . . . . . . . .26,100 | | 425. | 675. | 1,950. | 3,250. | 14,500. | 28,500. | |
| 1879 . . . .(30) . . . .384,740 | | 325. | 335. | 350. | 425. | 650. | 4,500. | 25,000. |
| 1879CC . . . . . . . . . . . .1,762 | | 9,500. | 14,500. | 26,000. | 31,000. | | | |
| 1879O . . . . . . . . . . . . .1,500 | | 2,500. | 4,500. | 10,500. | 15,000. | 35,000. | | |
| 1879S . . . . . . . . . . .224,000 | | 325. | 335. | 350. | 475. | 1,100. | 6,000. | |
| 1880 . . . . .(36) . . .1,644,840 | | 325. | 335. | 350. | 365. | 400. | 3,750. | 20,000. |
| 1880CC . . . . . . . . . . .11,190 | | 625. | 950. | 1,750. | 4,000. | 15,000. | | |
| 1880O . . . . . . . . . . . . .9,200 | | 425. | 775. | 1,500. | 2,350. | 8,750. | | |
| 1880S . . . . . . . . . . .506,250 | | 325. | 335. | 350. | 365. | 475. | 4,750. | |
| 1881 . . . .(40) . . .3,877,220 | | 325. | 335. | 350. | 365. | 400. | 1,350. | 20,000. |
| 1881CC . . . . . . . . . . .24,015 | | 550. | 850. | 1,200. | 1,450. | 7,000. | | |
| 1881O . . . . . . . . . . . . .8,350 | | 400. | 700. | 1,300. | 2,100. | 8,500. | | |
| 1881S . . . . . . . . . . .970,000 | | 325. | 335. | 350. | 365. | 400. | 4,750. | |
| 1882 . . . . .(40) . . .2,324,440 | | 325. | 335. | 350. | 365. | 400. | 1,350. | 20,000. |
| 1882CC . . . . . . . . . . . .6,764 | | 725. | 1,300. | 3,250. | 7,000. | 14,000. | | |
| 1882O . . . . . . . . . . . .10,820 | | 375. | 600. | 1,250. | 2,250. | 7,000. | 17,500. | |
| 1882S . . . . . . . . . . .132,000 | | 325. | 335. | 350. | 365. | 475. | 3,500. | |
| 1883 . . . .(40) . . . .208,700 | | 325. | 335. | 350. | 365. | 400. | 2,850. | 20,000. |

# EAGLES

| | Mintage | VF-20 | EF-40 | AU-50 | AU-55 | MS-60 | MS-63 | PF-63 |
|---|---|---|---|---|---|---|---|---|
| 1883CC | . . . . . . . . . . . .12,000 | $550. | $850. | $2,350. | $4,600. | $14,500. | | |
| 1883O | . . . . . . . . . . . . .800 | 4,000. | 7,500. | 12,500. | 15,000. | 37,500. | | |
| 1883S | . . . . . . . . . . . .38,000 | 325. | 335. | 350. | 475. | 1,150. | $11,500. | |
| 1884 | . . . . .(45) . . . . . .76,860 | 325. | 335. | 350. | 365. | 750. | 4,000. | $20,000. |
| 1884CC | . . . . . . . . . . . . .9,925 | 650. | 1,100. | 2,500. | 4,500. | 12,000. | 32,500. | |
| 1884S | . . . . . . . . . . . .124,250 | 325. | 335. | 350. | 365. | 600. | 4,750. | |
| 1885 | . . . . .(65) . . . . .253,462 | 325. | 335. | 350. | 365. | 405. | 4,000. | 17,500. |
| 1885S | . . . . . . . . . . . .228,000 | 325. | 335. | 350. | 365. | 400. | 5,250. | |
| 1886 | . . . . .(60) . . . . .236,100 | 325. | 335. | 350. | 365. | 400. | 4,750. | 17,500. |
| 1886S | . . . . . . . . . . . .826,000 | 325. | 335. | 350. | 365. | 400. | 1,650. | |
| 1887 | . . . . .(80) . . . . .53,600 | 325. | 335. | 350. | 450. | 850. | 4,500. | 17,000. |
| 1887S | . . . . . . . . . . . .817,000 | 325. | 335. | 350. | 365. | 400. | 3,500. | |
| 1888 | . . . . .(75) . . . . .132,921 | 325. | 335. | 360. | 425. | 800. | 4,750. | 17,000. |
| 1888O | . . . . . . . . . . . .21,335 | 325. | 335. | 350. | 365. | 625. | 5,500. | |
| 1888S | . . . . . . . . . . . .648,700 | 325. | 335. | 350. | 365. | 400. | 3,250. | |
| 1889 | . . . . .(45) . . . . . .4,440 | 345. | 425. | 875. | 1,500. | 2,800. | 6,750. | 17,000. |
| 1889S | . . . . . . . . . . . .425,400 | 325. | 335. | 350. | 365. | 400. | 1,850. | |
| 1890 | . . . . .(63) . . . . . .57,980 | 325. | 335. | 350. | 365. | 850. | 5,000. | 15,000. |
| 1890CC | . . . . . . . . . . . .17,500 | 400. | 550. | 800. | 1,200. | 2,450. | 14,500. | |
| 1891 | . . . . .(48) . . . . . .91,820 | 325. | 335. | 350. | 365. | 400. | 4,000. | 15,000. |
| 1891CC | . . . . . . . . . . . .103,732 | 375. | 625. | 750. | 800. | 975. | 6,000. | |
| 1892 | . . . . .(72) . . . . .797,480 | 325. | 335. | 350. | 365. | 400. | 1,500. | 15,000. |
| 1892CC | . . . . . . . . . . . .40,000 | 475. | 600. | 850. | 1,250. | 3,750. | 9,500. | |
| 1892O | . . . . . . . . . . . .28,688 | 325. | 335. | 350. | 375. | 525. | 6,000. | |
| 1892S | . . . . . . . . . . . .115,500 | 325. | 335. | 350. | 365. | 400. | 4,000. | |
| 1893 | . . . . .(55) . . .1,840,840 | 325. | 335. | 350. | 365. | 400. | 1,250. | 15,000. |
| 1893CC | . . . . . . . . . . . .14,000 | 500. | 750. | 1,500. | 2,750. | 7,750. | | |
| 1893O | . . . . . . . . . . . .17,000 | 325. | 335. | 395. | 450. | 675. | 5,750. | |
| 1893S | . . . . . . . . . . . .141,350 | 325. | 335. | 350. | 365. | 400. | 4,500. | |
| 1894 | . . . . .(43) . . .2,470,735 | 325. | 335. | 350. | 365. | 400. | 1,250. | 15,000. |
| 1894O | . . . . . . . . . . . .107,500 | 325. | 340. | 400. | 600. | 1,100. | 5,000. | |
| 1894S | . . . . . . . . . . . .25,000 | 325. | 365. | 750. | 1,100. | 3,500. | | |
| 1895 | . . . . .(56) . . . . .567,770 | 325. | 335. | 350. | 365. | 400. | 1,250. | 15,000. |
| 1895O | . . . . . . . . . . . .98,000 | 325. | 340. | 365. | 400. | 550. | 5,250. | |
| 1895S | . . . . . . . . . . . .49,000 | 350. | 375. | 700. | 1,100. | 2,500. | 9,500. | |
| 1896 | . . . . .(78) . . . . . .76,270 | 325. | 335. | 350. | 365. | 400. | 2,500. | 15,000. |
| 1896S | . . . . . . . . . . . .123,750 | 325. | 340. | 500. | 550. | 2,500. | 11,000. | |
| 1897 | . . . . .(69) . . .1,000,090 | 325. | 340. | 350. | 365. | 400. | 1,250. | 15,000. |
| 1897O | . . . . . . . . . . . .42,500 | 325. | 340. | 375. | 400. | 800. | 5,000. | |
| 1897S | . . . . . . . . . . . .234,750 | 325. | 335. | 350. | 400. | 800. | 4,750. | |
| 1898 | . . . . .(67) . . . . .812,130 | 325. | 335. | 350. | 365. | 400. | 1,300. | 15,000. |
| 1898S | . . . . . . . . . . . .473,600 | 325. | 335. | 350. | 365. | 400. | 4,750. | |
| 1899 | . . . . .(86) . . .1,262,219 | 325. | 335. | 350. | 365. | 400. | 1,250. | 12,500. |
| 1899O | . . . . . . . . . . . .37,047 | 325. | 335. | 375. | 400. | 700. | 5,500. | |
| 1899S | . . . . . . . . . . . .841,000 | 325. | 335. | 350. | 375. | 405. | 3,500. | |
| 1900 | . . . .(120) . . . . .293,840 | 325. | 335. | 350. | 365. | 400. | 1,250. | 12,500. |
| 1900S | . . . . . . . . . . . .81,000 | 325. | 340. | 360. | 375. | 900. | 5,500. | |
| 1901 | . . . . .(85) . . .1,718,740 | 325. | 335. | 350. | 365. | 400. | 1,250. | 12,500. |
| 1901O | . . . . . . . . . . . .72,041 | 325. | 335. | 350. | 385. | 475. | 3,500. | |
| 1901S | . . . . . . . . . .2,812,750 | 325. | 335. | 350. | 365. | 400. | 1,250. | |
| 1902 | . . . .(113) . . . . . .82,400 | 325. | 335. | 350. | 365. | 400. | 2,500. | 12,500. |

*Chart continued on next page.*

| | Mintage | VF-20 | EF-40 | AU-50 | AU-55 | MS-60 | MS-63 | PF-63 |
|---|---|---|---|---|---|---|---|---|
| 1902S | ...........469,500 | $325. | $335. | $350. | $365. | $400. | $1,250. | |
| 1903 | .....(96).....125,830 | 325. | 335. | 350. | 365. | 400. | 1,250. | $12,500. |
| 1903O | ............112,771 | 335. | 365. | 385. | 400. | 475. | 3,750. | |
| 1903S | ...........538,000 | 325. | 335. | 350. | 365. | 400. | 1,250. | |
| 1904 | ....(108).....161,930 | 325. | 335. | 350. | 365. | 400. | 1,250. | 12,500. |
| 1904O | ...........108,950 | 335. | 365. | 385. | 400. | 475. | 3,750. | |
| 1905 | .....(86).....200,992 | 335. | 365. | 385. | 400. | 450. | 1,500. | 12,500. |
| 1905S | ...........369,250 | 335. | 365. | 395. | 405. | 1,150. | 5,500. | |
| 1906 | .....(77).....165,420 | 325. | 335. | 350. | 365. | 400. | 2,500. | 12,500. |
| 1906D | ............981,000 | 325. | 335. | 350. | 365. | 400. | 1,250. | |
| 1906O | .............86,895 | 325. | 345. | 365. | 385. | 450. | 4,500. | |
| 1906S | ...........457,000 | 325. | 340. | 360. | 375. | 450. | 4,750. | |
| 1907 | .....(74)...1,203,899 | 325. | 335. | 350. | 365. | 400. | 1,250. | 12,500. |
| 1907D | ..........1,030,000 | 325. | 335. | 350. | 365. | 400. | 2,000. | |
| 1907S | ...........210,500 | 325. | 335. | 350. | 400. | 600. | 5,500. | |

# INDIAN HEAD (1907–1933)

Augustus Saint-Gaudens, considered by many the greatest of modern sculptors, introduced a new high standard of art in United States coins evidenced by his eagle and double eagle types of 1907. The obverse of the eagle shows the head of Liberty crowned with an Indian war bonnet while an impressively majestic eagle dominates the reverse side. A departure from older standards is found on the edge of the piece, where 46 raised stars (48 stars in 1912 and later) are arranged signifying the states of the Union, instead of there being a lettered or reeded edge.

The first of these coins struck had no motto IN GOD WE TRUST as had the later issues, starting in 1908. President Theodore Roosevelt personally objected to the use of the Deity's name on coins. The motto was restored to the coins by an act of Congress in 1908.

*Designer Augustus Saint-Gaudens; standards same as for previous issue; edge: (1907–1911) 46 raised stars, (1912–1933) 48 raised stars; mints: Philadelphia, Denver, San Francisco.*

**VF-20 VERY FINE**—Bonnet feathers worn near band. Wear visible on high points of hair.

**EF-40 EXTREMELY FINE**—Slight wear on cheekbone and headdress feathers. Slight wear visible on eagle's eye and left wing.

**AU-50 ABOUT UNCIRCULATED**—Trace of wear on hair above eye and on forehead.

**AU-55 CHOICE ABOUT UNCIRCULATED**—Evidence of friction on design high points. Much of original mint luster present.

**MS-60 UNCIRCULATED**—No trace of wear. Light blemishes.

**MS-63 CHOICE UNCIRCULATED**—Some distracting contact marks or blemishes in prime focal areas. Impaired luster possible.

## Variety 1 – No Motto on Reverse (1907–1908)

*Mintmark is above left tip of branch on 1908-D No Motto, and at left of arrow points thereafter.*

# EAGLES

*Gem Uncirculated (MS-65) coins are rare and worth substantial premiums.*

| | Mintage | VF-20 | EF-40 | AU-50 | AU-55 | MS-60 | MS-63 | PF-63 |
|---|---|---|---|---|---|---|---|---|
| 1907, Wire Rim, Periods . . . . . .500 | | | $14,500. | $16,500. | $18,500. | $22,000. | $30,000. | |
| 1907, Rounded Rim, Periods Before and After •E•PLURIBUS• UNUM• (a) . . . . . . . . . . . . .42 | | | 37,500. | 42,500. | 47,500. | 55,000. | 80,000. | — |
| 1907, No Periods . . . . . . . .239,406 | $400. | 450. | 500. | 550. | 650. | 2,800. | |
| 1908, No Motto . . . . . . . . . .33,500 | 425. | 500. | 550. | 600. | 1,050. | 4,000. | |
| 1908D, No Motto . . . . . . .210,000 | 400. | 450. | 500. | 550. | 800. | 6,250. | |

a. 20,000 were minted; all but 42 were melted at the mint.

## Variety 2 – Motto on Reverse (1908–1933)

| | Mintage | VF-20 | EF-40 | AU-50 | AU-55 | MS-60 | MS-63 | MATTE PF-63 |
|---|---|---|---|---|---|---|---|---|
| 1908 . . . . . . . .(116) . . . .341,370 | $400. | $425. | $475. | $500. | $600. | $1,850. | $16,000. |
| 1908D . . . . . . . . . . . . . . .836,500 | 400. | 425. | 475. | 500. | 800. | 6,750. | |
| 1908S . . . . . . . . . . . . . . . .59,850 | 500. | 550. | 700. | 1,000. | 2,750. | 8,750. | |
| 1909 . . . . . . . . .(74) . . . .184,789 | 400. | 425. | 475. | 500. | 600. | 2,250. | 16,500. |
| 1909D . . . . . . . . . . . . . . .121,540 | 400. | 425. | 485. | 550. | 900. | 4,000. | |
| 1909S . . . . . . . . . . . . . . . .292,350 | 400. | 425. | 475. | 500. | 750. | 4,000. | |
| 1910 . . . . . . . .(204) . . . .318,500 | 400. | 425. | 475. | 500. | 600. | 1,300. | 16,500. |
| 1910D . . . . . . . . . . . . . .2,356,640 | 400. | 425. | 475. | 500. | 600. | 1,300. | |
| 1910S . . . . . . . . . . . . . . .811,000 | 400. | 450. | 500. | 525. | 850. | 6,750. | |
| 1911 . . . . . . . . .(95) . . . .505,500 | 400. | 425. | 475. | 500. | 600. | 1,300. | 15,500. |
| 1911D . . . . . . . . . . . . . . .30,100 | 500. | 800. | 1,100. | 1,750. | 4,250. | 18,500. | |
| 1911S . . . . . . . . . . . . . . . .51,000 | 425. | 525. | 700. | 900. | 1,250. | 7,500. | |
| 1912 . . . . . . . . .(83) . . . .405,000 | 400. | 425. | 475. | 500. | 600. | 1,550. | 15,500. |
| 1912S . . . . . . . . . . . . . . .300,000 | 425. | 435. | 500. | 525. | 1,000. | 5,000. | |
| 1913 . . . . . . . . .(71) . . . .442,000 | 400. | 425. | 475. | 500. | 600. | 1,550. | 15,500. |
| 1913S . . . . . . . . . . . . . . . .66,000 | 500. | 750. | 950. | 1,750. | 4,250. | 26,500. | |
| 1914 . . . . . . . . .(50) . . . .151,000 | 400. | 425. | 475. | 500. | 600. | 1,750. | 16,500. |
| 1914D . . . . . . . . . . . . . . .343,500 | 400. | 425. | 475. | 500. | 600. | 1,750. | |
| 1914S . . . . . . . . . . . . . . .208,000 | 400. | 425. | 475. | 500. | 600. | 6,000. | |
| 1915 . . . . . . . . .(75) . . . .351,000 | 400. | 425. | 475. | 500. | 600. | 1,750. | 16,000. |
| 1915S . . . . . . . . . . . . . . . .59,000 | 425. | 675. | 850. | 1,500. | 3,250. | 12,500. | |
| 1916S . . . . . . . . . . . . . . .138,500 | 400. | 450. | 500. | 525. | 900. | 4,500. | |
| 1920S . . . . . . . . . . . . . . .126,500 | 9,500. | 12,000. | 14,500. | 16,500. | 26,500. | 75,000. | |
| 1926 . . . . . . . . . . . . . . .1,014,000 | 400. | 450. | 500. | 525. | 600. | 1,450. | |
| 1930S . . . . . . . . . . . . . . . .96,000 | 8,000. | 9,500. | 10,500. | 12,000. | 14,500. | 28,500. | |
| 1932 . . . . . . . . . . . . . . .4,463,000 | 400. | 450. | 500. | 525. | 600. | 1,450. | |
| 1933 (a) . . . . . . . . . . . . .312,500 | | | | | 180,000. | 225,000. | |

*$718,750, Unc, Stack's auction, Oct-04*

a. Nearly all were melted at the mint.

*Note: Values of common gold coins have been based on the current bullion price of gold, $550 per ounce, and may vary with the prevailing spot price. The net weight and content listed may be used to recalculate bullion value.*

## TYPE COIN VALUES

| | F-12 | VF-20 | EF-40 | MS-60 | MS-63 | MS-65 | PF-63 | PF-65 |
|---|---|---|---|---|---|---|---|---|
| Liberty Head, No Motto, 1849–1866 | $600.+ | $750.+ | $775.+ | $3,250.+ | $12,500.+ | $14,000.+ | $65,000. | $225,000.+ |
| Liberty Head, 1866–1876 | 525.+ | 650.+ | 675.+ | 1,050.+ | 12,000.+ | 95,000.+ | 47,500.+ | 180,000.+ |
| Liberty Head, 1877–1907 | 500.+ | 615.+ | 625.+ | 750.+ | 1,050.+ | 5,750.+ | 22,500.+ | 75,000.+ |
| Saint-Gaudens, RN, HR, 1907 | 6,250.+ | 9,500.+ | 11,500.+ | 17,500.+ | 29,500.+ | 47,500.+ | 32,500.+ | 65,000.+ |
| Saint-Gaudens, 1907–1933 | 560.+ | 625.+ | 635.+ | 700.+ | 900.+ | 1,600.+ | 22,500.+ | 62,500.+ |
| + or – indicates change from previous year | | | | | | | | |

# LIBERTY HEAD (1849–1907)

This largest denomination of all regular United States issues was authorized to be coined by the Act of March 3, 1849. Its weight was 516 grains, .900 fine. The 1849 double eagle is a unique pattern and reposes in the Smithsonian. The 1861 reverse design by Anthony C. Paquet was withdrawn soon after being struck. Very few pieces are known.

*Designer James B. Longacre; weight 33.436 grams; composition .900 gold, .100 copper (net weight: .96750 oz. pure gold); diameter 34 mm; reeded edge; mints: Philadelphia, Carson City, Denver, New Orleans, San Francisco.*

**VF-20 VERY FINE**—LIBERTY on crown bold; prongs on crown defined; lower half worn flat. Hair worn about ear.
**EF-40 EXTREMELY FINE**—Trace of wear on rounded prongs of crown and down hair curls. Minor bagmarks.
**AU-50 ABOUT UNCIRCULATED**—Trace of wear on hair over eye and on coronet.
**AU-55 CHOICE ABOUT UNCIRCULATED**—Evidence of friction on design high points. Some of original mint luster present.
**MS-60 UNCIRCULATED**—No trace of wear. Light blemishes.
**MS-63 CHOICE UNCIRCULATED**—Some distracting contact marks or blemishes in prime focal areas. Impaired luster possible.
**PF-63 CHOICE PROOF**—Reflective surfaces with only a few blemishes in secondary focal areas. No major flaws.

## Without Motto on Reverse (1849–1866)

Mintmark is below eagle.

1853, 3 Over 2

| | Mintage | VF-20 | EF-40 | AU-50 | AU-55 | MS-60 | MS-63 | PF-63 |
|---|---|---|---|---|---|---|---|---|
| 1849 (pattern) | 1 | *(Smithsonian Collection)* | | | | | | |
| 1850 | 1,170,261 | $800. | $1,200. | $2,750. | $4,250. | $10,000. | $52,500. | |
| 1850O | 141,000 | 1,150. | 2,750. | 9,500. | 19,500. | 45,000. | | |
| 1851 | 2,087,155 | 750. | 850. | 1,150. | 1,550. | 4,000. | 22,000. | |
| 1851O | 315,000 | 1,150. | 1,350. | 3,000. | 10,000. | 27,500. | 65,000. | |
| 1852 | 2,053,026 | 725. | 775. | 1,050. | 1,600. | 4,250. | 15,000. | |
| 1852O | 190,000 | 1,150. | 1,300. | 4,250. | 8,000. | 25,000. | 55,000. | |
| 1853, All kinds | 1,261,326 | | | | | | | |
| 1853, 3 Over 2 | | 950. | 1,500. | 4,250. | 7,500. | 32,500. | | |
| 1853 | | 750. | 775. | 1,100. | 1,600. | 5,500. | 28,500. | |
| 1853O | 71,000 | 1,150. | 2,250. | 4,500. | 11,000. | 37,500. | | |

| | Mintage | VF-20 | EF-40 | AU-50 | AU-55 | MS-60 | MS-63 | PF-63 |
|---|---|---|---|---|---|---|---|---|
| 1854, All kinds . . . . . .757,899 | | | | | | | | |
| 1854, Small Date . . . . . . . . . | | $700. | $775. | $1,100. | $1,650. | $6,500. | $30,000. | |
| 1854, Large Date . . . . . . . . . | | 700. | 1,750. | 5,000. | 10,000. | 25,000. | | |
| 1854O . . . . . . . . . . . . .3,250 | | 85,000. | 150,000. | 250,000. | 400,000. | 675,000. | | |
| *$431,250, AU-58, Heritage auction, Jul-05* | | | | | | | | |
| 1854S . . . . . . . . . . . . .141,468 | | 750. | 1,000. | 1,900. | 3,000. | 6,500. | 17,500. | |
| 1855 . . . . . . . . . . . . .364,666 | | 725. | 800. | 1,600. | 2,750. | 11,000. | 42,500. | |
| 1855O . . . . . . . . . . . . . .8,000 | | 4,000. | 9,500. | | | 95,000. | | |
| 1855S . . . . . . . . . . . . .879,675 | | 800. | 900. | 1,500. | 2,500. | 7,000. | 20,000. | |
| 1856 . . . . . . . . . . . . .329,878 | | 700. | 875. | 1,500. | 3,000. | 9,500. | 30,000. | |
| 1856O . . . . . . . . . . . . . .2,250 | | 95,000. | 150,000. | 300,000. | 425,000. | | | |
| *$542,800, SP-63, Heritage auction, Jun-04* | | | | | | | | |
| 1856S . . . . . . . . . . .1,189,750 | | 775. | 850. | 1,400. | 2,500. | 5,500. | 13,500. | |
| 1857 . . . . . . . . . . . . .439,375 | | 725. | 775. | 1,250. | 1,750. | 4,000. | 32,500. | |
| 1857O . . . . . . . . . . . . . .30,000 | | 1,200. | 2,500. | 6,000. | 15,000. | 35,000. | 150,000. | |
| 1857S . . . . . . . . . . . . .970,500 | | 750. | 850. | 1,200. | 2,000. | 4,250. | 7,500. | |
| 1858 . . . . . . . . . . . . .211,714 | | 775. | 900. | 1,400. | 3,000. | 6,000. | 40,000. | |
| 1858O . . . . . . . . . . . . . .35,250 | | | 2,500. | 8,000. | 17,500. | 37,500. | | |
| 1858S . . . . . . . . . . . . .846,710 | | 725. | 1,100. | 1,750. | 3,000. | 10,000. | 42,500. | |
| 1859 . . . . . . . .(80) . . . 43,597 | | 1,000. | 2,500. | 4,500. | 8,000. | 32,500. | | $100,000. |
| 1859O . . . . . . . . . . . . . .9,100 | | 6,000. | 12,500. | 30,000. | 45,000. | 115,000. | | |
| 1859S . . . . . . . . . . . . .636,445 | | 725. | 800. | 1,850. | 3,000. | 6,500. | 65,000. | |
| 1860 . . . . . . .(59) . . 577,670 | | 725. | 800. | 1,100. | 1,450. | 4,000. | 21,000. | 75,000. |
| 1860O . . . . . . . . . . . . . .6,600 | | 5,750. | 12,500. | 30,000. | 45,000. | 125,000. | | |
| 1860S . . . . . . . . . . . . .544,950 | | 975. | 1,500. | 2,000. | 4,000. | 9,000. | 27,500. | |
| 1861 . . . . . . . .(66) 2,976,453 | | 750. | 775. | 1,000. | 1,450. | 3,250. | 12,500. | 75,000. |
| 1861O . . . . . . . . . . . . . .17,741 | | 3,500. | 7,500. | 30,000. | 45,000. | 95,000. | | |
| 1861S . . . . . . . . . . . . .768,000 | | 800. | 1,000. | 2,500. | 4,000. | 12,500. | 60,000. | |

**1861, Normal Obverse**

**1861, Paquet Reverse**

| | Mintage | VF-20 | EF-40 | AU-50 | AU-55 | MS-60 | MS-63 | PF-63 |
|---|---|---|---|---|---|---|---|---|
| 1861, Paquet Rev (Tall Ltrs) | | | | | | $1,000,000. | | |
| *$660,000, MS-67, B&M auction, Nov-88* | | | | | | | | |
| 1861S, Paquet Rev (Tall Ltrs) | | $25,000. | $37,500. | $67,500. | $75,000. | 120,000. | | |
| 1862 . . . . . . .(35) . . . .92,133 | | 1,100. | 2,500. | 6,000. | 8,500. | 20,000. | $42,500. | $65,000. |
| 1862S . . . . . . . . . . . . .854,173 | | 800. | 1,350. | 2,200. | 4,000. | 13,000. | 40,000. | |
| 1863 . . . . . . .(30) . . .142,790 | | 750. | 1,300. | 3,750. | 8,000. | 21,500. | 47,500. | 65,000. |
| 1863S . . . . . . . . . . . . 966,570 | | 750. | 1,000. | 2,250. | 3,000. | 9,000. | 34,500. | |
| 1864 . . . . . . .(50) . . .204,235 | | 750. | 1,000. | 2,750. | 5,000. | 14,500. | 30,000. | 65,000. |
| 1864S . . . . . . . . . . . . .793,660 | | 725. | 900. | 2,250. | 3,500. | 8,500. | 32,500. | |
| 1865 . . . . . . .(25) . . .351,175 | | 725. | 900. | 1,100. | 2,000. | 7,000. | 25,000. | 65,000. |
| 1865S . . . . . . . . . . .1,042,500 | | 725. | 775. | 1,200. | 2,000. | 4,000. | 8,500. | |
| 1866S . . . . . . . . . . . . . *12,000* | | 4,000. | 11,500. | 37,500. | 77,500. | 150,000. | | |

## Motto Above Eagle
### *Value TWENTY D. (1866–1876)*

| | Mintage | VF-20 | EF-40 | AU-50 | AU-55 | MS-60 | MS-63 | PF-63 |
|---|---|---|---|---|---|---|---|---|
| 1866 . . . . . . .(30). . . 698,745 | | $750. | $850. | $1,400. | $2,500. | $6,000. | $32,500. | $50,000. |
| 1866S (a) . . . . . . . . . 842,250 | | 650. | 750. | 2,000. | 5,000. | 18,500. | | |
| 1867 . . . . . . .(50). . . 251,015 | | 650. | 675. | 900. | 1,750. | 2,500. | 19,500. | 50,000. |
| 1867S . . . . . . . . . . . 920,750 | | 650. | 775. | 1,500. | 3,400. | 15,500. | | |
| 1868 . . . . . .(25). . . 98,575 | | 800. | 1,000. | 1,900. | 3,250. | 10,000. | 37,500. | 50,000. |
| 1868S . . . . . . . . . . . 837,500 | | 650. | 750. | 1,250. | 2,400. | 10,000. | | |
| 1869 . . . . . .(25). . . 175,130 | | 700. | 800. | 1,200. | 2,400. | 6,500. | 20,000. | 50,000. |
| 1869S . . . . . . . . . . . 686,750 | | 650. | 750. | 1,150. | 1,950. | 6,500. | 37,500. | |
| 1870 . . . . . . .(35). . . 155,150 | | 700. | 850. | 1,900. | 2,750. | 9,500. | | 50,000. |
| 1870CC. . . . . . . . . . . . 3,789 | | 135,000. | 185,000. | 275,000. | 400,000. | 600,000. | | |
| 1870S . . . . . . . . . . . 982,000 | | 675. | 725. | 900. | 1,300. | 5,250. | 28,500. | |
| 1871 . . . . . . .(30). . . 80,120 | | 725. | 850. | 1,500. | 1,950. | 4,350. | 25,000. | 45,000. |
| 1871CC. . . . . . . . . . . 17,387 | | 7,500. | 11,500. | 25,000. | 35,000. | 55,000. | | |
| 1871S . . . . . . . . . . . 928,000 | | 700. | 750. | 800. | 1,100. | 4,500. | 22,500. | |
| 1872 . . . . . . .(30). . . 251,850 | | 700. | 750. | 800. | 1,200. | 3,250. | 24,500. | 45,000. |
| 1872CC. . . . . . . . . . . 26,900 | | 2,200. | 2,850. | 7,250. | 12,500. | 32,500. | | |
| 1872S . . . . . . . . . . . 780,000 | | 700. | 750. | 775. | 1,150. | 3,100. | 24,500. | |
| 1873, Cl 3 . . .(25) 1,709,800 | | 725. | 800. | 1,100. | 1,350. | 2,850. | | 45,000. |
| 1873, Open 3. . . . . . . . . . .* | | 700. | 750. | 775. | 850. | 1,200. | 12,500. | |
| 1873CC, Close 3 . . . . . 22,410 | | 2,300. | 4,500. | 7,000. | 13,000. | 37,500. | | |
| 1873S, Close 3 . . . . 1,040,600 | | 675. | 700. | 725. | 775. | 1,700. | 21,000. | |
| 1873S, Open 3. . . . . . . . . . .* | | 725. | 775. | 900. | 2,250. | 5,750. | | |
| 1874 . . . . . . .(20). . . 366,780 | | 675. | 700. | 725. | 750. | 1,400. | 19,500. | 50,000. |
| 1874CC. . . . . . . . . . . 115,085 | | 1,300. | 1,600. | 2,500. | 3,500. | 8,500. | | |
| 1874S . . . . . . . . . . . 1,214,000 | | 650. | 675. | 700. | 750. | 1,600. | 27,500. | |
| 1875 . . . . . . .(20). . . 295,720 | | 650. | 675. | 700. | 725. | 1,050. | 12,500. | 85,000. |
| 1875CC. . . . . . . . . . . 111,151 | | 1,250. | 1,500. | 1,850. | 2,150. | 2,950. | 18,500. | |
| 1875S . . . . . . . . . . . 1,230,000 | | 650. | 675. | 700. | 725. | 1,050. | 17,500. | |
| 1876 (b) . . . .(45). . . 583,860 | | 650. | 675. | 700. | 725. | 1,050. | 12,500. | 47,500. |
| 1876CC. . . . . . . . . . . 138,441 | | 1,250. | 1,450. | 1,750. | 2,600. | 5,750. | 33,500. | |
| 1876S . . . . . . . . . . . 1,597,000 | | 650. | 675. | 700. | 725. | 1,050. | 12,000. | |

* Included in number above. **a.** See page 255. **b.** A transitional Proof pattern also exists dated 1876 but of the type of 1877.

### *Value TWENTY DOLLARS (1877–1907)*

# DOUBLE EAGLES

| | Mintage | VF-20 | EF-40 | AU-50 | AU-55 | MS-60 | MS-63 | PF-63 |
|---|---|---|---|---|---|---|---|---|
| 1877 . . . . . . .(20) . . . 397,650 | | $615. | $625. | $635. | $645. | $900. | $11,000. | $32,500. |
| 1877CC. . . . . . . . . . . . 42,565 | | 1,350. | 1,750. | 2,600. | 4,500. | 16,500. | | |
| 1877S . . . . . . . . . . 1,735,000 | | 615. | 625. | 635. | 645. | 850. | 15,000. | |
| 1878 . . . . . . .(20) . . . 543,625 | | 615. | 625. | 635. | 645. | 800. | 9,500. | 35,000. |
| 1878CC. . . . . . . . . . . . 13,180 | | 2,000. | 3,250. | 5,500. | 10,500. | 26,500. | | |
| 1878S . . . . . . . . . . 1,739,000 | | 615. | 625. | 635. | 645. | 850. | 20,000. | |
| 1879 . . . . . . .(30) . . . 207,600 | | 615. | 625. | 635. | 645. | 1,050. | 13,500. | 35,000. |
| 1879CC. . . . . . . . . . . . 10,708 | | 2,100. | 3,750. | 6,500. | 11,000. | 32,500. | | |
| 1879O . . . . . . . . . . . . . 2,325 | | 8,500. | 11,500. | 27,500. | 37,500. | 77,500. | 120,000. | |
| 1879S . . . . . . . . . . 1,223,800 | | 615. | 625. | 635. | 645. | 1,400. | | |
| 1880 . . . . . . .(36) . . . . 51,420 | | 615. | 625. | 635. | 750. | 2,850. | 18,500. | 33,500. |
| 1880S . . . . . . . . . . . 836,000 | | 615. | 625. | 635. | 645. | 1,050. | 15,000. | |
| 1881 . . . . . . .(61) . . . . . 2,199 | | 5,500. | 7,750. | 13,500. | 19,500. | 47,500. | | 33,500. |
| 1881S . . . . . . . . . . . 727,000 | | 615. | 625. | 635. | 645. | 900. | 20,000. | |
| 1882 . . . . . . .(59) . . . . . . 571 | | 9,500. | 23,500. | 39,500. | 43,500. | 75,000. | 125,000. | 33,500. |
| 1882CC. . . . . . . . . . . . 39,140 | | 1,200. | 1,450. | 2,000. | 3,000. | 8,000. | | |
| 1882S . . . . . . . . . . 1,125,000 | | 615. | 625. | 635. | 645. | 825. | 16,000. | |
| 1883, Pf only (92) . . . . . . . . | | | | | | | | 75,000. |
| 1883CC. . . . . . . . . . . . 59,962 | | 1,250. | 1,450. | 2,100. | 2,350. | 5,250. | 21,000. | |
| 1883S . . . . . . . . . . 1,189,000 | | 615. | 625. | 635. | 645. | 800. | 11,500. | |
| 1884, Pf only (71) . . . . . . . . | | | | | | | | 75,000. |
| 1884CC. . . . . . . . . . . . 81,139 | | 1,200. | 1,350. | 1,500. | 1,850. | 2,950. | 23,500. | |
| 1884S . . . . . . . . . . . 916,000 | | 615. | 625. | 635. | 645. | 800. | 6,500. | |
| 1885 . . . . . . .(77) . . . . . . 751 | | 7,750. | 11,000. | 14,500. | 16,500. | 42,500. | 57,500. | 33,500. |
| 1885CC. . . . . . . . . . . . . 9,450 | | 2,250. | 3,250. | 5,250. | 6,750. | 12,500. | 52,500. | |
| 1885S . . . . . . . . . . . 683,500 | | 615. | 625. | 635. | 645. | 750. | 6,500. | |
| 1886 . . . . . .(106) . . . . 1,000 | | 11,500. | 18,000. | 29,500. | 32,500. | 47,500. | 77,500. | 30,000. |
| 1887, Pf only(121) . . . . . . . . | | | | | | | | 45,000. |
| 1887S . . . . . . . . . . . 283,000 | | 615. | 625. | 635. | 645. | 750. | 16,500. | |
| 1888 . . . . . .(105) . . . 226,161 | | 615. | 625. | 635. | 645. | 750. | 6,000. | 24,500. |
| 1888S . . . . . . . . . . . 859,600 | | 615. | 625. | 635. | 645. | 750. | 5,500. | |
| 1889 . . . . . . .(41) . . . . 44,070 | | 615. | 625. | 635. | 650. | 800. | 11,000. | 23,500. |
| 1889CC. . . . . . . . . . . . 30,945 | | 1,300. | 1,450. | 2,350. | 2,500. | 4,250. | 17,500. | |
| 1889S . . . . . . . . . . . 774,700 | | 615. | 625. | 635. | 645. | 750. | 6,750. | |
| 1890 . . . . . . .(55) . . . . 75,940 | | 615. | 625. | 635. | 645. | 750. | 8,000. | 23,000. |
| 1890CC. . . . . . . . . . . . 91,209 | | 1,150. | 1,250. | 1,450. | 1,750. | 2,750. | 32,500. | |
| 1890S . . . . . . . . . . . 802,750 | | 615. | 625. | 635. | 645. | 750. | 9,000. | |
| 1891 . . . . . . .(52) . . . . . 1,390 | | 3,600. | 5,250. | 9,750. | 17,500. | 35,000. | | 23,500. |
| 1891CC. . . . . . . . . . . . . 5,000 | | 3,500. | 7,500. | 9,500. | 11,000. | 19,000. | 45,000. | |
| 1891S . . . . . . . . . . 1,288,125 | | 615. | 625. | 635. | 645. | 750. | 4,000. | |
| 1892 . . . . . . .(93) . . . . . 4,430 | | 1,250. | 1,600. | 2,350. | 3,000. | 6,750. | 19,500. | 22,500. |
| 1892CC. . . . . . . . . . . . 27,265 | | 1,250. | 1,450. | 1,950. | 2,500. | 4,500. | 28,000. | |
| 1892S . . . . . . . . . . . 930,150 | | 615. | 625. | 635. | 645. | 750. | 4,250. | |
| 1893 . . . . . . .(59) . . . 344,280 | | 615. | 625. | 635. | 645. | 750. | 2,500. | 22,500. |
| 1893CC. . . . . . . . . . . . 18,402 | | 1,500. | 1,850. | 2,350. | 2,500. | 4,500. | 21,000. | |
| 1893S . . . . . . . . . . . 996,175 | | 615. | 625. | 635. | 645. | 750. | 3,750. | |
| 1894 . . . . . . .(50) . 1,368,940 | | 615. | 625. | 635. | 645. | 750. | 1,500. | 22,500. |
| 1894S . . . . . . . . . . 1,048,550 | | 615. | 625. | 635. | 645. | 750. | 3,250. | |
| 1895 . . . . . . .(51) . 1,114,605 | | 615. | 625. | 635. | 645. | 750. | 1,300. | 22,500. |
| 1895S . . . . . . . . . . 1,143,500 | | 615. | 625. | 635. | 645. | 750. | 3,250. | |
| 1896 . . . . . .(128) . . . 792,535 | | 615. | 625. | 635. | 645. | 750. | 1,850. | 22,500. |
| 1896S . . . . . . . . . . 1,403,925 | | 615. | 625. | 635. | 645. | 750. | 3,150. | |
| 1897 . . . . . . .(86) . 1,383,175 | | 615. | 625. | 635. | 645. | 750. | 1,250. | 22,500. |
| 1897S . . . . . . . . . . 1,470,250 | | 615. | 625. | 635. | 645. | 750. | 1,350. | |
| 1898 . . . . . . .(75) . . . 170,395 | | 615. | 625. | 635. | 645. | 750. | 6,500. | 22,500. |
| 1898S . . . . . . . . . . 2,575,175 | | 615. | 625. | 635. | 645. | 750. | 1,250. | |
| 1899 . . . . . . .(84) . 1,669,300 | | 615. | 625. | 635. | 645. | 750. | 1,050. | 22,500. |
| 1899S . . . . . . . . . . 2,010,300 | | 615. | 625. | 635. | 645. | 750. | 2,000. | |
| 1900 . . . . . .(124) . 1,874,460 | | 615. | 625. | 635. | 645. | 750. | 1,050. | 22,500. |
| 1900S . . . . . . . . . . 2,459,500 | | 615. | 625. | 635. | 645. | 750. | 2,250. | |
| 1901 . . . . . . .(96) . . . 111,430 | | 615. | 625. | 635. | 645. | 750. | 1,050. | 22,500. |
| 1901S . . . . . . . . . . 1,596,000 | | 615. | 625. | 635. | 645. | 750. | 4,500. | |
| 1902 . . . . . .(114) . . . . 31,140 | | 615. | 625. | 635. | 645. | 950. | 11,500. | 22,500. |
| 1902S . . . . . . . . . . 1,753,625 | | 615. | 625. | 635. | 645. | 750. | 4,250. | |
| 1903 . . . . . .(158) . . . 287,270 | | 615. | 625. | 635. | 645. | 750. | 1,050. | 22,500. |

*Chart continued on next page.*

# DOUBLE EAGLES FEDERAL ISSUES

| | Mintage | VF-20 | EF-40 | AU-50 | AU-55 | MS-60 | MS-63 | PF-63 |
|---|---|---|---|---|---|---|---|---|
| 1903S . . . . . . . . . . . . 954,000 | | $615. | $625. | $635. | $645. | $750. | $1,850. | |
| 1904 . . . . .(98). . . . 6,256,699 | | 615. | 625. | 635. | 645. | 750. | 1,050. | $22,500. |
| 1904S . . . . . . . . . . 5,134,175 | | 615. | 625. | 635. | 645. | 750. | 1,050. | |
| 1905 . . . . .(92) . . . . . .58,919 | | 615. | 625. | 650. | 800. | 1,250. | 13,500. | 22,500. |
| 1905S . . . . . . . . . .1,813,000 | | 615. | 625. | 635. | 645. | 750. | 3,750. | |
| 1906 . . . . .(94) . . . . . .69,596 | | 615. | 625. | 635. | 645. | 850. | 6,500. | 22,500. |
| 1906D. . . . . . . . . . . 620,250 | | 615. | 625. | 635. | 645. | 750. | 3,000. | |
| 1906S . . . . . . . . . .2,065,750 | | 615. | 625. | 635. | 645. | 750. | 2,500. | |
| 1907 . . . . .(78). . . . 1,451,786 | | 615. | 625. | 635. | 645. | 750. | 1,050. | 22,500. |
| 1907D. . . . . . . . . . . 842,250 | | 615. | 625. | 635. | 645. | 750. | 2,250. | |
| 1907S . . . . . . . . . .2,165,800 | | 615. | 625. | 635. | 645. | 750. | 2,250. | |

## SAINT-GAUDENS (1907–1933)

Many consider the twenty-dollar gold piece designed by Augustus Saint-Gaudens to be the most beautiful U.S. coin. The first coins issued were slightly more than 12,000 high-relief pieces struck for general circulation. The relief is much higher than for later issues, and the date 1907 is in Roman numerals (MCMVII). A few of the Proof coins were made using the lettered-edge collar from the ultra high relief version. These can be distinguished by a pronounced bottom left serif on the N in UNUM, and other minor differences. High-relief Proofs are trial or experimental pieces. Flat-relief double eagles were issued later in 1907 with Arabic numerals, and continued through 1933.

The field of the rare, ultra high relief experimental pieces is excessively concave and connects directly with the edge without any border, giving it a sharp, knifelike appearance; Liberty's skirt shows two folds on the side of her right leg; the Capitol building in the background at left is very small; the sun, on the reverse side, has 14 rays, as opposed to the 13 rays on regular high-relief coins.

The Proof finish of 1908 and 1911 through 1915 coins was originally referred to as Sand Blast Proof by the Mint. Proof coins minted in 1909 and 1910 have a different finish described as Satin Proof. In addition, double eagles from 1907 through 1911 have 46 stars on the obverse; and from 1912 through 1933, 48 stars.

*Designer Augustus Saint-Gaudens; standards same as for previous issue; edge: E PLURIBUS UNUM with words divided by stars (one specimen of the high-relief variety with plain edge is known); mints: Philadelphia, Denver, San Francisco.*

**VF-20 VERY FINE**—Minor wear on Liberty's legs and toes. Eagle's left wing and breast feathers worn.
**EF-40 EXTREMELY FINE**—Drapery lines on chest visible. Wear on left breast, knee, and below. Eagle's feathers on breast and right wing bold.
**AU-50 ABOUT UNCIRCULATED**—Trace of wear on nose, breast, and knee. Wear visible on eagle's wings.
**MS-60 UNCIRCULATED**—No trace of wear. Light marks or blemishes.

## Ultra High Relief Pattern, MCMVII (1907)

| | PF-67 |
|---|---|
| 1907, Ultra High Relief, Plain Edge *(unique)* . . . . . . . . . . . . . . . . . . . . . . . . . . . . . . . . . . . | — |
| 1907, Ultra High Relief, Lettered Edge  *$2,990,000, PF-69, Heritage auction, Nov-05* . . . . . | $2,000,000. |

# Without Motto IN GOD WE TRUST (1907–1908)
## *High Relief, MCMVII (1907)*

| | Mintage | VF-20 | EF-40 | AU-50 | AU-55 | MS-60 | MS-63 |
|---|---|---|---|---|---|---|---|
| 1907, High Relief, Roman Numerals (MCMVII), Wire Rim . .12,367 | | $9,500. | $11,500. | $12,500. | $13,500. | $17,500. | $29,500. |
| *$575,000, MS-69, Heritage auction, Nov-05* | | | | | | | |
| 1907, Same, Flat Rim . . . . . . . . .* | | 9,500. | 11,500. | 12,500. | 13,500. | 17,500. | 29,500. |

\* Included in number above.

## *Arabic Numerals, No Motto (1907–1908)*

*Mintmark is on obverse, above date.*

| | Mintage | VF-20 | EF-40 | AU-50 | AU-55 | MS-60 | MS-63 |
|---|---|---|---|---|---|---|---|
| 1907, Arabic Numerals . . .361,667 | | $625. | $635. | $645. | $655. | $725. | $1,250. |
| 1908 . . . . . . . . . . . . . . .4,271,551 | | 625. | 635. | 645. | 655. | 700. | 900. |
| 1908D . . . . . . . . . . . . . .663,750 | | 625. | 635. | 645. | 655. | 700. | 1,150. |

# With Motto IN GOD WE TRUST (1908–1933)

1909, 9 Over 8

# DOUBLE EAGLES

| | Mintage | VF-20 | EF-40 | AU-50 | AU-55 | MS-60 | MS-63 | MATTE PF-63 |
|---|---|---|---|---|---|---|---|---|
| 1908 . . . . . . . .(101) . . . . 156,258 | | $625. | $635. | $645. | $655. | $750. | $1,900. | $22,500. |
| 1908D . . . . . . . . . . . . . .349,500 | | 625. | 635. | 645. | 655. | 725. | 1,450. | |
| 1908S . . . . . . . . . . . . . . .22,000 | | 1,250. | 1,850. | 2,800. | 4,000. | 7,750. | 18,500. | |
| 1909, All kinds . .(67) . . . 161,282 | | | | | | | | |
| 1909, 9 Over 8 . . . . . . . . . . . . | | 625. | 635. | 700. | 800. | 1,400. | 7,500. | |
| 1909 . . . . . . . . . . . . . . . . . . . . | | 625. | 635. | 645. | 655. | 750. | 4,000. | 22,500. |
| 1909D . . . . . . . . . . . . . .52,500 | | 625. | 635. | 825. | 1,050. | 1,800. | 8,000. | |
| 1909S . . . . . . . . . . . . .2,774,925 | | 625. | 635. | 645. | 655. | 700. | 900. | |
| 1910 . . . . . . . .(167) . . . 482,000 | | 625. | 635. | 645. | 655. | 700. | 900. | 22,500. |
| 1910D . . . . . . . . . . . . . .429,000 | | 625. | 635. | 645. | 655. | 700. | 900. | |
| 1910S . . . . . . . . . . . . .2,128,250 | | 625. | 635. | 645. | 655. | 700. | 1,000. | |
| 1911 . . . . . . . .(100) . . . 197,250 | | 625. | 650. | 655. | 675. | 725. | 2,450. | 22,500. |
| 1911D . . . . . . . . . . . . . .846,500 | | 625. | 635. | 645. | 655. | 700. | 900. | |
| 1911S . . . . . . . . . . . . . .775,750 | | 625. | 635. | 645. | 655. | 700. | 900. | |
| 1912 . . . . . . . . .(74) . . . 149,750 | | 625. | 635. | 645. | 655. | 700. | 1,750. | 22,500. |
| 1913 . . . . . . . . .(58) . . . 168,780 | | 625. | 635. | 645. | 655. | 700. | 3,250. | 22,500. |
| 1913D . . . . . . . . . . . . . .393,500 | | 625. | 635. | 645. | 655. | 700. | 900. | |
| 1913S . . . . . . . . . . . . . . .34,000 | | 700. | 850. | 950. | 1,050. | 1,400. | 4,500. | |
| 1914 . . . . . . . . .(70) . . . .95,250 | | 625. | 635. | 645. | 655. | 725. | 2,750. | 22,500. |
| 1914D . . . . . . . . . . . . . .453,000 | | 625. | 635. | 645. | 655. | 700. | 900. | |
| 1914S . . . . . . . . . . . . .1,498,000 | | 625. | 635. | 645. | 655. | 700. | 900. | |
| 1915 . . . . . . . . .(50) . . . 152,000 | | 625. | 635. | 645. | 655. | 875. | 2,450. | 22,500. |
| 1915S . . . . . . . . . . . . . .567,500 | | 625. | 635. | 645. | 655. | 700. | 900. | |
| 1916S . . . . . . . . . . . . . .796,000 | | 625. | 635. | 645. | 655. | 700. | 1,050. | |
| 1920 . . . . . . . . . . . . . . .228,250 | | 625. | 635. | 645. | 655. | 700. | 1,050. | |
| 1920S . . . . . . . . . . . . . .558,000 | | 11,000. | 16,500. | 23,500. | 28,500. | 39,500. | 72,500. | |
| 1921 . . . . . . . . . . . . . . .528,500 | | 18,500. | 25,000. | 32,500. | 40,000. | 85,000. | 175,000. | |
| *$1,092,500, MS-66, Heritage auction, Nov-05* | | | | | | | | |
| 1922 . . . . . . . . . . . . .1,375,500 | | 625. | 635. | 645. | 655. | 700. | 900. | |
| 1922S . . . . . . . . . . . . .2,658,000 | | 750. | 850. | 1,100. | 1,350. | 2,250. | 4,000. | |
| 1923 . . . . . . . . . . . . . . .566,000 | | 625. | 635. | 645. | 655. | 700. | 900. | |
| 1923D . . . . . . . . . . . . .1,702,250 | | 625. | 635. | 645. | 655. | 700. | 900. | |
| 1924 . . . . . . . . . . . . .4,323,500 | | 625. | 635. | 645. | 655. | 700. | 900. | |
| 1924D . . . . . . . . . . . . .3,049,500 | | 1,100. | 1,500. | 1,750. | 2,000. | 3,000. | 8,000. | |
| 1924S . . . . . . . . . . . . .2,927,500 | | 1,100. | 1,500. | 1,750. | 2,100. | 3,000. | 8,000. | |
| 1925 . . . . . . . . . . . . .2,831,750 | | 625. | 635. | 645. | 655. | 700. | 900. | |
| 1925D . . . . . . . . . . . . .2,938,500 | | 1,600. | 2,400. | 2,600. | 2,800. | 3,750. | 11,000. | |
| 1925S . . . . . . . . . . . . .3,776,500 | | 1,500. | 2,300. | 2,500. | 3,250. | 8,500. | 24,500. | |
| 1926 . . . . . . . . . . . . . . .816,750 | | 625. | 635. | 645. | 655. | 700. | 900. | |
| 1926D . . . . . . . . . . . . . .481,000 | | 3,500. | 5,500. | 9,000. | 10,000. | 13,500. | 30,000. | |
| 1926S . . . . . . . . . . . . .2,041,500 | | 1,200. | 1,500. | 2,000. | 2,250. | 2,500. | 5,000. | |
| 1927 . . . . . . . . . . . . .2,946,750 | | 625. | 635. | 645. | 655. | 700. | 900. | |
| 1927D . . . . . . . . . . . . . .180,000 | | | | 500,000. | 600,000. | 750,000. | 1,000,000. | |
| *$1,897,500, MS-67, Heritage auction, Nov-05* | | | | | | | | |
| 1927S . . . . . . . . . . . . .3,107,000 | | | | 8,000. | 9,000. | 15,000. | 52,500. | |
| 1928 . . . . . . . . . . . . .8,816,000 | | 625. | 635. | 645. | 655. | 700. | 900. | |
| 1929 . . . . . . . . . . . . .1,779,750 | | | | 9,500. | 11,500. | 14,500. | 25,000. | |
| 1930S . . . . . . . . . . . . . . .74,000 | | | | 25,000. | 27,500. | 37,500. | 95,000. | |
| 1931 . . . . . . . . . . . . .2,938,250 | | | | 13,500. | 16,000. | 23,500. | 47,500. | |
| 1931D . . . . . . . . . . . . . .106,500 | | | | 14,000. | 16,000. | 26,500. | 47,500. | |
| 1932 . . . . . . . . . . . . .1,101,750 | | | | 15,000. | 17,500. | 25,000. | 40,000. | |
| 1933 *(ex. rare)* **(a)** . . . . . .445,500 | | | | | | | | |
| *$7,590,020, Gem BU, Sotheby's/Stack's auction, Jul-02* | | | | | | | | |

a. All were to have been melted at the mint. Today 13 are known to have survived. Only one has ever been on the market.

Commemorative coins have been popular since the days of the Greeks and Romans. In the beginning they served to record and honor important events, and in the absence of newspapers they proved highly useful in passing along news of the day.

Many modern nations have issued commemorative coins, and such pieces are highly esteemed by collectors. No nation has surpassed the United States when it comes to commemorative coins.

The unique position occupied by commemoratives in United States coinage is largely due to the fact that, with few exceptions, all commemorative coins have real historical significance. The progress and advance of people in the New World are presented in an interesting and instructive manner on the commemorative issues. Such a record of facts artistically presented on U.S. gold and silver memorial issues appeals strongly to the collector who favors the historical side of numismatics. It is the historical features of the commemoratives, in fact, that create interest among many people who would otherwise have little interest in coins.

Commemorative issues are considered for coinage by two committees of Congress: the Committee on Banking, Housing, and Urban Affairs; and the Committee on Banking and Financial Services of the House; as well as the Citizens Coin Advisory Committee. Congress is guided to a great extent by the reports of these committees when passing upon bills authorizing commemorative coins.

These special coins are usually issued either to commemorate events or to help pay for monuments or celebrations that commemorate historical persons, places, or things. A commemorative coin is offered in most instances by a commission in charge of the event to be commemorated, and sold at a price in advance of the face value of the piece. All are of the standard weight and fineness of traditional gold, silver, or clad coins, and all are legal tender.

Commemorative coins are popularly collected either by major types or in sets with mintmark varieties. During many years, no special commemorative coins were issued. Some regular coins, such as the Lincoln cent of 1909, Washington quarter of 1932 and 1999 through 2008; nickels of 2004 through 2005; and Bicentennial issues of 1976 are also commemorative in nature.

Unless otherwise stated, the coinage figures given represent the total outstanding mintage. In many cases, larger quantities were minted but were not all sold. The unsold coins were usually returned to the mint and melted, although some were placed in circulation at face value. A limited number of Proof strikings or presentation pieces were made for some of the 1892 through 1954 issues. All are very rare and valuable.

## Alphabetical Reference to Dates for Commemoratives and Sets

Edison, Thomas A., 2004*
Eisenhower Centennial, 1990
Elgin, IL, Centennial, 1936
Ericson, Leif, Millennium, 2000*
First Flight Bicentennial, 2003
Fort Vancouver Centennial, 1925
Franklin, Benjamin, 2006*
Gettysburg, Battle of, 1936
Grant Memorial, 1922
Hawaiian Sesquicentennial, 1928
Hudson, NY, Sesquicentennial, 1935
Huguenot-Walloon Tercentenary, 1924
Illinois Centennial, 1918
Iowa Centennial, 1946
Isabella Quarter Dollar, 1893
Jefferson, Thomas, 1993 (1994)*
Kennedy, Robert F., 1998*
Korean War Memorial, 1991
Lafayette Dollar, 1900
Lewis and Clark Bicentennial, 2004*
Lewis and Clark Exposition, 1904–1905
Lexington-Concord Sesquicentennial, 1925
Library of Congress Bicentennial, 2000
Long Island Tercentenary, 1936
Louisiana Purchase Exposition, 1903
Lynchburg, VA, Sesquicentennial, 1936
Madison, Dolley, 1999*
Maine Centennial, 1920
Marine Corps 230th Anniversary, 2005*
Marshall, John, 2005*
Maryland Tercentenary, 1934
McKinley Memorial, 1916–1917
Missouri Centennial, 1921
Monroe Doctrine Centennial, 1923
Mt. Rushmore Golden Anniversary, 1991*
National Law Enforcement Officers, 1997*
National Community Service, 1996*
National Prisoners of War, 1994
New Rochelle, NY, 250th, 1938
Norfolk, VA, Bicentennial, 1936
Old Spanish Trail, 1935

Olympics:
 1983–1984 (Los Angeles)*
 1988 (Seoul)*
 1992 (XXV/25th)*
 1995 (Centennial)*
 2002 (Salt Lake)*
Oregon Trail Memorial, 1926–1939
Panama-Pacific Exposition, 1915
Pilgrim Tercentenary, 1920–1921
Police Memorial, 1997
P.O.W.s, U.S., 1994
Providence, RI, Tercentenary, 1936
Roanoke Island, NC, 350th, 1937
Robinson, Jackie, 1997*
Robinson–Arkansas Centennial, 1936
Roosevelt, Franklin D. 1997
San Francisco–Oakland Bay Bridge, 1936
Shriver / Special Olympics, 1995*
Smithsonian 150th Anniversary, 1996*
Spanish Trail, Old, 1935
Special Olympics, 1995*
Statue of Liberty, 1986*
Stone Mountain Memorial, 1925
Texas Centennial, 1934–1938
U.S. Capitol Bicentennial, 1994
United Service Organizations, 1991
Vermont Sesquicentennial, 1927
Vietnam Veterans, 1994*
Washington, Booker T., 1946–1951; 1951–1954
Washington, George, 1982
 Bicentennial of Death, 1999*
West Point Bicentennial, 2002
White House 200th Anniversary, 1992
Wisconsin Territorial Centennial, 1936
Women in Military Service, 1994
World Cup (Soccer) Tournament, 1994*
World War II 50th Anniversary, 1991–1995
World War II, 1993*
Yellowstone National Park, 1999*
York County, ME, Tercentenary, 1936

* See also in "Government Commemorative Sets."

## PRICE PERFORMANCE

Few people would ever guess, or even believe, that this country once issued an official half dollar bearing the portrait of P.T. Barnum, the famous impresario to whom the saying "There's a sucker born every minute" was misattributed. He had nothing to do with the coins, which were made in 1936 (long after his death), but the exceptional honor and the fact that the fifty-cent coins were sold to the public for $2 each would have made him smile about bilking the public one last time.

Barnum did not have the last laugh in this matter. Those people who were fortunate enough to buy one of the original coins in 1936, and to save it in Mint State, find that today their treasure is worth more than $200! Only 25,000 of the pieces were made, and at the time they were not very popular even with the few people who ever heard about them.

The Bridgeport commemorative half dollar with P.T. Barnum's portrait is but one of many different designs that have been used on special coins made for collectors since 1892. During that time, commemorative coins have been issued to celebrate the founding of cities, to mark expositions, to honor famous citizens and presidents, and even to promote Olympic contests in recent years. These coins are not normally placed in circulation, and are usually distributed by some agency at a price over face value with the surplus going to fund the event being celebrated. All commemorative coins made since 1982 have been distributed through the Mint with proceeds going directly to the government, and from there, to the various sponsoring organizations.

It has mostly been in recent years that the general public has learned about commemorative coins. They have long been popular with coin collectors who enjoy the artistry and history associated with them, as well as the tremendous profit that they have made from owning these rare pieces. Very few of them ever reached circulation because they were all originally sold above face value, and because they are all so rare. Most of the early issues were of the half dollar denomination, and were usually made in quantities of fewer than 20,000 pieces. This is minuscule when compared to the regular half dollar pieces that are made by the millions each year, and still rarely seen in circulation.

At the beginning of 1988, prices of commemoratives in MS-65 condition had risen so high that most collectors had to content themselves with pieces in lower grades. Investors continued to apply pressure to the high-quality pieces, driving prices even higher, while the collector community went after coins in grades from About Uncirculated to MS-63. For several months the pressure from both influences caused prices to rise very rapidly for all issues and grades of commemoratives without even taking the price-adjustment breather that usually goes along with such activity.

By 1990, prices dropped to the point that several of the commemoratives began to look like bargains once again. Many of the MS-65 pieces held firm at price levels above the $3,000 mark, but others were still available at under $500 even for coins of similar mintage. Coins in MS-63 or MS-64 were priced at but a fraction of the MS-65 prices, which would seem to make them reasonably priced because the demand for these pieces is universal, and not keyed simply to grade, rarity, or speculator pressure.

Historically, the entire series of commemorative coins has frequently undergone a roller-coaster cycle of price adjustments. These cycles have usually been of short duration, lasting from months to years, with prices always recovering and eventually exceeding previous levels.

## CLASSIC COMMEMORATIVE SILVER AND GOLD
### (1892–1893) World's Columbian Exposition

The first United States commemorative coin was the Columbian half dollar designed by Olin Lewis Warner. Charles E. Barber engraved the obverse, showing the bust of Columbus; and George T. Morgan engraved the reverse, a representation of Columbus's flagship the *Santa Maria* above two hemispheres. The coins were sold for $1 each at the World's Columbian Exposition in Chicago during 1893. A great many remained unsold and a substantial quantity was later released for circulation at face value. Approximately 100 brilliant Proofs were struck for each date.

| | Mintage | AU-50 | MS-60 | MS-63 | MS-65 |
|---|---|---|---|---|---|
| 1892, Columbian Exposition | 950,000 | $15. | $32. | $85. | $710. |
| 1893, Same type | 1,550,405 | 14. | 28. | 80. | 850. |

## (1893) World's Columbian Exposition, Isabella Quarter

In 1893, the Board of Lady Managers of the Columbian Exposition petitioned for a souvenir quarter dollar. Authority was granted March 3, 1893. The coin known as the *Isabella quarter* was designed by Charles E. Barber. These souvenir quarters were sold for $1. The obverse has the crowned bust of Queen Isabella of Spain. The kneeling female on the reverse with distaff and spindle is emblematic of women's industry.

| | Mintage | AU-50 | MS-60 | MS-63 | MS-65 |
|---|---|---|---|---|---|
| 1893, Columbian Exposition, Chicago | 24,214 | $575. | $685. | $900. | $3,250. |

## (1900) Lafayette Dollar

The heads of Washington and Lafayette appear on this issue, which was the first commemorative coin of one-dollar denomination, and the first authorized United States coin to bear a portrait of a U.S. president. The dies were prepared by Charles E. Barber. The statue on the reverse is similar to the monument of General Lafayette that was erected in Paris as a gift of the American people. The coins were sold by the Lafayette Memorial Commission for $2 each.

| | Mintage | AU-50 | MS-60 | MS-63 | MS-65 |
|---|---|---|---|---|---|
| 1900, Lafayette | 36,026 | $575. | $850. | $1,950. | $9,500. |

## (1903) Louisiana Purchase Exposition

The first souvenir gold coins were authorized for the Louisiana Purchase Exposition, held in St. Louis in 1904. There are two varieties of the gold dollar—one with the head of Jefferson, who was president when the Louisiana Territory was purchased from France, and the other with President William McKinley, who sanctioned the exposition. The reverse is the same for each variety. The designs were by Charles E. Barber.

| | Mintage | AU-50 | MS-60 | MS-63 | MS-65 |
|---|---|---|---|---|---|
| 1903, Louisiana Purchase/Thomas Jefferson .........17,500 | | $650. | $750. | $1,000. | $3,200. |
| 1903, Louisiana Purchase/William McKinley ..........17,500 | | 650. | 750. | 1,000. | 3,200. |

*Note: Proofs exist of each type.*

## (1904–1905) Lewis and Clark Exposition

The Lewis and Clark Centennial Exposition was held in Portland, Oregon, in 1905. A souvenir issue of gold dollars was struck to mark the event with the dates 1904 and 1905. The two famous explorers are represented on either side of the coin, which was designed by Charles E. Barber. A bronze memorial of the Indian guide, Sacagawea, who assisted in the famous expedition, was erected in Portland, Oregon, and financed by the sale of these coins.

| | Mintage | AU-50 | MS-60 | MS-63 | MS-65 |
|---|---|---|---|---|---|
| 1904, Lewis and Clark Exposition .......10,025 | | $950. | $1,000. | $2,200. | $10,000. |
| 1905, Lewis and Clark Exposition .......10,041 | | 1,200. | 1,400. | 2,700. | 18,000. |

## (1915) Panama-Pacific Exposition

This half dollar was designed by Charles E. Barber (obverse) and George T. Morgan (reverse). The exposition held in San Francisco in 1915 celebrated the opening of the Panama Canal. The coins were struck at the San Francisco Mint and were sold at $1 each during the exposition. A representation of Columbia with the golden gate in the background is the principal feature of the obverse. The Panama-Pacific coins were the first commemorative coins to carry the motto IN GOD WE TRUST, which appears above the eagle.

| | Mintage | AU-50 | MS-60 | MS-63 | MS-65 |
|---|---|---|---|---|---|
| 1915S, Panama-Pacific Exposition .......27,134 | | $425. | $500. | $725. | $2,600. |

Charles Keck designed the gold dollar, the obverse of which has the head of a man, representing a Panama Canal laborer. Two dolphins encircle ONE DOLLAR on the reverse.

The quarter eagle was the work of Charles E. Barber and George T. Morgan. The obverse shows Columbia with a caduceus in her left hand seated on a hippocampus, signifying the use of the Panama Canal. An American eagle with raised wings is shown on the reverse.

| | Mintage | AU-50 | MS-60 | MS-63 | MS-65 |
|---|---|---|---|---|---|
| 1915S, Panama-Pacific Exposition, $1 ....15,000 | | $625. | $700. | $900. | $2,800. |
| 1915S, Panama-Pacific Exposition, $2.50 ...6,749 | | 1,550. | 1,800. | 3,800. | 7,000. |

The fifty-dollar gold piece was designed by Robert Aitken and was issued in both round and octagonal form. The obverse bears a helmeted head of Minerva; the owl, symbol of wisdom, is on the reverse. The octagonal issue has eight dolphins in the angles on both sides. Other devices are smaller on the octagonal variety.

| | Mintage | AU-50 | MS-60 | MS-63 | MS-65 |
|---|---|---|---|---|---|
| 1915S, Panama-Pacific, Round ...........483 | | $30,000. | $42,500. | $65,000. | $135,000. |

| | Mintage | AU-50 | MS-60 | MS-63 | MS-65 |
|---|---|---|---|---|---|
| 1915S, Panama-Pacific, Octagonal .........645 | | $28,000. | $40,000. | $60,000. | $120,000. |

## (1916–1917) McKinley Memorial

The sale of the McKinley dollars aided in paying for a memorial building at Niles, Ohio, the martyred president's birthplace. The obverse, showing a profile of McKinley, was designed by Charles E. Barber; the reverse, with the memorial building, was designed by George T. Morgan.

| | Mintage | AU-50 | MS-60 | MS-63 | MS-65 |
|---|---|---|---|---|---|
| 1916, McKinley Memorial . . . . . . . . . . . . .15,000 | $625. | $675. | $800. | $2,800. |
| 1917, McKinley Memorial . . . . . . . . . . . . .5,000 | 700. | 750. | 1,100. | 3,750. |

## (1918) Illinois Centennial

This coin was authorized to commemorate the 100th anniversary of the admission of Illinois into the Union, and was the first souvenir piece for such an event. The obverse was designed by George T. Morgan and the reverse by J.R. Sinnock. The obverse shows the head of Lincoln taken from the statue by Andrew O'Connor in Springfield, Illinois. The reverse is based on the Illinois State Seal.

| | Mintage | AU-50 | MS-60 | MS-63 | MS-65 |
|---|---|---|---|---|---|
| 1918, Illinois Centennial . . . . . . . . . . . . . .100,058 | $125. | $145. | $160. | $475. |

## (1920) Maine Centennial

Congress authorized the Maine Centennial half dollar on May 10, 1920, to be sold at the centennial celebration at Portland. They were received too late for this event and were sold by the state treasurer for many years. Anthony de Francisci modeled this coin from a design by Harry H. Cochrane. The obverse device is the arms of the state of Maine; the Latin word DIRIGO means "I Direct."

| | Mintage | AU-50 | MS-60 | MS-63 | MS-65 |
|---|---|---|---|---|---|
| 1920, Maine Centennial . . . . . . . . . . . . . .50,028 | $125. | $155. | $195. | $550. |

## (1920–1921) Pilgrim Tercentenary

To commemorate the landing of the Pilgrims at Plymouth, Massachusetts, in 1620, Congress authorized a special half dollar on May 12, 1920. Cyrus E. Dallin, a Boston sculptor, executed the designs furnished to him by the commission. His initial D is placed below Bradford's elbow. The obverse has a portrait of Governor Bradford; the reverse shows the *Mayflower*. The first issue had no date on the obverse. The coins struck in 1921 show that date in addition to 1620–1920. There was a large coinage of both issues, and not all were sold. A total of 128,000 were returned to the mint and melted.

**With 1921 in Field on Obverse**

| | Mintage | AU-50 | MS-60 | MS-63 | MS-65 |
|---|---|---|---|---|---|
| 1920, Pilgrim Tercentenary . . . . . . . . . . . .152,112 | | $80. | $100. | $120. | $450. |
| 1921, Same, With Date Added in Field . . . .20,053 | | 165. | 195. | 200. | 580. |

## (1921) Missouri Centennial

The 100th anniversary of the admission of Missouri to the Union was celebrated at Sedalia during August 1921. To mark the occasion, Congress authorized the coinage of a fifty-cent piece. Robert Aitken designed the coin, which shows the bust of a frontiersman on the obverse, and another frontiersman and Indian on the reverse. The first coins struck show 2★4 incused, indicating that Missouri was the 24th star in the flag. The type without this marking was struck later, but was the first to be sold.

**2★4 in Field**

| | Mintage | AU-50 | MS-60 | MS-63 | MS-65 |
|---|---|---|---|---|---|
| 1921, Missouri Centennial, "2★4" in Field . .5,000 | | $580. | $725. | $1,050. | $5,100. |
| 1921, Missouri Centennial, Plain . . . . . . . . .15,428 | | 375. | 575. | 875. | 5,200. |

## (1921) Alabama Centennial

The Alabama half dollars were authorized in 1920 for the centennial, which was celebrated in 1919, but they were not struck until 1921. The coins, designed by Laura Gardin Fraser, were offered first during President Harding's visit to Birmingham, October 26, 1921. The St. Andrew's cross, an emblem on the state flag,

**2X2 in Field**

appears on a part of the issue between the two's in "2X2," indicating the 22nd state of the Union. The obverse has busts of William Wyatt Bibb, first governor of Alabama, and T.E. Kilby, governor at the time of the centennial. This is the first instance of the use of a living person's portrait on a United States coin.

*See next page for chart.*    

| | Mintage | AU-50 | MS-60 | MS-63 | MS-65 |
|---|---|---|---|---|---|
| 1921, Alabama Centennial, Plain . . . . . . . . .59,038 | | $180. | $230. | $500. | $2,100. |
| 1921, Alabama Centennial, With "2X2" in Field of Obverse . . . . . . . . . . . . . . . .6,006 | | 280. | 325. | 600. | 2,400. |

## (1922) Grant Memorial

This coin was struck during 1922 as a centenary souvenir of Ulysses S. Grant's birth. A star that appeared on the first issues was later removed, creating a second variety. The star has no particular significance. Laura Gardin Fraser designed both the Grant half dollar and gold dollar. The reverse shows the frame house in Point Pleasant, Ohio, where Grant was born on April 27, 1822.

**Stars in Obverse Field**
*Fake stars usually have flattened spot on reverse.*

| | Mintage | AU-50 | MS-60 | MS-63 | MS-65 |
|---|---|---|---|---|---|
| 1922, Grant Memorial, Star in Obv Field . . . .4,256 | | $900. | $1,300. | $1,800. | $7,500. |
| 1922, Same type, No Star in Field . . . . . . .67,405 | | 110. | 125. | 160. | 785. |

Like the half-dollar commemorative coins, the gold dollars were first issued with a star which was removed for the later issues. The designs by Laura Gardin Fraser are the same as for the half-dollar coinage.

*Star*

| | Mintage | AU-50 | MS-60 | MS-63 | MS-65 |
|---|---|---|---|---|---|
| 1922, Grant Memorial, With Star . . . . . . . . .5,016 | | $1,700. | $1,800. | $2,100. | $4,300. |
| 1922, Grant Memorial, No Star . . . . . . . . . .5,000 | | 1,700. | 1,800. | 2,100. | 4,300. |

## (1923) Monroe Doctrine Centennial

The motion picture industry promoted this issue in conjunction with a motion picture exposition in June 1923. The obverse shows the heads of James Monroe and John Quincy Adams, who were identified with the Monroe Doctrine. The Western Hemisphere is portrayed on the reverse in forms that suggest two female figures. Chester Beach prepared the models for this coin.

| | Mintage | AU-50 | MS-60 | MS-63 | MS-65 |
|---|---|---|---|---|---|
| 1923S, Monroe Doctrine Centennial . . . . .274,077 | | $54. | $72. | $150. | $3,000. |

## **(1924) Huguenot-Walloon Tercentenary**

Settling of the Huguenots and Walloons in the New World was the occasion commemorated by this issue. New Netherland, now New York, was founded in 1624 by a group of Dutch colonists. The persons represented on the obverse were not directly concerned with the occasion, however. They are Admiral Coligny and William the Silent. The reverse shows the vessel *Nieuw Nederland*. George T. Morgan prepared the models for this coin.

| | Mintage | AU-50 | MS-60 | MS-63 | MS-65 |
|---|---|---|---|---|---|
| 1924, Huguenot-Walloon Tercentenary . . .142,080 | | $130. | $140. | $185. | $520. |

## **(1925) Lexington-Concord Sesquicentennial**

The two famous battles fought in 1775 are commemorated on this coin. A statue of the familiar Minute Man is depicted on the obverse, and the Old Belfry at Lexington is the reverse device. Chester Beach designed the coin. The famous statue by Daniel Chester French located in Concord was used for the design.

| | Mintage | AU-50 | MS-60 | MS-63 | MS-65 |
|---|---|---|---|---|---|
| 1925, Lexington-Concord Sesquicentennial . . . . . . . . . . . . . . .162,013 | | $85. | $100. | $120. | $600. |

## **(1925) Stone Mountain Memorial**

The models for this coin were prepared by Gutzon Borglum. The first coins were struck at Philadelphia on January 21, 1925, General Thomas "Stonewall" Jackson's birthday. Generals Robert E. Lee and Jackson, mounted, are shown on the obverse. The funds received from the sale of this large issue of half dollars were devoted to the expense of carving figures of Confederate leaders and soldiers

on Stone Mountain in Georgia. The carving was completed and dedicated in 1970. Some of these coins were counterstamped on the reverse by the issuing commission, with letters and numbers for distribution to individual state sales agencies. These are valued much higher than normal coins.

| | Mintage | AU-50 | MS-60 | MS-63 | MS-65 |
|---|---|---|---|---|---|
| 1925, Stone Mountain Memorial . . . . . .1,314,709 | | $63. | $75. | $90. | $250. |

## (1925) California Diamond Jubilee

The California half dollar was designed by Jo Mora, a noted California sculptor. The obverse bears a kneeling figure of a Forty-Niner. The reverse shows a walking grizzly bear, the state emblem. The celebration for which these coins were struck marked the 75th anniversary of the admission of California into the Union.

| | Mintage | AU-50 | MS-60 | MS-63 | MS-65 |
|---|---|---|---|---|---|
| 1925S, California Diamond Jubilee | 86,394 | $160. | $200. | $230. | $1,100. |

## (1925) Fort Vancouver Centennial

John McLoughlin, shown on the obverse of this coin, built Fort Vancouver (Washington) on the Columbia River in 1825. The sale of the coins at $1 each helped to finance the pageant staged for the celebration. Laura Gardin Fraser prepared the models for this coin, which was minted in San Francisco. The S mintmark was omitted. The reverse has a pioneer settler in buckskin suit with a musket in his hands. Fort Vancouver is in the background.

| | Mintage | AU-50 | MS-60 | MS-63 | MS-65 |
|---|---|---|---|---|---|
| 1925, Fort Vancouver Centennial | 14,994 | $300. | $400. | $425. | $1,450. |

## (1926) Sesquicentennial of American Independence

The 150th anniversary of the signing of the Declaration of Independence was the occasion for an international fair held in Philadelphia in 1926. To help raise funds for financing the fair, special issues of half dollars and quarter eagles were authorized by Congress. For the first time, a portrait of a president appeared on a coin struck during his own

lifetime. Presidents Coolidge and Washington are depicted on the obverse of the half dollar. The reverse bears an accurate model of the Liberty Bell. John R. Sinnock, chief engraver of the United States Mint, modeled the sesquicentennial coins from designs by John Frederick Lewis. The dies were in very low relief, causing much loss of detail.

| | Mintage | AU-50 | MS-60 | MS-63 | MS-65 |
|---|---|---|---|---|---|
| 1926, Sesquicentennial of American Independence | 141,120 | $90. | $105. | $160. | $4,750. |

The obverse of this special gold quarter eagle has a standing female figure symbolic of Liberty, holding in one hand a scroll representing the Declaration of Independence and in the other the Torch of Freedom. The reverse bears a representation of Independence Hall in Philadelphia. The coin was designed by John R. Sinnock.

| | Mintage | AU-50 | MS-60 | MS-63 | MS-65 |
|---|---|---|---|---|---|
| 1926, Sesquicentennial of American Independence . . . . . . . . . . .46,019 | | $475. | $525. | $800. | $5,000. |

## (1926–1939) Oregon Trail Memorial

This memorial coin was struck in commemoration of the Oregon Trail and in memory of the pioneers, many of whom lie buried along the famous 2,000-mile highway of history. James Earle Fraser and his wife, Laura Gardin Fraser, prepared the designs. The original issue was struck at Philadelphia and San Francisco in 1926. Coinage was resumed in 1928 (released in 1933), and in 1933, 1934, and 1936 through 1939. The 1933 half dollar was the first commemorative coin struck at the Denver Mint.

| | Mintage | AU-50 | MS-60 | MS-63 | MS-65 |
|---|---|---|---|---|---|
| 1926, Oregon Trail Memorial . . . . . . . . . . .47,955 | | $130. | $160. | $175. | $300. |
| 1926S, Same type, S mint . . . . . . . . . . . . .83,055 | | 130. | 160. | 175. | 300. |
| 1928, Oregon Trail Memorial (same as 1926) . . . . . . . . . . . . . . . . .6,028 | | 200. | 230. | 260. | 350. |
| 1933D, Oregon Trail Memorial . . . . . . . . . . .5,008 | | 380. | 400. | 415. | 590. |
| 1934D, Oregon Trail Memorial . . . . . . . . . . .7,006 | | 185. | 200. | 225. | 320. |
| 1936, Oregon Trail Memorial . . . . . . . . . . .10,006 | | 145. | 175. | 190. | 285. |
| 1936S, Same type, S mint . . . . . . . . . . . . . .5,006 | | 160. | 175. | 200. | 340. |
| 1937D, Oregon Trail Memorial . . . . . . . . . . .12,008 | | 165. | 190. | 210. | 290. |
| 1938, Oregon Trail Memorial (same as 1926) . . . . . . . . . . . . . . . . .6,006 | | | | | |
| 1938D, Same type, D mint . . . . . . . . . . . . . .6,005 | | *Set* | 520. | 615. | 850. |
| 1938S, Same type, S mint . . . . . . . . . . . . . .6,006 | | | | | |
| 1939, Oregon Trail Memorial (same as 1926) . . . . . . . . . . . . . . . . .3,004 | | | | | |
| 1939D, Same type, D mint . . . . . . . . . . . . . .3,004 | | *Set* | 1,600. | 1,700. | 2,200. |
| 1939S, Same type, S mint . . . . . . . . . . . . . .3,005 | | | | | |
| Oregon Trail Memorial, single type coin . . . . . . . . . | | 130. | 160. | 175. | 300. |

## (1927) Vermont Sesquicentennial

This souvenir issue commemorates the 150th anniversary of the Battle of Bennington and the independence of Vermont. Authorized in 1925, it was not coined until 1927. The models were prepared by Charles Keck. The obverse shows the head of Ira Allen, founder of Vermont. The reverse bears a catamount on a pedestal.

| | Mintage | AU-50 | MS-60 | MS-63 | MS-65 |
|---|---|---|---|---|---|
| 1927, Vermont Sesquicentennial (Battle of Bennington) ............28,142 | | $240. | $270. | $280. | $925. |

## (1928) Hawaiian Sesquicentennial

This small issue was struck to commemorate the 150th anniversary of the arrival on the Hawaiian Islands of Captain James Cook in 1778. The design was sketched by Juliette May Fraser of Honolulu and executed by Chester Beach. Captain Cook is shown on the obverse and a native chief on the reverse. The coins were distributed in 1928 and sold for $2 each, the highest initial sale price up to that time.

| | Mintage | AU-50 | MS-60 | MS-63 | MS-65 |
|---|---|---|---|---|---|
| 1928, Hawaiian Sesquicentennial ..........9,958 | | $1,500. | $2,375. | $2,950. | $6,000. |
| 1928, Hawaiian Sesquicentennial Sandblast Proof Presentation Piece .....(50) | | | | | 25,000. |

## (1934) Maryland Tercentenary

The 300th anniversary of the founding of the Maryland Colony by Cecil Calvert (known as Lord Baltimore) was the occasion for this special coin. The profits from the sale of this issue were used to finance the celebration in Baltimore during 1934. Hans Schuler designed the coin, which shows the facing head of Lord Baltimore on the obverse and the arms of Maryland on the reverse, reminiscent of the Maryland colonial pieces.

| | Mintage | AU-50 | MS-60 | MS-63 | MS-65 |
|---|---|---|---|---|---|
| 1934, Maryland Tercentenary ...........25,015 | | $145. | $165. | $180. | $340. |

## (1934-1938) Texas Independence Centennial

This issue commemorated the independence of Texas in 1836. The first of several dates was offered in 1934. The later dates were struck at all three mints. The models were prepared by Pompeo Coppini. The reverse shows the kneeling figure of winged Victory, and on each side, medallions with portraits of General Sam Houston and Stephen Austin, founders of the Republic and State of Texas. The large five-pointed star behind the eagle on the obverse carries out the Lone Star tradition.

| | Mintage | AU-50 | MS-60 | MS-63 | MS-65 |
|---|---|---|---|---|---|
| 1934, Texas Centennial ...............61,463 | | $125. | $140. | $150. | $230. |
| 1935, Texas Centennial (same as 1934) ....9,996<br>1935D, Same type, D mint .............10,007<br>1935S, Same type, S mint .............10,008 | | Set | 375. | 425. | 575. |
| 1936, Texas Centennial (same as 1934) ....8,911<br>1936D, Same type, D mint .............9,039<br>1936S, Same type, S mint .............9,055 | | Set | 375. | 425. | 575. |
| 1937, Texas Centennial (same as 1934) ....6,571<br>1937D, Same type, D mint .............6,605<br>1937S, Same type, S mint .............6,637 | | Set | 375. | 425. | 575. |
| 1938, Texas Centennial (same as 1934) ....3,780<br>1938D, Same type, D mint .............3,775<br>1938S, Same type, S mint .............3,814 | | Set | 650. | 750. | 1,500. |
| Texas Centennial, single type coin ............ | | 125. | 140. | 150. | 230. |

## (1934-1938) Daniel Boone Bicentennial

This coin type, which was minted for five years, was first struck in 1934 to commemorate the 200th anniversary of the famous frontiersman's birth. The change of date to 1935 for the second year's coinage brought about the addition of the commemorative date 1934 above the words PIONEER YEAR. Coinage covered several years, similar to the schedule for the Texas issues. The models for this coin were prepared by Augustus Lukeman. The obverse bears a portrait of Daniel Boone; the reverse shows Boone with Chief Black Fish.

Date Added in Field

| | Mintage | AU-50 | MS-60 | MS-63 | MS-65 |
|---|---|---|---|---|---|
| 1934, Daniel Boone Bicentennial ........10,007 | | $115. | $125. | $135. | $200. |

*Chart continued on next page.*

| | Mintage | AU-50 | MS-60 | MS-63 | MS-65 |
|---|---|---|---|---|---|
| 1935, Same type | 10,010 | | | | |
| 1935D, Same type, D mint | 5,005 | Set | $375. | $400. | $625. |
| 1935S, Same type, S mint | 5,005 | | | | |
| 1935, Same as 1934, Same 1934 on Rev | 10,008 | | | | |
| 1935D, Same type, D mint | 2,003 | Set | 850. | 950. | 2,000. |
| 1935S, Same type, S mint | 2,004 | | | | |
| 1936, Daniel Boone (same as above) | 12,012 | | | | |
| 1936D, Same type, D mint | 5,005 | Set | 375. | 400. | 625. |
| 1936S, Same type, S mint | 5,006 | | | | |
| 1937, Daniel Boone (same as above) | 9,810 | | | | |
| 1937D, Same type, D mint | 2,506 | Set | 825. | 875. | 1,300. |
| 1937S, Same type, S mint | 2,506 | | | | |
| 1938, Daniel Boone (same as above) | 2,100 | | | | |
| 1938D, Same type, D mint | 2,100 | Set | 950. | 1,100. | 1,700. |
| 1938S, Same type, S mint | 2,100 | | | | |
| Daniel Boone Bicentennial, single type coin | | $115. | 125. | 135. | 200. |

## (1935) Connecticut Tercentenary

In commemoration of the 300th anniversary of the founding of the colony of Connecticut, a souvenir half dollar was struck. Henry Kreis designed the coin. The famous Charter Oak is the main device on the reverse—according to legend, the Royal Charter was secreted in the tree during the reign of James II, who wished to revoke it. The charter was produced after the king's overthrow in 1688, and the colony continued under its protection.

| | Mintage | AU-50 | MS-60 | MS-63 | MS-65 |
|---|---|---|---|---|---|
| 1935, Connecticut Tercentenary | 25,018 | $225. | $265. | $300. | $575. |

## (1935–1939) Arkansas Centennial

This souvenir issue marked the 100th anniversary of the admission of Arkansas into the Union. Edward Everett Burr designed the piece, and models were prepared by Emily Bates of Arkansas. Although 1936 was the centennial year, the first of several issues was brought out in 1935 from all three mints. The 1936 through 1939 issues were the same as those of

1935 except for the dates. They were sold by the distributors at $8.75 per set of three coins. The reverse shows accolated heads of an Indian chief of 1836 and an American girl of 1936. During 1936, a second design was authorized by Congress. Senator Joseph T. Robinson consented to have his portrait placed on the reverse side of the coins, which were struck at the Philadelphia Mint (see listing on next page).

| | Mintage | AU-50 | MS-60 | MS-63 | MS-65 |
|---|---|---|---|---|---|
| 1935, Arkansas Centennial ...............3,012 | | | | | |
| 1935D, Same type, D mint ..............5,505 | | *Set* | $300. | $350. | $800. |
| 1935S, Same type, S mint ..............5,506 | | | | | |
| | | | | | |
| 1936, Arkansas Centennial (same as 1935; | | | | | |
|     date 1936 on reverse) ..............9,660 | | | | | |
| 1936D, Same type, D mint ..............9,660 | | *Set* | 300. | 350. | 850. |
| 1936S, Same type, S mint ..............9,662 | | | | | |
| | | | | | |
| 1937, Arkansas Centennial (same as 1935) ...5,505 | | | | | |
| 1937D, Same type, D mint ..............5,505 | | *Set* | 300. | 375. | 1,100. |
| 1937S, Same type S mint ................5,506 | | | | | |
| | | | | | |
| 1938, Arkansas Centennial (same as 1935) ...3,156 | | | | | |
| 1938D, Same type, D mint ..............3,155 | | *Set* | 500. | 550. | 2,000. |
| 1938S, Same type, S mint ..............3,156 | | | | | |
| | | | | | |
| 1939, Arkansas Centennial (same as 1935) ...2,104 | | | | | |
| 1939D, Same type, D mint ..............2,104 | | *Set* | 850. | 1,000. | 3,250. |
| 1939S, Same type, S mint ..............2,105 | | | | | |
| | | | | | |
| Arkansas Centennial, single type coin ........... | | $80. | 100. | 120. | 275. |

## *(1936) Arkansas Centennial – Robinson*

A new reverse design for the Arkansas Centennial coin (see facing page) was authorized by the Act of June 26, 1936. Senator Joseph T. Robinson, still living at the time his portrait was used, was the subject for the new issue engraved by Henry Kreis. The obverse, designed by Everett Burr, was unchanged. The law specified a change in the reverse, because of the fact that the obverse side is that which bears the date. From a numismatic viewpoint, however, the side that has the portrait is usually considered the obverse. Thus, in this instance, the side with the eagle device is often considered the reverse.

| | Mintage | AU-50 | MS-60 | MS-63 | MS-65 |
|---|---|---|---|---|---|
| 1936, Arkansas Centennial (Robinson) ......25,265 | | $135. | $145. | $160. | $395. |

## (1935) Hudson, New York, Sesquicentennial

This souvenir half dollar marked the 150th anniversary of the founding of Hudson, New York, which was named after the explorer Henry Hudson. The designs, by Chester Beach, show Hudson's flagship, the *Half Moon*, on the obverse and the seal of the City of Hudson on the reverse. Details of the seal include representations of Neptune with trident on a spouting whale and a mermaid blowing a conch shell.

| | Mintage | AU-50 | MS-60 | MS-63 | MS-65 |
|---|---|---|---|---|---|
| 1935, Hudson, NY, Sesquicentennial | 10,008 | $650. | $775. | $950. | $1,850. |

## (1935–1936) California Pacific International Exposition

Congress approved the coinage of souvenir half dollars for the exposition on May 3, 1935. Robert Aitken designed the coin, which was struck at the San Francisco Mint. The same type with date 1936 was struck at the Denver Mint, under authority of the special Recoinage Act of May 6, 1936, which specified that 180,000 pieces could be recoined with the date 1936 irrespective of the year of issue. The obverse displays a seated female with spear and a bear in the left background. The reverse shows the observation tower and the State of California building at the exposition.

| | Mintage | AU-50 | MS-60 | MS-63 | MS-65 |
|---|---|---|---|---|---|
| 1935S, California-Pacific Exposition | 70,132 | $95. | $120. | $135. | $170. |
| 1936D, California-Pacific Exposition | 30,092 | 95. | 140. | 155. | 180. |

## (1935) Old Spanish Trail

This coin commemorated the 400th anniversary of the overland trek of the Cabeza de Vaca Expedition through the Gulf states in 1535. The coin was designed by L.W. Hoffecker, and models were prepared by Edmund J. Senn. The explorer's name literally translated means "head of a cow"; therefore this device was chosen for the obverse. The reverse bears a yucca tree and a map showing the Old Spanish Trail.

| | Mintage | AU-50 | MS-60 | MS-63 | MS-65 |
|---|---|---|---|---|---|
| 1935, Old Spanish Trail | 10,008 | $1,050. | $1,200. | $1,300. | $1,550. |

## (1936) Providence, Rhode Island, Tercentenary

The 300th anniversary of Roger Williams's founding of Providence was the occasion for this special half dollar in 1936. The designs were the work of Arthur Graham Carey and John Howard Benson. The obverse shows Roger Williams in a canoe, being welcomed by an Indian. The reverse has the anchor of Hope with a shield and mantling in the background. Although the founding of Providence was being celebrated, no mention of the city is to be found on the coin.

| | Mintage | AU-50 | MS-60 | MS-63 | MS-65 |
|---|---|---|---|---|---|
| 1936, Rhode Island Tercentenary ........20,013 | | | | | |
| 1936D, Same type, D mint ..............15,010 | | *Set* | $300. | $340. | $760. |
| 1936S, Same type, S mint ..............15,011 | | | | | |
| Rhode Island Tercentenary, single type coin ...... | | $80. | 100. | 115. | 255. |

## (1936) Cleveland Centennial / Great Lakes Exposition

A special coinage of fifty-cent pieces was authorized in commemoration of the centennial celebration of Cleveland, Ohio, on the occasion of the Great Lakes Exposition held there in 1936. The designs were prepared by Brenda Putnam. Although half the coinage was struck in 1937, all were dated 1936. The obverse has a bust of Moses Cleaveland, and the reverse displays a map of the Great Lakes region with a compass point at the city of Cleveland. Nine Great Lakes cities are marked by stars.

| | Mintage | AU-50 | MS-60 | MS-63 | MS-65 |
|---|---|---|---|---|---|
| 1936, Cleveland Centennial/ | | | | | |
| Great Lakes Exposition ...........50,030 | | $123. | $130. | $150. | $240. |

## (1936) Wisconsin Territorial Centennial

The 100th anniversary of the Wisconsin Territorial government was the occasion for this issue. The original design was made by David Parsons, a University of Wisconsin student. Benjamin Hawkins, a New York artist, made changes to conform with technical requirements. The reverse has the Territorial Seal, which includes a forearm holding a pickaxe over a mound of lead ore, and the inscription 4TH DAY OF JULY ANNO DOMINI 1836. The obverse shows a badger on a log, the state emblem, and arrows representing the Black Hawk War of the 1830s.

| | Mintage | AU-50 | MS-60 | MS-63 | MS-65 |
|---|---|---|---|---|---|
| 1936, Wisconsin Centennial . . . . . . . . . . . .25,015 | | $220. | $240. | $260. | $340. |

## (1936) Cincinnati Music Center

Although the head of Stephen Foster, "America's Troubadour," dominates the obverse of this special issue, the anniversary celebrated bears no relation to him. The coins, designed by Constance Ortmayer of Washington, DC, were supposedly struck to commemorate the 50th anniversary in 1936 of Cincinnati as a center of music. The coins were struck at the three mints and were sold only in sets at $7.75, the highest initial cost of a new type at that time.

| | Mintage | AU-50 | MS-60 | MS-63 | MS-65 |
|---|---|---|---|---|---|
| 1936, Cincinnati Music Center . . . . . . . . . . .5,005 | | | | | |
| 1936D, Same type, D mint . . . . . . . . . . . . . .5,005 | | *Set* | $930. | $1,000. | $2,600. |
| 1936S, Same type, S mint . . . . . . . . . . . . . .5,006 | | | | | |
| Cincinnati Music Center, single type coin . . . . . . . . | | $260. | 310. | 335. | 875. |

## (1936) Long Island Tercentenary

This souvenir issue was author-ized to commemorate the 300th anniversary of the first white settlement on Long Island, which was made at Jamaica Bay by Dutch colonists. The design was prepared by Howard Kenneth Weinman, son of the sculptor A.A. Weinman, who designed the regular Liberty Walking type half dollar. Accolated heads depicting

a Dutch settler and an Indian are shown on the obverse, while a Dutch sailing vessel is the reverse device. This was the first issue for which a date was specified (1936) irre-spective of the year minted or issued, as a safeguard against extending the coinage over a period of years.

| | Mintage | AU-50 | MS-60 | MS-63 | MS-65 |
|---|---|---|---|---|---|
| 1936, Long Island Tercentenary . . . . . . . . .81,826 | | $85. | $95. | $110. | $400. |

## (1936) York County, Maine, Tercentenary

A souvenir half dollar was author-ized by Congress upon the 300th anniversary of the founding of York County, Maine. Brown's Garrison on the Saco River was the site of a town that was settled in 1636. The designs were made by Walter H. Rich of Portland. The obverse design shows a stock-ade, and the reverse has an adap-tation of the York County seal.

| | Mintage | AU-50 | MS-60 | MS-63 | MS-65 |
|---|---|---|---|---|---|
| 1936, York County,<br>Maine, Tercentenary . . . . . . . . . . . . . .25,015 | | $210. | $220. | $240. | $300. |

## (1936) Bridgeport, Connecticut, Centennial

In commemoration of the 100th anniversary of the incorporation of the city of Bridgeport, a special fifty-cent piece was authorized on May 15, 1936. Henry Kreis designed this coin. The head of P.T. Barnum, Bridgeport's best known citizen, occupies the obverse. An art deco eagle domi-nates the reverse.

| | Mintage | AU-50 | MS-60 | MS-63 | MS-65 |
|---|---|---|---|---|---|
| 1936, Bridgeport, CT, Centennial . . . . . . . .25,015 | | $155. | $170. | $185. | $270. |

## (1936) Lynchburg, Virginia, Sesquicentennial

The issuance of a charter to the city of Lynchburg in 1786 was commemorated in 1936 by a special coinage of half dollars. The models for the coin were prepared by Charles Keck. The obverse bears a portrait of Senator Carter Glass, a native of Lynchburg and former secretary of the Treasury, who objected to the idea of using portraits of living men on coins. Despite his mild protests, his likeness was incorporated on the coin. The reverse shows Liberty standing, with the old Lynchburg courthouse in the background.

| | Mintage | AU-50 | MS-60 | MS-63 | MS-65 |
|---|---|---|---|---|---|
| 1936, Lynchburg, VA, Sesquicentennial . . . .20,013 | | $220. | $250. | $275. | $345. |

## (1936) Elgin, Illinois, Centennial

The 100th anniversary of the founding of Elgin was marked by a special issue of half dollars in 1936. The proceeds were devoted to financing a Pioneer Memorial statue, which is depicted on the reverse of the coin. The year 1673 bears no relation to the event but refers to the year in which Joliet and Marquette entered Illinois Territory. The designs were prepared by Trygve Rovelstad, who also designed the Pioneer Memorial (which was not dedicated until 2001).

| | Mintage | AU-50 | MS-60 | MS-63 | MS-65 |
|---|---|---|---|---|---|
| 1936, Elgin, Illinois, Centennial . . . . . . . . .20,015 | | $220. | $240. | $260. | $300. |

## (1936) Albany, New York, Charter

The 250th anniversary of the granting of a charter to the city of Albany was the occasion for this commemorative half dollar. The reverse design shows Governor Dongan, Peter Schuyler, and Robert Livingston. The obverse depicts a beaver gnawing on a maple branch. Gertrude K. Lathrop of Albany was the designer.

| | Mintage | AU-50 | MS-60 | MS-63 | MS-65 |
|---|---|---|---|---|---|
| 1936, Albany, New York, Charter . . . . . . . .17,671 | | $290. | $310. | $330. | $380. |

# COMMEMORATIVES

## (1936) San Francisco – Oakland Bay Bridge Opening

The opening of the San Francisco Bay Bridge was the occasion for a special souvenir fifty-cent piece. The designs were the work of Jacques Schnier, a San Francisco artist. A California grizzly bear dominates the obverse. The famous landmark bridge is shown on the reverse. The coins were struck at the San Francisco Mint in November 1936. The bear depicted was a composite of animals in local zoos.

| | Mintage | AU-50 | MS-60 | MS-63 | MS-65 |
|---|---|---|---|---|---|
| 1936S, San Francisco–Oakland Bay Bridge . .71,424 | | $150. | $170. | $200. | $300. |

## (1936) Columbia, South Carolina, Sesquicentennial

Souvenir half dollars were authorized to help finance the extensive celebrations marking the sesquicentennial of the founding of Columbia in 1786. A. Wolfe Davidson designed the coin, which was struck at all three mints and sold in sets. The obverse bears the figure of Justice with sword and scales. At the left is the capitol of 1786, and at the right, the capitol of 1936. A palmetto tree, the state emblem, is the reverse device.

| | Mintage | AU-50 | MS-60 | MS-63 | MS-65 |
|---|---|---|---|---|---|
| 1936, Columbia, SC, Sesquicentennial . . . . .9,007 | | | | | |
| 1936D, Same type, D mint . . . . . . . . . . . . . .8,009 | | Set | $775. | $875. | $950. |
| 1936S, Same type, S mint . . . . . . . . . . . . . .8,007 | | | | | |
| Columbia, SC, Sesqui, single type coin . . . . . . . . . | | $240. | 250. | 290. | 315. |

## (1936) Delaware Tercentenary

The 300th anniversary of the landing of the Swedes in Delaware was the occasion for a souvenir issue of half dollars. The colonists landed on the spot that is now Wilmington and established a church, which is the oldest Protestant church still used for worship. Their ship, *Kalmar Nyckel*, is shown on the reverse of the coin, and the Old Swedes Church is on the obverse.

Designs were chosen from a competition that was won by Carl L. Schmitz. This coin was authorized in 1936, struck in 1937, and dated 1938 on the reverse and 1936 on the obverse. The anniversary was celebrated in 1938 in both Sweden and the United States. A two-krona coin was issued in Sweden to commemorate the same event.

| | Mintage | AU-50 | MS-60 | MS-63 | MS-65 |
|---|---|---|---|---|---|
| 1936, Delaware Tercentenary . . . . . . . . . . .20,993 | | $300. | $320. | $350. | $435. |

## (1936) Battle of Gettysburg Anniversary

On June 16, 1936, Congress authorized a coinage of fifty-cent pieces in commemoration of the 1863 Battle of Gettysburg. The models were prepared by Frank Vittor, a Pittsburgh sculptor. Portraits of a Union and a Confederate veteran are shown on the obverse. On the reverse are two shields, representing the Union and Confederate armies, separated by a double-bladed fasces.

| | Mintage | AU-50 | MS-60 | MS-63 | MS-65 |
|---|---|---|---|---|---|
| 1936, Battle of Gettysburg Anniversary . . . .26,928 | | $375. | $415. | $450. | $700. |

## (1936) Norfolk, Virginia, Bicentennial

To provide funds for the celebration of Norfolk's anniversary of its growth from a township in 1682 to a royal borough in 1736, Congress first passed a law for the striking of medals. The proponents, however, being dissatisfied, finally succeeded in winning authority for half dollars commemorating the 300th anniversary of the original Norfolk land grant and the 200th anniversary of the establishment of the

borough. William Marks Simpson and his wife, Marjorie Emory Simpson, designed the piece. The obverse shows the Seal of the City of Norfolk with a three-masted ship as the central device. The reverse features the Royal Mace of Norfolk, presented by Lieutenant Governor Dinwiddie in 1753.

| | Mintage | AU-50 | MS-60 | MS-63 | MS-65 |
|---|---|---|---|---|---|
| 1936, Norfolk, VA, Bicentennial . . . . . . . . .16,936 | | $475. | $500. | $525. | $550. |

## (1937) Roanoke Island, North Carolina, 350th Anniversary

A celebration was held in Old Fort Raleigh in 1937 to commemorate the 350th anniversary of Sir Walter Raleigh's "Lost Colony" and the birth of Virginia Dare, the first white child born in British North America. A special half dollar for the occasion was designed by William Marks Simpson of Baltimore. The obverse bears a portrait of Sir Walter Raleigh, and the reverse has a figure representing Ellinor Dare holding the child Virginia.

| | Mintage | AU-50 | MS-60 | MS-63 | MS-65 |
|---|---|---|---|---|---|
| 1937, Roanoke Island, NC . . . . . . . . . . . . .29,030 | | $230. | $275. | $290. | $325. |

## (1937) Battle of Antietam Anniversary

A souvenir half dollar was designed by William Marks Simpson and struck in 1937 to commemorate the 75th anniversary of the famous Civil War battle to thwart Lee's invasion of Maryland. The opposing generals McClellan and Lee are featured on the obverse, while the Burnside Bridge, an important tactical objective, is shown on the reverse. The Battle of Antietam, on September 17, 1862, was one of the bloodiest single-day battles of the war, with more than 23,000 men killed, wounded, or missing.

| | Mintage | AU-50 | MS-60 | MS-63 | MS-65 |
|---|---|---|---|---|---|
| 1937, Battle of Antietam Anniversary .....18,028 | | $600. | $625. | $650. | $775. |

## (1938) New Rochelle, New York, 250th Anniversary

To observe the founding of New Rochelle in 1688 by French Huguenots, a special half dollar was issued in 1938. The title to the land that the Huguenots purchased from John Pell provided that a fattened calf be given away every year on June 20. This is represented by a calf and figure of John Pell on the obverse of the coin. The fleur-de-lis, which is shown on the reverse, is adopted from the seal of the city. Both sides of the coin were designed by Gertrude K. Lathrop.

| | Mintage | AU-50 | MS-60 | MS-63 | MS-65 |
|---|---|---|---|---|---|
| 1938, New Rochelle, New York .........15,266 | | $370. | $390. | $410. | $500. |

## (1946) Iowa Centennial

This half dollar, commemorating the 100th anniversary of Iowa's statehood, was designed by Adam Pietz of Philadelphia. The reverse shows the Iowa state seal, and the obverse shows the first stone capitol building at Iowa City. This issue was sold first to the residents of Iowa and only a small remainder to others. Nearly all of the issue was disposed of within several months, except for some that were held back by the state for sale at future anniversary dates.

| | Mintage | AU-50 | MS-60 | MS-63 | MS-65 |
|---|---|---|---|---|---|
| 1946, Iowa Centennial ...............100,057 | | $100. | $115. | $130. | $200. |

## (1946–1951) Booker T. Washington Memorial

This commemorative coin was issued to perpetuate the ideals and teachings of Booker T. Washington and to construct memorials to his memory. Issued from all mints, it received wide distribution from the start. The reverse has the legend FROM SLAVE CABIN TO HALL OF FAME. His log-cabin birthplace is shown beneath. This coin was designed by Isaac Scott Hathaway, as was the Carver/Washington half dollar.

| | Mintage | AU-50 | MS-60 | MS-63 | MS-65 |
|---|---|---|---|---|---|
| 1946, Booker T Washington (a) | 1,000,546 | | | | |
| 1946D, Same type, D mint | 200,113 | Set | $50. | $70. | $150. |
| 1946S, Same type, S mint | 500,279 | | | | |
| 1947, Same type as 1946 | 100,017 | | | | |
| 1947D, Same type, D mint | 100,017 | Set | 70. | 82. | 275. |
| 1947S, Same type, S mint | 100,017 | | | | |
| 1948, Same type as 1946 | 20,005 | | | | |
| 1948D, Same type, D mint | 20,005 | Set | 150. | 165. | 210. |
| 1948S, Same type, S mint | 20,005 | | | | |
| 1949, Same type as 1946 | 12,004 | | | | |
| 1949D, Same type, D mint | 12,004 | Set | 220. | 240. | 340. |
| 1949S, Same type, S mint | 12,004 | | | | |
| 1950, Same type as 1946 | 12,004 | | | | |
| 1950D, Same type, D mint | 12,004 | Set | 125. | 140. | 225. |
| 1950S, Same type, S mint | 512,091 | | | | |
| 1951, Same type as 1946 | 510,082 | | | | |
| 1951D, Same type, D mint | 12,004 | Set | 110. | 130. | 200. |
| 1951S, Same type, S mint | 12,004 | | | | |
| BT Washington Memorial, single type coin | | $14. | 17. | 23. | 50. |

a. Minted; quantity melted unknown.

## (1951–1954) Carver/Washington Commemorative

Designed by Isaac Scott Hathaway, this coin portrays the conjoined busts of two prominent black Americans. Booker T. Washington was a lecturer, educator, and principal of Tuskegee Institute. He urged training to advance independence and efficiency for his race. George Washington Carver was an agricultural chemist who worked to improve the economy of the south. He spent part of his life teaching crop improvement and new uses for soybeans, peanuts, sweet potatoes, and cotton waste. Money obtained from the sale of these commemoratives was to be used "to oppose the spread of communism among Negroes in the interest of national defense."

# COMMEMORATIVES

| | Mintage | AU-50 | MS-60 | MS-63 | MS-65 |
|---|---|---|---|---|---|
| 1951, Carver/Washington ............110,018 | | | | | |
| 1951D, Same type, D mint ............10,004 | | Set | $85. | $95. | $525. |
| 1951S, Same type, S mint ............10,004 | | | | | |
| 1952, Same type as 1951 ..........2,006,292 | | | | | |
| 1952D, Same type, D mint ..............8006 | | Set | 85. | 110. | 360. |
| 1952S, Same type, S mint ..............8006 | | | | | |
| 1953, Same type as 1951 ..............8,003 | | | | | |
| 1953D, Same type, D mint ..............8,003 | | Set | 85. | 110. | 525. |
| 1953S, Same type, S mint ............108,020 | | | | | |
| 1954, Same type as 1951 ............12,006 | | | | | |
| 1954D, Same type, D mint ............12,006 | | Set | 85. | 100. | 400. |
| 1954S, Same type, S mint ............122,024 | | | | | |
| Carver/Washington, single type coin ........... | | $15. | 20. | 22. | 50. |

## MODERN COMMEMORATIVES
### (1982) George Washington

This coin, the first commemorative half dollar issued since 1954, commemorated the 250th anniversary of the birth of George Washington. It was also the first 90% silver coin produced by the U.S. Mint since 1964. Designed by Elizabeth Jones, chief sculptor and engraver of the United States, the obverse features George Washington astride a horse. The reverse depicts the eastern facade of Mount Vernon. The Uncirculated version was struck at Denver and the Proof at San Francisco.

| | Mintage | MS-67 | PF-67 |
|---|---|---|---|
| 1982D, George Washington, 250th Anniv half dollar ......2,210,458 | | $6.50 | |
| 1982S, Same, Proof ................(4,894,044)............ | | | $6.50 |

### (1983–1984) Los Angeles Olympiad

Three distinctive coins were issued to commemorate the 1984 Los Angeles Summer Olympic Games. The silver dollar dated 1983 was designed by Elizabeth Jones, chief engraver of the Mint. On the obverse is a representation of the traditional Greek discus thrower inspired by the ancient work of the sculptor Myron. The reverse depicts the head and upper body of an American eagle.

| | Mintage | MS-67 | PF-67 |
|---|---|---|---|
| 1983P, Discus Thrower silver dollar ...................294,543 | | $12. | |
| 1983D, Same type, D mint............................174,014 | | 12. | |
| 1983S, Same type, S mint ..........(1,577,025) .......174,014 | | 12. | $13. |

The 1984 Olympic silver dollar was designed by Robert Graham, an American sculptor who created the sculpture placed at the entrance to the Los Angeles Memorial Coliseum. The obverse depicts Graham's sculpture with the coliseum in the background. The reverse features an American eagle.

| | Mintage | MS-67 | PF-67 |
|---|---|---|---|
| 1984P, Olympic Coliseum silver dollar................ 217,954 | | $14. | |
| 1984D, Same type, D mint........................... 116,675 | | 21. | |
| 1984S, Same type, S mint .............(1,801,210).. 116,675 | | 20. | $13. |

The commemorative gold coin minted for the 1984 Olympics was the first U.S. gold piece issued in more than 50 years. The weight, size, and fineness are the same as for the previous ten-dollar coin, issued in 1933. It is the first coin ever to bear the W mintmark for West Point.

The obverse depicts two runners bearing the Olympic torch aloft, and was designed by John Mercanti from a concept by James Peed, an artist at the Mint. The eagle on the reverse is modeled after that on the Great Seal.

| | Mintage | MS-67 | PF-67 |
|---|---|---|---|
| 1984P, Olympic gold $10 ....................(33,309) ........ | | | $300. |
| 1984D, Same type, D mint ...................(34,533) ........ | | | 320. |
| 1984S, Same type, S mint ...................(48,551) ........ | | | 250. |
| 1984W, Same type, W mint ................(381,085)... 75,886 | | $240. | 260. |

## (1986) Statue of Liberty

The first copper-nickel clad half dollar commemorative depicts the United States' heritage as a nation of immigrants. The obverse, designed by Edgar Steever, pictures a ship of immigrants steaming into New York harbor, with the Statue of Liberty greeting them in the foreground and the New York skyline in the distance. The reverse, designed by Sherl Joseph Winter, has a scene of an immigrant family with their belongings on the threshold of America.

| | Mintage | MS-67 | PF-67 |
|---|---|---|---|
| 1986D, Statue of Liberty half dollar .....................928,008 | | $6.75 | |
| 1986S, Same type, S mint, Proof ..........(6,925,627) ........ | | | $7.00 |

Designed by Mint artist John Mercanti, this .900 fine silver dollar commemorates Ellis Island as the "Gateway to America." The obverse features a classic pose of Liberty in the foreground, with the Ellis Island Immigration Center behind her. On the reverse is a depiction of Liberty's torch,  along with the words GIVE ME YOUR TIRED, YOUR POOR, YOUR HUDDLED MASSES YEARNING TO BREATHE FREE.

| | Mintage | MS-67 | PF-67 |
|---|---|---|---|
| 1986P, Statue of Liberty silver dollar . . . . . . . . . . . . . . . . . .723,635 | | $12. | |
| 1986S, Same type, S mint, Proof . . . . . . . . . . . . . . . . . .(6,414,638) | | | $16. |

The commemorative half eagle is also the first of this denomination to be minted in more than 50 years. Standards for weight and size are the same as for previous half eagle gold coins. The design is the creation of the Mint's chief engraver, Elizabeth Jones. The obverse features a compelling close-up view of Liberty's face in sharp relief, with the inscription 1986 LIBERTY. An eagle in flight adorns the reverse. All were minted at West Point and bear the W mintmark.

| | Mintage | MS-67 | PF-67 |
|---|---|---|---|
| 1986W, Statue of Liberty gold $5 . . . .(404,013) . . . . . . . . . .95,248 | | $145. | $145. |

## (1987) Constitution Bicentennial

The silver dollar commemorating the 200th anniversary of the United States Constitution was designed by Patricia Lewis Verani using standard weight, size, and fineness. A quill pen, a sheaf of parchment, and the words WE THE PEOPLE are depicted on the obverse. The  reverse portrays a cross-section of Americans from various periods representing contrasting lifestyles.

| | Mintage | MS-67 | PF-67 |
|---|---|---|---|
| 1987P, U.S. Constitution silver dollar . . . . . . . . . . . . . . . . . .723,635 | | $14. | |
| 1987S, Same type, S mint, Proof . . . . . . . . . .(2,747,116) . . . . . . . . | | | $14. |

A modernistic design by Marcel Jovine was selected for the five-dollar gold coin of standard weight, size, and fineness commemorating the bicentennial of the United States Constitution. The obverse portrays a stylized eagle holding a massive quill pen. Another large quill pen is featured on the reverse. To the left are nine stars, signifying the first colonies that ratified the Constitution. Four stars to the right represent the remaining original states. Both Uncirculated and Proof versions were minted at West Point.

| | Mintage | MS-67 | PF-67 |
|---|---|---|---|
| 1987W, U.S. Constitution gold $5 ......(651,659) .......214,225 | | $150. | $150. |

## (1988) Seoul Olympiad

The 1988 Olympic silver dollar commemorates U.S. participation in the Seoul Olympiad. Its size and weight are identical to those of other silver dollars. Design of the obverse is by Patricia Lewis Verani. The reverse is by Mint sculptor-engraver Sherl Joseph Winter.

| | Mintage | MS-67 | PF-67 |
|---|---|---|---|
| 1988D, Olympiad silver dollar .........................191,368 | | $14. | |
| 1988S, Same type, S mint, Proof ..........(1,359,366) ........ | | | $14. |

The 1988 five-dollar gold Olympic coin was designed by Elizabeth Jones, chief sculptor and engraver of the U.S. Mint. The obverse features Nike, goddess of Victory, wearing a crown of olive leaves. The reverse features Marcel Jovine's stylized Olympic flame, evoking the spectacle of the Olympic Games and the renewal of the Olympic spirit every four years.

| | Mintage | MS-67 | PF-67 |
|---|---|---|---|
| 1988W, Olympiad gold $5 .................(281,465)... 62,913 | | $150. | $150. |

## (1989) Congress Bicentennial

The obverse was designed by sculptor Patricia L. Verani and features a detailed bust of the Statue of Freedom. The reverse, designed by William Woodward, offers a full view of the Capitol Building accented by a wreath of stars. The clad composition is approximately 92% copper, 8% nickel.

| | Mintage | MS-67 | PF-67 |
|---|---|---|---|
| 1989D, Congress Bicentennial half dollar ...............163,753 | | $8.50 | |
| 1989S, Same type, S mint, Proof ...........(767,897) ........ | | | $8.50 |

Designed by muralist William Woodward, the obverse of the dollar features the Statue of Freedom that towers atop the Capitol dome. The reverse shows the Mace of the House of Representatives, which resides in the House Chamber whenever the House is in session. The mace's staff is topped by an eagle astride a globe. A scarce variety of the 1989-D dollar shows the dies rotated 360 degrees, rather than the normal "coin turn" of 180 degrees.

| | Mintage | MS-67 | PF-67 |
|---|---|---|---|
| 1989D, Congress Bicentennial silver dollar ...............135,203 | | $18. | |
| 1989S, Same type, S mint, Proof ...................(762,198) | | | $22. |

The Capitol dome is depicted on the obverse of the five-dollar gold coin. The design is the work of Mint engraver John Mercanti. The reverse features a majestic eagle atop the canopy overlooking the Old Senate Chamber.

| | Mintage | MS-67 | PF-67 |
|---|---|---|---|
| 1989W, Congress Bicentennial gold $5 ........(164,690)... 46,899 | | $165. | $165. |

## (1990) Eisenhower Centennial

The unusual design on this coin features the profile of President Eisenhower facing right, which is superimposed over his own left-facing profile as a five-star general. It is the creation of Mint engraver John Mercanti. The reverse shows the Eisenhower home at Gettysburg, a national historic site, and was designed by Marcel Jovine. The coin was issued to celebrate the 100th anniversary of the birth of the 34th president.

| | Mintage | MS-67 | PF-67 |
|---|---|---|---|
| 1990W, Eisenhower Centennial silver dollar . . . . . . . . . . . . . .241,669 | | $20. | |
| 1990P, Same type, P mint, Proof . . . . . . . . . .(1,144,461) . . . . . . . . | | | $23. |

## (1991) Mount Rushmore Golden Anniversary

The 50th anniversary of the Mount Rushmore National Memorial was commemorated on three coins. Surcharges from the sale of these pieces were divided between the Treasury Department and the Mount Rushmore National Memorial Society of Black Hills, South Dakota, with money going to finance restoration work on the national landmark. The obverse of the copper-nickel half dollar was designed by New Jersey artist Marcel Jovine, and features a view of the famous carving by Gutzon Borglum. The reverse, designed by Mint sculptor-engraver James Ferrell, shows an American bison with the words GOLDEN ANNIVERSARY.

| | Mintage | MS-67 | PF-67 |
|---|---|---|---|
| 1991D, Mount Rushmore half dollar . . . . . . . . . . . . . . . . . . .172,754 | | $22. | |
| 1991S, Same type, S mint, Proof . . . . . . . . . . .(753,257) . . . . . . . . | | | $21. |

The Mount Rushmore Golden Anniversary silver dollar obverse was designed by Marika Somogyi. It displays the traditional portraits of presidents George Washington, Thomas Jefferson, Theodore Roosevelt, and Abraham Lincoln as sculptured on the mountain by Gutzon Borglum, who earlier had modeled the figures shown on the Stone Mountain commemorative coin. The reverse, which was designed by former chief sculptor-engraver of the Mint Frank Gasparro, features a small outline map of the United States with the Great Seal above.

| | Mintage | MS-67 | PF-67 |
|---|---|---|---|
| 1991P, Mount Rushmore silver dollar . . . . . . . . . . . . . . . . . . 133,139 | | $36. | |
| 1991S, Same type, S mint, Proof . . . . . . . . . . . (738,419) . . . . . . . | | | $40. |

The five-dollar gold coin commemorating the 50th anniversary of the Mount Rushmore National Memorial features an American eagle flying above the monument with LIBERTY and the date in the field. The obverse was designed by Mint sculptor-engraver John Mercanti, and the reverse was designed by Rhode Island artist Robert Lamb, and engraved by Mint sculptor-engraver William Cousins. The size, weight, and fineness are the same as for all other half eagle coins.

| | Mintage | MS-67 | PF-67 |
|---|---|---|---|
| 1991W, Mount Rushmore gold $5 . . . . . . . . . . . (111,991) . . . 31,959 | | $190. | $175. |

## (1991) Korean War Memorial

The 38th anniversary of the end of the Korean War was the occasion for striking this coin, which honors the end of the conflict and those who served in combat. The design has been criticized as being cluttered, and the occasion no more than a fund-raising opportunity for the creation of a national monument in Washington. The obverse, designed by sculptor-engraver of the U.S. Mint John Mercanti, features an Army infantryman in full gear. On the reverse is an outline map of Korea with North and South divided at the 38th parallel, designed by Mint sculptor-engraver James Ferrell.

| | Mintage | MS-67 | PF-67 |
|---|---|---|---|
| 1991D, Korean War silver dollar . . . . . . . . . . . . . . . . . . . . . . . 213,049 | | $16.50 | |
| 1991P, Same type, P mint, Proof . . . . . . . . . . . (618,488) . . . . . . . | | | $19.00 |

## (1991) United Service Organizations

A special commemorative silver dollar was struck to honor the 50th anniversary of United Service Organizations. The group was founded in 1941 to supply social, recreational, welfare, and spiritual facilities to armed services personnel. Surcharges on sales of the coins were divided equally between the USO and the Department of the Treasury. The coins were launched on Flag Day, June 14, using designs selected in a limited competition between Mint staff and five outside, invited artists. The obverse uses a banner inscribed USO, designed by Rhode Island artist Robert Lamb. On the reverse is a globe with an eagle on top, the work of Mint sculptor-engraver John Mercanti.

| | Mintage | MS-67 | PF-67 |
|---|---|---|---|
| 1991D, USO silver dollar .......................124,958 | | $17. | |
| 1991S, Same type, S mint, Proof ...................(321,275) | | | $23. |

## (1992) XXV Olympiad

The XXV Olympiad held Winter Olympic games in Albertville and Savoie, France, and Summer Olympic games in Barcelona, Spain. United States commemorative coins were issued to honor the participation of American athletes and to finance their training. Competitive designs were selected from 1,107 entries.

The clad half dollar obverse, designed by Mint sculptor-engraver William Cousins, depicts a gymnast in motion. The reverse, by Steven M. Bieda, has the inscription CITIUS, ALTIUS, FORTIUS (the Olympic motto: "Faster, Higher, Stronger") with an olive branch crossing the Olympic torch.

| | Mintage | MS-67 | PF-67 |
|---|---|---|---|
| 1992P, XXV Olympiad clad half dollar ..................161,607 | | $8.50 | |
| 1992S, Same type, S mint, Proof ...........(519,645) ........ | | | $8.50 |

# COMMEMORATIVES

The 1992 Olympic silver dollar obverse is a rendering by John R. Deecken of a pitcher firing a ball to home plate. The reverse, by sculptor Marcel Jovine, combines the Olympic rings, olive branches, and stars and stripes with a bold USA. Uncirculated dollars minted at Denver have the phrase XXV OLYMPIAD impressed four times around the edge, alternately inverted, on a reeded background.

| | Mintage | MS-67 | PF-67 |
|---|---|---|---|
| 1992D, XXV Olympiad silver dollar . . . . . . . . . . . . . . . . . . . . .187,552 | | $25. | |
| 1992S, Same type, S mint, Proof . . . . . . . . . . . . . . . . . . . .(504,505) | | | $28. |

The obverse of the 1992 Olympic five-dollar gold was designed by James Sharpe, and modeled by T. James Ferrell. It depicts a sprinter in a burst of speed. The reverse, by James Peed, unites two impressive symbols, the Olympic rings and the American bald eagle. Size and fineness of these coins is the same as for other United States commemorative issues of this denomination.

| | Mintage | MS-67 | PF-67 |
|---|---|---|---|
| 1992W, XXV Olympiad gold $5 . . . . . . . . . . . . .(77,313). . . 27,732 | | $175. | $160. |

## (1992) White House 200th Anniversary

The obverse of this coin, designed by Mint sculptor Edgar Z. Steever IV, depicts the north portico of the White House. The reverse, by Mint sculptor Chester Y. Martin, features a bust of James Hoban, the original architect, and the main entrance he designed.

| | Mintage | MS-67 | PF-67 |
|---|---|---|---|
| 1992D, White House silver dollar . . . . . . . . . . . . . . . . . . . .123,803 | | $36. | |
| 1992W, Same type, W mint, Proof . . . . . . . . . . . . . . . . .(375,849) | | | $41. |

## (1992) Christopher Columbus Quincentenary

This copper-nickel half dollar, designed by Mint sculptor T. James Ferrell, depicts Columbus landing in the New World on the obverse, and his three ships on the reverse.

| | Mintage | MS-67 | PF-67 |
|---|---|---|---|
| 1992D, Columbus Quincentenary half dollar . . . . . . . . . . . . .135,702 | | $12. | |
| 1992S, Same type, S mint, Proof . . . . . . . . . . .(390,154) . . . . . . . | | | $12. |

Mint sculptor John Mercanti designed this silver dollar obverse, which features a full-length figure of Columbus beside a globe, with his ships above. The reverse, by Mint sculptor Thomas D. Rogers Sr., is a split image of the *Santa Maria* and the U.S. space shuttle *Discovery*.

| | Mintage | MS-67 | PF-67 |
|---|---|---|---|
| 1992D, Columbus Quincentenary silver dollar . . . . . . . . . . . .106,949 | | $32. | |
| 1992P, Same type, P mint, Proof . . . . . . . . . . . .(385,241) . . . . . . . | | | $42. |

The five-dollar gold coin obverse, designed by Mint sculptor T. James Ferrell, bears a portrait of Columbus facing a map of the New World. The reverse, by Mint sculptor Thomas D. Rogers Sr. shows the Crest of the Admiral of the Ocean Sea.

| | Mintage | MS-67 | PF-67 |
|---|---|---|---|
| 1992W, Columbus Quincentenary gold $5 . . . . . . .(79,730). . . 24,329 | | $230. | $195. |

## (1993) Bill of Rights

The silver half dollar in this series depicts James Madison penning the Bill of Rights. It was designed by Mint sculptor T. James Ferrell. The reverse, by Dean McMullen, displays the torch of freedom. Some 9,656 of the Uncirculated version were privately marked on the edge with a serial number and the initials of the Madison Foundation and the American Numismatic Association.

| | Mintage | MS-67 | PF-67 |
|---|---|---|---|
| 1993W, Bill of Rights silver half dollar . . . . . . . . . . . . . . . . . . .173,224 | | $22. | |
| 1993S, Same type, S mint, Proof . . . . . . . . . . .(559,758) . . . . . . . . | | | $19. |

A portrait of James Madison is shown on the obverse of this silver dollar, designed by William Krawczewicz. Dean McMullen designed the reverse, which shows Montpelier, the Virginia home of James and Dolley Madison.

| | Mintage | MS-67 | PF-67 |
|---|---|---|---|
| 1993D, Bill of Rights silver dollar . . . . . . . . . . . . . . . . . . . . . .98,383 | | $20. | |
| 1993S, Same type, S mint, Proof . . . . . . . . . . .(534,001) . . . . . . . . | | | $22. |

The obverse of the five-dollar gold coin was designed by Scott R. Blazek. It features Madison studying the Bill of Rights. On the reverse, by Joseph D. Peña, is a quotation by Madison, accented by an eagle, torch, and laurel branch.

| | Mintage | MS-67 | PF-67 |
|---|---|---|---|
| 1993W, Bill of Rights gold $5 . . . . . . . . . . . . . . .(78,651) . . . 23,266 | | $220. | $195. |

# COMMEMORATIVES

## (1991–1995) 50th Anniversary of World War II

Each of the three coins in this series is dated 1991–1995, and commemorates the 50th anniversary of U.S. involvement in World War II, which lasted from 1941 to 1945. Pieces were coined and issued in 1993. The obverse of the clad half dollar was designed by George Klauba. It depicts the faces of three members of the armed services superimposed upon the "V for victory" symbol. The reverse, by Bill J. Leftwich, portrays a Pacific island battle scene.

| | Mintage | MS-67 | PF-67 |
|---|---|---|---|
| (1993P), 1991–1995 World War II clad half dollar ......................(290,343).. 192,968 | | $35. | $37. |

U.S. Mint sculptor-engraver Thomas D. Rogers Sr. designed the silver dollar showing an American soldier on the beach at Normandy. The reverse depicts the shoulder sleeve insignia of Supreme Headquarters Allied Expeditionary Force, with a quotation from Dwight D. Eisenhower.

| | Mintage | MS-67 | PF-67 |
|---|---|---|---|
| (1993D), 1991–1995 World War II silver dollar ...........94,708 | | $33. | |
| (1993W), Same type, W mint, Proof .........(322,422) ....... | | | $43. |

Both Proof and Uncirculated versions of the five-dollar gold coin were struck at the West Point Mint. The obverse, designed by Charles J. Madsen, depicts an American serviceman with rifle raised in victory. The reverse, by Edward Southworth Fisher, features a "V for victory" in the center with Morse code for the letter superimposed.

| | Mintage | MS-67 | PF-67 |
|---|---|---|---|
| (1993W), 1991–1995 World War II gold $5 .....(65,461)... 23,089 | | $230. | $220. |

## (1994) World Cup Tournament

The 1994 World Cup Tournament was the culmination of soccer games among 141 nations. The United States was selected to host the XV FIFA World Cup playoff, and three commemorative coins were issued to celebrate the event. Each of the coins employs a shared design on the reverse.

The obverse of the clad half dollar depicts a soccer player in action. It was designed by Richard T. LaRoche. The reverse, designed by Dean McMullen, features the official World Cup USA 1994 logo flanked by laurel branches.

| | Mintage | MS-67 | PF-67 |
|---|---|---|---|
| 1994D, World Cup Tournament clad half dollar . . . . . . . . . . .168,208 | | $13. | |
| 1994P, Same type, P mint, Proof . . . . . . . . . . . .(609,354) . . . . . . . | | | $11. |

The obverse of the silver dollar coin features two competing players converging on a soccer ball. It was designed by Dean McMullen, who also executed the reverse design, the official logo that is used on all of the World Cup coins.

| | Mintage | MS-67 | PF-67 |
|---|---|---|---|
| 1994D, World Cup Tournament silver dollar . . . . . . . . . . . . . .81,524 | | $28. | |
| 1994S, Same type, S mint, Proof . . . . . . . . . . .(577,090) . . . . . . . | | | $32. |

Both Proof and Uncirculated versions of the five-dollar gold coin were struck at the West Point Mint. The obverse, designed by William J. Krawczewicz, depicts the modernistic gold World Cup trophy. The reverse was designed by Dean McMullen and shows the same logo used on other World Cup coins.

| | Mintage | MS-67 | PF-67 |
|---|---|---|---|
| 1994W, World Cup Tournament gold $5 . . . . . . . .(89,614). . . 22,447 | | $220. | $190. |

## (1993 [1994]) Thomas Jefferson

| | Mintage | MS-67 | PF-67 |
|---|---|---|---|
| 1993 (1994), Jefferson silver dollar, P mint . . . . . . . . . . . . . .266,927 | | $26. | |
| 1993 (1994), Same type, S mint, Proof . . . . . . . .(332,891) . . . . . . . . | | | $32. |

## (1994) Vietnam Veterans Memorial

| | Mintage | MS-67 | PF-67 |
|---|---|---|---|
| 1994W, Vietnam Veterans Memorial silver dollar . . . . . . . . . . .57,317 | | $92. | |
| 1994P, Same type, P mint, Proof . . . . . . . . . . . .(226,262) . . . . . . . . | | | $100. |

## (1994) U.S. Prisoner of War Memorial

| | Mintage | MS-67 | PF-67 |
|---|---|---|---|
| 1994W, POW Museum silver dollar . . . . . . . . . . . . . . . . . . . . .54,790 | | $95. | |
| 1994P, Same type, P mint, Proof . . . . . . . . . . . .(220,100) . . . . . . . . | | | $77. |

## (1994) Women in Military Service Memorial

| | Mintage | MS-67 | PF-67 |
|---|---|---|---|
| 1994W, Women in Military Service silver dollar . . . . . . . . . . .53,054 | | $65. | |
| 1994P, Same type, P mint, Proof . . . . . . . . . . . . .(213,201) . . . . . . . . | | | $60. |

## (1994) U.S. Capitol Bicentennial

| | Mintage | MS-67 | PF-67 |
|---|---|---|---|
| 1994D, U.S. Capitol Bicentennial silver dollar . . . . . . . . . . . . .68,352 | | $24. | |
| 1994S, Same type, S mint, Proof . . . . . . . . . . . .(279,416) . . . . . . . . | | | $30. |

## (1995) Civil War Battlefields

| | Mintage | MS-67 | PF-67 |
|---|---|---|---|
| 1995S, Civil War Battlefield Preservation clad half dollar . . . . . . . . . . . . . . . . . . . . . . . . . . . . . . . .119,520 | | $50. | |
| 1995S, Same type, S mint, Proof . . . . . . . . . . .(226,632) . . . . . . . . | | | $48. |

| | Mintage | MS-67 | PF-67 |
|---|---|---|---|
| 1995P, Civil War Battlefield Preservation silver dollar ........45,866 | | $75. | |
| 1995S, Same type, S mint, Proof ............(437,114) ........ | | | $95. |

| | Mintage | MS-67 | PF-67 |
|---|---|---|---|
| 1995W, Civil War Battlefield gold $5 ....................12,735 | | $585. | |
| 1995W, Same type, W mint, Proof ............(55,246) ........ | | | $400. |

## (1995) Centennial Olympic Games

| | Mintage | MS-67 | PF-67 |
|---|---|---|---|
| 1995S, 100th Olympics, Basketball clad half dollar ........171,001 | | $24. | |
| 1995S, Same type, S mint, Proof ............(169,655) ........ | | | $19. |
| 1995S, 100th Olympics, Baseball clad half dollar ..........164,605 | | 24. | |
| 1995S, Same type, S mint, Proof ............(118,087) ........ | | | 20. |
| 1996S, 100th Olympics, Swimming clad half dollar ........49,533 | | 175. | |
| 1996S, Same type, S mint, Proof ............(114,315) ........ | | | 50. |
| 1996S, 100th Olympics, Soccer clad half dollar ...........52,836 | | 100. | |
| 1996S, Same type, S mint, Proof ............(112,412) ........ | | | 100. |

| | Mintage | MS-67 | PF-67 |
|---|---|---|---|
| 1995D, 100th Olympics, Gymnastics silver dollar . . . . . . . . . .42,497 | | $85. | |
| 1995P, Same type, P mint, Proof . . . . . . . . . . . .(182,676) . . . . . . . | | | $60. |
| 1995D, 100th Olympics, Paralympics silver dollar . . . . . . . . .28,649 | | 95. | |
| 1995P, Same type, P mint, Proof . . . . . . . . . . . .(138,337) . . . . . . . | | | 63. |
| 1995D, 100th Olympics, Track and Field silver dollar . . . . . . .24,976 | | 92. | |
| 1995P, Same type, P mint, Proof . . . . . . . . . . . .(136,935) . . . . . . . | | | 55. |
| 1995D, 100th Olympics, Cycling silver dollar . . . . . . . . . . . . .19,662 | | 165. | |
| 1995P, Same type, P mint, Proof . . . . . . . . . . . .(118,795) . . . . . . . | | | 47. |
| 1996D, 100th Olympics, Tennis silver dollar . . . . . . . . . . . . . .15,983 | | 300. | |
| 1996P, Same type, P mint, Proof . . . . . . . . . . . .(92,016) . . . . . . . | | | 100. |
| 1996D, 100th Olympics, Paralympics silver dollar . . . . . . . . . .14,497 | | 375. | |
| 1996P, Same type, P mint, Proof . . . . . . . . . . . .(84,280) . . . . . . . | | | 90. |
| 1996D, 100th Olympics, Rowing silver dollar . . . . . . . . . . . . .16,258 | | 325. | |
| 1996P, Same type, P mint, Proof . . . . . . . . . . . .(151,890) . . . . . . . | | | 75. |
| 1996D, 100th Olympics, High Jump silver dollar . . . . . . . . . . .15,697 | | 350. | |
| 1996P, Same type, P mint, Proof . . . . . . . . . . . .(124,502) . . . . . . . | | | 65. |

| | Mintage | MS-67 | PF-67 |
|---|---|---|---|
| 1995W, 100th Olympics, Torch Runner gold $5 . . . . . . . . . . . .14,675 | | $390. | |
| 1995W, Same type, W mint, Proof . . . . . . . . . . .(57,442) . . . . . . . | | | $275. |
| 1995W, 100th Olympics, Stadium gold $5 . . . . . . . . . . . . . . .10,579 | | 420. | |
| 1995W, Same type, W mint, Proof . . . . . . . . . . .(43,124) . . . . . . . | | | 325. |
| 1996W, 100th Olympics, Flag Bearer gold $5 . . . . . . . . . . . . . .9,174 | | 500. | |
| 1996W, Same type, W mint, Proof . . . . . . . . . . .(32,886) . . . . . . . | | | 400. |
| 1996W, 100th Olympics, Cauldron gold $5 . . . . . . . . . . . . . . . .9,210 | | 500. | |
| 1996W, Same type, W mint, Proof . . . . . . . . . . .(38,555) . . . . . . . | | | 400. |

## (1995) Special Olympics Games

| | Mintage | MS-67 | PF-67 |
|---|---|---|---|
| 1995W, Special Olympics silver dollar .................. .89,301 | | $30. | |
| 1995P, Same type, P mint, Proof ............(351,764) ........ | | | $28. |

## (1996) National Community Service

| | Mintage | MS-67 | PF-67 |
|---|---|---|---|
| 1996S, National Community Service silver dollar ..........23,468 | | $285. | |
| 1996S, Same type, S mint, Proof ...........(100,787) ........ | | | $100. |

## (1996) Smithsonian Institution 150th Anniversary

| | Mintage | MS-67 | PF-67 |
|---|---|---|---|
| 1996D, Smithsonian silver dollar ......................31,320 | | $150. | |
| 1996P, Same type, P mint, Proof ..........(126,616) .......... | | | $70. |

| | Mintage | MS-67 | PF-67 |
|---|---|---|---|
| 1996W, Smithsonian gold $5 . . . . . . . . . . . . . . . . . . . . . . . . . . . . . .9,068 | | $950. | |
| 1996W, Same type, W mint, Proof . . . . . . . . . . . .(21,840) . . . . . . . | | | $425. |

## (1997) Botanic Garden

| | Mintage | MS-67 | PF-67 |
|---|---|---|---|
| 1997P, Botanic Garden silver dollar . . . . . . . . . . . . . . . . . . . . . .57,272 | | $50. | |
| 1997P, Same type, P mint, Proof . . . . . . . . . . . .(264,528) . . . . . . . | | | $50. |

## (1997) Jackie Robinson

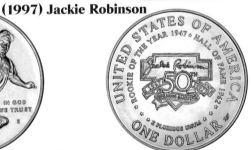

| | Mintage | MS-67 | PF-67 |
|---|---|---|---|
| 1997S, Jackie Robinson silver dollar . . . . . . . . . . . . . . . . . . . . .30,180 | | $100. | |
| 1997S, Same type, S mint, Proof . . . . . . . . . . . .(110,002) . . . . . . . | | | $85. |

| | Mintage | MS-67 | PF-67 |
|---|---|---|---|
| 1997W, Jackie Robinson gold $5 . . . . . . . . . . . . . . . . . . . . . . . .5,174 | | $2,750. | |
| 1997W, Same type, W mint, Proof . . . . . . . . . . . .(24,072) . . . . . . . | | | $600. |

## (1997) Franklin D. Roosevelt

| | Mintage | MS-67 | PF-67 |
|---|---|---|---|
| 1997W, Franklin D. Roosevelt gold $5 . . . . . . . . . . . . . . . . . . . .11,805 | | $370. | |
| 1997W, Same type, W mint, Proof . . . . . . . . . . . .(29,233) . . . . . . . . | | | $320. |

## (1997) National Law Enforcement Officers Memorial

| | Mintage | MS-67 | PF-67 |
|---|---|---|---|
| 1997P, Law Enforcement silver dollar . . . . . . . . . . . . . . . . . . . .30,007 | | $190. | |
| 1997P, Same type, P mint, Proof . . . . . . . . . . . . .(110,428) . . . . . . . . | | | $165. |

## (1998) Robert F. Kennedy

| | Mintage | MS-67 | PF-67 |
|---|---|---|---|
| 1998S, Robert F. Kennedy silver dollar . . . . . . . . . . . . . . . . .106,422 | | $35. | |
| 1998S, Same type, S mint, Proof . . . . . . . . . . . .(99,020) . . . . . . . . | | | $50. |

# COMMEMORATIVES

## (1998) Black Revolutionary War Patriots

| | Mintage | MS-67 | PF-67 |
|---|---|---|---|
| 1998S, Black Patriots silver dollar . . . . . . . . . . . . . . . . . . . . . . .37,210 | | $160. | |
| 1998S, Same type, S mint, Proof . . . . . . . . . . . . .(75,070) . . . . . . . . | | | $120. |

## (1999) Dolley Madison Commemorative

| | Mintage | MS-67 | PF-67 |
|---|---|---|---|
| 1999P, Dolley Madison silver dollar . . . . . . . . . . . . . . . . . . . . . .89,104 | | $55. | |
| 1999P, Same type, P mint, Proof . . . . . . . . . . . . .(224,403) . . . . . . . . | | | $60. |

## (1999) George Washington Death Bicentennial

| | Mintage | MS-67 | PF-67 |
|---|---|---|---|
| 1999W, George Washington gold $5 . . . . . . . . . . . . . . . . . . . . .22,511 | | $320. | |
| 1999W, Same type, W mint, Proof . . . . . . . . . . . .(41,693) . . . . . . . . | | | $320. |

## (1999) Yellowstone National Park

| | Mintage | MS-67 | PF-67 |
|---|---|---|---|
| 1999P, Yellowstone silver dollar .....................23,614 | | $56. | |
| 1999P, Same type, P mint, Proof ............(128,646) ........ | | | $50. |

## (2000) Library of Congress Bicentennial

| | Mintage | MS-67 | PF-67 |
|---|---|---|---|
| 2000P, Library of Congress silver dollar .................52,771 | | $47. | |
| 2000P, Same type, P mint, Proof ............(196,900) ........ | | | $47. |

| | Mintage | MS-67 | PF-67 |
|---|---|---|---|
| 2000W, Library of Congress bimetallic (gold/platinum) $10 ............................6,683 | | $1,450. | |
| 2000W, Same type, W mint, Proof ............(27,167) ........ | | | $650. |

## (2000) Leif Ericson Millennium

| | Mintage | MS-67 | PF-67 |
|---|---|---|---|
| 2000P, Leif Ericson silver dollar . . . . . . . . . . . . . . . . . . . . . . . .28,150 | | $90. | |
| 2000P, Same type, P mint, Proof . . . . . . . . . . . . .(144,748) . . . . . . . | | | $80. |

## (2001) American Buffalo Commemorative

| | Mintage | MS-67 | PF-67 |
|---|---|---|---|
| 2001D, American Buffalo silver dollar . . . . . . . . . . . . . . . . .227,131 | | $150. | |
| 2001P, Same type, P mint, Proof . . . . . . . . . . . . .(272,869) . . . . . . . | | | $150. |

## (2001) Capitol Visitor Center

| | Mintage | MS-67 | PF-67 |
|---|---|---|---|
| 2001P, Capitol Visitor Center clad half dollar . . . . . . . . . . . . . .99,157 | | $16. | |
| 2001P, Same type, P mint, Proof . . . . . . . . . . . . .(77,962) . . . . . . . | | | $21. |

| | Mintage | MS-67 | PF-67 |
|---|---|---|---|
| 2001P, Capitol Visitor Center silver dollar | 35,380 | $45. | |
| 2001P, Same type, P mint, Proof | (143,793) | | $50. |

| | Mintage | MS-67 | PF-67 |
|---|---|---|---|
| 2001W, Capitol Visitor Center gold $5 | 6,761 | $675. | |
| 2001W, Same type, W mint, Proof | (27,652) | | $350. |

## (2002) Salt Lake City Olympic Games

| | Mintage | MS-67 | PF-67 |
|---|---|---|---|
| 2002D, Salt Lake Olympics silver dollar | 40,257 | $42. | |
| 2002P, Same type, P mint, Proof | (166,864) | | $42. |

| | Mintage | MS-67 | PF-67 |
|---|---|---|---|
| 2002W, Salt Lake Olympics gold $5 | 10,585 | $375. | |
| 2002W, Same type, W mint, Proof | (32,877) | | $315. |

# COMMEMORATIVES

## (2002) West Point Bicentennial

| | Mintage | MS-67 | PF-67 |
|---|---|---|---|
| 2002W, West Point Bicentennial silver dollar . . . . . . . . . . . .103,201 | | $40. | |
| 2002W, Same type, W mint, Proof . . . . . . . . . .(288,293) . . . . . . . . | | | $45. |

## (2003) First Flight Centennial

| | Mintage | MS-67 | PF-67 |
|---|---|---|---|
| 2003P, First Flight Centennial clad half dollar . . . . . . . . . . . . .57,726 | | $17. | |
| 2003P, Same type, P mint, Proof . . . . . . . . . .(111,569) . . . . . . . . . . . | | | $20. |
| 2003P First Flight Centennial silver dollar . . . . . . . . . . . . . . . .53,761 | | 40. | |
| 2003P, Same type, P mint, Proof . . . . . . . . . .(193,086) . . . . . . . . . . . | | | 40. |
| 2003W First Flight Centennial gold $10 . . . . . . . . . . . . . . . . . .10,129 | | 430. | |
| 2003W, Same type, W mint, Proof . . . . . . . . . .(21,846) . . . . . . . . . . . | | | 430. |

## (2004) Thomas Alva Edison

| | Mintage | MS-67 | PF-67 |
|---|---|---|---|
| 2004P, Thomas Alva Edison silver dollar . . . . . . . . . . . . . . . . . 68,031 | | $45. | |
| 2004P, Same type, P mint, Proof . . . . . . . . . . . .(213,409) . . . . . . . . | | | $50. |

## (2004) Lewis and Clark Bicentennial

| | Mintage | MS-67 | PF-67 |
|---|---|---|---|
| 2004P, Lewis and Clark silver dollar . . . . . . . . . . . . . . . . . . .90,323 | | $38. | |
| 2004P, Same type, P mint, Proof . . . . . . . . . . . .(288,492) . . . . . . . . | | | $39. |

## (2005) Chief Justice John Marshall

| | Mintage | MS-67 | PF-67 |
|---|---|---|---|
| 2005P, John Marshall silver dollar . . . . . . . . . . . . . . . . . . . . . .48,953 | | $35. | |
| 2005P, Same type, P mint, Proof . . . . . . . . . . . .(141,993) . . . . . . . . | | | $40. |

## (2005) Marine Corps 230th Anniversary

| | Mintage | MS-67 | PF-67 |
|---|---|---|---|
| 2005P, Marine Corps 230th Anniversary silver dollar . . . . . . .130,000 | | $40. | |
| 2005P, Same type, P mint, Proof . . . . . . . . . . . . .(370,000) . . . . . . . . | | | $45. |

## (2006) Benjamin Franklin

| | Mintage | MS-67 | PF-67 |
|---|---|---|---|
| 2006P, Benjamin Franklin "Scientist" silver dollar . . . . . . . . . . .58,000 | | $40. | |
| 2006P, Same type, P mint, Proof . . . . . . . . . . . .(142,000) | | | $45. |
| 2006P, Benjamin Franklin "Founding Father" silver dollar . . . . .58,000 | | 40. | |
| 2006P, Same type, P mint, Proof . . . . . . . . . . . .(142,000) . . . . . . . . | | | 45. |

# GOVERNMENT COMMEMORATIVE SETS

*Values are for commemorative coins and sets in their original packaging.*

## (1983–1984) Los Angeles Olympiad

|  | Price |
|---|---|
| 1983 and 1984 Proof dollars . . . . . . . . . . . . . . . . . . . . . . . . . . . . . . . . . . . . . . . . . . . . . . . . . . . . . . . . . | $24. |
| 1983 and 1984 6-coin set. One each of 1983 and 1984 dollars, both Proof and Uncirculated gold $10 **(a)** . . . . . . . . . . . . . . . . . . . . . . . . . . . . . . . . . . . . . . . . . . . . . | 600. |
| 1983 3-piece collector set. 1983 P, D, and S Uncirculated dollars. . . . . . . . . . . . . . . . . . . . . . . | 35. |
| 1984 3-piece collector set. 1984 P, D, and S Uncirculated dollars. . . . . . . . . . . . . . . . . . . . . . . | 50. |
| 1983 and 1984 gold and silver Uncirculated set. One each of 1983 and 1984 Uncirculated dollar and one 1984 Uncirculated gold $10 . . . . . . . . . . . . . . . . . . . . . . . . . | 300. |
| 1983 and 1984 gold and silver Proof set. One each of 1983 and 1984 Proof dollars and one 1984 Proof gold $10 . . . . . . . . . . . . . . . . . . . . . . . . . . . . . . . . . . . . . . . . . | 300. |

## (1986) Statue of Liberty

|  | Price |
|---|---|
| 2-coin set. Proof silver dollar and clad half dollar . . . . . . . . . . . . . . . . . . . . . . . . . . . . . . . . . . . | $23. |
| 3-coin set. Proof silver dollar, clad half dollar, and gold $5 . . . . . . . . . . . . . . . . . . . . . . . . . | 170. |
| 2-coin set. Uncirculated silver dollar and clad half dollar . . . . . . . . . . . . . . . . . . . . . . . . . . . . | 23. |
| 2-coin set. Uncirculated and Proof gold $5 . . . . . . . . . . . . . . . . . . . . . . . . . . . . . . . . . . . . . . . . | 320. |
| 3-coin set. Uncirculated silver dollar, clad half dollar, and gold $5 . . . . . . . . . . . . . . . . . . . . . | 170. |
| 6-coin set. One each of Proof and Uncirculated half dollar, silver dollar, and gold $5 **(a)** . . . . . . | 340. |

## (1987) Constitution

|  | Price |
|---|---|
| 2-coin set. Uncirculated silver dollar and gold $5 . . . . . . . . . . . . . . . . . . . . . . . . . . . . . . . . . . . | $165. |
| 2-coin set. Proof silver dollar and gold $5 . . . . . . . . . . . . . . . . . . . . . . . . . . . . . . . . . . . . . . . . . | 165. |
| 4-coin set. One each of Proof and Uncirculated silver dollar and gold $5 **(a)** . . . . . . . . . . . . . . | 330. |

**a.** Packaged in cherrywood box.

# COMMEMORATIVES

## (1988) Seoul Olympiad

| | Price |
|---|---|
| 2-coin set. Uncirculated silver dollar and gold $5 ................................... | $165. |
| 2-coin set. Proof silver dollar and gold $5 ...................................... | 165. |
| 4-coin set. One each of Proof and Uncirculated silver dollar and gold $5 **(a)** ............... | 340. |

## (1989) Congress

| | Price |
|---|---|
| 2-coin set. Proof clad half dollar and silver dollar .................................... | $24. |
| 3-coin set. Proof clad half dollar, silver dollar, and gold $5 ........................ | 170. |
| 2-coin set. Uncirculated clad half dollar and silver dollar ............................. | 24. |
| 3-coin set. Uncirculated clad half dollar, silver dollar, and gold $5 ..................... | 180. |
| 6-coin set. One each of Proof and Uncirculated clad half dollar, silver dollar, and gold $5 **(a)** .. | 336. |

## (1991) Mount Rushmore

| | Price |
|---|---|
| 2-coin set. Uncirculated clad half dollar and silver dollar ........................... | $50. |
| 2-coin set. Proof clad half dollar and silver dollar .................................... | 58. |
| 3-coin set. Uncirculated clad half dollar, silver dollar, and gold $5 ..................... | 240. |
| 3 coin set: Proof half dollar, silver dollar, and gold $5 ............................... | 225. |
| 6-coin set. One each of Proof and Uncirculated clad half dollar, silver dollar, and gold $5 **(a)** .. | 470. |

## (1992) XXV Olympiad

| | Price |
|---|---|
| 2-coin set. Uncirculated clad half dollar and silver dollar ........................... | $30. |
| 2-coin set. Proof clad half dollar and silver dollar .................................... | 34. |
| 3-coin set. Uncirculated clad half dollar, silver dollar, and gold $5 ..................... | 200. |
| 3-coin set. Proof clad half dollar, silver dollar, and gold $5 ........................ | 180. |
| 6-coin set. One each of Proof and Uncirculated clad half dollar, silver dollar, and gold $5 **(a)** .. | 360. |

## (1992) Christopher Columbus

| | Price |
|---|---|
| 2-coin set. Uncirculated clad half dollar and silver dollar ........................... | $36. |
| 2-coin set. Proof clad half dollar and silver dollar .................................... | 50. |
| 3-coin set. Uncirculated clad half dollar, silver dollar, and gold $5 ..................... | 280. |
| 3-coin set. Proof half dollar, silver dollar, and gold $5 ............................. | 230. |
| 6-coin set. One each of Proof and Uncirculated clad half dollar, silver dollar, and gold $5 **(a)** | 450. |

## (1993) Bill of Rights

| | Price |
|---|---|
| 2-coin set. Uncirculated silver half dollar and silver dollar ........................... | $45. |
| 2-coin set. Proof silver half dollar and silver dollar .................................. | 45. |
| 3-coin set. Uncirculated silver half dollar, silver dollar, and gold $5 ..................... | 250. |
| 3-coin set. Proof half dollar, silver dollar, and gold $5 .............................. | 220. |
| 6-coin set. One each of Proof and Uncirculated silver half dollar, silver dollar, and gold $5 **(a)** | 450. |
| "Young Collector" set. Silver half dollar ........................................ | 20. |
| "Educational" set. Silver half dollar and James Madison medal ..................... | 16. |
| Proof silver half dollar and 25-cent stamp ...................................... | 25. |

**a.** Packaged in cherrywood box.

## (1993) Thomas Jefferson

| | Price |
|---|---|
| 3-piece set (issued in 1994). Silver dollar, Jefferson nickel, and $2 note . . . . . . . . . . . . . . . . . | $95. |

## (1993) World War II

| | Price |
|---|---|
| 2-coin set. Uncirculated clad half dollar and silver dollar . . . . . . . . . . . . . . . . . . . . . . . . . . . . | $56. |
| 2-coin set. Proof clad half dollar and silver dollar . . . . . . . . . . . . . . . . . . . . . . . . . . . . . . . . . | 60. |
| 3-coin set. Uncirculated clad half dollar, silver dollar, and gold $5 . . . . . . . . . . . . . . . . . . . . . | 270. |
| 3-coin set. Proof clad half dollar, silver dollar, and gold $5 . . . . . . . . . . . . . . . . . . . . . . . . . | 270. |
| 6-coin set. One each of Proof and Uncirculated clad half dollar, silver dollar, and gold $5 (a) . . | 550. |
| "Young Collector" set. Clad half dollar . . . . . . . . . . . . . . . . . . . . . . . . . . . . . . . . . . . . . . . . | 24. |
| "Victory" set. Silver dollar and French franc . . . . . . . . . . . . . . . . . . . . . . . . . . . . . . . . . . . . | 24. |
| Victory Medal set. Uncirculated clad half dollar and reproduction medal . . . . . . . . . . . . . . . . . | 30. |

## (1994) World Cup Soccer

| | Price |
|---|---|
| 2-coin set. Uncirculated clad half dollar and silver dollar . . . . . . . . . . . . . . . . . . . . . . . . . . . . | $35. |
| 2-coin set. Proof clad half dollar and silver dollar . . . . . . . . . . . . . . . . . . . . . . . . . . . . . . . . . | 38. |
| 3-coin set. Uncirculated clad half dollar, silver dollar, and gold $5 . . . . . . . . . . . . . . . . . . . . . | 224. |
| 3-coin set. Proof clad half dollar, silver dollar, and gold $5 . . . . . . . . . . . . . . . . . . . . . . . . . | 200. |
| 6-coin set. One each of Proof and Uncirculated clad half dollar, silver dollar, and gold $5 . . . . . | 400. |
| "Young Collector" set. Uncirculated clad half dollar . . . . . . . . . . . . . . . . . . . . . . . . . . . . . . . | 12. |
| "Special Edition" set. Proof clad half dollar and silver dollar . . . . . . . . . . . . . . . . . . . . . . . . . | 40. |

## (1994) U.S. Veterans

| | Price |
|---|---|
| 3-coin set. Uncirculated POW, Vietnam, and Women in Military Service silver dollars . . . . . . . . | $225. |
| 3-coin set. Proof POW, Vietnam, and Women in Military Service silver dollars . . . . . . . . . . . . | 200. |

## (1995) Special Olympics

| | Price |
|---|---|
| 2-coin set. Proof Special Olympics silver dollar, 1995S Kennedy half dollar . . . . . . . . . . . . . . | $120. |

## (1995) Civil War Battlefield Preservation

| | Price |
|---|---|
| 2-coin set. Uncirculated clad half dollar and silver dollar . . . . . . . . . . . . . . . . . . . . . . . . . . . . | $125. |
| 2-coin set. Proof clad half dollar and silver dollar . . . . . . . . . . . . . . . . . . . . . . . . . . . . . . . . . | 150. |
| 3-coin set. Uncirculated clad half dollar, silver dollar, and gold $5 . . . . . . . . . . . . . . . . . . . . . | 675. |
| 3-coin set. Proof clad half dollar, silver dollar, and gold $5 . . . . . . . . . . . . . . . . . . . . . . . . . | 525. |
| 6-coin set. One each of Proof and Uncirculated clad half dollar, silver dollar, and gold $5 (a) . . | 1,200. |
| "Young Collector" set. Uncirculated clad half dollar . . . . . . . . . . . . . . . . . . . . . . . . . . . . . . . | 35. |
| 2-coin "Union" Set. Clad half dollar and silver dollar . . . . . . . . . . . . . . . . . . . . . . . . . . . . . . | 65. |
| 3-coin "Union" Set. Clad half dollar, silver dollar, and gold $5 . . . . . . . . . . . . . . . . . . . . . . . . | 400. |

a. Packaged in cherrywood box.

## (1995–1996) Centennial Olympic Games

| | Price |
|---|---|
| 4-coin set #1. Uncirculated half dollar (Basketball), dollars (Gymnast, Paralympics), gold $5 (Torch Bearer) | $575. |
| 4-coin set #2. Proof half dollar (Basketball), dollars (Gymnast, Paralympics), gold $5 (Torch Bearer) | 350. |
| 2-coin set #1. Proof silver dollars (Gymnast, Paralympics) | 75. |
| "Young Collector" set. Uncirculated Basketball, Swimming, or Soccer half dollar | 28. |
| 1995–1996 16-coin Uncirculated set. One each of all Uncirculated coins **(a)** | 2,100. |
| 1995–1996 16-coin Proof set. One each of all Proof coins **(a)** | 2,000. |
| 1995–1996 32-coin set. One each of all Uncirculated and Proof coins **(a)** | 5,500. |

## (1996) National Community Service

| | Price |
|---|---|
| Proof silver dollar and Saint-Gaudens stamp | $120. |

## (1996) Smithsonian Institution 150th Anniversary

| | Price |
|---|---|
| 2-coin set. Proof silver dollar and $5 gold | $500. |
| 4-coin set. One each of Proof and Uncirculated silver dollar and $5 gold **(a)** | 1,500. |
| "Young Collector" set. Proof silver dollar | 70. |

## (1997) Botanic Garden

| | Price |
|---|---|
| "Coinage and Currency" set. Uncirculated silver dollar, Jefferson nickel, and $1 note | $265. |

## (1997) Jackie Robinson

| | Price |
|---|---|
| 2-coin set. Proof silver dollar and gold $5 | $700. |
| 4-coin set. One each of Proof and Uncirculated silver dollar and gold $5 **(a)** | 3,500. |
| 3-piece "Legacy" set. Baseball card, pin, and gold $5 | 625. |

## (1997) National Law Enforcement Officers Memorial

| | Price |
|---|---|
| Insignia set. Silver dollar, lapel pin, and patch | $210. |

## (1998) Robert F. Kennedy

| | Price |
|---|---|
| 2-coin set. RFK silver dollar and JFK silver half dollar | $420. |
| 2-coin set. RFK silver dollar, Proof and Uncirculated | 85. |

## (1998) Black Revolutionary War Patriots

| | Price |
|---|---|
| 2-coin set. Uncirculated and Proof silver dollars | $280. |
| "Young Collector" set. Uncirculated silver dollar | 175. |
| Black Revolutionary War Patriots set. Silver dollar and four stamps | 160. |

**a.** Packaged in cherrywood box.

## (1999) Dolley Madison Commemorative

| | Price |
|---|---|
| 2-coin set. Proof and Uncirculated silver dollars | $120. |

## (1999) George Washington Death

| | Price |
|---|---|
| 2-coin set. One each of Proof and Uncirculated gold $5 | $650. |

## (1999) Yellowstone National Park

| | Price |
|---|---|
| 2-coin set. One each of Proof and Uncirculated silver dollars | $115. |

## (2000) Leif Ericson Millennium

| | Price |
|---|---|
| 2-coin set. Proof silver dollar and Icelandic 1,000 kronur | $110. |

## (2001) American Buffalo

| | Price |
|---|---|
| 2-coin set. One each of Proof and Uncirculated silver dollars | $300. |
| "Coin and Currency" set. Uncirculated American Buffalo silver dollar, face reprint of 1899 $5 Indian Chief Silver Certificate, 1987 Chief Red Cloud 10¢ stamp, 2001 Bison 21¢ stamp | 175. |

## (2001) Capitol Visitor Center

| | Price |
|---|---|
| 3-coin set. Proof clad half dollar, silver dollar, and gold $5 | $350. |

## (2002) Salt Lake Olympic Games

| | Price |
|---|---|
| 2-coin set. Proof silver dollar and gold $5 | $400. |
| 4-coin set. One each of Proof and Uncirculated silver dollar and gold $5 | 775. |

## (2004) Thomas Alva Edison

| | Price |
|---|---|
| Edison set. Uncirculated silver dollar and light bulb | $60. |

## (2004) Lewis and Clark

| | Price |
|---|---|
| Coin and Pouch set. Proof silver dollar and beaded pouch | $200. |
| "Coinage and Currency" set. Uncirculated silver dollar, Sacagawea golden dollar, two 2005 nickels, replica 1901 $10 Bison note, silver-plated Peace Medal replica, three stamps, two booklets | 100. |
| Westward Journey Nickel Series™ Coin and Medal Set. Proof Sacagawea golden dollar, two 2005 Proof nickels, silver-plated Peace Medal | 40. |

## (2005) Chief Justice John Marshall

| | Price |
|---|---|
| Coin and Chronicles Set. Uncirculated silver dollar, booklet, BEP intaglio portrait . . . . . . . . . . . | $60. |
| American Legacy Collection. Proof Marine Corps dollar, | |
| Proof John Marshall dollar, 10-piece Proof set . . . . . . . . . . . . . . . . . . . . . . . . . . . . . . . . . | 150. |

## (2005) Marine Corps 230th Anniversary

| | Price |
|---|---|
| Marine Corps Uncirculated silver dollar and Stamp set . . . . . . . . . . . . . . . . . . . . . . . . . . . . . | $85. |
| American Legacy Collection. Proof Marine Corps dollar, | |
| Proof John Marshall dollar, 10-piece Proof set . . . . . . . . . . . . . . . . . . . . . . . . . . . . . . . . . | 150. |

## (2006) Benjamin Franklin

| | Price |
|---|---|
| Coin and Chronicles Set. Uncirculated "Scientist" silver dollar, four stamps, | |
| *Poor Richard's Almanack* replica, intaglio print . . . . . . . . . . . . . . . . . . . . . . . . . . . . . . . . . | $65. |

## PROOF COINS AND SETS

A *Proof* is a specimen striking of coinage for presentation, souvenir, exhibition, or numismatic purposes. Pre-1968 Proofs were made only at the Philadelphia Mint, except in a few rare instances in which presentation pieces were struck at branch mints. Current Proofs are made at San Francisco and West Point.

The term *Proof* refers to the method of manufacture and not the condition of a coin. Regular production coins in Mint State have coruscating, frosty luster; soft details; and minor imperfections. A Proof coin can usually be distinguished by its sharpness of detail, high wire edge, and extremely brilliant, mirrorlike surface. All Proofs are originally sold by the Mint at a premium.

Very few Proof coins were made prior to 1856. Because of their rarity and infrequent sales, they are not all listed in this catalog.

*Frosted Proofs* were issued prior to 1936 and starting again in the late 1970s. These have a brilliant, mirrorlike field with contrasting dull or frosted design.

*Matte Proofs* have a granular, "sandblast" surface instead of the mirror finish. Matte Proof cents, nickels, and gold coins were issued from 1908 to 1916; a few 1921 and 1922 silver dollars and a 1998-S silver half dollar were also struck in this manner.

*Brilliant Proofs* have been issued from 1936 to date. These have a uniformly brilliant, mirrorlike surface and sharp, high-relief details.

"Prooflike" coins are occasionally seen. These are examples from dies that have been lightly polished, often inadvertently during the removal of lines, contact marks, or other marks in the fields. In other instances, such as with certain New Orleans gold coins of the 1850s, the dies were polished in the machine shop of the mint. They are not true Proofs, but may have most of the characteristics of a Proof coin and generally command a premium. Collectors should beware of coins that have been buffed to look like Proofs; magnification will reveal polishing lines and lack of detail.

### How a Proof Coin Is Made

Selected dies are inspected for perfection and are highly polished and cleaned. They are again wiped clean or polished after every 15 to 25 impressions and are replaced frequently to avoid imperfections from worn dies. Coinage blanks are polished and cleaned to assure high quality in striking. They are then hand fed into the coinage press one at a time, each blank receiving two or more blows from the dies to bring up sharp, high relief details. The coinage operation is done at slow speed with extra pressure. Finished Proofs are individually inspected and are handled by gloves or tongs. They also receive a final inspection by packers before being sonically sealed in special plastic cases.

After a lapse of 20 years, Proof coins were struck at the Philadelphia Mint from 1936 to 1942, inclusive. In 1942, when the composition of the five-cent piece was changed, there were two types of this denomination available to collectors. The striking of Proof coins was temporarily suspended from 1943 through 1949, and again from 1965 through 1967; during the latter period, special Mint sets were struck. Proof sets were resumed in 1968.

Sets from 1936 through 1972 include the cent, nickel, dime, quarter, and half; from 1973 through 1981 the dollar was also included, and again from 2000 on. Regular Proof sets issued from 1982 to 1998 contain the cent through half dollar. Special Prestige sets containing commemorative coins were sold from 1983 through 1997 at an additional premium. Beginning in 1999, sets contain five different statehood quarters. 1999 Proof dollars were sold separately.

## *Proof Set Values*

Values are for sets in average unspotted condition and in original government packaging. Figures in parentheses are the total number of full sets minted.

| Year | Mintage | Issue Price | Current Value |
|---|---|---|---|
| 1936 | (3,837) | $1.89 | $7,250.00 |
| 1937 | (5,542) | 1.89 | 4,150.00 |
| 1938 | (8,045) | 1.89 | 2,000.00 |
| 1939 | (8,795) | 1.89 | 1,900.00 |
| 1940 | (11,246) | 1.89 | 1,600.00 |
| 1941 | (15,287) | 1.89 | 1,600.00 |
| 1942, Both nickels | (21,120) | 1.89 | 1,500.00 |
| 1942, One nickel | * | 1.89 | 1,400.00 |
| 1950 | (51,386) | 2.10 | 725.00 |
| 1951 | (57,500) | 2.10 | 650.00 |
| 1952 | (81,980) | 2.10 | 400.00 |
| 1953 | (128,800) | 2.10 | 325.00 |
| 1954 | (233,300) | 2.10 | 175.00 |
| 1955, Box pack | (378,200) | 2.10 | 150.00 |
| 1955, Flat pack | * | 2.10 | 175.00 |
| 1956 | (669,384) | 2.10 | 75.00 |
| 1957 | (1,247,952) | 2.10 | 35.00 |
| 1958 | (875,652) | 2.10 | 75.00 |
| 1959 | (1,149,291) | 2.10 | 30.00 |
| 1960, With Large Date cent | (1,691,602) | 2.10 | 22.00 |
| 1960, With Small Date cent | * | 2.10 | 38.00 |
| 1961 | (3,028,244) | 2.10 | 11.00 |
| 1962 | (3,218,019) | 2.10 | 11.00 |
| 1963 | (3,075,645) | 2.10 | 16.00 |
| 1964 | (3,950,762) | 2.10 | 12.00 |
| 1968S | (3,041,506) | 5.00 | 7.50 |
| 1968S, With No S dime | * | 5.00 | 10,000.00 |
| 1969S | (2,934,631) | 5.00 | 8.00 |
| 1970S | (2,632,810) | 5.00 | 15.00 |
| 1970S, With Small Date cent | * | 5.00 | 110.00 |
| 1970S, With No S dime (est 2,200) | * | 5.00 | 1,600.00 |
| 1971S | (3,220,733) | 5.00 | 6.00 |
| 1971S, With No S nickel (est 1,655) | * | 5.00 | 1,450.00 |
| 1972S | (3,260,996) | 5.00 | 5.50 |
| 1973S | (2,760,339) | 7.00 | 12.00 |
| 1974S | (2,612,568) | 7.00 | 8.00 |
| 1975S, With 1976 quarter, half, and dollar | (2,845,450) | 7.00 | 15.00 |
| 1975S, With No S dime | * | 7.00 | 46,000.00 |
| 1976S | (4,149,730) | 7.00 | 10.00 |
| 1976S, 3-piece set | (3,998,621) | 15.00 | 19.00 |
| 1977S | (3,251,152) | 9.00 | 8.00 |
| 1978S | (3,127,781) | 9.00 | 9.00 |
| 1979S, Filled S **(a)** | (3,677,175) | 9.00 | 8.00 |
| 1979S, Clear S **(a)** | * | 9.00 | 130.00 |
| 1980S | (3,554,806) | 10.00 | 7.00 |
| 1981S, First S **(a)** | (4,063,083) | 11.00 | 9.00 |
| 1981S, Clear S (all coins) **(a)** | * | 11.00 | 390.00 |
| 1982S | (3,857,479) | 11.00 | 5.00 |
| 1983S | (3,138,765) | 11.00 | 6.00 |
| 1983S, With No S dime | * | 11.00 | 1,200.00 |
| 1983S, Prestige Set (Olympic dollar) | (140,361) | 59.00 | 120.00 |
| 1984S | (2,748,430) | 11.00 | 8.00 |
| 1984S, Prestige Set (Olympic dollar) | (316,680) | 59.00 | 30.00 |

* Included in number above. **a.** See illustrations at top of page 219 for clarification.

*Chart continued on next page.*

| Year | Mintage | Issue Price | Current Value |
|---|---|---|---|
| 1985S | (3,362,821) | $11.00 | $7.00 |
| 1986S | (2,411,180) | 11.00 | 18.00 |
| 1986S, Prestige Set (Statue of Liberty half, dollar) | (599,317) | 48.50 | 43.00 |
| 1987S | (3,792,233) | 11.00 | 5.00 |
| 1987S, Prestige Set (Constitution dollar) | (435,495) | 45.00 | 30.00 |
| 1988S | (3,031,287) | 11.00 | 8.00 |
| 1988S, Prestige Set (Olympic dollar) | (231,661) | 45.00 | 38.00 |
| 1989S | (3,009,107) | 11.00 | 8.00 |
| 1989S, Prestige Set (Congressional half, dollar) | * | 45.00 | 48.00 |
| 1990S | (2,793,433) | 11.00 | 9.00 |
| 1990S, With No S cent (Proof Set) | (3,555) | 11.00 | 7,000.00 |
| 1990S, With No S cent (Prestige Set) | * | 45.00 | 7,200.00 |
| 1990S, Prestige Set (Eisenhower dollar) | (506,126) | 45.00 | 30.00 |
| 1991S | (2,610,833) | 11.00 | 14.00 |
| 1991S, Prestige Set (Mt. Rushmore half, dollar) | (256,954) | 59.00 | 75.00 |
| 1992S | (26,756,118) | 11.00 | 8.00 |
| 1992S, Prestige Set (Olympic half, dollar) | (183,293) | 56.00 | 100.00 |
| 1992S, Silver | (1,009,586) | 21.00 | 16.50 |
| 1992S, Silver Premier Set | (308,055) | 37.00 | 17.00 |
| 1993S | (2,409,394) | 12.50 | 15.00 |
| 1993S, Prestige Set (Madison half, dollar) | (224,045) | 57.00 | 50.00 |
| 1993S, Silver | (570,213) | 21.00 | 42.00 |
| 1993S, Silver Premier Set | (191,140) | 37.50 | 43.00 |
| 1994S | (2,308,701) | 12.50 | 15.00 |
| 1994S, Prestige Set (World Cup half, dollar) | (175,893) | 57.00 | 60.00 |
| 1994S, Silver | (636,009) | 21.00 | 50.00 |
| 1994S, Silver Premier Set | (149,320) | 37.50 | 52.00 |
| 1995S | (2,010,384) | 12.50 | 60.00 |
| 1995S, Prestige Set (Civil War half, dollar) | (107,112) | 57.00 | 230.00 |
| 1995S, Silver | (549,878) | 21.00 | 120.00 |
| 1995S, Silver Premier Set | (130,107) | 37.50 | 120.00 |
| 1996S | (1,695,244) | 12.50 | 20.00 |
| 1996S, Prestige Set (Olympic half, dollar) | (55,000) | 57.00 | 700.00 |
| 1996S, Silver | (623,655) | 21.00 | 60.00 |
| 1996S, Silver Premier Set | (151,366) | 37.50 | 62.00 |
| 1997S | (1,975,000) | 12.50 | 50.00 |
| 1997S, Prestige Set (Botanic dollar) | (80,000) | 48.00 | 250.00 |
| 1997S, Silver | (605,473) | 21.00 | 100.00 |
| 1997S, Silver Premier Set | (136,205) | 37.50 | 110.00 |
| 1998S | (2,086,507) | 12.50 | 30.00 |
| 1998S, Silver | (638,134) | 21.00 | 50.00 |
| 1998S, Silver Premier Set | (240,658) | 37.50 | 52.00 |
| 1999S, 9-piece set | (2,543,401) | 19.95 | 80.00 |
| 1999S, 5-piece quarter set | (1,169,958) | 13.95 | 70.00 |
| 1999S, Silver 9-piece set | (804,565) | 31.95 | 385.00 |
| 2000S, 10-piece set | (3,082,572) | 19.95 | 24.00 |
| 2000S, 5-piece quarter set | (937,600) | 13.95 | 15.00 |
| 2000S, Silver 10-piece set | (965,421) | 31.95 | 39.00 |
| 2001S, 10-piece set | (2,294,909) | 19.95 | 150.00 |
| 2001S, 5-piece quarter set | (799,231) | 13.95 | 60.00 |
| 2001S, Silver 10-piece set | (889,697) | 31.95 | 175.00 |
| 2002S, 10-piece set | (2,319,766) | 19.95 | 45.00 |
| 2002S, 5-piece quarter set | (764,479) | 13.95 | 27.50 |
| 2002S, Silver 10-piece set | (892,229) | 31.95 | 80.00 |
| 2003S, 10-piece set | (2,172,684) | 19.95 | 32.00 |
| 2003S, 5-piece quarter set | (1,235,832) | 13.95 | 25.00 |

* Included in number above.

| Year | Mintage | Issue Price | Current Value |
|------|--------:|------------:|--------------:|
| 2003S, Silver 10-piece set . . . . . . . . . . . . . . . . . . . . . . . . . . . . . . . . . . . . . .(1,125,755) | | $31.95 | $38.00 |
| 2004S, 11-piece set . . . . . . . . . . . . . . . . . . . . . . . . . . . . . . . . . . . . . . . . . .(1,804,396) | | 22.95 | 70.00 |
| 2004S, 5-piece quarter set . . . . . . . . . . . . . . . . . . . . . . . . . . . . . . . . . . . .(956,767) | | 15.95 | 40.00 |
| 2004S, Silver 11-piece set . . . . . . . . . . . . . . . . . . . . . . . . . . . . . . . . . . . .(1,187,673) | | 37.95 | 50.00 |
| 2004S, Silver 5-piece quarter set . . . . . . . . . . . . . . . . . . . . . . . . . . . . . . .(601,671) | | 23.95 | 36.00 |
| 2005S, 11-piece set . . . . . . . . . . . . . . . . . . . . . . . . . . . . . . . . . . . . . . . . . .(2,275,000) | | 22.95 | 30.00 |
| 2005S, 5-piece quarter set . . . . . . . . . . . . . . . . . . . . . . . . . . . . . . . . . . . .(987,000) | | 15.95 | 20.00 |
| 2005S, Silver 11-piece set . . . . . . . . . . . . . . . . . . . . . . . . . . . . . . . . . . . .(998,000) | | 37.95 | 40.00 |
| 2005S, Silver 5-piece quarter set . . . . . . . . . . . . . . . . . . . . . . . . . . . . . . .(608,970) | | 23.95 | 25.00 |
| 2006S, 11-piece set . . . . . . . . . . . . . . . . . . . . . . . . . . . . . . . . . . . . . . . . . . | | | |
| 2006S, 5-piece quarter set . . . . . . . . . . . . . . . . . . . . . . . . . . . . . . . . . . . . | | | |
| 2006S, Silver 11-piece set . . . . . . . . . . . . . . . . . . . . . . . . . . . . . . . . . . . . | | | |
| 2006S, Silver 5-piece quarter set . . . . . . . . . . . . . . . . . . . . . . . . . . . . . . . | | | |

**2005 Silver Proof Set**

## UNCIRCULATED MINT SETS

Official Uncirculated Mint sets are specially packaged by the government for sale to collectors. They contain uncirculated specimens of each year's coins for every denomination issued from each mint. In previous years, the coins were the same as those normally intended for circulation and were not minted with any special consideration for quality. Since 2005, however, Mint sets have been made with a satin finish rather than the traditional Uncirculated luster. As in the past, coins struck only as Proofs are not included.

Uncirculated Mint sets sold by the Treasury from 1947 through 1958 contained two examples of each regular-issue coin. These were packaged in cardboard holders that did not protect the coins from tarnish. Nicely preserved early sets generally command a 10 to 20% premium above listed values. No official Uncirculated Mint sets were produced in 1950, 1982, or 1983.

Since 1959, sets have been sealed in protective plastic envelopes. In 1965, 1966, and 1967, Special Mint sets of higher-than-normal quality were made to substitute for Proof sets, which were not made during that period. Similar sets dated 1964 are reported to exist. The 1966 and 1967 sets were packaged in hard plastic holders. Sets issued from 2005 onward have a special Satin Finish that is somewhat different from the finish on Uncirculated coins made for general circulation.

Privately assembled Mint sets, and Souvenir sets produced for sale at the Philadelphia or Denver mints or for special occasions, are valued according to the individual pieces they contain. Only the official, government-sealed full sets are included in the following list.

Current-year sets may be ordered by telephoning 1-800-USA MINT.

*See next page for chart.*

## *Uncirculated Mint Set Values*

| Year | Mintage | Issue Price | Face Value | Current Value |
|---|---|---|---|---|
| 1947 P-D-S | 5,000 | $4.87 | $4.46 | $1,300. |
| 1948 P-D-S | 6,000 | 4.92 | 4.46 | 650. |
| 1949 P-D-S | 5,000 | 5.45 | 4.96 | 900. |
| 1951 P-D-S | 8,654 | 6.75 | 5.46 | 950. |
| 1952 P-D-S | 11,499 | 6.14 | 5.46 | 800. |
| 1953 P-D-S | 15,538 | 6.14 | 5.46 | 600. |
| 1954 P-D-S | 25,599 | 6.19 | 5.46 | 300. |
| 1955 P-D-S | 49,656 | 3.57 | 2.86 | 200. |
| 1956 P-D | 45,475 | 3.34 | 2.64 | 180. |
| 1957 P-D | 34,324 | 4.40 | 3.64 | 290. |
| 1958 P-D | 50,314 | 4.43 | 3.64 | 185. |
| 1959 P-D | 187,000 | 2.40 | 1.82 | 55. |
| 1960 P-D | 260,485 | 2.40 | 1.82 | 30. |
| 1961 P-D | 223,704 | 2.40 | 1.82 | 50. |
| 1962 P-D | 385,285 | 2.40 | 1.82 | 20. |
| 1963 P-D | 606,612 | 2.40 | 1.82 | 15. |
| 1964 P-D | 1,008,108 | 2.40 | 1.82 | 13. |
| 1968 P-D-S | 2,105,128 | 2.50 | 1.33 | 5. |
| 1969 P-D-S | 1,817,392 | 2.50 | 1.33 | 7. |
| 1970 P-D-S, With Large Date cent | 2,038,134 | 2.50 | 1.33 | 25. |
| 1970 P-D-S, With Small Date cent | * | 2.50 | 1.33 | 55. |
| 1971 P-D-S | 2,193,396 | 3.50 | 1.83 | 6. |
| 1972 P-D-S | 2,750,000 | 3.50 | 1.83 | 6. |
| 1973 P-D-S | 1,767,691 | 6.00 | 3.83 | 25. |
| 1974 P-D-S | 1,975,981 | 6.00 | 3.83 | 8. |
| 1975 P-D, With 1976 quarter, half, dollar | 1,921,488 | 6.00 | 3.82 | 12. |
| 1776–1976, 3-piece set | 4,908,319 | 9.00 | 1.75 | 18. |
| 1976 P-D | 1,892,513 | 6.00 | 3.82 | 9. |
| 1977 P-D | 2,006,869 | 7.00 | 3.82 | 8. |
| 1978 P-D | 2,162,609 | 7.00 | 3.82 | 9. |
| 1979 P-D (a) | 2,526,000 | 8.00 | 3.82 | 7. |
| 1980 P-D-S | 2,815,066 | 9.00 | 4.82 | 7. |
| 1981 P-D-S | 2,908,145 | 11.00 | 4.82 | 16. |
| 1984 P-D | 1,832,857 | 7.00 | 1.82 | 7. |
| 1985 P-D | 1,710,571 | 7.00 | 1.82 | 8. |
| 1986 P-D | 1,153,536 | 7.00 | 1.82 | 20. |
| 1987 P-D | 2,890,758 | 7.00 | 1.82 | 7. |
| 1988 P-D | 1,646,204 | 7.00 | 1.82 | 7. |
| 1989 P-D | 1,987,915 | 7.00 | 1.82 | 7. |
| 1990 P-D | 1,809,184 | 7.00 | 1.82 | 7. |
| 1991 P-D | 1,352,101 | 7.00 | 1.82 | 10. |
| 1992 P-D | 1,500,143 | 7.00 | 1.82 | 7. |
| 1993 P-D | 1,297,431 | 8.00 | 1.82 | 10. |
| 1994 P-D | 1,234,813 | 8.00 | 1.82 | 10. |
| 1995 P-D | 1,038,787 | 8.00 | 1.82 | 25. |
| 1996 P-D, Plus 1996W dime | 1,457,949 | 8.00 | 1.92 | 30. |
| 1997 P-D | 950,473 | 8.00 | 1.82 | 39. |
| 1998 P-D | 1,187,325 | 8.00 | 1.82 | 15. |
| 1999 P-D (18 pieces) (b) | 1,243,867 | 14.95 | 3.82 | 30. |
| 2000 P-D (20 pieces) | 1,490,160 | 14.95 | 5.82 | 16. |
| 2001 P-D (20 pieces) | 1,116,915 | 14.95 | 5.82 | 22. |
| 2002 P-D (20 pieces) | 1,139,388 | 14.95 | 5.82 | 16. |

* Included in number above. **a.** S-mint dollar not included. **b.** Dollar not included.

| Year | Mintage | Issue Price | Face Value | Current Value |
|------|---------|-------------|------------|---------------|
| 2003 P-D (20 pieces) .................................1,001,532 | | $14.95 | $5.82 | $23. |
| 2004 P-D (22 pieces) ..................................844,484 | | 16.95 | 5.92 | 75. |
| 2005 P-D (22 pieces) .................................1,160,000 | | 16.95 | 5.92 | 30. |
| 2006 P-D (22 pieces) ..................................... | | | | |

*Note:* Sets issued from 2005 onward have a special Satin Finish that is somewhat different from the finish on Uncirculated coins made for general circulation.

**1967 Special Mint Set**

## Special Mint Sets

| Year | Mintage | Issue Price | Face Value | Current Value |
|------|---------|-------------|------------|---------------|
| 1965 ...................................................2,360,000 | | $4.00 | $0.91 | $14. |
| 1966 ...................................................2,261,583 | | 4.00 | 0.91 | 15. |
| 1967 ...................................................1,863,344 | | 4.00 | 0.91 | 21. |

## Souvenir Sets

Uncirculated Souvenir sets were packaged and sold at Philadelphia and Denver gift shops in 1982 and 1983 in place of the "official Mint sets," which were not made in those years. A bronze Mint medal is packaged with each set. Similar sets were also made in other years.

| Year | Issue Price | Face Value | Current Value |
|------|-------------|------------|---------------|
| 1982P .......................................................... | $4.00 | $0.91 | $37. |
| 1982D .......................................................... | 4.00 | 0.91 | 35. |
| 1983P .......................................................... | 4.00 | 0.91 | 66. |
| 1983D .......................................................... | 4.00 | 0.91 | 37. |

# SILVER EAGLES

The silver eagle is a 1-oz. bullion coin with a face value of one dollar. The obverse has Adolph A. Weinman's Liberty Walking design used on the half dollar coins from 1916 through 1947. His initials are on the hem of the gown. The reverse design is a rendition of a heraldic eagle by John Mercanti.

Since 2001, regular-strike silver eagles have been produced at West Point (without mintmarks), and Proofs have been produced at West Point (with mintmarks). The U.S. Mint does not release bullion mintage data on a regular basis; the numbers below are the most recent official mintages.

*Designers Adolph A. Weinman (obv) and John Mercanti (rev); composition .9993 silver, .0007 copper (net weight 1 oz. pure silver); weight 31.101 grams; diameter 40.6 mm; reeded edge; mints: Philadelphia, San Francisco, West Point.*

| | Mintage | Unc. | PF | | Mintage | Unc. | PF |
|---|---|---|---|---|---|---|---|
| $1 1986 | 5,393,005 | $20. | | $1 1996P | (500,000) | | $75. |
| $1 1986S | (1,446,778) | | $38. | $1 1997 | 4,295,004 | $20. | |
| $1 1987 | 11,442,335 | 14. | | $1 1997P | (435,368) | | 100. |
| $1 1987S | (904,732) | | 38. | $1 1998 | 4,847,549 | 14. | |
| $1 1988 | 5,004,646 | 14. | | $1 1998P | (450,000) | | 68. |
| $1 1988S | (557,370) | | 75. | $1 1999 | 7,408,640 | 14. | |
| $1 1989 | 5,203,327 | 14. | | $1 1999P | (549,769) | | 77. |
| $1 1989S | (617,694) | | 50. | $1 2000(W) | 9,239,132 | 14. | |
| $1 1990 | 5,840,210 | 14. | | $1 2000P | (600,000) | | 42. |
| $1 1990S | (695,510) | | 45. | $1 2001(W) | 9,001,711 | 14. | |
| $1 1991 | 7,191,066 | 14. | | $1 2001W | | | 42. |
| $1 1991S | (511,925) | | 70. | $1 2002(W) | 10,539,026 | 14. | |
| $1 1992 | 5,540,068 | 14. | | $1 2002W | | | 42. |
| $1 1992S | (498,654) | | 60. | $1 2003(W) | 8,495,008 | 14. | |
| $1 1993 | 6,763,762 | 14. | | $1 2003W | | | 40. |
| $1 1993P | (405,913) | | 200. | $1 2004(W) | (8,882,754) | 14. | |
| $1 1994 | 4,227,319 | 14. | | $1 2004W | | | 40. |
| $1 1994P | (372,168) | | 200. | $1 2005(W) | | 14. | |
| $1 1995 | 4,672,051 | 14. | | $1 2005W | 8,891,025 | | 40. |
| $1 1995P | (438,511) | | 200. | $1 2006(W) | | 14. | |
| $1 1995W | (30,125) | | 5,100. | $1 2006W | | | 40. |
| $1 1996 | 3,603,386 | 43. | | | | | |

# AMERICAN EAGLE GOLD BULLION

The gold American Eagle bullion coins are made in four denominations that contain 1 oz., 1/2 oz., 1/4 oz., and 1/10 oz. of gold. The obverse features a modified rendition of the Augustus Saint-Gaudens design used on U.S. twenty-dollar gold pieces from 1907 until 1933. The reverse displays a "family of eagles" motif designed by Miley Busiek.

Uncirculated American Eagles, unlike their Proof counterparts, are not sold directly to the general public, but to a series of authorized buyers. These buyers obtain the uncirculated bullion coins from the Mint based on the current spot price of the metal plus a small premium. The coins are then sold to secondary distributors for sale to other dealers and the general public.

## Tenth-Ounce Gold

### *Design similar to other American Eagle gold bullion coins.*

*Designers Augustus Saint-Gaudens (obv), Miley Busiek (rev); weight 3.393 grams; composition .9167 gold, .03 silver, .0533 copper (net weight 1/10 oz. pure gold); diameter 16.5 mm; reeded edge; mints: Philadelphia, West Point.*

| | Mintage | Unc. | PF | | Mintage | Unc. | PF |
|---|---|---|---|---|---|---|---|
| $5 MCMLXXXVI | | | | $5 1995W ......(62,673) | | | $100. |
| (1986) ......912,609 | | $65. | | $5 1996 ........401,964 | | $70. | |
| $5 MCMLXXXVII | | | | $5 1996W ......(56,700) | | | 100. |
| (1987) ......580,266 | | 65. | | $5 1997 ........528,266 | | 65. | |
| $5 MCMLXXXVIII | | | | $5 1997W ......(34,984) | | | 110. |
| (1988) ......159,500 | | 190. | | $5 1998 ......1,344,520 | | 65. | |
| $5 MCMLXXXVIII | | | | $5 1998W ......(20,000) | | | 100. |
| (1988)P ....(143,881) | | | $100. | $5 1999 ......2,750,338 | | 65. | |
| $5 MCMLXXXIX | | | | $5 1999W ......(48,426) | | | 100. |
| (1989) ......264,790 | | 95. | | $5 1999W, Unc made from | | | |
| $5 MCMLXXXIX | | | | unpolished Proof dies | | 450. | |
| (1989)P .....(84,647) | | | 100. | $5 2000 ........569,153 | | 70. | |
| $5 MCMXC (1990) 210,210 | | 75. | | $5 2000W ......(49,970) | | | 100. |
| $5 MCMXC | | | | $5 2001 ........269,147 | | 65. | |
| (1990)P .....(99,349) | | | 100. | $5 2001W ......(37,547) | | | 100. |
| $5 MCMXCI (1991) 165,200 | | 115. | | $5 2002 ........230,027 | | 65. | |
| $5 MCMXCI | | | | $5 2002W ......(40,864) | | | 100. |
| (1991)P .....(70,334) | | | 100. | $5 2003 ........245,029 | | 65. | |
| $5 1992 ........209,300 | | 75. | | $5 2003W ......(46,000) | | | 100. |
| $5 1992P ......(64,874) | | | 100. | $5 2004 ........250,016 | | 65. | |
| $5 1993 ........210,709 | | 75. | | $5 2004W .............. | | | 100. |
| $5 1993P ......(58,649) | | | 100. | $5 2005 ........300,043 | | 65. | |
| $5 1994 ........206,380 | | 75. | | $5 2005W .............. | | | 100. |
| $5 1994W ......(62,849) | | | 100. | $5 2006 .............. | | 65. | |
| $5 1995 ........223,025 | | 70. | | $5 2006W .............. | | | 100. |

## Quarter-Ounce Gold

*Designers Augustus Saint-Gaudens (obv), Miley Busiek (rev); weight 8.483 grams; composition .9167 gold, .03 silver, .0533 copper (net weight 1/4 oz. pure gold); diameter 22 mm; reeded edge; mints: Philadelphia, West Point.*

*See next page for chart.*      **327** ▬▬

| | Mintage | Unc. | PF | | Mintage | Unc. | PF |
|---|---|---|---|---|---|---|---|
| $10 MCMLXXXVI | | | | $10 1995W .....(47,484) | | | $200. |
| (1986) .......726,031 | | $170. | | $10 1996 .........60,318 | | $160. | |
| $10 MCMLXXXVII | | | | $10 1996W .....(37,900) | | | 200. |
| (1987) .......269,255 | | 170. | | $10 1997 ........108,805 | | 160. | |
| $10 MCMLXXXVIII | | | | $10 1997W .....(29,808) | | | 200. |
| (1988) .......49,000 | | 180. | | $10 1998 .......309,829 | | 160. | |
| $10 MCMLXXXVIII | | | | $10 1998W .....(29,733) | | | 200. |
| (1988)P .....(98,028) | | | $200. | $10 1999 .......564,232 | | 160. | |
| $10 MCMLXXXIX | | | | $10 1999W .....(34,416) | | | 200. |
| (1989) .......81,789 | | 170. | | $10 1999W, Unc made from | | | |
| $10 MCMLXXXIX | | | | unpolished Proof dies | | 500. | |
| (1989)P ....(54,170) | | | 200. | $10 2000 .......128,964 | | 160. | |
| $10 MCMXC (1990) 41,000 | | 170. | | $10 2000W .....(36,033) | | | 200. |
| $10 MCMXC | | | | $10 2001 .........71,280 | | 160. | |
| (1990)P ....(62,674) | | | 200. | $10 2001W .....(25,630) | | | 200. |
| $10 MCMXCI (1991) 36,100 | | 325. | | $10 2002 .........62,027 | | 160. | |
| $10 MCMXCI | | | | $10 2002W .....(29,242) | | | 200. |
| (1991)P ....(50,839) | | | 200. | $10 2003 .........74,029 | | 160. | |
| $10 1992 ........59,546 | | 160. | | $10 2003W .....(31,000) | | | 200. |
| $10 1992P ......(46,269) | | | 200. | $10 2004 .........72,014 | | 160. | |
| $10 1993 ........71,864 | | 160. | | $10 2004W ............ | | | 200. |
| $10 1993P ......(46,464) | | | 200. | $10 2005 .........72,015 | | 160. | |
| $10 1994 ........72,650 | | 160. | | $10 2005W ............ | | | 200. |
| $10 1994W .....(48,172) | | | 200. | $10 2006 ............ | | 160. | |
| $10 1995 ........83,752 | | 160. | | $10 2006W ............ | | | 200. |

## Half-Ounce Gold

### *Design similar to other American Eagle gold bullion coins.*

*Designers Augustus Saint-Gaudens (obv), Miley Busiek (rev); weight 16.966 grams; composition .9167 gold, .03 silver, .0533 copper (net weight 1/2 oz. pure gold); diameter 27 mm; reeded edge; mints: Philadelphia, West Point.*

| | Mintage | Unc. | PF | | Mintage | Unc. | PF |
|---|---|---|---|---|---|---|---|
| $25 MCMLXXXVI | | | | $25 1994W .....(44,584) | | | $400. |
| (1986) .......599,566 | | $410. | | $25 1995 ........53,474 | | $350. | |
| $25 MCMLXXXVII | | | | $25 1995W .....(45,442) | | | 400. |
| (1987) .......131,255 | | 325. | | $25 1996 ........39,287 | | 425. | |
| $25 MCMLXXXVII | | | | $25 1996W .....(34,700) | | | 400. |
| (1987)P ....(143,398) | | | $400. | $25 1997 ........79,605 | | 300. | |
| $25 MCMLXXXVIII | | | | $25 1997W .....(26,801) | | | 400. |
| (1988) .......45,000 | | 450. | | $25 1998 .......169,029 | | 300. | |
| $25 MCMLXXXVIII | | | | $25 1998W .....(25,549) | | | 400. |
| (1988)P .....(76,528) | | | 400. | $25 1999 .......263,013 | | 300. | |
| $25 MCMLXXXIX | | | | $25 1999W .....(30,452) | | | 400. |
| (1989) .......44,829 | | 550. | | $25 2000 ........79,287 | | 300. | |
| $25 MCMLXXXIX | | | | $25 2000W .....(32,027) | | | 400. |
| (1989)P ....(44,798) | | | 400. | $25 2001 ........48,047 | | 375. | |
| $25 MCMXC (1990) 31,000 | | 675. | | $25 2001W .....(23,261) | | | 400. |
| $25 MCMXC | | | | $25 2002 ........70,027 | | 300. | |
| (1990)P ....(51,636) | | | 400. | $25 2002W .....(26,646) | | | 400. |
| $25 MCMXCI (1991) 24,100 | | 1,000. | | $25 2003 ........79,029 | | 300. | |
| $25 MCMXCI | | | | $25 2003W .....(33,000) | | | 400. |
| (1991)P ....(53,125) | | | 400. | $25 2004 ........98,040 | | 300. | |
| $25 1992 ........54,404 | | 400. | | $25 2004W ............ | | | 400. |
| $25 1992P ......(40,976) | | | 400. | $25 2005 ........80,023 | | 300. | |
| $25 1993 ........73,324 | | 300. | | $25 2005W ............ | | | 400. |
| $25 1993P ......(43,319) | | | 400. | $25 2006 ............ | | 300. | |
| $25 1994 ........62,400 | | 300. | | $25 2006W ............ | | | 400. |

# One-Ounce Gold

*Designers Augustus Saint-Gaudens (obv), Miley Busiek (rev); weight 33.931 grams; composition .9167 gold, .03 silver, .0533 copper (net weight 1 oz. pure gold); diameter 32.7 mm; reeded edge; mints: Philadelphia, West Point.*

| | Mintage | Unc. | PF | | Mintage | Unc. | PF |
|---|---|---|---|---|---|---|---|
| $50 MCMLXXXVI (1986) | 1,362,650 | $600. | | $50 1994 | 221,633 | 575. | |
| $50 MCMLXXXVI (1986)W | (446,290) | | $800. | $50 1994W | (46,674) | | $800. |
| $50 MCMLXXXVII (1987) | 1,045,500 | 600. | | $50 1995 | 200,636 | 575. | |
| $50 MCMLXXXVII (1987)W | (147,498) | | 800. | $50 1995W | (46,484) | | 800. |
| $50 MCMLXXXVIII (1988) | 465,000 | 600. | | $50 1996 | 189,148 | 575. | |
| $50 MCMLXXXVIII (1988)W | (87,133) | | 800. | $50 1996W | (36,000) | | 800. |
| $50 MCMLXXXIX (1989) | 415,790 | 600. | | $50 1997 | 664,508 | 575. | |
| $50 MCMLXXXIX (1989)W | (54,570) | | 800. | $50 1997W | (27,554) | | 800. |
| $50 MCMXC (1990) | 373,210 | 600. | | $50 1998 | 1,468,530 | 575. | |
| $50 MCMXC (1990)W | (62,401) | | 800. | $50 1998W | (26,060) | | 800. |
| $50 MCMXCI (1991) | 243,100 | 600. | | $50 1999 | 1,505,026 | 575. | |
| $50 MCMXCI (1991)W | (50,411) | | 800. | $50 1999W | (31,446) | | 800. |
| $50 1992 | 275,000 | 575. | | $50 2000 | 433,319 | 575. | |
| $50 1992W | (44,826) | | 800. | $50 2000W | (33,006) | | 800. |
| $50 1993 | 480,192 | 575. | | $50 2001 | 143,605 | 575. | |
| $50 1993W | (34,389) | | 800. | $50 2001W | (24,580) | | 800. |
| | | | | $50 2002 | 222,029 | 575. | |
| | | | | $50 2002W | (27,499) | | 800. |
| | | | | $50 2003 | 416,032 | 575. | |
| | | | | $50 2003W | (33,000) | | 800. |
| | | | | $50 2004 | 417,019 | 575. | |
| | | | | $50 2004W | | | 800. |
| | | | | $50 2005 | 356,555 | 575. | |
| | | | | $50 2005W | | | 800. |
| | | | | $50 2006 | | 575. | |
| | | | | $50 2006W | | | 775. |

## Gold Bullion Sets

| | PF | | PF |
|---|---|---|---|
| 1987 Gold Set. $50, $25 | $1,650. | 1996 Gold Set. $50, $25, $10, $5 | $1,600. |
| 1988 Gold Set. $50, $25, $10, $5 | 1,600. | 1997 Gold Set. $50, $25, $10, $5 | 1,600. |
| 1989 Gold Set. $50, $25, $10, $5 | 1,600. | 1997 Impressions of Liberty Set. | |
| 1990 Gold Set. $50, $25, $10, $5 | 1,600. |    $100 platinum, $50 gold, $1 silver | 2,200. |
| 1991 Gold Set. $50, $25, $10, $5 | 1,600. | 1998 Gold Set. $50, $25, $10, $5 | 1,600. |
| 1992 Gold Set. $50, $25, $10, $5 | 1,600. | 1999 Gold Set. $50, $25, $10, $5 | 1,600. |
| 1993 Gold Set. $50, $25, $10, $5 | 1,600. | 2000 Gold Set. $50, $25, $10, $5 | 1,650. |
| 1993 Bicentennial Gold Set. $25, $10, | | 2001 Gold Set. $50, $25, $10, $5 | 1,600. |
|    $5, $1 silver eagle, and medal | 900. | 2002 Gold Set. $50, $25, $10, $5 | 1,600. |
| 1994 Gold Set. $50, $25, $10, $5 | 1,600. | 2003 Gold Set. $50, $25, $10, $5 | 1,600. |
| 1995 Gold Set. $50, $25, $10, $5 | 1,600. | 2004 Gold Set. $50, $25, $10, $5 | 1,600. |
| 1995 Anniversary Gold Set. $50, $25, | | 2005 Gold Set. $50, $25, $10, $5 | 1,600. |
|    $10, $5, and $1 silver eagle | 5,500. | 2006 Gold Set. $50, $25, $10, $5 | 1,600. |

## AMERICAN EAGLE PLATINUM BULLION

American Eagle platinum coins are made in four denominations different from the similar gold coins. The $100 coin contains one ounce of pure platinum. Fractional denominations containing 1/2 oz., 1/4 oz., and 1/10 oz. are denominated fifty, twenty-five, and ten dollars, respectively. In 1997, Proof platinum coins had the same reverse design as regular strikes. Since then, regular strikes have continued with the 1997 reverse design, while the Proofs have featured a different reverse design each year. From 1998 through 2002, these special Proof designs displayed American eagles flying through various "Vistas of Liberty."

## Vistas of Liberty Reverse Designs

**1998**
**Eagle Over**
**New England**

**1999**
**Eagle Above**
**Southeastern Wetlands**

**2000**
**Eagle Above**
**America's Heartland**

**2001**
**Eagle Above**
**America's Southwest**

**2002**
**Eagle Fishing in**
**America's Northwest**

## Tenth-Ounce Platinum

*Designers John M. Mercanti (obv), Thomas D. Rogers Sr. (orig rev); weight 0.10005 oz.; composition .9995 platinum; diameter 16.5 mm; reeded edge; mints: Philadelphia, West Point.*

| | Mintage | Unc. | PF |
|---|---|---|---|
| 1997 | 70,250 | $150. | |
| 1997W | (37,025) | | $175. |
| 1998 | 39,525 | 170. | |
| 1998W | (19,832) | | 175. |
| 1999 | 55,955 | 150. | |
| 1999W | (19,123) | | 175. |
| 2000 | 34,027 | 150. | |
| 2000W | (15,651) | | 175. |
| 2001 | 52,017 | 150. | |
| 2001W | (12,193) | | 175. |

| | Mintage | Unc. | PF |
|---|---|---|---|
| 2002 | 23,005 | $175. | |
| 2002W | (12,365) | | $175. |
| 2003 | 22,007 | 160. | |
| 2003W | (9,249) | | 185. |
| 2004 | | 160. | |
| 2004W | | | 185. |
| 2005 | 14,013 | 175. | |
| 2005W | | | 190. |
| 2006 | | 175. | |
| 2006W | | | 190. |

## Quarter-Ounce Platinum
### *Design similar to other American Eagle platinum bullion coins.*

*Designers John M. Mercanti (obv), Thomas D. Rogers Sr. (orig rev); weight 0.2501 oz.; composition .9995 platinum; diameter 22 mm; reeded edge; mints: Philadelphia, West Point.*

| | Mintage | Unc. | PF |
|---|---|---|---|
| 1997 | 27,100 | $350. | |
| 1997W | (18,661) | | $400. |
| 1998 | 38,887 | 350. | |
| 1998W | (14,860) | | 400. |
| 1999 | 39,734 | 350. | |
| 1999W | (13,514) | | 400. |
| 2000 | 20,054 | 350. | |
| 2000W | (11,995) | | 400. |
| 2001 | 21,815 | 375. | |
| 2001W | (8,858) | | 400. |

| | Mintage | Unc. | PF |
|---|---|---|---|
| 2002 | 27,405 | $375. | |
| 2002W | (9,282) | | $400. |
| 2003 | 25,207 | 350. | |
| 2003W | (6,829) | | 450. |
| 2004 | | 365. | |
| 2004W | | | 450. |
| 2005 | 12,013 | 365. | |
| 2005W | | | 450. |
| 2006 | | 350. | |
| 2006W | | | 450. |

## Half-Ounce Platinum

*Designers John M. Mercanti (obv), Thomas D. Rogers Sr. (orig rev); weight 0.5003 oz.; composition .9995 platinum; diameter 27 mm; reeded edge; mints: Philadelphia, West Point.*

| | Mintage | Unc. | PF |
|---|---|---|---|
| 1997 | 20,500 | $675. | |
| 1997W | (15,463) | | $750. |
| 1998 | 32,415 | 675. | |
| 1998W | (13,821) | | 750. |
| 1999 | 32,309 | 675. | |
| 1999W | (11,098) | | 750. |
| 2000 | 18,892 | 675. | |
| 2000W | (11,049) | | 750. |
| 2001 | 12,815 | 675. | |
| 2001W | (8,268) | | 750. |

| | Mintage | Unc. | PF |
|---|---|---|---|
| 2002 | 24,005 | $650. | |
| 2002W | (8,772) | | $750. |
| 2003 | 17,409 | 650. | |
| 2003W | (6,963) | | 750. |
| 2004 | | 675. | |
| 2004W | | | 750. |
| 2005 | 9,013 | 650. | |
| 2005W | | | 750. |
| 2006 | | 650. | |
| 2006W | | | 750. |

# One-Ounce Platinum

*Designers John M. Mercanti (obv), Thomas D. Rogers Sr. (orig rev); weight 1.0005 oz.; composition .9995 platinum; diameter 32.7 mm; reeded edge; mints: Philadelphia, West Point.*

| | Mintage | Unc. | PF | | Mintage | Unc. | PF |
|---|---|---|---|---|---|---|---|
| 1997 | 56,000 | $1,350. | | 2002 | 11,502 | $1,350. | |
| 1997W | (18,000) | | $1,500. | 2002W | (9,834) | | $1,500. |
| 1998 | 133,002 | 1,350. | | 2003 | 8,007 | 1,350. | |
| 1998W | (14,203) | | 1,500. | 2003W | (8,106) | | 1,500. |
| 1999 | 56,707 | 1,350. | | 2004 | | 1,350. | |
| 1999W | (12,351) | | 1,500. | 2004W | | | 1,500. |
| 2000 | 10,003 | 1,350. | | 2005 | 6,310 | 1,350. | |
| 2000W | (12,453) | | 1,500. | 2005W | | | 1,500. |
| 2001 | 14,070 | 1,350. | | 2006 | | 1,350. | |
| 2001W | (8,990) | | 1,500. | 2006W | | | 1,500. |

**2003 Proof Design**       **2004 Proof Design**       **2005 Proof Design**

*Designs for Proofs 1998 through 2002 appear on page 330.*

# Platinum Bullion Sets

| | PF | | PF |
|---|---|---|---|
| 1997 Platinum Set. | | 2002 Platinum Set. | |
| $100, $50, $25, $10 | $2,500. | $100, $50, $25, $10 | $2,500. |
| 1998 Platinum Set. | | 2003 Platinum Set. | |
| $100, $50, $25, $10 | 2,500. | $100, $50, $25, $10 | 2,500. |
| 1999 Platinum Set. | | 2004W Platinum Set. | |
| $100, $50, $25, $10 | 2,500. | $100, $50, $25, $10 | 2,500. |
| 2000 Platinum Set. | | 2005W Platinum Set. | |
| $100, $50, $25, $10 | 2,500. | $100, $50, $25, $10 | 2,500. |
| 2001 Platinum Set. | | 2006W Platinum Set. | |
| $100, $50, $25, $10 | 2,500. | $100, $50, $25, $10 | 2,500. |

United States patterns are a fascinating part of numismatics that encompass a myriad of designs and experimental pieces made by the U.S. Mint to test new concepts and motifs, to provide coins for numismatists, and for other reasons. The book *United States Pattern Coins*, by J. Hewitt Judd, gives extensive details of the history and characteristics of more than 2,000 different pattern varieties from 1792 to the present era.

Patterns provide students and collectors a chronology of the continuing efforts of engravers and artists to present their work for approval. Throughout the 200+ years of federal coinage production, concepts meant to improve various aspects of circulating coins have been proposed and incorporated into representative patterns. In some instances, changes have been prompted by an outcry for higher aesthetics, a call for a more convenient denomination, or a need to overcome striking deficiencies. In many other instances, the Mint simply created special coins for the numismatic trade—often controversial in their time, but enthusiastically collected today. Certain patterns, bearing particular proposed designs or innovations, provided tangible examples for Mint and Treasury Department officials or members of Congress to evaluate. If adopted, the pattern design became a familiar regular-issue motif; those that were rejected have become part of American numismatic history.

The patterns listed and illustrated in this section are representative of a much larger group. Such pieces generally include die and hub trials, off-metal Proof strikings of regular issues, and various combinations of dies that were sometimes struck at a later date. Certain well-known members of this extended pattern family historically have been included with regular issues in many popular, general-circulation numismatic reference books. The four-dollar gold Stellas of 1879 and 1880; certain Gobrecht dollars of 1836, 1838, and 1839; and the Flying Eagle cents of 1856 are such examples. No official mintage figures of patterns and related pieces were recorded in most instances, and the number extant of each can usually only be estimated from auction appearances and from those found in museum holdings and important private collections. Although most patterns are very rare, the 2,000+ distinct varieties make them unexpectedly collectible—not by one of each, but by selected available examples from favorite types or categories.

Unlike regular coin issues that were emitted through the usual channels of commerce, and Proofs of regular issues that were struck expressly for sale to collectors, patterns were not intended to be officially sold. Yet as a matter of Mint policy in accordance with certain previously established restrictions, countless patterns were secretly and unofficially sold and traded to favorite dealers and collectors, disseminated to government officials, and occasionally made available to numismatic societies. Not until mid-1887 did the Mint enforce stringent regulations prohibiting their sale and distribution, although there had been several misleading statements to this effect earlier. In succeeding decades the Mint, while not making patterns available to numismatists, did place certain examples in the Mint Collection, now called the National Numismatic Collection, in the Smithsonian Institution. On other occasions, selected patterns were obtained by Mint and Treasury officials, or otherwise spared from destruction. Today, with the exception of certain cents and five-cent pieces of 1896, all pattern coins dated after 1885 are extremely rare.

The private possession of patterns has not been without its controversy. Most significant was the 1910 seizure by government agents of a parcel containing some 23 "pattern pieces" belonging to John W. Haseltine, a leading Philadelphia coin dealer with undisclosed private ties to Mint officials. The government asserted that the patterns had been removed from the Mint without authority, and that they remained the property of the United States. Haseltine's attorney successfully used the Mint's pre-1887 policies in his defense, and recovered the patterns a year after their confiscation. This set precedent for ownership, at least for the patterns minted prior to 1887, as all of the pieces in question predated that year. Today, pattern coins can be legally held.

Among the grandest impressions ever produced at the U.S. Mint are the two varieties of pattern fifty-dollar gold pieces of 1877. Officially titled *half unions*, these large patterns were created at the request of certain politicians with interests tied to the gold-producing state of California. Specimens were struck in copper, and one of each variety was struck in gold. Both of the gold pieces were purchased around 1908 by numismatist William H. Woodin (who, years later, in 1933, served as President Franklin D. Roosevelt's first secretary of the Treasury). The Mint desired to re-obtain the pieces for its own collection, and through a complex trade deal for quantities of other patterns, did so, adding them to the Mint Collection. Now preserved in the Smithsonian Institution, these half unions are regarded as national treasures.

Special credit is due to the following individuals for contributing to this feature: Q. David Bowers, Marc Crane, Robert Hughes, Julian Leidman, Andy Lustig, and Saul Teichman. The following sources are recommended for additional information, descriptions, and complete listings:

- *United States Pattern Coins*, 9th ed., J. Hewitt Judd, edited by Q. David Bowers, 2005.
- *United States Patterns and Related Issues*, Andrew W. Pollock III, 1994. (Out of print)
- www.harrybassfoundation.org
- www.uspatterns.com

**Judd-52**

**J-67**

|  | PF-60 | PF-63 | PF-65 |
|---|---|---|---|
| **1836 Two-cent piece (J-52, billon)** This proposal for a two-cent coin is one of the earliest collectible patterns. It was designed by Christian Gobrecht. *(21–30 known)* . . . . . . . . | $2,400. | $4,250. | $7,750. |
| **1836 Gold dollar (J-67, gold)** Gobrecht styled the first gold dollar pattern after the familiar Mexican "cap and rays" design, then legal tender in this country. *(31–75 known)* . . . . . . . . . . . . . | 9,500. | 15,750. | 25,000. |

**J-93**

**J-115**

|  | PF-60 | PF-63 | PF-65 |
|---|---|---|---|
| **1839 Half dollar (J-93, silver)** Christian Gobrecht designed this proposed, but rejected, successor to the long-running Capped Bust half dollar design. *(7 known)* . . . . . . . . . . . . . . . . . . . . . . . . . . . . | $14,000. | $27,500. | $45,000. |
| **1849 Gold dollar (J-115, gold)** Various pattern ring dollars were produced in 1849 and after. This piece was hand engraved (not die struck) by James Longacre *(4–6 known)*. . . . . . . . . . . . . . . . | 16,000. | 23,000. | 45,000. |

J-119
J-125

|  | PF-60 | PF-63 | PF-65 |
|---|---|---|---|
| **1850 Cent (J-119, billon)** This was the first attempt by the Mint to reduce the size of the copper cent by creating a holed silver-copper cent. *(21–30 known)* . . . . . . . . . . . . . . . . . . . . . . | $1,200. | $1,750. | $3,000. |
| **1850 Trime (J-125, silver)** A year before the first three-cent piece was issued, these attractive patterns revived the earlier "cap and rays" dollar design. *(76–200 known)* . . . . . . . . . . . . . . . . . . . . . . | 1,400. | 2,200. | 4,000. |

J-164
J-177

|  | PF-60 | PF-63 | PF-65 |
|---|---|---|---|
| **1854 Cent (J-164, bronze)** Beginning in 1850, the Mint produced patterns for a reduced-weight cent. Among the designs were ring-style, Liberty Head, and Flying Eagle motifs. These experiments culminated with the 1856 Flying Eagle cent. *(31–75 known)* . . . . . | $1,500. | $2,750. | $5,000. |
| **1856 Half cent (J-177, copper-nickel)** Before producing copper-nickel small-size cents in 1856, the Mint experimented with that alloy using half-cent dies. *(31–75 known)* . . . . . . . . . . . . . . . . . . | 2,500. | 4,000. | 7,000. |

J-204
J-239

|  | PF-60 | PF-63 | PF-65 |
|---|---|---|---|
| **1858 Cent (J-204, copper-nickel)** This cent pattern features a flying eagle different from the one eventually adopted on regular coinage. *(31–75 known)* . . . . . . . . . . . . . . . . . . . . . . . . . . . . . . | $1,600. | $2,500. | $4,500. |
| **1859 Half dollar (J-239)** This design for a new half dollar features Longacre's French Liberty Head design. *(76–200 known)*. . . . . . . . | 1,500. | 2,500. | 4,500. |

J-305

J-329

| | PF-60 | PF-63 | PF-65 |
|---|---|---|---|
| **1863 Washington two-cent piece (J-305, copper)** Before introduction of the two-cent coin in general circulation, two basic designs were considered. If the Washington design had been adopted, it would have been the first to depict a historical figure. *(76–200 known)* .......... | $1,550. | $2,150. | $3,250. |
| **1863 Postage Currency dime (J-329, tin)** A shortage of silver coins prompted the Mint to consider redeeming Postage Currency (the predecessor of Fractional Currency) with a reduced-weight silver coin. Various alloys and weights were used for these patterns. *(21–30 known)* | 1,750. | 3,150. | 4,750. |

J-349

J-407

J-470

| | PF-60 | PF-63 | PF-65 |
|---|---|---|---|
| **1863 Eagle (J-349, gold)** This unique gold piece features GOD OUR TRUST on a scroll on the reverse. The obverse is from the regular 1863 die. . . . . . . . . . . . . . . . . . . . . . . . . . . . . . . . . . . . . . . . . . | — | $325,000. | — |
| **1865 Bimetallic two-cent piece (J-407)** This experimental piece is the first "clad" coin. It consists of an irregular and streaky layer of silver fused to copper. The experiment was unsuccessful. *(4–6 known)* .. | $5,500. | 10,250. | $18,500. |
| **1866 Five-cent piece (J-470, nickel)** Another of George Washington's early pattern appearances was on five-cent pieces of 1866. *(21–30 known)* | 1,500. | 2,250. | 3,750. |

J-486

| | PF-60 | PF-63 | PF-65 |
|---|---|---|---|
| **1866 Lincoln five-cent piece (J-486, nickel)** A number of pattern nickels were produced in 1866, including one designed to depict the recently assassinated president. *(7–12 known)* . . . . . . . . . . . . | $4,000. | $8,500. | $15,000. |

**J-561**

|  | PF-60 | PF-63 | PF-65 |
|---|---|---|---|
| **1867 Five-cent piece (J-561, aluminum)** Aluminum, earlier considered to be a semiprecious metal (before low-cost refining methods were developed), was used in the 1860s to make certain patterns, mostly as numismatic delicacies. *(31–75 known)* ...... | $1,750. | $3,500. | $5,750. |

**J-611**

|  | PF-60 | PF-63 | PF-65 |
|---|---|---|---|
| **1868 Cent (J-611, copper)** There is no known reason for the minting of this unusual piece, which mimics the original large cents that had last been made in 1857. There was no intent to resume the coinage of old-style copper "large" cents in 1868. Accordingly, this variety is regarded as a rarity created for collectors. Fewer than 15 are believed to exist. .............................................. | $19,000. | $26,500. | $36,500. |

**J-1096**

|  | PF-60 | PF-63 | PF-65 |
|---|---|---|---|
| **1871 Standard Silver quarter (J-1096, silver)** This lightweight pattern is one of many produced in the Standard Silver series, from 1869 to 1871. It was thought that lightweight coins would not be hoarded. The concept never went beyond the pattern stage. *(7–12 known)* ........................................ | $3,200. | $4,750. | $8,500. |

J-1195          J-1235

| | PF-60 | PF-63 | PF-65 |
|---|---|---|---|
| **1872 Amazonian quarter (J-1195, silver)** Many of the most popular patterns have been given colorful nicknames by collectors in appreciation of their artistry. This design is by Chief Engraver William Barber. *(7–12 known)* | $22,500. | $35,000. | $60,000. |
| **1872 Amazonian gold $3 (J-1235, gold)** This unique piece was contained in the Mint's only uniform gold set using the same design from the gold dollar to the double eagle. | — | — | 1,000,000. |

J-1281

| | PF-60 | PF-63 | PF-65 |
|---|---|---|---|
| **1873 Bailly trade dollar (J-1281, silver)** Several different pattern trade dollars were produced from 1871 to 1873, prior to selection of the Liberty Seated design by William Barber. *(76–200 known)* | $2,500. | $6,000. | $11,500. |

J-1373

| | PF-60 | PF-63 | PF-65 |
|---|---|---|---|
| **1874 Bickford eagle (J-1373, gold)** Dana Bickford, a manufacturer, proposed a ten-dollar gold coin that would be exchangeable at set rates with other world currencies. Patterns were made, but the idea proved impractical. *(2 known)* | — | $350,000. | $500,000. |

**J-1392**

| | PF-60 | PF-63 | PF-65 |
|---|---|---|---|
| **1875 Sailor Head twenty-cent piece (J-1392, silver)** William Barber's "Sailor Head" is one of the most elegant of several rejected designs for a twenty-cent coin. The same head was used on other patterns, including trade dollars. *(21–30 known)* . . . . . . . | $2,500. | $5,000. | $10,000. |

**J-1507**          **J-1512**          **J-1528**

| | PF-60 | PF-63 | PF-65 |
|---|---|---|---|
| **1877 Morgan half dollar (J-1507, copper)** A year before his famous Morgan dollar design was adopted, designer George Morgan's Liberty Head appeared on several varieties of pattern half dollar, all of which are rare today. This one pairs the well-known obverse with an indented shield design. *(2 known)* . . . . . . | — | — | $40,000. |
| **1877 Morgan half dollar (J-1512, silver)** This half dollar pattern pairs Morgan's "silver dollar style" obverse with a dramatic "Defiant Eagle" reverse. *(6 known)* . . . . . . . . . . . . . . . . . . . . . . . . | $13,000. | $26,000. | 42,000. |
| **1877 Half dollar (J-1528, silver)** This is one of several 1877 pattern half dollars by Chief Engraver William Barber. *(4 known)* | 16,000. | 31,000. | 45,000. |

J-1548

| | PF-60 | PF-63 | PF-65 |
|---|---|---|---|

**1877 Half union (J-1548, gold)** This famous fifty-dollar pattern by
William Barber would have been the highest denomination ever
issued by the Mint up to that time. The gold impression is unique
(residing in the Smithsonian), but copper specimens (which are
priced here), sometimes gilt, occasionally come to the market.
Varieties exist with a somewhat larger or smaller head. . . . . . . . .   $110,000.   $180,000.   $280,000.

J-1590

| | PF-60 | PF-63 | PF-65 |
|---|---|---|---|

**1879 Quarter dollar (J-1590, silver)** Referred to as the
"Washlady" design, this was Charles Barber's first attempt
at a uniform silver design. *(13–20 known)* . . . . . . . . . . . . . . . . . .   $7,000.   $11,500.   $20,000.

J-1609

| | PF-60 | PF-63 | PF-65 |
|---|---|---|---|

**1879 Dollar (J-1609, copper)** The "Schoolgirl" design by George T.
Morgan is a widespread favorite among pattern collectors, although
examples are rare. *(7–12 known)* . . . . . . . . . . . . . . . . . . . . . . . .   $23,000.   $47,500.   $90,000.

J-1617

| | PF-60 | PF-63 | PF-65 |
|---|---|---|---|

**1879 Goloid metric dollar (J-1617, goloid)** In 1878 through 1880, an ill-fated attempt to settle the rivalry between silver and gold resulted in small-sized pattern dollars containing both metals, a composition designated as *goloid*. The alloy is visually indistinguishable at sight from silver. *(76–200 known)* ... $1,550. $3,000. $4,250.

J-1669

J-1698

| | PF-60 | PF-63 | PF-65 |
|---|---|---|---|

**1881 One-, three- (J-1669, pictured, copper), and five-cent pieces.** These patterns represent an attempt at a uniform set of minor coins struck in nickel. $2,000. $3,500. $5,500.
**1882 Quarter dollar (J-1698, silver)** The "Shield Earring" design by George T. Morgan was made in quarter, half, and dollar denominations. *(7–12 known)* .. 15,000. 30,000. 50,000.

J-1761

| | PF-60 | PF-63 | PF-65 |
|---|---|---|---|

**1891 Barber quarter (J-1761, silver)** Charles Barber prepared various pattern dimes, quarters, and half dollars in 1891. The piece illustrated is similar to the adopted design. Two pieces are known, both in the Smithsonian. .......... — — —

J-1770

| | PF-60 | PF-63 | PF-65 |
|---|---|---|---|

**1896 Shield nickel (J-1770, nickel)** The Mint struck experimental cents and nickels with similar designs in 1896. *(21–30 known)* ................... $1,250. $2,200. $3,500.

J-1905

| | PF-60 | PF-63 | PF-65 |
|---|---|---|---|
| **1907 Indian Head double eagle (J-1905, gold)** Designed by Augustus Saint-Gaudens, this pattern is unique and extremely valuable. A variation of the reverse of this design was eventually used on the twenty-dollar gold coins of 1907 through 1933. | — | — | $5,250,000. |

J-1992

| | PF-60 | PF-63 | PF-65 |
|---|---|---|---|
| **1916 Liberty Walking half dollar (J-1992, silver)** Various pattern Mercury dimes, Standing Liberty quarters, and Liberty Walking half dollars were struck, all dated 1916. All are extremely rare, but a few found their way into circulation. | $40,000. | $72,500. | $130,000. |

J-2063

| | PF-60 | PF-63 | PF-65 |
|---|---|---|---|
| **1942 Experimental cent (J-2063, light tan plastic)** Before settling on the zinc-coated steel composition used for the Lincoln cents of 1943, the Mint considered various alternative compositions, including plastics. Most were struck by outside contractors using specially prepared dies provided by the Mint. *(7–12 known)* | — | — | $4,000. |

The expression *private gold*, used with reference to coins struck outside the United States Mint, is a general term. In the sense that no state or territory had authority to coin money, *private gold* simply refers to those interesting necessity pieces of various shapes, denominations, and degrees of intrinsic worth that were circulated in isolated areas of the United States by individuals, assayers, bankers, and so on. Some will use the words *territorial* and *state* to cover certain issues because they were coined and circulated in a territory or state. While the state of California properly sanctioned the ingots stamped by F.D. Kohler as state assayer, in no instance were any of the gold pieces struck by authority of any of the territorial governments.

The stamped fifty-dollar and other gold coins, sometimes called *ingots*, but in coin form, were made by Augustus Humbert, the United States Assayer of Gold, but were not receivable at face value for government payments, despite the fact that Humbert was an official agent. However, such pieces circulated widely in commerce.

Private coins were circulated in most instances because of a shortage of regular coinage. In the western states particularly, money became so scarce that the very commodity that the pioneers had come so far to acquire was converted into a local medium of exchange.

Ephraim Brasher's New York doubloon of 1787 is also a private American gold issue and is described on page 61.

# TEMPLETON REID
## Georgia Gold 1830

The first private gold coinage in the 19th century was struck by Templeton Reid, a jeweler and gunsmith, in Milledgeville, Georgia, in July 1830. To be closer to the mines, he moved to Gainesville, where most of his coins were made. Although weights were accurate, Reid's assays were not and his coins were slightly short of claimed value. Accordingly, he was severely attacked in the newspapers and soon lost the public's confidence. He closed his mint before the end of October in 1830; his output had amounted to only about 1,600 coins. Denominations struck were $2.50, $5, and $10.

| | VF | EF |
|---|---|---|
| 1830 $2.50 . . . . . . . . . . . . . | $60,000. | $85,000. |

| | VF | EF |
|---|---|---|
| 1830 $5 . . . . . . . . . . . . . . . | $175,000. | $240,000. |

| | VG | VF |
|---|---|---|
| 1830 TEN DOLLARS . . . . . . | $200,000. | $325,000. |

| | VG | VF |
|---|---|---|
| (No Date) TEN DOLLARS . . . | $175,000. | $250,000. |

## California Gold 1849

The enigmatic later issues of Templeton Reid were probably made from California gold. Reid, who never went to California, was then a cotton-gin maker in Columbus, Georgia, where he died in 1851. The coins were in denominations of ten and twenty-five dollars. Struck copies of both exist in various metals.

The only example known of the twenty-five-dollar piece was stolen from the cabinet of the U.S. Mint on August 16, 1858. It was never recovered.

1849 TEN DOLLAR CALIFORNIA GOLD *(unique, in Smithsonian Collection)* . . . . . . . . . . . . . .
1849 TWENTY-FIVE DOLLARS CALIFORNIA GOLD *(unknown)* . . . . . . . . . . . . . . . . . . . . . . . . .

## THE BECHTLERS
## RUTHERFORD COUNTY, NC, 1830–1852

A skilled German metallurgist, Christopher Bechtler, assisted by his son August and his nephew, also named Christopher, operated a private mint in Rutherford County, North Carolina. Rutherford County and other areas in the Piedmont region of North Carolina and Georgia were the principal sources of the nation's gold supply from 1790 until the California gold strikes in 1848.

The coins minted by the Bechtlers were of only three denominations, but they covered a wide variety of weights and sizes. Rotated dies are common throughout the series. In 1831, the Bechtlers produced the first gold dollar in the United States. The U.S. Mint struck its first circulating gold dollar in 1849. Bechtler coins were well accepted by the public and circulated widely in the Southeast.

The inscription AUGUST 1. 1834 on several varieties of five-dollar pieces has a special significance. The secretary of the Treasury recommended to the Mint director that gold coins of the reduced weight bear the authorization date. This was not done on federal gold coinage, but the elder Christopher Bechtler evidently acted on the recommendation to avoid difficulty with Treasury authorities.

### Christopher Bechtler

| | VF | EF | AU | Unc. |
|---|---|---|---|---|
| ONE GOLD DOLLAR N. CAROLINA, 30.G. . . . . . . . . . | $2,400. | $3,700. | $5,500. | $14,250. |
| ONE GOLD DOLLAR N. CAROLINA, 28.G Centered, No Star . . . . . . . . . . . . . . . . . . . . . . . . . . | 3,500. | 4,800. | 8,500. | 18,500. |
| ONE GOLD DOLLAR N. CAROLINA, 28.G High, No Star | 7,500. | 11,500. | 17,500. | 27,500. |

| | VF | EF | AU | Unc. |
|---|---|---|---|---|
| ONE DOLLAR CAROLINA, 28.G., N Reversed . . . . . . . | $1,800. | $2,600. | $3,750. | $7,000. |
| 2.50 CAROLINA, 67.G., 21 CARATS . . . . . . . . . . . . . | 5,500. | 9,500. | 12,000. | 22,000. |

| | VF | EF | AU | Unc. |
|---|---|---|---|---|
| 2.50 CAROLINA, 70.G, 20 CARATS . . . . . . . . . . . . . | $5,500. | $9,750. | $12,500. | $25,000. |
| 2.50 GEORGIA, 64.G, 22 CARATS . . . . . . . . . . . . . | 5,500. | 9,750. | 12,500. | 25,000. |
| 2.50 GEORGIA, 64.G, 22 CARATS (Even "22") . . . . . | 7,500. | 12,000. | 16,000. | 35,000. |

| | VF | EF | AU | Unc. |
|---|---|---|---|---|
| 2.50 NORTH CAROLINA, 75.G., 20 CARATS. RUTHERFORD in a Circle. Border of Large Beads | $15,000. | $22,500. | $30,000. | $50,000. |
| 2.50 NORTH CAROLINA, Without 75.G. . . . . . . . . . . | 15,000. | 22,500. | 30,000. | 50,000. |
| 2.50 NORTH CAROLINA, Without 75.G., CAROLINA Above 250 Instead of GOLD *(unique)* | | | | — |
| 2.50 NORTH CAROLINA, 20 CARATS on Obverse, 75.G. on Reverse. Border Finely Serrated . . . . . . | — | — | — | |

| | VF | EF | AU | Unc. |
|---|---|---|---|---|
| 5 DOLLARS NORTH CAROLINA GOLD, 150.G., 20.CARATS . . . . . . . . . . . . . . . . . . . | $15,000. | $20,000. | $32,500. | $56,000. |
| Similar, Without 150.G. . . . . . . . . . . . . . . . . . . | | — | — | |

| | VF | EF | AU | Unc. |
|---|---|---|---|---|
| 5 DOLLARS CAROLINA, RUTHERFORD, 140.G., 20 CARATS, Plain Edge ................. | $6,000. | $8,000. | $12,000. | $24,000. |
| 5 DOLLARS CAROLINA, RUTHERFORD, 140.G., 20 CARATS, Reeded Edge ............... | 12,500. | 20,000. | 32,500. | 45,000. |
| 5 DOLLARS BECHTLER, Without Star and C. ..... | — | | | |
| 5 DOLLARS CAROLINA GOLD, 134.G., 21 CARATS, With Star ................. | 5,400. | 7,500. | 11,000. | 18,500. |

| | VF | EF | AU | Unc. |
|---|---|---|---|---|
| 5 DOLLARS GEORGIA GOLD, RUTHERFORD, 128.G., 22 CARATS .................... | $6,500. | $9,000. | $13,000. | $26,500. |
| 5 DOLLARS GEORGIA GOLD, RUTHERFORD, 128.G:, 22 CARATS, With Colon ........... | — | — | | |
| 5 DOLLARS GEORGIA GOLD, RUTHERF, 128.G., 22 CARATS .................... | 6,500. | 9,000. | 13,000. | 26,500. |
| 5 DOLLARS CAROLINA GOLD, RUTHERF., 140.G., 20 CARATS, AUGUST 1, 1834 ....... | 6,000. | 8,250. | 11,500. | 24,000. |
| Similar, but "20" Distant From CARATS ........ | 6,750. | 11,000. | 16,000. | 24,000. |

## August Bechtler

| | VF | EF | AU | Unc. |
|---|---|---|---|---|
| 1 DOL:, CAROLINA GOLD, 27.G., 21.C. .......... | $1,300. | $1,900. | $2,800. | $4,500. |
| 5 DOLLARS, CAROLINA GOLD, 134.G:, 21 CARATS | 5,500. | 7,500. | 11,000. | 27,500. |
| 5 DOLLARS, CAROLINA GOLD, 128.G., 22 CARATS | 11,000. | 14,000. | 20,000. | 34,000. |

| | VF | EF | AU | Unc. |
|---|---|---|---|---|
| 5 DOLLARS, CAROLINA GOLD, 141.G., 20 CARATS | $9,000. | $13,000. | $18,000. | $30,000. |
| 5 DOLLARS CAROLINA 134 gr. 21 CARATS, Reverse of C. Bechtler as Shown on Facing Page . . . . . | — | — | | |

*Note:* Restrikes in "Proof" using original dies were made about 1920.

## NORRIS, GREGG & NORRIS
## SAN FRANCISCO 1849

Collectors consider this piece the first of the California private gold coins. A newspaper account dated May 31, 1849, described a five-dollar gold coin, struck at Benicia City, though with the imprint San Francisco. It mentioned the private stamp of Norris, Gregg & Norris. The initials N.G.&N. were not identified until 1902, when the coins of Augustus Humbert were sold.

| | F | VF | EF | AU | Unc. |
|---|---|---|---|---|---|
| 1849 Half Eagle, Plain Edge . . . . . . . . | $3,900. | $5,900. | $10,000. | $13,000. | $27,500. |
| 1849 Half Eagle, Reeded Edge . . . . . . | 3,900. | 5,900. | 10,000. | 13,000. | 27,500. |
| 1850 Half Eagle, With STOCKTON Beneath Date *(unique)* . . . . . . . . | | | | | |

## MOFFAT & CO.
## SAN FRANCISCO 1849–1853

The firm of Moffat & Co. was perhaps the most important of the California private coiners. The assay office they conducted was semi-official in character. The successors to this firm, Curtis, Perry and Ward, later established the United States Branch mint of San Francisco.

In June or July 1849, Moffat & Co. began to issue small, rectangular pieces of gold owing to lack of coin in the locality, in values from $9.43 to $264. The $9.43, $14.25, and $16.00 varieties are the only types known today.

The unique examples of the $9.43 and $14.25 ingots are in the National Coin Collection in the Smithsonian.

*See next page for chart.*

| | |
|---|---|
| $9.43 Ingot *(unique)* ............. | — |
| $14.25 Ingot *(unique)* ............. | — |

| | |
|---|---|
| $16.00 Ingot .................... | $43,000. |

The dies for the ten-dollar piece were cut by a Bavarian, Albert Kuner. On the coronet of Liberty appear the words MOFFAT & CO., instead of the word LIBERTY as in regular United States issues.

| | F | VF | EF | AU | Unc. |
|---|---|---|---|---|---|
| 1849 FIVE DOL. *(all varieties)* ....... | $1,400. | $2,200. | $3,650. | $5,800. | $13,000. |
| 1850 FIVE DOL. *(all varieties)* ....... | 1,450. | 2,300. | 3,800. | 6,250. | 13,500. |
| 1849 TEN DOL. ................. | 2,800. | 4,300. | 9,000. | 16,500. | 30,000. |
| 1849 TEN D. ................... | 2,850. | 4,400. | 11,000. | 18,500. | 36,000. |

## UNITED STATES ASSAY OFFICE
### Augustus Humbert
### United States Assayer of Gold, 1851

Augustus Humbert, a New York watchcase maker, was appointed United States assayer, and he placed his name and the government stamp on the ingots of gold issued by Moffat & Co. The assay office, a provisional government mint, was a temporary expedient to accommodate the Californians until the establishment of a permanent branch mint.

The fifty-dollar gold piece was accepted as legal tender on a par with standard U.S. gold coins and was known variously as a *slug*, *quintuple eagle*, or *five-eagle* piece. It was officially termed an *ingot*.

### *Lettered-Edge Varieties*

| | F | VF | EF | AU | Unc. |
|---|---|---|---|---|---|
| 1851 50 D C 880 THOUS., No 50 on Reverse. Sunk in Edge: AUGUSTUS HUMBERT UNITED STATES ASSAYER OF GOLD CALIFORNIA 1851 .......... | $13,000. | $19,000. | $27,500. | $38,000. | $70,000. |

| | F | VF | EF | AU | Unc. |
|---|---|---|---|---|---|
| 1851 50 D C, Similar to Last Variety, but 50 on Reverse . . . . . . . . . . . | $15,500. | $26,000. | $37,500. | $52,000. | $80,000. |
| 1851 50 D C, 887 THOUS., With 50 on Reverse . . . . . . . . . . | 14,000. | 25,000. | 35,000. | 45,000. | 74,000. |

## *Reeded-Edge Varieties*

| | F | VF | EF | AU | Unc. |
|---|---|---|---|---|---|
| 1851 FIFTY DOLLS, 880 THOUS., "Target" Reverse . . . . . . . . . . . . | $9,500. | $13,000. | $19,500. | $27,500. | $48,000. |
| 1851 FIFTY DOLLS, 887 THOUS., "Target" Reverse . . . . . . . . . . . . | 9,500. | 13,000. | 19,500. | 27,500. | 48,000. |
| 1852 FIFTY DOLLS, 887 THOUS. . . . . | 9,500. | 13,000. | 19,500. | 27,500. | 48,000. |

*Note:* A unique Proof of the 1851 with 887 THOUS. was sold at the Garrett II auction in 1980 for $500,000.

## *Moffat-Humbert*

The withdrawal of the discredited private coins of five-, ten-, and twenty-dollar denominations as a result of the new U.S. Assay operations caused a new turn of affairs for Californians. Fractional currency coins of almost every nation were pressed into service by the Californians, but the supply was too small to help to any extent. Moffat & Co. proceeded in January 1852 to issue a new ten-dollar gold piece bearing the stamp MOFFAT & CO.

| | | **Close Date** | | **Wide Date** | | |

| | F | VF | EF | AU | Unc. |
|---|---|---|---|---|---|
| 1852 TEN D. MOFFAT & CO. (Close Date) | $3,200. | $5,000. | $10,000. | $25,000. | $55,000. |
| 1852 TEN D. MOFFAT & CO. (Wide Date) | 3,200. | 5,000. | 10,000. | 25,000. | 55,000. |

| | F | VF | EF | AU | Unc. |
|---|---|---|---|---|---|
| 1852 TEN DOLS. 1852, 2 Over 1 | $2,300. | $3,800. | $6,750. | $11,000. | $22,500. |
| 1852 TEN DOLS. | 2,000. | 3,000. | 4,800. | 8,750. | 19,000. |

| | F | VF | EF | AU | Unc. |
|---|---|---|---|---|---|
| 1852 TWENTY DOLS., 1852, 2 Over 1 | $5,400. | $8,300. | $16,000. | $28,500. | $67,500. |

## United States Assay Office of Gold – 1852

The firm of Moffat & Co. was dissolved in 1852 and a newly reorganized company known as the United States Assay Office of Gold took over the contract. Principals were Curtis, Perry, and Ward.

| | F | VF | EF | AU | Unc. |
|---|---|---|---|---|---|
| 1852 FIFTY DOLLS., 887 THOUS. ... | $9,500. | $13,000. | $20,000. | $29,000. | $48,000. |
| 1852 FIFTY DOLLS., 900 THOUS. ... | 9,500. | 13,000. | 20,000. | 30,000. | 50,000. |

| | F | VF | EF | AU | Unc. |
|---|---|---|---|---|---|
| 1852 TEN DOLS., 884 THOUS. ...... | $1,650. | $2,700. | $4,000. | $7,000. | $16,000. |
| 1853 TEN D., 884 THOUS. ......... | 6,000. | 11,500. | 22,000. | 30,000. | 65,000. |
| 1853 TEN D., 900 THOUS. ......... | 3,750. | 5,700. | 9,000. | 14,500. | 22,000. |

| | F | VF | EF | AU | Unc. |
|---|---|---|---|---|---|
| 1853 TWENTY D., 884 THOUS. ..... | $6,500. | $11,500. | $17,000. | $25,000. | $41,000. |

| | F | VF | EF | AU | Unc. |
|---|---|---|---|---|---|
| 1853 TWENTY D., 900 THOUS. . . . . . | $1,900. | $2,750. | $4,000. | $6,000. | $11,000. |

## United States Assay Office of Gold – Moffat

The last Moffat issue, an 1853 twenty-dollar piece, is very similar to the U.S. double eagle of that period. It was struck after John L. Moffat retired from the Assay Office.

| | F | VF | EF | AU | Unc. |
|---|---|---|---|---|---|
| 1853 TWENTY D. . . . . . . . . . . . . . . | $3,750. | $4,750. | $7,000. | $11,000. | $25,000. |

## J.H. BOWIE

Joseph H. Bowie joined his cousins in San Francisco in 1849 and possibly produced a limited coinage of gold pieces. A trial piece of the dollar denomination is known in copper, but may never have reached the coinage stage. Little is known about the company or the reason for issuing these pieces.

| | | | |
|---|---|---|---|
| 1849 1 DOL. (Copper) . . . . . . . . . . . | — | 1849 5 DOL. . . . . . . . . . . . . . . . . . . . . | — |

## CINCINNATI MINING & TRADING CO. (1849)

The origin and location of this company are unknown.

| | EF | Unc. |
|---|---|---|
| 1849 FIVE DOLLARS *(unique)* . . . . . . . . . . . . . . . . . . . . . . . . . . . . . | | |
| 1849 TEN DOLLARS *(7 known)* $431,250, EF, Stack's auction, May-04 | $500,000. | — |

*Note: Beware of spurious specimens cast in base metal with the word TRACING in place of TRADING.*

## MASSACHUSETTS AND CALIFORNIA COMPANY

This company was believed to have been organized in Northampton, Massachusetts, in May 1849. Pieces with 5D are not genuine.

| | VF | EF |
|---|---|---|
| 1849 FIVE D. . . . . . . . . . . . . . . . . . . . . . . . . . . . . . . . . . . . . . . . . | $140,000. | $200,000. |

## MINERS' BANK
## SAN FRANCISCO 1849

The institution of Wright & Co., exchange brokers located in Portsmouth Square, San Francisco, was known as the Miners' Bank.

A ten-dollar piece was issued in the autumn of 1849, but the coins were not readily accepted because they were worth less than face value. The firm was dissolved on January 14, 1850. Unlike the gold in most California issues, the gold in these coins was alloyed with copper.

| **Plain Border** | | | **Crimped Border** | |
|---|---|---|---|---|
| | VF | EF | AU | Unc. |
| (1849) TEN D., Normal Border . . . . . . . . . . . . . . . | $14,000. | $24,000. | $35,000. | $70,000. |
| (1849) TEN D., Crimped Border . . . . . . . . . . . . . . | 15,000. | 26,000. | 36,000. | 75,000. |

## J.S. ORMSBY
## SACRAMENTO 1849

The initials J.S.O., which appear on certain issues of California privately coined gold pieces, represent the firm of J.S. Ormsby & Co. They struck both five- and ten-dollar denominations, all undated.

| | VF |
|---|---|
| (1849) 5 DOLLS, Plain Edge *(possibly unique)* .................................... | — |
| (1849) 5 DOLLS, Reeded Edge *(unique, in Smithsonian Collection)* ................... | — |
| (1849) 10 DOLLS *(4 known)* ................................................ | $225,000. |

## PACIFIC COMPANY, SAN FRANCISCO 1849

The origin of the Pacific Company is very uncertain. All data regarding the firm are based on conjecture.

Edgar H. Adams wrote that he believed that the coins bearing the stamp of the Pacific Company were produced by the coining firm of Broderick and Kohler. The coins were probably hand struck with the aid of a sledgehammer.

| | EF | AU |
|---|---|---|
| 1849 1 DOLLAR *(2 known)* ................................ | | |
| 1849 5 DOLLARS ....................................... | $250,000. | $325,000. |
| 1849 10 DOLLARS ...................................... | 300,000. | 400,000. |

## F.D. KOHLER
## CALIFORNIA STATE ASSAYER 1850

The State Assay Office was authorized on April 12, 1850. That year, Governor Burnett appointed F.D. Kohler, who thereupon sold his assaying business to Baldwin & Co. He served at both the San Francisco and Sacramento offices. The State Assay Offices were discontinued at the time the U. S. Assay Office was established, on February 1, 1851.

Ingots issued ranged from $36.55 to $150. An Extremely Fine specimen sold in the Garrett Sale, 1980, for $200,000. Each is unique.

| | | | | |
|---|---|---|---|---|
| $36.55 Sacramento .............. | — | $45.34 San Francisco .............. | — |
| $37.31 San Francisco .............. | — | $50.00 San Francisco .............. | — |
| $40.07 San Francisco .............. | — | $54.09 San Francisco .............. | — |

*Note:* A $40.07 ingot was stolen from the Mint Cabinet in 1858 and never recovered.

## DUBOSQ & COMPANY
## SAN FRANCISCO 1850

Theodore Dubosq, a Philadelphia jeweler, took melting and coining machinery to San Francisco in 1849.

| | VF | | VF |
|---|---|---|---|
| 1850 FIVE D. .................... | $90,000. | 1850 TEN D. .................... | $100,000. |

## BALDWIN & CO.
## SAN FRANCISCO 1850

George C. Baldwin and Thomas S. Holman were in the jewelry business in San Francisco and were known as Baldwin & Co. They were the successors to F.D. Kohler & Co., taking over its machinery and other equipment in May 1850.

| | F | VF | EF | AU | Unc. |
|---|---|---|---|---|---|
| 1850 FIVE DOL. ................. | $5,500. | $10,000. | $19,000. | $25,000. | $35,000. |
| 1850 TEN DOLLARS, Horseman Type | 28,000. | 50,000. | 75,000. | 100,000. | 150,000. |

| | F | VF | EF | AU | Unc. |
|---|---|---|---|---|---|
| 1851 TEN D. .................... | $8,000. | $18,000. | $30,000. | $45,000. | $95,000. |

The Baldwin & Co. twenty-dollar piece was the first of that denomination issued in California. Baldwin coins are believed to have contained about 2% copper alloy.

| | EF | Unc. |
|---|---|---|
| 1851 TWENTY D. | $200,000. | — |

## SCHULTZ & COMPANY
## SAN FRANCISCO 1851

The firm of Schultz & Co., a brass foundry, was operated by Judge G.W. Schultz and William T. Garratt.  The surname is misspelled *Shultz* on the coins.

| | F | VF | EF | AU |
|---|---|---|---|---|
| 1851 FIVE D. | $22,000. | $42,000. | $59,000. | $85,000. |

## DUNBAR & COMPANY
## SAN FRANCISCO 1851

Edward E. Dunbar operated the California Bank in San Francisco. Dunbar later returned to New York and organized the famous Continental Bank Note Co.

| | EF |
|---|---|
| 1851 FIVE D. | $200,000. |

## WASS, MOLITOR & CO.
## SAN FRANCISCO 1852–1855

The gold-smelting and assaying plant of Wass, Molitor & Co. was operated by two Hungarian patriots, Count S.C. Wass and A.P. Molitor. They maintained an excellent laboratory and complete apparatus for analysis and coinage of gold.

The company struck five-, ten-, twenty-, and fifty-dollar coins. In 1852 they produced a ten-dollar piece similar in design to the five-dollar denomination. The difference is in the reverse legend, which reads: S.M.V. [Standard Mint Value] CALIFORNIA GOLD TEN D.

No pieces were coined in 1853 or 1854, but they brought out the twenty- and fifty-dollar pieces in 1855. A considerable number of the fifty-dollar coins were made. There was a ten-dollar piece issued in 1855 also, with the Liberty head and small close date.

**Large Head, Pointed Bust**

| | F | VF | EF | AU | Unc. |
|---|---|---|---|---|---|
| 1852 FIVE DOLLARS, Small Head, With Rounded Bust .......... | $3,500. | $7,000. | $15,000. | $22,500. | $50,000. |
| 1852 FIVE DOLLARS, Large Head, With Pointed Bust ............ | 3,200. | 6,500. | 13,500. | 19,500. | 42,500. |

**Large Head**       **Small Head**

**Small Date**       **1855**

| | F | VF | EF | AU | Unc. |
|---|---|---|---|---|---|
| 1852 TEN D., Large Head .......... | $2,400. | $3,800. | $6,500. | $12,000. | $20,000. |
| 1852 TEN D., Small Head .......... | 5,500. | 7,250. | 16,500. | 27,500. | 65,000. |
| 1852 TEN D., Small Closed Date .... | 9,500. | 20,000. | 37,500. | 75,000. | |
| 1855 TEN D. ................... | 10,000. | 16,000. | 22,000. | 30,000. | 55,000. |

**Large Head**                **Small Head**

| | F | VF | EF | AU | Unc. |
|---|---|---|---|---|---|
| 1855 TWENTY DOL., Large Head .... | — | — | $260,000. | — | — |
| 1855 TWENTY DOL., Small Head .... | $11,000. | $24,000. | 36,000. | $55,000. | $100,000. |

| | F | VF | EF | AU | Unc. |
|---|---|---|---|---|---|
| 1855 50 DOLLARS ............... | $20,000. | $26,500. | $37,500. | $70,000. | $150,000. |

## KELLOGG & CO.
## SAN FRANCISCO 1854–1855

John G. Kellogg went to San Francisco on October 12, 1849, from Auburn, New York. At first he was employed by Moffat & Co., and remained with that organization when control passed to Curtis, Perry, and Ward. When the U.S. Assay Office was discontinued, December 14, 1853, Kellogg became associated with G.F. Richter, who had been an assayer in the government assay office. These two set up business as Kellogg & Richter on December 19, 1853.

When the U.S. Assay Office ceased operations, a period ensued during which no private firm was striking gold. The new San Francisco branch mint did not produce coins for some months after Curtis & Perry took the contract for the government (Ward having died). The lack of coin was again keenly felt by businessmen, who petitioned Kellogg & Richter to "supply the vacuum" by issuing private coin. Their plea was soon answered: on February 9, 1854, Kellogg & Co. placed their first twenty-dollar piece in circulation.

The firm dissolved late in 1854 and reorganized as Kellogg & Humbert. The latter partner was Augustus Humbert, for some time identified as U.S. assayer of gold in California. Regardless of the fact that the branch mint was then producing coins, Kellogg & Humbert issued twenty-dollar coins in 1855 in a quantity greater than before.

| | F | VF | EF | AU | Unc. |
|---|---|---|---|---|---|
| 1854 TWENTY D. | $2,200. | $3,000. | $4,850. | $7,000. | $17,000. |

The 1855 twenty-dollar piece is similar to that of 1854. The letters on the reverse are larger and the arrows longer on one 1854 variety. There are die varieties of both.

| | F | VF | EF | AU | Unc. |
|---|---|---|---|---|---|
| 1855 TWENTY D. | $2,200. | $3,000. | $5,500. | $7,750. | $19,000. |

In 1855, Ferdinand Grüner cut the dies for a round-format fifty-dollar gold coin for Kellogg & Co., but coinage seems to have been limited to presentation pieces. Only 10 to 12 pieces are known to exist. A "commemorative restrike" was made in 2001 using transfer dies made from the original and gold recovered from the SS *Central America*. These pieces have the inscription S.S. CENTRAL AMERICA GOLD, C.H.S. on the reverse ribbon.

| | PF |
|---|---|
| 1855 FIFTY DOLLS. | $250,000. |

## OREGON EXCHANGE COMPANY
## OREGON CITY 1849
### The Beaver Coins of Oregon

Upon the discovery of gold in California, a great exodus of settlers joined in the hunt for the precious metal. Soon, returning gold seekers offered their gold dust, which became the accepted medium of exchange. As in other western areas at that time, the uncertain qualities of the gold and weighing devices tended to irk the trades-people, and petitions were made to the legislature for a standard gold coin issue.

On February 16, 1849, the legislature passed an act providing for a mint and spec-ified five- and ten-dollar gold coins without alloy. Oregon City, the largest city in the territory with a population of about 1,000, was designated as the location for the mint. At the time this act was passed, Oregon had been brought into the United States as a territory by act of Congress. When the new governor arrived on March 2, he declared the coinage act unconstitutional.

The public-spirited people, however, continued to work for a convenient medium of exchange and soon took matters into their own hands by starting a private mint. Eight men of affairs, whose names were Kilborne, Magruder, Taylor, Abernethy, Willson, Rector, Campbell, and Smith, set up the Oregon Exchange Company.

The coins struck were of virgin gold as specified in the original act. Ten-dollar dies were made later, and were of finer design and workmanship.

| | Mintage | F | VF | EF | AU | Unc. |
|---|---|---|---|---|---|---|
| 1849 5 D. | 6,000 | $20,000. | $30,000. | $45,000. | $75,000. | — |

| | Mintage | F | VF | EF | AU | Unc. |
|---|---|---|---|---|---|---|
| 1849 TEN.D | 2,850 | $45,000. | $80,000. | $150,000. | $225,000. | — |

## MORMON GOLD PIECES
## SALT LAKE CITY, UTAH, 1849–1860

The first name given to the organized Mormon Territory was the "State of Deseret," the last word meaning "honeybee." The beehive, which is shown on the reverse of the five-dollar 1860 piece, was a favorite device of the followers of Joseph Smith and Brigham Young. The clasped hands appear on most Mormon coins and exemplify strength in unity. HOLINESS TO THE LORD was an inscription frequently used.

# PRIVATE AND TERRITORIAL GOLD

Brigham Young was the instigator of the coinage system and personally supervised the mint, which was housed in a little adobe building in Salt Lake City. The mint was inaugurated late in 1849 as a public convenience.

| | F | VF | EF | AU | Unc. |
|---|---|---|---|---|---|
| 1849 TWO.AND.HALF.DO. . . . . . . . . | $9,250. | $15,000. | $24,000. | $37,500. | $55,000. |
| 1849 FIVE.DOLLARS . . . . . . . . . . . . | 6,750. | 12,500. | 19,000. | 25,000. | 43,000. |

| | F | VF | EF | AU |
|---|---|---|---|---|
| 1849 TEN.DOLLARS . . . . . . . . . . . . . . . . . . . . . . . | $140,000. | $185,000. | $225,000. | $300,000. |

*The first of the twenty-dollar denomination to be coined in the United States.*

| | F | VF | EF | AU |
|---|---|---|---|---|
| 1849 TWENTY.DOLLARS . . . . . . . . . . . . . . . . . . . | $50,000. | $90,000. | $125,000. | $165,000. |

| | F | VF | EF | AU | Unc. |
|---|---|---|---|---|---|
| 1850 FIVE DOLLLARS . . . . . . . . . . . . | $7,500. | $13,500. | $22,000. | $34,000. | $62,500. |

| | F | VF | EF | AU | Unc. |
|---|---|---|---|---|---|
| 1860 5.D. . . . . . . . . . . . . . . . . . . . . | $12,500. | $25,000. | $33,000. | $45,000. | $55,000. |

## COLORADO GOLD PIECES
### Clark, Gruber & Co.
### Denver 1860–1861

Clark, Gruber & Co. was a well-known private minting firm in Denver, Colorado, in the early 1860s.

| | F | VF | EF | AU | Unc. |
|---|---|---|---|---|---|
| 1860 2 1/2 D. . . . . . . . . . . . . . . . . | $1,500. | $2,250. | $3,750. | $5,000. | $13,000. |
| 1860 FIVE D. . . . . . . . . . . . . . . . . . | 1,900. | 2,750. | 4,000. | 5,500. | 14,000. |

| | F | VF | EF | AU | Unc. |
|---|---|---|---|---|---|
| 1860 TEN D. . . . . . . . . . . . . . . . . . | $6,250. | $8,500. | $13,500. | $19,500. | $35,000. |
| 1860 TWENTY D. . . . . . . . . . . . . . . | 35,000. | 60,000. | 100,000. | 140,000. | — |
| *$690,000, MS-64, Heritage auction, Jan-06* | | | | | |

The $2.50 and $5 pieces of 1861 follow closely the designs of the 1860 issues. The main difference is found in the legends. The reverse side now has CLARK GRUBER & CO. DENVER. PIKES PEAK now appears on the coronet of Liberty.

|  | F | VF | EF | AU | Unc. |
|---|---|---|---|---|---|
| 1861 2 1/2 D. . . . . . . . . . . . . . . . . | $1,600. | $2,500. | $3,900. | $7,000. | $13,500. |
| 1861 FIVE D. . . . . . . . . . . . . . . | 2,000. | 3,000. | 4,750. | 8,250. | 30,000. |
| 1861 TEN D. . . . . . . . . . . . . . . . | 2,000. | 3,200. | 5,000. | 8,500. | 22,500. |

|  | F | VF | EF | AU | Unc. |
|---|---|---|---|---|---|
| 1861 TWENTY D. . . . . . . . . . . . . . | $7,500. | $15,000. | $35,000. | $52,500. | $125,000. |

## John Parsons & Company
## Tarryall Mines – Colorado, 1861

Very little is known regarding the mint of John Parsons and Co., although it is reasonably certain that it operated in the South Park section of Park County, Colorado near the original town of Tarryall, in the summer of 1861.

**Pikes Peak Gold**

|  | VF | EF |
|---|---|---|
| (1861) Undated 2 1/2 D. . . . . . . . . . . . . . . . . . . . . . . . . . . . . . . . . | $150,000. | $200,000. |
| (1861) Undated FIVE D. . . . . . . . . . . . . . . . . . . . . . . . . . . . . . . . . | 200,000. | 250,000. |

## J.J. Conway & Co.
## Georgia Gulch, Colorado, 1861

Records show that the Conway mint operated for a short while in 1861. As in all gold-mining areas the value of gold dust caused disagreement among the merchants and the miners. The firm of J.J. Conway & Co. solved this difficulty by bringing out its gold pieces in August 1861.

|  | VF | EF |
|---|---|---|
| (1861) Undated 2 1/2 DOLL'S . . . . . . . . . . . . . . . . . . . . . . . . . . . . | $100,000. | $125,000. |
| (1861) Undated FIVE DOLLARS . . . . . . . . . . . . . . . . . . . . . . . . . . | 155,000. | 210,000. |

(1861) Undated TEN DOLLARS . . . . . . . . . . . . . . . . . . . . . . . . . . . . . . . . . . . . . . . . . . . . . . . . . . . . . .    —

## CALIFORNIA SMALL-DENOMINATION GOLD

There was a scarcity of small coins during the California gold rush, and starting in 1852, quarter, half, and dollar coins were privately minted from native gold to alleviate the shortage. The acceptability of these hard-to-handle and underweight coins was always limited, but they soon became popular as souvenirs. Early coins contained up to 85% of face value in gold. The amount and quality of gold in the coins soon decreased, and some are merely gold plated.

The Coinage Act of April 22, 1864, made private coinage illegal, but the law was not fully enforced until 1883. In compliance with the law, non-denominated tokens were made, and from 1872 until 1883 both coins and tokens were produced. After 1883, most of the production was tokens. To circumvent the law, and to make them more acceptable, some pieces made after 1881 were backdated to the 1850s or 1860s.

Early issues have Liberty heads; later issues have Indian heads and are often prooflike. Most have a wreath on the reverse, but some have original designs. About 35,000 pieces are believed to exist. More than 570 different varieties have been identified, many of them very rare. The quality of strike and edge treatment is inconsistent. Many bear their makers' initials: D, DERI, DERIB, DN, FD, G, GG, GL, H, L, N, or NR. Major denominated coins are listed below; values are for the most common variety of each type. Non-denominated tokens are not included in these listings. They are much less valuable. *Beware of extremely common modern replicas* (often having a bear in the design), which have little numismatic value.

The values in the following charts are only for coins made before 1883 with the denomination on the reverse expressed as CENTS, DOL., DOLL., or DOLLAR.

### *Quarter Dollar – Octagonal*

|  | EF | AU | Unc. |
|---|---|---|---|
| Large Liberty Head/Value and Date in Wreath . . . . . . . . . . . . . . . | $170. | $250. | $400. |
| Large Liberty Head/Value and Date in Beaded Circle . . . . . . . . . . . | 170. | 275. | 450. |
| Large Liberty Head/Value and CAL in Wreath . . . . . . . . . . . . . . . . . | 170. | 225. | 300. |
| Small Liberty Head/Value and Date in Wreath . . . . . . . . . . . . . . . . | 170. | 225. | 300. |
| Small Liberty Head/Value and Date in Beaded Circle . . . . . . . . . . . | 175. | 250. | 325. |
| Small Liberty Head/Value in Shield, Date in Wreath . . . . . . . . . . . . | 175. | 250. | 350. |
| Small Liberty Head/Value and CAL in Wreath . . . . . . . . . . . . . . . . . | 175. | 250. | 400. |
| Large Indian Head/Value in Wreath . . . . . . . . . . . . . . . . . . . . . . . . . | 210. | 300. | 450. |
| Large Indian Head/Value and CAL in Wreath . . . . . . . . . . . . . . . . . | 190. | 275. | 425. |
| Small Indian Head/Value in Wreath . . . . . . . . . . . . . . . . . . . . . . . . . | 210. | 275. | 475. |
| Small Indian Head/Value and CAL in Wreath . . . . . . . . . . . . . . . . . | 485. | 600. | 875. |
| Washington Head 1872/Value and CAL in Wreath . . . . . . . . . . . . . | 500. | 800. | 1,250. |

## Quarter Dollar – Round

| | EF | AU | Unc. |
|---|---|---|---|
| Large Liberty Head/Value and Date in Wreath | $180. | $300. | $375. |
| Large Liberty Head/Value and CAL in Wreath | 150. | 240. | 350. |
| Large Liberty Head/25 CENTS in Wreath | 275. | 400. | 600. |
| Small Liberty Head/Value and Date in Wreath | 175. | 280. | 400. |
| Small Liberty Head/Value in Shield, Date in Wreath | 175. | 310. | 500. |
| Small Liberty Head/Value and CAL in Wreath | 175. | 310. | 350. |
| Large Indian Head/Value in Wreath | 350. | 500. | 775. |
| Large Indian Head/Value and CAL in Wreath | 320. | 415. | 650. |
| Small Indian Head/Value in Wreath | 180. | 290. | 500. |
| Small Indian Head/Value and CAL in Wreath | 350. | 500. | 775. |
| Washington Head 1872/Value and CAL in Wreath | 650. | 900. | 1,400. |

## Half Dollar – Octagonal

| | EF | AU | Unc. |
|---|---|---|---|
| Large Liberty Head/Value and Date in Wreath | $275. | $350. | $600. |
| Large Liberty Head/Value and Date in Beaded Circle | 150. | 200. | 400. |
| Large Liberty Head/Value and CAL in Wreath | 200. | 400. | 575. |
| Large Liberty Head/Legend Surrounds Wreath | 375. | 575. | 900. |
| Small Liberty Head/Value and Date in Wreath | 190. | 350. | 500. |
| Small Liberty Head/Value and CAL in Wreath | 175. | 300. | 420. |
| Small Liberty Head/Small Eagle With Rays | 1,000. | 1,250. | 2,200. |
| Small Liberty Head/Large Eagle With Raised Wings | 950. | 1,250. | 2,200. |
| Large Indian Head/Value in Wreath | 200. | 375. | 575. |
| Large Indian Head/Value and CAL in Wreath | 220. | 340. | 520. |
| Small Indian Head/Value in Wreath | 225. | 410. | 625. |
| Small Indian Head/Value and CAL in Wreath | 425. | 570. | 875. |

## Half Dollar – Round

| | EF | AU | Unc. |
|---|---|---|---|
| Liberty Head/Value and Date in Wreath | $175. | $300. | $430. |
| Liberty Head/Value and CAL in Wreath | 200. | 325. | 510. |
| Liberty Head/CALIFORNIA GOLD Around Wreath | 200. | 325. | 525. |
| Large Indian Head/Value in Wreath | 200. | 300. | 450. |
| Large Indian Head/Value and CAL in Wreath | 175. | 275. | 425. |
| Small Indian Head/Value in Wreath | 200. | 325. | 550. |
| Small Indian Head/Value and CAL in Wreath | 180. | 300. | 450. |

## Dollar – Octagonal

| | EF | AU | Unc. |
|---|---|---|---|
| Liberty Head/Value and Date in Wreath | $450. | $650. | $1,050. |
| Liberty Head/Value in Beaded Circle | 475. | 700. | 1,200. |
| Liberty Head/Legend Around Wreath | 485. | 725. | 1,300. |
| Liberty Head/Large Eagle | 2,000. | 3,000. | 4,750. |
| Large Indian Head/Value and Date in Wreath | 600. | 900. | 1,600. |
| Large Indian Head/Value in Wreath | 700. | 1,000. | 1,800. |
| Small Indian Head/Value and CAL in Wreath | 700. | 1,000. | 1,800. |

## *Dollar – Round*

|  | EF | AU | Unc. |
|---|---|---|---|
| Liberty Head/Value and Date in Wreath .................... | $1,500. | $2,100. | $3,500. |
| Liberty Head/Date Beneath Head .......................... | 2,200. | 3,000. | 4,500. |
| Indian Head/Date Beneath Head .......................... | 1,800. | 2,600. | 4,300. |

## CALIFORNIA GOLD INGOT BARS

During the Gold Rush era, gold coins, ingots, and "dust" were sent by steamship from San Francisco to other ports, most importantly to New York City and London, where the gold was sold or, in some instances, sent to mints for conversion into coins. The typical procedure in the mid-1850s was to send the gold by steamship from San Francisco to Panama, where it was sent across 48 miles of land on the Panama Railroad, then loaded aboard another ship at the town of Aspinwall on the Atlantic side. On September 12, 1857, the SS *Central America*, en route from Aspinwall to New York City with more than 475 passengers, over 100 crew members, and an estimated $1.6 million in gold (in an era in which pure gold was valued at $20.67 per ounce) was lost at sea. Miraculously, more than 150 people, including all but one of the women and children, were rescued by passing ships. The SS *Central America* went to the bottom of the Atlantic Ocean off the Carolina coast.

In the 1980s a group of researchers in Ohio formed the Columbus-America Discovery Group and secured financing to search for the long-lost ship. After much study and many explorations, they discovered the wreck of the SS *Central America* 7,200 feet below the surface. Tommy Thompson, Bob Evans, and others from C-ADG used the robotic Nemo, a sophisticated device weighing several tons, to photograph the wreck and to carefully bring to the surface many artifacts. A king's ransom in gold ingots was found, along with more than 7,500 coins, the latter mostly consisting of Mint State 1857-S double eagles.

The 500-plus gold ingots furnished a unique opportunity to study specimens that, after conservation, were essentially in the same condition as they had been in 1857. These bore the imprints of five different California assayers, who operated seven offices. With few exceptions, each ingot bears individual stamps, indicating its maker, a serial number, the weight in ounces, the fineness (expressed in thousandths, e.g., .784 indicating 784/1000 pure gold), and the 1857 value in dollars. The smallest bar found was issued by Blake & Co., weighed 4.95 ounces, was .795 fine, and was stamped with a value of $81.34. The largest ingot, dubbed the *Eureka bar*, bore the imprint of Kellogg & Humbert, and was stamped with a weight of 933.94 ounces, .903 fine, and a value of $17,433.57.

**Blake & Co., Sacramento, California:** From December 28, 1855, to May 1858, Blake & Co. was operated by Gorham Blake and W.R. Waters. • 34 ingots recovered. Serial numbers in the 5,100 and 5,200 series. Lowest weight and value: 4.95 ounces, $81.34. Highest weight and value: 157.40 ounces, $2,655.05. These bars have beveled or "dressed" edges and may have seen limited use in California commerce.

**Harris, Marchand & Co., Sacramento and Marysville:** Founded in Sacramento in 1855 by Harvey Harris and Desiré Marchand, with Charles L. Farrington as the "& Co." The Marysville office was opened in January 1856. Serial numbers in the 6,000 series are attributed to Sacramento, comprising 36 bars; a single bar in the 7,000 series (7095) is attributed to Marysville. The Marchand bars each have a circular coin-style counterstamp on the face. Lowest weight and value (Sacramento): 9.87 ounces, $158.53. Highest weight and value (Sacramento): 295.20 ounces, $5,351.73. • Unique Marysville bar: 174.04 ounces, $3,389.06.

**Henry Hentsch, San Francisco:** Henstch, a Swiss, was an entrepreneur involved in banking, real estate, assaying, and other ventures. In February 1856, he opened an assay office as an annex to his bank. It is likely that many of his ingots were exported to Europe, where he had extensive banking connections. • 33 ingots recovered. Lowest weight and value: 12.52 ounces, $251.82. Highest weight and value: 238.84 ounces, $4,458.35.

**Justh & Hunter, San Francisco and Marysville:** Emanuel Justh, a Hungarian, was a lithographer in San Francisco in the early 1850s. In 1854 and 1855 he worked as assistant assayer at the San Francisco Mint. Solomon Hillen Hunter came to California from Baltimore. The Justh & Hunter partnership was announced in May 1855. • Although study is continuing, the 60 ingots in the 4,000 series are tentatively attributed to San Francisco, and the 26 ingots in the 9,000 series are attributed to Marysville. • San Francisco—Lowest weight and value: 5.24 ounces, $92.18. Highest weight and value: 866.19 ounces, $15,971.93. • Marysville—Lowest weight and value: 19.34 ounces, $356.21. Highest weight and value: 464.65 ounces, $8,759.90.

**Kellogg & Humbert, San Francisco:** John Glover Kellogg and Augustus Humbert, two of the most famous names in the minting of California gold coins, formed the partnership of Kellogg & Humbert in spring 1855. The firm was one of the most active of all California assayers during the mid-1850s. • 346 ingots recovered, constituting the majority of those found. • Lowest weight and value: 5.71 ounces, $101.03. Highest weight and value: 933.94 ounces, $17,433.57.

A selection of gold ingots from the SS *Central America* treasure (with an 1857S-S $20 double eagle shown for scale, near lower left). (1) Harris, Marchand & Co., Marysville office, serial number 7095, 174.04 ounces, .942 fine, $3,389.06 (all values as stamped in 1857). (2) Henry Henstch, San Francisco, serial number 3120, 61.93 ounces, .886 fine, $1,134.26. (3) Kellogg & Humbert, San Francisco, serial number 215, .944 fine, $1,045.96. (4) Blake & Co., Sacramento, 19.30 ounces, .946 fine, $297.42. (5) Another Blake & Co. ingot, serial number 5216, .915 fine, $266.12. (6) Justh & Hunter, Marysville office, serial number 9440, 41.79 ounces, $761.07. (7) Justh & Hunter, San Francisco office, serial number 4243, 51.98 ounces, .916 fine, $984.27. (8) Harris, Marchand & Co., Sacramento office, serial number 6514, 35.33 ounces, .807 fine, $589.38. (9) Harris, Marchand & Co., Sacramento office, serial number 6486, 12.64 ounces, .950 fine, $245.00.

# HARD TIMES TOKENS (1832-1844)

We are indebted to the following contributors who initially helped bring the first Hard Times token special section together in the 1978 Red Book: Edward Janis, Gil Steinberg, Joseph Levine, and Paul Koppenhaver. Larry Johnson revised the text and updated the valuations to reflect current token prices.

"The issues commonly called Hard Times tokens mark a period of peculiar interest in the Numismatic history of the United States. They form a group by themselves as distinct as the Colonial Series so-called, or the State Issues which followed the Revolution. Unlike those, they had no semblance of authority behind them, and they combine, therefore, the character of Political pieces with the catch-words of party cries; of Satirical pieces with sarcastic allusions to the sentiments or speeches of the leaders of opposing parties; and in some degree also of Necessity pieces, in a time when, to use one of the phrases of the day, 'money was a cash article,' hard to get for daily needs; and though the dearth of a circulating medium, was not quite so great as it occasionally seems to have been over the border, when even buttons were made to do duty, not alone as is jestingly said, for the contribution-box, yet currency was difficult to obtain for the small change of petty expenses." This quotation is the introduction to Lyman Haynes Low's *Hard Times Tokens*, second edition, published in 1906. Low's token-numbering system of the 183 types of Hard Times token known to him has been expanded to more than 500 different types identified in Russell Rulau's *Standard Catalog of United States Tokens, 1700–1900*.

Prior to Andrew Jackson's election as president of the United States in 1828, the Second Bank of the United States operated under a 20-year charter that granted it complete control over the currency system of the United States. Jackson disliked this bank not only for economic reasons, but also because of political considerations. In 1832 Jackson vetoed a bill rechartering the bank, preferring instead to order the transfer of government deposits to state banks, many of which were owned by political cronies.

This action unfortunately also took away some stability from an already shaky economy and created a growing climate of mistrust. Jackson's economic policies contributed to a nationwide financial collapse. By 1837, hundreds of banks and large businesses had closed; the nation was gripped by a severe depression. Specie payments (disbursements in gold and silver) were suspended on May 10, 1837, in an attempt to stop the outflow of scarce reserves. Even the small change needed for everyday necessities was hoarded, and large cent–sized tokens quickly appeared as substitutes for coins to fill this compelling need, circulating freely at the value of one cent. The Gresham principle of Gresham's Law (bad money drives the good from circulation) was again proven to be reliable.

The primary attraction of Hard Times tokens is the wide variety of styles and themes used to reflect the passions of the day. Many are satirical pieces produced by Jackson's political enemies to lampoon the president's economic policies. Some voice anti-slavery sentiments. Legends on these pieces often made use of popular slogans, such as the most famous battle cry of the United States naval battle with Tripoli: MILLIONS FOR DEFENSE—NOT ONE CENT FOR TRIBUTE. Most are store cards used to promote various enterprises. It must be noted that a token could be produced for as little as half a cent each, which could result in a nice profit when used in place of a cent when making change. It is estimated that 10 to 20 million tokens were produced during this era. Many common varieties can be found in inexpensive lower grades at most coin shows, while some are quite rare and elusive. The collecting challenge is to find choice examples in any grade; outstanding examples in both color and strike will command large premiums. Many large coin collections also contain examples of Hard Times tokens because of their important role in U.S. monetary history.

# PRIVATE TOKENS

This special section is intended to be an introduction to the series, once described by Neil Carothers as "quaint and curious relics of our currency history." Store cards/political mules, as well as those pieces dedicated entirely to advertising, are omitted because of space limitations. Interested collectors are encouraged to obtain a reprint of Low's reference book as well as the Rulau *Standard Catalog* to gain a better appreciation and understanding of this fascinating series.

| | VF | EF | AU |
|---|---|---|---|
| L1, HT1. Andrew Jackson. Copper. | $5,750. | $9,000. | — |
| L57, HT76. Van Buren, facing left. Brass. | 2,500. | 3,500. | $4,500. |
| L4, HT6. Jackson President of the U.S. Brass. | 125. | 300. | 800. |
| L56, HT75. Van Buren facing left. Copper. | 75. | 150. | 400. |
| L66, HT24. Agriculture. Copper. | 200. | 275. | 700. |
| L54, HT81. A Woman & A Sister. Copper. | 175. | 250. | 500. |
| L55, HT63. Loco Foco, 1838. Copper. | 40. | 100. | 200. |
| L31, HT46. Not One Cent, Motto. Copper. | 20. | 40. | 75. |

L8, HT9

L18, HT32

L51, HT70

L47, HT66

L60, HT18

L44, HT69

L59, HT17

L65, HT23

|  | VF | EF | AU |
|---|---|---|---|
| L8, HT9. My Victory/Jackson. Copper. | $35. | $85. | $140. |
| L18, HT32. Executive Experiment. Copper. | 25. | 60. | 85. |
| L51, HT70. Roman Firmness. Copper. | 25. | 60. | 90. |
| L47, HT66. Phoenix/May Tenth. Copper. | 20. | 45. | 80. |
| L60, HT18. Ship/Lightning. Copper. | 22. | 50. | 90. |
| L44, HT69. Ship/Jackson. Copper. | 25. | 70. | 110. |
| L59, HT17. Ship/Wreath Border | 20. | 50. | 100. |
| L65, HT23. Ship/Liberty Head. Copper. | 75. | 175. | 225. |

## FEUCHTWANGER TOKENS (1837–1864)

Lewis Feuchtwanger produced a metal that was really a variety of German silver consisting of nickel, copper, and some zinc. He suggested as early as 1837 to Congress that his metal be substituted for copper, and he made one-cent and three-cent trial pieces that circulated freely during the coin shortage of 1836 through 1844.

|  | F | EF | AU | Unc. |
|---|---|---|---|---|
| 1837 One Cent, Eagle | $90. | $210. | $325. | $500. |
| 1837 Three-Cent, New York Coat of Arms | 350. | 1,350. | 2,250. | 7,500. |
| 1837 Three-Cent, Eagle | 700. | 3,250. | 4,750. | 12,000. |
| 1864 Three-Cent, Eagle |  | 2,400. | 4,000. | 7,800. |

## LESHER REFERENDUM DOLLARS (1900–1901)

Distributed in 1900 and 1901 by Joseph Lesher of Victor, Colorado, these private tokens were used in trade to some extent, and stocked by various merchants who redeemed them in goods. Coins were numbered and a blank space left at bottom of 1901 issues, in which were stamped names of businessmen who bought them. All are quite rare; many varieties are extremely rare. Composition is .950 fine silver (alloyed with copper).

|  | EF | AU | Unc. |
|---|---|---|---|
| 1900 First type, no business name | $2,000. | $2,750. | $4,500. |
| 1900 A.B. Bumstead, with or without scrolls | 1,200. | 1,600. | 2,750. |
| 1900 Bank type | 12,000. | 15,000. | — |
| 1901 Imprint type, no name | 1,300. | 1,900. | 3,000. |
| 1901 Imprint type, Boyd Park | 1,450. | 2,000. | 3,000. |
| 1901 Imprint type, Slusher | 1,750. | 2,500. | 3,500. |
| 1901 Imprint type, Mullen | 3,100. | 5,000. | 7,750. |
| 1901 Imprint type, Cohen, Klein | 5,250. | 6,800. | — |
| 1901 Imprint type, Alexander | 5,750. | 7,750. | — |
| 1901 Imprint type, White | 11,000. | 15,000. | — |
| 1901 Imprint type, Goodspeeds, Nelson | 11,500. | 15,000. | — |
| 1901 Imprint type, A.W. Clark *(unique)* |  | 300,000. | — |

## CIVIL WAR TOKENS (1860s)

Civil War Tokens are generally divided into two groups: tradesmen's tokens, and anonymously issued pieces with political or patriotic themes. They came into existence only because of the scarcity of government coins and disappeared as soon as the bronze coins of 1864 met the public demand for small copper change.

From the outset of the Civil War, government cents were insufficient in number, widely hoarded, and worth a premium over all other currencies. As a result of this scarcity of cent pieces, private copper coins were issued by many individuals. Their wide circulation was made possible by the scarcity of copper-nickel cents and the public dislike of fractional paper money.

The tradesmen's tokens were issued by various firms to provide change and advertise the dealers' wares. They usually bore implied or explicit promises of redemption in goods or money. The second type were simply unauthorized substitutes for government coins, produced at a profit by private manufacturers and put into general circulation through various agencies.

These tokens are of great variety in composition and design. A number were more or less faithful imitations of the copper-nickel cent. A few of this type have the word NOT in very small letters above the words ONE CENT.

Many pieces, especially of the tradesmen's-token type, were individual in device and size, representing any caprice of design or slogan that appealed to the maker. Some were political or patriotic in character, carrying the likeness of some military leader such as McClellan or bearing such inscriptions as "Millions for contractors, not one cent for the widows." An estimated 50,000,000 or more of these pieces were issued. Approximately 10,000 different varieties have been recorded.

The legal status of the Civil War tokens was uncertain. Mint Director Pollock thought they were illegal; however, there was no law prohibiting the issue of tradesmen's tokens or of private coins not in imitation of United States coins. A law was passed April 22, 1864, prohibiting the issue of any one- or two-cent coins, tokens, or devices for use as money, and on June 8 another law was passed that abolished private coinage of every kind.

*Values shown are for the most common tokens in each composition.*

|  | F | VF | EF | Unc. |
|---|---|---|---|---|
| Copper or brass tokens | $14. | $18. | $22. | $50. |
| Nickel or German silver tokens | 35. | 50. | 75. | 135. |
| White metal tokens | 40. | 60. | 85. | 150. |
| Copper-nickel tokens | 50. | 70. | 100. | 185. |
| Silver tokens | 150. | 200. | 250. | 500. |

## Patriotics

Patriotic Civil War tokens feature leaders such as Abraham Lincoln; military images such as cannons or ships; and sociopolitical themes from both sides, such as flags and slogans. Thousands of varieties are known.

|  | VG | VF | AU | MS-63 |
|---|---|---|---|---|
| Lincoln | $30. | $50. | $65. | $150. |
| Monitor | 20. | 40. | 75. | 150. |
| "Wealth of the South" | 150. | 300. | 400. | 550. |

# Store Cards

Tradesmen's tokens of the Civil War era are often called *store cards*. These are typically collected by geographical location or by topic. The Fuld text catalogs store cards by state, city, merchant, die combination, and metal. Values shown below are for the most common tokens for each state.

| | VG | VF | AU | MS-63 | | VG | VF | AU | MS-63 |
|---|---|---|---|---|---|---|---|---|---|
| Alabama | $1,500. | $3,000. | $4,000. | $5,500. | Minnesota | $150. | $450. | $550. | $750. |
| Connecticut | 10. | 15. | 20. | 40. | Missouri | 40. | 100. | 125. | 250. |
| Washington, DC | — | 1,000. | 1,250. | 1,750. | New Hampshire | 65. | 100. | 150. | 250. |
| Idaho | 400. | 700. | 1,300. | — | New Jersey | 10. | 15. | 20. | 40. |
| Illinois | 10. | 15. | 20. | 40. | New York | 10. | 15. | 20. | 30. |
| Indiana | 10. | 15. | 25. | 45. | Ohio | 10. | 15. | 20. | 40. |
| Iowa | 150. | 400. | 550. | 900. | Pennsylvania | 10. | 15. | 20. | 35. |
| Kansas | 900. | 2,500. | 3,500. | 5,000. | Rhode Island | 10. | 15. | 20. | 35. |
| Kentucky | 50. | 125. | 200. | 350. | Tennessee | 300. | 650. | 1,100. | 1,650. |
| Louisiana | — | 3,500. | 4,500. | — | Virginia | 250. | 500. | 1,000. | — |
| Maine | 50. | 100. | 150. | 250. | West Virginia | 45. | 90. | 165. | 300. |
| Maryland | 150. | 350. | 550. | 1,000. | Wisconsin | 15. | 25. | 40. | 75. |
| Massachusetts | 15. | 25. | 45. | 65. | Sutlers **(a)** | 100. | 200. | 250. | 350. |
| Michigan | 10. | 15. | 20. | 40. | | | | | |

**a.** Sutlers' tokens were issued by registered contractors who operated camp stores that traveled with the military.

**DC500A-1h (Red)**          **IN190D-3a**

| | VG | VF | AU | MS-63 |
|---|---|---|---|---|
| DC500a-1h (Red). H. A. Hall, Washington, DC | — | $1,000. | $1,400. | $2,000. |
| IN190D-3a. J.L. & G.F. Rowe, Corunna, IN, 1863 | $15. | 40. | 65. | 150. |

**MI865A-1a**

**MN980A-1a**

**MO910A-4a**

**NY630AQ-4a**

**NY630Z-1a**

**OH165M-1a**

**NY630BJ-1a**

**WI510M-1a**

**PA750F-1a**

**WV890D-4a**

|  | VG | VF | AU | MS-63 |
|---|---|---|---|---|
| MI865A-1a. W. Darling, Saranac, MI, 1864 . . . . . . . | $7,500. | $12,000. | $15,000. | — |
| MN980A-1a. C. Benson, Druggist, Winona, MN . . . . | 300. | 600. | 900. | 1,500. |
| MO910A-4a. Drovers Hotel, St. Louis, MO, 1863 . . . | 125. | 300. | 600. | 1,250. |
| NY630AQ-4a. Gustavus Lindenmueller, New York, 1863 | 10. | 15. | 20. | 35. |
| NY630Z-1a. Fr. Freise, Undertaker, New York, 1863 | 15. | 25. | 45. | 75. |
| OH165M-1a. B.P. Belknp.,"Teeth Extracted Without Pain" | 125. | 250. | 350. | 600. |
| NY630BJ-1a. Sanitary Commission, New York, 1864 | 400. | 850. | 1,100. | 1,750. |
| WI510M-1a. Goes & Falk Malt House & Brewery, | | | | |
|   Milwaukee, WI, 1863 . . . . . . . . . . . . . . . . . . . . . . | 20. | 45. | 75. | 150. |
| PA750F-1a. M.C. Campbell's Dancing Academy, | | | | |
|   Philadelphia, PA . . . . . . . . . . . . . . . . . . . . . . . . . | 15. | 30. | 45. | 100. |
| WV890D-4a. R.C. Graves, Wheeling, WV, 1863 . . . . | 45. | 90. | 165. | 300. |

# CONFEDERATE CENTS

An order to make cents for the Confederacy was placed with Robert Lovett Jr., an engraver and diesinker of Philadelphia, through a jewelry firm of that city. Fearing arrest by the United States government for assisting the enemy, Lovett decided against delivering the coins and hid them, and the dies, in his cellar.

The original dies were later purchased by Captain John W. Haseltine, who used them to make restrikes. In 1960 the dies were copied and additional pieces made by Robert Bashlow. These show die cracks and rust marks that distinguish them from earlier copies. They have very little numismatic value.

| | Mintage | Unc. | PF |
|---|---|---|---|
| 1861 Cent, Original, Copper-Nickel, Unc ................. 12 | | $120,000. | |
| 1861 Cent, Restrike, Copper, Proof ..........(55).......... | | | $8,000. |
| 1861 Cent, Restrike, Gold, Proof .............(7)......... | | | 35,000. |
| 1861 Cent, Restrike, Silver, Proof ...........(12).......... | | | 9,000. |

# CONFEDERATE HALF DOLLARS

According to records, only four original Confederate half dollars were struck (on a hand press). Original silver planchets were used, as well as a regular obverse die. One of the coins was given to Secretary of the Confederacy Memminger, who passed it on to President Jefferson Davis for his approval. Another was given to Professor J.L. Riddell of the University of Louisiana. E. Ames of New Orleans received a third specimen. The last was kept by chief coiner B.F. Taylor. Lack of bullion prevented the Confederacy from coining more pieces.

The Confederate half dollar was unknown to collectors until 1879, when a specimen and its die were found in Taylor's possession in New Orleans. E. Mason Jr., of Philadelphia, purchased both and later sold them to J.W. Scott and Company of New York. J.W. Scott acquired 500 genuine 1861 half dollars from the New Orleans Mint, smoothed the reverses, and then restamped them with the Confederate die. Known as *restrikes*, these usually have slightly flattened obverses. Scott also struck some tokens in white metal using the Confederate reverse die and an obverse die bearing this inscription: 4 ORIGINALS STRUCK BY ORDER OF C.S.A. IN NEW ORLEANS 1861 / ******* / REV. SAME AS U.S. (FROM ORIGINAL DIE•SCOTT)

Confederate Reverse     Scott Obverse

| | Mintage | VF-20 | EF-40 | Unc. |
|---|---|---|---|---|
| 1861 HALF DOL. *(4 known) $632,500, VF, Stack's auction, Oct-03* | — | — | — | — |
| 1861 HALF DOL., Restrike ...........................500 | | $5,000. | $6,000. | $8,000. |
| 1861 Scott token Obverse, Confederate Reverse ..........500 | | 2,000. | 3,000. | 3,750. |

There are only five official coins that were issued by the Kingdom of Hawaii. These include the 1847 cent issued by King Kamehameha III and the 1883 silver dimes, quarters, halves, and dollars of King Kalakaua I, which bear his portrait. The 1883 eighth-dollar is a pattern, while the 1881 five-cent piece was an unofficial issue. After Hawaii became a U.S. territory in 1900, the legal tender status of these coins was removed and most were withdrawn and melted. Owing to a lack of small change on the islands, the early tokens were widely accepted and circulated freely.

**One Cent (1847)**              **Ten Cents (1883)**

| | Mintage | F-12 | VF-20 | EF-40 | AU-50 | MS-60 | MS-63 | PF |
|---|---|---|---|---|---|---|---|---|
| 1847 Cent | 100,000 | $400. | $500. | $750. | $950. | $1,250. | $2,500. | |
| 1881 Five Cents | | 6,000. | 8,000. | 14,000. | 16,000. | 17,000. | 25,000. | — |
| 1883 Ten Cents .....(26) | 249,974 | 70. | 120. | 300. | 450. | 1,500. | 3,000. | $12,500. |
| 1883 Eighth Dollar ...(20) | | | | | | | | 55,000. |
| 1883 Quarter Dollar .(26) | 499,974 | 65. | 90. | 150. | 200. | 275. | 500. | 12,500. |
| 1883 Half Dollar ....(26) | 699,974 | 100. | 150. | 300. | 500. | 1,400. | 3,000. | 15,000. |
| 1883 Dollar ........(26) | 499,974 | 400. | 500. | 750. | 1,500. | 4,500. | 11,000. | 20,000. |

**Thomas Hobron Token (1879)**

**Wailuku Plantation (1871)**

**Wailuku Plantation (1880)**       **Haiku Plantation (1882)**

| | F-12 | VF-20 | EF-40 | AU-50 |
|---|---|---|---|---|
| Waterhouse token, 1860. Title of Kamehameha IV ... | $1,500. | $2,200. | $4,000. | |
| Wailuku Plantation token, 12 1/2 (cents), 1871 ..... | 600. | 900. | 2,000. | |
| Wailuku Plantation token, 1 Real, 1880 ........... | 550. | 850. | 1,800. | |
| Wailuku Plantation token, Half Real, 1871 and 1880 .. | 1,000. | 1,800. | 2,750. | |
| Thomas Hobron token, 12 1/2 (cents), 1879 ....... | 550. | 650. | 1,000. | |
| Haiku Plantation token, One Real, 1882 ........... | 600. | 800. | 1,100. | |
| Grove Ranch Plantation token, 12 1/2 (cents), 1886 .. | 900. | 1,200. | 2,200. | |
| Grove Ranch Plantation token, 12 1/2 (cents), 1887 .. | 1,200. | 1,800. | 2,700. | |
| Kahului Railroad token, 10 cents, 1891 ........... | 800. | 1,200. | 2,500. | $3,500. |
| Kahului Railroad token, 15 cents, 1891 ........... | 800. | 1,200. | 2,500. | 3,500. |
| Kahului Railroad token, 20 cents, 1891 ........... | 800. | 1,200. | 2,500. | 3,500. |
| Kahului Railroad token, 25 cents, 1891 ........... | 800. | 1,200. | 2,500. | 3,500. |
| Kahului Railroad token, 35 cents, 1891 ........... | 800. | 1,200. | 2,500. | 3,500. |
| Kahului Railroad token, 75 cents, 1891 ........... | 800. | 1,200. | 2,500. | 3,500. |

The Philippine Islands were acquired by the United States in 1899 as part of a treaty with Spain ending the Spanish-American War of the previous year. A military government was replaced with a civil administration in 1901, and one of its first tasks was to sponsor a new coinage that was compatible with the old Spanish issues, yet was also legally exchangeable for American money at the rate of two Philippine pesos to the U.S. dollar.

The resulting coins were introduced in 1903 and bear the identities of both the Philippines (Filipinas in Spanish) and the United States of America. Following Spanish custom, the peso was divided into 100 centavos. A dollar-size coin valued at one peso was the principal issue in this series, but silver fractions were also minted in values of 50, 20, and 10 centavos. Minor coins included the copper-nickel five-cent piece, as well as one-centavo and half-centavo coins of bronze.

A rise in the price of silver forced the reduction of the fineness and weight for each silver denomination beginning in 1907, and subsequent issues are smaller in diameter. The smaller size of the new silver issues led to confusion between the silver 20-centavo piece and the copper-nickel five-centavo piece, resulting in a mismatching of dies for these two denominations in 1918 and again in 1928. A solution was found by reducing the diameter of the five-centavo piece beginning in 1930.

In 1935, the Commonwealth of the Philippines was established by an act of Congress, and a three-piece set of commemorative coins was issued the following year to mark this transition. Despite the popularity of United States commemoratives at that time, these sets sold poorly, and thousands remained within the Philippine Treasury at the onset of World War II. The commonwealth arms were adapted to all circulating issues beginning in 1937.

The advance on the Philippines by Japanese forces in 1942 prompted removal of much of the Treasury's bullion to the United States. More than 15 million pesos' worth of silver remained, mostly in the form of one-peso pieces of 1907 through 1912 and the ill-fated 1936 commemoratives. These coins were hastily crated and dumped into Manila's Caballo Bay to prevent their capture. Partially recovered after the war, these coins were badly corroded from their exposure to saltwater, adding further to the scarcity of high-grade prewar silver coins.

The Philippines became an independent republic on July 4, 1946, ending a historic and colorful chapter in U.S. history and numismatics.

## PHILIPPINES UNDER U.S. SOVEREIGNTY
### Bronze Coinage

Philippine coins dated from 1903 to 1919 were struck at the Philadelphia and San Francisco Mints. Those dated after 1920 were made in Manila. During World War II, coins of 1944 and 1945 were made at Philadelphia, Denver, and San Francisco.

*Price contributors to the Philippine listings are Lyman Allen and Raymond Czahor.*

**Half Centavo**

|  | Mintage | EF | MS-63 | MS-65 | PF-65 |
|---|---|---|---|---|---|
| 1903 | 12,084,000 | $1.00 | $2.25 | $15. | $25. |
| 1903, Proof | (2,558) |  |  |  | 65. |
| 1904 | 5,654,000 | 1.25 | 3.00 | 30. | 40. |
| 1904, Proof | (1,355) |  |  |  | 100. |
| 1905, Proof only | (471) |  | 75.00 |  | 200. |
| 1906, Proof only | (500) |  | 50.00 |  | 200. |
| 1908, Proof only | (500) |  | 50.00 |  | 200. |

**One Centavo**

| | Mintage | VF | EF | MS-60 | MS-63 |
|---|---|---|---|---|---|
| 1903 | 10,790,000 | $1.00 | $2.50 | $17.50 | $25. |
| 1903, Proof .....(2,558) | | | | 40.00 | 85. |
| 1904 | 17,040,400 | 1.00 | 3.00 | 18.00 | 25. |
| 1904, Proof .....(1,355) | | | | 50.00 | 100. |
| 1905 | 10,000,000 | 1.50 | 3.00 | 25.00 | 40. |
| 1905, Proof .......(471) | | | 75.00 | 100.00 | 225. |
| 1906, Proof only ...(500) | | | | 125.00 | 200. |
| 1908, Proof only ...(500) | | | | 125.00 | 200. |
| 1908S | 2,187,000 | 4.00 | 12.00 | 60.00 | 90. |
| 1909S | 1,737,612 | 12.50 | 30.00 | 90.00 | 140. |
| 1910S | 2,700,000 | 4.00 | 10.00 | 60.00 | 100. |
| 1911S | 4,803,000 | 3.00 | 5.00 | 50.00 | 90. |
| 1912S | 3,001,000 | 5.00 | 12.00 | 75.00 | 110. |
| 1913S | 5,000,000 | 2.00 | 6.00 | 40.00 | 70. |
| 1914S | 5,000,500 | 2.00 | 6.00 | 40.00 | 75. |
| 1915S | 2,500,000 | 40.00 | 95.00 | 500.00 | 900. |
| 1916S | 4,330,000 | 10.00 | 25.00 | 100.00 | 175. |
| 1917S | 7,070,000 | 4.00 | 10.00 | 45.00 | 90. |
| 1918S | 1,160,000 | 4.00 | 12.50 | 50.00 | 95. |
| 1918S, Large S | * | 125.00 | 300.00 | 1,000.00 | 1,750. |
| 1919S | 454,000 | 2.00 | 6.00 | 45.00 | 70. |
| 1920S | 2,500,000 | 10.00 | 25.00 | 175.00 | 250. |
| 1920 | 3,552,259 | 6.00 | 10.00 | 50.00 | 80. |
| 1921 | 7,282,673 | 3.50 | 8.00 | 40.00 | 70. |
| 1922 | 3,519,100 | 2.50 | 6.00 | 40.00 | 60. |
| 1925M | 9,325,000 | 2.00 | 6.00 | 35.00 | 50. |
| 1926M | 9,000,000 | 2.00 | 6.00 | 35.00 | 50. |
| 1927M | 92,700,000 | 2.00 | 6.00 | 35.00 | 45. |
| 1928M | 91,500,000 | 1.50 | 5.00 | 35.00 | 45. |
| 1929M | 5,657,161 | 2.50 | 8.00 | 40.00 | 65. |
| 1930M | 5,577,000 | 1.50 | 4.00 | 25.00 | 50. |
| 1931M | 5,659,355 | 1.50 | 5.00 | 30.00 | 50. |
| 1932M | 4,000,000 | 3.00 | 8.00 | 40.00 | 60. |
| 1933M | 8,392,692 | 1.50 | 3.50 | 25.00 | 40. |
| 1934M | 3,179,000 | 2.00 | 4.00 | 40.00 | 60. |
| 1936M | 17,455,463 | 1.00 | 4.00 | 30.00 | 40. |

\* Included in number above.

## Copper-Nickel Coinage

**Large-Size Five Centavos
(1903–1928)**

**Reduced-Size Five Centavos
(1930–1935)**

|  | Mintage | VF | EF | MS-60 | MS-63 |
|---|---|---|---|---|---|
| 1903 | 8,910,000 | $1.00 | $2.00 | $15. | $30. |
| 1903, Proof (2,558) | | | | 40. | 75. |
| 1904 | 1,075,000 | 2.00 | 3.00 | 30. | 65. |
| 1904, Proof (1,355) | | | | 45. | 85. |
| 1905, Proof only (471) | | | | 135. | 225. |
| 1906, Proof only (500) | | | | 125. | 200. |
| 1908, Proof only (500) | | | | 125. | 195. |
| 1916S | 300,000 | 55.00 | 85.00 | 600. | 900. |
| 1917S | 2,300,000 | 4.00 | 10.00 | 125. | 200. |
| 1918S | 2,780,000 | 3.00 | 12.50 | 100. | 200. |
| 1918S, Mule (Small-Date Reverse of 20 centavos) | | 450.00 | 1,300.00 | 3,500. | 5,500. |
| 1919S | 1,220,000 | 6.00 | 15.00 | 100. | 175. |
| 1920 | 1,421,078 | 10.00 | 17.50 | 125. | 175. |
| 1921 | 2,131,529 | 7.00 | 13.00 | 100. | 175. |
| 1925M | 1,000,000 | 12.50 | 40.00 | 125. | 200. |
| 1926M | 1,200,000 | 7.00 | 15.00 | 75. | 130. |
| 1927M | 1,000,000 | 6.00 | 12.00 | 50. | 90. |
| 1928M | 1,000,000 | 6.00 | 12.00 | 50. | 90. |
| 1930M | 2,905,182 | 2.50 | 5.00 | 50. | 65. |
| 1931M | 3,476,790 | 2.50 | 5.00 | 50. | 80. |
| 1932M | 3,955,861 | 2.00 | 4.00 | 30. | 65. |
| 1934M | 2,153,729 | 3.00 | 9.00 | 90. | 150. |
| 1935M | 2,754,000 | 2.50 | 5.00 | 65. | 100. |

## Silver Coinage

**Large-Size Ten Centavos**
**(1903–1906)**

**Reduced-Size Ten Centavos**
**(1907–1935)**

|  | Mintage | VF | EF | MS-60 | MS-63 |
|---|---|---|---|---|---|
| 1903 | 5,102,658 | $2.50 | $5.00 | $30. | $50. |
| 1903, Proof (2,558) | | | | 50. | 95. |
| 1903S | 1,200,000 | 16.00 | 35.00 | 250. | 500. |
| 1904 | 10,000 | 20.00 | 35.00 | 80. | 130. |
| 1904, Proof (1,355) | | | | 75. | 120. |
| 1904S | 5,040,000 | 2.50 | 5.00 | 35. | 65. |
| 1905, Proof only (471) | | | | 160. | 225. |
| 1906, Proof only (500) | | | | 130. | 190. |
| 1907 | 1,500,781 | 3.00 | 7.50 | 45. | 70. |
| 1907S | 4,930,000 | 2.25 | 3.50 | 40. | 65. |
| 1908, Proof only (500) | | | | 120. | 175. |
| 1908S | 3,363,911 | 2.50 | 5.00 | 45. | 65. |
| 1909S | 312,199 | 30.00 | 60.00 | 325. | 500. |
| 1911S | 1,000,505 | 5.00 | 25.00 | 75. | 130. |
| 1912S | 1,010,000 | 5.00 | 20.00 | 100. | 175. |
| 1913S | 1,360,693 | 4.00 | 9.00 | 60. | 90. |
| 1914S | 1,180,000 | 6.00 | 10.00 | 175. | 300. |
| 1915S | 450,000 | 17.50 | 50.00 | 300. | 450. |
| 1917S | 5,991,148 | 2.00 | 5.00 | 35. | 60. |
| 1918S | 8,420,000 | 1.50 | 2.50 | 30. | 55. |
| 1919S | 1,630,000 | 2.00 | 7.50 | 45. | 80. |

*Chart continued on next page.*

| | Mintage | VF | EF | MS-60 | MS-63 |
|---|---|---|---|---|---|
| 1920 | .520,000 | $5.00 | $12.00 | $90. | $160. |
| 1921 | .3,863,038 | 1.50 | 2.50 | 20. | 35. |
| 1929M | .1,000,000 | 1.50 | 2.50 | 15. | 40. |
| 1935M | .1,280,000 | 1.50 | 2.50 | 15. | 30. |

**Large-Size Twenty Centavos (1903–1906)**

**Reduced-Size Twenty Centavos (1907–1929)**

| | Mintage | VF | EF | MS-60 | MS-63 |
|---|---|---|---|---|---|
| 1903 | .5,350,231 | $3.50 | $4.00 | $40. | $75. |
| 1903, Proof | (2,558) | | | 65. | 125. |
| 1903S | .150,080 | 20.00 | 60.00 | 500. | 1,500. |
| 1904 | .10,000 | 30.00 | 45.00 | 90. | 150. |
| 1904, Proof | (1,355) | | | 90. | 150. |
| 1904S | .2,060,000 | 4.00 | 7.00 | 60. | 120. |
| 1905, Proof only | (471) | | | 200. | 325. |
| 1905S | .420,000 | 10.00 | 30.00 | 175. | 300. |
| 1906, Proof only | (500) | | | 175. | 275. |
| 1907 | .1,250,651 | 4.00 | 10.00 | 80. | 125. |
| 1907S | .3,165,000 | 3.00 | 5.00 | 45. | 75. |
| 1908, Proof only | (500) | | | 175. | 275. |
| 1908S | .1,535,000 | 3.50 | 10.00 | 60. | 90. |
| 1909S | .450,000 | 20.00 | 45.00 | 275. | 500. |
| 1910S | .500,259 | 20.00 | 60.00 | 325. | 550. |
| 1911S | .505,000 | 12.00 | 30.00 | 225. | 500. |
| 1912S | .750,000 | 10.00 | 25.00 | 200. | 300. |
| 1913S | .795,000 | 5.00 | 17.50 | 140. | 200. |
| 1914S | .795,000 | 5.00 | 17.50 | 150. | 250. |
| 1915S | .655,000 | 15.00 | 50.00 | 300. | 500. |
| 1916S | .1,435,000 | 6.00 | 20.00 | 100. | 160. |
| 1917S | .3,150,655 | 3.00 | 5.00 | 50. | 125. |
| 1918S | .5,560,000 | 2.50 | 4.00 | 40. | 60. |
| 1919S | .850,000 | 5.00 | 7.50 | 60. | 90. |
| 1920 | .1,045,415 | 5.00 | 10.00 | 100. | 150. |
| 1921 | .1,842,631 | 3.00 | 4.00 | 50. | 85. |
| 1928M, Mule (Reverse of 1903–1928 5 centavos) | .100,000 | 15.00 | 50.00 | 500. | 800. |
| 1929M | .1,970,000 | 3.00 | 4.00 | 35. | 60. |

**Large-Size Fifty Centavos (1903–1906)**

| | Mintage | VF | EF | MS-60 | MS-63 |
|---|---|---|---|---|---|
| 1903 | 3,099,061 | $8. | $15. | $65. | $100. |
| 1903, Proof | (2,558) | | | 100. | 170. |
| 1903S | | | 22,000. | | |
| 1904 | 10,000 | 35. | 50. | 110. | 185. |
| 1904, Proof | (1,355) | | | 125. | 190. |
| 1904S | 216,000 | 10. | 20. | 100. | 150. |
| 1905, Proof only | (471) | | | 250. | 425. |
| 1905S | 852,000 | 15. | 40. | 275. | 600. |
| 1906, Proof only | (500) | | | 225. | 400. |

**Reduced-Size Fifty Centavos
(1907–1921)**

| | Mintage | VF | EF | MS-60 | MS-63 |
|---|---|---|---|---|---|
| 1907 | 1,200,625 | $8.00 | $25. | $125. | $250. |
| 1907S | 2,112,000 | 6.00 | 20. | 100. | 200. |
| 1908, Proof only | (500) | | | 250. | 375. |
| 1908S | 1,601,000 | 8.00 | 15. | 250. | 600. |
| 1909S | 528,000 | 10.00 | 40. | 250. | 400. |
| 1917S | 674,369 | 8.00 | 25. | 120. | 225. |
| 1918S | 2,202,000 | 5.00 | 10. | 70. | 125. |
| 1919S | 1,200,000 | 5.00 | 12. | 100. | 150. |
| 1920 | 420,000 | 5.00 | 10. | 40. | 90. |
| 1921 | 2,316,763 | 3.50 | 4. | 30. | 55. |

**Large-Size One Peso
(1903–1906)**

**Reduced-Size One Peso
(1907–1912)**

*See next page for chart.*

| | Mintage | VF | EF | MS-60 | MS-63 |
|---|---|---|---|---|---|
| 1903 | 2,788,901 | $18. | $25. | $150. | $225. |
| 1903, Proof | (2,558) | | | 150. | 300. |
| 1903S | 11,361,000 | 15. | 22. | 100. | 175. |
| 1904 | 11,355 | 85. | 110. | 200. | 300. |
| 1904, Proof | (1,355) | | | 200. | 350. |
| 1904S | 6,600,000 | 18. | 25. | 125. | 175. |
| 1905, Proof only | (471) | | | 600. | 1,000. |
| 1905S | 6,056,000 | 20. | 35. | 275. | 450. |
| 1906, Proof only | (500) | | | 500. | 800. |
| 1906S | 201,000 | 1,400. | 2,500. | 9,000. | 20,000. |
| 1907S | 10,278,000 | 6. | 10. | 70. | 140. |
| 1908, Proof only | (500) | | | 500. | 800. |
| 1908S | 20,954,944 | 6. | 10. | 70. | 140. |
| 1909S | 7,578,000 | 7. | 12. | 90. | 175. |
| 1910S | 3,153,559 | 10. | 20. | 175. | 400. |
| 1911S | 463,000 | 20. | 40. | 650. | 1,400. |
| 1912S | 680,000 | 25. | 50. | 700. | 1,750. |

## COMMONWEALTH ISSUES
### Bronze Coinage

**One Centavo**

| | Mintage | VF | EF | MS-60 | MS-63 |
|---|---|---|---|---|---|
| 1937M | 15,790,492 | $1.00 | $3.00 | $15.00 | $40.00 |
| 1938M | 10,000,000 | 0.75 | 2.00 | 15.00 | 25.00 |
| 1939M | 6,500,000 | 1.00 | 2.50 | 15.00 | 30.00 |
| 1940M | 4,000,000 | 0.75 | 2.00 | 10.00 | 15.00 |
| 1941M | 5,000,000 | 2.50 | 4.00 | 15.00 | 25.00 |
| 1944S | 58,000,000 | 0.10 | 0.25 | 1.25 | 2.50 |

### Copper-Nickel Coinage

**Five Centavos**

| | Mintage | VF | EF | MS-60 | MS-63 |
|---|---|---|---|---|---|
| 1937M | 2,493,872 | $3.00 | $6.00 | $45. | $90. |
| 1938M | 4,000,000 | 1.00 | 2.50 | 15. | 30. |
| 1941M | 2,750,000 | 3.00 | 6.00 | 35. | 60. |

## Copper-Nickel-Zinc Alloy

| | Mintage | VF | EF | MS-60 | MS-63 |
|---|---|---|---|---|---|
| 1944 | 21,198,000 | $0.20 | $0.30 | $1.25 | $2.50 |
| 1944S | 14,040,000 | 0.20 | 0.30 | 1.25 | 3.00 |
| 1945S | 72,796,000 | 0.20 | 0.25 | 0.75 | 3.00 |

## Silver Coinage

### Ten Centavos

| | Mintage | VF | EF | MS-60 | MS-63 |
|---|---|---|---|---|---|
| 1937M | 3,500,000 | $2.00 | $4.00 | $10.00 | $25.00 |
| 1938M | 3,750,000 | 1.00 | 2.00 | 10.00 | 25.00 |
| 1941M | 2,500,000 | 1.25 | 2.50 | 10.00 | 15.00 |
| 1944D | 31,592,000 | 0.30 | 0.50 | 1.25 | 5.00 |
| 1945D | 137,208,000 | 0.30 | 0.50 | 1.00 | 4.00 |

### Twenty Centavos

| | Mintage | VF | EF | MS-60 | MS-63 |
|---|---|---|---|---|---|
| 1937M | 2,665,000 | $2.00 | $3.50 | $17.50 | $25.00 |
| 1938M | 3,000,000 | 1.50 | 2.00 | 9.00 | 15.00 |
| 1941M | 1,500,000 | 2.00 | 3.00 | 9.00 | 15.00 |
| 1944D | 28,596,000 | 0.50 | 0.75 | 1.75 | 3.00 |
| 1944D, D Over S | 82,804,000 | 10.00 | 20.00 | 40.00 | 70.00 |
| 1945D | * | 0.40 | 0.50 | 1.25 | 2.50 |

* Included in number above.

### Fifty Centavos

| | Mintage | VF | EF | MS-60 | MS-63 |
|---|---|---|---|---|---|
| 1944S | 19,187,000 | $1.25 | $2.00 | $4.50 | $6.00 |
| 1945S | 18,120,000 | 1.25 | 2.00 | 4.00 | 5.00 |

# COMMEMORATIVE ISSUES

**Silver Fifty Centavos**

| | Mintage | VF | EF | MS-60 | MS-63 |
|---|---|---|---|---|---|
| 1936M ............................20,000 | | $30. | $50. | $95. | $150. |

**Silver One Peso**
**Busts of Murphy and Quezon**

| | Mintage | VF | EF | MS-60 | MS-63 |
|---|---|---|---|---|---|
| 1936M ............................10,000 | | $50. | $75. | $150. | $225. |

**Silver One Peso**
**Busts of Roosevelt and Quezon**

| | Mintage | VF | EF | MS-60 | MS-63 |
|---|---|---|---|---|---|
| 1936M ............................10,000 | | $50. | $75. | $150. | $225. |

# The Official RED BOOK®

## #1 Selling Price Guide for 60 Years

---

## FREE Gift!

In Celebration of the 60th Anniversary of
*The Official Red Book® A Guide Book of United States Coins*

Complete and mail this card to receive 1 free custom snaplock with 2 Uncirculated Lewis & Clark nickels. Go to www.whitmanbooks.com to see our complete line of hobby products.

1. Are you a collector, investor, both, or none?

2. How many hours per month do you devote to collecting? 5 hrs or less • 6-14 hrs • 15 hrs or more

3. In the past year, how much did you spend on collecting? $999 or less • $1,000-$4,999 • $5,000 or more

Brilliant
Uncirculated!

PLEASE PRINT

Name_____

Address_____

City_____

State_____ Zip_____

Email_____

Phone_____

## FREE Gift!

### FREE LEWIS & CLARK NICKELS IN A CUSTOM SNAPLOCK. A $5 VALUE!

Offer good in USA only. Postcard must be fully completed to receive a free gift. Limit one gift per address. Please allow 4-6 weeks for delivery. Offer expires 4/9/07. No cash value. Void where prohibited by law.

## ALASKA RURAL REHABILITATION
## CORPORATION TOKENS OF 1935

These tokens were issued by the U.S. government for the use of the colonists of the Matanuska Valley Colonization Project, to supply them with much-needed federal aid. They were redeemable only at the ARRC stores. The "Bingles," as they were called, were in use only about six months during 1935 and 1936, after which they were redeemed for regular U.S. money and destroyed. They were issued on a basis of family dependents. Each token is similar in size to the corresponding U.S. coin, with the exception of the one-cent piece, which is octagonal. The design is the same on both sides of each denomination.

### Aluminum

| | Mintage | EF | Unc. | | Mintage | EF | Unc. |
|---|---|---|---|---|---|---|---|
| One Cent | 5,000 | $72. | $135. | Twenty-Five Cents | 3,000 | $100. | $200. |
| Five Cents | 5,000 | 72. | 135. | Fifty Cents | 2,500 | 100. | 200. |
| Ten Cents | 10 | 72. | 135. | One Dollar | 2,500 | 200. | 270. |

### Brass

| | Mintage | EF | Unc. | | Mintage | EF | Unc. |
|---|---|---|---|---|---|---|---|
| Five Dollars | 1,000 | $175. | $300. | Ten Dollars | 1,000 | $200. | $375. |

## Misstruck Coins and Error Pieces

With the production of millions of coins each year, it is natural that a few abnormal pieces escape inspection and are inadvertently released for circulation, usually in original bags or rolls of new coins. These are not considered regular issues because they were not made intentionally. They are all eagerly sought by collectors for the information they shed on minting techniques, and as a variation from normal date and mint series collecting.

Nearly every misstruck or error coin is unique in some way, and prices may vary from coin to coin. They may all be classified in general groups related to the kinds of errors or manufacturing malfunctions involved. Collectors value these pieces according to the scarcity of each kind of error for each type of coin. Non-collectors usually view them as curios, and often believe that they must be worth much more than normal coins because they look so strange. In reality, the value assigned to various types of errors by collectors and dealers reflects both supply and demand, and is based on recurring transactions between willing buyers and sellers.

The following listings show current average values for the most frequently encountered kinds of error coins. In each case, the values shown are for coins that are unmarred by serious marks or scratches, and in Uncirculated condition for modern issues, and Extremely Fine condition for obsolete types. Exceptions are valued higher or lower. Error coins of rare date issues generally do not command a premium beyond their normal values. In most cases each of these coins is unique in some respect and must be valued according to its individual appearance, quality, and eye appeal.

There are many other kinds of errors and misstruck coins beyond those listed in this guide book. Some are more valuable, and others less valuable, than the most popular pieces that are listed here as examples of what this interesting field contains. The pieces illustrated are general examples of the types described.

Early in 2002 the mints changed their production methods to a new system designed to eliminate deformed planchets, off-center strikes, and similar errors. They also changed the delivery system of bulk coin, and no longer shipped loose coins in sewn bags to be counted and wrapped by banks or counting rooms, where error coins were often found and sold to collectors. Under the new system, coins are packaged in large quantities and go directly to automated counters that filter out deformed coins. The result has been that very few error coins have entered the market since late 2002, and almost none after that date. The values shown in these listings are for pre-2002 coins; those dated after that, with but a few exceptions, are valued considerably higher.

For additional details and information about these coins, the following books are recommended:

- Margolis, Arnold, and Weinberg, Fred. *The Error Coin Encyclopedia* (4th ed.), 2004.

- Herbert, Alan. *Official Price Guide to Minting Varieties and Errors*, New York, 1991.

- Fivaz, Bill, and Stanton, J.T. *The Cherrypickers' Guide to Rare Die Varieties* (4th ed.), Atlanta, GA, 2006.

The coins discussed in this section must not be confused with others that have been mutilated or damaged after leaving the mint. Examples of such pieces include coins that have been scratched, hammered, engraved, impressed, acid etched, or plated by individuals to simulate something other than a normal coin. Those pieces have no numismatic value, and can only be considered as altered coins not suitable for a collection.

# MISSTRIKES AND ERRORS

## Types of Error Coins

**1. *Clipped Planchet*—An incomplete coin, missing 10 to 25% of the metal.** Incomplete planchets result from accidents when the steel rods used to punch out blanks from the metal strip overlap a portion of the strip already punched. There are curved, straight, ragged, incomplete, and elliptical clips. Values may be greater or less depending on the nature and size of the clip. Coins with more than one clip usually command higher values.

**2. *Multiple Strike*—A coin with at least one additional image from being struck again off center.** Value increases with the number of strikes. These minting errors occur when a finished coin goes back into the press and is struck again with the same dies. The presence or absence of a date will also affect values.

**3. *Blank or Planchet*—A blank disc of metal intended for coinage but not struck with dies.** In the process of preparation for coinage, the blanks are first punched from a strip of metal and then milled to upset the rim. In most instances, first-process pieces (blanks without upset rim) are slightly more valuable than the finished planchets. Values shown are for the most common pieces.

**No Rim**     **With Rim**

**4. *Defective Die*—A coin showing raised metal from a large die crack, or small rim break.** Coins that show evidence of light die cracks, polishing, or very minor die damage are generally of little or no value. Prices shown here are for coins with very noticeable, raised die-crack lines, or those for which the die broke away, producing an unstruck area known as a *cud*.

**5. *Off Center*—A coin that has been struck out of collar and incorrectly centered with part of the design missing.** Values are for coins with approximately 10 to 20% of design missing from obsolete coins, or 20 to 60% missing from modern coins. These are misstruck coins that were made when the planchet did not enter the coinage press properly. Coins that are struck only slightly off center, with none of the design missing, are called *broadstrikes* (see the next category). Those with nearly all of the impression missing are generally worth more, but those with a readable date and mint are the most valuable.

**6.** *Broadstrike*—**A coin that was struck outside the retaining collar.** When coins are struck without being contained in the collar die, they spread out larger than normal pieces. All denominations have a plain edge.

**7.** *Lamination*—**A flaw whereby a fragment of metal has peeled off the coin's surface.** This defect occurs when a foreign substance, such as gas oxides or dirt, becomes trapped in the strip as it is rolled out to the proper thickness. Lamination flaws may be missing or still attached to the coin's surface. Minor flaws may only decrease a coin's value, while a clad coin that is missing the full surface of one or both sides is worth more than the values listed here.

**8.** *Brockage*—**A mirror image of the design impressed on the opposite side of the same coin.** These errors are caused when a struck coin remains on either die after striking, and impresses its image into the next blank planchet as it is struck, leaving a negative or mirror image. Off-center and partial Brockage coins are worth less than those with full impression. Coins with negative impressions on both sides are usually mutilated pieces made outside the mint by the pressing together of coins.

**9.** *Wrong Planchet*—**A coin struck on a planchet intended for another denomination or of the wrong metal.** Examples of these are cents struck on dime planchets, nickels on cent planchets, or quarters on dime planchets. Values vary depending on the type of error involved. Those struck on coins of a different denomination that were previously struck normally are of much greater value.

## Waffled Coins

In mid-2003, the U.S. Mint acquired machines to eliminate security concerns and the cost associated with providing Mint police escorts to private vendors for the melting of scrap, substandard struck coins, planchets, and blanks. Under high pressure, the rollers and blades of these machines cancel the coins and blanks in a manner similar in appearance to the surface of a waffle, and they are popularly known by that term. This process has effectively kept most misstruck coins produced after 2003 from becoming available to collectors. Waffled examples are known for all six 2003-dated coin denominations, from the Lincoln cent through the Sacagawea dollar. The Mint has not objected to these pieces' trading in the open market because they are not considered coins with legal tender status.

389

## Misstruck and Error Pieces

| Misstruck and Error Pieces | 1 | 2 | 3 | 4 | 5 | 6 | 7 | 8 |
|---|---|---|---|---|---|---|---|---|
| Large Cent | $50.00 | $450.00 | $100.00 | $15. | $225. | $40. | $18. | $350. |
| Indian 1¢ | 25.00 | 300.00 | — | 10. | 100. | 50. | 10. | 250. |
| Lincoln 1¢ (95% copper) | 4.00 | 35.00 | 3.00 | 10. | 5. | 6. | 2. | 25. |
| Steel 1¢ | 18.00 | 200.00 | 20.00 | 15. | 70. | 35. | 15. | 100. |
| Lincoln 1¢ zinc | 2.00 | 28.00 | 2.00 | 15. | 5. | 4. | 15. | 38. |
| Liberty 5¢ | 30.00 | 500.00 | — | 30. | 125. | 100. | 20. | 325. |
| Buffalo 5¢ | 35.00 | 900.00 | — | 25. | 300. | 200. | 25. | 750. |
| Jefferson 5¢ | 6.50 | 30.00 | 60.00 | 15. | 10. | 10. | 20. | 60. |
| Wartime 5¢ | 15.00 | 350.00 | 350.00 | 25. | 150. | 70. | 15. | 400. |
| Barber 10¢ | 60.00 | 300.00 | 10.00 | 75. | 200. | 100. | 15. | 150. |
| Mercury 10¢ | 40.00 | 200.00 | 10.00 | 25. | 150. | 75. | 14. | 150. |
| Roosevelt 10¢ (S) | 7.00 | 100.00 | 10.00 | 35. | 100. | 65. | 15. | 120. |
| Roosevelt 10¢ (C) | 4.00 | 30.00 | 3.50 | 15. | 8. | 10. | 16. | 50. |
| Washington 25¢ (S) | 15.00 | 250.00 | 85.00 | 20. | 150. | 100. | 10. | 200. |
| Washington 25¢ (C) | 5.00 | 100.00 | 6.00 | 10. | 30. | 15. | 25. | 55. |
| Bicentennial 25¢ | 25.00 | 350.00 | — | 50. | 150. | 65. | 50. | 200. |
| Statehood 25¢ | 50.00 | 450.00 | — | 25. | 150. | 125. | 30. | 350. |
| Franklin 50¢ | 50.00 | 800.00 | 60.00 | 100. | 600. | 450. | 30. | 650. |
| Kennedy 50¢ (S) | 25.00 | 800.00 | 60.00 | 70. | 350. | 250. | 40. | 400. |
| Kennedy 50¢ (C) | 20.00 | 350.00 | 40.00 | 50. | 100. | 75. | 25. | 300. |
| Bicentennial 50¢ | 40.00 | 450.00 | — | 75. | 250. | 75. | 25. | — |
| Silver $1 | 50.00 | 3,000.00 | 1,000.00 | 900. | 1,500. | 1,200. | 50. | |
| Eisenhower $1 | 50.00 | 1,200.00 | 50.00 | 500. | 700. | 200. | 50. | 1,200. |
| Bicentennial $1 | 50.00 | 2,000.00 | — | 1,000. | 800. | 200. | 50. | 1,500. |
| Anthony $1 | 40.00 | 800.00 | 85.00 | 100. | 300. | 75. | 30. | 350. |
| Sacagawea $1 | 100.00 | 900.00 | 125.00 | 50. | 600. | 300. | 50. | 650. |

Note: 1 = Clipped Planchet; 2 = Multiple Strike; 3 = Blank Planchet; 4 = Defective Die; 5 = Off Center; 6 = Broadstrike; 7 = Lamination; 8 = Brockage.

## Wrong Metals

| | 1¢ ZN | 1¢ CU | 1¢ Steel | 5¢ | (S)10¢ | (C)10¢ | (S) 25¢ | (C)25¢ | (C) 50¢ |
|---|---|---|---|---|---|---|---|---|---|
| Indian 1¢ | np | — | np | np | $3,600. | np | np | np | np |
| Lincoln 1¢ | — | — | np | np | 1,000. | $250. | np | np | np |
| Buffalo 5¢ | np | $3,000. | np | — | 1,200. | np | np | np | np |
| Jefferson 5¢ | $95. | 175. | $900. | — | 250. | 200. | np | np | np |
| Wartime 5¢ | np | 1,500. | 2,000. | — | 2,000. | np | np | np | np |
| Wash 25¢ (S) | np | 900. | 4,000. | $450. | 250. | — | — | — | np |
| Wash 25¢ (C) | — | 800. | np | 200. | — | 350. | — | — | np |
| 1976 25¢ | np | 900. | np | 1,000. | — | 600. | — | — | np |
| Statehood 25¢ | — | 2,000. | np | 800. | np | 1,500. | np | — | np |
| Walking 50¢ | np | — | — | — | — | np | — | np | np |
| Franklin 50¢ | np | 5,000. | np | 5,000. | 7,000. | np | $1,500. | np | np |
| Kennedy 50¢ | np | 5,000. | np | 1,000. | 2,000. | 2,500. | 350. | $650. | — |
| 1976 50¢ | np | — | np | 1,250. | — | — | — | 800. | — |
| Eisenhower $1 | np | 9,500. | np | 8,000. | — | 9,000. | — | 6,000. | $5,000. |
| Anthony $1 | np | 3,000. | np | — | np | — | — | 1,500. | np |
| Sacagawea $1 | 2,500. | np | np | 2,500. | np | 1,500. | np | 900. | np |

Note: ZN = Zinc; CU = Copper; S = Silver; C + Copper-Nickel Clad; np = not possible.
  The Kennedy fifty-cent piece struck on an Anthony one-dollar planchet is very rare. Coins struck over other coins of different denominations are usually valued three to five times higher than these prices. Values for statehood quarter errors vary with each type and state, and are generally much higher than for other quarters. Coins made from mismatched dies (statehood quarter obverse combined with Sacagawea dollar reverse) are extremely rare.

A *Guide Book of United States Coins* has long held the record for being the longest-running annual retail coin-price guide. It has now passed its 50th anniversary, and collectors seem to be almost as interested in assembling sets of old Red Books as of old coins. The reason for this popularity seems to be that collectors have a penchant for completing sets of many things. The demand for old editions of the Red Book that are still in existence has created a solid market for them.

Those who save old editions of the Red Book seem to do so for many reasons. Some maintain reference libraries of all kinds of coin publications. To them, having one of each edition is essential, because that is the way old books are collected. Others are speculators who believe that the value of old editions will go up as interest and demand increase. The great majority of people who save old Red Books do so to maintain a record of coin prices going back further than any other source.

Following price trends in old Red Books is a good indicator of how well coins of any date or denomination are doing in comparison to each other. The price information published in this book each year is an average of what the entire market is paying for each coin. As such, it is a valuable benchmark, showing how prices have gone up or down over the years. It is information like this that often gives investors an edge in predicting what the future may hold.

Old Red Books are also a handy source of information about collecting trends. They show graphically how grading has changed over the years, what new coins have been discovered and added to the listings, and which areas are growing in popularity. Studying these old books can be educational as well as nostalgic. It's great fun to see what your favorite coins sold for 15 or 25 years ago or more. It can also be a bit frustrating to realize what might have been if we had only bought the right coins at the right time in years past.

Many collectors have asked about the quantities printed of each edition. Unfortunately, that information has never been published, and now even the manufacturer has no records of how many were made. The original author, R.S. Yeoman, told inquirers that the first press run in November 1946 was for 9,000 copies. In February 1947 an additional 9,000 copies were printed to satisfy the unexpected demand.

There was a slight difference between the first and second printings. The wording in the first printing, at the bottom of page 135, reads, "which probably accounts for the scarcity of *this date*." Those last few words were changed to "the scarcity of *1903 O*" in the second printing.

The second edition had a press run of 22,000. The printing of each edition thereafter gradually increased, with the highest number ever being reached with the 18th edition, dated 1965. In that year, at the top of a booming coin market, a whopping 1,200,000 copies were produced. Since that time the numbers have decreased in proportion to the market, but still maintain a record of being the world's largest selling coin publication each year.

In some years a very limited number of Red Books were made for use by price contributors. Those were interleaved with blank pages. No more than 50 copies were ever made for any one year. Perhaps fewer than 20 were made in the first few years. Three of these of the first edition, and one of the second edition, are currently known. Their value is now in four figures. Those made in the 1960s sell for around $50 each today.

There are other unusual Red Books that command exceptional prices. One of the most popular is the 1987 special edition that was made for, and distributed only to, people who attended the 1986 ANA banquet in Milwaukee. Only 500 of those were printed with a special commemorative cover. Copies have sold for $100 to $750 each and are always in demand.

Error books are also popular with collectors. The most common is one with double-stamped printing on the cover. The second most frequently seen are those with the cover put on upside down. Probably the best known of the error books is the 1963 16th edition with a missing page. For some uncanny reason, page 239 is duplicated in some of those books, and page 237 is missing. The error was corrected on most of the printing.

Those who collect old Red Books find them in the strangest places—everywhere from flea markets to hospital libraries. Garage sales are the most fruitful source. We have heard many stories of collectors finding first or second editions in garage sales for 10¢ or 25¢. Others come from book stores at 50¢ or $1, but if you want to collect these books seriously you will probably have to look for them in numismatic book auctions. There you will compete with others, and probably have to pay prices close to those shown in the accompanying chart.

The terminology used to describe book condition differs from that utilized in grading coins. A "Very Fine" book is one that is nearly new, with minimal signs of use. Early editions of the Red Book are rarely if ever found in anything approaching "New" condition. Exceptionally well-preserved older editions command a substantial premium and are in great demand. Nice used copies that are still clean and in good shape, but slightly worn from use, are also desirable. Perhaps the gilt stamping on the front cover and spine is a bit indistinct; someone may have added his or her name, or made notes, inside. Only the early editions are worth a premium in badly worn condition.

## *Valuation Guide for Past Editions of the Red Book*

| YEAR/EDITION | Issue Price | VG | F | VF | NEW |
|---|---|---|---|---|---|
| 1947 (1st ed.), 1st Printing | $1.50 | $300.00 | $500.00 | $1,000.00 | |
| 1947 (1st ed.), 2nd Printing | 1.50 | 250.00 | 450.00 | 850.00 | |
| 1948 (2nd ed.) | 1.50 | 75.00 | 150.00 | 250.00 | |
| 1949 (3rd ed.) | 1.50 | 75.00 | 125.00 | 175.00 | |
| 1951/52 (4th ed.) | 1.50 | 50.00 | 100.00 | 150.00 | |
| 1952/53 (5th ed.) | 1.50 | 125.00 | 250.00 | 350.00 | |
| 1953/54 (6th ed.) | 1.50 | 40.00 | 60.00 | 90.00 | |
| 1954/55 (7th ed.) | 1.75 | 40.00 | 60.00 | 85.00 | |
| 1955 (8th ed.) | 1.75 | 25.00 | 40.00 | 70.00 | |
| 1956 (9th ed.) | 1.75 | 25.00 | 30.00 | 50.00 | |
| 1957 (10th ed.) | 1.75 | 20.00 | 30.00 | 40.00 | |
| 1958 (11th ed.) | 1.75 | | 10.00 | 15.00 | $35.00 |
| 1959 (12th ed.) | 1.75 | | 15.00 | 25.00 | 35.00 |
| 1960 (13th ed.) | 1.75 | | 6.00 | 8.00 | 18.00 |
| 1961 (14th ed.) | 1.75 | | 4.00 | 6.00 | 15.00 |
| 1962 (15th ed.) | 1.75 | | 4.00 | 5.00 | 8.00 |
| 1963 (16th ed.) | 1.75 | | 4.00 | 5.00 | 8.00 |
| 1964 (17th ed.) | 1.75 | | 4.00 | 5.00 | 7.00 |
| 1965 (18th ed.) | 1.75 | | 3.00 | 4.00 | 6.00 |
| 1966 (19th ed.) | 1.75 | | 3.00 | 4.00 | 6.00 |
| 1967 (20th ed.) | 1.75 | | 3.00 | 5.00 | 8.00 |
| 1968 (21st ed.) | 1.75 | | 3.00 | 5.00 | 10.00 |
| 1969 (22nd ed.) | 2.00 | | 3.00 | 5.00 | 10.00 |
| 1970 (23rd ed.) | 2.00 | | 3.00 | 6.00 | 11.00 |
| 1971 (24th ed.) | 2.50 | | 3.00 | 4.00 | 6.00 |
| 1972 (25th ed.) | 2.50 | | 6.00 | 9.00 | 12.00 |
| 1973 (26th ed.) | 2.50 | | 4.00 | 5.00 | 7.00 |
| 1974 (27th ed.) | 2.50 | | 2.00 | 4.00 | 6.00 |
| 1975 (28th ed.) | 3.00 | | | 4.00 | 5.00 |
| 1976 (29th ed.) | 3.95 | | | 4.00 | 5.00 |
| 1977 (30th ed.) | 3.95 | | | 4.00 | 6.00 |
| 1978 (31st ed.) | 3.95 | | | 4.00 | 5.00 |
| 1979 (32nd ed.) | 3.95 | | | 4.00 | 6.00 |

| YEAR/EDITION | Issue Price | VG | F | VF | NEW |
|---|---|---|---|---|---|
| 1980 (33rd ed.) . . . . . . . . . . . . . . . . . . . . . .$3.95 | | | | $4.00 | $10.00 |
| 1981 (34th ed.) . . . . . . . . . . . . . . . . . . . . . .4.95 | | | | 2.00 | 5.00 |
| 1982 (35th ed.) . . . . . . . . . . . . . . . . . . . . . .4.95 | | | | 2.00 | 5.00 |
| 1983 (36th ed.) . . . . . . . . . . . . . . . . . . . . . .5.95 | | | | 2.00 | 5.00 |
| 1984 (37th ed.) . . . . . . . . . . . . . . . . . . . . . .5.95 | | | | 2.00 | 5.00 |
| 1985 (38th ed.) . . . . . . . . . . . . . . . . . . . . . .5.95 | | | | 2.00 | 5.00 |
| 1986 (39th ed.) . . . . . . . . . . . . . . . . . . . . . .5.95 | | | | 2.50 | 5.00 |
| 1987 (40th ed.), Special ANA Cover . . . . . . . . . . . | | $100.00 | | 200.00 | 750.00 |
| 1987 (40th ed.) . . . . . . . . . . . . . . . . . . . . . .6.95 | | | | 3.00 | 6.00 |
| 1988 (41st ed.) . . . . . . . . . . . . . . . . . . . . . .6.95 | | | | 3.00 | 5.00 |
| 1989 (42nd ed.) . . . . . . . . . . . . . . . . . . . . . .6.95 | | | | 3.00 | 8.00 |
| 1990 (43rd ed.) . . . . . . . . . . . . . . . . . . . . . .7.95 | | | | 2.00 | 7.00 |
| 1991 (44th ed.) . . . . . . . . . . . . . . . . . . . . . .8.95 | | | | 2.00 | 5.00 |
| 1992 (45th ed.) . . . . . . . . . . . . . . . . . . . . . .8.95 | | | | 2.00 | 6.00 |
| 1992 (45th ed.), Special ANA Cover . . . . . . . . . . . | | 20.00 | | 75.00 | 250.00 |
| 1993 (46th ed.), Hardbound . . . . . . . . . . . . .9.95 | | | | 2.25 | 7.00 |
| 1993 (46th ed.), Softbound . . . . . . . . . . . . .6.95 | | | | 1.00 | 5.00 |
| 1994 (47th ed.), Hardbound . . . . . . . . . . . . .9.95 | | | | 1.50 | 4.00 |
| 1994 (47th ed.), Softbound . . . . . . . . . . . . .7.95 | | | | 1.00 | 4.00 |
| 1995 (48th ed.), Hardbound . . . . . . . . . . . . .10.95 | | | | 1.50 | 4.00 |
| 1995 (48th ed.), Softbound . . . . . . . . . . . . .7.95 | | | | 1.00 | 3.00 |
| 1996 (49th ed.), Hardbound . . . . . . . . . . . . .10.95 | | | | 1.50 | 4.00 |
| 1996 (49th ed.), Softbound . . . . . . . . . . . . .7.95 | | | | 1.00 | 3.00 |
| 1997 (50th ed.), Hardbound . . . . . . . . . . . . .11.95 | | | | 1.50 | 5.00 |
| 1997 (50th ed.), Coilbound . . . . . . . . . . . . .8.95 | | | | 1.00 | 5.00 |
| 1997 (50th ed.), Special Anniversary Cover . .24.95 | | | | 50.00 | 120.00 |
| 1998 (51st ed.), Hardbound . . . . . . . . . . . . .11.95 | | | | | 3.00 |
| 1998 (51st ed.), Softbound . . . . . . . . . . . . .8.95 | | | | | 2.00 |
| 1999 (52nd ed.), Hardbound . . . . . . . . . . . . .11.95 | | | | | 2.00 |
| 1999 (52nd ed.), Coilbound . . . . . . . . . . . . .8.95 | | | | | 2.00 |
| 2000 (53rd ed.), Hardbound . . . . . . . . . . . . .12.95 | | | | | 2.00 |
| 2000 (53rd ed.), Coilbound . . . . . . . . . . . . .8.95 | | | | | 2.00 |
| 2001 (54th ed.), Hardbound . . . . . . . . . . . . .13.95 | | | | | 2.00 |
| 2001 (54th ed.), Coilbound . . . . . . . . . . . . .9.95 | | | | | 2.00 |
| 2002 (55th ed.), Hardbound . . . . . . . . . . . . .14.95 | | | | | 2.00 |
| 2002 (55th ed.), Coilbound . . . . . . . . . . . . .10.95 | | | | | 2.00 |
| 2002 ANA Special Edition . . . . . . . . . . . . . .100.00 | | | | 80.00 | 125.00 |
| 2002 *S.S. Central America* . . . . . . . . . . . . . . . . . | | | | 35.00 | 40.00 |
| 2003 (56th ed.), Hardbound . . . . . . . . . . . . .15.95 | | | | | 2.00 |
| 2003 (56th ed.), Coilbound . . . . . . . . . . . . .11.95 | | | | | 2.00 |
| 2003 (56th ed.), Softbound . . . . . . . . . . . . .11.95 | | | | | 2.00 |
| 2004 (57th ed.), Hardbound . . . . . . . . . . . . .15.95 | | | | | |
| 2004 (57th ed.), Coilbound . . . . . . . . . . . . .12.95 | | | | | |
| 2004 (57th ed.), Softbound . . . . . . . . . . . . .11.95 | | | | | |
| 2005 (58th ed.), Hardbound . . . . . . . . . . . . .15.95 | | | | | |
| 2005 (58th ed.), Coilbound . . . . . . . . . . . . .12.95 | | | | | |
| 2005 (58th ed.), Softbound . . . . . . . . . . . . .11.95 | | | | | |
| 2005 (58th ed.), Special Leather Bound . . . .69.95 | | | | | 75.00 |
| 2005 (58th ed.), F.U.N. Special Edition . . . . . . . . . | | | | | 75.00 |
| 2006 (59th ed.), Hardbound . . . . . . . . . . . . .16.95 | | | | | |
| 2006 (59th ed.), Coilbound . . . . . . . . . . . . .14.95 | | | | | |
| 2006 (59th ed.), Softbound . . . . . . . . . . . . .12.95 | | | | | |
| 2006 (59th ed.), Special Leather Bound . . . . . . . . | | | | | 75.00 |

These charts show the bullion values of common-date circulation-strike silver and gold coins. These are intrinsic values and do not reflect any numismatic premium a coin might have. The weight attached to each denomination is its actual silver weight (ASW) or actual gold weight (AGW).

## Bullion Values of Silver Coins

| Silver Price Per Ounce | Wartime Nickel .05626 oz. | Dime .07234 oz. | Quarter .18084 oz. | Half Dollar .36169 oz. | Silver Clad Half Dollar .14792 oz. | Silver Dollar .77344 oz. |
|---|---|---|---|---|---|---|
| $5.00 | $0.28 | $0.36 | $0.90 | $1.81 | $0.74 | $3.87 |
| 5.50 | 0.31 | 0.40 | 0.99 | 1.99 | 0.81 | 4.25 |
| 6.00 | 0.34 | 0.43 | 1.09 | 2.17 | 0.89 | 4.64 |
| 6.50 | 0.37 | 0.47 | 1.18 | 2.35 | 0.96 | 5.03 |
| 7.00 | 0.39 | 0.51 | 1.27 | 2.53 | 1.04 | 5.41 |
| 7.50 | 0.42 | 0.54 | 1.36 | 2.71 | 1.11 | 5.80 |
| 8.00 | 0.45 | 0.58 | 1.45 | 2.89 | 1.18 | 6.19 |
| 8.50 | 0.48 | 0.61 | 1.54 | 3.07 | 1.26 | 6.57 |
| 9.00 | 0.51 | 0.65 | 1.63 | 3.26 | 1.33 | 6.96 |
| 9.50 | 0.53 | 0.69 | 1.72 | 3.44 | 1.41 | 7.35 |
| 10.00 | 0.56 | 0.72 | 1.81 | 3.62 | 1.48 | 7.73 |
| 10.50 | 0.59 | 0.76 | 1.90 | 3.80 | 1.55 | 8.12 |
| 11.00 | 0.62 | 0.80 | 1.99 | 3.98 | 1.63 | 8.51 |
| 11.50 | 0.65 | 0.83 | 2.08 | 4.16 | 1.70 | 8.89 |
| 12.00 | 0.68 | 0.87 | 2.17 | 4.34 | 1.78 | 9.28 |

## Bullion Values of Gold Coins

| Gold Price Per Ounce | $5.00 Liberty Head 1839–1908 Indian Head 1908–1929 .24187 oz. | $10.00 Liberty Head 1838–1907 Indian Head 1907–1933 .48375 oz. | $20.00 1849–1933 .96750 oz. |
|---|---|---|---|
| $350.00 | $84.65 | $169.31 | $338.63 |
| 375.00 | 90.70 | 181.41 | 362.81 |
| 400.00 | 96.75 | 193.50 | 387.00 |
| 425.00 | 102.79 | 205.59 | 411.19 |
| 450.00 | 108.84 | 217.69 | 435.38 |
| 475.00 | 114.89 | 229.78 | 459.56 |
| 500.00 | 120.94 | 241.88 | 483.75 |
| 525.00 | 126.98 | 253.97 | 507.94 |
| 550.00 | 133.03 | 266.06 | 532.13 |
| 575.00 | 139.08 | 278.16 | 556.31 |
| 600.00 | 145.12 | 290.25 | 580.50 |
| 625.00 | 151.17 | 302.34 | 604.69 |
| 650.00 | 157.22 | 314.44 | 628.88 |
| 675.00 | 163.26 | 326.53 | 653.06 |
| 700.00 | 169.31 | 338.63 | 677.25 |
| 725.00 | 175.36 | 350.72 | 701.44 |
| 750.00 | 181.40 | 362.81 | 725.63 |

Note: The U.S. bullion coins first issued in 1986 are unlike the older regular issues. They contain the following amounts of pure metal: silver $1, 1 oz.; gold $50, 1 oz.; gold $25, 1/2 oz.; gold $10, 1/4 oz.; gold $5, 1/10 oz.

# GREAT COLLECTORS

## GREAT COLLECTORS AND COLLECTIONS OF THE PAST
### by Ron Guth and Jeff Garrett

**Appleton, William Sumner**—William Sumner Appleton was an active buyer in the latter half of the 19th century, purchasing J.J. Mickley's 1804 silver dollar, Mickley's entire gold coin collection, and virtually all of Lorin G. Parmelee's collection. He authored several works, including one on Washington-related coins and medals.

**Bass, Harry W.**—Harry W. Bass Jr. did what most collectors can only dream of—he built a nearly complete collection of United States gold coins, with an emphasis on superb quality. A true numismatist in the classic sense, Bass collected by die variety, both major and minor. The bulk of his collection was sold over a series of four auctions from 1999 to 2000, but the core collection of gold types and three-dollar gold pieces (including the unique 1870-S) is now on display at the Money Museum of the American Numismatic Association in Colorado Springs, Colorado.

**Boyd, Frederick C.C.**—F.C.C. Boyd was active as a coin dealer and collector during the first half of the 20th century. He acquired many great rarities, including an 1894-S dime, an 1876-CC twenty-cent piece, a 1927-D double eagle, and many others; for a short time, he owned an 1804 silver dollar. His silver and gold coins were sold at auction in 1946, with the silver portion billed as "The World's Greatest Collection." His U.S. colonial coins have recently come onto the market, via the John J. Ford collection.

**Brand, Virgil M.**—Virgil Brand was a Chicago brewer, and used his fortune to amass one of the largest coin collections of all time. Active from 1879 until his death in 1926, Brand was not averse to buying multiple items of great rarities (he owned six of the ten 1884 trade dollars, 30 four-dollar gold Stellas, five 1792 silver-center cents, etc. but only one 1804 silver dollar). At his death, his collection contained more than 350,000 coins, which required several decades to disperse completely.

**Browning, Jeff**—Jeff Browning was the name behind the Dallas Bank Collection of gold coins, sold at auction in 2001. Collecting during the 1960s and 1970s, Browning acquired a complete set of Liberty Head double eagles, a complete set of four-dollar Stellas, and a 1907 Ultra High Relief double eagle.

**Carter, Amon, Sr. and Jr.**—Amon Carter Sr. was a Texas oilman and cofounder of American Airlines. In the 1930s, he was introduced to coins by B. Max Mehl and went on a two-decade buying binge that netted him fabulous rarities such as an 1804 silver dollar, an 1884 trade dollar, an 1885 trade dollar, an 1822 half eagle, and many other rarities. Upon his death, Carter's collection passed to his son, who developed his own reputation as a top-ranked collector of United States currency.

**Dunham, William F.**—William Dunham was a Chicago druggist who was an active collector in the first half of the 20th century. His collection included one of the finest known 1802 half dimes, an 1804 silver dollar, and an 1822 half eagle. Following Dunham's death, Texas coin dealer B. Max Mehl purchased the collection intact. Mehl's 1941 Mail Bid Sale of the Dunham collection, offered in a lavish catalog, was a deception, as many of the best coins had already been sold privately!

**Eckfeldt, Adam**—A Mint employee for many years, Adam Eckfeldt was instrumental in building the Mint Cabinet that is now part of the National Numismatic Collection at the Smithsonian Institution. Beginning with the Mint's inception in 1792, Eckfeldt set aside coins each year with an eye to someday establishing a conservatory of coins. His dream was realized in 1838, when Mint Director Robert Maskell Patterson established a national collection at the Philadelphia Mint. Thanks to Adam Eckfeldt's foresight, collectors of today can enjoy many rarities that might otherwise have been lost forever.

**Eliasberg, Louis E., Sr.**—Louis Eliasberg is famous in numismatic circles for having assembled the only complete collection of federally issued United States coins. In 1942, Eliasberg purchased John Clapp's comprehensive collection intact, reducing his want list to a mere handful of coins. In 1950 Eliasberg achieved his goal of completion with the purchase of the unique 1873-CC No Arrows dime. His gold coins were sold at auction in 1982 and the balance of the collection was sold at auction in 1996 and 1997. The combined sales reached a total of $44 million.

**Ellsworth, Colonel James W.**—James Ellsworth's collection, begun during the late 1800s and continued through 1923, included many important rarities, such as a 1787 Brasher doubloon and two (!) 1804 silver dollars. Unlike most collectors, Ellsworth sold his collection during his lifetime, sharing many of the most significant coins with another famous collector, John Work Garrett.

**King Farouk of Egypt**—Farouk was a flamboyant king who used the Egyptian treasury to build a fabulous collection of U.S. and world coins. Farouk was deposed in 1952 and the sale of his collection in 1954 was one of the great numismatic events of history. The 1933 double eagle he once held reappeared in 2002, selling for a record price of $7.59 million!

**Garrett, John Work**—In 1919, John Work Garrett acquired a collection, built by his father and brother, that was already one of the most celebrated in America. While not as complete as Louis Eliasberg's U.S. coin collection, Garrett's included U.S. colonial and pre-federal issues, plus rarities from around the world. The sale of his U.S. coins (from 1979 through 1981) realized more than $25 million, setting a modern record for a single coin collection. In adjusted dollars, it would still be the most valuable collection today.

**Green, Colonel Edward Howland Robinson**—Colonel E.H.R. Green was a prolific collector, thanks to the fortune left him by his mother, Hetty Green (the "Witch of Wall Street"). He once owned all five of the 1913 Liberty Head nickels, an 1804 silver dollar, several 1838-O half dollars, and more than two hundred 1796 Draped Bust quarter dollars. In 1939, his coin collection was appraised at over $1.2 million, a staggering figure at the time.

**Lilly, Josiah K.**—Josiah K. Lilly amassed a huge collection of U.S. and world gold coins during the 1950s and 1960s. After his death, the Smithsonian Institution accepted the donation of the collection in exchange for a $5 million estate tax credit (worth roughly $50 million today). The U.S. section was virtually complete and included such rarities as the 1787 Brasher half doubloon, an 1822 half eagle, and a 1907 Ultra High Relief twenty-dollar gold piece. His collection was formerly exhibited in a special room in the National Museum of American History.

**Mickley, Joseph J.**—Joseph Mickley was one of the pioneer collectors of American coins, beginning a quest for a cent of his birth year (1799) in the early 1800s. Legend had Mickley visiting the U.S. Mint in 1827 to purchase four of the rare quarter dollars of that date; however, that legend has been debunked in recent years. Mickley is best known for the restrikes that he made of certain U.S. coins (1811 half cent, 1804 large cent, and 1823 large cent) using dies that the Mint had sold years earlier as scrap metal. Most of Mickley's dies were bought back by the U.S. government when they appeared in an auction of Mickley's estate in 1878.

**Mitchelson, John C.**—In December 1911, Joseph Mitchelson donated his collection of more than 10,000 U.S. and world coins to the Connecticut State Library in Hartford, where the bulk of the collection remains to this day. Provisions were made for the addition of new U.S. coins as they were minted in subsequent years. Highlights of the collection include a 1907 Ultra High Relief double eagle, a 1737 Higley copper, and many other fabulous rarities, few of which have been seen by the general public. In 1995, selected duplicates from the Connecticut State Library's collection were sold at auction, including a 1927-D double eagle.

**Newcomer, Waldo**—Waldo Newcomer began collecting in the 1890s and quickly built one of the largest and most complete collections of American colonial and federal coins. His collection of U.S. gold coins was said to be complete except for one half eagle and one double eagle. Newcomer also owned examples of such great rarities as two 1787 Brasher doubloons, an 1802 half dime, an 1838-O half dollar, an 1853 half dollar (without rays and arrowheads), and an 1804 silver dollar. Newcomer's coins were sold at auction over nearly a decade, from 1932 to 1941.

**Norweb, Mrs. R. Henry**—Over the course of many decades in the late 1800s, and throughout the 20th century, the Norweb family built an extensive collection of rare colonials and superb-quality U.S. coins. Mrs. Norweb acquired the love of numismatics at her father's feet and continued adding coins after his death. Highlights of the collection included a 1787 Brasher doubloon, a 1792 pattern quarter dollar, a 1913 nickel, an 1815 half eagle, and the finest known 1861 Paquet Reverse double eagle. The Norweb collection realized $20 million at auction in 1987 and 1988, despite the previous gifting-away of the Brasher doubloon and the 1913 nickel!

**Parmelee, Lorin G.**—Lorin Parmelee, a Boston bean-baker, started collecting coins in the 1850s, when U.S. colonial copper coins and large cents still circulated at face value. As his taste and fortunes advanced, he began purchasing coins at auction, then began buying entire collections, taking what he wanted and selling off the duplicates. The remainders, from the Charles Bushnell collection (purchased by Parmelee in 1880) alone, represented one of the finest coin auctions of the 19th century. In its time, Parmelee's collection was generally perceived to be the finest and most complete collection of coins ever assembled. Included were great rarities such as the 1796 and 1797 half dollars, an 1804 silver dollar, and a set of 1783 Nova Constellatio pattern coins in silver.

**Pittman, John Jay**—Unlike most of the collectors in this section, John Jay Pittman had limited resources with which to buy rare coins. However, through shrewd purchases, Pittman amassed a collection that realized more than $30 million when it was sold between 1997 and 1998. Some of his best purchases were made at the 1954 sale of King Farouk's coin collection.

**Reed, Byron**—A real estate operator in Omaha, Nebraska, Byron Reed built a fine collection of American coins, books, and autographs. Reed worked on his collection from the 1880s until his death in 1891. Reed bequeathed his coins and library to the city of Omaha, along with a plot of land for a building that would eventually house both collections. In 1996, selections from his coin collection were sold at auction to raise money for the city. However, the majority of Reed's collection, including his 1804 silver dollar and rare U.S. patterns, remains largely intact, with many of the coins now on display at the Western Heritage Museum in Omaha.

**Sheldon, William H.**—William Sheldon collected large cents by die variety, and in 1949 he wrote *Early American Cents* (renamed *Penny Whimsy* in 1958), the standard reference book on the 1793 through 1814 cent varieties. The 70-point grading system used by numismatists today was developed by Sheldon.

**Snowden, James Ross**—James Snowden served as director of the Mint from 1853 to 1861, and was a serious numismatist as well. He built the cabinet of Washington coins, tokens, and medals that went on display at the Philadelphia Mint in 1860. Snowden acquired many of the items in the display by trading restrikes of rare United States coins.

**Stickney, Matthew Adams**—Matthew Stickney was a contemporary of Joseph J. Mickley and thus among the first truly serious collectors of American coins. Stickney acquired many of his best coins directly from the Mint: some through trades and some through an annual purchase of Proof coins beginning in 1845. Other rarities came from his special relationship with a New York bullion firm, which sent him gold rarities for their intrinsic metal value. Around 1843, Stickney traded a gold 1785 Immune Columbia colonial coin for one of the Mint's 1804 silver dollars! Other highlights from his collection include the unique 1776 New Hampshire cent and a 1776 Massachusetts "Janus Head" copper.

**Trompeter, Ed**—Ed Trompeter built a collection of Proof U.S. gold coins, complete for the period from 1858 through 1915 (save for the 1858 double eagle), plus extra rarities such as an 1855 Proof gold dollar, a complete set of four-dollar gold Stellas, a quintuple "Stella," a 1907 Ultra High Relief double eagle, and more. Trompeter's Proof gold dollars through three-dollar gold pieces were sold at auction in 1992; his Proof half eagles through double eagles were sold privately for more than $15 million in 1998. The Trompeter pedigree is one of the most desirable of modern times.

**Wilkison, John**—John Wilkison built the finest collection of U.S. gold pattern coins ever assembled outside the Mint. His collection included unique rarities such as the 1907 Indian Head double eagle and the complete set of gold 1872 "Amazonian"one-through twenty-dollar patterns. The collection formed the basis for David Akers's 1975 book *United States Gold Patterns*, a modern numismatist's "wish book."

**Woodin, William H.**—William Woodin once owned the unique 1870-S three-dollar piece. In 1909, he acquired the two known gold 1877 fifty-dollar half unions, prompting an outrage that the government had allowed them to be released. Shortly thereafter, Woodin traded them for a "trunkful" of patterns that served as the basis for the first book on U.S. pattern coins. The half unions are now in the Smithsonian Institution, and Woodin's patterns represent the majority of the pieces that appear on the market today.

## TOP 250 COIN PRICES REALIZED AT AUCTION

| Rank | Price | Class | Coin | Grade | Firm | Date |
|------|-------|-------|------|-------|------|------|
| 1 | 7,590,020 | $20 | 1933 | Gem BU | Soth/Stack's | Jul-02 |
| 2 | 4,140,000 | Silver $ | 1804 Class I | PCGS PF-68 | B&M | Aug-99 |
| 3 | 2,990,000 | $20 | MCMVII Ultra HR LE | PCGS PF-69 | Heritage | Nov-05 |
| 4 | 2,990,000 | Pre-Fed | 1787 Brasher, EB on Breast (A) | NGC EF-45 | Heritage | Jan-05 |
| 5 | 2,415,000 | Pre-Fed | 1787 Brasher, EB on Wing | NGC AU-55 | Heritage | Jan-05 |
| 6 | 1,897,500 | $20 | 1927-D (I) | PCGS MS-67 | Heritage | Nov-05 |
| 7 | 1,840,000 | 5¢ | 1913 Liberty Head | NGC PF-66 | Superior | Mar-01 |
| 8 | 1,840,000 | Silver $ | 1804 Class I (B) | PCGS PF-64 | Stack's | Oct-00 |
| 9 | 1,815,000 | Silver $ | 1804 Class I | PF-63 | B&M/Stack's | Apr-97 |
| 10 | 1,485,000 | 5¢ | 1913 Liberty Head | Gem PF-66 | B&M/Stack's | May-96 |
| 11 | 1,380,000 | $2.50 | 1796 No Stars | PCGS MS-65 | ANR | Jun-05 |
| 12 | 1,322,500 | $20 | 1927-D | NGC MS-65 | Heritage | Jan-06 |
| 13 | 1,322,500 | 10¢ | 1894-S (L) | NGC PF-66 | DLRC | Mar-05 |
| 14 | 1,265,000 | Silver $ | 1795 Flowing Hair B-7 | V Ch Gem MS | Bullowa | Dec-05 |
| 15 | 1,210,000 | $20 | MCMVII Ultra HR LE (J) | PCGS PF-67 | Goldberg | May-99 |
| 16 | 1,207,500 | Silver $ | 1866 No Motto | NGC PF-63 | ANR | Jan-05 |
| 17 | 1,207,500 | Silver $ | 1804 Class III (C) | PCGS PF-58 | B&M | Jul-03 |
| 18 | 1,150,000 | Silver $ | 1794 | NGC MS-64 | ANR | Jun-05 |
| 19 | 1,092,500 | $20 | 1921 | PCGS MS-66 | Heritage | Nov-05 |
| 20 | 1,092,500 | Silver $ | 1870-S | BU PL | Stack's | May-03 |
| 21 | 1,035,000 | 10¢ | 1894-S | PCGS PF-65 | Heritage | Jan-05 |
| 22 | 1,006,250 | Trade $ | 1885 | NGC PF-62 | DLRC | Nov-04 |
| 23 | 990,000 | Silver $ | 1804 Class I (B) | Choice Proof | Rarcoa | Jul-89 |
| 24 | 977,500 | $4 | 1880 Coiled Hair | NGC PF-66 Cam | Heritage | Jan-05 |
| 25 | 977,500 | $5 | 1833 Large Date (G) | PCGS PF-67 | Heritage | Jan-05 |
| 26 | 966,000 | 50¢ | 1797 O-101a | NGC MS-66 | ANR | Mar-04 |
| 27 | 962,500 | 5¢ | 1913 Liberty Head | Proof | Stack's | Oct-93 |
| 28 | 920,000 | $20 | 1907 Small Edge Letters | PCGS PF-68 | Heritage | Nov-05 |
| 29 | 920,000 | Trade $ | 1885 | NGC PF-61 | Stack's | May-03 |
| 30 | 907,500 | Trade $ | 1885 | Gem PF-65 | B&M/Stack's | Apr-97 |
| 31 | 891,250 | 10¢ | 1873-CC No Arrows (D) | NGC MS-65 | B&M | Jul-04 |
| 32 | 874,000 | Silver $ | 1804 Class III (C) | PCGS PF-58 | B&M | Nov-01 |
| 33 | 825,000 | $20 | MCMVII Ultra HR LE (M) | Proof | Sotheby's | Dec-96 |
| 34 | 805,000 | $20 | 1921 | PCGS MS-65 | Heritage | Nov-05 |
| 35 | 747,500 | Silver $ | 1794 | NGC MS-61 | Heritage | Jun-05 |
| 36 | 725,000 | Pre-Fed | 1787 Brasher, EB on Wing | MS-63 | B&R | Nov-79 |
| 37 | 718,750 | $10 | 1933 | Unc | Stack's | Oct-04 |
| 38 | 690,000 | Terr | 1860 Clark, Gruber Pikes Peak $20 | NGC MS-64 | Heritage | Jan-06 |
| 39 | 690,000 | Pre-Fed | 1742 (1786) Lima Brasher | NGC EF-40 | Heritage | Jan-05 |
| 40 | 690,000 | $5 | 1835 (H) | PCGS PF-67 | Heritage | Jan-05 |
| 41 | 690,000 | Gold $ | 1849-C Open Wreath | NGC MS-63 PL | DLRC | Jul-04 |
| 42 | 690,000 | $20 | MCMVII Ultra HR LE | Proof | Soth/Stack's | Oct-01 |
| 43 | 687,500 | $3 | 1870-S | EF-40 | B&R | Oct-82 |
| 44 | 687,500 | $5 | 1822 | VF-30/EF-40 | B&R | Oct-82 |
| 45 | 661,250 | 1/2 Dime | 1870-S (E) | NGC MS-63 | B&M | Jul-04 |
| 46 | 660,000 | $20 | MCMVII Ultra HR LE (J) | PF-67 | B&M | Jan-97 |
| 47 | 660,000 | $20 | 1861 Paquet Reverse | MS-67 | B&M | Nov-88 |
| 48 | 655,500 | $4 | 1879 Coiled Hair | NGC PF-67 Cam | Heritage | Jan-05 |
| 49 | 632,500 | Pre-Fed | 1652 Willow Tree Threepence N-I-A | VF | Stack's | Oct-05 |
| 50 | 632,500 | 50¢ | 1838-O | PCGS PF-64 BM | Heritage | Jun-05 |
| 51 | 632,500 | Confed | 1861 Original 50¢ | VF | Stack's | Oct-03 |
| 52 | 632,500 | 10¢ | 1873-CC No Arrows (D) | PCGS MS-64 | Heritage | Apr-99 |
| 53 | 625,000 | Pre-Fed | 1787 Brasher, EB on Breast (A) | VF | B&R | Mar-81 |
| 54 | 618,125 | $4 | 1880 Coiled Hair | NGC PF-63 | Superior | Jul-05 |

| Rank | Price | Class | Coin | Grade | Firm | Date |
|---|---|---|---|---|---|---|
| 55 | 605,000 | $2.50 | 1796 No Stars | Choice BU | Stack's | Nov-95 |
| 56 | 603,750 | Trade $ | 1884 | PCGS PF-65 | Heritage | Nov-05 |
| 57 | 577,500 | $20 | 1927-D | PCGS MS-65 | Akers | May-98 |
| 58 | 577,500 | Silver $ | 1794 | Gem BU | Stack's | Nov-95 |
| 59 | 575,000 | Silver $ | 1895-O | PCGS MS-67 | Heritage | Nov-05 |
| 60 | 575,000 | $20 | MCMVII HR WR | PCGS MS-69 | Heritage | Nov-05 |
| 61 | 575,000 | $20 | 1927-D | NGC MS-62 | DLRC | Jul-04 |
| 62 | 550,000 | $10 | 1838 | Ch Proof | Akers | May-98 |
| 63 | 550,000 | 10¢ | 1873-CC No Arrows (D) | Gem MS-65 | B&M/Stack's | May-96 |
| 64 | 550,000 | 25¢ | 1901-S | NGC MS-68 | Superior | May-90 |
| 65 | 542,800 | $20 | 1856-O | NGC SP-63 | Heritage | Jun-04 |
| 66 | 534,750 | $20 | MCMVII HR FR | NGC PF-69 | Heritage | Nov-05 |
| 67 | 529,000 | Silver $ | 1889-CC | PCGS MS-68 | B&M | Jan-01 |
| 68 | 522,500 | $20 | 1927-D (I) | Gem BU | Stack's | Mar-91 |
| 69 | 517,500 | $10 | 1933 | PCGS MS-65 | Heritage | Nov-05 |
| 70 | 517,500 | $20 | 1920-S | PCGS MS-66 | Heritage | Nov-05 |
| 71 | 517,000 | 50¢ | 1797 O-102a | Gem BU | Stack's | Nov-95 |
| 72 | 510,600 | Trade $ | 1884 | PCGS PF-67 | Goldberg | Oct-00 |
| 73 | 506,000 | $10 | 1795 13 Leaves T-1 | PCGS MS-65 | B&M | Jul-03 |
| 74 | 506,000 | 1/2¢ | 1796 No Pole | MS-65 RB PL | B&M/Stack's | May-96 |
| 75 | 506,000 | Silver $ | 1794 | PCGS MS-65 | Superior | May-91 |
| 76 | 500,000 | Terr | 1851 Humbert $50 | Proof | B&R | Mar-80 |
| 77 | 488,750 | $20 | MCMVII Ultra HR LE of '06 | Proof EF | Stack's | Mar-05 |
| 78 | 475,000 | Silver $ | 1804 Class I | AU | Stack's | Oct-93 |
| 79 | 475,000 | Pattern | 1907 $20 J-1776 (F) | Proof | B&R | Jul-81 |
| 80 | 467,500 | $5 | 1833 Large Date (G) | Gem Proof | Akers | Oct-97 |
| 81 | 467,500 | Pattern | 1907 $20 J-1776 (F) | PF-67 | Paramount | Jul-84 |
| 82 | 462,000 | Silver $ | 1889-CC | MS-66 PL | B&M/Stack's | Apr-97 |
| 83 | 462,000 | Silver $ | 1870-S | Unc | Stack's | Mar-95 |
| 84 | 460,000 | $10 | 1933 | NGC MS-65 | Goldberg | May-05 |
| 85 | 460,000 | $10 | 1795 13 Leaves T-1 | PCGS MS-64 | Heritage | Jan-05 |
| 86 | 460,000 | 50¢ | 1796 16 Stars O-102a | Specimen 66 | Stack's | May-99 |
| 87 | 451,000 | 10¢ | 1894-S | Gem PF-64 | B&M/Stack's | May-96 |
| 88 | 440,000 | $4 | 1880 Coiled Hair | PCGS PF-66 | Superior | Aug-91 |
| 89 | 437,000 | Pattern | 1792 No Silver Center Cent J-2 | PCGS VF-30 PQ | Goldberg | Feb-05 |
| 90 | 434,500 | Terr | 1852/1 Humbert $20 | NGC PF-64 | Superior | Oct-90 |
| 91 | 431,250 | Silver $ | 1794 | NGC AU-55 | Heritage | Nov-05 |
| 92 | 431,250 | $20 | 1854-O | NGC AU-58 | Heritage | Jul-05 |
| 93 | 431,250 | $20 | 1856-O | PCGS AU-55 | Heritage | Jul-05 |
| 94 | 431,250 | 1¢ | 1793 Chain AMERICA S-2 | PCGS MS-65 BR | ANR | Jan-05 |
| 95 | 431,250 | Terr | 1849 Cincinnati Mining & Trading $10 | EF | Stack's | May-04 |
| 96 | 431,250 | 10¢ | 1894-S | Gem Proof | Stack's | Oct-00 |
| 97 | 430,000 | Pre-Fed | 1787 Brasher, EB on Wing | AU | Rarcoa | Jul-79 |
| 98 | 425,500 | Pre-Fed | 1776 Cont. $1 Silver N-3-D | EF | Stack's | Oct-03 |
| 99 | 414,000 | $10 | 1795 13 Leaves B 1-A T-1 | PCGS MS-64 | ANR | Jun-05 |
| 100 | 414,000 | 1¢ | 1793 Strawberry Leaf NC-3 | NGC Fine-12 | ANR | Nov-04 |
| 101 | 414,000 | Silver $ | 1870-S | NGC EF-40 | DLRC | Nov-04 |
| 102 | 414,000 | Pattern | 1792 Silver Center Cent J-1 | BU | Stack's | Jan-02 |
| 103 | 414,000 | Silver $ | 1893-S | Superb Gem BU | Stack's | Nov-01 |
| 104 | 402,500 | $2.50 | 1848 "CAL" | NGC MS-68 | Heritage | Jan-06 |
| 105 | 402,500 | Silver $ | 1896-S | PCGS MS-69 | Heritage | Nov-05 |
| 106 | 402,500 | $20 | 1921 | PCGS MS-64 | Heritage | Nov-05 |
| 107 | 402,500 | Pattern | 1875 20¢ J-1443 | NGC PF-64 | Heritage | May-05 |
| 108 | 402,500 | $10 | 1839/8 Type of 1838 | PCGS MS-66 | Heritage | Jan-05 |

# TOP 250 AUCTION PRICES

| Rank | Price | Class | Coin | Grade | Firm | Date |
|------|-------|-------|------|-------|------|------|
| 109 | 402,500 | $4 | 1880 Coiled Hair | NGC PF-62 | DLRC | Jul-04 |
| 110 | 402,500 | $20 | 1927-D | Unc | Soth/Stack's | Oct-01 |
| 111 | 400,000 | Pattern | 1865 $20 J-452 | PCGS PF-64 | Superior | Aug-90 |
| 112 | 400,000 | Silver $ | 1804 Class III | EF-40 | B&R | Mar-80 |
| 113 | 396,000 | $10 | 1857 | NGC PF-66 | Goldberg | May-99 |
| 114 | 396,000 | Trade $ | 1884 | Sup Gem PF-66+ | B&M/Stack's | Apr-97 |
| 115 | 391,000 | Silver $ | 1795 Flowing Hair BB-21 B-1 | NGC MS-65 | Heritage | Nov-05 |
| 116 | 391,000 | 1¢ | 1793 Chain AMERICA S-4 | PCGS MS-65 BR | ANR | Jul-04 |
| 117 | 391,000 | Pre-Fed | 1792 Getz 50¢ Silver B-24A | Gem BU PL | Stack's | May-04 |
| 118 | 390,500 | $20 | 1927-D | NGC MS-66 | Heritage | Jun-95 |
| 119 | 385,000 | 5¢ | 1913 Liberty Head | PF-63 | Superior | Jan-85 |
| 120 | 379,500 | $4 | 1880 Coiled Hair | NGC PF-61 | B&M | Mar-04 |
| 121 | 374,000 | $5 | 1909-O | Gem Unc | Akers | May-98 |
| 122 | 374,000 | $5 | 1829 Small Date | V Choice Unc | Christie's | Oct-96 |
| 123 | 374,000 | Terr | 1852/1 Humbert $20 | PCGS PF-65 | Superior | May-92 |
| 124 | 368,000 | $20 | 1854-O | PCGS AU-53 | Heritage | Jan-05 |
| 125 | 368,000 | $20 | 1870-CC | PCGS AU-53 | Heritage | Jan-04 |
| 126 | 368,000 | $4 | 1880 Coiled Hair | NGC PF-65 | Stack's | Oct-00 |
| 127 | 357,500 | Silver $ | 1893-S | Gem MS-65 | B&M | Nov-88 |
| 128 | 352,000 | $5 | 1829 Small Date | Proof 64-65 | B&M | Oct-87 |
| 129 | 345,000 | Silver $ | 1896-O | PCGS MS-66 | Heritage | Nov-05 |
| 130 | 345,000 | $20 | 1926-D | PCGS MS-66 | Heritage | Nov-05 |
| 131 | 345,000 | $20 | 1927-S | PCGS MS-67 | Heritage | Nov-05 |
| 132 | 345,000 | Pre-Fed | Undated (1652) NE Shilling N-III-B | VF | Stack's | Oct-05 |
| 133 | 345,000 | Pre-Fed | 1776 Cont. $1 Silver N-1-C | VF | Stack's | Jan-05 |
| 134 | 345,000 | $2.50 | 1796 No Stars | PCGS MS-62 | ANR | Jul-04 |
| 135 | 345,000 | Pattern | 1878 Eagle J-1579 | Gem Proof | Stack's | Oct-03 |
| 136 | 345,000 | Terr | 1855 Wass, Molitor & Co. $50 (N) | Gem BU | Stack's | Oct-03 |
| 137 | 345,000 | $4 | 1879 Coiled Hair | Proof | Soth/Stack's | Oct-01 |
| 138 | 345,000 | $20 | 1861 Paquet Reverse | AU | Soth/Stack's | Oct-01 |
| 139 | 333,500 | Pattern | 1792 Half Disme J-7 | NGC MS-63 | Heritage | Jul-05 |
| 140 | 333,500 | 50¢ | 1817/4 O-102a | PCGS AU-50 | DLRC | Nov-04 |
| 141 | 333,500 | $4 | 1879 Flowing Hair | NGC PF-67 | Superior | Apr-04 |
| 142 | 330,000 | 50¢ | 1796 16 Stars O-102/102a | Gem BU | Stack's | Nov-95 |
| 143 | 325,000 | Terr | 1852/1 Humbert $20 | Proof | B&R | Mar-80 |
| 144 | 322,000 | $20 | MCMVII HR Partial Wire Rim PE | Ch AU | Stack's | Jan-06 |
| 145 | 322,000 | Silver $ | 1892-S | PCGS MS-68 | Heritage | Nov-05 |
| 146 | 322,000 | Pre-Fed | Undated (1652) NE Shilling N-III-C | EF | Stack's | Oct-05 |
| 147 | 322,000 | Silver $ | 1795 Draped Bust BB-52 B-15 | PCGS MS-65 | ANR | Jun-05 |
| 148 | 322,000 | $2.50 | 1808 | PCGS MS-63 | ANR | Jul-04 |
| 149 | 322,000 | Pre-Fed | 1786 NJ, Date Under Plow M-7-E | Ch AU | Stack's | Oct-03 |
| 150 | 319,000 | 1¢ | 1793 Liberty Cap S-13 | MS-64+ BR | B&M/Stack's | May-96 |
| 151 | 316,250 | Silver $ | 1802 Restrike | PCGS PF-64 | Heritage | Nov-05 |
| 152 | 316,250 | Pattern | 1792 Half Disme J-7 | NGC MS-63 | Heritage | Nov-05 |
| 153 | 312,000 | Pattern | 1916 25¢ J-1989 | NGC PF-65 | Heritage | Jan-04 |
| 154 | 310,500 | 50¢ | 1796 15 Stars O-101a | NGC MS-64 | ANR | Sep-05 |
| 155 | 310,500 | Trade $ | 1884 | NGC PF-64 | DLRC | Nov-04 |
| 156 | 310,500 | 50¢ | 1853-O No Arrows | PCGS VF-35 | B&M | Jul-04 |
| 157 | 310,500 | $20 | 1856-O | SP-65 | Heritage | Jan-02 |
| 158 | 310,500 | $4 | 1879 Coiled Hair | NGC PF-66 | Stack's | Oct-00 |
| 159 | 310,000 | $4 | 1879 Flowing Hair | NGC PF-67 Cam | Heritage | Jan-05 |
| 160 | 310,000 | 25¢ | 1873-CC No Arrows | Superb Gem BU | Rarcoa | Aug-90 |
| 161 | 308,000 | Pattern | 1792 Half Disme J-7 | Gem Unc | Akers | Oct-97 |
| 162 | 308,000 | $5 | 1835 (H) | Gem Proof | Akers | Oct-97 |
| 163 | 308,000 | Silver $ | 1795 Draped Bust BB-51 B-14 | MS-67 PL | B&M/Stack's | Apr-97 |

| Rank | Price | Class | Coin | Grade | Firm | Date |
|------|-------|-------|------|-------|------|------|
| 164 | 308,000 | $4 | 1880 Coiled Hair | Proof | Stack's | Oct-95 |
| 165 | 308,000 | $10 | 1795 9 Leaves T-3 | NGC MS-63 | Superior | Jul-89 |
| 166 | 308,000 | Silver $ | 1804 Class III | MS-60+ | Superior | Jan-85 |
| 167 | 304,750 | $20 | 1854-O | NGC AU-53 | DLRC | Jul-04 |
| 168 | 304,750 | Terr | 1855 Kellogg & Co. $50 | Gem Proof | Stack's | Oct-03 |
| 169 | 300,000 | Terr | 1855 Kellogg & Co. $50 | Proof | B&R | Mar-80 |
| 170 | 299,000 | $20 | 1891 | NGC PF-68 U Cam | Heritage | Jan-06 |
| 171 | 299,000 | Pre-Fed | 1787 MA 1¢ Trans Arrs R-2a-F | Unc | Stack's | Oct-04 |
| 172 | 299,000 | $4 | 1879 Coiled Hair | NGC PF-63 | DLRC | Jul-04 |
| 173 | 299,000 | $10 | 1907 Rounded Rim | PCGS MS-66 | ANR | Jul-04 |
| 174 | 299,000 | $5 | 1795 Small Eagle B-1A | NGC MS-65 | B&M | May-04 |
| 175 | 299,000 | Pattern | 1792 Half Disme J-7 | PCGS MS-64 PQ | Goldberg | Jan-04 |
| 176 | 299,000 | Pattern | 1878 Half Eagle J-1575 | Gem Proof | Stack's | Oct-03 |
| 177 | 299,000 | $2.50 | 1796 No Stars | Unc | Stack's | May-99 |
| 178 | 297,000 | $5 | 1832 Curved Base 2 12 Star | Unc | Christie's | Oct-96 |
| 179 | 297,000 | $4 | 1880 Flowing Hair | PF-65 | Superior | Oct-89 |
| 180 | 294,320 | Pattern | 1863 Eagle J-351 | PCGS PF-63 | Heritage | Jan-05 |
| 181 | 293,250 | $4 | 1879 Flowing Hair | PCGS PF-67 | ANR | Jul-03 |
| 182 | 291,500 | $2.50 | 1798 | PCGS MS-65 | Superior | Aug-91 |
| 183 | 289,671 | Comm | 1915-S Pan Pac $50 Oct | NGC MS-67 | Heritage | May-05 |
| 184 | 288,500 | 50¢ | 1794 O-101a | PCGS MS-63 | B&M | Jan-99 |
| 185 | 287,500 | $20 | 1925-S | PCGS MS-67 | Heritage | Nov-05 |
| 186 | 287,500 | Pattern | 1875 $3 J-1438 | NGC PF-65 | Heritage | May-05 |
| 187 | 287,500 | Silver $ | 1893-S | PCGS MS-64 | Superior | Jan-05 |
| 188 | 287,500 | Gold $ | 1855 Type 2 | PCGS PF-63 | Heritage | Jan-05 |
| 189 | 287,500 | $4 | 1879 Coiled Hair | NGC PF-63 | Heritage | Jan-05 |
| 190 | 287,500 | 5¢ | 1918/7-D | PCGS MS-65 | B&M | Jul-04 |
| 191 | 287,500 | Terr | 1852/1 Humbert $20 | PF-64 | Stack's | May-04 |
| 192 | 287,500 | Pre-Fed | 1776 Cont. $1 Silver N-1-C | F/VG+ | Stack's | Oct-03 |
| 193 | 287,500 | 1/2¢ | 1796 No Pole | MS-64 | Stack's | May-99 |
| 194 | 286,000 | 25¢ | 1873-CC No Arrows | PCGS MS-65 | Superior | Aug-91 |
| 195 | 286,000 | $20 | MCMVII Ultra HR LE | PF-65+ | Superior | Jul-85 |
| 196 | 280,000 | Silver $ | 1804 Class I (**B**) | Proof | Stack's | Oct-81 |
| 197 | 276,000 | $2.50 | 1797 | NGC MS64 | Superior | Nov-05 |
| 198 | 276,000 | $20 | 1908 Roman Finish (**K**) | PCGS PF-64 | Heritage | Nov-05 |
| 199 | 276,000 | Pre-Fed | Undated (1652) NE Shilling N-III-C | EF | Stack's | Oct-05 |
| 200 | 276,000 | Pre-Fed | 1652 Willow Tree Shilling N-I-A | EF | Stack's | Oct-05 |
| 201 | 276,000 | Silver $ | 1893-S | PCGS MS-64 | ANR | Jan-05 |
| 202 | 276,000 | $10 | 1933 | NGC MS-64 | DLRC | Jul-04 |
| 203 | 276,000 | $20 | 1856-O | NGC AU-50 | DLRC | Jul-04 |
| 204 | 276,000 | 50¢ | 1796 16 Stars O-102 | NGC MS-64 | ANR | Mar-04 |
| 205 | 276,000 | Pattern | 1874 Eagle J-1373 | Gem Proof | Stack's | Oct-03 |
| 206 | 276,000 | $10 | 1798/7 7x6 Stars T-10 | PCGS MS-62 | B&M | Jul-03 |
| 207 | 275,000 | $2.50 | 1866 | PCGS PF-66 | Rarcoa/Akers | Jul-96 |
| 208 | 275,000 | 10¢ | 1894-S (**L**) | Proof | Stack's | Jan-90 |
| 209 | 275,000 | $20 | 1927-D | Unc | Stack's | Oct-85 |
| 210 | 275,000 | Terr | 1855 Wass, Molitor & Co. $50 (**N**) | Unc | B&R | Mar-80 |
| 211 | 270,250 | 50¢ | 1919-D | PCGS MS-66 | Heritage | Nov-04 |
| 212 | 270,000 | Terr | 1849 Cincinnati Mining & Trading $10 | EF-40 | B&R | Mar-80 |
| 213 | 268,500 | $2.50 | 1798 | PCGS MS-65 | Sotheby's | Jun-00 |
| 214 | 264,500 | $20 | MCMVII HR FR | PCGS MS-68 | Heritage | Nov-05 |
| 215 | 264,500 | $20 | 1931 | PCGS MS-67 | Heritage | Nov-05 |
| 216 | 264,500 | 5¢ | 1916 Dbl Die | PCGS MS-64 | Heritage | Sep-05 |
| 217 | 264,500 | $4 | 1880 Flowing Hair | NGC PF-65 | Heritage | Jan-05 |

# TOP 250 AUCTION PRICES

| Rank | Price | Class | Coin | Grade | Firm | Date |
|------|-------|-------|------|-------|------|------|
| 218 | 264,500 | $20 | 1865 | PCGS PF-65 DC | ANR | Aug-04 |
| 219 | 264,500 | Silver $ | 1795 Flowing Hair BB-27 B-5 | NGC MS-65 | ANR | Mar-04 |
| 220 | 264,500 | Trade $ | 1884 | PCGS PF-65 | Sotheby's | Oct-01 |
| 221 | 264,500 | $5 | 1798 Small Eagle B-1A | PCGS EF-40 | Goldberg | Jun-00 |
| 222 | 264,500 | $4 | 1880 Coiled Hair | Proof | Stack's | Mar-99 |
| 223 | 264,000 | $5 | 1835 | Gem Proof | Akers | May-98 |
| 224 | 264,000 | $10 | 1933 | V Choice Unc | Akers | May-98 |
| 225 | 264,000 | Silver $ | 1870-S | EF-45/AU-50 | B&M/Stack's | Apr-97 |
| 226 | 264,000 | $4 | 1880 Coiled Hair | Gem Proof | Superior | Feb-92 |
| 227 | 264,000 | Silver $ | 1803 Proof Restrike | PCGS PF-66 | Superior | May-91 |
| 228 | 264,000 | $20 | MCMVII Ultra HR LE (M) | PF-65 | B&M | Nov-85 |
| 229 | 264,000 | Silver $ | 1794 | Unc | Stack's | Jan-84 |
| 230 | 258,750 | Silver $ | 1893-O | PCGS MS-65 DM | Heritage | Nov-05 |
| 231 | 258,750 | Trade $ | 1884 | PF-63 | Stack's | May-03 |
| 232 | 253,000 | $10 | 1907 Rounded Rim | PCGS MS-66 | Stack's | Jan-06 |
| 233 | 253,000 | 50¢ | 1817/4 O-102a | ANACS EF Corroded | Heritage | Jan-06 |
| 234 | 253,000 | $2.50 | 1805 | V Ch MS | Bullowa | Dec-05 |
| 235 | 253,000 | $20 | 1930-S | PCGS MS-66 | Heritage | Dec-05 |
| 236 | 253,000 | Pre-Fed | Undated (1652) NE Shilling N-I-A | VF | Stack's | Nov-05 |
| 237 | 253,000 | Pre-Fed | 1652 Willow Tree Sixpence N-I-A | Unc | Stack's | Nov-05 |
| 238 | 253,000 | Silver $ | 1893-S | PCGS MS-64 | Heritage | Nov-05 |
| 239 | 253,000 | Silver $ | 1895-O | PCGS MS-65 DM | Heritage | Nov-05 |
| 240 | 253,000 | $2.50 | 1854-S | NGC EF45 | ANR | Aug-05 |
| 241 | 253,000 | Terr | 1855 Kellogg & Co. $50 | Brill Proof | Stack's | Mar-05 |
| 242 | 253,000 | 1¢ | 1793 Wreath S-9 | PCGS MS-66 | B&M | Jan-05 |
| 243 | 253,000 | $2.50 | 1841 | NGC PF-65 DC | Heritage | Jun-04 |
| 244 | 253,000 | Pre-Fed | Undated Washington NJ M-4-C | AU | Stack's | Oct-03 |
| 245 | 253,000 | Terr | 1849 J.H. Bowie $5 | PCGS AU-58 | Stack's | Jan-01 |
| 246 | 253,000 | $4 | 1880 Coiled Hair | NGC PF-64 | B&M | Jan-00 |
| 247 | 253,000 | $10 | 1839/8 Type of 1838 | MS-65 PL | Superior | Feb-98 |
| 248 | 253,000 | $20 | 1908 With Motto (K) | Roman Proof | Sotheby's | Dec-97 |
| 249 | 253,000 | Silver $ | 1895-O | MS-66/67 | B&M/Stack's | Apr-97 |
| 250 | 253,000 | 1/2 Dime | 1870-S (E) | Unc | Superior | Jul-86 |

## Key

**Price:** The sale price of the coin, including the appropriate buyer's fee.

**Class:** The denomination or classification of the coin.

Confed = Confederate States of America issue; Terr = territorial issue; Pattern = a pattern, experimental, or trial piece; Pre-Fed = pre-federal issue.

**Coin:** The date and description of the coin, along with pertinent catalog or reference numbers.

B = Baker (for pre-federal), Bolender (for silver dollars), Breen (for gold), Browning (for quarter dollars); Barry = Barry doubloon; BB = Bowers/Borckardt; Brasher = Brasher doubloon; C = Cohen (for half cents), Crosby (for pre-federal); J = Judd; M = Maris; N = Newman; NC = Non-Collectible; O = Overton; R = Ryder; S = Sheldon; T = Taraszka; Ultra HR LE = Ultra High Relief, Lettered Edge. Letters in parentheses, **(A)** through **(N)**, note instances in which multiple sales of the same coin rank within the Top 250.

**Grade:** The grade of the coin, plus the name of the grading firm (if independently graded).

NGC = Numismatic Guaranty Corporation of America; PCGS = Professional Coin Grading Service.

**Firm:** The auction firm (or firms) that sold the coin.

ANR = American Numismatic Rarities; B&M = Bowers & Merena; B&R = Bowers & Ruddy; DLRC = David Lawrence Rare Coins; Soth = Sotheby's.

**Date:** The month and year of the auction.

*Auction records compiled and edited by P. Scott Rubin and Richard A. Bagg, Ph. D.*

Over the years coin collectors have developed a special jargon to describe their coins. The following list includes terms that are used frequently by coin collectors or that have a special meaning other than their ordinary dictionary definitions. You will find them useful when you want to discuss or describe your coins.

*alloy*—A combination of two or more metals.

*altered date*—A false date on a coin; a date altered to make a coin appear to be one of a rarer or more valuable issue.

*bag mark*—A surface mark, usually a small nick, acquired by a coin through contact with others in a mint bag.

*billon*—A low-grade alloy of silver (usually less than 50%) mixed with another metal, typically copper.

*blank*—The formed piece of metal on which a coin design will be stamped.

*bronze*—An alloy of copper, zinc, and tin.

*bullion*—Uncoined gold or silver in the form of bars, ingots, or plate.

*cast coins*—Coins that are made by pouring molten metal into a mold, instead of in the usual manner of striking with dies.

*cent*—One one-hundredth of the standard monetary unit. Also known as a *centavo*, *centimo*, or *centesimo* in some Central American and South American countries; *centime* in France and various former colonies in Africa; and other variations.

*certified coin*—A coin that has been graded, authenticated, and encapsulated in plastic by an independent grading service.

*cherrypicker*—A collector who finds scarce and unusual coins by carefully searching through old accumulations or dealers' stocks.

*circulation strike*—An Uncirculated coin intended for eventual use in commerce, as opposed to a Proof coin.

*clad coinage*—Issues of the United States dimes, quarters, halves, and dollars made since 1965. Each coin has a center core of pure copper and a layer of copper-nickel or silver on both sides.

*collar*—The outer ring, or die chamber, that holds a blank in place in the coinage press while the coin is impressed with the obverse and reverse dies.

*contact marks*—Minor abrasions on an uncirculated coin, made by contact with other coins in a bag or roll.

*countermark*—A stamp or mark impressed on a coin to verify its use by another government or to indicate revaluation.

*crack-out*—A coin that has been removed from an encapsulated grading service holder.

*crown*—Any dollar-size coin (c. 38 mm in diameter) in general, often struck in silver; specifically, one from the United Kingdom and some Commonwealth countries.

*designer*—The artist who creates a coin's design. An engraver is the person who cuts a design into a coinage die.

*die*—A piece of metal engraved with a design and used for stamping coins.

*die crack*—A fine, raised line on a coin, caused by a broken die.

*die defect*—An imperfection on a coin, caused by a damaged die.

*die variety*—Any minor alteration in the basic design of a coin.

*dipped, dipping*—Refers to chemical cleaning of a coin with diluted acid.

*double eagle*—The United States twenty-dollar gold coin.

*doubled die*—A die that that been given two misaligned impressions from a hub; also, a coin made from such a die.

*doubloon*—Popular name for a Spanish gold coin originally valued at $16.

**eagle**—A United States ten-dollar gold coin; also refers to U.S. silver, gold, and platinum bullion pieces made from 1986 to the present.

**edge**—Periphery of a coin, often containing a series of reeds, lettering, or other decoration.

**electrotype**—A reproduction of a coin or medal made by the electrodeposition process. Electrotypes are frequently used in museum displays.

**electrum**—A naturally occurring mixture of gold and silver. Some of the world's first coins were made of this alloy.

**encapsulated coins**—Coins that have been authenticated, graded, and sealed in plastic by a professional service.

**engraver**—The person who cuts the design into a coinage die.

**error**—A mismade coin not intended for circulation.

**exergue**—That portion of a coin beneath the main design, often separated from it by a line, and typically bearing the date.

**field**—The background portion of a coin's surface not used for a design or inscription.

**filler**—A coin in worn condition but rare enough to be included in a collection.

**fineness**—The purity of gold, silver, or any other precious metal, expressed in terms of one thousand parts. A coin of 90% pure silver is expressed as .900 fine.

**flan**—A blank piece of metal in the size and shape of a coin; also called a *planchet*.

**gem**—A coin of exceptionally high quality.

**half eagle**—The United States five-dollar gold coin minted from 1795 to 1929.

**hub**—A positive-image punch to impress the coin's design into a die for coinage.

**incuse**—The design of a coin which has been impressed below the coin's surface. A design raised above the coin's surface is in relief.

**inscription**—The legend or lettering on a coin.

**intrinsic value**—Bullion or "melt" value of the actual precious metal in a numismatic item.

**investment grade**—Promotional term; generally, a coin in grade MS-65 or better.

**junk silver**—Common-date silver coins taken from circulation; worth only bullion value.

**key coin**—The scarcest or most valuable coin or coins in a series.

**laureate**—Head crowned with a laurel wreath.

**legal tender**—Money that is officially issued and recognized for redemption by an authorized agency or government.

**legend**—The principal inscription on a coin.

**lettered edge**—The narrow edge of a coin bearing an inscription, found on some foreign and some older United States coins.

**luster**—The brilliant or "frosty" surface quality of an Uncirculated (Mint State) coin.

**milled edge**—The raised rim around the outer surface of a coin, not to be confused with the reeded or serrated narrow edge of a coin.

**mint error**—Any mismade or defective coin produced by a mint.

**mint luster**—Shiny "frost" or brilliance on the surface of an Uncirculated or Mint State coin.

**mintmark**—A small letter on a coin, indicating the mint at which it was struck.

**Mint set**—A set of Uncirculated coins packaged and sold by the Mint. Each set contains one of each of the coins made for circulation at each of the mints.

**motto**—An inspirational word or phrase used on a coin.

**mule**—A coin struck from two dies not originally intended to be used together.

# GLOSSARY

*obverse*—The front or face side of a coin.

*overdate*—Date made by superimposing one or more numerals on a previously dated die.

*over graded*—A coin in poorer condition than stated.

*overstrike*—An impression made with new dies on a previously struck coin.

*patina*—The green or brown surface film found on ancient copper and bronze coins, caused by oxidation over a long period of time.

*pattern*—Experimental or trial coin, generally of a new design, denomination, or metal.

*pedigree*—The record of previous owners of a rare coin.

*planchet*—The blank piece of metal on which a coin design is stamped.

*Proofs*—Coins struck for collectors by the Mint using specially polished dies and planchets.

*Proof set*—A set of each of the Proof coins made during a given year, packaged by the Mint and sold to collectors.

*quarter eagle*—The United States $2.50 gold coin.

*raw*—A coin that has not been encapsulated by an independent grading service.

*reeded edge*—The edge of a coin with grooved lines that run vertically around its perimeter, as seen on modern United States silver and clad coins.

*relief*—Any part of a coin's design that is raised above the coin's field is said to be in relief. The opposite of relief is incuse, meaning sunk into the field.

*restrike*—A coin struck from genuine dies at a later date than the original issue.

*reverse*—The back side of a coin.

*rim*—The raised portion of a coin that protects the design from wear.

*round*—A round one-ounce silver medal or bullion piece.

*series*—A set of one coin of each year of a specific design and denomination issued from each mint. For example, Lincoln cents from 1909 to 1959.

*slab*—A hard plastic case containing a coin that has been graded and encapsulated by a professional service.

*spot price*—The daily quoted market value of precious metals in bullion form.

*token*—A privately issued piece, typically with an exchange value for goods or services, but not an official government coin.

*trade dollar*—Silver dollar issued especially for trade with a foreign country. In the United States, trade dollars were first issued in 1873 to stimulate commerce with the Orient. Many other countries have also issued trade dollars.

*truncation*—The sharply cut-off bottom edge of a bust or portrait.

*type*—A series of coins defined by a shared distinguishing design, composition, denomination, and other elements. For example, Barber dimes or Franklin half dollars.

*type set*—A collection consisting of one representative coin of each type, of a particular series or period.

*Uncirculated*—A circulation-strike coin that has never been used in commerce, and has retained its original surface and luster; also called Mint State.

*unique*—An item of which only one specimen is known to exist.

*variety*—A coin's design that sets it apart from the normal issue of that type.

*wheaties*—Lincoln cents with the wheat ears reverse, issued from 1909 to 1958.

*year set*—A set of coins for any given year, consisting of one of each denomination issued that year.

# BIBLIOGRAPHY

## COLONIAL ISSUES

Breen, Walter. *Walter Breen's Complete Encyclopedia of U.S. and Colonial Coins,* New York, 1988.
Carlotto, Tony. *The Copper Coins of Vermont,* Chelsea, MI, 1998.
Crosby, S.S. *The Early Coins of America,* Boston, 1875 (reprinted 1945, 1965, 1974, 1983).
Kessler, Alan. *The Fugio Cents,* Newtonville, MA, 1976.
Maris, Edward. *A Historic Sketch of the Coins of New Jersey,* Philadelphia, 1881 (reprinted 1925, 1974, 1987).
Miller, Henry C., and Hillyer, Ryder. *The State Coinages of New England,* New York, 1920.
Nelson, Philip. *The Coinage of William Wood 1722–1733,* London, 1903 (reprinted 1959).
Newman, Eric P. *Coinage for Colonial Virginia,* New York, 1956.
Newman, Eric P., and Doty, Richard G. *Studies on Money in Early America,* New York, 1976.
Noe, Sydney P. *The New England and Willow Tree Coinage of Massachusetts,* New York, 1943; *The Oak Tree Coinage of Massachusetts,* New York, 1947; and *The Pine Tree Coinage of Massachusetts,* New York, 1952 (all reprinted 1973).
Rulau, Russell, and Fuld, George. *Medallic Portraits of Washington,* Iola, WI, 1999.
Vlack, Robert. *An Illustrated Catalogue of the French Billon Coinage in the Americas,* Boston, 2004.
Wurtzbach, Carl. *Massachusetts Colonial Silver Money 1937.*

## HISTORY OF THE U.S. MINT

Lange, David W. *History of the United States Mint and Its Coinage,* Atlanta, GA, 2005.

## HALF CENTS

Breen, Walter. *Walter Breen's Encyclopedia of United States Half Cents 1793–1857,* South Gate, CA, 1983.
Cohen, Roger S., Jr. *American Half Cents—The "Little Half Sisters"* (2nd ed.), 1982.
Manley, Ronald P. *The Half Cent Die State Book, 1793–1857,* United States, 1998.

## LARGE CENTS

Breen, Walter. *Walter Breen's Encyclopedia of Early United States Cents 1793–1814,* Wolfeboro, NH, 2001.
Grellman, J.R. *Attribution Guide for United States Large Cents 1840–1857* (3rd ed.), Bloomington, MN, 2002.
Newcomb, H.R. *United States Copper Cents 1816–1857,* New York, 1944 (reprinted 1983).
Noyes, William C. *United States Large Cents 1793–1814,* Bloomington, MN, 1991.
Noyes, William C. *United States Large Cents 1816–1839,* Bloomington, MN, 1991.
*PENNY-WISE,* official publication of Early American Coppers, Inc.
Sheldon, William H. *Penny Whimsy (1793–1814),* New York, 1958 (reprinted 1965, 1976).
Wright, John D. *The Cent Book 1816–1839,* Bloomington, MN, 1992.

## SMALL CENTS

Lange, David W. *The Complete Guide to Lincoln Cents,* Wolfeboro, NH, 1996.
Snow, Richard. *A Guide Book of Flying Eagle and Indian Head Cents,* Atlanta, GA, 2006.
Steve, Larry, and Flynn, Kevin. *Flying Eagle and Indian Cent Die Varieties,* Jarretteville, MD, 1995.
Taylor, Sol. *The Standard Guide to the Lincoln Cent,* Anaheim, CA, 1999.
Wexler, John, and Flynn, Kevin. *The Authoritative Reference on Lincoln Cents,* Rancocas, NJ, 1996.

## TWO-CENT PIECES

Flynn, Kevin. *Getting Your Two Cents Worth,* Rancocas, NJ, 1994.
Kliman, Myron M. *The Two Cent Piece and Varieties,* South Laguna, CA, 1977.
Leone, Frank. *Longacre's Two Cent Piece Die Varieties and Errors,* College Point, NY, 1991.

## NICKEL FIVE-CENT PIECES

Bowers, Q. David. *A Guide Book of Shield and Liberty Head Nickels,* Atlanta, GA, 2006.
Fletcher, Edward L., Jr. *The Shield Five Cent Series,* Ormond Beach, FL, 1994.
Lange, David W. *The Complete Guide to Buffalo Nickels,* Virginia Beach, VA, 2000.
Nagengast, Bernard. *The Jefferson Nickel Analyst* (2nd ed.), Sidney, Ohio, 1979.
Peters, Gloria, and Mahon, Cynthia. *The Complete Guide to Shield and Liberty Head Nickels,* Virginia Beach, VA, 1995.
Wescott, Michael. *The United States Nickel Five-Cent Piece,* Wolfeboro, NH, 1991.

# BIBLIOGRAPHY

## HALF DIMES

Blythe, Al. *The Complete Guide to Liberty Seated Half Dimes,* Virginia Beach, VA, 1992.
Breen, Walter. *United States Half Dimes: A Supplement,* New York, 1958.
Logan, Russell, and McClosky, John. *Federal Half Dimes 1792–1837,* Manchester, MI, 1998.
Newlin, H.P. *The Early Half-Dimes of the United States,* Philadelphia, 1883 (reprinted 1933).
Valentine, D.W. *The United States Half Dimes,* New York, 1931 (reprinted 1975).

## DIMES

Ahwash, Kamal M. *Encyclopedia of United States Liberty Seated Dimes 1837–1891,* Kamal Press, 1977.
Davis, David; Logan, Russell; Lovejoy, Allen; McCloskey, John; and Subjack, William. *Early United States Dimes 1796–1837,* Ypsilanti, MI, 1984.
Flynn, Kevin. *The 1894-S Dime: A Mystery Unraveled,* Rancocas, NJ, 2005.
Flynn, Kevin. *The Authoritative Reference on Roosevelt Dimes,* Brooklyn, NY, 2001.
Greer, Brian. *The Complete Guide to Liberty Seated Dimes,* Virginia Beach, VA, 1992.
Kosoff, A. *United States Dimes From 1796,* New York, 1945.
Lange, David W. *The Complete Guide to Mercury Dimes* (2nd ed.), Virginia Beach, VA 1993.
Lawrence, David. *The Complete Guide to Barber Dimes,* Virginia Beach, VA 1991.

## QUARTER DOLLARS

Bowers, Q. David. *A Guide Book of Washington and State Quarters,* Atlanta, GA, 2006.
Bressett, Kenneth. *The Official Whitman Statehood Quarters Collector's Handbook,* New York, 2000.
Briggs, Larry. *The Comprehensive Encyclopedia of United States Seated Quarters,* Lima, Ohio, 1991.
Browning, A.W. *The Early Quarter Dollars of the United States 1796–1838.* New York, 1925 (reprinted 1992)
Cline, J.H. *Standing Liberty Quarters* (3rd ed.), 1996.
Duphorne, R. *The Early Quarter Dollars of the United States,* 1975.
Fivaz, Bill, and Stanton, J.T. *The Cherrypickers' Guide to Rare Die Varieties,* Atlanta, GA, 2006.
Haseltine, J.W. *Type Table of United States Dollars, Half Dollars and Quarter Dollars,* Philadelphia, 1881 (reprinted 1927, 1968).
Kelman, Keith N. *Standing Liberty Quarters,* 1976.
Lawrence, David. *The Complete Guide to Barber Quarters,* Virginia Beach, VA, 1989.

## HALF DOLLARS

Flynn, Kevin. *The Authoritative Reference on Barber Half Dollars,* Brooklyn, NY, 2005.
Fox, Bruce. *The Complete Guide to Walking Liberty Half Dollars,* Virginia Beach, VA, 1993.
Lawrence, David. *The Complete Guide to Barber Halves,* Virginia Beach, VA, 1991.
Overton, Al C. *Early Half Dollar Die Varieties 1794–1836,* Colorado Springs, CO, 1967 (3rd ed., 1990, edited by Donald Parsley).
Peterson, Glenn R. *The Ultimate Guide to Attributing Bust Half Dollars,* Rocky River, OH, 2000.
Wiley, Randy, and Bugert, Bill. *The Complete Guide to Liberty Seated Half Dollars,* Virginia Beach, VA, 1993.

## SILVER DOLLARS

Bolender, M.H. *The United States Early Silver Dollars From 1794 to 1803* (3rd ed.), Iola, WI, 1982 (reprinted 1987).
Bowers, Q. David. *The Rare Silver Dollars Dated 1804,* Wolfeboro, NH, 1999.
Bowers, Q. David. *Silver Dollars and Trade Dollars of the United States: A Complete Encyclopedia,* Wolfeboro, NH, 1993.
Bowers, Q. David. *A Guide Book of Morgan Silver Dollars: A Complete History and Price Guide* (2nd ed.), Atlanta, GA, 2005.
Fey, Michael S., and Oxman, Jeff. *The Top 100 Morgan Dollar Varieties,* Morris Planes, NJ, 1997.
Haseltine, J.W. *Type Table of United States Dollars, Half Dollars and Quarter Dollars,* Philadelphia, 1881 (reprinted 1927, 1968).
Newman, Eric P., and Bressett, Kenneth E. *The Fantastic 1804 Dollar,* Racine, WI, 1962.
Van Allen, Leroy C., and Mallis, A. George. *Comprehensive Catalogue and Encyclopedia of U.S. Morgan and Peace Silver Dollars,* New York, 1997.
Willem, John M. *The United States Trade Dollar* (2nd ed.), Racine, WI, 1965.

## GOLD PIECES ($1 THROUGH $20)

Akers, David W. *Gold Dollars (and Other Gold Denominations)*, Englewood, OH, 1975–1982.
Bowers, Q. David. *A Guide Book of Double Eagle Gold Coins*, Atlanta, GA, 2004.
Bowers, Q. David. *United States Gold Coins: An Illustrated History*, Wolfeboro, NH, 1982.
Breen, Walter. *Major Varieties of U.S. Gold Dollars (and Other Gold Denominations)*, Chicago, 1964.
Fivaz, Bill, *United States Gold Counterfeit Detection Guide*, Atlanta, GA, 2005.
Garrett, Jeff, and Guth, Ron. *Encyclopedia of United States Gold Coins*, Atlanta, GA, 2006.

## COMMEMORATIVES

Bowers, Q. David. *A Guide Book of United States Commemorative Coins*, Atlanta, GA, 2006.
Bullowa, David M. *The Commemorative Coinage of the United States 1892–1938*, New York, 1938.
Mosher, Stuart. *The Commemorative Coinage of the United States 1892–1938*, New York, 1940.
Slabaugh, Arlie. *United States Commemorative Coinage*, Racine, WI, 1975.
Swiatek, Anthony, and Breen, Walter. *The Encyclopedia of United States Silver and Gold Commemorative Coins 1892–1954*, New York, 1981.
Taxay, Don. *An Illustrated History of U.S. Commemorative Coinage*, New York, 1967.

## TOKENS

Fuld, George, and Fuld, Melvin. *U.S. Civil War Store Cards*, Lawrence, MA, 1975.
Jaeger, Katherine. *A Guide Book of United States Tokens and Medals*, Atlanta, GA, 2006.
Rulau, Russell. *Standard Catalog of United States Tokens 1700–1900*, Iola, WI, 1997.

## PATTERNS

Judd, J. Hewitt. *United States Pattern Coins* (9th ed., edited by Q. David Bowers), Atlanta, GA, 2005.

## PRIVATE AND TERRITORIAL GOLD

Adams, Edgar H. *Official Premium Lists of Private and Territorial Gold Coins*, Brooklyn, NY, 1909.
Adams, Edgar H. *Private Gold Coinage of California 1849–1855*, Brooklyn, NY, 1913.
Bowers, Q. David. *A California Gold Rush History Featuring Treasure from the* S.S. Central America, Wolfeboro, NH, 2001.
Bowers, Q. David. *The History of United States Coinage as Illustrated by the Garrett Collection*, Los Angeles, 1979.
Breen, Walter, and Gillio, Ronald. *California Pioneer Fractional Gold* (2nd ed.), Santa Barbara, CA, 1983.
Clifford, Henry H. "Pioneer Gold Coinage in the West—1848–1861," reprint from *The Westerners Brand Book—Book Nine*, Los Angeles, 1961.
Doering, David. *California Fractional Gold*, Seal Beach, CA, 1982.
Griffin, Clarence. *The Bechtlers and Bechtler Coinage and Gold Mining in North Carolina 1814–1830*, Spindale, NC, 1929.
Kagin, Donald H. *Private Gold Coins and Patterns of the United States*, New York, 1981.
Lee, Kenneth W. *California Gold—Dollars, Half Dollars, Quarter Dollars*, Santa Ana, CA, 1979.
Leonard, Robert D., Jr., et al. *California Pioneer Fractional Gold by Walter Breen and Ronald J. Gillio* (2nd ed.), Wolfeboro, NH, 2003.
Owens, Dan. *California Coiners and Assayers*, Wolfeboro, NH, and New York, 2000.
Seymour, Dexter C. *The 1830 Coinage of Templeton Reid*, American Numismatic Society Museum Notes No. 22, New York, 1977.

## PHILIPPINE ISSUES

Allen, Lyman L. *U.S. Philippine Coins*, Lyman Allen Numismatic Services, Oakland Park, FL, 1998.
Shafer, Neil. *United States Territorial Coinage for the Philippine Islands*, Whitman Publishing Company, 1961.

## PROOF COINS AND PROOF SETS

Lange, David W. *A Guide Book of Modern United States Proof Coin Sets*, Atlanta, GA, 2005.

## TYPE COINS

Bowers, Q. David. *A Guide Book of United States Type Coins*, Atlanta, GA, 2005.
Garrett, Jeff, and Guth, Ron. *100 Greatest U.S. Coins* (2nd ed.), Atlanta, GA, 2005.
Guth, Ron, and Garrett, Jeff. *United States Coinage: A Study by Type*. Atlanta, GA, 2005.